Modern Times
Transatlantic Encounters in the 1920s

THE ADA PUBLICATIONS SERIES At the Archiv der Avantgarden – Egidio Marzona (ADA) research, exhibitions, events, and education are all uniquely combined. At the core of the ADA are Egidio Marzona's remarkably diverse collection of artworks, objects, and documents relating to the twentieth-century avant-gardes, and also his comprehensive library. The latter contains scholarly and artistic publications as well as works of literature. This enormous store of knowledge will be made accessible and subject to critical reflection, and linked up with contemporary discourses via the ADA publications series. Complementing our exhibitions and events, these publications will present a long-term perspective that facilitates the dissemination of avant-garde ideas. While the publications accompanying exhibitions will focus on specific themes from the archive, the ADA publications series will also offer international authors a platform where they can access and undertake more in-depth work on related themes. In line with the interdisciplinary and hybrid nature of the archive, this platform will connect diverse fields and formats, with academic research and essays sitting alongside artistic approaches. In this way, the radical utopias of the avant-gardes and the ideas of modernism can be made widely visible and serve as new impulses for the present and the future.

Modern Times Transatlantic Encounters in the 1920s

Staatliche Kunstsammlungen Dresden
Archiv der Avantgarden – Egidio Marzona

Przemysław Strożek, Rudolf A. Fischer, Antonella B. Meloni in collaboration with David Wittinghofer

Spector Books

Contents

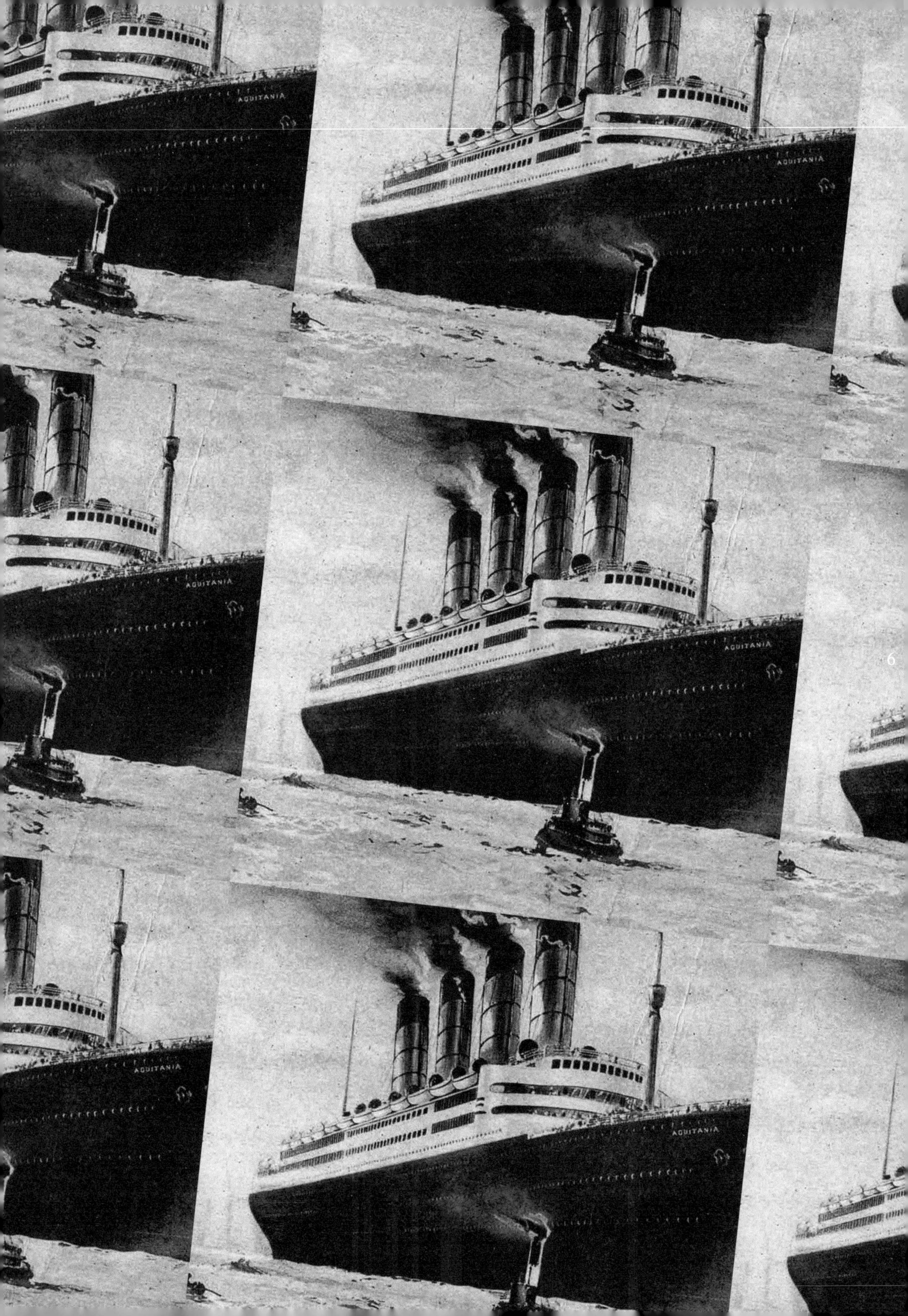
AQUITANIA

Greetings

With the exhibition *Modern Times. The American Dream and the Avant-Gardes of the 1920s*, the Archiv der Avantgarden – Egidio Marzona (ADA) demonstrates, for the third time since its opening in May 2024, that it is established as a driving force in its role as a hybrid between archive and museum within the Staatliche Kunstsammlungen Dresden.

We are delighted that this newly-established institution was named Museum of the Year 2024 in its inaugural year by the members of the German section of AICA (Association Internationale des Critiques d'Art).

Modern Times unlocks a new potential for the ADA. Both the exhibition and its catalog celebrate the numerous artistic milestones of the 1920s and, a century on, engage in a dialogue with them within its own collection.

Parallel to the avant-garde movements in 1920s Europe, an unprecedented economic prosperity developed in the United States. In Europe, "America" at that time stood as a cultural concept symbolizing an urban lifestyle, efficient work systems, and accessible entertainment. The label "Made in America" permeated every aspect of life while also defining what it meant to be modern.

The exhibition highlights the encounters between Europe and the United States which occurred in the 1920s across art, technology, literature, and music—an exchange that was widely popularized. Hollywood's film industry, Henry Ford's assembly line-produced Ford Model-T car, and Josephine Baker's frenzied dance performances are notable examples from the American side. Equally, the European side captured significant attention: in the United States, there was considerable interest in European art and its newly-emergent movements, such as Dadaism, Futurism, and Constructivism. The American audience discovered these through magazines like *The Little Review* and exhibitions by the Société Anonyme. Music, which was arguably the most intercontinentally influential force, is also well represented here, with Ernst Křenek's time opera *Jonny spielt auf*, which tells the story of a jazz violinist. It premiered in Leipzig in 1927 and was first performed at the Metropolitan Opera in New York in 1929.

It was primarily the transcontinental networks forged between the avant-garde groups that laid the foundation for this thriving exchange. Therefore, the main section of the exhibition focuses on the dissemination of the images and ideas that shaped what we now know as "Modernity." Printed magazines of the 1920s played a crucial role in transferring new ideas and movements between Europe and the USA.

I would like to thank the ADA team most sincerely for their accomplishments. In particular, I wish to thank Przemysław Strożek and David Wittinghofer, the two curators of the exhibition, the art handling team led by Joachim Kleinert and Ilka Stern, Clemens A. Ottenhausen as project coordinator, Antonella B. Meloni as editorial director and co-editor of the ADA publication series and, of course, Rudolf A. Fischer, who as head of the ADA has accompanied the team and the development of the new institution from the very beginning.

Marius Winzeler
General Director ad interim of
Staatliche Kunstsammlungen Dresden

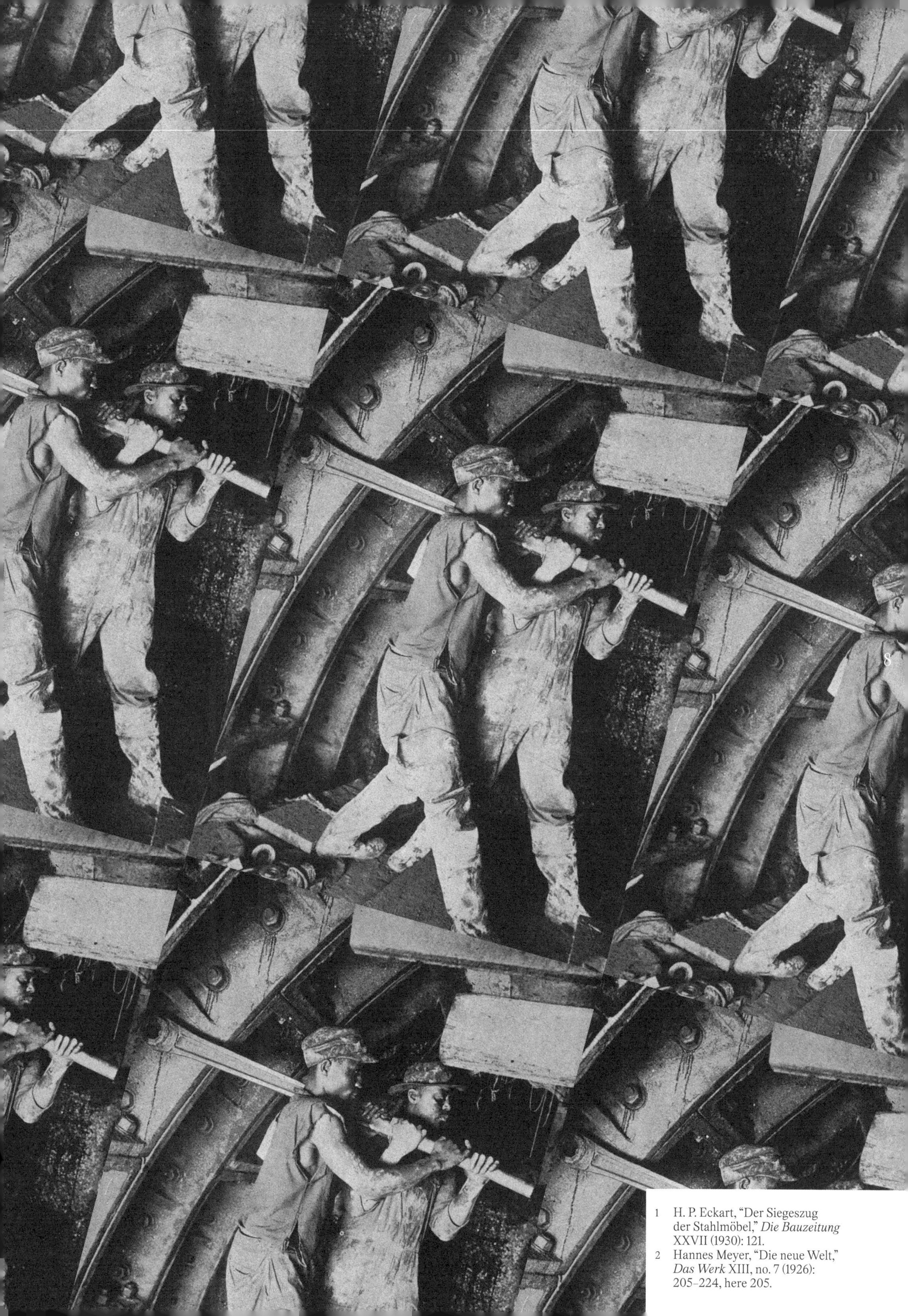

1 H. P. Eckart, “Der Siegeszug der Stahlmöbel,” *Die Bauzeitung* XXVII (1930): 121.

2 Hannes Meyer, “Die neue Welt,” *Das Werk* XIII, no. 7 (1926): 205–224, here 205.

Foreword
Modern Times: Transatlantic Interplay

The arts and culture of the 1920s has been the subject of ongoing worldwide fascination which, one hundred years on, has now reached its peak. In contemporary literature and film, the Roaring Twenties shine as a glamorous decade of rapid progress, passion, and the relaxing of social norms. The upheaval was particularly striking in European countries, whose populations yearned for a period of stability and improvement following the brutality of the First World War and the ensuing political turmoil of its aftermath. An inclination towards consumerism and leisure was mixed with notions of international unity, as demonstrated at the time by the popularity of Esperanto, the "international language" developed in Poland as early as 1887. Society became more libertine—especially in the Weimar Republic's metropolitan cities, where new liberal and even queer lifestyles became possible that would have been inconceivable in the Wilhelmine Empire. Media inventions such as radio, film, and the illustrated press contributed to the rapidly accelerating modernization of post-war European society.

This context was an ideal hotbed for artistic creativity that also had politically effects in the ever-fiercer struggle for cultural identity and power between the rising National Socialists and the left-wing labor organizations in Germany in the 1920s. Political artists and intellectuals such as George Grosz and John Heartfield relentlessly exposed the social stereotypes of the post-imperial era, strategically utilizing the potential of dissemination through the magazines and new media of their day. After all, socio-political criticism in artistic packaging was now legal. Freedom of art, science, and teaching was granted for the first time in Germany under Article 142 of the Weimar Constitution.

ALL NEW

The "New" was celebrated everywhere, as was reflected in new terminologies, for example in the New Objectivity with the exhibition of the same name in Mannheim in 1925, in Neues Bauen with the Stuttgart Weißenhofsiedlung in 1927, and in Neues Frankfurt with the CIAM (Congrès Internationaux d'Architecture Moderne) exhibition on housing for living wage workers in 1929. After decades of fighting for women's rights, the "New Woman" finally secured legal rights in Europe. Following the example of the Scandinavian countries, women were at last granted universal suffrage in major European countries such as Great Britain, Poland, and Germany from 1918 onwards. The momentum began to build and women all over Europe broke away from their traditional and discriminatory gender roles, becoming the "New Woman" who "played sports, drove cars and occasionally got on an airplane."[1]

In his 1926 essay "Die Neue Welt" the Swiss architect and second Bauhaus director Hannes Meyer gave a prime example of how creative people in major cities lived. The audience was now the cosmopolitan community: "Cars invade our streets: around us, on the insular sidewalks of the Avenue des Champs Elysees in Paris, the greatest possible fortissimo of metropolitan dynamism plays from 6–8 p.m. 'Ford' and 'Rolls-Royce' blast through the city center blurring the distance and boundaries between city and countryside. Airplanes glide through the airspace: 'Fokker' and 'Farman' increase our freedom of movement as well as the distance to the earth; they disobey national borders and reduce the distance between peoples. [...] We live faster and therefore longer."[2]

We had arrived in the middle of the Roaring Twenties, a decade of international awakening that still fascinates us today, and which we all believe we know. Recent literature, film adaptations, and television series such as *The Great Gatsby* and *Babylon Berlin* are responsible for this, providing us with voyeuristic but not always historically-balanced perspectives on urban society in the 1920s.

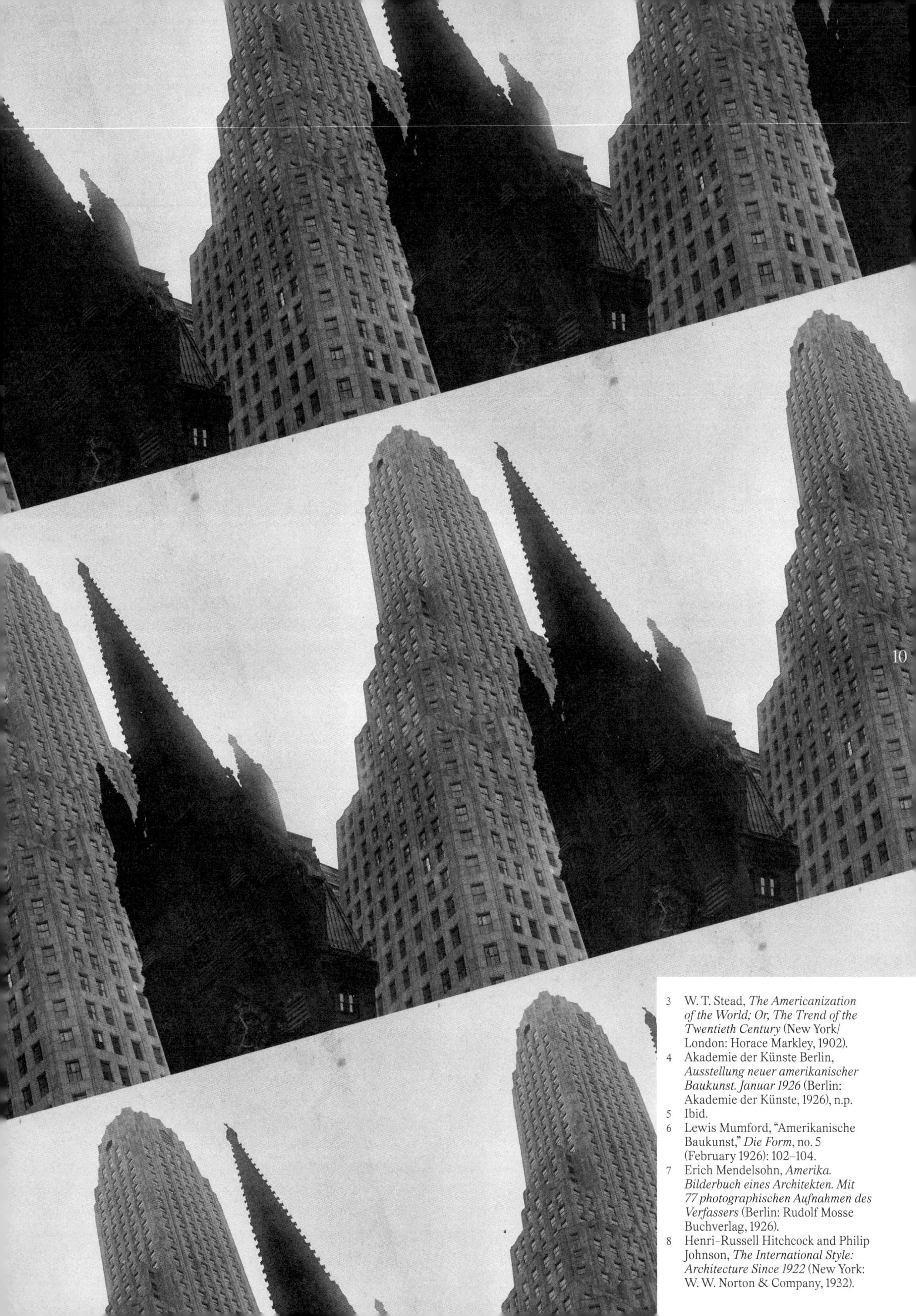

3 W. T. Stead, *The Americanization of the World; Or, The Trend of the Twentieth Century* (New York/ London: Horace Markley, 1902).
4 Akademie der Künste Berlin, *Ausstellung neuer amerikanischer Baukunst. Januar 1926* (Berlin: Akademie der Künste, 1926), n.p.
5 Ibid.
6 Lewis Mumford, "Amerikanische Baukunst," *Die Form*, no. 5 (February 1926): 102–104.
7 Erich Mendelsohn, *Amerika. Bilderbuch eines Architekten. Mit 77 photographischen Aufnahmen des Verfassers* (Berlin: Rudolf Mosse Buchverlag, 1926).
8 Henri-Russell Hitchcock and Philip Johnson, *The International Style: Architecture Since 1922* (New York: W. W. Norton & Company, 1932).

AMERICANIZATION—A EUROPEAN PHENOMENON

Literature on the Roaring Twenties in Europe often fails to mention a phenomenon known as "Americanization", a concept referring to the European fascination with the United States. The term is borrowed from the 1902 book *The Americanization of the World* by the British journalist and pacifist William T. Stead, who predicted that this movement would be trailblazing for European modernization in the decades to come.[3]

The interest of European countries in the US was massive. Cultural imports from the United States were ubiquitous—visible and audible everywhere, especially in urban areas, they included swing and jazz on the radio, boxing events and six-day races in sport, and automobiles and the latest consumer products in public life. New industrial forms of production from the US were just as widely appreciated as the resulting political formations of the trade union movements.

A great deal of curiosity was also apparent in the field of architecture. In 1924, the Akademie der Künste zu Berlin, in cooperation with the Prussian Ministry of Science, Art and National Education and the Foreign Office, invited "the architectural artists of the United States of America to organize an exhibition of their works [...] in Berlin". The intention was "to show in Germany the new American architecture of the last ten to fifteen years."[4] As Academy President, the artist Max Liebermann noted in the catalog of the exhibition, which opened in January 1926, that the architecture on display revealed the "American people's living conditions from which their architectural culture for public and private life would emerge."[5] As expected, the exhibition was a great success, but it also triggered a fierce debate—drawing upon an article by US-American architect Lewis Mumford[6]—among German modernist and conservative artists about the image of North America and the future of architecture and art in Germany. Powerful publications such as Erich Mendelsohn's *Amerika. Bilderbuch eines Architekten* from 1926 followed in efforts to construct the image of the United States as one of enthusiasm and superlatives.[7]

TRANSATLANTIC INTERPLAY

Contrary to popular belief, this was not a one-sided relationship. In the field of art and architecture, American artists and curators looked to Europe and were equally captivated as Europeans looking the other way. Therefore, we should speak of interconnections, or even of interplay. Two of the most important figures in importing European art to America were the American artist Katherine S. Dreier and the founding director of the Museum of Modern Art (MoMA), Alfred H. Barr.

In 1920, together with Marcel Duchamp and Man Ray, Dreier founded a completely new artists' organization in New York, called Société Anonyme Inc. Through exhibitions, the well-connected artist brought the European avant-garde movements closer to the North American public. She traveled to Europe as preparation, where she visited many of the modern protagonists of the avant-garde, establishing an intensive exchange across the Atlantic. MoMA also named a new shared European architectural "language" of the 1920s. Towards the end of the decade, the New York-based curator and later architect Philip Johnson travelled repeatedly to Europe, intensively studying the European avant-gardes and meeting the new architectural movement's key protagonists, including Le Corbusier, Mies van der Rohe, and J. J. P. Oud. However, the concept of an "international style" for the European architectural avant-garde was born in the US, and specifically, due to an exhibition curated by Philip Johnson together with the architectural historian Henry-Russell Hitchcock at MoMA in 1932. The publication accompanying the exhibition, *The International Style: Architecture Since 1922*, gave its name to an entire movement in modernism.[8]

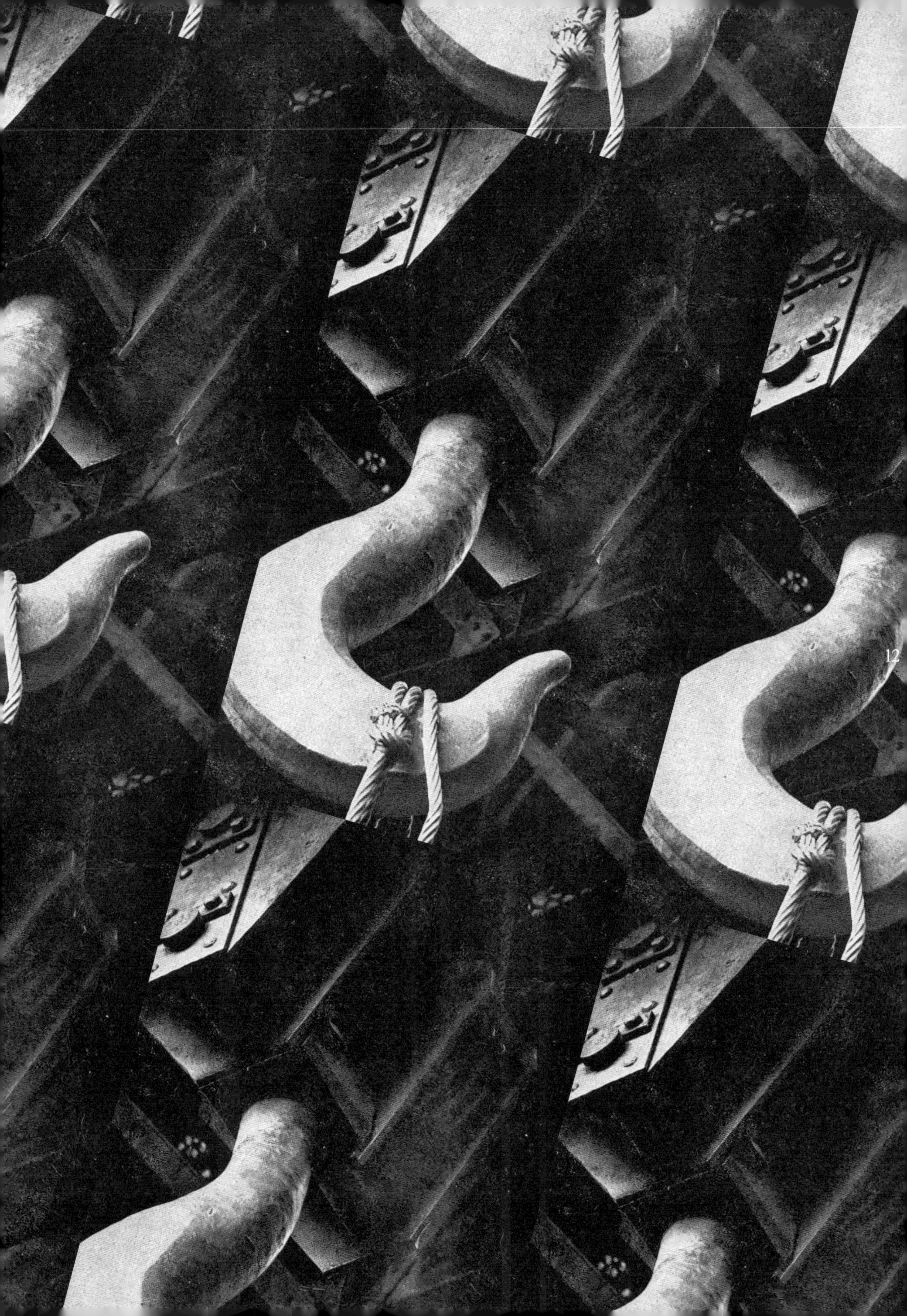

MODERN TIMES: ADA'S THIRD EXHIBITION

The Archiv der Avantgarden — Egidio Marzona (ADA) in Dresden, is a unique institution with a collection of around 1.5 million works of art, objects and documents pertaining to the artistic avant-garde movements of the twentieth century. The collection was amassed by a single person, Egidio Marzona, whose attention reaches far beyond individual artworks.

Through Marzona's collection practice of focusing on density, his archive of archives reveals a comprehensive view of all areas of the avant-gardes, from the visual arts to design and architecture, to theater, film, dance, and poetry. The collector regards all materials made in the context of art production to be of equal value. For him, this means that a typed letter is just as important as a painting; a small sketch on a napkin just as important as a watercolor; a record just as important as a printed book or an artist's magazine. Due to its structure, ADA is a democratic collection that goes hand in hand with the historical avant-garde movements' aim of merging art and life. Likewise, in the 1920s, the Société Anonyme Inc. mentioned above forged connections between avant-gardes and the public.

In May 2024, ADA moved into its new home in the so-called Blockhaus on the banks of the Elbe in Dresden, where it acts as a newly-conceived institution with a hybrid function: it operates both as a progressive museum and as an international, interdisciplinary research center. With its wide-ranging program, it also acts as a place for personal encounters and discursive exchange in Dresden. The opening exhibition *Archive of Dreams. A Surrealist Impulse* in May 2024 and the second presentation *Building worlds. Visionary architecture in the 20th century* is now followed by *Modern Times. The American Dream and the Avant-Gardes of the 1920s*, which marks ADA's third exhibition entirely compiled from the collection's own artworks and objects.

With *Modern Times* and the accompanying catalog, ADA once again becomes a platform for discourse on modern art in the first half of the twentieth century—this time, specifically the 1920s. The displayed selection reveals the traces of artistic ideas, the numerous utopias, and the astonishing networks between artists. In a way, moments of radical change in art and society reflect similar challenges in our present moment. Indeed, *Modern Times*'s range of works contains numerous links to the present day. Take, for example, the ambivalent entrepreneurial personality of Henry Ford. Back then, architects and entrepreneurs from all over the world visited and praised Ford's new, bright, and clean factories in Detroit. The humanitarian and social effects of his mass production and Fredericks Taylor's "scientific management", as well as the controversial beliefs figure of the avowed anti-Semite Henry Ford, represented the dark side of this unrestrained push for modernity. They have been met with fierce criticism from trade unions, social movements, artists, and intellectuals for decades. Together with the avant-gardes, the workers' movement sought (or rather formed) its own icons as counter-positions, for example in the figure of Charlie Chaplin, who is also central to *Modern Times*.

We are now living in the new twenties, the 2020s. There are many similarities and parallels to what happened one hundred years ago. The American mass media and pop culture with its new films and music, continue to influence Europe, but under new conditions. Increasingly instead of cinema, there are now streaming services, and instead of the Model-T Ford, there are now electric cars on the streets of big cities. Today, just like Henry Ford back then, a car manufacturer and the richest man in the world appears ambivalently, both as a hip visionary and darling of a global design community, and at the same time as a politician to be viewed critically. Just as in the 1920s, politically disruptive factors can be felt on both sides of the Atlantic. An iconic antagonist of Charlie Chaplin's stature has yet to emerge.

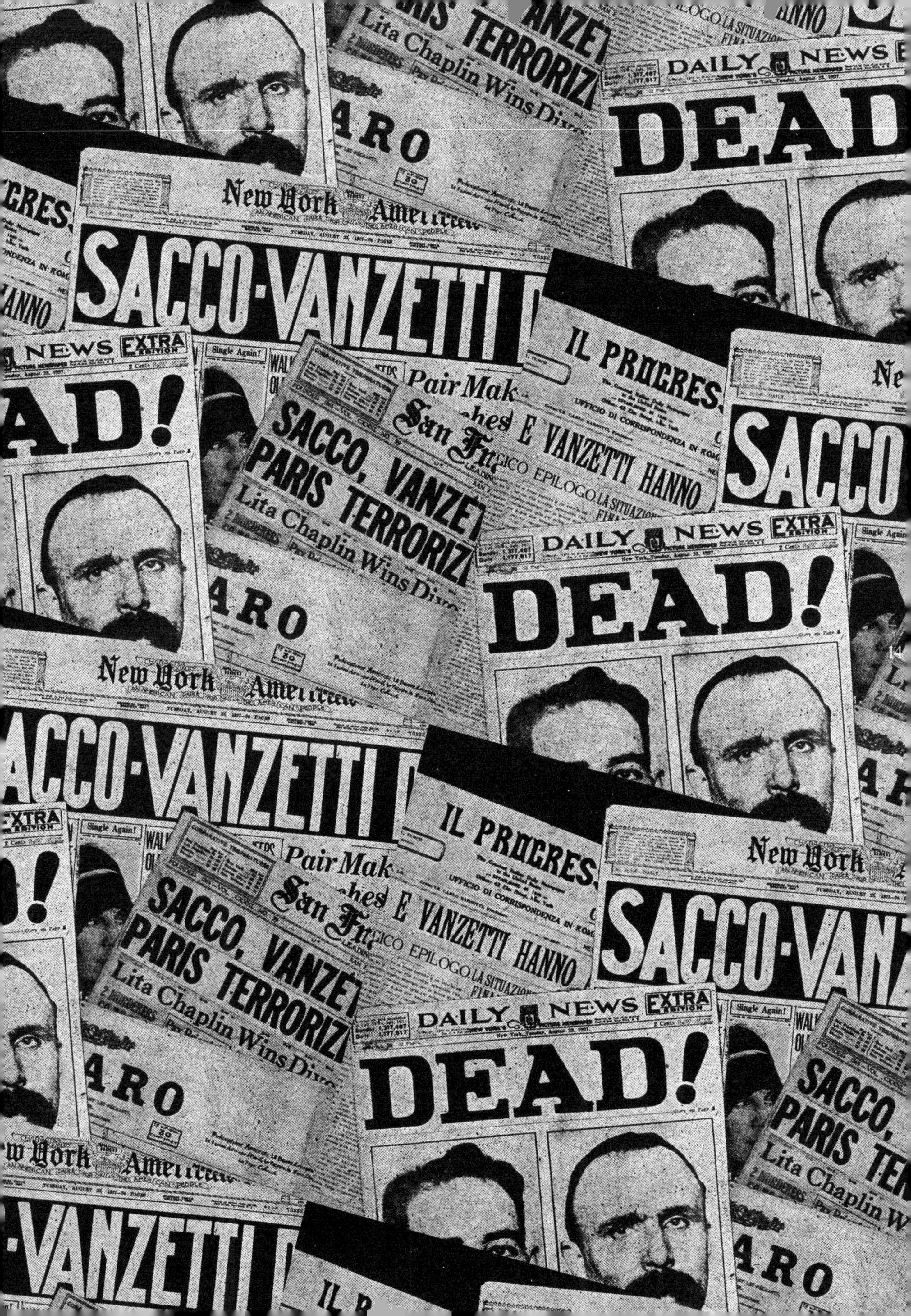
New York American
SACCO-VANZETTI
DAILY NEWS EXTRA EDITION
DEAD!
IL PROGRESSO
E VANZETTI HANNO
EPILOGO LA SITUAZIONE
UFFICIO DI CORRISPONDENZA IN ROMA
San Fr
Pair Mak
SACCO, VANZE
PARIS TERRORIZ
Lita Chaplin Wins Divo
Single Again!
ARO

The archive can be particularly helpful in dealing with the social positions of the twenty-first century by highlighting the forgotten and hidden, asking questions, and inviting visitors to engage in further discussion. This brings one of ADA's greatest potentials into focus: the ability to retrieve knowledge and objects from the past, to situate them in contemporary discourse, and to develop new perspectives and ideas for the future. I would like to take this opportunity to thank my team at ADA, in particular the curatorial duo Przemysław Strożek and David Wittinghofer, for making the ADA's potential visible.

Rudolf A. Fischer
Director Archiv der Avantgarden (ADA)

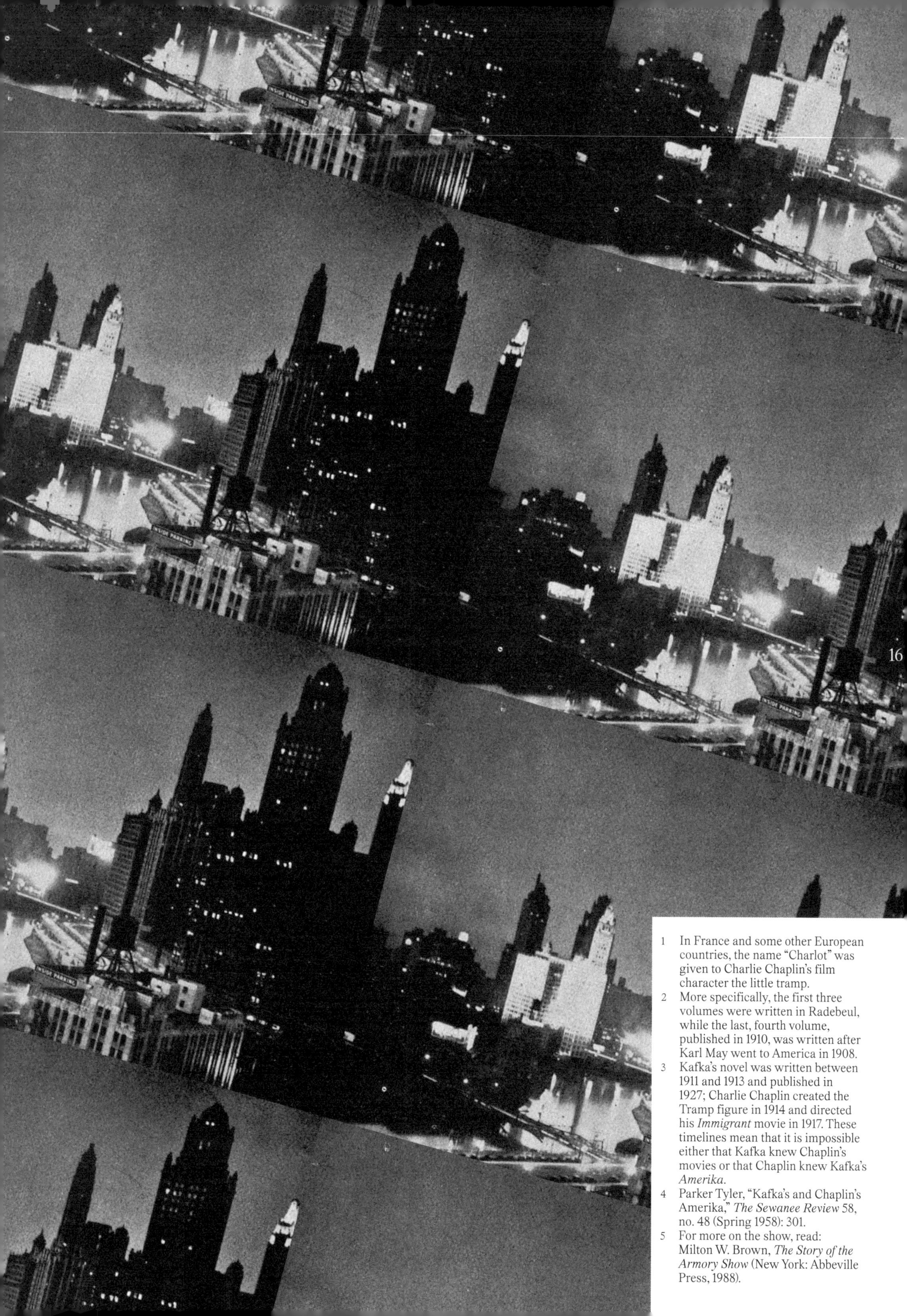

1 In France and some other European countries, the name "Charlot" was given to Charlie Chaplin's film character the little tramp.
2 More specifically, the first three volumes were written in Radebeul, while the last, fourth volume, published in 1910, was written after Karl May went to America in 1908.
3 Kafka's novel was written between 1911 and 1913 and published in 1927; Charlie Chaplin created the Tramp figure in 1914 and directed his *Immigrant* movie in 1917. These timelines mean that it is impossible either that Kafka knew Chaplin's movies or that Chaplin knew Kafka's *Amerika*.
4 Parker Tyler, "Kafka's and Chaplin's Amerika," *The Sewanee Review* 58, no. 48 (Spring 1958): 301.
5 For more on the show, read: Milton W. Brown, *The Story of the Armory Show* (New York: Abbeville Press, 1988).

Transatlantic Encounters in the 1920s: European Avant-Gardes, American Popular Culture and New Systems of Work

Przemysław Strożek

In 1920, the Rudolf Kraemmerer Verlag in Dresden published *Die Chapliniade* (The Chapliniade) by Ivan Goll, which included four avant-garde images designed by Fernand Léger depicting Charlie Chaplin, titled *Charlot Cubiste* (Cubist Chaplin).[1] In the same year, Katherine S. Dreier, Man Ray, and Marcel Duchamp founded the Société Anonyme, Inc.: Museum of Modern Art, which was the first institution in the US devoted to popularizing, collecting, and exhibiting the works of diverse European avant-garde movements. The Year 1920 also saw the Ford Motor Company reorganized in the US by the Delaware Charter, making Henry Ford the sole manager and owner of his automobile company. Never before had one man controlled such a huge business enterprise alone. Still in 1920, on the other side of the Atlantic, the Fiat factory in Turin witnessed a huge wave of workers' protests in the famous "clock hand strike". This general strike began after a worker was dismissed for turning back the clock, an act breaking the rules of the time-management system used to control the workflow in the factory. All these events, which happened more or less simultaneously on each side of the Atlantic in the same year, announced the beginnings of the new decade commonly known as The Roaring Twenties, The Golden Twenties, and The Jazz Age. For many, this decade was a time of joy, optimism, hedonism, cheerfulness, and entertainment. It emerged within a new geopolitical order, when Europe was recovering from the destruction of the First World War, and the United States had begun to be recognized as a growing global superpower.

In the 1920s, the term "America" became a synonym for an important cultural concept of the Roaring Twenties which was inseparably linked with modernization processes, popular culture, and the Machine Age in the United States. From the perspective of ruined Europe, the post-war US was commonly viewed as a promised land of democracy, unprecedented economic prosperity, and celebrity culture, but at the same time, also as a symbol of capitalist exploitation. It was viewed as a true model for the Machine Age, both utopian and dystopian, with the ultra-modern cityscape of New York, neon lights, cocktails, jazz, and Hollywood. In this way, the Roaring Twenties America markedly differed from the myth of Old America which had been popularized by adventure fiction in Europe at the turn of the 20th century.

Before the arrival of film and the establishment of cinema culture, adventure fiction had stimulated Europe's collective imagination about the American Wild West. These mental images were most notably shaped by the four volumes of *Winnetou* (1893–1910) by Karl May, one of the best-selling books of all time, with total sales exceeding 100 million copies. All Europe read the thrilling adventures of Old Shatterhand, a brave and skilled adventurer, and Winnetou, a noble and wise Apache, who together overcome challenges and dangers to maintain peace between cowboys and native communities. The series was actually mostly written in Radebeul, a town close to Dresden,[2] and envisioned America as a natural landscape of the mythic Wild West. *Winnetou* inspired a whole generation of German-speaking writers, among whom was Prague-based Franz Kafka, whose unfinished novel *Amerika* (written in German between 1911 and 1914 under the title *Der Verschollene* [*The Missing Person*] and published posthumously in Munich in 1927) linked the images of the natural landscape of Old America (Wild West) with the envisioned cityscape of New York as known from the 1910s illustrated press.

Amerika described the story of a fictional character, Karl Rossmann, who arrived in New York on a transatlantic ocean liner, reflecting the mass immigration across the Atlantic. The transatlantic journey from Europe to the US was by then a crucial theme in Charlie Chaplin's movie *The Immigrant* (1917), which drew on his own experiences of arriving in the United States. By approaching the New World by boat, the first image of America that both Karl Rossmann in Kafka's literary work and the little tramp in Chaplin's film encounter is the Statue of Liberty, a symbol of freedom and democracy. Even if there are no direct links between Kafka's novel and Chaplin's movie,[3] an American avant-garde writer and critic, Parker Tyler, later claimed that those "two immigrant heroes [...] Karl and Charlie the Tramp are heroes of the identical international myth: the great adventure of the young foreigner coming head-on to the United States to start a new life and rise level beyond any available to him in his native land."[4]

Between 1850 and 1915, more than 28 million Europeans migrated to the United States. Among these masses were a few avant-garde artists and architects who had decided to cross the Atlantic. Those who arrived in the 1910s had either fled war-torn Europe and remained in New York for a short period or wanted to stay longer and achieve commercial success there. European art was always in favor in the US, and the market for modern art was beginning to grow, most notably after European Cubism gained wide recognition and success at the 1913 Armory Show in New York.[5] However, in general, the avant-garde "isms" were still not generally known by American society, except in the hermetic circles of the photographer and

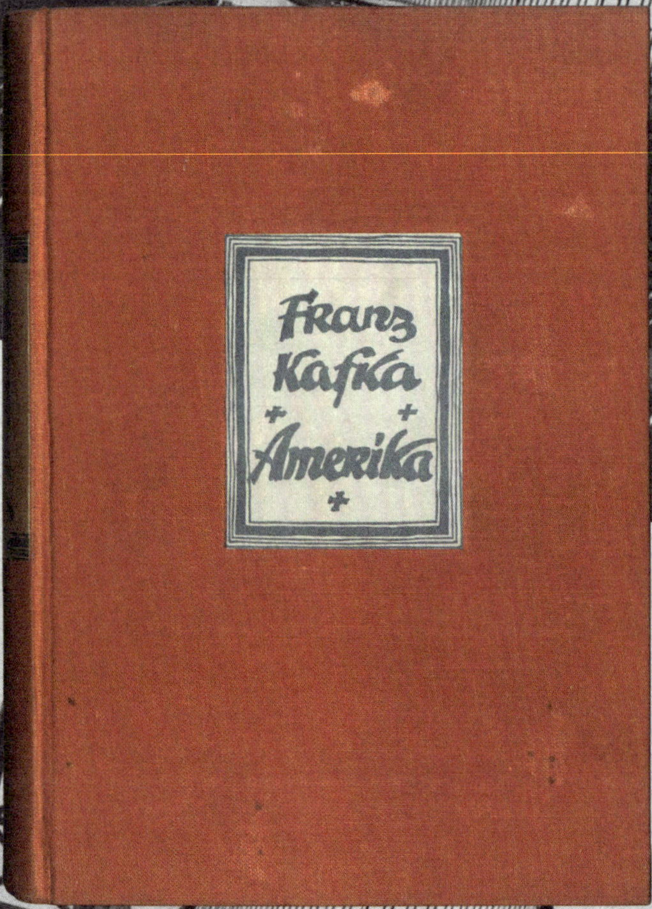

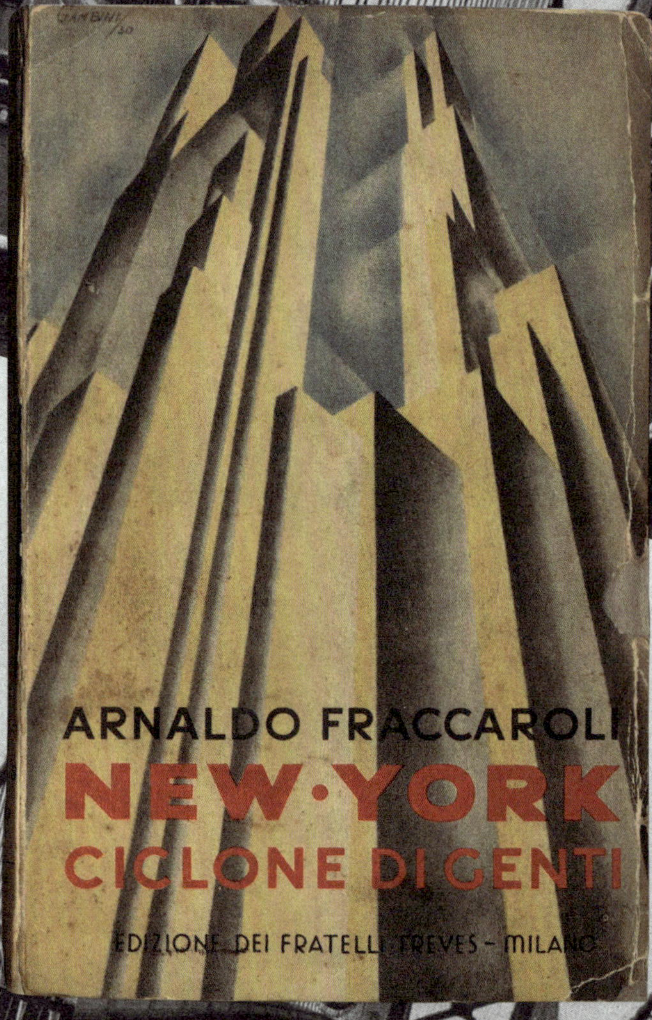

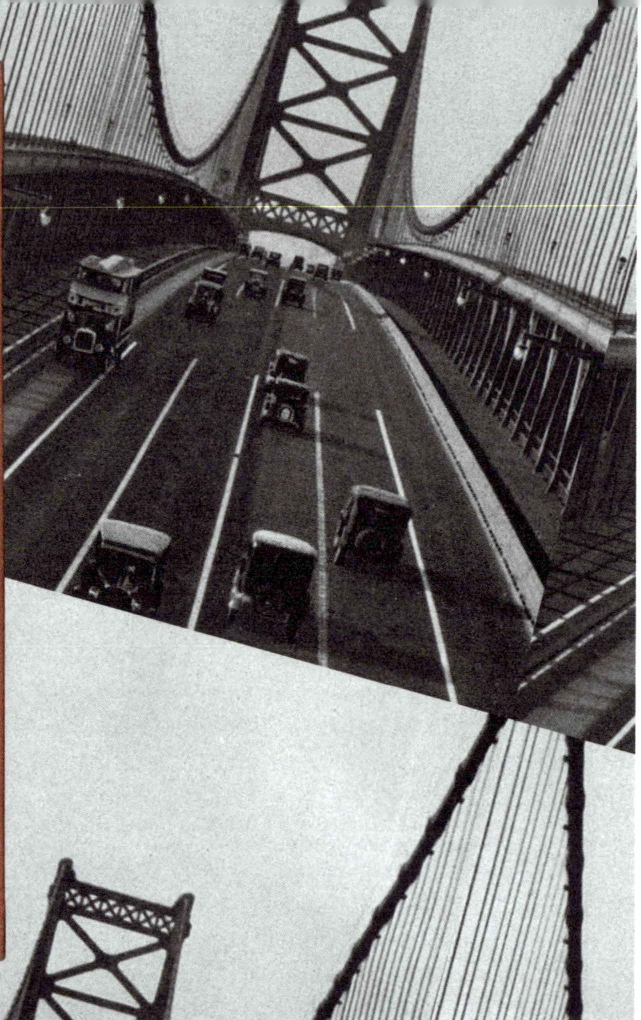

001 Franz Kafka, *Amerika [Der Verschollene]*, Munich: Kurt Wolff Verlag 1927
002 Arnaldo Fraccaroli, *New York. Ciclone di Genti*, Milan: Fratelli Treves Editori 1929, cover by Ivanhoe Gambini

6 For more on New York Dada, read: *New York Dada*, ed. Rudolf E. Kuenzli (New York: Willis Locker & Owens, 1986).
7 [Katherine S. Dreier's letter to schools in New York city in 1920], quoted after, [Editors] "Introduction," in *The Société Anonyme and the Dreier Bequest at Yale University. A Catalogue Raisonnée*, eds. Robert L. Herbert, Eleanor S. Apter, Elise K. Kenney, (New Haven: Yale University Press, 1984), 4.
8 Sybil Kantor, *Alfred H. Barr, Jr. and the Intellectual Origins of the Museum of Modern Art* (Cambridge, MA: MIT Press, 2003), 111.
9 Blaise Cendrars, quoted in *Henry Poulaille, Charles Chaplin, précédé de Un Soir Avec Charlot à New York*, par Paul Morand (Paris: Bernard Grasset, 1927), 114–115.
10 Georges Antheil, quoted in Douglas Kahn, *Noise, Water, Meat: A History of Sound in the Arts* (Cambridge, MA: MIT Press, 2001), 66.
11 The three volumes in 1893.
12 Rudolf Kayser, "Americanism," in *The Weimar Republic Sourcebook*, eds. Anton Kaes, Martin Jay, Dward Dimendberg, (Berkeley: University of California Press, 1994), 395.
13 Read also Adolf Halfeld, *Amerika und der Amerikanismus* (Jena: Eugen Diedrichs, 1927).
14 American artists such as Man Ray, Alexander Calder, Berenice Abbott, George Antheil, and Josephine Baker, who moved in the 1920s to Paris, gained much more notoriety in Europe because they were active in France and not in the US.

↑001

gallerist Alfred Stieglitz and art collector Walter C. Arensberg. Stieglitz founded a magazine, and a gallery named *291* in New York and worked there with, among others, Francis Picabia and Marcel Duchamp, who had arrived in the city in 1913 and 1915, respectively. Their collaboration gave an impulse to the short-lived phenomenon of New York Dada.[6]

In 1920, an American artist, Katherine S. Dreier, engaged Duchamp and Man Ray to establish a new institution called Société Anonyme, Inc.: Museum of Modern Art in New York. It was the first avant-garde institution to introduce a wide array of European movements to the US audience, from Expressionism, Cubism, Futurism, and Dada to Constructivism and Purism. Its primary goal was to popularize European avant-gardes through providing exhibitions, lectures, and dedicated publications. According to Dreier, it was a "circulating museum" without a permanent exhibition site. She wrote: "We are not a Museum along the old lines of collecting and conserving art, but are acting as a circulating museum where the movements in contemporary art may be studied."[7] Thanks to her curatorial work, publications, and collecting practices, the European "isms" became institutionalized and commercialized in the US, becoming a model for practices for experimental American artists to follow. Even if the impact of Société Anonyme was limited as it did not have a permanent exhibition space, Dreier's groundbreaking efforts from the 1920s prepared the fertile ground for the establishment of another venue, the Museum of Modern Art (MoMA) in New York in 1929, directed by Alfred H. Barr. The founding of MoMA, independently from Société Anonyme, signaled the arrival of New York as a major player in the global modern art scene. It soon became one of the most influential museums in the world, having followed Dreier's strategies to institutionalize and canonize avant-garde movements.[8]

By the mid-1910s, the first Charlie Chaplin movies made in Hollywood and American jazz bands arrived in Europe along with the First World War. An avant-garde poet, Blaise Cendrars, wrote that the iconic figure of Chaplin was born at the military front,[9] and an American avant-garde musician, George Antheil, recalled that: "Black music made us remember at least that we still had bodies which had not been explored by shrapnel."[10] In the following decade, the Roaring Twenties, both Chaplin and jazz became inseparably associated with the American lifestyle, reflecting the joy and optimism of the Machine Age. In his influential essay, *Amerikanismus* (Americanism, 1925), Rudolf Kayser listed skyscrapers, commercial offices, film, technical inventions, jazz, boxing, illustrated magazines, and business and management, asking "Is that America?" "Perhaps."—was his answer without being quite sure, because in reality he had never been there. When

↑002

Karl May wrote subsequent volumes of *Winnetou*[11] and Franz Kafka drafts of *Amerika*, they visualized the US as an adventurous land fuelled with literary imagination. Kayser, in turn, associated America more with the socio-political changes that occurred in the 1920s. His essay expressed significant awareness that "*Amerikanismus* is the European new catchword [...] the more it is used, the less one knows what it means."[12] He saw Americanism as a "new orientation" and a "European method", manifesting itself in a common ideal of a new industrial society free from the burdens of the past. This new "method" originated in Weimar Germany in around 1924 and was an integral element of Weimar culture linked to a preoccupation with American values, lifestyles, and economic systems as a basis upon which to reform and transform the country.[13]

As has been outlined above, the America of the Roaring Twenties was envisioned as embodying a modern lifestyle (urbanisation, a machine-driven cityscape), entertainment (jazz, Hollywood), and new rationalized systems of work (Taylorism, Fordism). These phenomena inspired many avant-garde European artists, who referred to them in artworks, publications, books, magazines, advertisements, music notes, manifestos, poetry, literature, posters, and collages. America was inseparably associated with skyscrapers, automobiles, neon city lights, jazz, Hollywood, Ford, prosperity, and business, all of which became viral images circulating across European countries, mainly through mass media. It appeared on the one hand as a synonym for the optimistic outcomes of the Machine Age, and on the other, as a pessimistic image of deep social issues, such as racism, political prosecutions, the exploitation of the working class, growing unemployment, and homelessness.

At first glance, transatlantic encounters in the 1920s can be framed by cultural interactions between the US and Europe. During that decade, diverse European avant-garde movements became popularized in New York, gaining increased attention and prestige and serving as a paradigm for new artistic practices (through Société Anonyme, for example). Meanwhile, European avant-gardes envisioned America as a modern concept of the Machine Age, linked with the technological advancements, prosperity, and overall excitement of popular culture. In other words, the progressive art world from the US absorbed avant-gardes from Europe as a model for modern art, while some artists connected to European avant-gardes embraced the lifestyle and pop-cultural phenomena emanating from America. This observation may lead to the conclusion that the European art world was primarily interested in jazz and Hollywood, but not in American art developments.[14] On the other hand, Americans were less interested in the new cinema and new music emerging in Europe. Some evidence of this

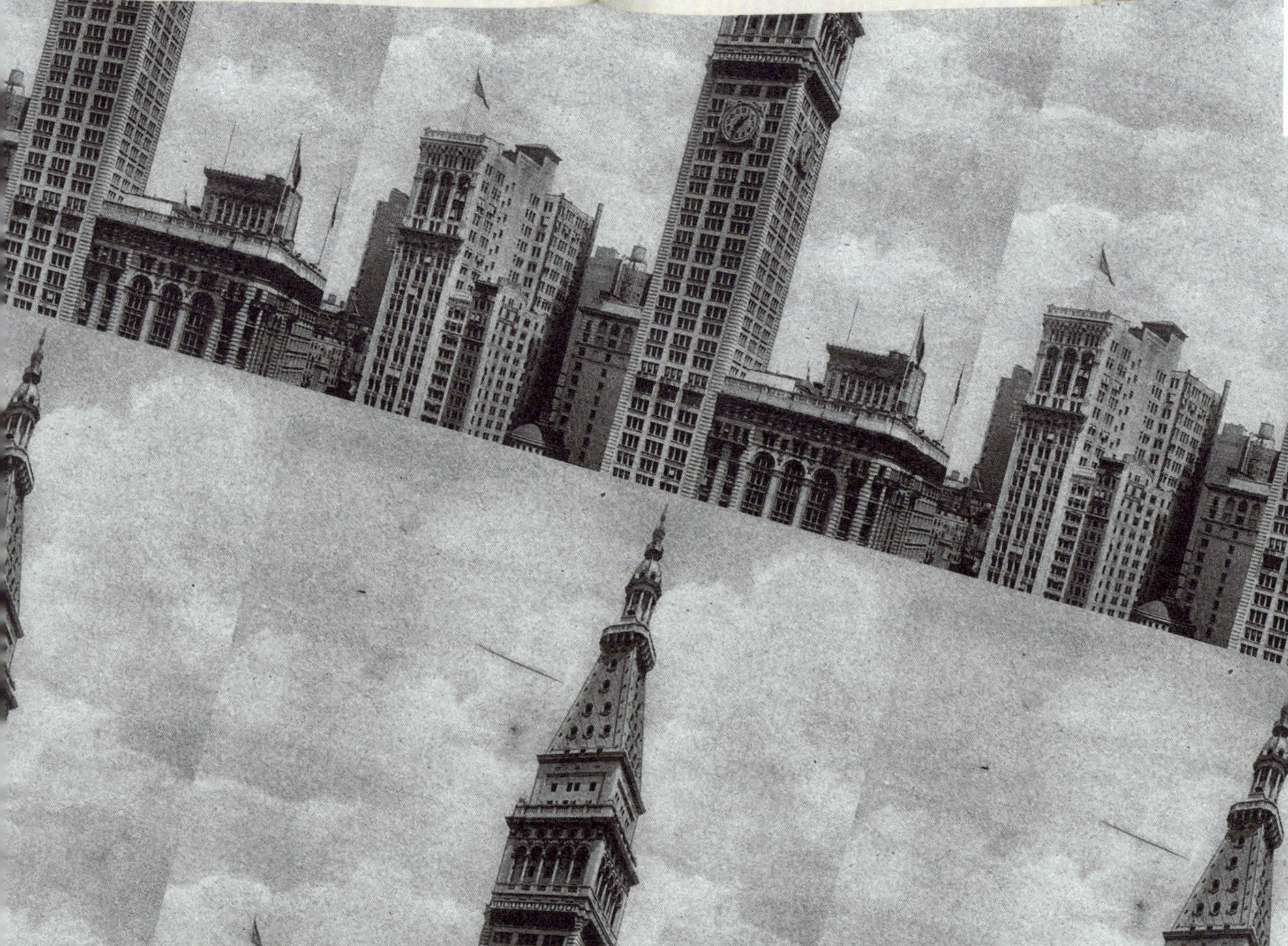

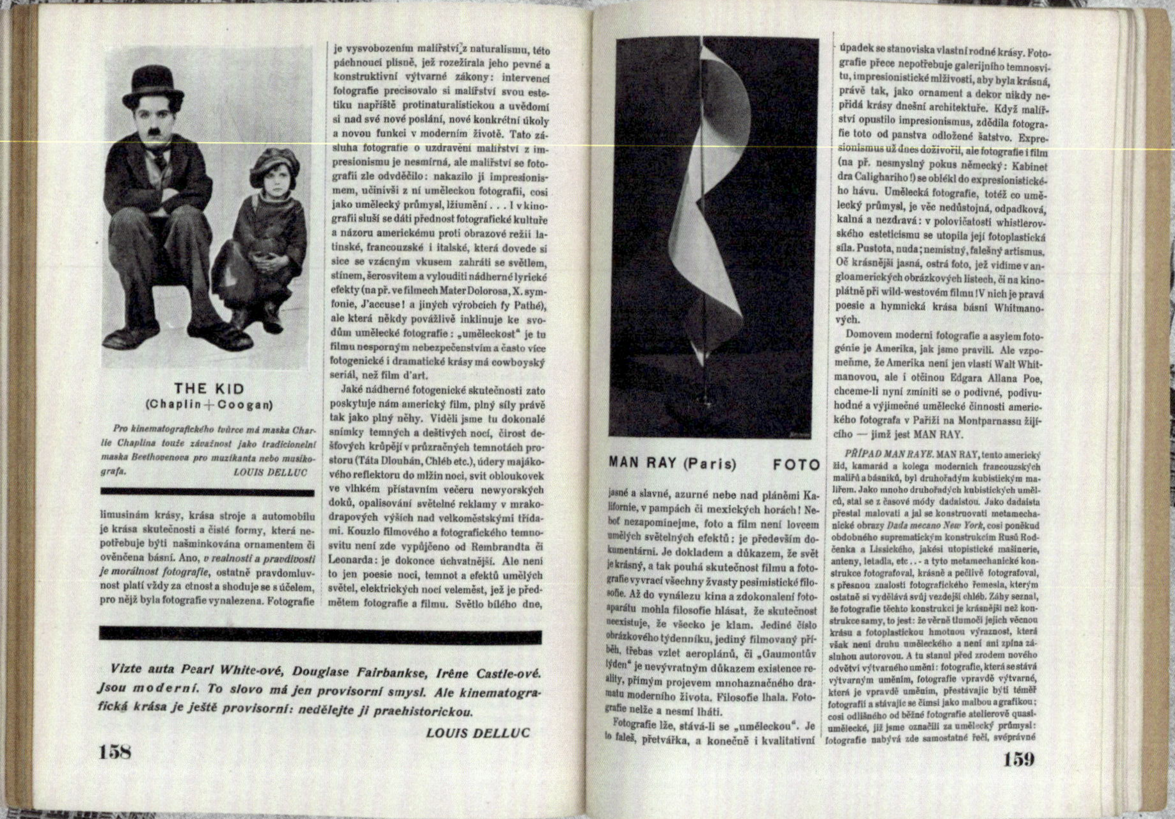

je vysvobozením malířství z naturalismu, této páchnoucí plísně, jež rozežírala jeho pevné a konstruktivní výtvarné zákony: intervencí fotografie precisovalo si malířství svou estetiku napříště protinaturalistickou a uvědomí si nad své nové poslání, nové konkrétní úkoly a novou funkci v moderním životě. Tato zásluha fotografie o uzdravení malířství z impresionismu je nesmírná, ale malířství se fotografii zle odvděčilo: nakazilo ji impresionismem, učinivši z ní uměleckou fotografii, cosi jako umělecký průmysl, lžiumění . . . I v kinografii sluší se dáti přednost fotografické kultuře a názoru americkému proti obrazové režii latinské, francouzské i italské, která dovede si sice se vzácným vkusem zahráti se světlem, stínem, šerosvitem a vylouditi nádherné lyrické efekty (na př. ve filmech Mater Dolorosa, X. symfonie, J'accuse! a jiných výrobcích fy Pathé), ale která někdy povážlivě inklinuje ke svodům umělecké fotografie: „uměleckost" je tu filmu nesporným nebezpečenstvím a často více fotogenické i dramatické krásy má cowboyský seriál, než film d'art.

Jaké nádherné fotogenické skutečnosti zato poskytuje nám americký film, plný síly právě tak jako plný něhy. Viděli jsme tu dokonalé snímky temných a deštivých nocí, čirost dešťových krůpějí v průzračných temnotách prostoru (Táta Dlouhán, Chléb etc.), údery majákového reflektoru do mlžin noci, svit obloukovek ve vlhkém přístavním večeru newyorských doků, opalisování světelné reklamy v mrakodrapových výších nad velkoměstskými třídami. Kouzlo filmového a fotografického temnosvitu není zde vypůjčeno od Rembrandta či Leonarda: je dokonce úchvatnější. Ale není to jen poesie noci, temnot a efektů umělých světel, elektrických nocí veleměst, jež je předmětem fotografie a filmu. Světlo bílého dne,

THE KID
(Chaplin + Coogan)

Pro kinematografického tvůrce má maska Charlie Chaplina touže závažnost jako tradicionelní maska Beethovenova pro muzikanta nebo musikografa. *LOUIS DELLUC*

limusinám krásy, krása stroje a automobilu je krása skutečnosti a čisté formy, která nepotřebuje býti našminkována ornamentem či ověnčena básní. Ano, *v realnosti a pravdivosti je morálnost fotografie*, ostatně pravdomluvnost platí vždy za ctnost a shoduje se s účelem, pro nějž byla fotografie vynalezena. Fotografie

Vizte auta Pearl White-ové, Douglase Fairbankse, Irêne Castle-ové. Jsou moderní. To slovo má jen provisorní smysl. Ale kinematografická krása je ještě provisorní: nedělejte ji praehistorickou.

LOUIS DELLUC

158

MAN RAY (Paris) FOTO

jasné a slavné, azurné nebe nad pláněmi Kalifornie, v pampách či mexických horách! Neboť nezapomínejme, foto a film není lovcem umělých světelných efektů: je především dokumentární. Je dokladem a důkazem, že svět je krásný, a tak pouhá skutečnost filmu a fotografie vyvrací všechny žvasty pesimistické filosofie. Až do vynálezu kina a zdokonalení fotoaparátu mohla filosofie hlásat, že skutečnost neexistuje, že všecko je klam. Jediné číslo obrázkového týdenníku, jediný filmovaný příběh, třebas vzlet aeroplánů, či „Gaumontův týden" je nevývratným důkazem existence reality, přímým projevem mnohaznačného dramatu moderního života. Filosofie lhala. Fotografie nelže a nesmí lháti.

Fotografie lže, stává-li se „uměleckou". Je to faleš, přetvářka, a konečně i kvalitativní úpadek se stanoviska vlastní rodné krásy. Fotografie přece nepotřebuje galerijního temnosvitu, impresionistické mlživosti, aby byla krásná, právě tak, jako ornament a dekor nikdy nepřidá krásy dnešní architektuře. Když malířství opustilo impresionismus, zdědila fotografie toto od panstva odložené šatstvo. Expresionismus už dnes doživořil, ale fotografie i film (na př. nesmyslný pokus německý: Kabinet dra Calighariho!) se oblékl do expresionistického hávu. Umělecká fotografie, totéž co umělecký průmysl, je věc nedůstojná, odpadková, kalná a nezdravá: v polovičatosti whistlerovského esteticismu se utopila její fotoplastická síla. Pustota, nuda; nemístný, falešný artismus. Oč krásnější jasná, ostrá foto, jež vidíme v angloamerických obrázkových listech, či na kinoplátně při wild-westovém filmu! V nich je pravá poesie a hymnická krása básní Whitmanových.

Domovem moderní fotografie a asylem fotogénie je Amerika, jak jsme pravili. Ale vzpomeňme, že Amerika není jen vlastí Walt Whitmanovou, ale i otčinou Edgara Allana Poe, chceme-li nyní zmíniti se o podivné, podivuhodné a výjimečné umělecké činnosti amerického fotografa v Paříži na Montparnassu žijícího — jímž jest MAN RAY.

PŘÍPAD MAN RAYE. MAN RAY, tento americký žid, kamarád a kolega moderních francouzských malířů a básníků, byl druhořadým kubistickým malířem. Jako mnoho druhořadých kubistických umělců, stal se z časové módy dadaistou. Jako dadaista přestal malovati a jal se konstruovati metamechanické obrazy *Dada mecano New York*, cosi poněkud obdobného suprematickým konstrukcím Rusů Rodčenka a Lissického, jakési utopistické mašinerie, anteny, letadla, etc . . . - a tyto metamechanické konstrukce fotografoval, krásně a pečlivě fotografoval, s přesnou znalostí fotografického řemesla, kterým ostatně si vydělává svůj vezdejší chléb. Záhy seznal, že fotografie těchto konstrukcí je krásnější než konstrukce samy, to jest: že věrně tlumočí jejich věcnou krásu a fotoplastickou hmotnou výraznost, která však není druhu uměleckého a není ani zplna zásluhou autorovou. A tu stanul před zrodem nového odvětví výtvarného umění: fotografie, která se stává výtvarným uměním, fotografie vpravdě výtvarné, která je vpravdě uměním, přestávajíc býti téměř fotografií a stávajíc se čímsi jako malbou a grafikou; cosi odlišného od běžné fotografie atelierově quasiumělecké, již jsme označili za umělecký průmysl: fotografie nabývá zde samostatné řeči, svéprávné

159

003 *Život. Nové umění—konstrukce, soudobá intelektuelní aktivita*, no. 2, 1922, ed. Jaromír Krejcar, Prague, 158–159

15 Laura McGuire, "A Movie House in Space and Time: Frederick Kiesler's Film Arts Guild Cinema, New York, 1929," *Studies in the Decorative Arts*, 14, no. 2 (Spring–Summer 2007): 70.

16 Ramón Gómez de la Serna, *Ismos*, (Madrid: Biblioteca nueva, 1931).

can, for example, be found in the failure of a promising Film Arts Guild Cinema project established in New York in 1929 with a focus on screening European avant-garde films. Austrian avant-garde artist Frederick Kiesler designed the screening rooms, which were open only briefly. A scholar, Laura M. McGuire, has noted that even if the Guild was primarily interested in promoting non-American cinema, it also screened some Hollywood films, and "Charlie Chaplin films appear to have been a favourite."[15]

The image of transatlantic encounters and exchanges between the European avant-garde, American art institutions, and American popular culture outlined above has still more layers. By digging deeper into those interconnections, a more complex and complicated idea can be unfolded of its socio-political impact. It is important to underline that some sections of the American art world, most notably its conservative officials and collectors, were not always uncritical towards the strategy of popularising avant-garde movements, which they argued was to the detriment of American national art. On the other hand, European artists, mainly those connected to the avant-garde left, often criticized the blind worship of the American Machine Age. The 1927 executions of two Italian anarchists, Nicola Sacco and Bartolomeo Vanzetti, who had been sentenced to death without proof of their guilt, sparked global outrage against the American system of justice. Two years later, on October 24, 1929, the New York Stock Exchange market on Wall Street crashed so drastically that the entire global economy soon collapsed along with it. The 1920s ended with the so-called Great Depression that completely changed the image of America which had been established in Europe across the entire decade. The Great Depression anticipated the ongoing economic instability of the 1930s, which came hand-in-hand with political instability in many parts of the world. The rise of a dictatorship in the Third Reich, fascism in Japan, Stalinism in the Soviet Union, and a more radicalized version of fascism in Italy (than it had initially been in the 1920s), defined the deeply troubled geopolitical situation of the 1930s. By then, the Roaring Twenties had become a memory of an optimistic, hedonistic decade gone by.

MODERN TIMES. THE CONCEPT OF THE EXHIBITION AND THE CATALOG

The thesis of *Modern Times*—both the exhibition project and the catalog—is to show that in the 1920s, for the first time on such a scale, and as never before, transatlantic cultural encounters between America (in the form of American popular culture and lifestyle) and Europe (via the European avant-gardes) defined what it really meant to be modern. These encounters embraced many significant, and sometimes contradictory, socio-political and cultural phenomena, such as Americanism, Hollywood, Jazz, Fordism, Taylorism, capitalism, communism, the Machine Age, art institutions, the art market, the mass media, utopia and dystopia, in a complex network of mutual impacts. In that context, European "isms", including Italian Futurism, French Purism, Czech Poetism, and Soviet and International Constructivism, along with Berlin and Paris Dada, were not detached, but were in fact strictly interconnected with the aesthetics of the Roaring Twenties.

The exhibition project is the third presentation of the vast Archiv der Avantgarden — Egidio Marzona collection. The first highlighted three hundred carefully selected objects displayed together as the *Archive of Dreams* and explored the Surrealist impulse in the 20th century (May to August 2024). The second project, *Building Worlds*, was devoted to visionary and utopian architecture in the 20th century (November 2024 to March 2025). The narrative of *Modern Times* (April to August 2025) again derives from the holdings of Archiv der Avantgarden, which mostly comprise works on paper, magazines, books, and photography. The central focus of this show and the catalog are not the artworks themselves, but the circulation of ideas, concepts, books, catalogs, mass media, images, and sound recordings between the US and Europe.

Similarly to the first exhibition, *Archive of Dreams*, *Modern Times* builds a specific dialogue with Egidio Marzona's system of organization by which Marzona divided the archive into particular "isms" using the book *Kunst-Ismen* (1925) by Hans Arp and El Lissitzky as a model. *Modern Times* expands this structure and looks to other "isms", introducing, among others, Jazzbandism and Charlotism (Chaplinism), as defined by a Spanish avant-garde writer Ramón Gómez de la Serna in 1931 as crucial avant-garde movements directed against the decadent culture of Old Europe.[16] On the other hand, the exhibition highlights the work of Société Anonyme, which was established in 1920 as a new form of a museum that institutionalized avant-garde movements and simultaneously acted as a space to study modern art with educational aims. It can be viewed as the first historical model for Archiv der Avantgarden, which opened its doors to the public last year, in 2024, with a similar aim.

The exhibition and catalog of *Modern Times* explore what kind of narratives waiting to come to light and be re-discovered are stored in the archive, and seek to enhance understanding of the complex history of the avant-gardes in the single decade of the 1920s. The 170 objects selected for the exhibition explore transatlantic encounters through journeys and migrations across the ocean, as well as through the ideas and concepts outlined in diverse mass media, which were appropriated, created, and re-used by avant-garde artists. The central mediums used to transmit these encounters were books, catalogs, posters, photographs, publications, magazines, and films.

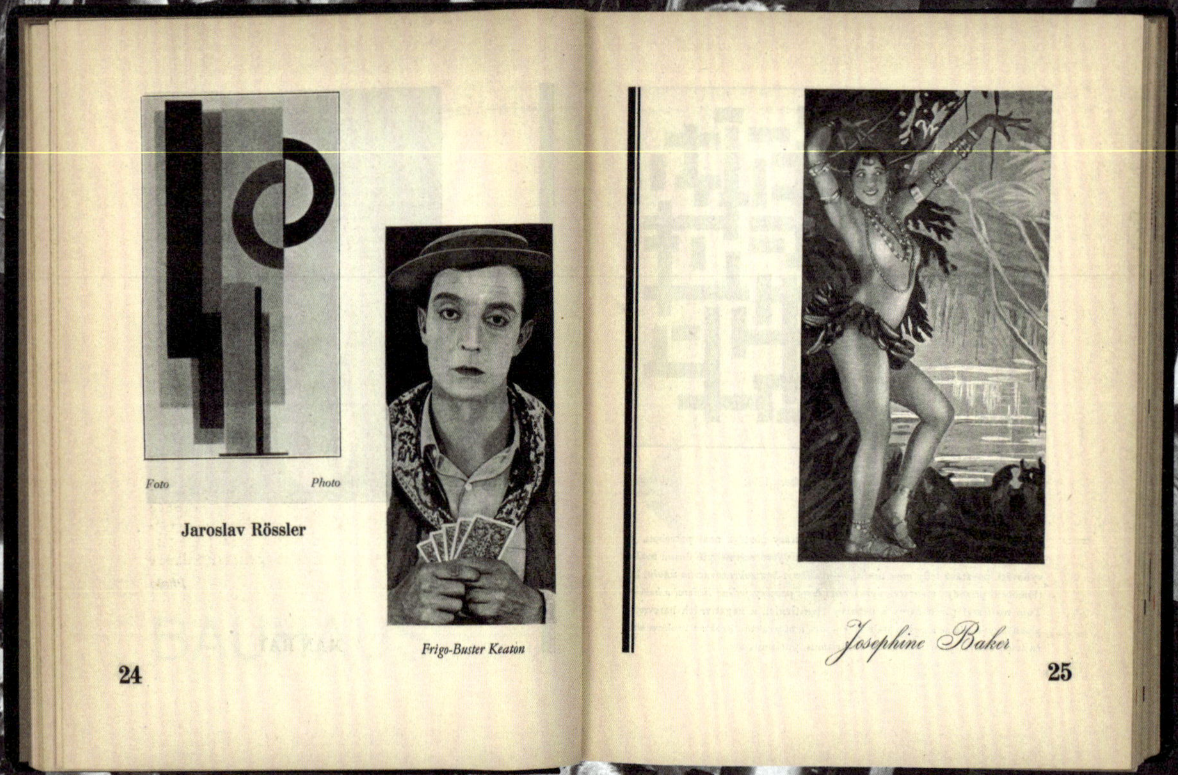

004 *ReD [Revue Devětsil]. Měsíčník pro moderní kulturu*, no. 1, October 1927, ed. Karel Teige, Prague, 24–25

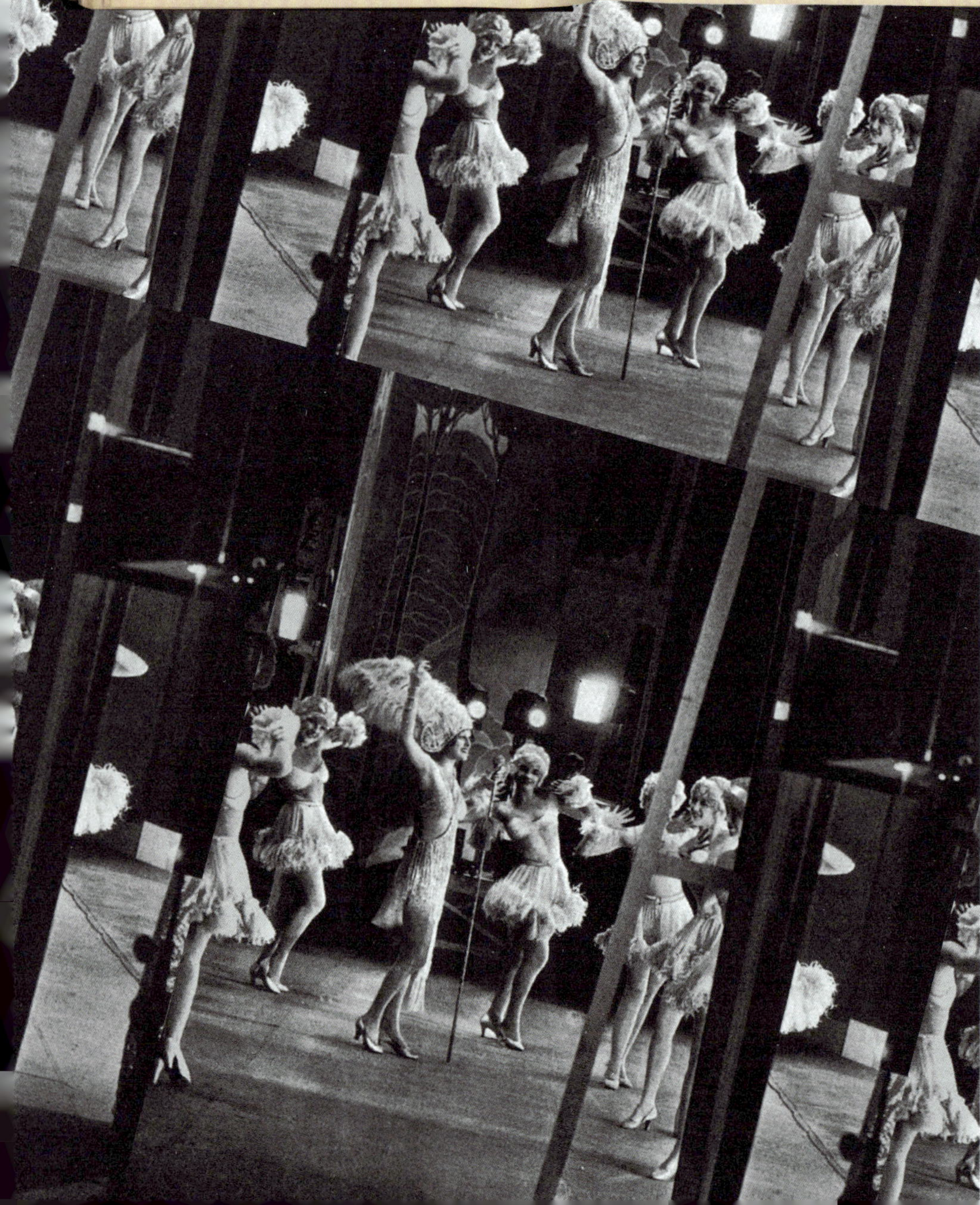

17 *Amerika: Traum und Depression, 1920–40*, ed. by Eckhart Gillen, Yvonne Leonard (Berlin: NGBK, 1980); *The Machine Age in America 1918–1941*, ed. Richard Guy Wilson, Dianne H. Pilgrim and Dickran Tashijian (New York: Abrams, 1986); *Envisioning America. Prints, Drawings and Photographs by George Grosz and His Contemporaries, 1915–1933*, ed. by Beeke Sell Tower (Cambridge, MA: Busch-Reisinger Museum, Harvard University, 1990); *The Société Anonyme: Modernism for America*, ed. Jennifer R. Gross (New Haven: Yale University Press, 2006).

18 "The Société Anonyme at 100," *Yale University Art Gallery Bulletin* [special issue] (2020–2021); Jed Rasula, "Jazzbandism," *Georgia Review* 60, no. 1 (Spring 2006): 61–124; Bojan Jovic, *Avangardni mit Čaplin* (Belgrade: Sluzbeni glasnik, 2018); David Gartman, *From Autos to Architecture. Fordism and Architectural Aesthetics in the Twentieth Century* (New York: Princeton Architectural Press, 2009); Owen Hatherley, *The Chaplin Machine. Slapstick, Fordism and the Communist Avant-Garde* (London: Pluto Press, 2016).

19 Walter Benjamin, "The Work of Art in the Age of its Technological Reproducibility," in Howard Eiland and Michael Jennings (eds.), *Walter Benjamin, Selected Writings*, vol. 4: 1938–1940 (Cambridge, MA: Harvard University Press, 2003), 264.

The exhibition project sheds new light on avant-garde historiography by connecting it directly to tight relations with American popular culture, the establishment of new institutions of modern art, artistic exchanges, and the new systems of work brought by Taylorism and Fordism. It draws on some similar projects undertaken from the 1980s onwards. In 1980, Eckhart Gillen und Yvonne Leonard prepared *Amerika: Traum und Depression, 1920–40* at the NGBK in West Berlin and edited a profound catalog on this subject. In 1986, Brooklyn Museum organized *The Machine Age in America 1918–1941* exploring the machine aesthetics of the wider interwar period, in which references to European avant-garde movements played a significant role. In 1990, LACMA in Los Angeles prepared *Envisioning America. Prints, Drawings and Photographs by George Grosz and His Contemporaries, 1915–1933,* which focused primarily on the connections between avant-garde artists active in Weimar Germany and the visions of America that fuelled imagination before 1933, and the mass exile of German intellectuals and artists to the US. More recently, in 2006, *The Société Anonyme: Modernism for America* at Yale University Art Gallery explored the impact and the reception of European "-isms" within America's first "experimental museum" for modern art.[17]

As well as the above-mentioned exhibitions and cat-a-logs, other books and articles by scholars have shaped the thinking underpinning the present project. Among these were books and publications on Société Anonyme, Chaplin, jazz, and the avant-gardes, as well as on Fordism and its impact on European experimental art of the 1920s.[18] In this way, *Modern Times* partly draws upon the previous research already present in the form of past exhibitions and publications. However, it also intends to outline a new approach towards avant-garde historiography within the context of the socio-political complexity of the Roaring Twenties.

This new perspective in this project focuses on incorporating diverse narratives into the subject framed around transatlantic encounters through the processes of institutionalization of European avant-gardes in the United States, by exploring how American popular culture affected European "isms", and by presenting the perceptions of new systems of work (Taylorism/Fordism) in the socio-political context of avant-garde practices. These topics are used to divide the exhibition and the catalog into three parts. First part investigates the transatlantic routes between Europe and the US as connections between avant-gardes, institutions, the art world, and modernist magazines. Second explores the impact of jazz music and dance, and Chaplin movies on the aesthetics of Dada, Futurism, Constructivism, and Purism. Third and last part presents the avant-garde fascination with capitalist modes developed by Taylorism–Fordism as well as the rejection of these concepts by the cultural leftist movements of the 1920s.

The *Modern Times* catalog comprises chapter introductions, short descriptions of selected objects and artworks, and examples of source texts that address exhibition's three central topics. It includes an introduction by the General Director ad interim of the SKD Marius Winzeler, the Director of ADA, Rudolf A. Fischer, and Przemysław Strożek, who conceived the project. Four scholarly texts were specially commissioned for this publication. The text by Przemysław Strożek explores the Machine Age aesthetics through the work of Louis Lozowick; Jed Rasula focuses on the recognition of American culture by European avant-gardes; Jennifer J. Wild analyses Fernand Léger's and Purist interest in Charlie Chaplin's figure; and Meghan Forbes reflects on labor movements in the United States, Mexico, and Czechoslovakia through modernist and avant-garde magazines. All these texts are framed around the transatlantic encounters that shaped the utopian and dystopian 1920s.

The emphasis of this catalog and exhibition is on the viral images, illustrated books and magazines that spread the image of America as a universal concept of modernisation in all spheres of life. These photographs and reports about Fifth Avenue in Manhattan, New York, with its famous fashion shops, as well as images of foxtrots, jazz, the Charleston, musicals, Hollywood, boxing champions, and of crowded and multicultural cities full of skyscrapers and automobiles, reached Europe primarily through the mass media of the time. In his influential essay *The Work of Art in the Age of Mechanical Reproduction* (1936), Walter Benjamin described the endless circulation of images disconnected from their source, which changed the approach of the masses towards art, stripping it of its initial museum context. He reflected on the film industry of the Roaring Twenties, stating that it is more accessible to the masses than, for example, traditional avant-garde Cubist paintings: "The technological reproducibility of the artwork changes the relation of the masses to art. The extremely backward attitude toward a Picasso painting changes into a highly progressive reaction to a Chaplin film."[19] This exhibition project intends to show that more traditional European avant-gardes such as Cubism were not, in fact, regressive in Benjamin's sense. They also recognized the importance of American popular culture and the power of mass media. A significant example is Fernand Léger's *Charlot Cubiste*, which linked the more progressive Cubist style (known as Purism) with modern cinematic culture and the endless reproduction of "viral" images (see pages: 150–153).

Modern Times show that 1920s art practices were shaped by the rhizomatic flow of ideas, reproducibility of viral images, and constitution of networks using transatlantic

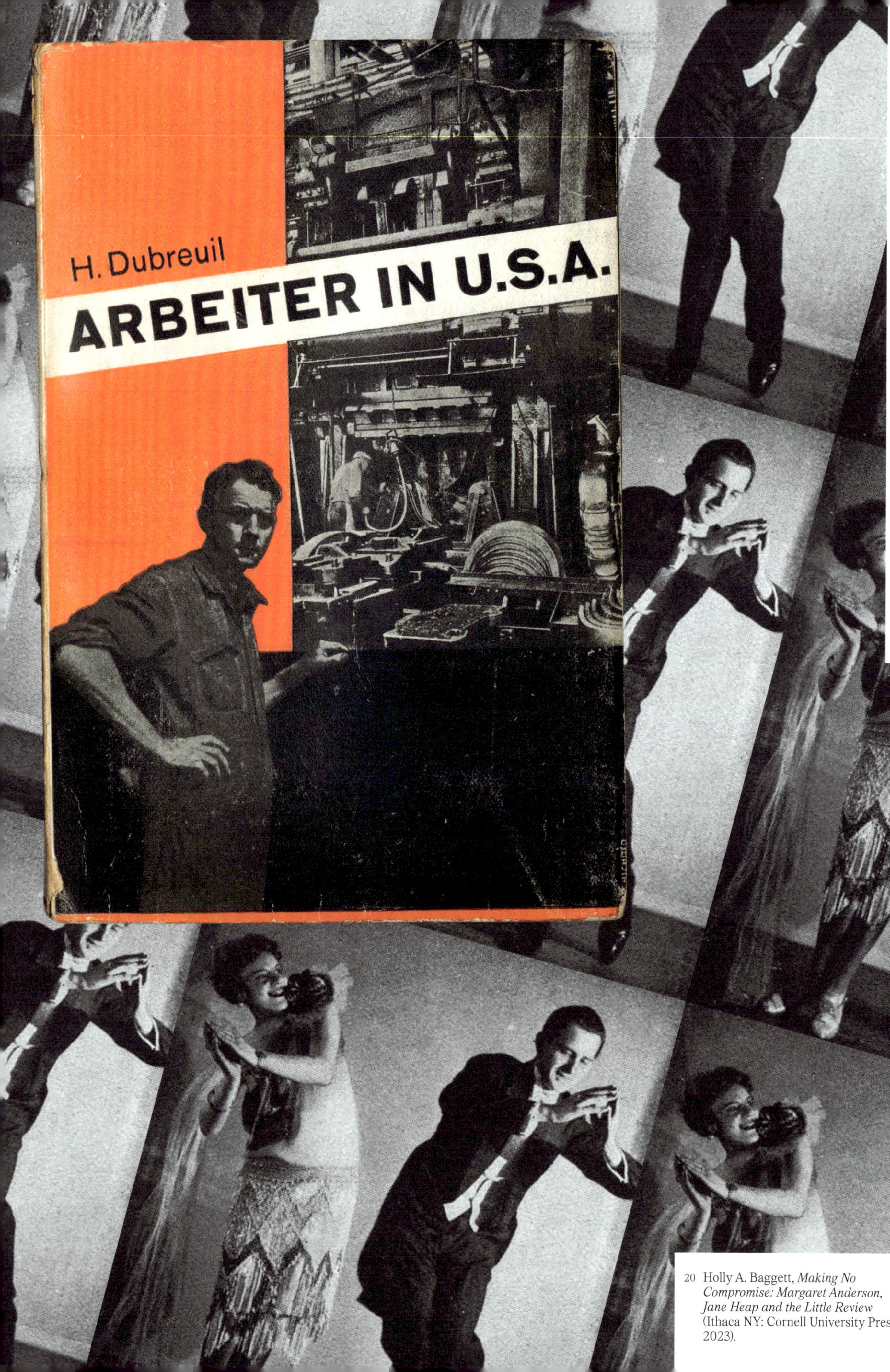

005 Hyacinthe Dubreuil, *Arbeiter in U.S.A.*, Leipzig: Bibliographisches Institut 1930 [French first edition 1929]

20 Holly A. Baggett, *Making No Compromise: Margaret Anderson, Jane Heap and the Little Review* (Ithaca NY: Cornell University Press, 2023).

routes between the Old Continent—Europe, and the New World—America. The focus on the extensive collections of Archiv der Avantgarden does not mean that the topic of transatlantic encounters is, or will ever be, exhausted. While the collection in Dresden holds extensive material on leftist books and magazines, such as those published by Malik Verlag and Neuer Deutscher Verlag, or the American *New Masses*, which addressed topics of racial and ethnical diversity, it holds a very limited collection of US-based Latin American, Asian American, and African American artists. There is, for example, a lack of material in ADA related to the Harlem Renaissance, an important cultural movement in 1920s Black America. Due to this awareness of the lack of books and works relating to that movement, it was important in the exhibition to mention Jean Toomer and Langston Hughes, both important African American poets, and to highlight Josephine Baker, who first performed in Harlem in around 1922 before coming to Paris in 1925. Regarding US-based Latin American artists, the covers which Rufino Tamayo designed for *New Masses* are also included in the show with the aim of highlighting the subject of the Mexican worker movement.

While at first sight, the exhibition and catalog might be critically viewed as showing only a few works produced by women artists, the project instead highlights the significance of the organizational work of two very influential women: Katherine S. Dreier and Jane Heap, whose exhibition concepts and publications were the major driving force behind the popularization of the European avant-gardes in America. The history of *The Little Review* magazine, which Heap co-edited with her lover and companion Margaret Anderson, was the focus of a full book-length monograph as recently as 2023, *Making No Compromise: Margaret Anderson, Jane Heap and the Little Review* by Holly A. Baggett.[20] This work is further evidence on the important actors behind the historical avant-gardes, who were often overlooked. Now is the ideal time to rediscover their work and bring it into wider focus.

The selected materials from ADA framed around transatlantic encounters show how many stories can be derived from the source materials stored in the Archiv der Avantgarden collection. These encounters reveal new perspectives on avant-garde historiography as a transcontinental phenomenon, and explore the complex connections between literary and artistic visions and the mass media, and between literary and artistic phantasies and the fact checks and actual events narrated in the illustrated press. *Modern Times* intends to show how the media shapes our understanding of the world, depicts geopolitical tensions, spreads propaganda, reproduce viral images, objectifies and subjectifies the news, and creates fake news. The works by avant-garde artists embedded in such a socio-political reality were, in fact, impacted by the creations of simulacra of "America" and the information mediated through the illustrated mass media of the 1920s. Framed in that way, they had already anticipated the divisions between American capitalism and its criticism by leftist and communist movements. These divisions found a fertile ground in Europe, where the geopolitical impact of, and tensions between, American capitalism, Italian fascism, Stalinism, and National Socialism in Germany would go on to shape and define the decades to come, with the Second World War and the Cold War, with their influence apparent right up to the present day.

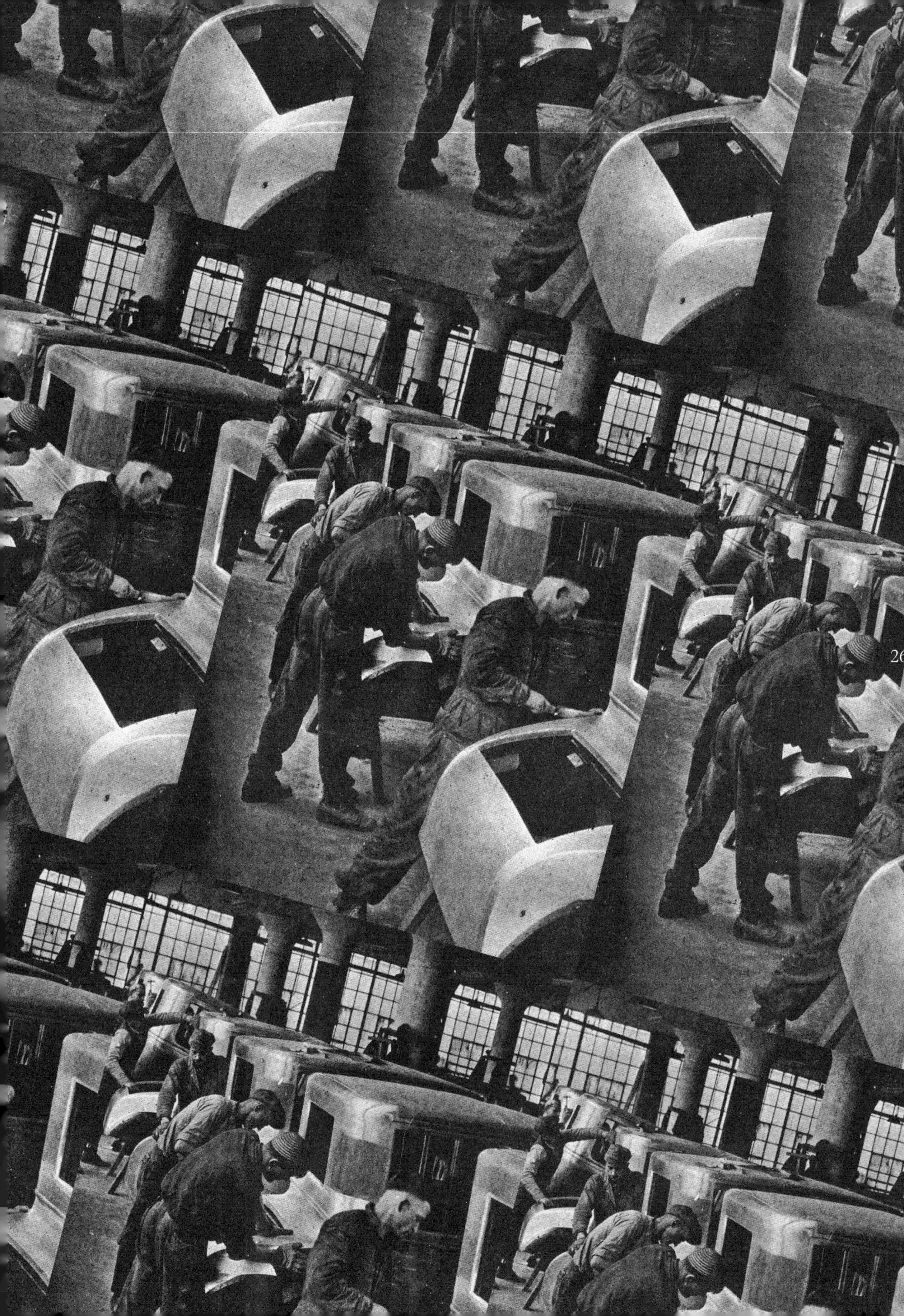

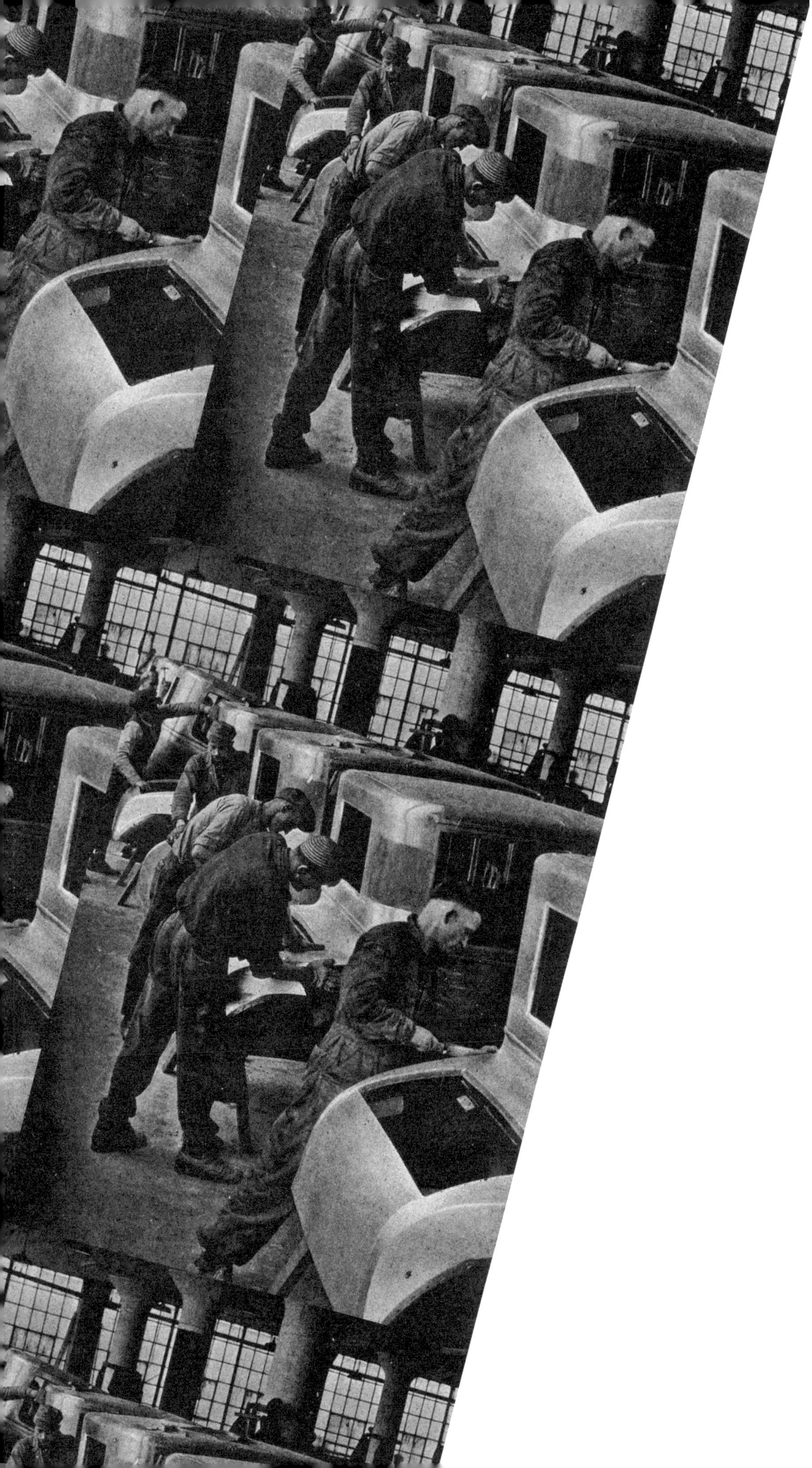

Transatlantic Encounters: Journeys, Magazines and Exhibition Projects

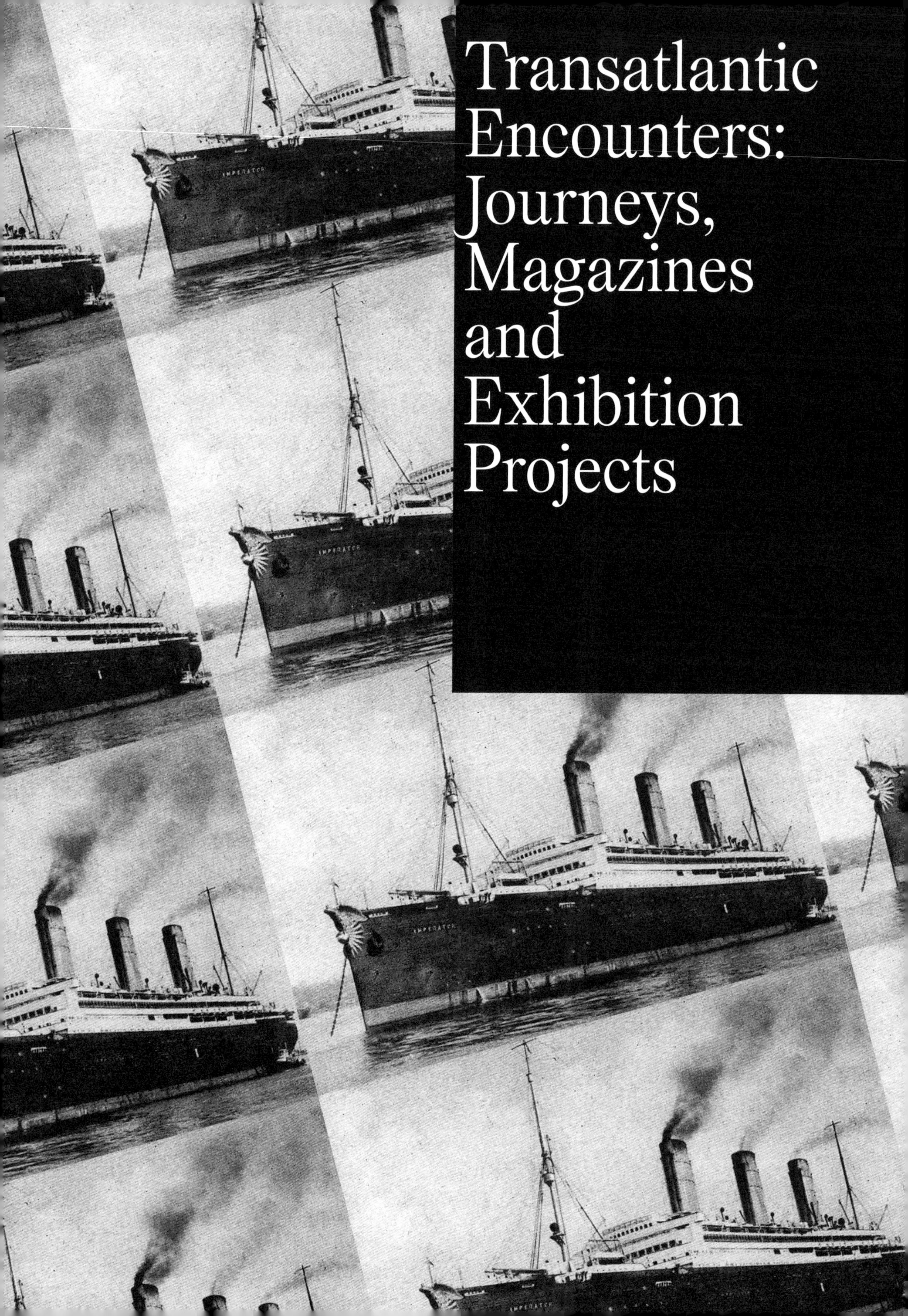

In the 1920s, European avant-garde movements reached America primarily through special exhibition projects, and a specialized network of cultural and modernist magazines, such as *Broom*, *The Little Review* and *transition*, which circulated across the Atlantic, disseminating information about the newest "-isms". The other means of dissemination were cross-continental journeys and migrations. American artists and collectors travelled to Europe after the First World War to make contact with avant-garde artists, or invited them to work for a more extended period in the US and supported their art in an American environment. Although America was also attractive to European avant-garde artists, not many decided to migrate there in the 1920s. A huge wave of European avant-garde artists migrated to the US eventually, but this was mainly in the 1930s and 1940s. By the time they arrived, the European avant-garde would already be popularized, institutionalized, and canonized thanks to the efforts of two institutions: Société Anonyme, led by Katherine S. Dreier from 1920, and the Museum of Modern Art, established in 1929 and directed by Alfred H. Barr.

"Ever since 1908 there appeared throughout Europe a new approach towards Art, referred to in this country by the rather vague term of "Modern Art" in England as "The Vortex Movement", in Italy as "The Futurist", in Germany as "Expressionismus" and in France as "Cubism". Except for a small group who had gathered around Mr. Alfred Stieglitz and his Gallery, 291 Fifth Avenue, these movements were practically unknown in this country until 1913"—wrote Katherine S. Dreier in the booklet *Its Why & Its Wherefore* published by Société Anonyme in 1923. She directed attention to the famous 1913 Armory Show in New York and exhibitions at the 291 Gallery (active between 1905 and 1917) as the major shows that had introduced European avant-garde currents to the US.

The 1910s movements of Expressionism, Cubism, and Futurism, as well as the first signs of Dada, were primarily promoted in New York by men such as Alfred Stieglitz, Marius de Zayas, and Walter C. Arensberg. But in the 1920s, the most significant promoters of the newest avant-garde tendencies, such as Constructivism and Purism, were two women: Katherine S. Dreier and Jane Heap. While Dreier's Société Anonyme remained interested in the painterly experiments of the 1910s Cubists and Expressionists, Heap's Little Review Gallery, *The Little Review* magazine, and the exhibitions she organized promoted those avant-garde movements that were connected with the aesthetics of the American Machine Age. In her exhibition projects and articles popularizing the avant-garde, she mainly focused on issues relating to industrialization and modern machinery beyond painting or sculpture, and explored the potential of mechanical art in theatre, stage design, and architecture.

Both Dreier and Heap were interested in presenting an entire range of European avant-garde art both from the West and from Central and Eastern European countries. Their activities peaked in 1926–1927 when Dreier and Heap organized very important large-scale exhibitions in New York. Dreier and her Société Anonyme prepared *The International Exhibition of Modern Art* at the Brooklyn Museum of Art, while Heap and her Little Review opened the *International Theatre Exposition* and *Machine-Age Exposition* at the Steinway Hall. Many artists, including members of avant-garde movements such as Futurism, Cubism, Purism, Dada, and Constructivism, and some American artists like Louis Lozowick, exhibited with both art institutions. However, there was no direct sign of Dreier and Heap joining forces, and the institutions they created remained separate in their parallel aims of collecting, exhibiting, and popularizing the European avant-garde.

Beyond the practices of exhibition-making, Dreier and Heap recognized the importance of producing publications to promote their efforts. And, while Société Anonyme published mainly catalogs, booklets, and brochures related to specific artists, movements, and exhibition topics, Heap co-edited *The Little Review* magazine together with Margaret Anderson and recognized its networking power. *The Little Review* had contacts with key players in the European scene, including, for example, London-based magazine *Egoist* edited by Ezra Pound.

Dreier's and Heap's initial mission, which was to popularize European avant-gardes in the 1920s through collecting and various exhibition projects, was taken over by the Museum of Modern Art, directed by Adolf H. Barr, from 1929. MoMA had sufficient operational funds and could afford a stable exhibition place, which was not the case with Société Anonyme or the exhibitions organized by The Little Review Gallery. MoMA opened its doors to the public on November 7, 1929, during the initial phase of the Great Depression. In the following decades it helped to define the nature of the modern art movement and to give it respectability, canonizing the European avant-garde movements.

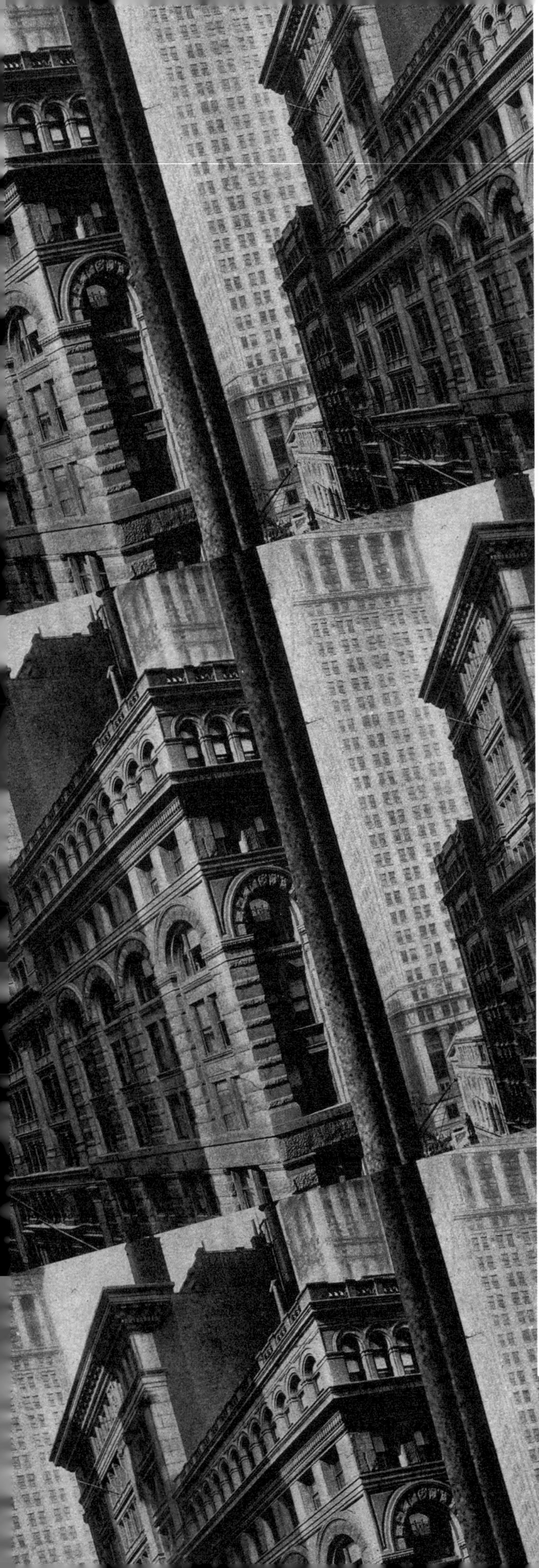

TRANSATLANTIC JOURNEYS AND MIGRATIONS IN THE 1920s

Between 1900 and 1929, the number of immigrants who arrived in the USA was estimated at just under 40 million, most of whom arrived on ocean liners across the Atlantic from Europe. Among the immigrants who came at the turn of the 20th century were Max Weber (1891), Louis Lozowick (1906), and Morris Kantor (1906) from what was then the Russian Empire, Joseph Stella (1896) from Italy, and Jan Matulka (1907) from the Habsburg Empire (later Czechoslovakia). They all arrived in the US as teenagers and were educated in the United States. In the coming years, most notably the 1910s–1920s, they played an important role in the development of modernist American painting. They were all inspired by European avant-garde movements, and were influenced either by Cubism, Futurism, or Constructivism.

Among those who migrated after the First World War in the 1920s and arrived in New York were only a few European avant-garde artists who had already established their careers. Among them was a Russian/Ukrainian Cubist sculptor, Alexander Archipenko (arrived in 1923), a Russian/Ukrainian Futurist painter, David Burluk (arrived in 1922), an Armenian avant-garde designer, Constantin Alajálov (arrived in 1923), an experimental designer and architect, Frederick Kiesler (arrived in 1926), and a modernist architect, Richard Neutra (arrived in 1923), the latter both from Austria. They remained in the US for the rest of their lives, and all of them had become American citizens by 1930. Still in the 1920s, Archipenko, Burluk and Alajálov would exhibit in New York with Société Anonyme. Kiesler, in turn, would collaborate with Jane Heap and The Little Review, organizing experimental shows in New York.

As the above examples show, only a few avant-garde artists migrated from Europe to the US in the 1920s. However, others also travelled to experience America first-hand, then soon after returned to their home countries. Among them were poets, musicians, painters, architects, and filmmakers, including Vladimir Mayakovsky from Georgia/Russia, Darius Milhaud from France, Nanni Leone Castelli and Fortunato Depero from Italy, and Erich Mendelsohn and Fritz Lang from Germany. The latter two decided to migrate to the US after the National Socialists came to power in Germany in 1933. Among German nationals, who visited the US in the 1920s, was also Otto Haeckel, who produced many photographs for the German press.

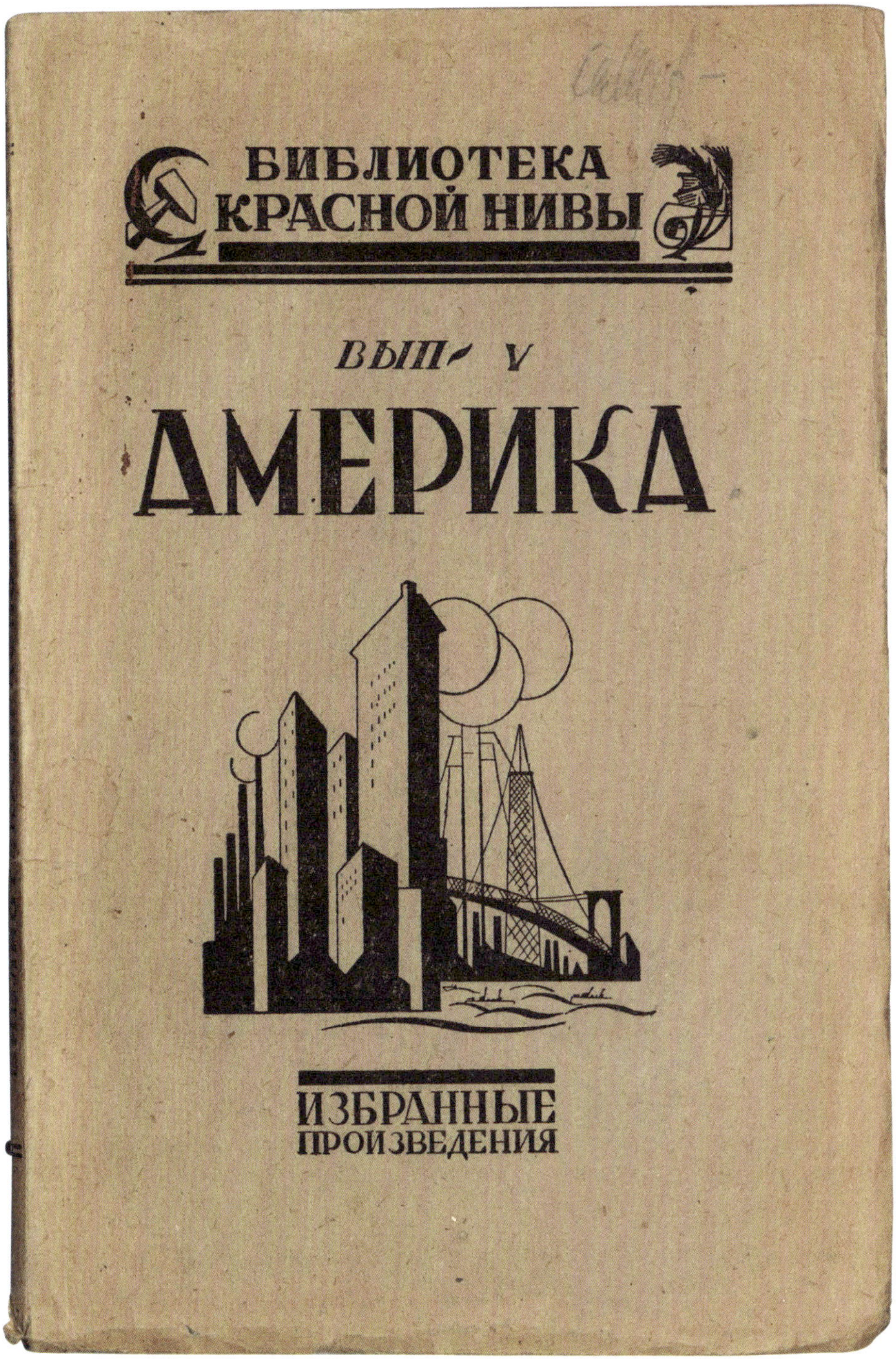

006 Америка [*America*], ed. R. A. Rosenthal, Moscow: Biblioteka Krasnoj Nivy 1924

RUSSIAN FUTURISTS IN NEW YORK David Burluk, who was a member of Futurist group in Russia, arrived in New York in 1922. But had lived for too short a time in America to be able to invite Mayakovsky in. Instead he asked one of his friends to send an invitation. On July 1925 Mayakovsky crossed the border into the United States from Mexico, and three days later he was in New York. The first person he contacted was Burluk. He helped to organize several of his readings and provided the illustrations for two of his poems, which were published as separate books during his stay in the US. Mayakovsky's poems on his experiences with America, including *Brooklyn Bridge* and *Broadway,* restrain his childlike enthusiasm for America's technological marvels. The trip to the US made a great impression on him, and after his return to the Soviet Union he gave many lectures about his encounter with the US.

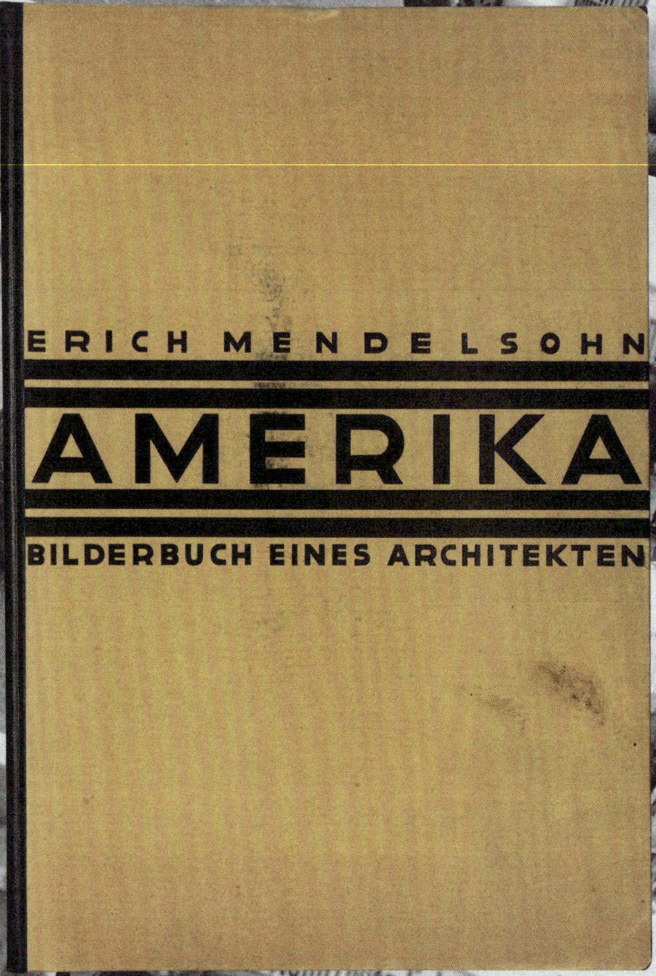

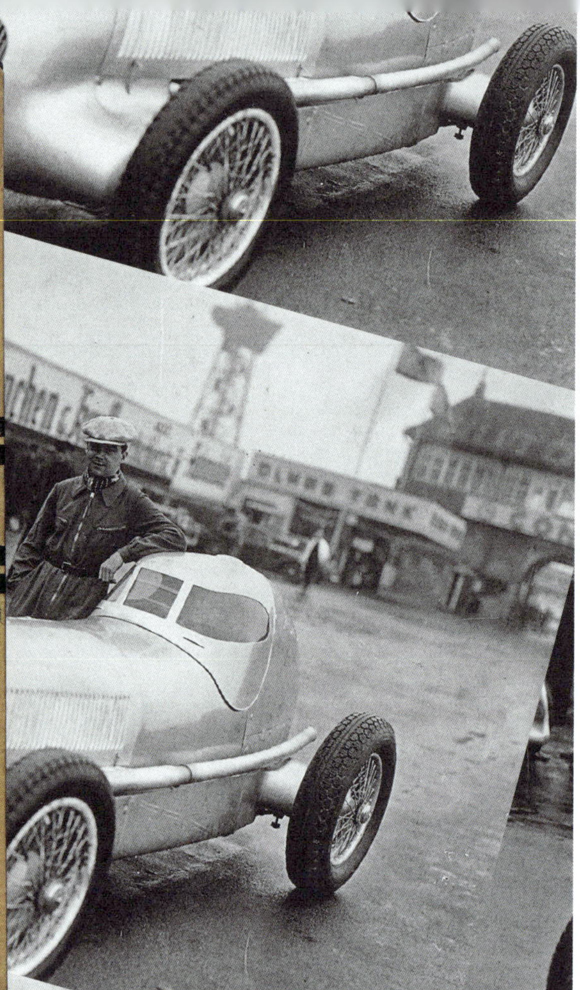

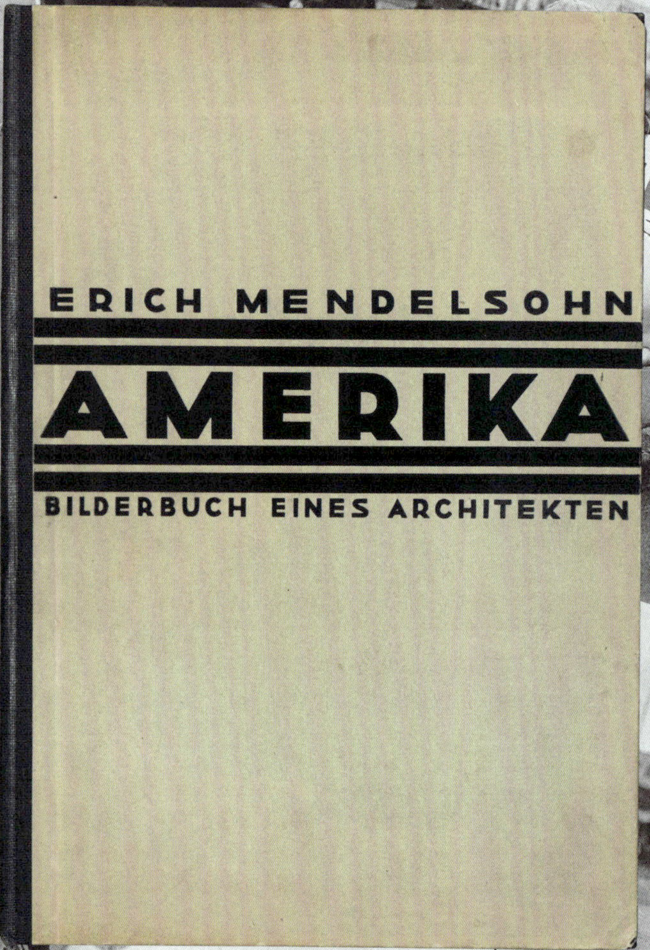

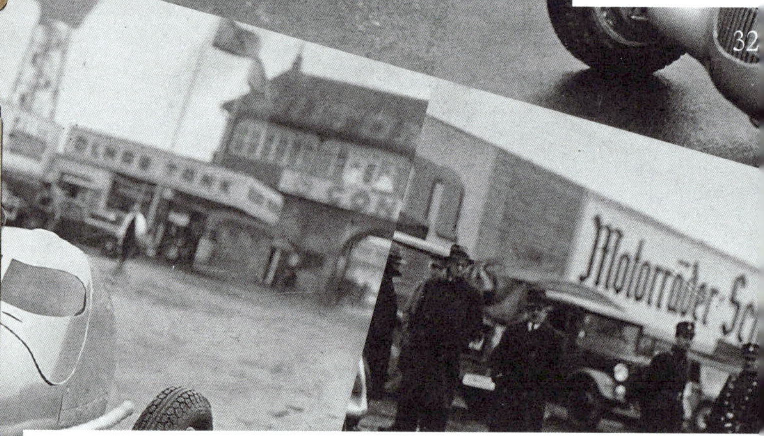

007 Erich Mendelsohn, *Amerika. Bilderbuch eines Architekten*, Berlin: Rudolf Mosse Buchverlag 1926 [3rd edition, first edition 1926], cover by Erich Mendelsohn

008 Erich Mendelsohn, *Amerika. Bilderbuch eines Architekten*, Berlin: Rudolf Mosse Buchverlag 1928 [6th modified edition, first edition 1926], cover presumably by Erich Mendelsohn

009 see 007, 44–45, photo by Erich Mendelsohn

010 see 008, 130–131, photo by Fritz Lang

PHOTOBOOKS ON AMERICA A German architect, Erich Mendelsohn, arrived in the US in October 1924, travelling with the filmmaker Fritz Lang. The photobook *Amerika* documented Mendelsohn's time in New York City, Buffalo, Detroit, Ann Arbor, and Chicago. In the first edition, he included 77 images, among them a photograph of lighted signs on Broadway reportedly taken by Fritz Lang, whose 1924 visit to Manhattan inspired his groundbreaking movie *Metropolis* (prem. 1927). Mendelsohn's book was a bestseller in Germany. In the following two years, five new editions appeared. One of the architects who, in 1926, witnessed the impact that Erich Mendelsohn's *Amerika* had had in Europe was Richard Neutra. He was an Austrian-born architect and designer who arrived in New York in 1923, and in 1930, he published a similar photobook in Vienna. His *Amerika*, which was the second part of a series of three books called *Neues Bauen in der Welt*, focused on new buildings in the United States. The photographs were taken by world-renowned photographers including Edward Weston, and the photomontage on the cover was created by El Lissitzky.

↓009 ↑007

NEW YORK
BROADWAY BEI NACHT

Unheimlich. Die Konturen der Häuser sind ausgewischt. Aber im Bewußtsein steigen sie noch, laufen einander nach, überrennen sich.
Das ist die Folie für die Flammenschriften, das Raketenfeuer der beweglichen Lichtreklame, auf- und untertauchend, verschwindend und ausbrechend über den Tausenden von Autos und dem Lustwirbel der Menschen.
Noch ungeordnet, weil übersteigert, aber doch schon voll von phantastischer Schönheit, die einmal vollendet sein wird.

44

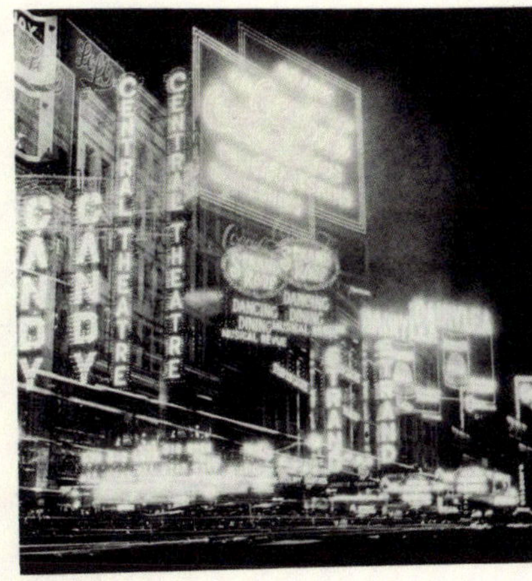

NEW YORK
BROADWAY BEI NACHT

Unheimlich. Die Konturen der Häuser sind ausgewischt. Aber im Bewußtsein steigen sie noch, laufen einander nach, überrennen sich.
Das ist die Folie für die Flammenschriften, das Raketenfeuer der beweglichen Lichtreklame, auf- und untertauchend, verschwindend und ausbrechend über den Tausenden von Autos und dem Lustwirbel der Menschen.
Noch ungeordnet, weil übersteigert, aber doch schon voll von phantastischer Schönheit, die einmal vollendet sein wird.

150

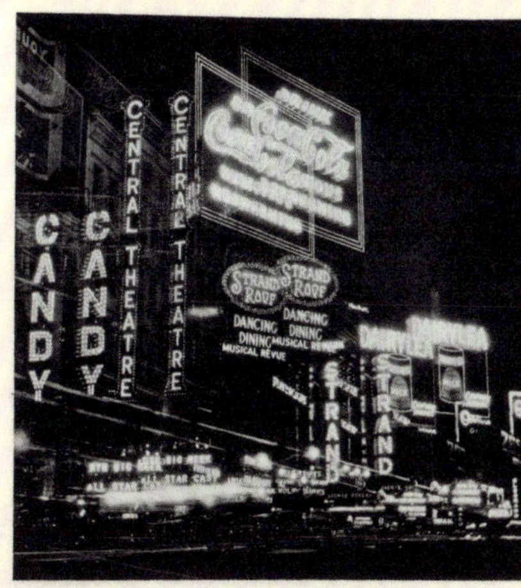

↓010 ↑008

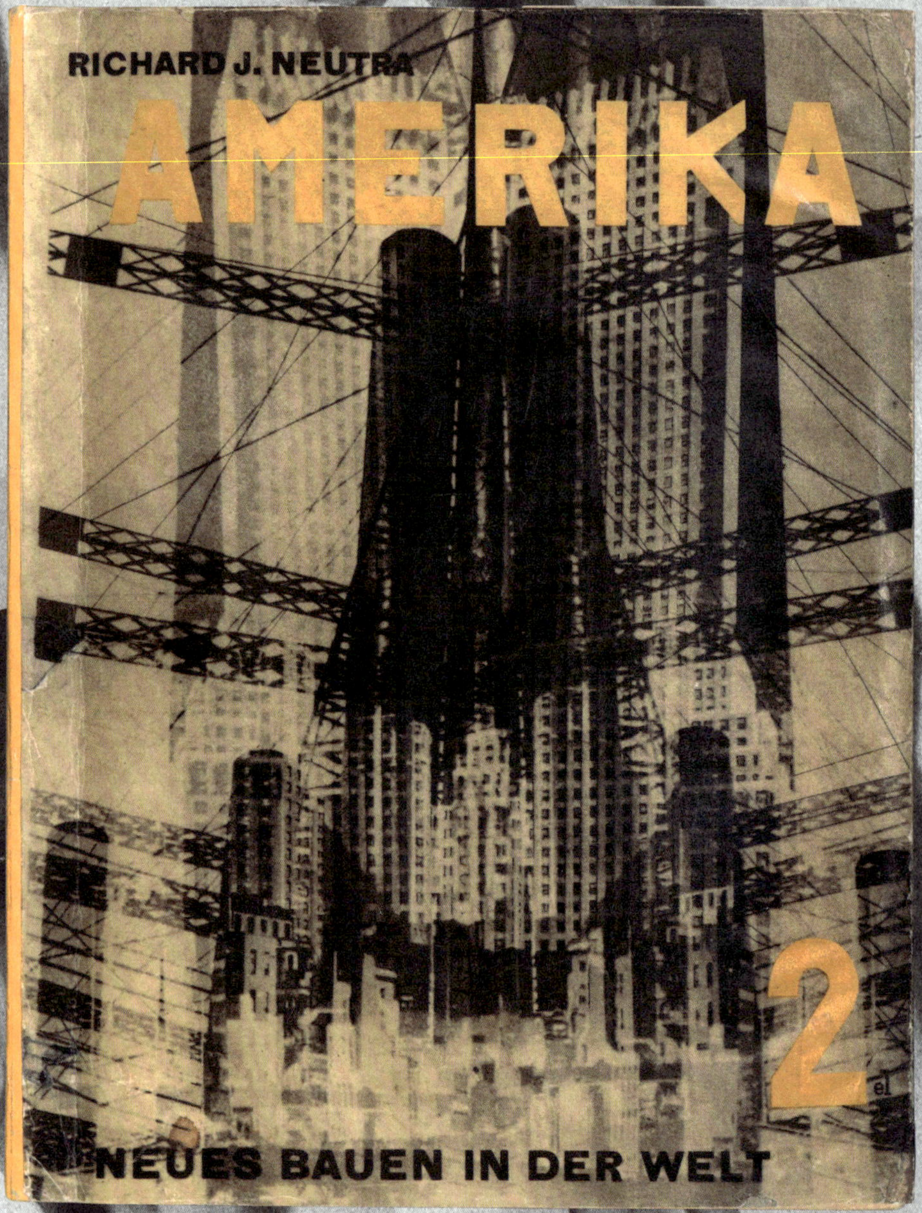

011 Richard J. Neutra, *Amerika. Die Stilbildung des neuen Bauens in den Vereinigten Staaten* [*Neues Bauen in der Welt. Band 2*], Vienna: Verlag Anton Schroll & Co 1930, cover by El Lissitzky

012 Otto Haeckel, *West 42te Strasse vom Broadway aus gesehen*, ca. 1924

013 Otto Haeckel, *Die Front eines der vielen Theater, hell erleuchtet*, ca. 1924

↓012 ↑011

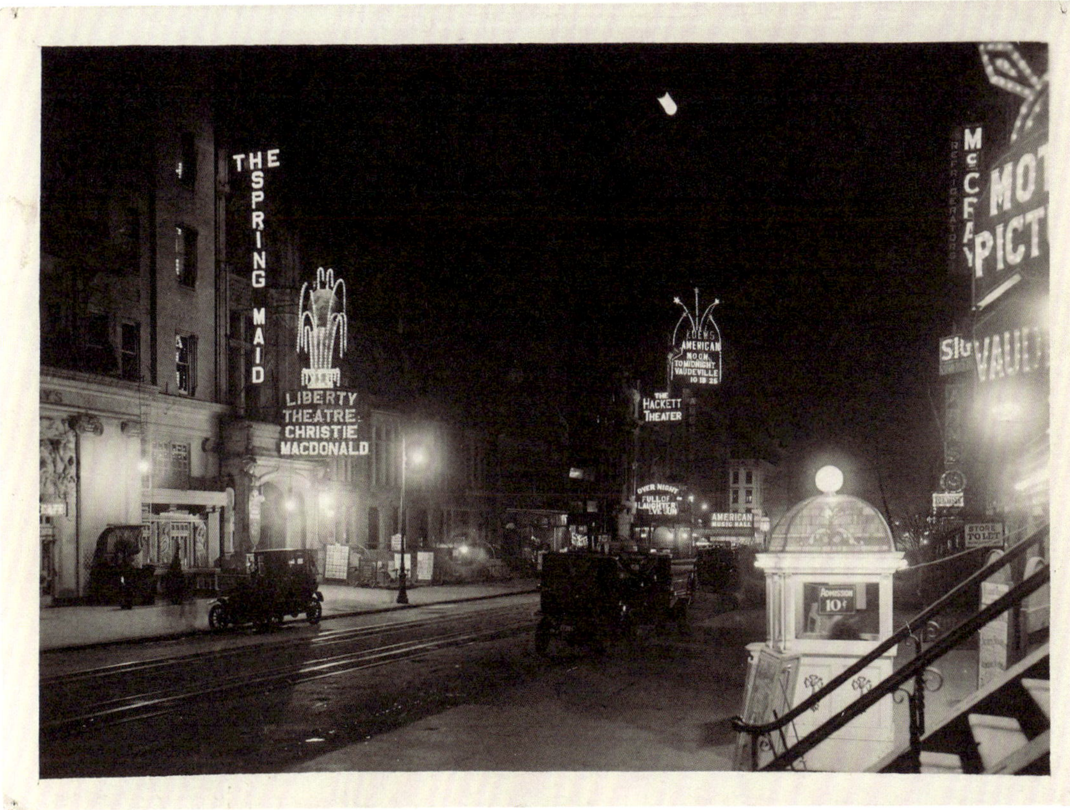
THE SPRING MAID
LIBERTY THEATRE CHRISTIE MACDONALD
THE HACKETT THEATER
AMERICAN
VAUDEVILLE
ADMISSION 10¢
STORE TO LET
MOT PICT
VAUD

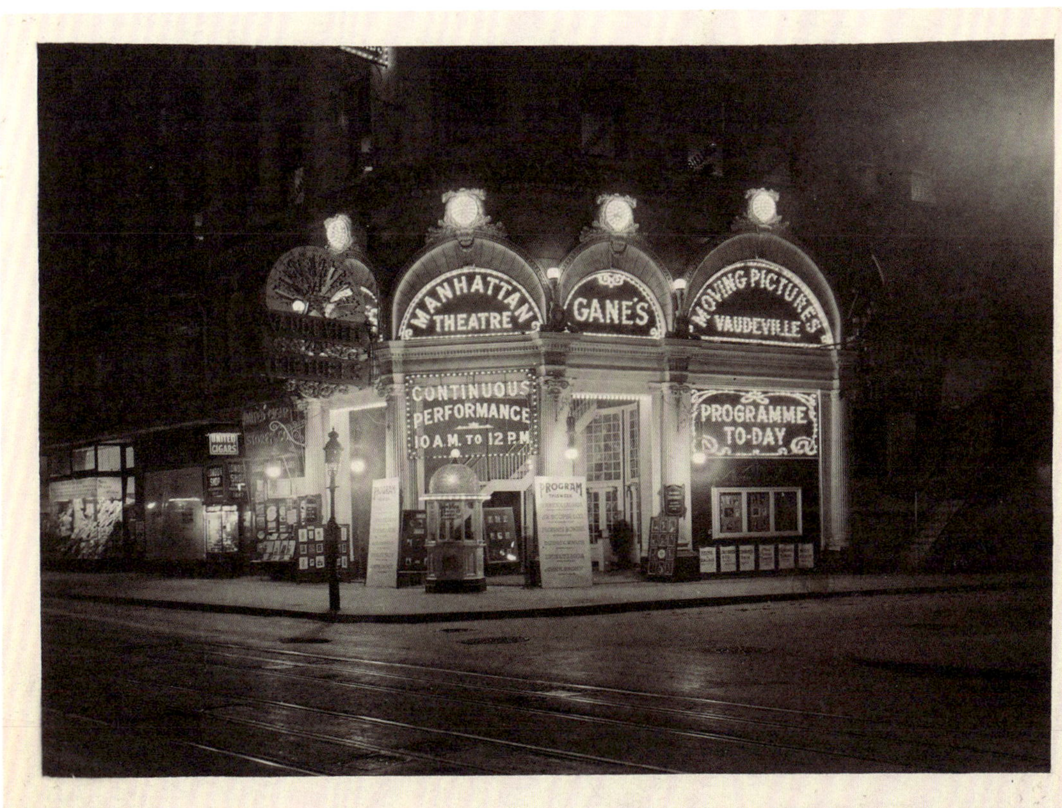
MANHATTAN THEATRE
GANE'S
MOVING PICTURES VAUDEVILLE
CONTINUOUS PERFORMANCE 10 A.M. TO 12 P.M.
PROGRAMME TO-DAY
PROGRAM
UNITED CIGARS

↓013

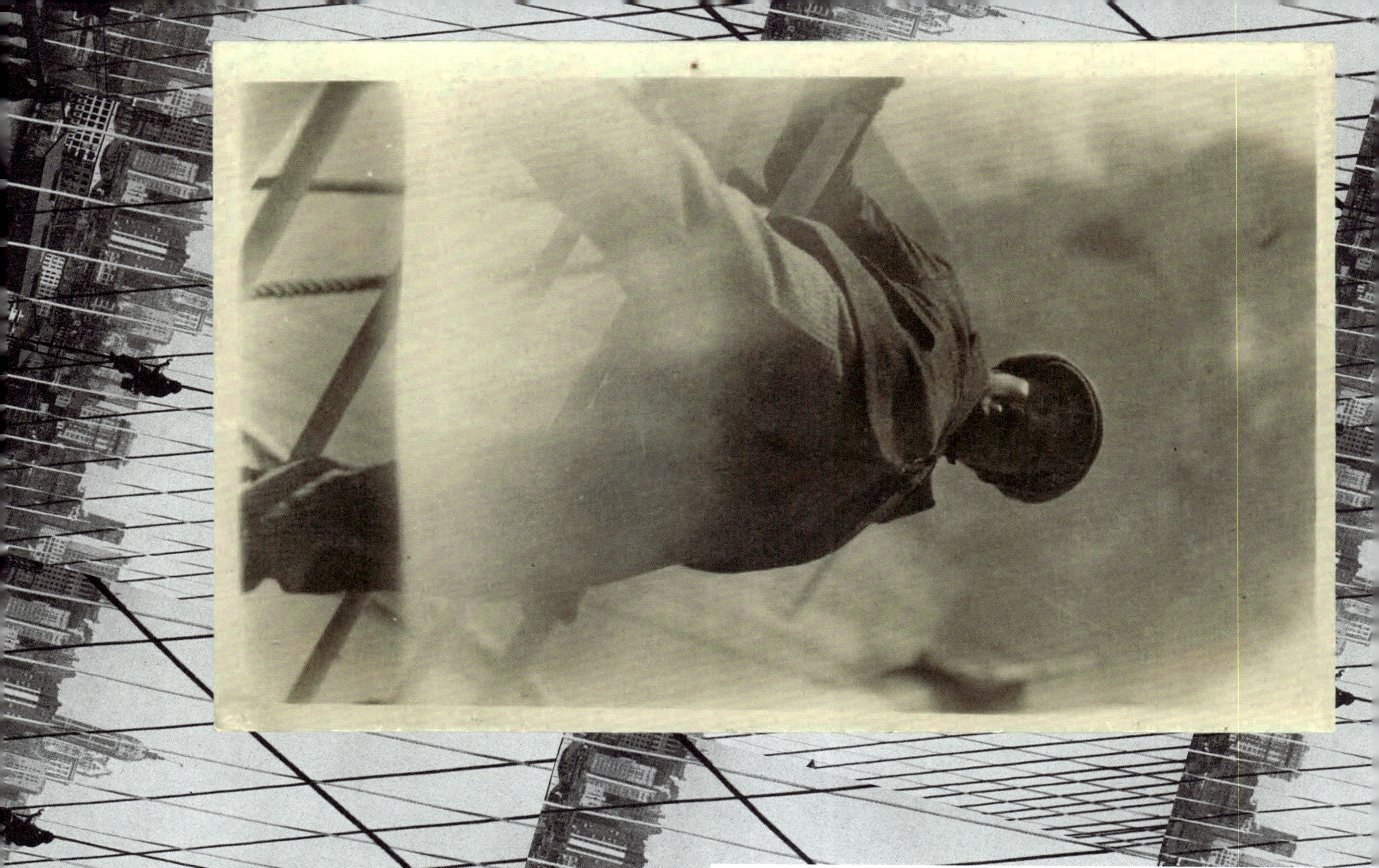

014 [Postcard] Fortunato Depero on the transatlantic ship Augustus, ca. 1928, photo presumably by Rosetta Depero
015 [Leaflet] *New-York. Film vissuto. Primo libro parolibero sonoro. Fortunato Depero 1931*, Rovereto 1931, photomontage by Mario Castagneri

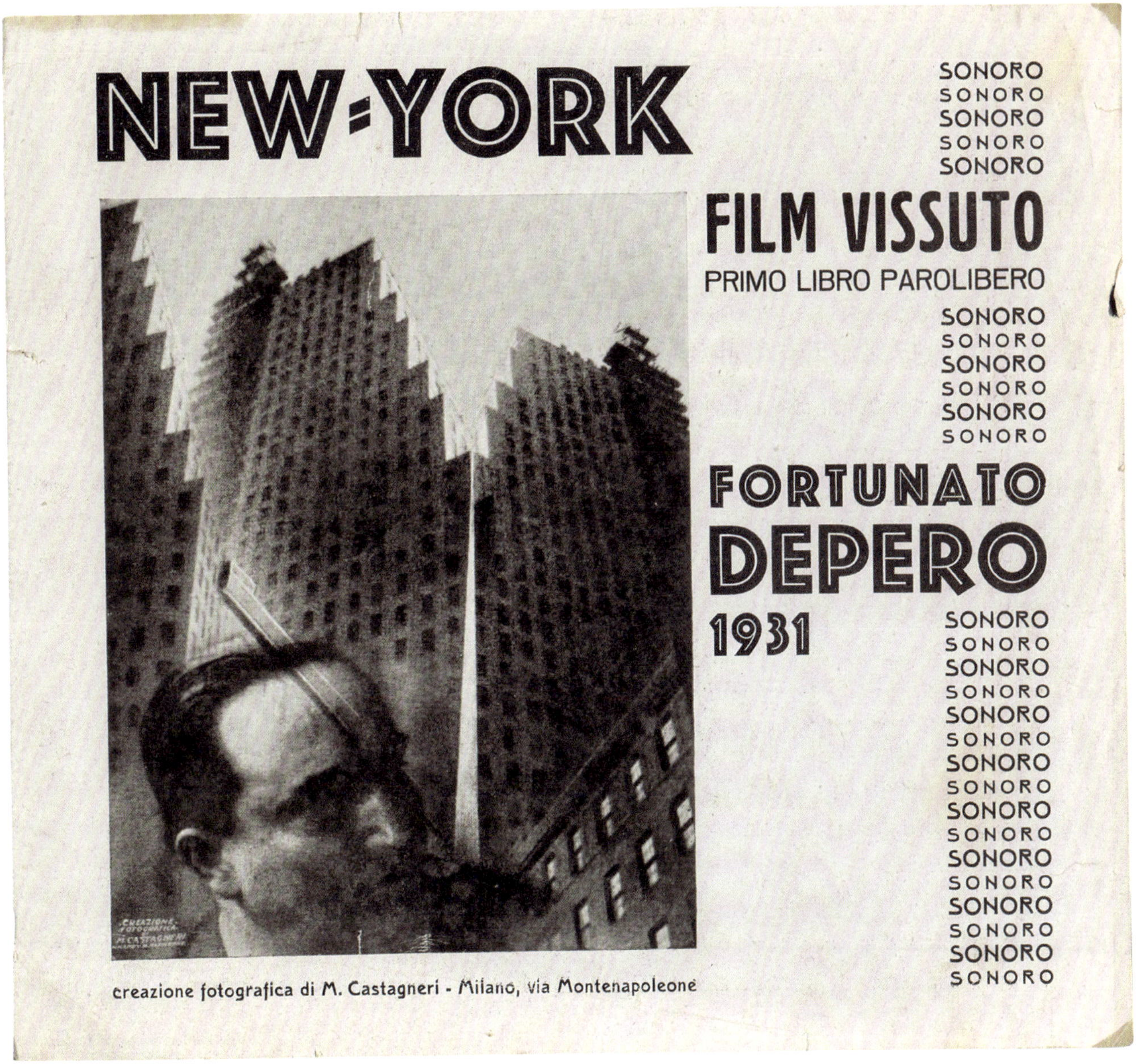

FORTUNATO DEPERO AND FUTURIST NEW YORK After enormous success at the Parisian World's Fair in 1925, Fortunato Depero decided to pursue a career in America. He travelled from Italy on the transatlantic liner Augustus and arrived in New York on October 13, 1928, with his wife Rosetta. He opened his Futurist House in the New Transit Hotel on 23rd Street to produce commercial paintings, sculptures, wall panels, posters, interior, graphics, and stage design. He organized some exhibitions, but soon encountered financial problems. The financial crisis of October 1929, which marked the beginning of the Great Depression, forced Depero to return to Italy the following year, in October 1930. A year after that, he prepared a book about his American experiences entitled *New York—Film Visutto* (New York—A Lived Film) accompanied by recordings of his voice, but it was never published. One of the chapters of this unpublished book focused on the work of Katherine S. Dreier and referred to the founder of Société Anonyme. She also praised Depero's oeuvre and reproduced some of his works in her *Brochure Quarterly* magazine (no. 2, 1928).

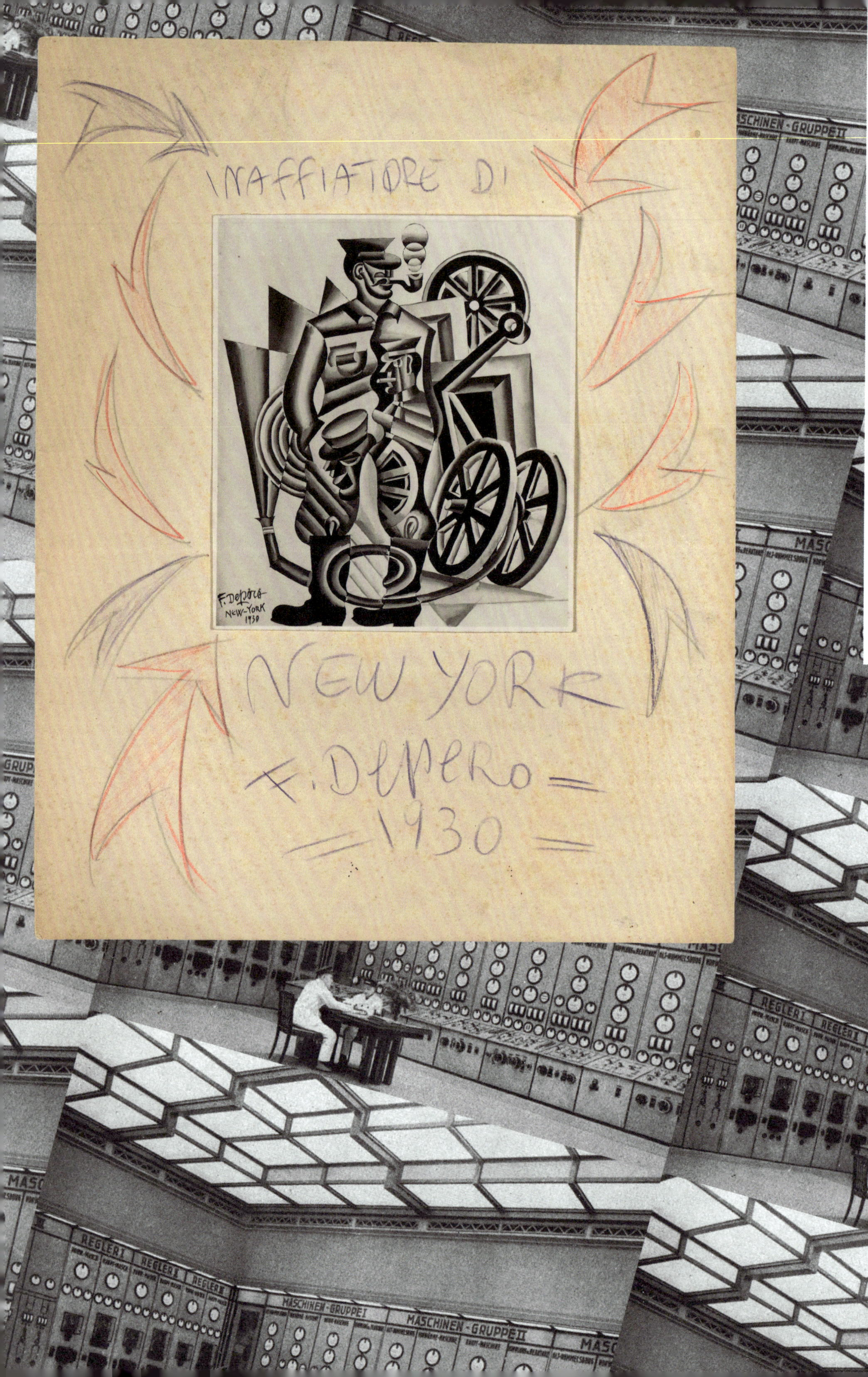

016 Fortunato Depero, *Inaffiatore* [delle strade] *di New York*, 1930
017 [Postcard] *Prenotazione libraria. New York film vissuto. Primo libro parolibero sonoro*, ca. 1931, front and back, photomontage by Mario Castagneri

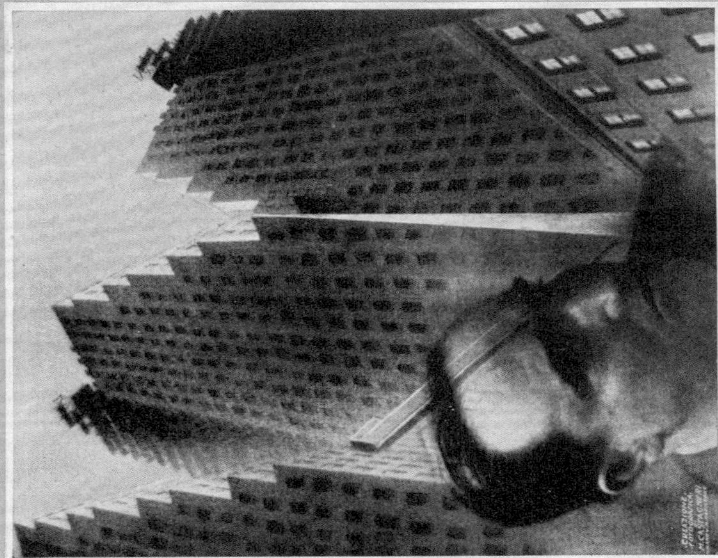

Creazione Fotografica M. CASTAGNERI - Milano - Montenapoleone

1000 copie numerate , firma e dedica dell'autore

al signor
cav. uff. FORTUNATO
DEPERO

ROVERETO
VIA 2 NOVEMBRE, 14
Trentino Italia

prenotazione libraria

li 1931

egregio signore,
appena pronto, pregovi spedirmi
contro assegno, copie n.° ....
del vostro annunciato volume:

NEW-YORK sonoro sonoro sonoro
film vissuto sonoro sonoro sonoro

primo libro parolibero
illustrazione dinamica
DUE DISCHI fuori testo
(incisi dall'autore)

al prezzo di lire it. 100
incl. spese post.

ringraziandovi

cognome :
nome :
indirizzo esatto :

uscirà improrogabilmente entro il 1931

NEW-YORK
film vissuto

primo libro parolibero sonoro sonoro sonoro

del pittore-poeta
DEPERO

due dischi fuori testo
(incisi dall'autore)

Lire ital.
100

ROVERETO
Via 2 Novembre, 14
Trentino Italia

A1/Fut.8, Nr.34

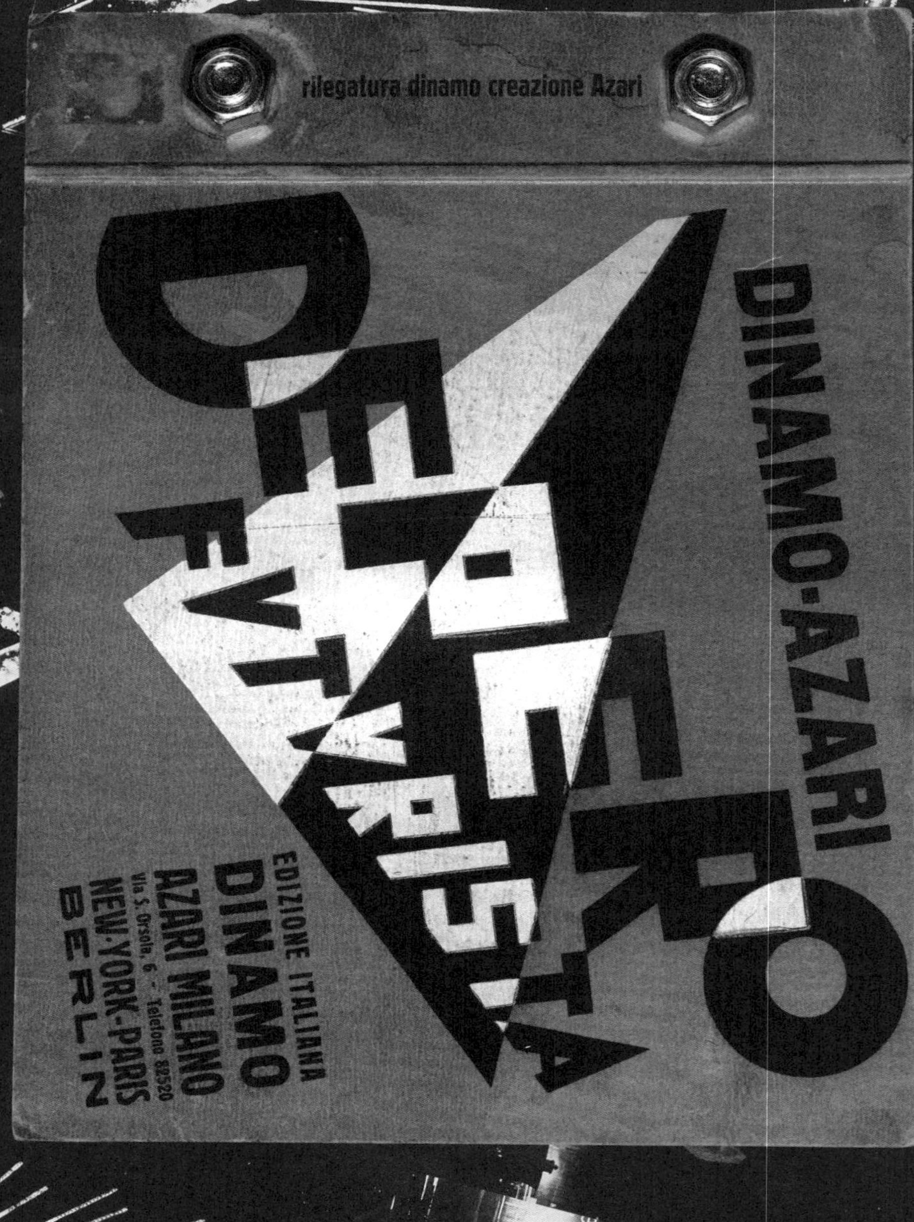

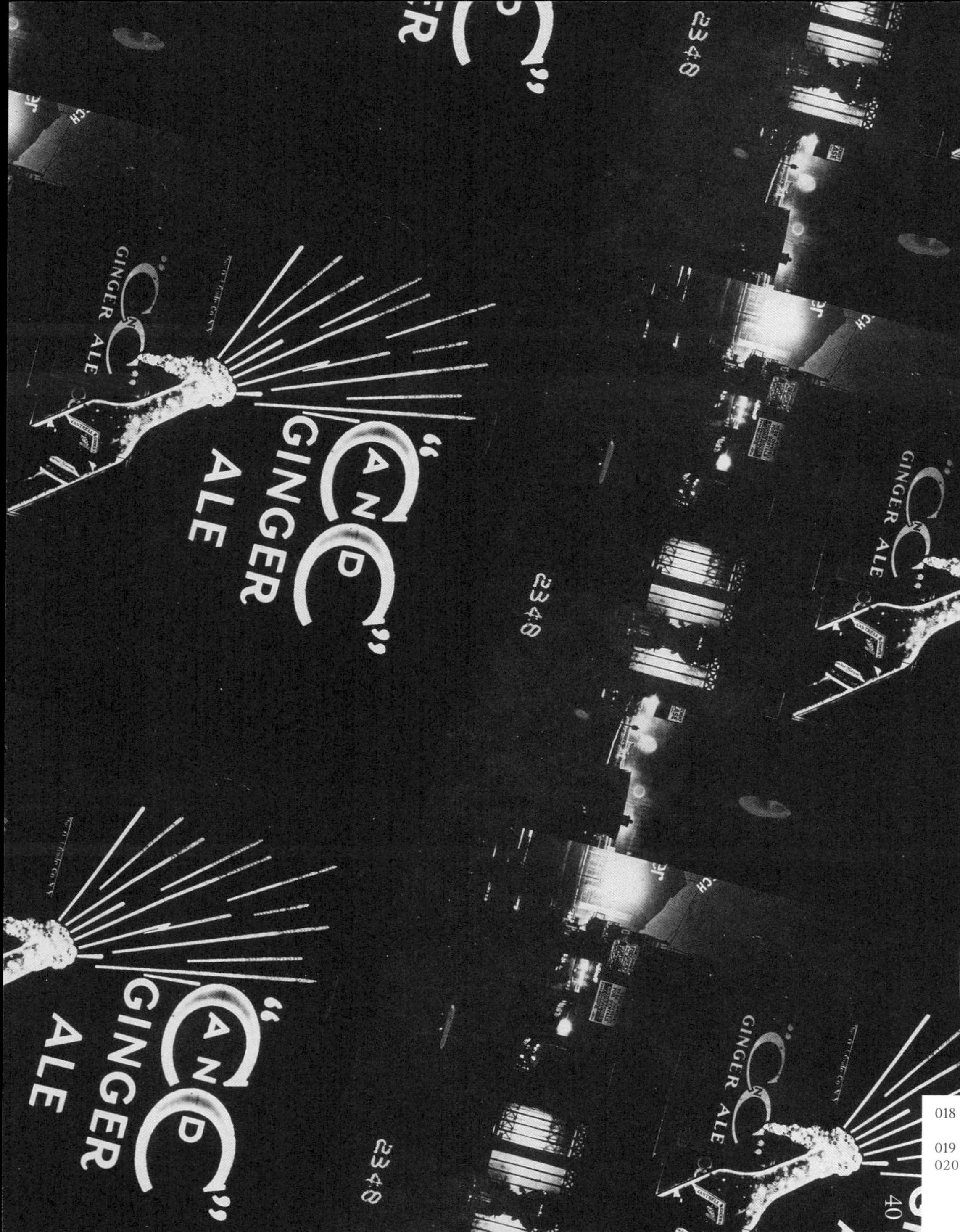

018 Fortunato Depero, *Depero Futurista. 1913–1927*, Milano: Edizione Italiana della Dinamo Azari [1927], cover by Fortunato Depero, no. 391/1000, signed
019 [Business card] *Depero. Futurist House. New York City*, New York 1929, designed by Fortunato Depero
020 [Invitation card] *Fortunato Depero. Opening New York Studio*, New York 1928–1930, signed by Fortunato Depero

↓019 ↑018

fortunato depero · 97 macdougal street · new york 12

it is with great pleasure that i announce the opening of my new york studio at 97 macdougal street, where i am exhibiting my latest paintings, drawings and examples of a new decorative art · i believe these works will interest you, and i am looking forward to your visit. Fortunato Depero

p.s. because of difficulties in getting telephone installations, i have arranged that any message left at or. 4-9456 will reach me.

OR-3-3385

↓020

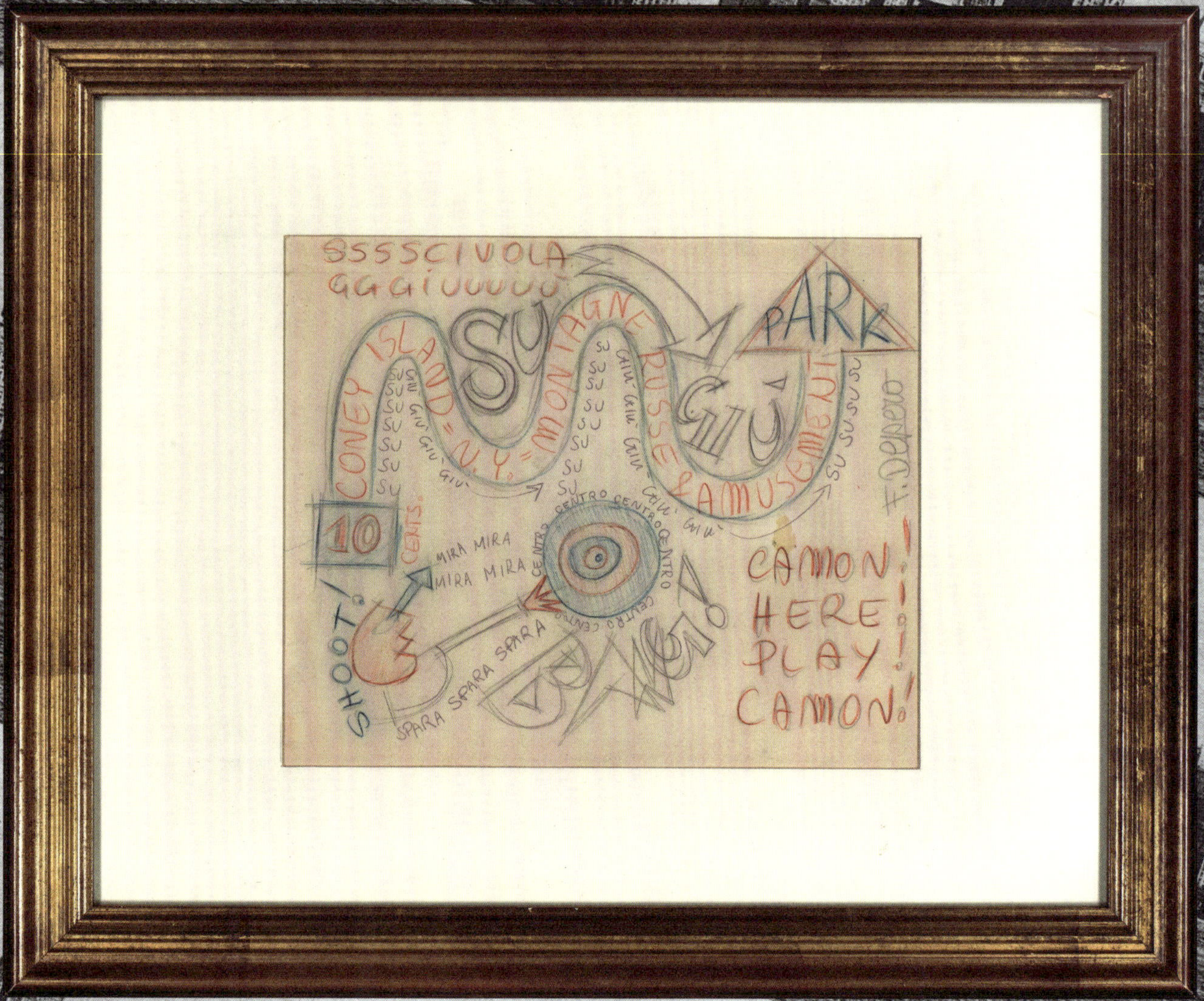

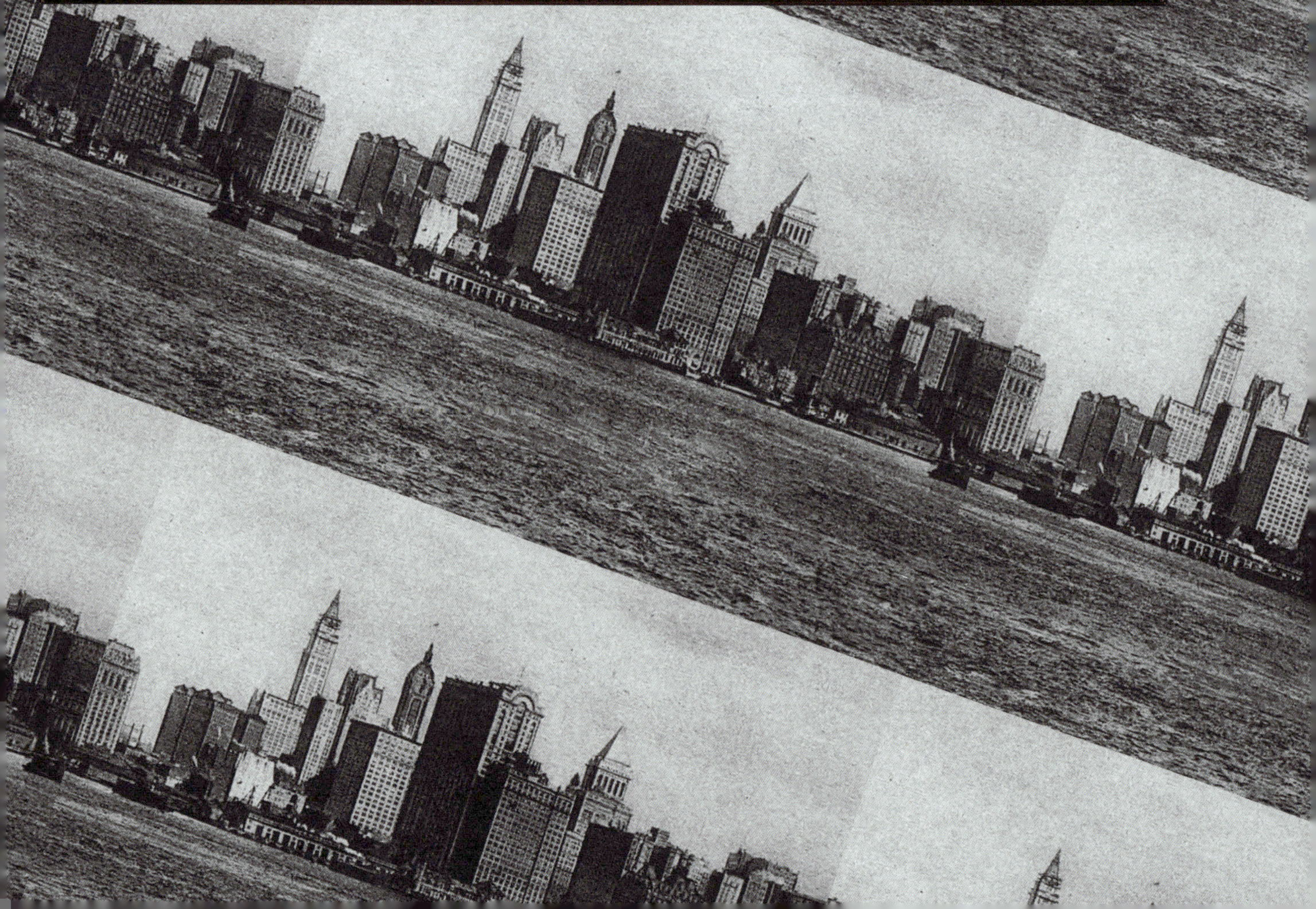

021 Fortunato Depero, *Coney Island N. Y.*, 1929
022 Fortunato Depero, [Variation of the poem *Subway*], ca. 1930

↓022 ↑021

Piedi Piedi Piedi Piedi Piedi
Piedi che scendono

Plicco ticco ticco Tikke Tak
Plicco Ticco Ticco Tikke Tak } assieme

Polpacci che salgono e si
rituffano nei fiumi neri del
le velocità sotterranee.
Sacchi di teste che si
rovesciano giù per le scale.
Ruote-controllo sgranano
la folla :
gran-gran-gran-gran —

Plicco ticco ticco Tikke-Tak
Plicco ticco ticco Tikke-Tak
Plicco ticco ticco Tikke-Tak } "assieme"

gran-gran-gran-gran-gran

accompagnamento.
piedi
piedi
piedi
piedi
piedi
piedi
piedi
piedi
piedi
piedi
piedi
piedi
piedi
piedi
piedi

Tere tenn zigzag

Tere-tenn sulla testa a <u>me</u>
Tere-tenn sulla testa a <u>te</u>
tere-Tenn sulla Testa a <u>tutti</u>.

ciuff
ciuff
ciuff
ciuff
ciuff
ciuff
ciuff
ciuff

Alla fine con
un potente

TATUM GRAN ← assieme

la SUBWAY da il colpo
di grazia a tutti.

Len ta men te,
ma cullati, pestati
insaccati —
usciamo in pasto ai
voraci rumori-cani delle
strade.

piedi
piedi
piedi
piedi
piedi
piedi
piedi
piedi
piedi
piedi

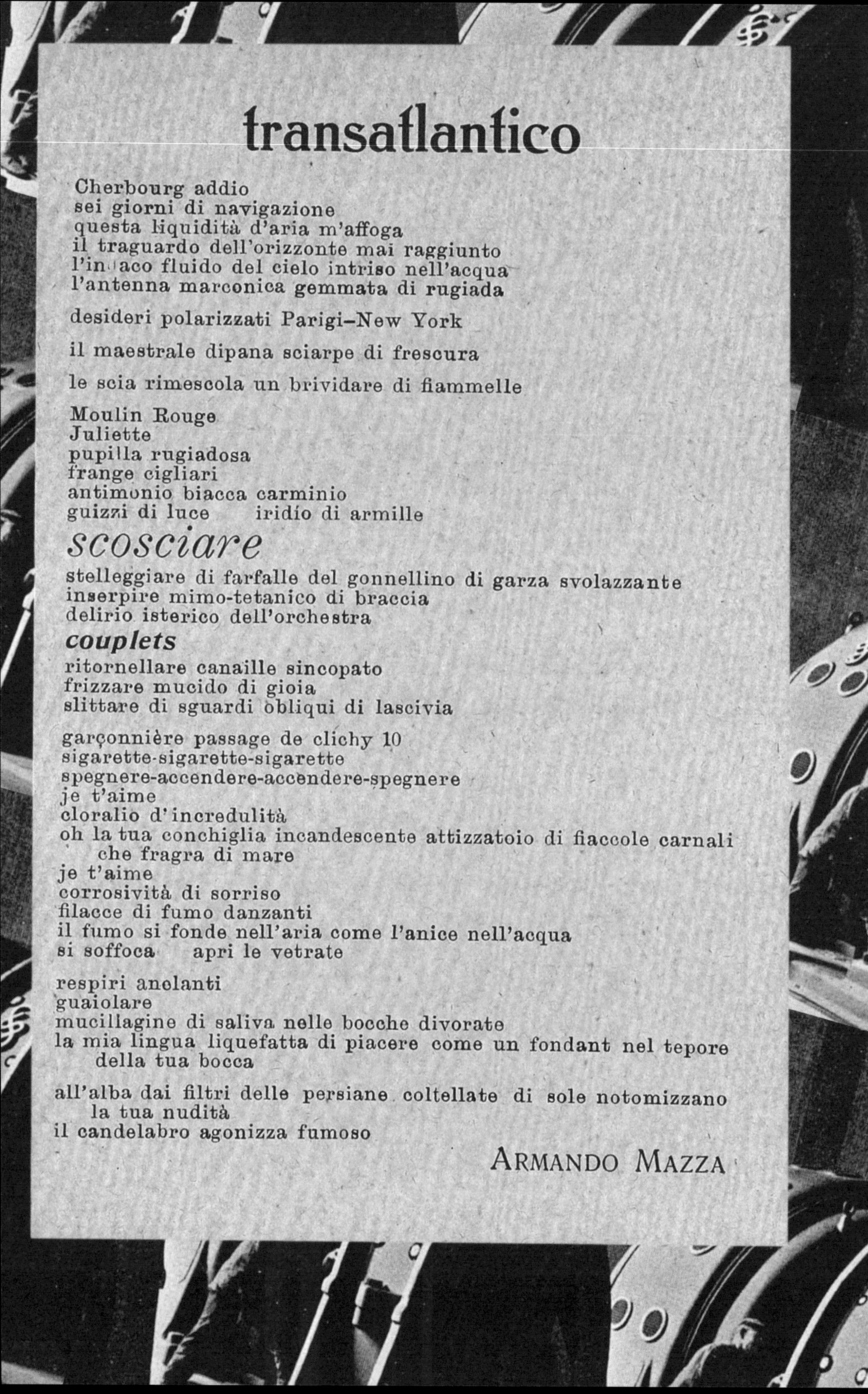

transatlantico

Cherbourg addio
sei giorni di navigazione
questa liquidità d'aria m'affoga
il traguardo dell'orizzonte mai raggiunto
l'in aco fluido del cielo intriso nell'acqua
l'antenna marconica gemmata di rugiada

desideri polarizzati Parigi–New York

il maestrale dipana sciarpe di frescura

le scia rimescola un brividare di fiammelle

Moulin Rouge
Juliette
pupilla rugiadosa
frange cigliari
antimonio biacca carminio
guizzi di luce   iridío di armille

scosciare

stelleggiare di farfalle del gonnellino di garza svolazzante
inserpire mimo-tetanico di braccia
delirio isterico dell'orchestra

couplets

ritornellare canaille sincopato
frizzare mucido di gioia
slittare di sguardi obliqui di lascivia

garçonnière passage de clichy 10
sigarette-sigarette-sigarette
spegnere-accendere-accendere-spegnere
je t'aime
cloralio d'incredulità
oh la tua conchiglia incandescente attizzatoio di fiaccole carnali
    che fragra di mare
je t'aime
corrosività di sorriso
filacce di fumo danzanti
il fumo si fonde nell'aria come l'anice nell'acqua
si soffoca   apri le vetrate

respiri anelanti
guaiolare
mucillagine di saliva nelle bocche divorate
la mia lingua liquefatta di piacere come un fondant nel tepore
    della tua bocca

all'alba dai filtri delle persiane coltellate di sole notomizzano
    la tua nudità
il candelabro agonizza fumoso

ARMANDO MAZZA

023 [Postcard] Armando Mazza, *Transatlantico*, Italy, 1930s
024 [Photographer unknown], *Golfspiel auf dem Sportdeck des neuen Hapagdampfer Hamburg*, Photographisches Atelier der Hamburg-Amerika Linie, 1920s

↓024 ↑023

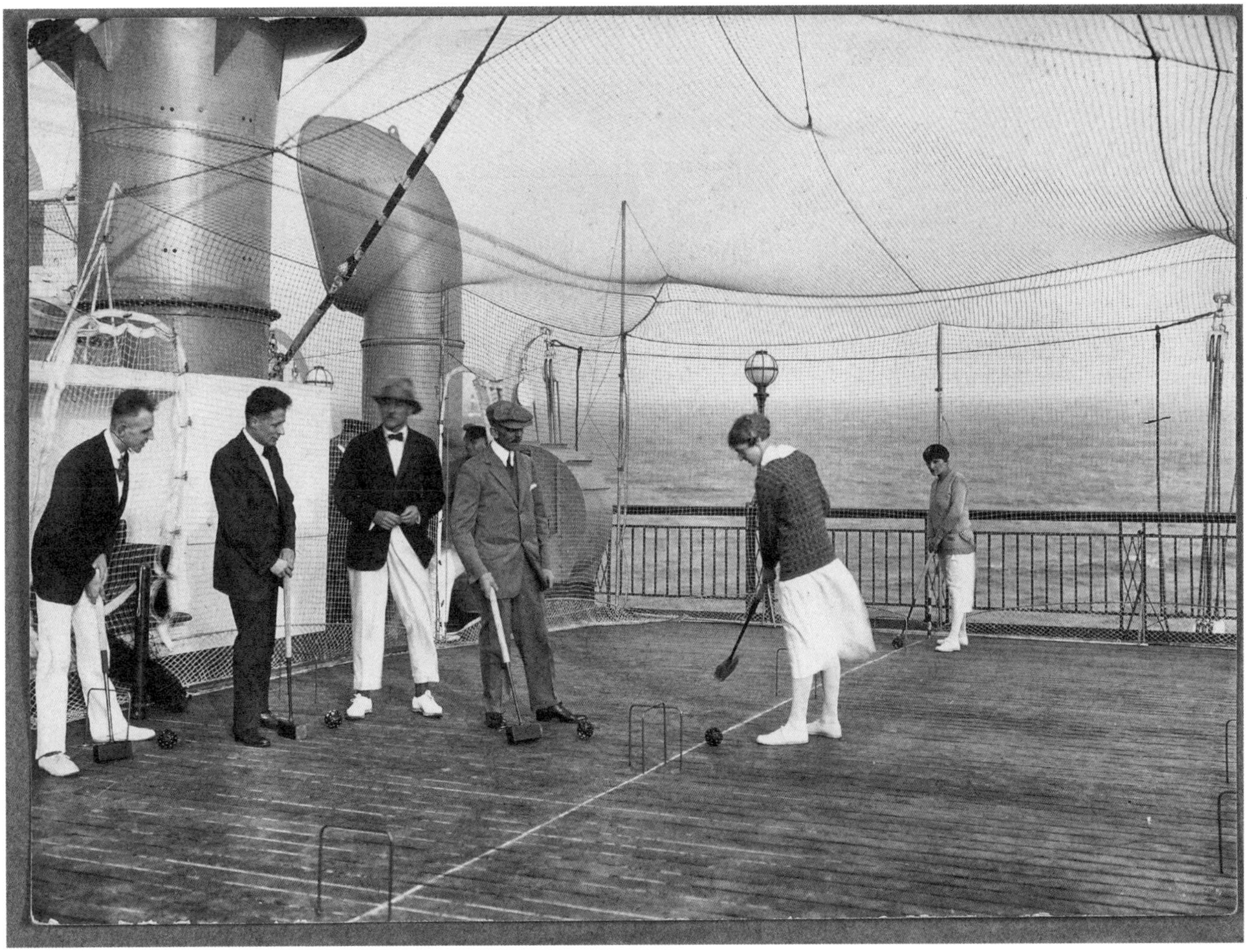

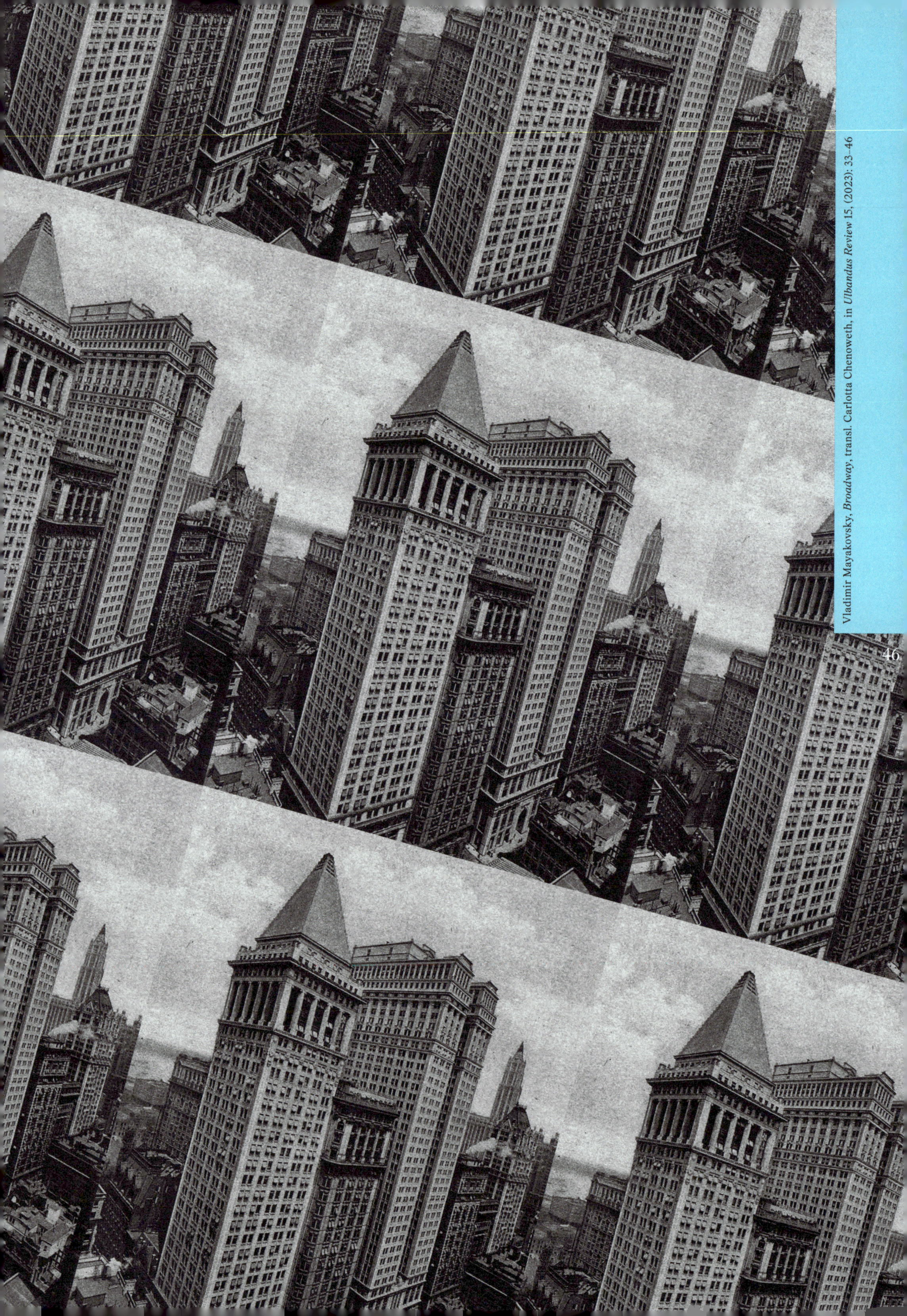

Vladimir Mayakovsky, *Broadway*, transl. Carlotta Chenoweth, in *Ulbandus Review* 15, (2023): 33–46

Vladimir Mayakovsky

Broadway

The asphalt—glass.
I walk and I clink.
The forests and grasses—
shaved clean.
To the north
from the south
run the avenues,
to the west from the east—
the streets.
But between them —
(where their builder has thrust them)
homes
of impossible height.
Some of them are
tall as the stars,
others —
tall as the moon.
For a Yankee,
too lazy to schlep with
his feet:
a simple
and high-speed lift.
At 7 o'clock —
the high tide of man,
at 5 o'clock
the low.
The machinery grinds,
the noise and racket,
and all are
mute in the clatter.
They slow down only
to chew chewing gum,
to ask:
"*Make money?*"
A mother
gave her breast
to her child.
The child,
with drops from its nose,
sucks
as if not
from a breast, but a dollar—
occupied with
a serious
business.
The work is done.
Entwine the body
in the continuous
electric wind.

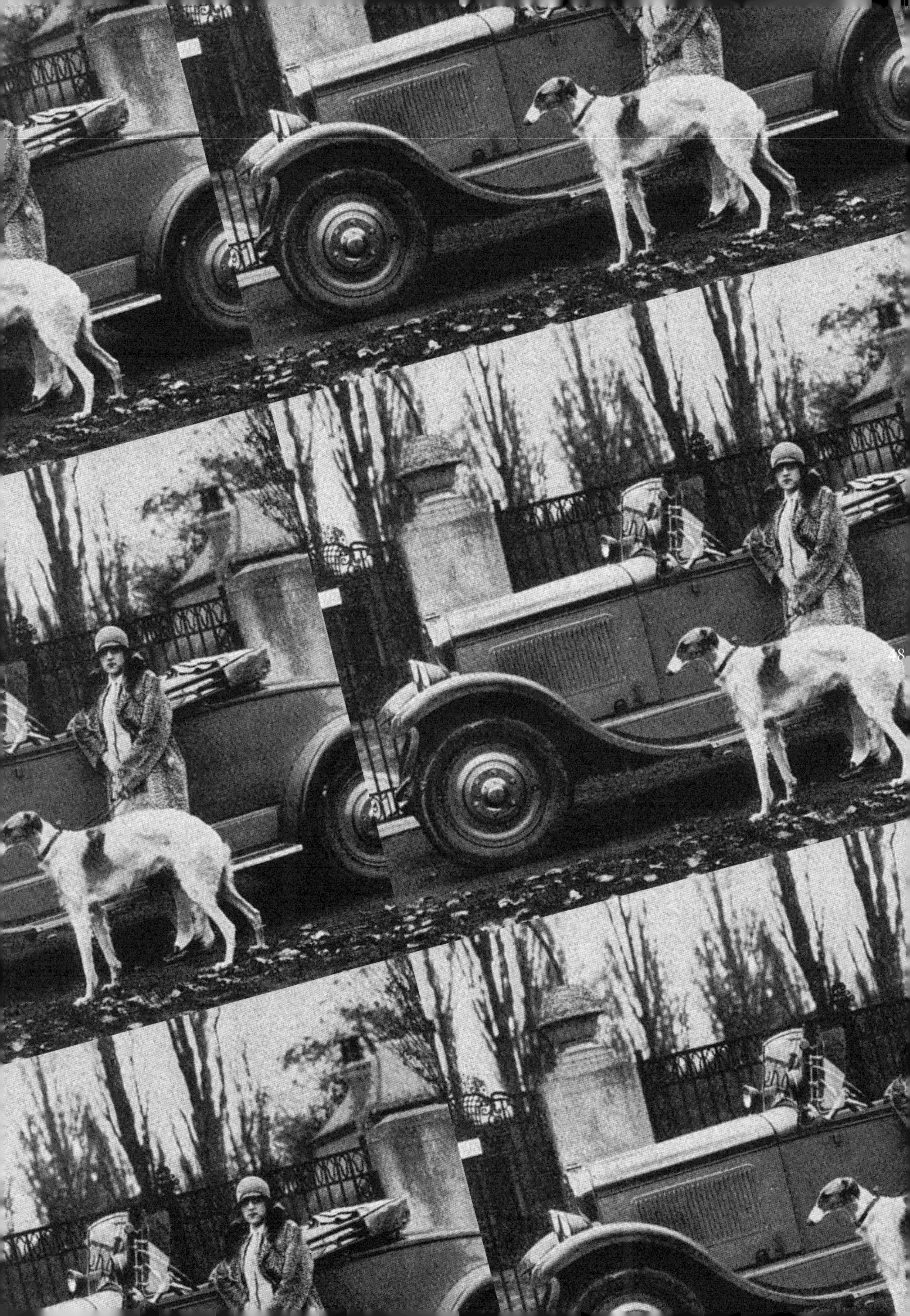

48

If you want to go below ground —
take the subway,
To the sky—
take an elevator.
The train cars
travel
beneath rising smoke,
and on the heels
of buddings,
bump shoulders,
and bring
a trail of smoke
to the Brooklyn Bridge,
and hide
in holes
under the Hudson.
You've gone blind,
stupid with sleep.
But,
like a drum beat,
from the darkness,
along the crown of your head:
"*Maxwell Coffee:*
good
to the last drop."
And the lights
how they
dig up the night,
well, I'll report to you –
a blaze!
You look to the left
— oh my god!
To the right
— my goodness!
There's something for a Muscovite to look at.
And in a day
you couldn't reach the end.
This is New York.
This is Broadway.
How do you do!
I am in ecstasy
from the city of New York.
But I will not
take the cap
from my head.
The Soviets have
their own pride:
on the bourgeoisie
we look from above.

SOCIÉTÉ ANONYME INC.: MUSEUM OF MODERN ART 1920

During the period between the 1913 Armory Show in New York and the founding of the Museum of Modern Art in 1929, the Société Anonyme (1920–1928/1950) was one of the most important institutions aiming at exhibiting and popularizing European avant-garde movements in the United States. Through its exhibitions, accompanying lecture series, and other events, the organization, led by Katherine S. Dreier, introduced more than 70 European artists to an American audience. In its major *International Exhibition of Modern Art* at the Brooklyn Museum (1926–1927), the entire spectrum of aesthetic and stylistically diverse avant-garde movements was shown: from Expressionism, Cubism, and Futurism to Bauhaus and De Stijl, and from International Constructivism, Dadaism, and Surrealism to modern American art.

When Dreier decided to found Société Anonyme in 1920 with Marcel Duchamp and Man Ray, she initially intended to create a space with permanent and temporary exhibitions, a room to hold lectures, and a library of books and periodicals on modern art. It was supposed to be named the Modern Ark, a play upon the symbolic implications of bringing art across the Ocean from Europe to the US. But the official name they ultimately chose was Société Anonyme, suggested by Man Ray (the French term for "Incorporated" and "Anonymous Society"), and Dreier added the subtitle "Museum of Modern Art".

The goal of Société Anonyme Inc. Museum of Modern Art was not only to organize exhibitions of international artists, but also to connect them with potential buyers. It intended to educate the public through staging exhibitions and talks, publications, and a library specializing in books on modern art. To support their endeavour, they charged an entrance fee, sold admission cards and accepted donations. Dreier was the chief (and increasingly, the main) organizer of the exhibitions. She pursued plans for a permanent building, an idea that was first broached in 1923. Société Anonyme's exhibitions were held in dealers' galleries, schools, colleges, private clubs, or in American and Canadian museums.

In 1928, Dreier closed its headquarters in New York and moved the library into storage. Société Anonyme then continued to operate throughout the 1930s and 1940s until 1950. The collection was donated to Yale University in 1941 because Dreier and Duchamp felt that an educational institution was best placed to continue their initial mission.

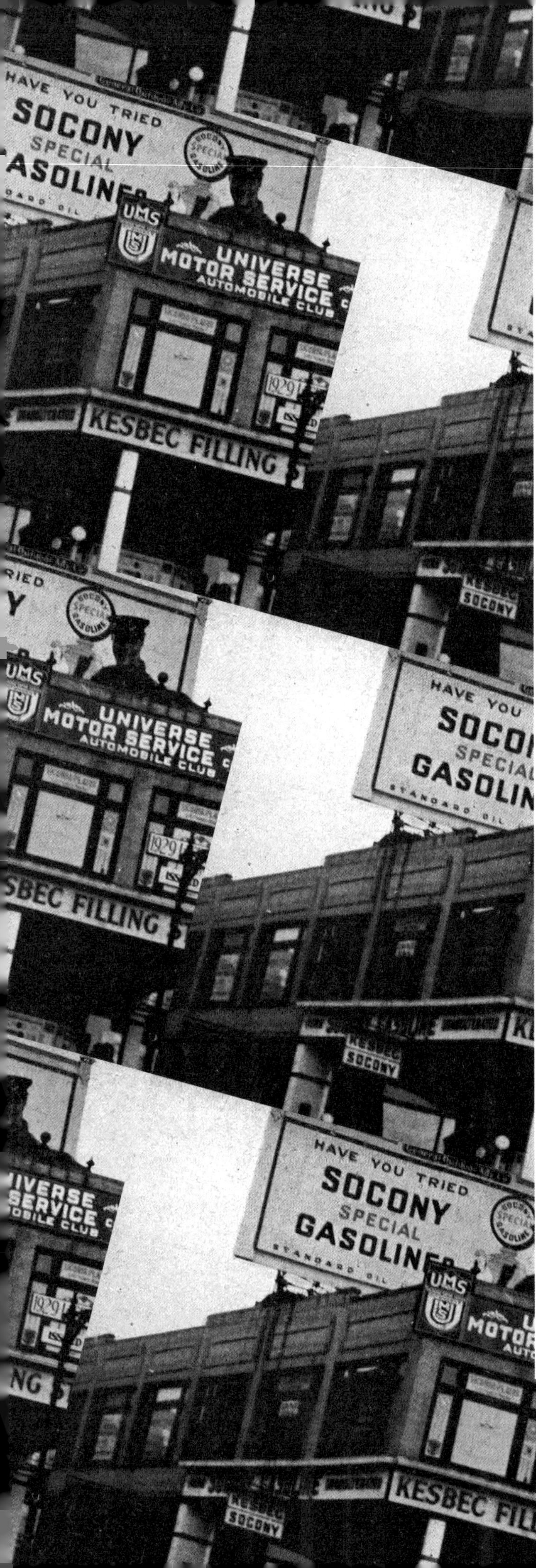

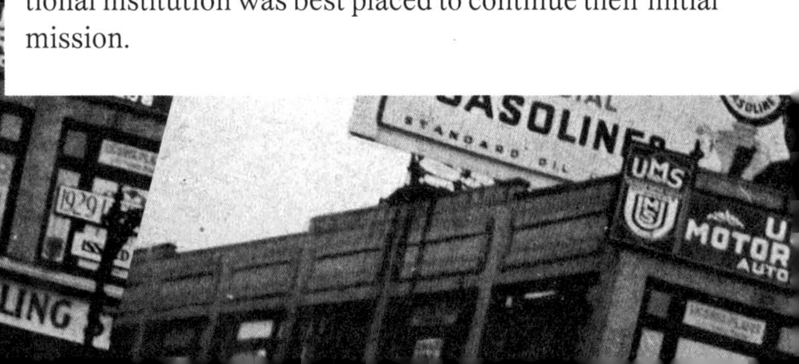

↓026 ↓025

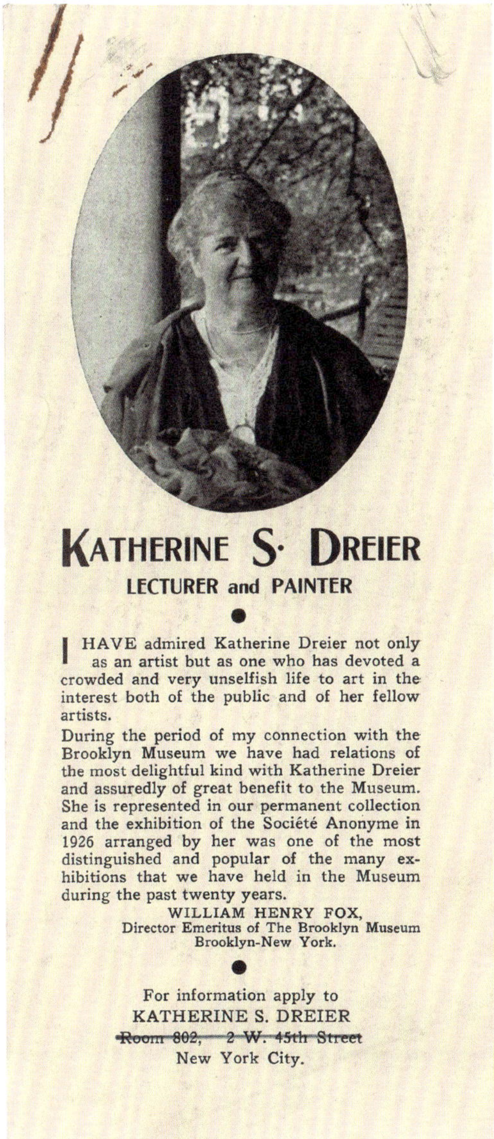

KATHERINE S· DREIER

LECTURER and PAINTER

I HAVE admired Katherine Dreier not only as an artist but as one who has devoted a crowded and very unselfish life to art in the interest both of the public and of her fellow artists.

During the period of my connection with the Brooklyn Museum we have had relations of the most delightful kind with Katherine Dreier and assuredly of great benefit to the Museum. She is represented in our permanent collection and the exhibition of the Société Anonyme in 1926 arranged by her was one of the most distinguished and popular of the many exhibitions that we have held in the Museum during the past twenty years.

WILLIAM HENRY FOX,
Director Emeritus of The Brooklyn Museum
Brooklyn-New York.

For information apply to
KATHERINE S. DREIER
~~Room 802, 2 W. 45th Street~~
New York City.

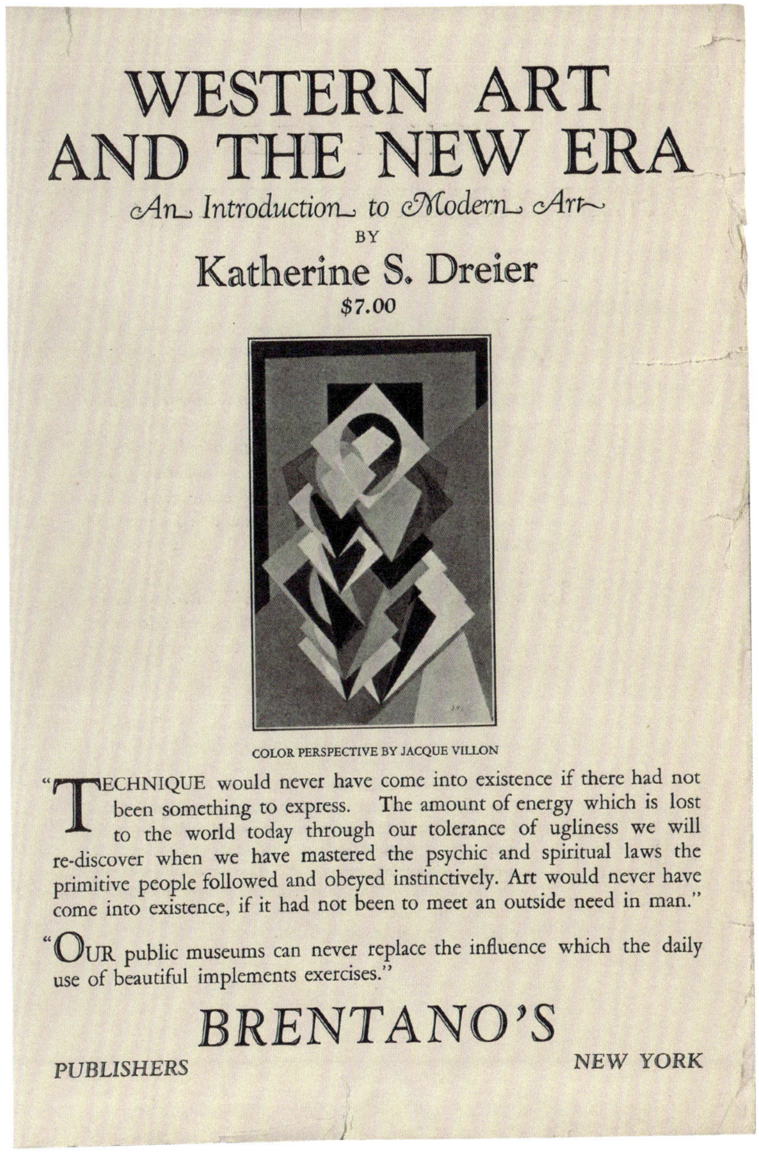

WESTERN ART AND THE NEW ERA

An Introduction to Modern Art

BY

Katherine S. Dreier

$7.00

COLOR PERSPECTIVE BY JACQUE VILLON

"TECHNIQUE would never have come into existence if there had not been something to express. The amount of energy which is lost to the world today through our tolerance of ugliness we will re-discover when we have mastered the psychic and spiritual laws the primitive people followed and obeyed instinctively. Art would never have come into existence, if it had not been to meet an outside need in man."

"OUR public museums can never replace the influence which the daily use of beautiful implements exercises."

PUBLISHERS **BRENTANO'S** NEW YORK

KATHERINE S. DREIER Katherine Sophie Dreier is still rarely mentioned in avant-garde historiography, but her efforts to popularize and institutionalize avant-garde movements are of the greatest importance. She was born in the United States to a family of German immigrants, and her sister, Dorothea, was a Post-Impressionist painter. Katherine S. Dreier was involved in the suffragette movement in New York, which ultimately gained votes for women in 1917. She studied at art academies in the US and Europe and exhibited her works at the 1913 Armory Show in New York, where she became fascinated with paintings by European avant-garde artists, including Wassily Kandinsky and Marcel Duchamp. In 1917, she was a co-founder of the Society of Independent Artists in New York City, where she exhibited with Duchamp. They both resigned from the Society in the fall of the same year. In 1919, she travelled again to Europe to encounter avant-garde movements and saw Dada exhibitions in Cologne and Paris. By early January 1920, both Dreier and Duchamp had returned to New York, where the idea of establishing a gallery to show modern art became the focus of her organizational abilities.

025 [Leaflet] *Katherine S. Dreier. Lecturer and Painter*, New York, after 1933
026 [Booklet] *Western Art and the New Era. An Introduction to Modern Art by Katherine S. Dreier*, New York: Bretano's Publishers 1923, cover with a painting by Jacques Villon: *Color Perspective*

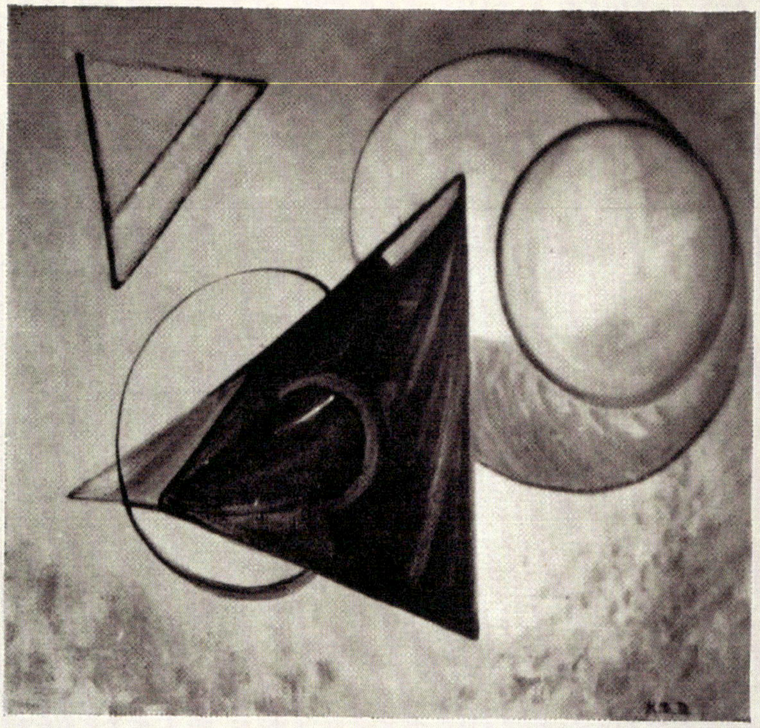

Katherine S. Dreier: The Blue Triangle

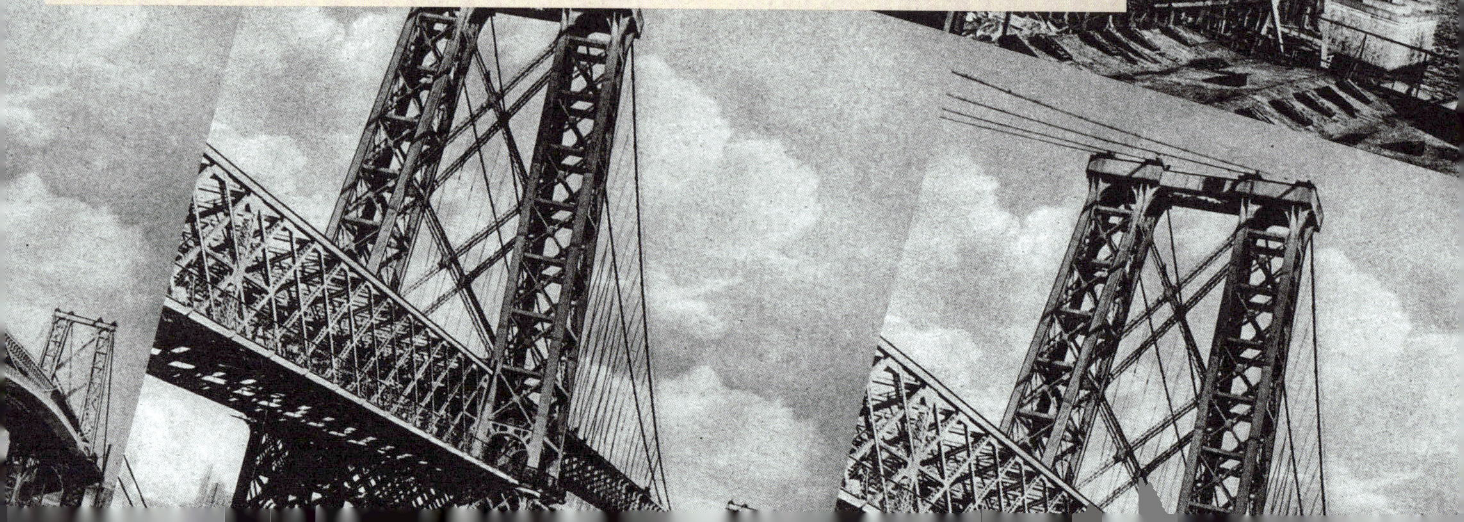

027 [Leaflet] *4 Painters. Albers, Dreier, Drewes, Kelpe*, presumably New York 1936, [unpaginated], Katherine S. Dreier; *The Blue Triangle*
028 Katherine S. Dreier, *Marcel Duchamp*, 1918

↓ 028 ↑ 027

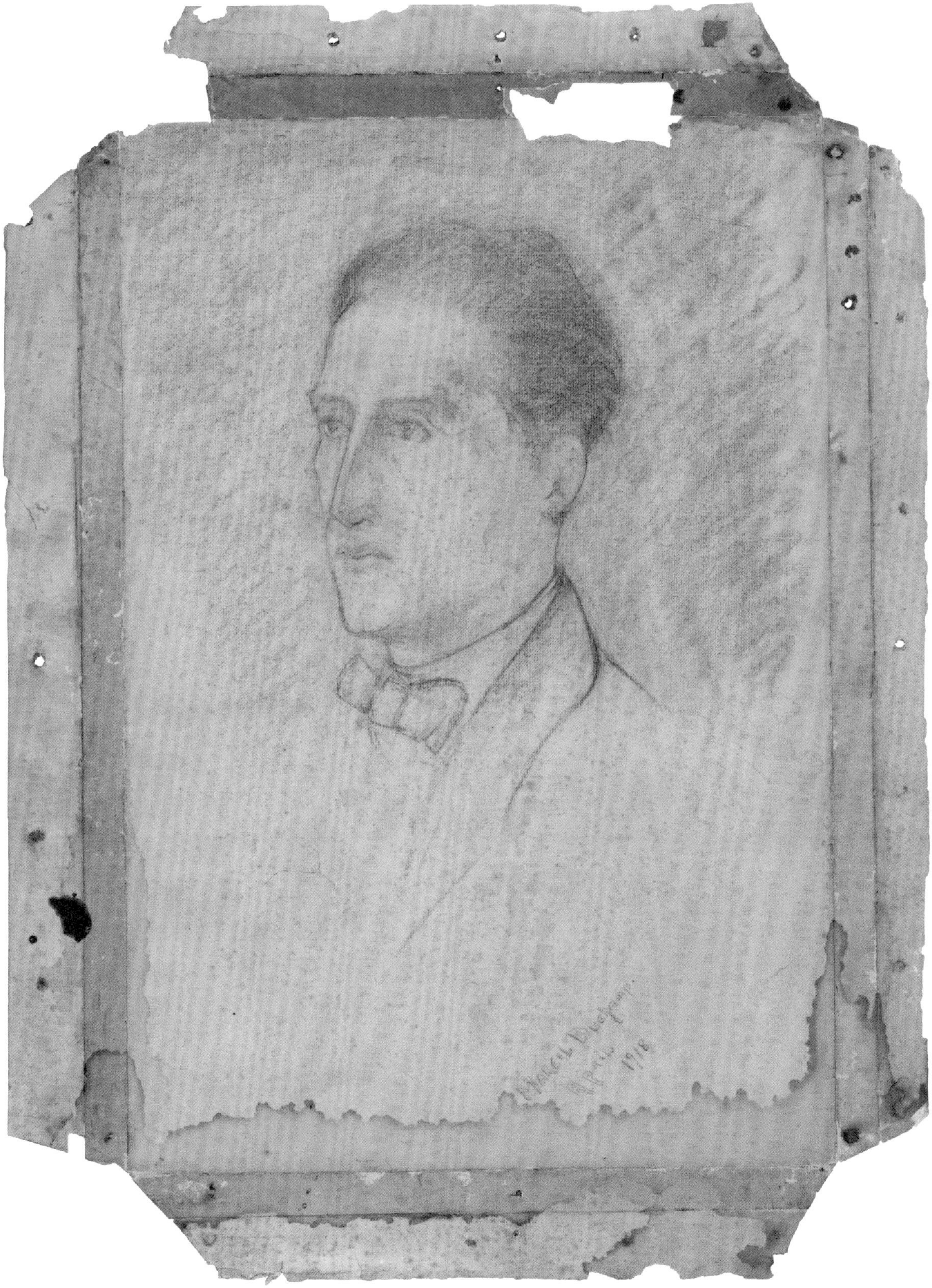

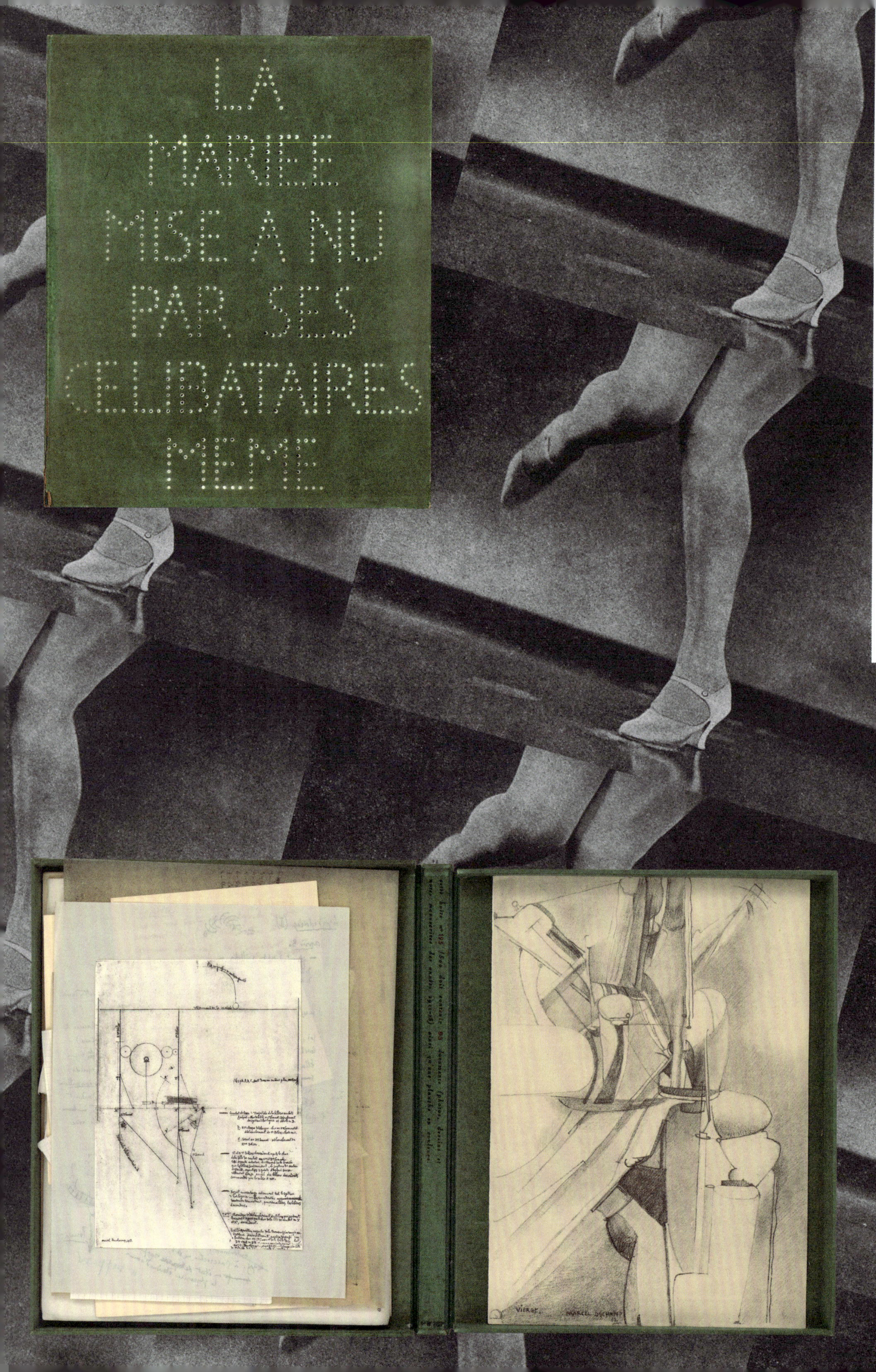

029 Marcel Duchamp, *La Mariée mise à nu par ses célibataires, même* (Boîte Verte), Paris: Editions Rrose Sélavy, 1934, no. 193/300, cover; open views

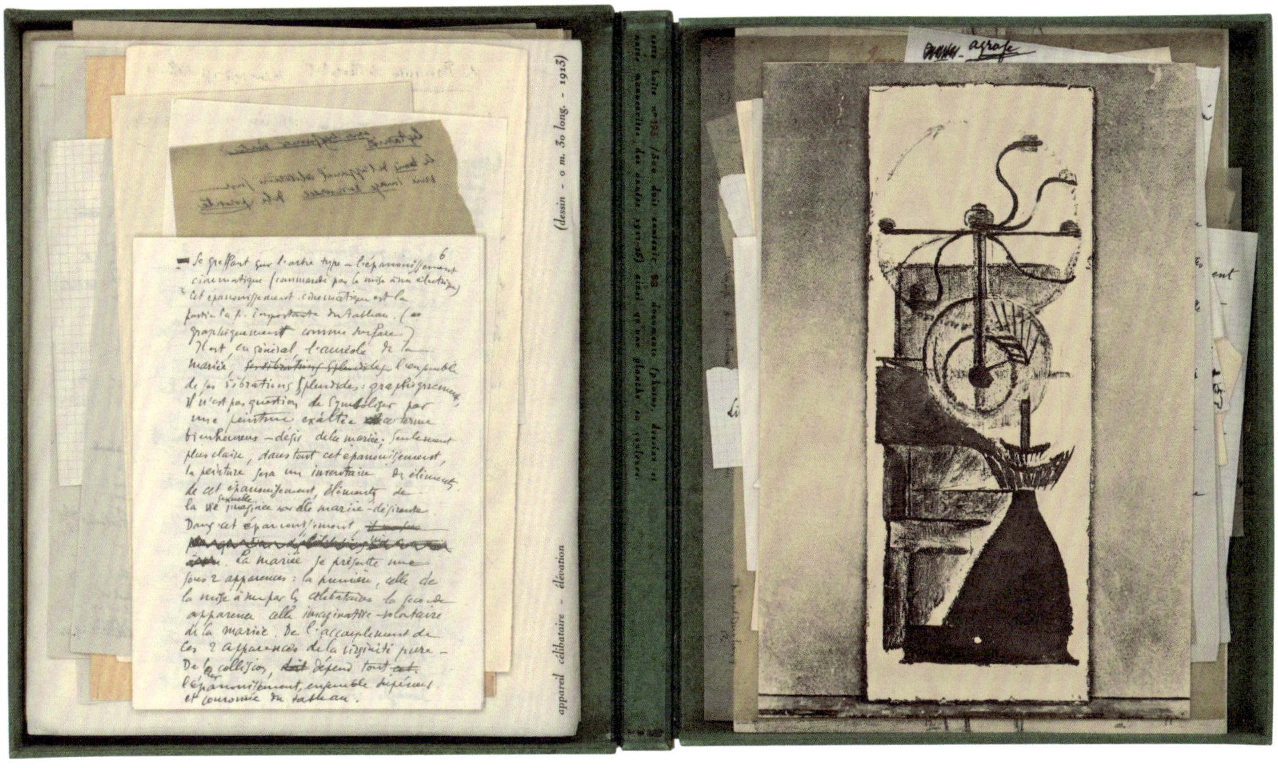

KATHERINE S. DREIER—MARCEL DUCHAMP—MAN RAY
Katherine S. Dreier met Marcel Duchamp in New York and began collecting his work in 1918. At around the same time she had plans to establish the first Museum of Modern Art to be created by artists. She asked Duchamp to collaborate with her, and he advised her to contact Man Ray for the project. Dreier rented a space near Fifth Avenue and asked them both to work on the first exhibition. Duchamp curated the show, and Man Ray took on the dual role of public relations agent and photographer of the museum's artworks. Among the works that are closely connected with the history of Société Anonyme are *Lampshade* by Man Ray and *The Large Glass* by Duchamp. *Lampshade* was the first mobile sculpture prepared for an exhibition at the Société Anonyme in 1921, while Duchamp's *The Large Glass* was shown publicly for the first time at the *International Exhibition of Modern Art*, which opened at the Brooklyn Museum in 1926. It was accidentally shattered in transit following the exhibition, a misfortune which was only discovered after it was removed from storage by Dreier several years later. In the 1930s, Duchamp spent some time at Dreier's home to photograph *The Large Glass* for *The Green Box* (1934) and *La Boîte-en-valise* (1935) before the work was ultimately moved to the Philadelphia Museum of Art in the 1950s.

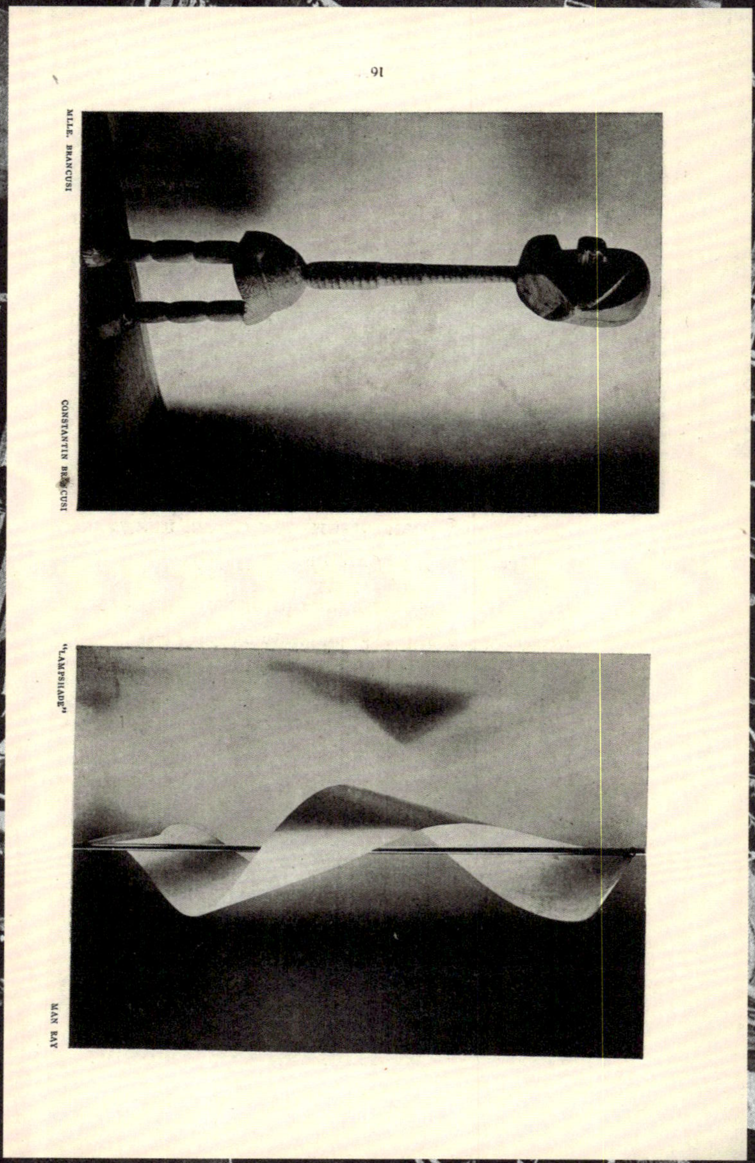

16

MLLE. BRANCUSI

CONSTANTIN BRANCUSI

"LAMPSHADE"

MAN RAY

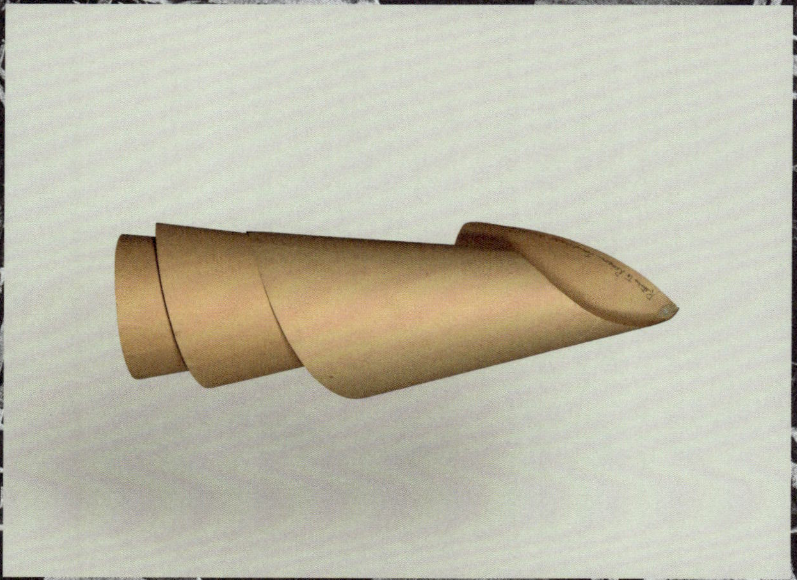

030 Société Anonyme, Inc., *Report 1920–1921*, New York: Société Anonyme, Inc. 1921, 16, sculptures by Constantin Brancusi: *Mille* and Man Ray: *Lampshade*

031 Man Ray, *Lampshade. Return to Reason*, 1920

032 *391*, no. 13, July 1920, ed. Francis Picabia, Paris, sculpture by Man Ray: *Lampshade*, [unpaginated]

EXTRAIT DE JÉSUS-CHRIST RASTAQUOUÈRE

LA PLUS BELLE DÉCOUVERTE DE L'HOMME EST LE BICARBONATE DE SOUDE.

IL N'Y A PAS D'INCONNUS EXCEPTÉ POUR MOI.

NOUS SOMMES DANS UN TUBE DIGESTIF.

EAU DE COLOGNE VERTÉBRALE.

DIEU ÉTAIT JUIF, IL FUT ROULÉ PAR LES CATHOLIQUES.

IL Y A BEAUCOUP MOINS DE CHOSES SUR TERRE QUE NE NOUS LE FAIT CROIRE NOTRE PHILOSOPHIE.

SPINOZA EST LE SEUL QUI N'AIT PAS LU SPINOZA.

LE SATYRE A QUEUE-DE-RAT.

NOTRE TÊTE A DEUX BESOINS COMME LE VENTRE.

LA PUDEUR SE CACHE DERRIÈRE NOTRE SEXE.

L'ŒIL FROID

Après notre mort, on devrait nous mettre dans une boule; cette boule serait en bois de plusieurs couleurs, on la roulerait pour nous conduire au cimetière et les croque-morts chargés de ce soin porteraient des gants transparents, afin de rappeler aux amants le souvenir des caresses. Pour ceux qui désireraient enrichir leur ameublement du plaisir objectif de l'être cher, il existerait des boules en cristal au travers desquelles on apercevrait la nudité définitive de son grand-père ou de son frère jumeau !

Il y a des gens qui ont la tête en bas, comme les plantes, et qui regardent avec leurs pieds.

La connaissance et la morale ne sont que papier à mouches, je conseille aux mouches de vivre dans les confessionnaux, les pêchés étant une nourriture bien plus agréable que le caca.

TOUT EST POISON, EXCEPTÉ NOS HABITUDES.

IL FAUT COMMUNIER AVEC DU CHEWING-GUM.

Francis PICABIA

57

LAMPSHADE

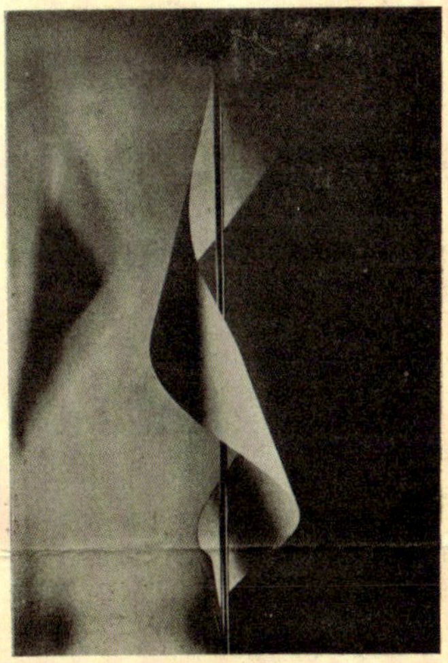

MAN RAY.

391

Numéro 13
JUILLET 1920
(5e Année)
Le Gérant : RIBEMONT-DESSAIGNES.

PRIX : 1 FR. 50 (PARIS)
Dépositaire : AU SANS-PAREIL
37, Avenue Kléber, PARIS

S.P.I. — 27, Rue Nicolo, PARIS (XVIe)

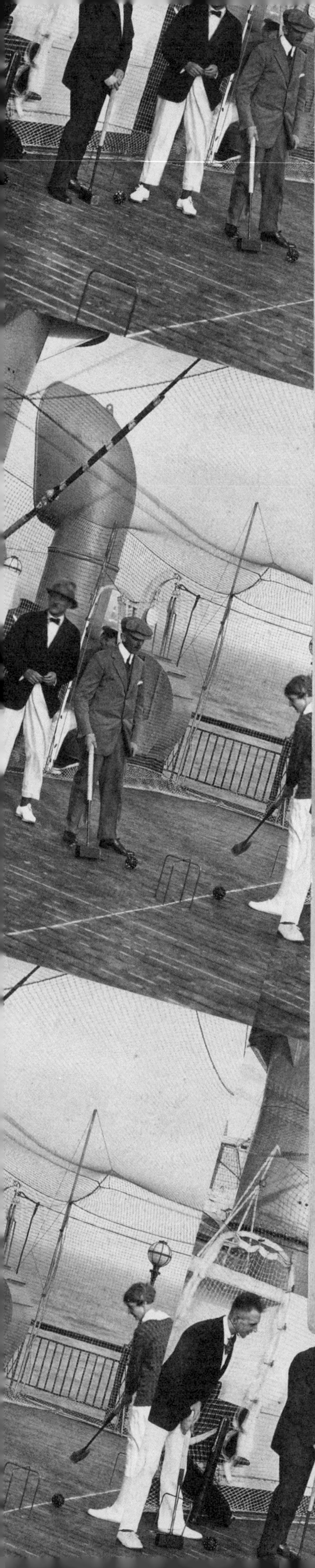

"You may not easily understand this exhibition as indeed another man's language or religion may not be comprehended without considerable study.

Yet we have a right to know what is going on in the art world and perhaps to discern for ourselves:

FIRST: That art has something else to do besides copying pretty things.

SECOND: That an artist has as much a right to use color and form abstractly as have the musician and the writer in their fields of sound and thought.

What is the Expressionist trying to do? He is trying to make us look within — to help us discern our souls.

We may laugh at his attempts in our ignorance, but we cannot escape the truth of their philosophy which is based on the Platonic conception that the world of ideas and not the world of things is the true primary sphere of man's highest activity.

Hence these various expressionists of Modern Art are the evidence of a world-wide effort in which all men are interested. They are records of man's search for his soul.

This journey into the studies of artists in America, France, Germany and Russia is made possible through the co-operation of the Société Anonyme of New York City."

Introduction to the Modern Section of Art in the catalogue presented by the Michigan Art Institute at the State Fair, Detroit, September, 1923.

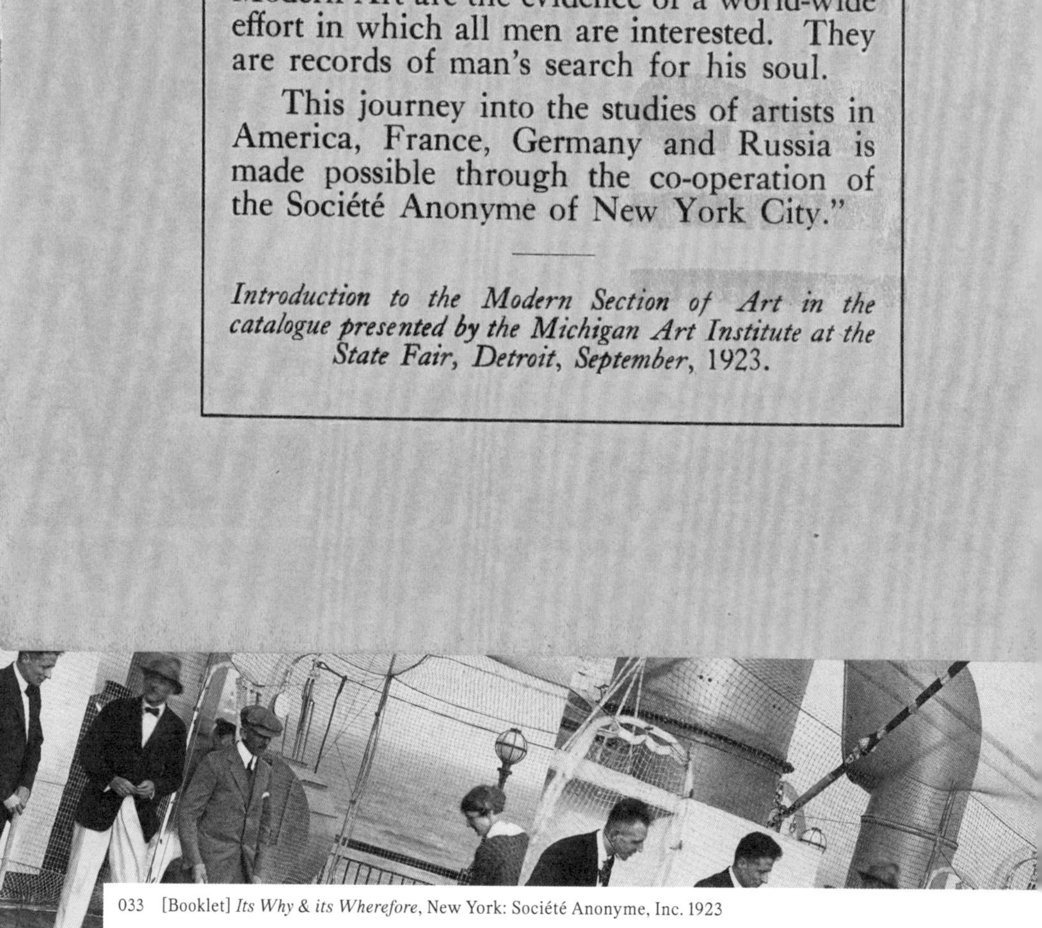

033 [Booklet] *Its Why & its Wherefore*, New York: Société Anonyme, Inc. 1923

EVER since 1908 there appeared throughout Europe a new approach towards Art, referred to in this country by the rather vague term of "Modern Art" in England as "The Vortex Movement," in Italy as "The Futurist," in Germany as "Expressionismus" and in France as "Cubism."

EXCEPT for a small group who had gathered around Mr. Alfred Stieglitz and his Gallery, 291 Fifth Avenue, these movements were practically unknown in this country until 1913, when several artists and laymen under the leadership of Mr. Arthur B. Davies arranged the now historic Exhibition, known as the Armory or International Exhibition. Here was seen for the first time in New York, or for that matter in the United States, not only the men who concern us today, but older men such as Cezanne, Gauguin and Van Gogh, who are now universally accepted by the public.

OUR backwardness seems almost incomprehensible when one considers that the Atlantic could be crossed in five days before the War! What blocked this movement from reaching us was the high duty which our Government had placed on the works of living artists. Dealers were unable to handle such men who left the beaten track, as they could not afford the duty without sales. This prohibitive duty was removed in 1912 through the efforts of Mr. John Quinn, making it

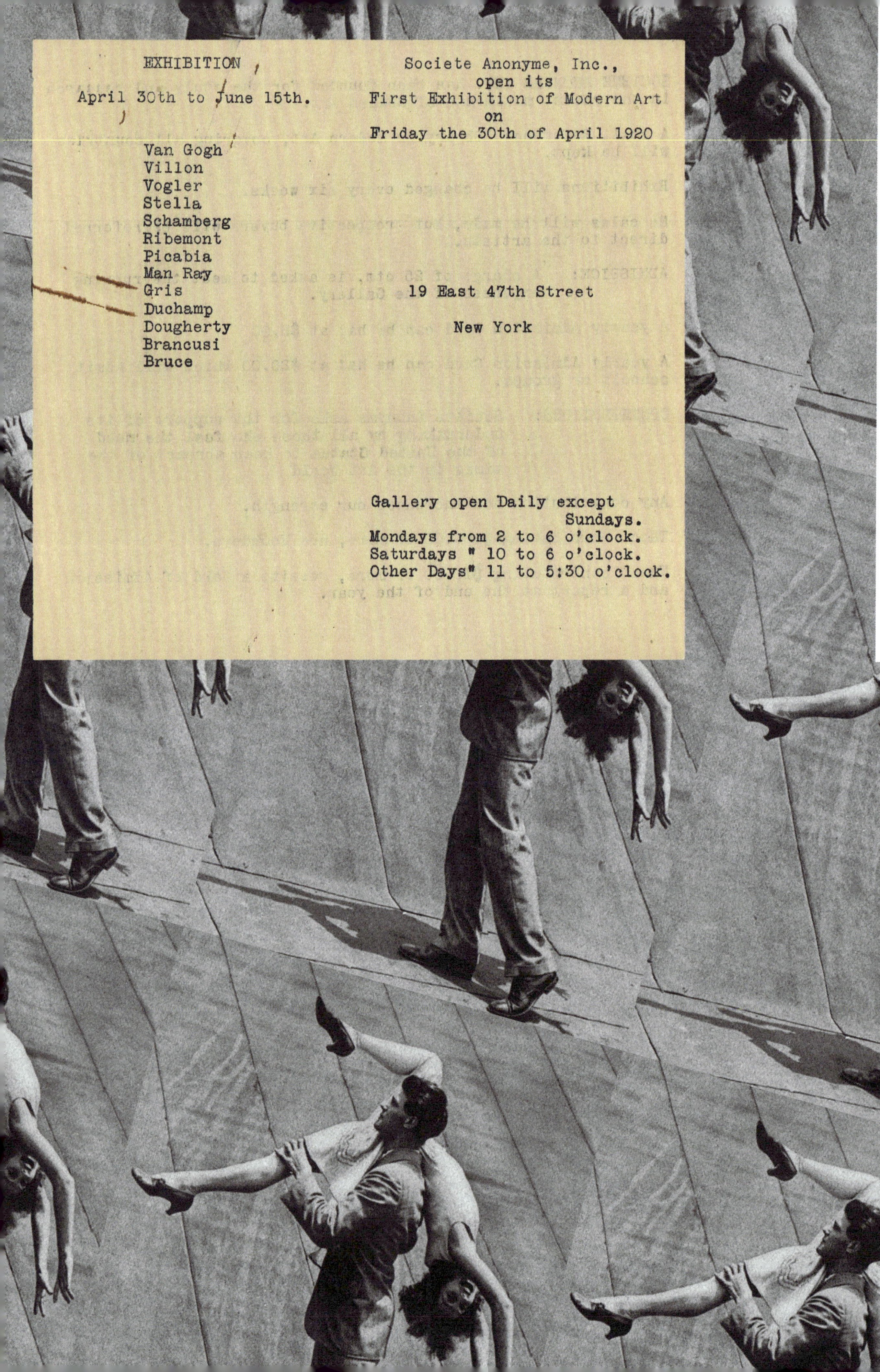

EXHIBITION

April 30th to June 15th.

Van Gogh
Villon
Vogler
Stella
Schamberg
Ribemont
Picabia
Man Ray
Gris
Duchamp
Dougherty
Brancusi
Bruce

Societe Anonyme, Inc.,
open its
First Exhibition of Modern Art
on
Friday the 30th of April 1920

19 East 47th Street

New York

Gallery open Daily except
Sundays.
Mondays from 2 to 6 o'clock.
Saturdays " 10 to 6 o'clock.
Other Days" 11 to 5:30 o'clock.

034 [Invitation card] *Societe Anonyme, Inc. open its First Exhibition of Modern Art* […], New York 1920
035 [Invitation card] *Société Anonyme, Inc. opens its 3rd Exhibition of Modern Art* […], New York 1920

↓035 ↑034

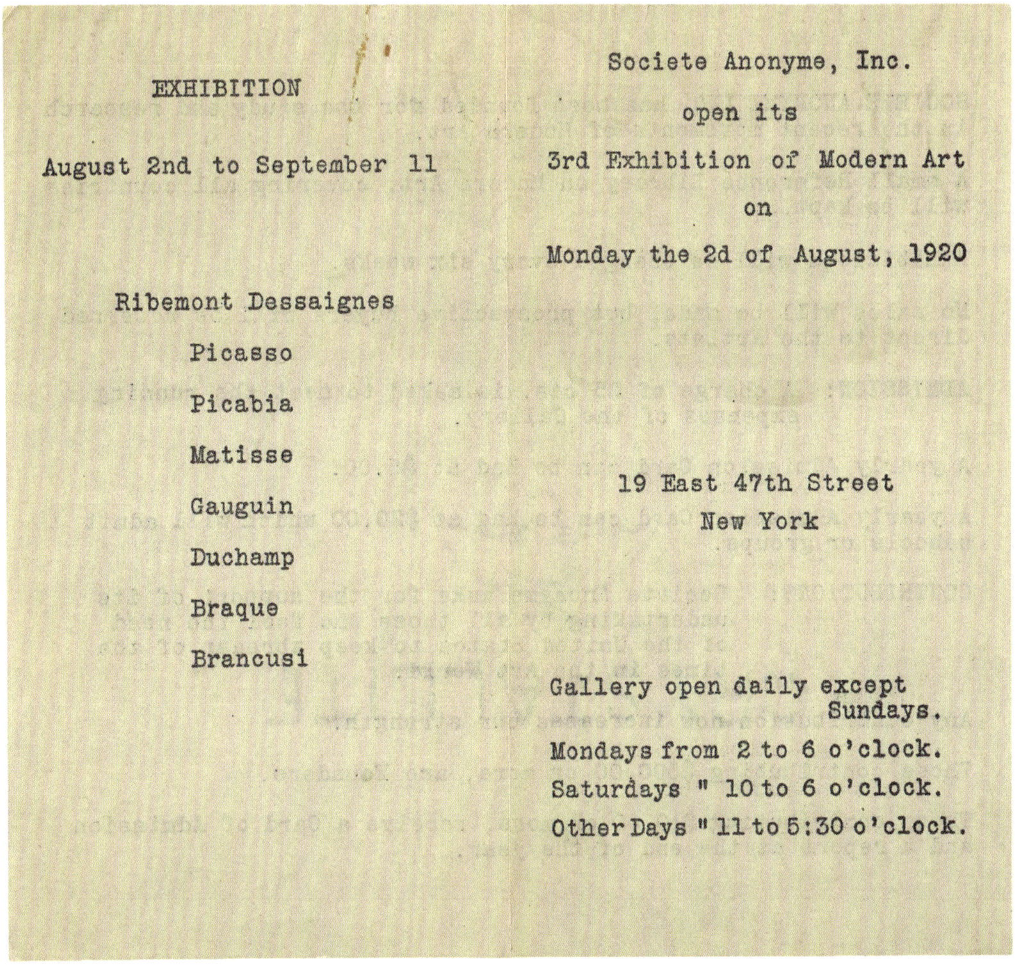

EXHIBITION

August 2nd to September 11

Ribemont Dessaignes

Picasso

Picabia

Matisse

Gauguin

Duchamp

Braque

Brancusi

Societe Anonyme, Inc.

open its

3rd Exhibition of Modern Art

on

Monday the 2d of August, 1920

19 East 47th Street

New York

Gallery open daily except Sundays.

Mondays from 2 to 6 o'clock.

Saturdays " 10 to 6 o'clock.

Other Days " 11 to 5:30 o'clock.

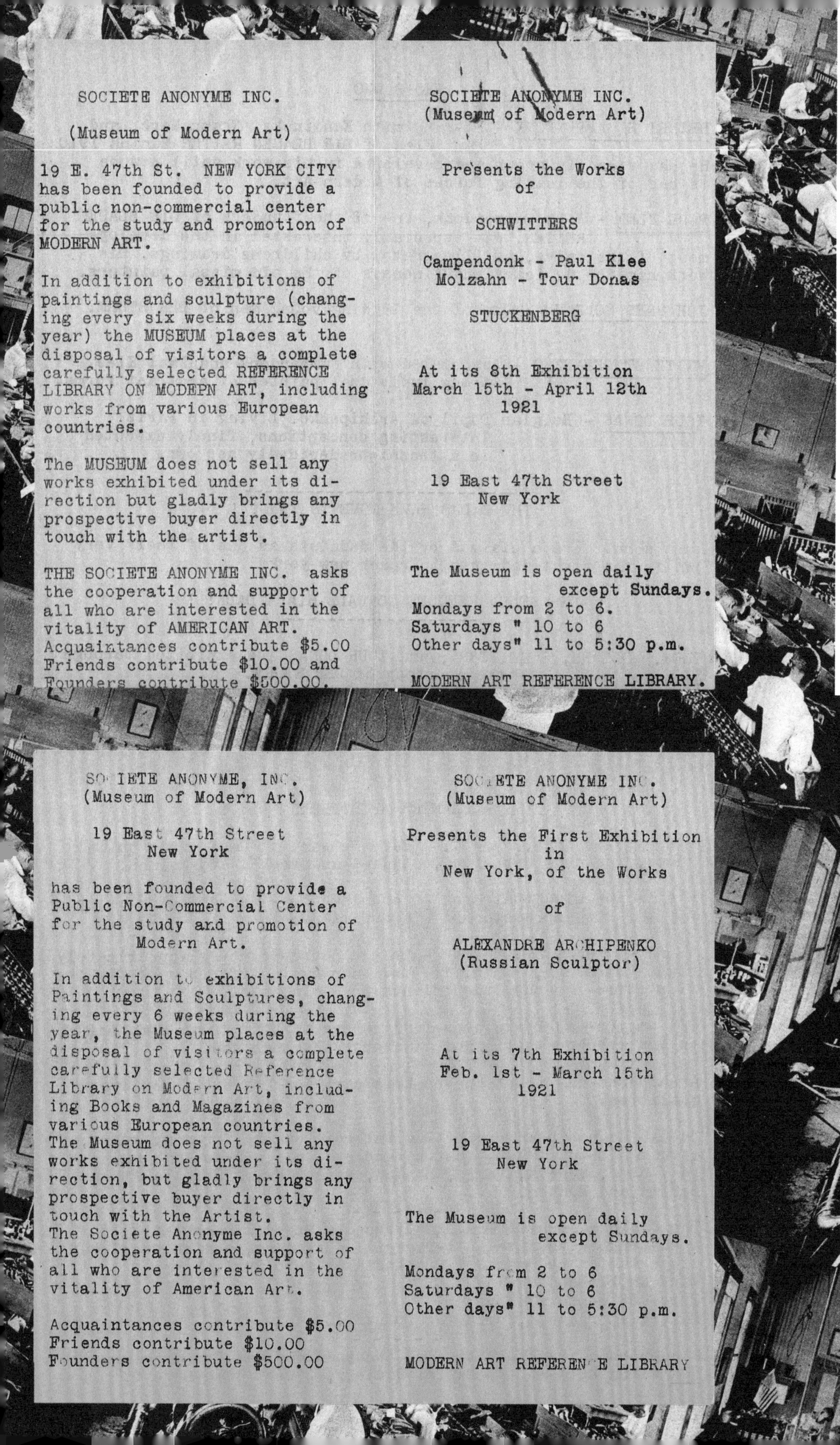

SOCIETE ANONYME INC.

(Museum of Modern Art)

19 E. 47th St. NEW YORK CITY has been founded to provide a public non-commercial center for the study and promotion of MODERN ART.

In addition to exhibitions of paintings and sculpture (changing every six weeks during the year) the MUSEUM places at the disposal of visitors a complete carefully selected REFERENCE LIBRARY ON MODEPN ART, including works from various European countries.

The MUSEUM does not sell any works exhibited under its direction but gladly brings any prospective buyer directly in touch with the artist.

THE SOCIETE ANONYME INC. asks the cooperation and support of all who are interested in the vitality of AMERICAN ART.
Acquaintances contribute $5.00
Friends contribute $10.00 and
Founders contribute $500.00.

SOCIETE ANONYME INC.
(Museum of Modern Art)

Presents the Works
of

SCHWITTERS

Campendonk - Paul Klee
Molzahn - Tour Donas

STUCKENBERG

At its 8th Exhibition
March 15th - April 12th
1921

19 East 47th Street
New York

The Museum is open daily
except Sundays.
Mondays from 2 to 6.
Saturdays " 10 to 6
Other days" 11 to 5:30 p.m.

MODERN ART REFERENCE LIBRARY.

SOCIETE ANONYME, INC.
(Museum of Modern Art)

19 East 47th Street
New York

has been founded to provide a Public Non-Commercial Center for the study and promotion of Modern Art.

In addition to exhibitions of Paintings and Sculptures, changing every 6 weeks during the year, the Museum places at the disposal of visitors a complete carefully selected Reference Library on Modern Art, including Books and Magazines from various European countries.
The Museum does not sell any works exhibited under its direction, but gladly brings any prospective buyer directly in touch with the Artist.
The Societe Anonyme Inc. asks the cooperation and support of all who are interested in the vitality of American Art.

Acquaintances contribute $5.00
Friends contribute $10.00
Founders contribute $500.00

SOCIETE ANONYME INC.
(Museum of Modern Art)

Presents the First Exhibition
in
New York, of the Works

of

ALEXANDRE ARCHIPENKO
(Russian Sculptor)

At its 7th Exhibition
Feb. 1st - March 15th
1921

19 East 47th Street
New York

The Museum is open daily
except Sundays.

Mondays from 2 to 6
Saturdays " 10 to 6
Other days" 11 to 5:30 p.m.

MODERN ART REFERENCE LIBRARY

036 [Invitation card] *Societe Anonyme Inc. (Museum of Modern Art) Presents the Works of Schwitters—Campendonk—Paul Klee—Molzahn—Tour Donas—Stuckenberg*, New York 1921

037 [Invitation card] *Societe Anonyme Inc. (Museum of Modern Art) Presents the First Exhibition in New York, of the Works of Alexandre Archipenko (Russian Sculptor)*, New York 1921

038 [Invitation card] *Societe Anonyme Inc. (Museum of Modern Art) Presents the First Exhibition in New York, of the Works of Dorothea A. Dreier (American Painter)*, New York 1921

039 [Invitation card] *Societe Anonyme Inc. (Museum of Modern Art) Announces its Last Exhibition For the Season 1920—1921* […], New York 1921

↓038 ↑036

SOCIETE ANONYME, INC.
(Museum of Modern Art)

19 East 47th Street
New York

has been founded to provide a Public Non-Commercial Center for the study and promotion of Modern Art.

In addition to exhibitions of Paintings and Sculptures, changing every 6 weeks during the year, the Museum places at the disposal of visitors a complete carefully selected Reference Library on Modern Art, including Books and Magazines from various European countries.
The Museum does not sell any works exhibited under its direction, but gladly brings any prospective buyer directly in touch with the Artist
The Societe Anonyme Inc. asks the cooperation and support of all who are interested in the vitality of American Art.

Acquaintances contribute $5.00
Friends contribute $10.00
Founders contribute $500.00

SOCIETE ANONYME INC.
(Museum of Modern Art)

Presents the First Exhibition
in
New York, of the Works
of

DOROTHEA A. DREIER
(American Painter)

At its 9th Exhibition
April 16th - May 15th
1921

19 East 47th Street
New York

The Museum is open daily
except Sundays.
Mondays from 2 to 6
Saturdays " 10 to 6
Other days" 11 to 5:30 p.m.

MODERN ART REFERENCE LIBRARY

63

SOCIETE ANONYME INC.

(Museum of Modern Art)

19 E. 47th St. NEW YORK CITY
has been founded to provide a public non-commercial center for the study and promotion of MODERN ART.

In addition to exhibitions of paintings and sculpture (changing every six weeks during the year) the MUSEUM places at the disposal of visitors a complete carefully selected REFERENCE LIBRARY ON MODERN ART, including works from various European countries.

The Museum does not sell any works exhibited under its direction but gladly brings any prospective buyer directly in touch with the artist.

THE SOCIETE ANONYME INC. asks the cooperation and support of all who are interested in the vitality of AMERICAN ART.
Acquaintances contribute $5.00
Friends contribute $10.00 and
Founders contribute $500.00.

SOCIETE ANONYME INC.
(Museum of Modern Art)

Announces its Last Exhibition
~~For the Season 1920-1921~~
and
Presents the Works
of

Villon-Duchamp-Katherine Dreier
Johannes Molzahn - George Muche
John Covert - L. Godewols
Arnold Topp - Joseph Garvey
Henry Fitch Taylor

At its 10th Exhibition
May 16th - June 15th
1921

19 East 47th Street
New York

The Museum is open daily
except Sundays.
Mondays from 2 to 6.
Saturdays " 10 to 9.
Other days" 11 to 5:30 p.m.

MODERN ART REFERENCE LIBRARY.

↓039 ↑037

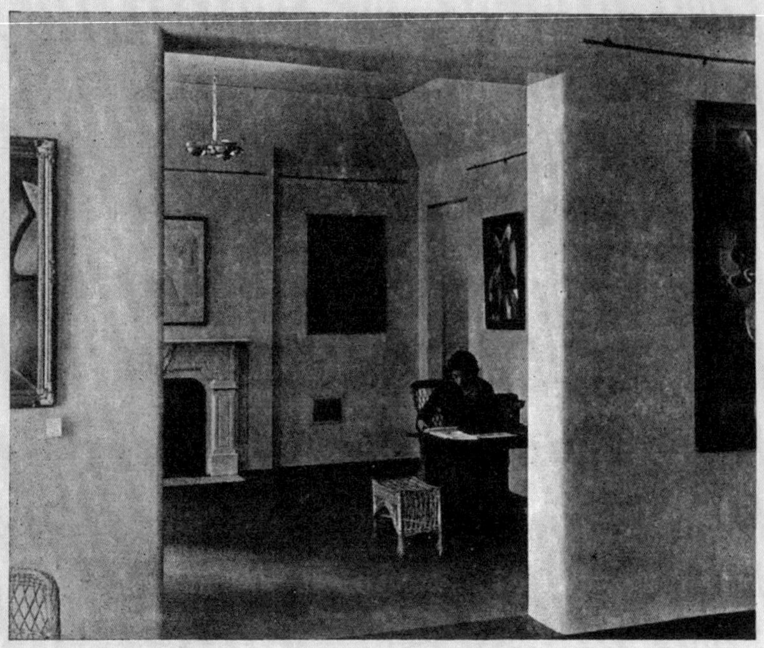

FRONTISPIECE

EXHIBITION ROOMS

of

THE SOCIÉTÉ ANONYME, INC.

(Museum of Modern Art)

19 E. 47th Street

New York

2

040 see 030, 2
041 [Booklet] Jennings Tofel, *Form in Painting*, New York: Société Anonyme, Inc. 1921
042 [Booklet] Jennings Tofel, *Expression*, New York: Société Anonyme, Inc. 1923

↓041 ↑040

FORM

Published by the

SOCIÉTÉ ANONYME, Inc.

19 East 47th St., New York

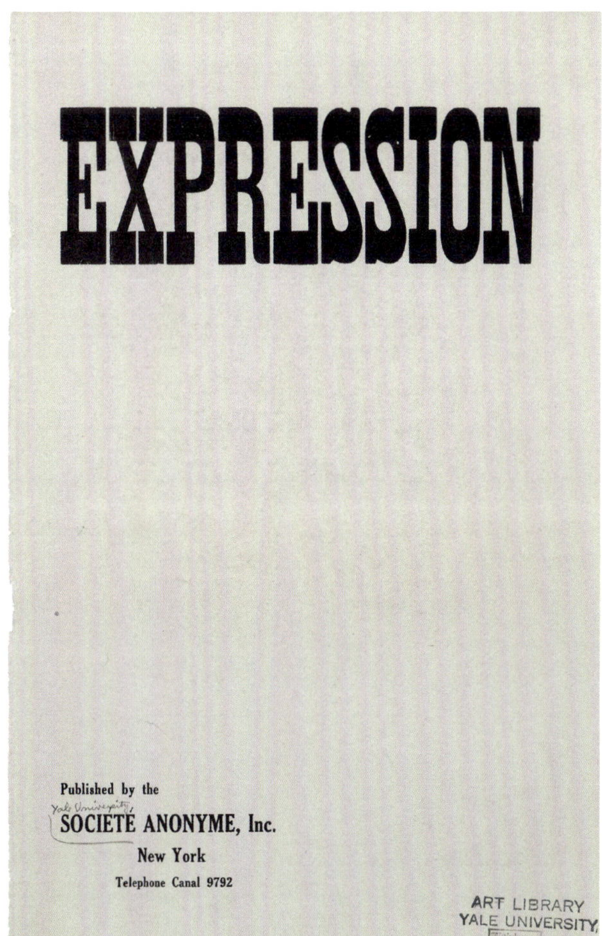
EXPRESSION

Published by the

SOCIÉTÉ ANONYME, Inc.

New York

Telephone Canal 9792

↓042

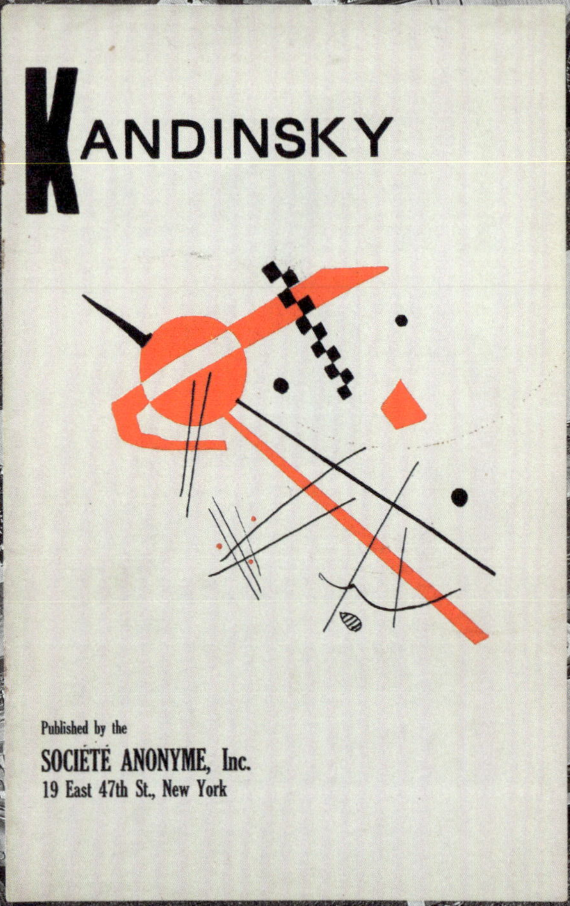

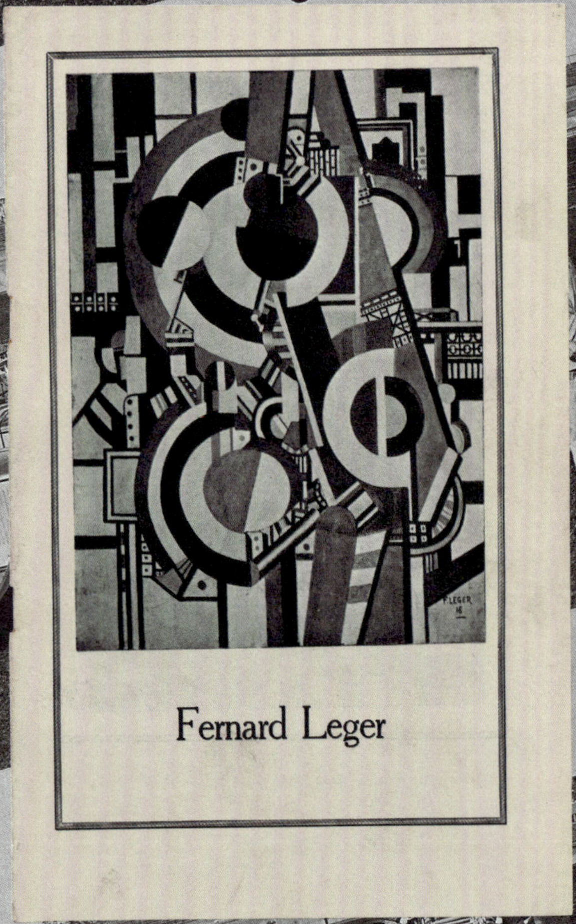

043 [Booklet] *Kandinsky*, New York: Société Anonyme, Inc. 1923, cover with an illustration by Wassily Kandinsky
044 [Booklet] *Fernand Leger, New York: Société Anonyme, Inc., Anderson Galleries 1925*, cover with a painting by Fernand Léger
045 [Booklet] *Archipenko*, New York: Société Anonyme. Inc. 1921, [unpaginated]
046 [Booklet] *Stella*, New York: Société Anonyme, Inc. 1923, 2–3, painting by Joseph Stella: *The Prow*

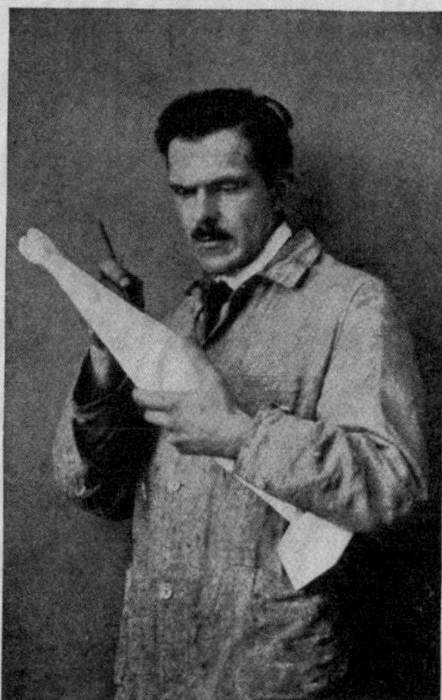

ARCHIPENKO

An Appreciation by IVAN GOLL

Translated from the French by Mary Knoblauch

Everyone knows of the egg
of Christopher Columbus,
It was an upright egg
fixed on its flattened base,
the egg of an inventor.
The sculpture of Archipenko
is the first ovoidal egg
Held in intense equilibrium,
Like a motionless top
On its animated point.
Blaise Cendrars.

THERE appeared in a concert hall the other day, above the brown violins, the black swallow tails, the red laughter, the white faces, an unexpected conductor, no—not a conductor of the orchestra, but a conductor of life.

IT was a work of art, a plastic figure by Archipenko, placed in the middle of the hall, like a window open to all the horizons of the world, like a diamond which consumes in itself all the flames from the seven colored source, a receiver of the external motion. That day a new art was born.

THAT misshapen form of polished white sheet iron, seemed to be the true reservoir of a life, which we round about: orchestra, auditors, halls, stained glass windows and pictures, believed to be alive. An enchanted mirror!

AND such is the mission of all works of art, to create an existence drawn from within ourselves, that is, from within the mind of him who looks, who reads, or who hears—to be the reflec-

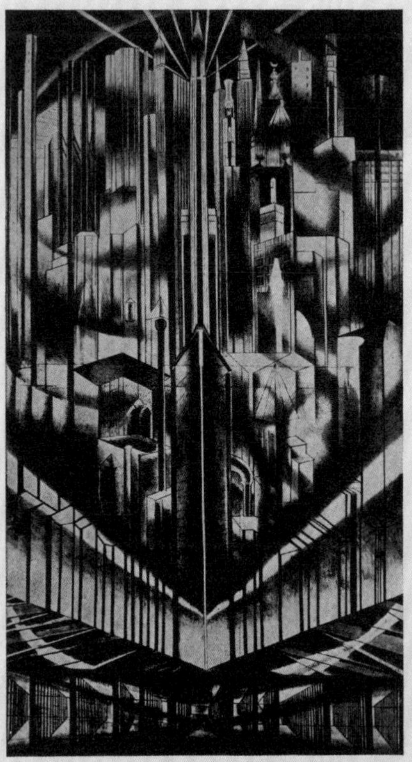

"THE PROW"

WHO is Joseph Stella?
Is he an American? An Italian? Who is he? And how comes it that he of all painters should be constantly interpreting New York?

I THINK New York can claim him for her own. For, though born in Italy, where he received his art education in Rome, and later joined the Italian Futurists — New York left her impress upon him so strongly, when on a visit here as a lad of fifteen — that he could never again escape her — for New York had chosen him — claimed him — as her interpreter.

AND New York was wise to claim him as her interpreter — for few painters have ever lived who had the amount of vitality to give that New York demands — and Stella is vital. Besides, Stella has given his all to this young giant throbbing, pulsating with life — not the life of flesh and blood — but of cold, hard steel. Cold, powerful steel girders — drilled, driven into rocks — and it is this very coldness which Stella emphasizes — Stella, who came from warm and sunny Italy — from the land of warmth and sunshine — the land of soft contours and gay, happy people — the land of dreams — not of hard, cold realities.

THIS son of Italy has left all the softness, all the warmth, for the call of the brilliancy that steel has to give — for the call of the brilliancy of the flare of the electric lights — which dazzle but never warm. He has brought out the hardness

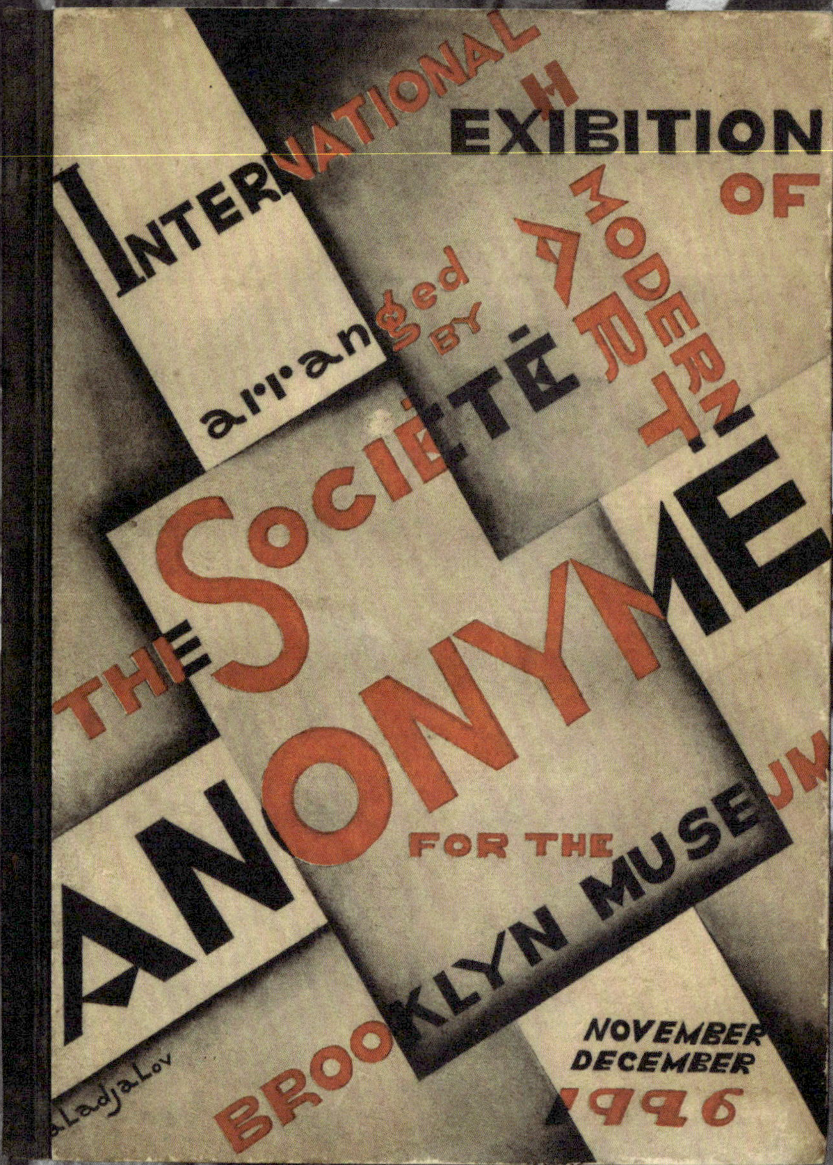

047 *International Exhibition of Modern Art, arranged by Société Anonyme for the Brooklyn Museum*, New York: Société Anonyme, Inc.–Museum of Modern Art 1926, cover by Constantin Alajálov; 42–43, portraits of and artworks by Edmund Kesting and Adolf Küthe; 56–57, portrait of László Moholy-Nagy and view of his exhibition at Galerie Fides Dresden, photo by Lucia Moholy

INTERNATIONAL EXHIBITION OF MODERN ART AT BROOKLYN MUSEUM The *International Exhibition of Modern Art* held between November 19, 1926 and January 9, 1927 at the Brooklyn Museum included more than 300 works by 60 artists representing a total of 19 countries. The co-curators of the show were Katherine S. Dreier and Marcel Duchamp. Preparations for this groundbreaking exhibition started in 1925, and Dreier decided to travel throughout Europe to meet with avant-garde artists and select artworks. In Paris, she met Fernand Léger, in Hannover, Kurt Schwitters, and she travelled to Dresden and Prague with Lucia Moholy. She also visited the Fides Gallery in Dresden and later included a Dresden-based artist, Edmund Kesting, in the show. After completing her list of artists and artworks, she opened the largest modern art exhibit to be held in the United States since the 1913 Armory Show. Over 52,000 visitors viewed the exhibition, and it travelled to three other venues: Anderson Galleries in New York, Albright Art Gallery in Buffalo, and the Art Gallery of Toronto.

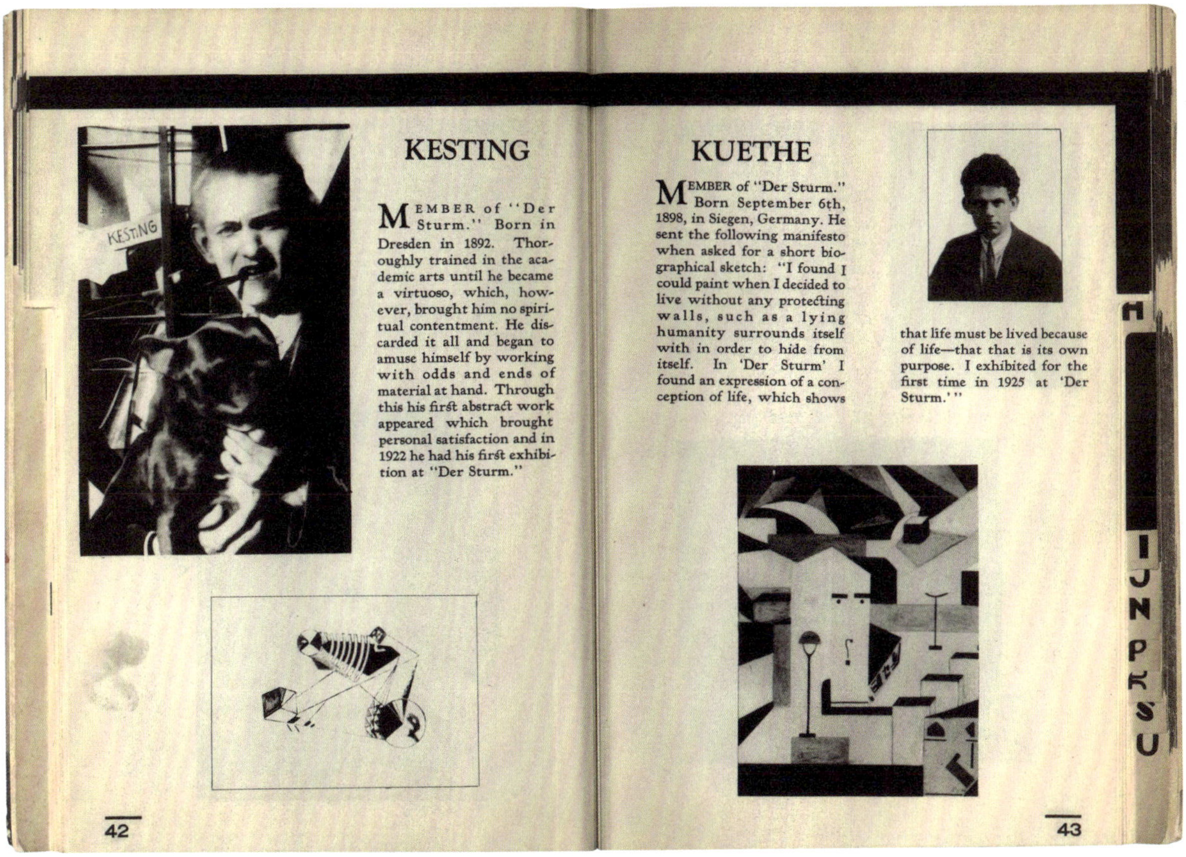

KESTING

MEMBER of "Der Sturm." Born in Dresden in 1892. Thoroughly trained in the academic arts until he became a virtuoso, which, however, brought him no spiritual contentment. He discarded it all and began to amuse himself by working with odds and ends of material at hand. Through this his first abstract work appeared which brought personal satisfaction and in 1922 he had his first exhibition at "Der Sturm."

KUETHE

MEMBER of "Der Sturm." Born September 6th, 1898, in Siegen, Germany. He sent the following manifesto when asked for a short biographical sketch: "I found I could paint when I decided to live without any protecting walls, such as a lying humanity surrounds itself with in order to hide from itself. In 'Der Sturm' I found an expression of a conception of life, which shows that life must be lived because of life—that that is its own purpose. I exhibited for the first time in 1925 at 'Der Sturm.'"

42

43

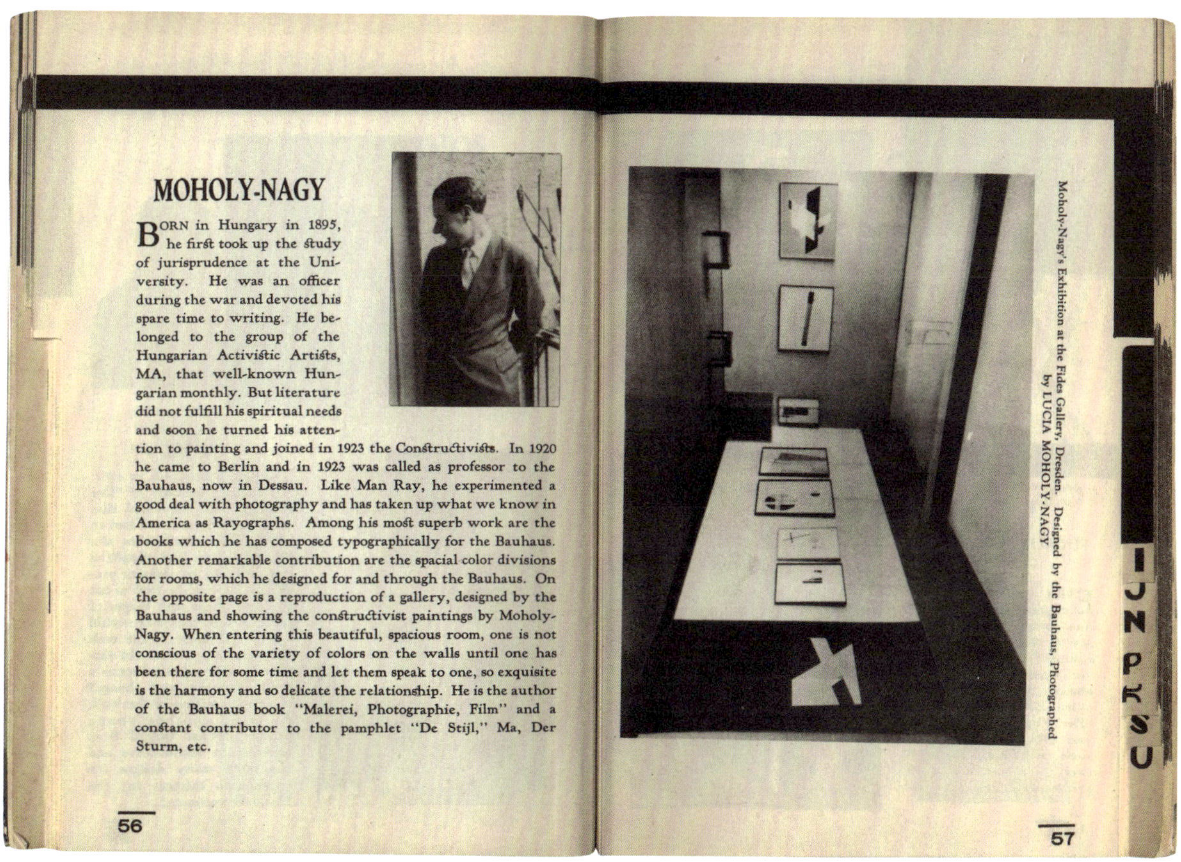

MOHOLY-NAGY

BORN in Hungary in 1895, he first took up the study of jurisprudence at the University. He was an officer during the war and devoted his spare time to writing. He belonged to the group of the Hungarian Activistic Artists, MA, that well-known Hungarian monthly. But literature did not fulfill his spiritual needs and soon he turned his attention to painting and joined in 1923 the Constructivists. In 1920 he came to Berlin and in 1923 was called as professor to the Bauhaus, now in Dessau. Like Man Ray, he experimented a good deal with photography and has taken up what we know in America as Rayographs. Among his most superb work are the books which he has composed typographically for the Bauhaus. Another remarkable contribution are the spacial color divisions for rooms, which he designed for and through the Bauhaus. On the opposite page is a reproduction of a gallery, designed by the Bauhaus and showing the constructivist paintings by Moholy-Nagy. When entering this beautiful, spacious room, one is not conscious of the variety of colors on the walls until one has been there for some time and let them speak to one, so exquisite is the harmony and so delicate the relationship. He is the author of the Bauhaus book "Malerei, Photographie, Film" and a constant contributor to the pamphlet "De Stijl," Ma, Der Sturm, etc.

Moholy-Nagy's Exhibition at the Fides Gallery, Dresden. Designed by the Bauhaus, Photographed by LUCIA MOHOLY-NAGY

56

57

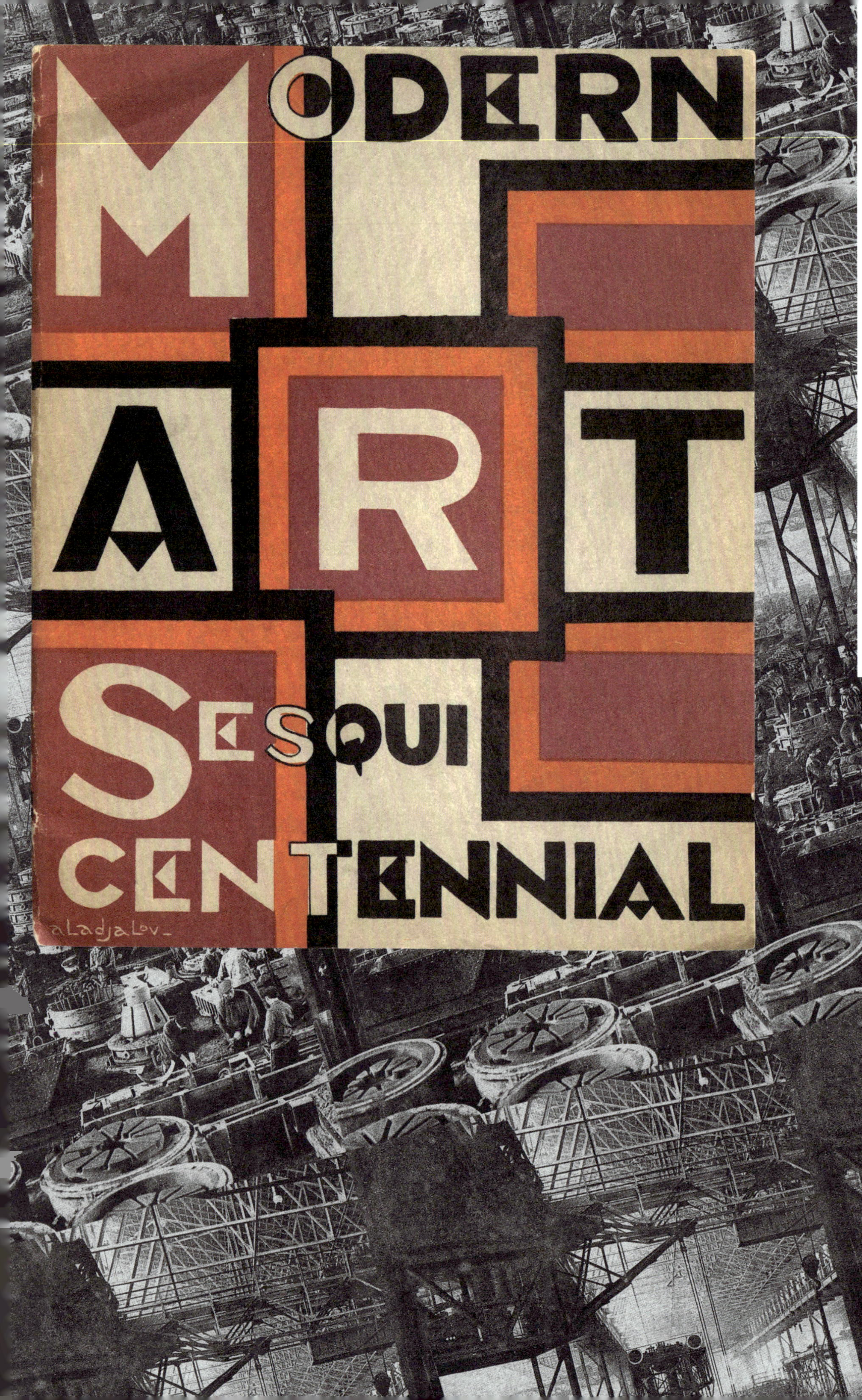

048 Société Anonyme, Inc., *Modern Art at the Sesqui-Centennial Exhibition*, New York: Société Anonyme, Inc.–Museum of Modern Art 1926, cover by Constantin Alajálov
049 *Brochure Quarterly*, no. 1, July 1928, ed. Société Anonyme, Inc., New York, cover by Constantin Alajálov
050 *Brochure Quarterly*, no. 2, October 1928–January 1929, ed. Société Anonyme, Inc., New York, cover by Constantin Alajálov

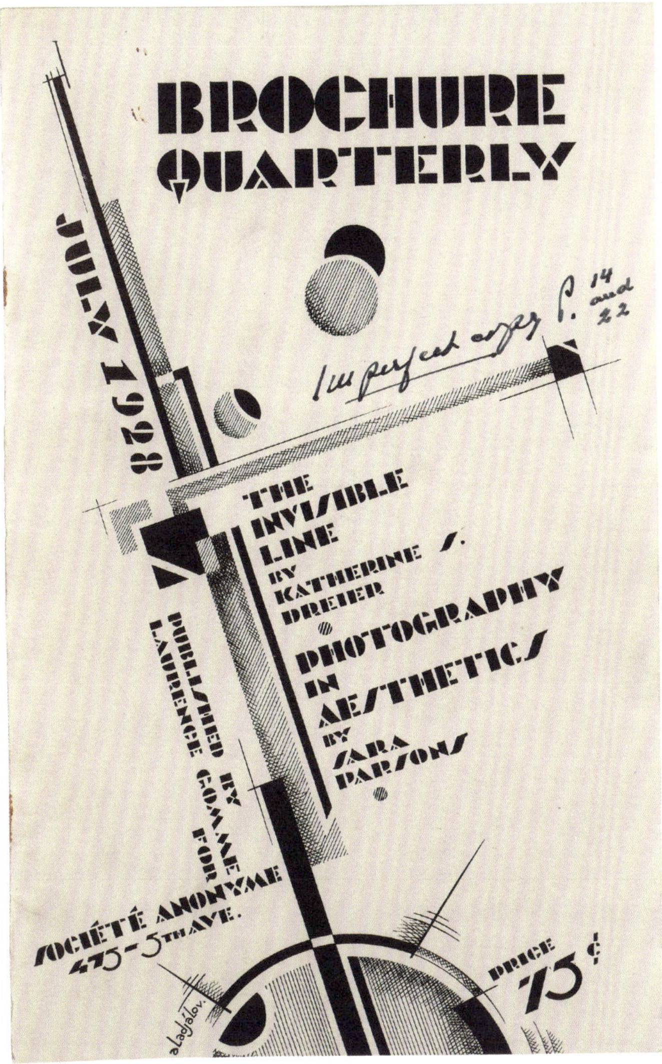
BROCHURE
QUARTERLY
JULY 1928
THE INVISIBLE LINE BY KATHERINE S. DREIER
PHOTOGRAPHY IN AESTHETICS BY SARA PARSONS
PUBLISHED BY LAURENCE GOMME FOR
SOCIÉTÉ ANONYME
475-5TH AVE.
PRICE 75¢

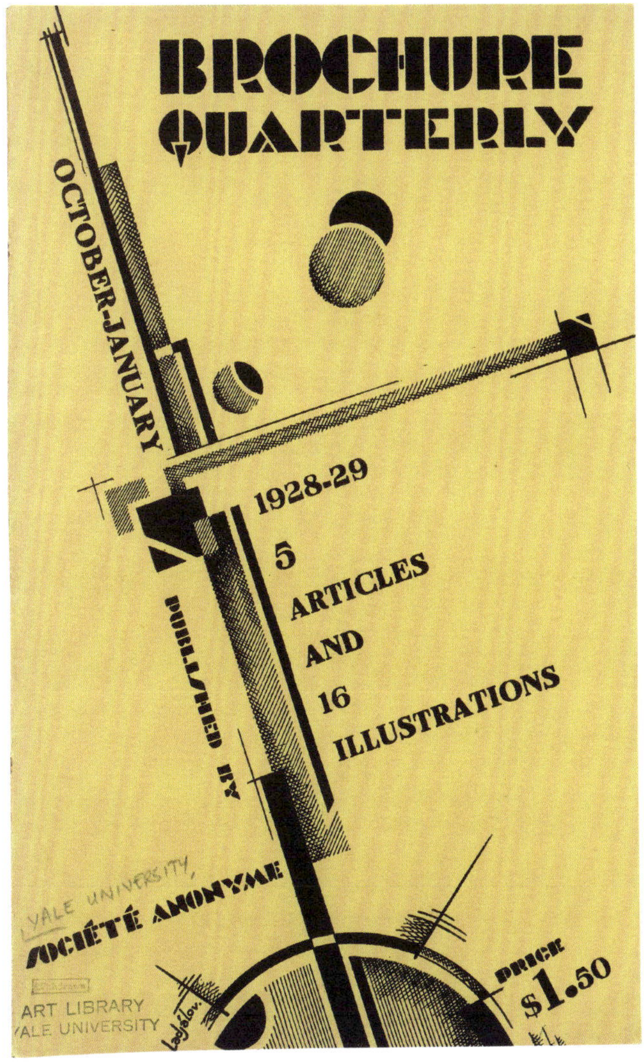
BROCHURE
QUARTERLY
OCTOBER-JANUARY
1928-29
5 ARTICLES AND 16 ILLUSTRATIONS
PUBLISHED BY
SOCIÉTÉ ANONYME
PRICE $1.50
ART LIBRARY
YALE UNIVERSITY

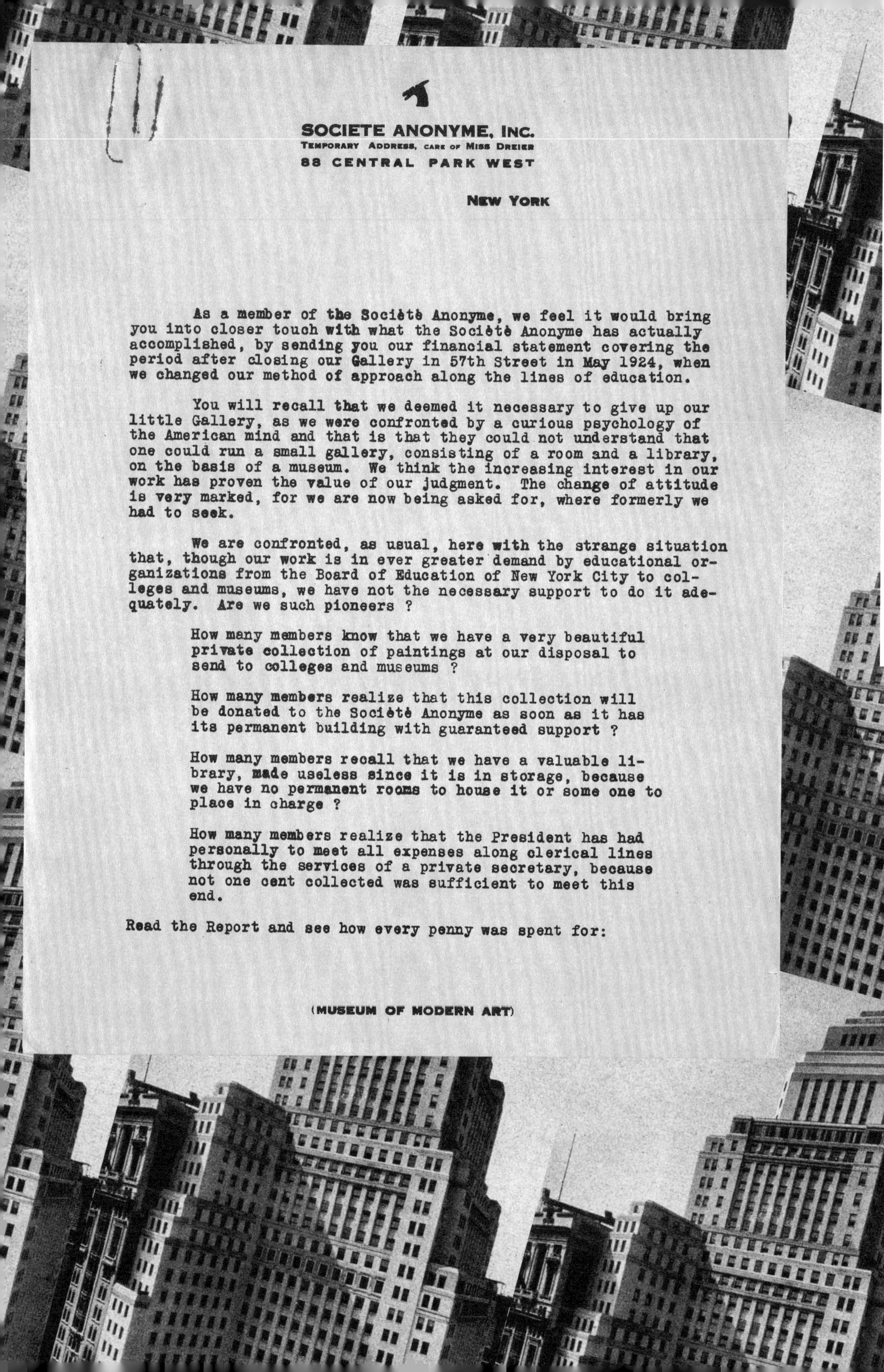

SOCIETE ANONYME, INC.
TEMPORARY ADDRESS, CARE OF MISS DREIER
88 CENTRAL PARK WEST

NEW YORK

As a member of the Sociètè Anonyme, we feel it would bring you into closer touch with what the Sociètè Anonyme has actually accomplished, by sending you our financial statement covering the period after closing our Gallery in 57th Street in May 1924, when we changed our method of approach along the lines of education.

You will recall that we deemed it necessary to give up our little Gallery, as we were confronted by a curious psychology of the American mind and that is that they could not understand that one could run a small gallery, consisting of a room and a library, on the basis of a museum. We think the increasing interest in our work has proven the value of our judgment. The change of attitude is very marked, for we are now being asked for, where formerly we had to seek.

We are confronted, as usual, here with the strange situation that, though our work is in ever greater demand by educational organizations from the Board of Education of New York City to colleges and museums, we have not the necessary support to do it adequately. Are we such pioneers ?

How many members know that we have a very beautiful private collection of paintings at our disposal to send to colleges and museums ?

How many members realize that this collection will be donated to the Sociètè Anonyme as soon as it has its permanent building with guaranteed support ?

How many members recall that we have a valuable library, made useless since it is in storage, because we have no permanent rooms to house it or some one to place in charge ?

How many members realize that the President has had personally to meet all expenses along clerical lines through the services of a private secretary, because not one cent collected was sufficient to meet this end.

Read the Report and see how every penny was spent for:

(MUSEUM OF MODERN ART)

051 [Typescript] [no title], New York: Société Anonyme, Inc., presumably 1927, 1–2/6

Printers' Bills,
Gallery Expenses,
Advertising,
Stamps,
Expressage, Freight or Insurance, and
Guides into the Realm of Modern Art.

Can this go on ? ? ?

We need a permanent home !

How can we achieve it ?

The Directors of the Sociètè Anonyme would appreciate very much any suggestion as to how to achieve this end and I would ask you to address such suggestions to me in writing, so that they may receive the proper consideration.

The present big International Exhibition, representing twenty-three countries, which was assembled by the Sociètè Anonyme for the Brooklyn Museum, will travel to the Albright Art Gallery, the Museum at Buffalo and from there to the Art Gallery of Toronto, Museum at Toronto, before being returned to Europe. A section will be sent to Vassar in connection with their Modern Language Week.

May we count on this year's contribution, not only for our current work, for we have the entire expense of the return of this Exhibition from New York to Europe. But, maybe, you will already begin to contribute a mite to our Building Fund, to which was donated the first $1000.00 by Miss Mary E. Dreier in memory of our sister, Dorothea A. Dreier, for which a special account has been arranged, so that the money may draw interest and not be used for other purposes.

See our deficit and help us if you want us to continue.

Do you not feel the need of our work and has our work not won enough friends to continue it ?

Faithfully yours,

OUR AIM.

The aim of the Societè Anonyme is educational. It is an international organization for the promotion of the study of the prophetic in art, based on the fundamental principles for students in America and renders aid to conserve the vigor and vitality of the new expressions of beauty in the art of to-day. One of its tenets is that it does not exhibit sketches, but only the complete expression of a thought.

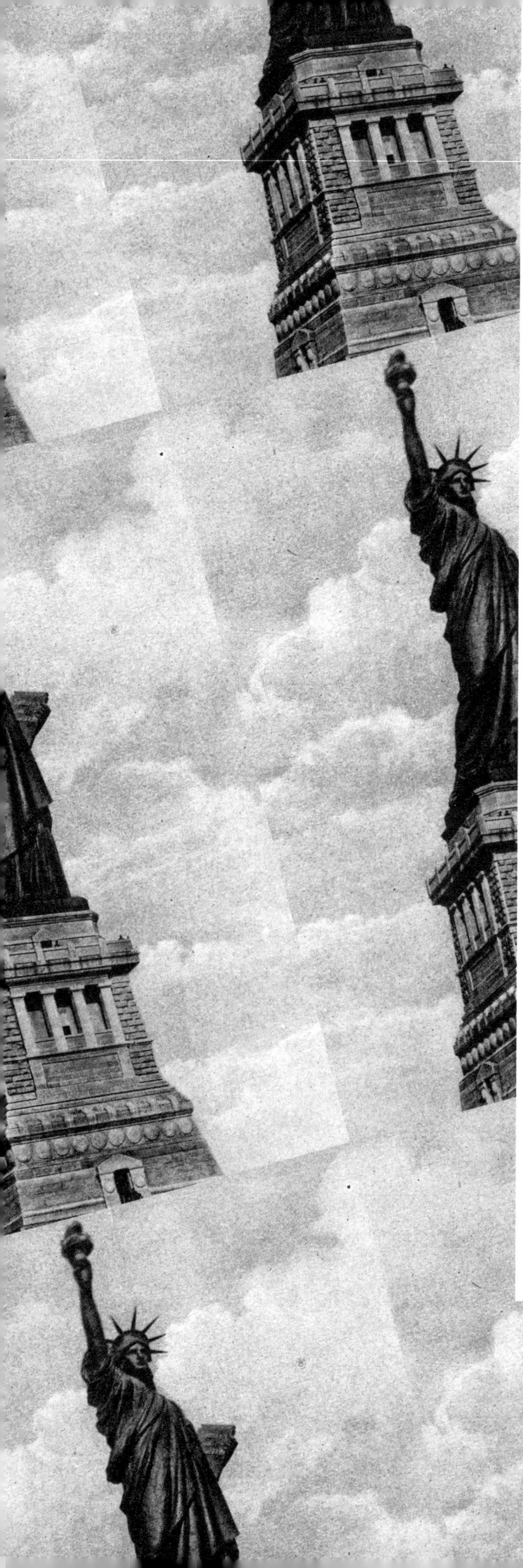

TRANSATLANTIC MAGAZINES AND EXHIBITIONS

News of Futurism, Expressionism and Cubism, as well as Dada, Purism and Constructivism, reached America in the 1920s not only through exhibitions but also through modernist magazines. Magazines such as *Broom* (1921–1924), *transition* (1927–1938) and *The Little Review* (1914–1929) all fostered transatlantic exchange and had editorial offices both in New York and on the European continent. *Broom* operated between Rome, Berlin, and New York. *The Little Review* was founded in Chicago and had a foreign editorship in London (Ezra Pound); it later moved to New York and to Paris, publishing its final number in 1929 with both New York and Paris editorial addresses. The magazine *transition*, founded in 1927, furthered the goals of its predecessors and provided a forum for transatlantic exchanges of art and literature in the English language with an editorial office in Paris and New York (from 1935). All three of these magazines were catalysts in disseminating reproductions of European avant-garde works and writings in the 1920s, and they all fostered specialized transnational discourse networks reaching beyond nation states and continents by straddling the Atlantic Ocean.

The Little Review played a double role, both as a magazine that promoted European avant-gardes and as an institution that initiated exhibitions on American and European modern art. It was founded in the 1910s as a literary magazine, but in the 1920s it began publishing special numbers devoted to artists (for example Francis Picabia and Constantin Brâncuşi), and organizing experimental exhibitions related to Machine Age aesthetics. When its founder, Margaret Anderson, moved to Paris, and the co-editor of the magazine, Jane Heap, became the sole editor, the latter shifted its focus from literature towards the visual arts. Inspired by the undertakings of Société Anonyme, Heap recognized the potential of exhibiting the newest avant-garde currents at The Little Review Gallery and organized large-scale exhibition projects with global avant-garde trends at the Steinway Building in New York. With her innovative practice of connecting exhibition-making with magazine publishing, two special numbers of *The Little Review* also served as exhibition catalogs. In this way, the exhibition could circulate in printed form within the specialized transatlantic avant-garde network of modernist and avant-garde magazines.

↓052

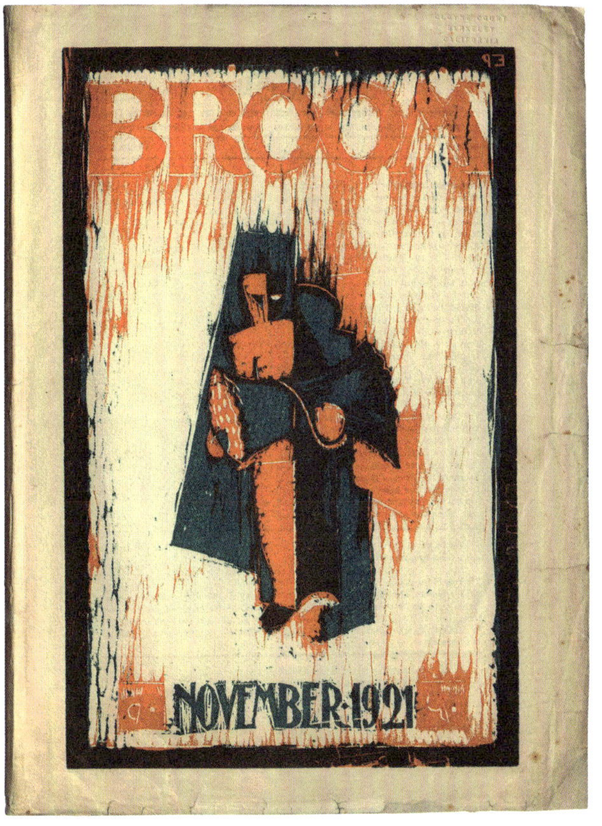

052 *Broom*, no. 1, November 1921, ed. Harold A. Loeb, Alfred Kreymborg, Rome/New York, cover by Enrico Prampolini

BROOM: BETWEEN AVANT-GARDES AND HARLEM RENAISSANCE *Broom* was a magazine primarily edited between 1921 and 1924 by Harold Loeb, a cousin of Peggy Guggenheim, a promising literary figure of the time. When he arrived in Rome in 1921, he decided to establish a magazine that would focus on the newest literature and art in the US and Europe. He was rather critical of American mass culture and debated it on the pages of the magazine with another *Broom* associate, Matthew Josephson. Covers of *Broom* were designed by prominent figures of diverse avant-garde "-isms", including Alicja Halicka and Louis Marcoussis (Cubism), El Lissitzky (Constructivism), Fernand Léger (Purism), Enrico Prampolini (Futurism), and Laszló Moholy-Nagy (Bauhaus). Although it had been established in Rome, *Broom* was an American magazine intended for the American audience. Lola Ridge became the American editor, based in New York City, and in October 1922, Loeb announced that the magazine was moving to Berlin. He continued to edit *Broom* until March 1923. It was later revived in New York City in August 1923, and ultimately ceased publication in January 1924 under Josephson's editorship. *Broom* not only printed examples of European literary and artistic avant-gardes, but also of socially-engaged American writers, including the left-leaning John dos Passos and an African American, Jean Toomer, an important figure of the Harlem Renaissance.

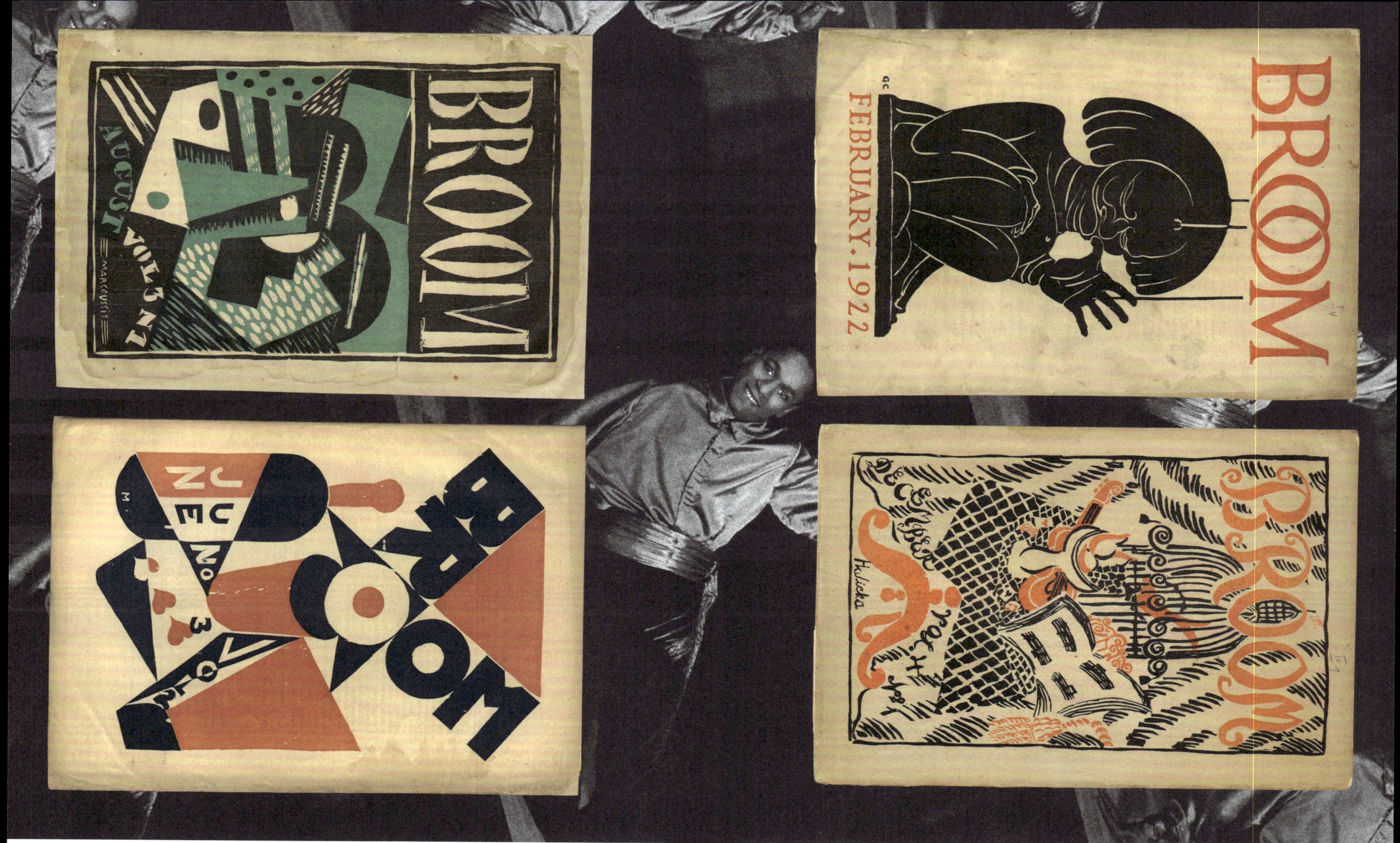

057 *Broom*, no. 2, September 1922, ed. Harold A. Loeb, Rome/New York/London, cover by Juan Gris
058 *Broom*, no. 1, April 1922, ed. Harold A. Loeb, Rome/New York/London, cover by unknown artist
059 *Broom*, no. 4, March 1923, ed. Harold A. Loeb, Berlin/New York, cover by Man Ray
060 *Broom*, no. 3, October 1923, ed. Harold A. Loeb, New York. cover by Edward Nagle

053 *Broom*, no. 4, February 1922, ed. Harold A. Loeb, Alfred Kreymborg, Rome/New York/London, cover by Gordon Craig
054 *Broom*, no. 1, December 1922, ed. Harold A. Loeb, Berlin/New York, cover by Alice Halicka
055 *Broom*, no. 1, August 1922, ed. Harold A. Loeb, Rome/New York/London, cover by Louis Marcoussis
056 *Broom*, no. 3, June 1922, ed. Harold A. Loeb, Rome/New York/London, cover by Ladislaw Medges

↓058 ↓057 ↑054 ↑053

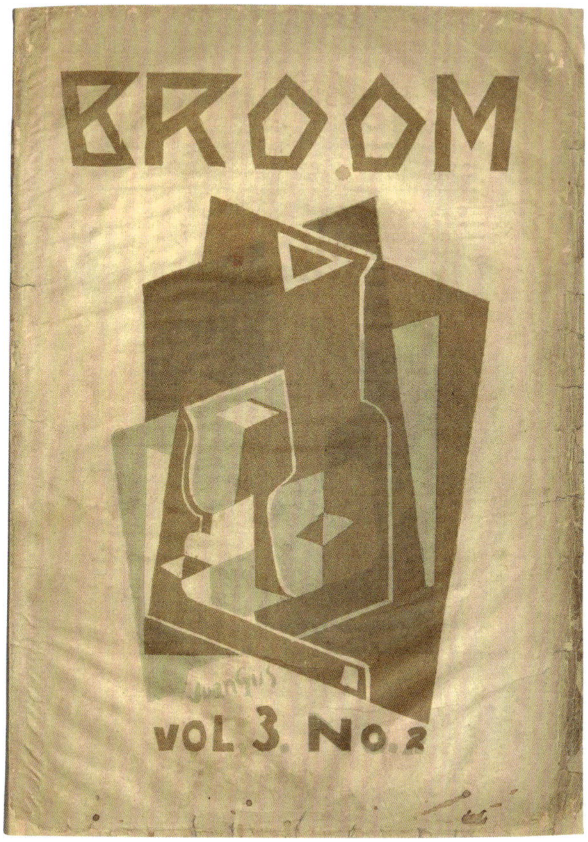

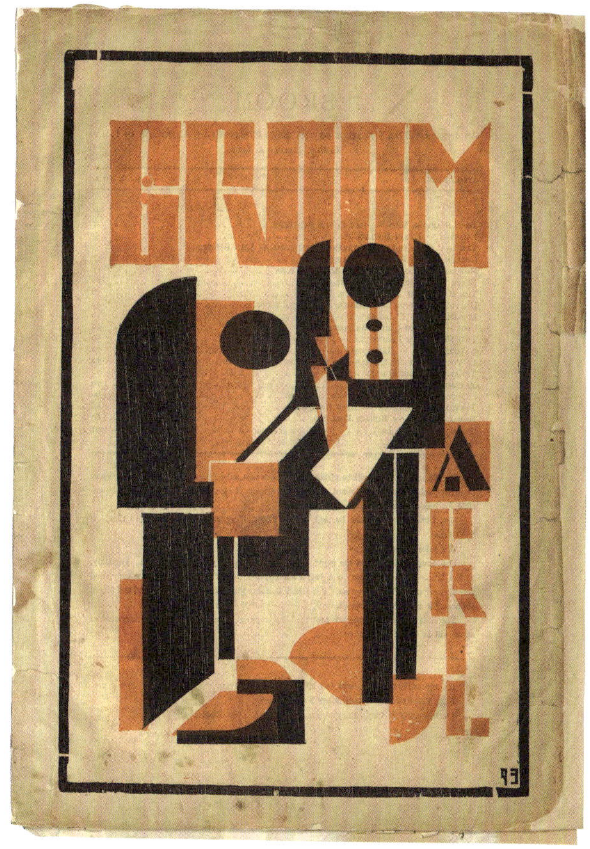

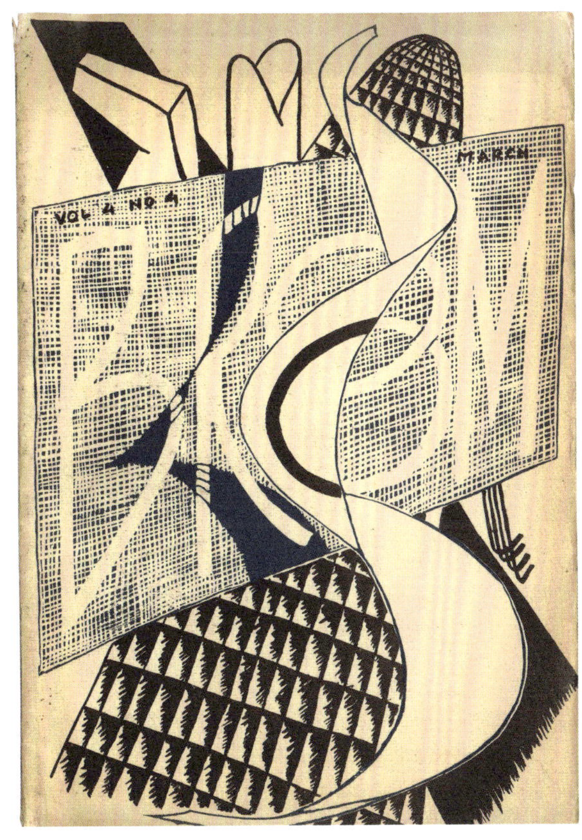

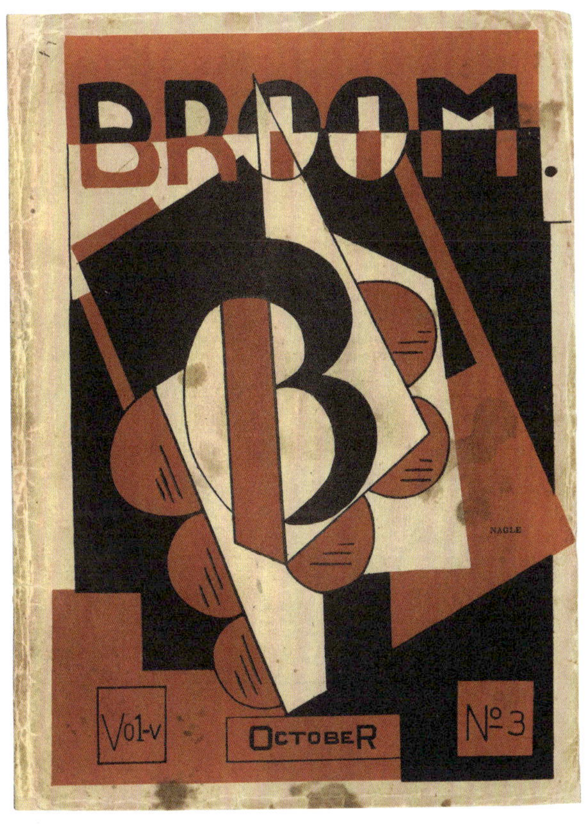

↓060 ↓059 ↑056 ↑055

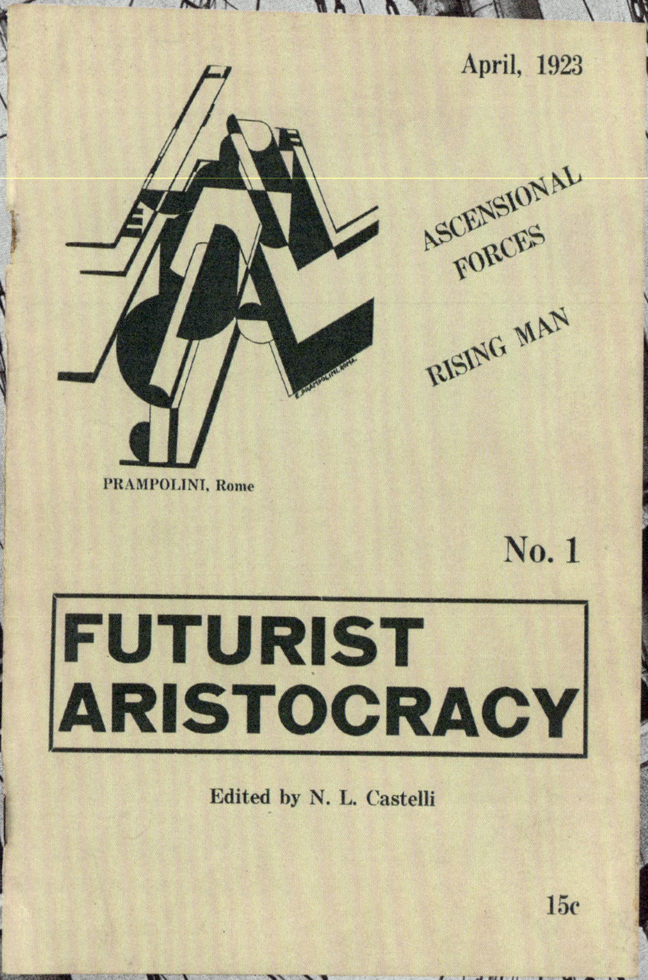

061 *Futurist Aristocracy*, no. 1, April 1923, ed. Nanni [Giovanni] Leone Castelli, New York, cover with an illustration by Enrico Prampolini; inside cover with a painting by Charles Sheeler: *Skyscrapers of New York*; 15–16 with a painting by John Marin: *New York*

FUTURIST ARISTOCRACY *Futurist Aristocracy* was a magazine seeking to popularize the postulates and works of the Italian Futurist movement in the US. It was edited by Nanni Leone Castelli, who arrived in New York in 1922 to open a Futurist art gallery. However, the project failed and he returned to Italy two years later. In 1923, he issued a magazine with only one number. *Futurist Aristocracy* was designed to bring the latest Futurist developments to the American artistic scene. It revealed the international potential of the Futurist movement and demonstrated its affinity with the American Machine Age. The cover was designed by Enrico Prampolini, the author of manifestos glorifying Mechanical Art in the 1920s. Among the artists whose works were reproduced in the magazine was Charles Sheeler, a representative of the painterly style known as Precisionism, which focused on the changing cityscapes of American cities.

190 ↓↑

CHARLES SHEELER

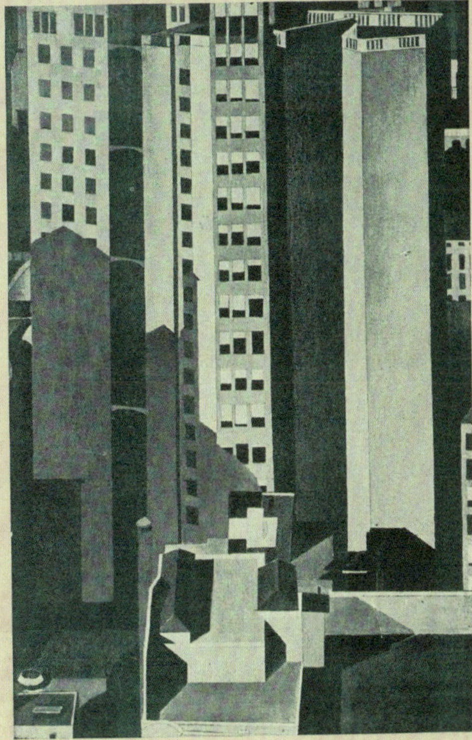

Skyscrapers of New York

SPEED CITY

On a morning of soul torturing wretchedness, while with my great friend Veniero d'Annunzio we were frantically rushing up the long straight majesty of Fifth Avenue in a magnificently powerful and proud "Isotta," I have hurled forth my great youthfully passionate love for the speed of this huge, boundless, unique Cosmopolis. Elated by the danger and the surprise of the policemen drawn up at each of those crossings swarming with thousands of bright human eyes, I felt a sense of mastery over the crowd swiftly disappearing behind the pulsating brightness of our car.

I asked Veniero to forget the colored signals and the energical gestures of those automatons trying to measure both danger and distance. Infernally we drove on, with a will ferociously bent upon the ever increasing speed of our race, happy of its danger!

Streets, streets, streets.

Ffffrrrrrrrrrrrrrr

A long bleating of the horn. Bevies of flappers hurriedly crossing the street.

SsssssssssszzzzzzzzzzzzsssssssssZZZ

Four brakes on each wheel. The "Isotta" had stopped. Veniero had the hard, steely look of the self-controlled aviator. The road stretched on and on, now uphill, now down. Long rows of modern buildings. The joy of high open space. Tall spires defying the blue sky.

Fffffffrrrrrrrrrr ffffffrrrrrrrr

A new flashing start. Smilingly, tensely we drank the strong whistling wind. The elevated droned its heavy metallic rythm on the aerial track of a side street. The muffled glide of the subway rose to a crash. Endless rows of automobiles.

Life—Speed—New York: the ideal city of gipsy poets and international dreamers, of the eternally young lovers clutching at all the strange passions of this convulsed world, of elegant passers-by from Parisian Montmartre or the Berlin of Unter den Linden, of London bohemians, Muscovite outlaws and Italian lovers.

To rent the darkly veiled future the unknown emigrant must fling the proud and tenacious audacity of his intelligence towards a victory against ignorance, over that yawning chasm: the Past and plunge himself headlong in the vortex of American speed, abandoning himself to the mad savage dance. Dominating old conventional forms and the mass steeped in commercialism he must reveal the strange glory of Life, the power of man's spirit and intelligence, the eternal aristocracy of thought, great beyond all the things of this world, reigning supreme on the highest summit of human destiny.

CASTELLI, futurist.

LIFE

We tank the press for its favorable comments on the beginnings of our artistic and literary battle.

The first article dealing with Marinetti, Castelli and the other Futurists was written in New York by Senorita Jesus Alfan (Beatriz Sandoval) and appeared in "La Prensa," the only Spanish daily in America.

The independent painter Robert Edwards, editor of "The Quill," the Old New York Greenwich Village review, has promised to write for "Futurist Aristocracy."

The "Greenwich Village Historical Society" still holds weekly meetings of which Mrs. Catherine Parker Clivette is president and in the course of which Juanita recites her spiritualized poetry.

The "International Club of the City of New York" has recently been formed as a meeting place for all intelligent foreigners and weekly entertainments are given in the shape of concerts, recitals, lectures, etc.

Another newcomer, the "Orient Society," has published the first issue of its official organ "Orient" of which Hari G. Govel is editor. Good! The West must know the East.

The "Union of East & West" is another association for the propagation of Eastern Culture in the West.

JOHN MARIN

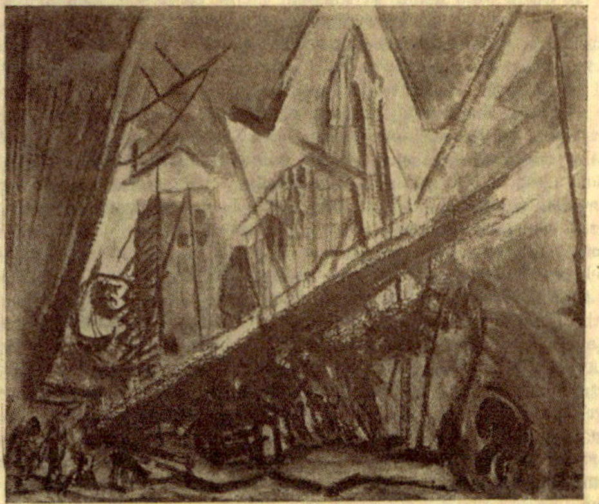

NEW YORK (water color)

INTERNATIONAL ACTIVITIES

Futurism created by the inexhaustible mind of the Italian poet F. T. Marinetti has its own reviews, papers and clubs in all parts of the world:

Germany, Berlin: "Der Futurismus," Director the poet R. Vasari.
France, Paris: "Le Futurisme," Director Marinetti.
Italy, Milan: "Il Futurismo," Director Marinetti.
Italy, Rome: "Noi," Director the great painter Prampolini.
Italy, Florence: "Firenze Futurista," Director Oscar Fusetti.
Italy, Messina: "Balza Futurista," Directors Guglielmo Jannelli and Luciano Nicastro.

Shortly an international review will be published in Italian, German, French and English under the name of "Dynamo." Director: Marinetti. Editors Vasari, Prampolini, Castelli. Editorial offices: Berlin, Germany; Paris, France; Milan, Italy; New York, U. S. A.

FUTURIST ARISTOCRACY

has secured the cooperation of the best advanced artists and writers.

It will be distributed in the leading world centers: London, Madrid, Barcellona, Paris, Berlin, Vienna, Prague, Tokio, Constantinople, Cairo, Mexico, &c.

It is published in simple form so that its circulation may be more rapidly increased among the best artistic and educational circles.

Our English articles will be translated in Italy and reproduced in Italian newspapers.

Marinetti will write special manifestos and articles for "Futurist Aristocracy."

FUTURIST ARISTOCRACY
POST OFFICE BOX 338
Grand Central Station
NEW YORK CITY

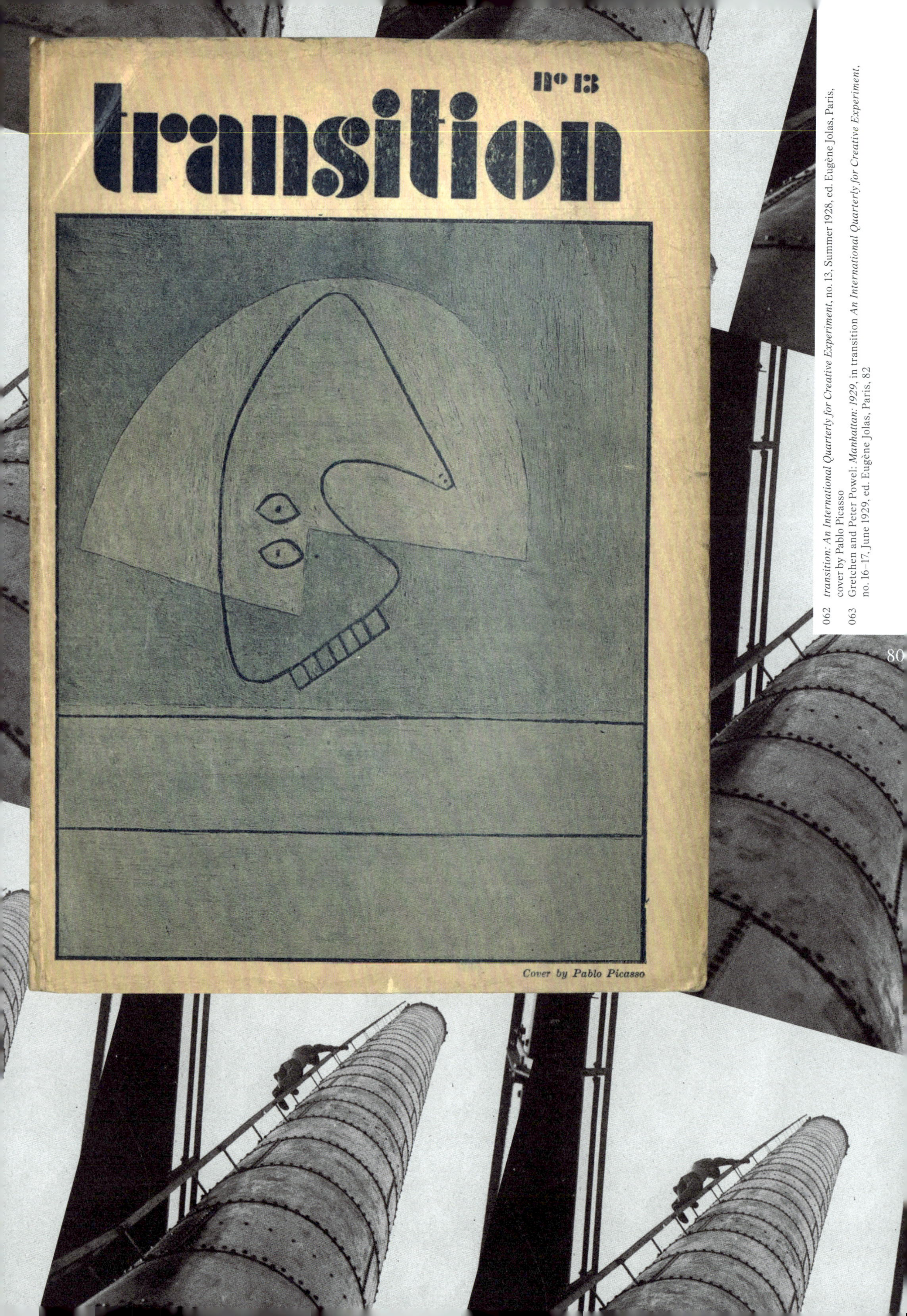

062 *transition: An International Quarterly for Creative Experiment*, no. 13, Summer 1928, ed. Eugène Jolas, Paris, cover by Pablo Picasso

063 Gretchen and Peter Powel: *Manhattan: 1929*, in transition *An International Quarterly for Creative Experiment*, no. 16–17, June 1929, ed. Eugène Jolas, Paris, 82

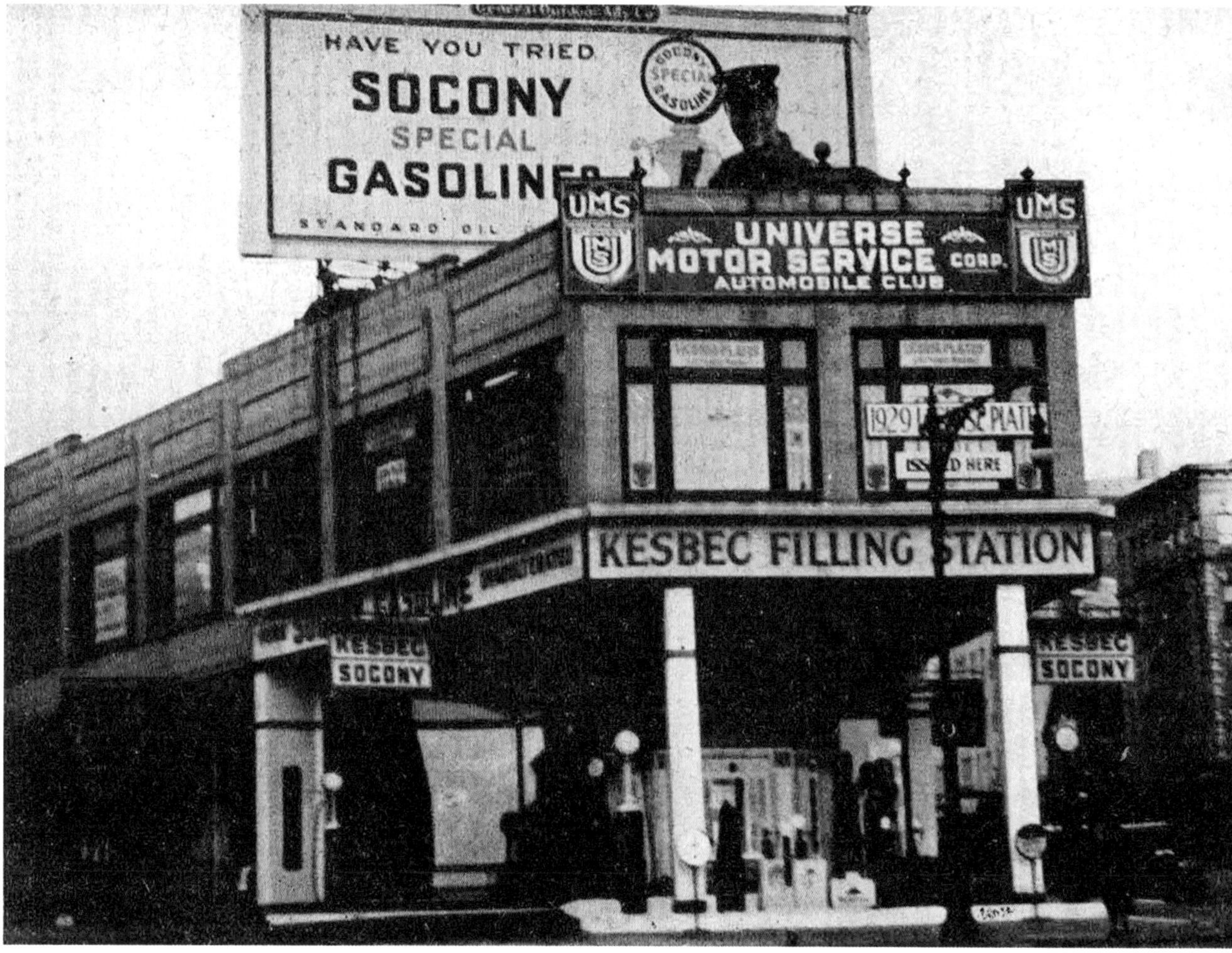

TRANSITION The magazine *transition* was founded in Paris by American-born Eugène Jolas, his wife Maria Jolas, and Elliot Paul in 1927, and ran until 1938. It provided a forum for the transatlantic exchange of art and literature, situating itself within the international avant-garde and championing Dada and Surrealism. It also featured photographs by Berenice Abbott, and reproductions of avant-garde works by Pablo Picasso, Man Ray, Marcel Duchamp, and Piet Mondrian. It published literary works by Gertrude Stein, Franz Kafka, and James Joyce. In the 12th issue from 1928, Jolas addressed the advancements of American literature, and underlined that: "While *transition* will continue to regard itself as a link between Europe and America [...] the emphasis in the future will be placed on American contributions, as we feel that our intensified inquiry into international writing is, for the moment, at a standstill." The magazine had a good reputation within progressive circles in the US, and among its admirers was Michael Gold, the editor of the pro-communist magazine *New Masses*, published in New York. He described *transition* as the magazine which "reflects the mind of the young writers [...] [and] is full of furious anarchistic spirit" (*New Masses*, no. 4, 1928).

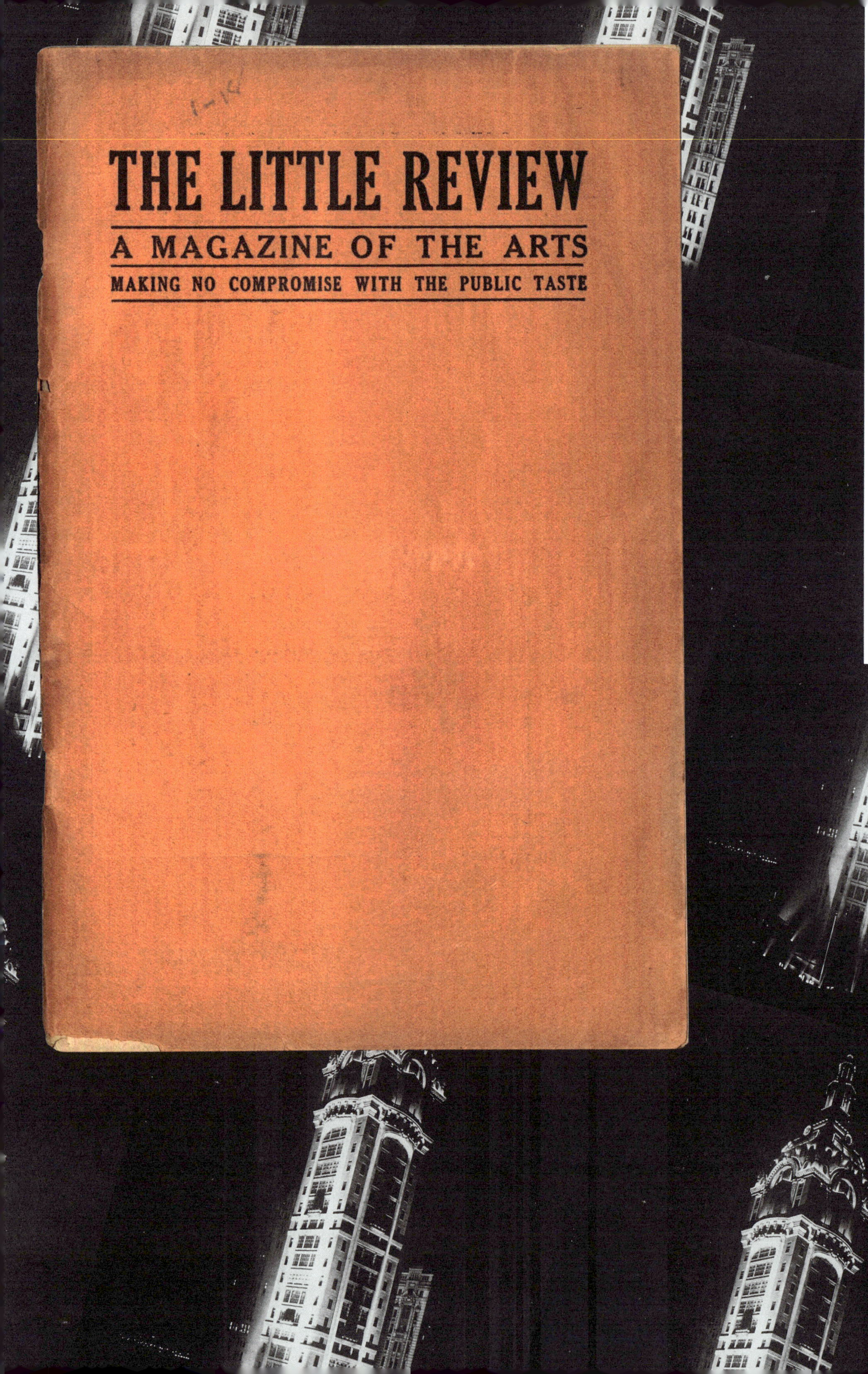

064 *The Little Review. A Magazine of the Arts*, no. 9, January 1918, ed. Margaret Anderson, Ezra Pound, New York/London
065 *The Little Review. Quarterly Journal of Art and Letters*, no. 2, Winter 1922, ed. Margaret Anderson, Jane Heap, Ezra Pound, Francis Picabia, 24–25

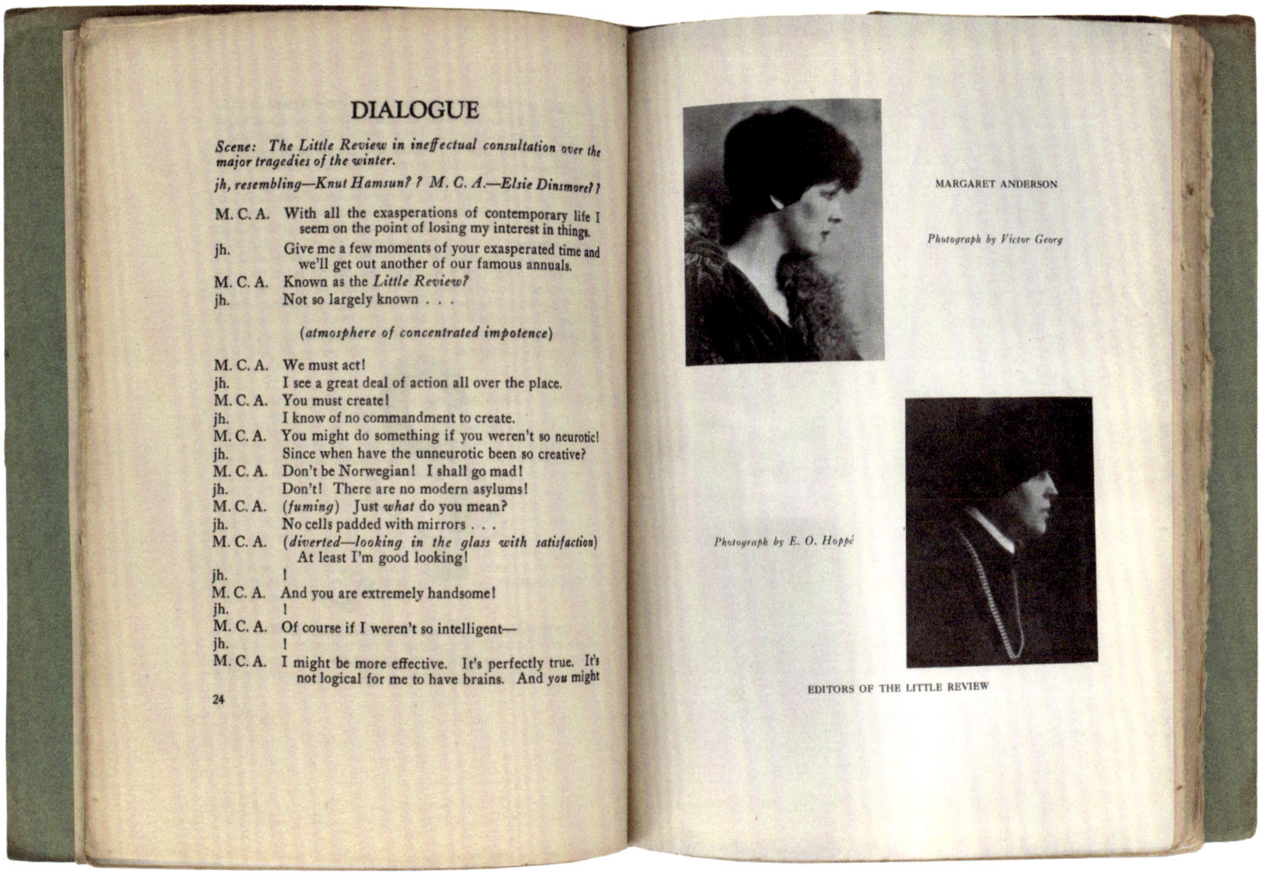

DIALOGUE

Scene: The Little Review in ineffectual consultation over the major tragedies of the winter.

jh, resembling—Knut Hamsun? ? M. C. A.—Elsie Dinsmore? ?

M. C. A.	With all the exasperations of contemporary life I seem on the point of losing my interest in things.
jh.	Give me a few moments of your exasperated time and we'll get out another of our famous annuals.
M. C. A.	Known as the *Little Review?*
jh.	Not so largely known . . .

(atmosphere of concentrated impotence)

M. C. A.	We must act!
jh.	I see a great deal of action all over the place.
M. C. A.	You must create!
jh.	I know of no commandment to create.
M. C. A.	You might do something if you weren't so neurotic!
jh.	Since when have the unneurotic been so creative?
M. C. A.	Don't be Norwegian! I shall go mad!
jh.	Don't! There are no modern asylums!
M. C. A.	*(fuming)* Just *what* do you mean?
jh.	No cells padded with mirrors . . .
M. C. A.	*(diverted—looking in the glass with satisfaction)* At least I'm good looking!
jh.	!
M. C. A.	And you are extremely handsome!
jh.	!
M. C. A.	Of course if I weren't so intelligent—
jh.	!
M. C. A.	I might be more effective. It's perfectly true. It's not logical for me to have brains. And *you* might

24

MARGARET ANDERSON

Photograph by Victor Georg

Photograph by E. O. Hoppé

EDITORS OF THE LITTLE REVIEW

THE *LITTLE REVIEW* MAGAZINE AND EXHIBITIONS ORGANIZED BY JANE HEAP *The Little Review* magazine's output falls into three distinct periods: the Chicago period from March 1914 to March 1917, the New York period from April 1917 to 1922, and the Paris period from 1923 to 1929. It was founded by Margaret Anderson in March 1914 in Chicago with the motto "Making No Compromise with the Public Taste." In 1916 Jane Heap became its co-editor, and one of her aims, similar to Alfred Stieglitz and Katherine S. Dreier, was to bring the European avant-garde to the attention of American audiences. On her first visit to Paris in 1923, Heap met Fernand Léger, Constantin Brâncuşi, and Tristan Tzara, whose work she would feature in the magazine. Later, she represented them in The Little Review Gallery, which was open from 1924 through 1927. In 1926, she invited Frederick Kiesler to co-organize the well-attended *International Theatre Exposition*. One year later, she opened the influential *Machine-Age Exposition* to illustrate the inter-relations and inter-influences of architecture, engineering, industrial arts, and modern art. However, the latter exhibition received limited attention, and Heap lost faith in the collective activity of artists and engineers. The Little Review Gallery closed in 1927, and *The Little Review* ceased publication in May 1929.

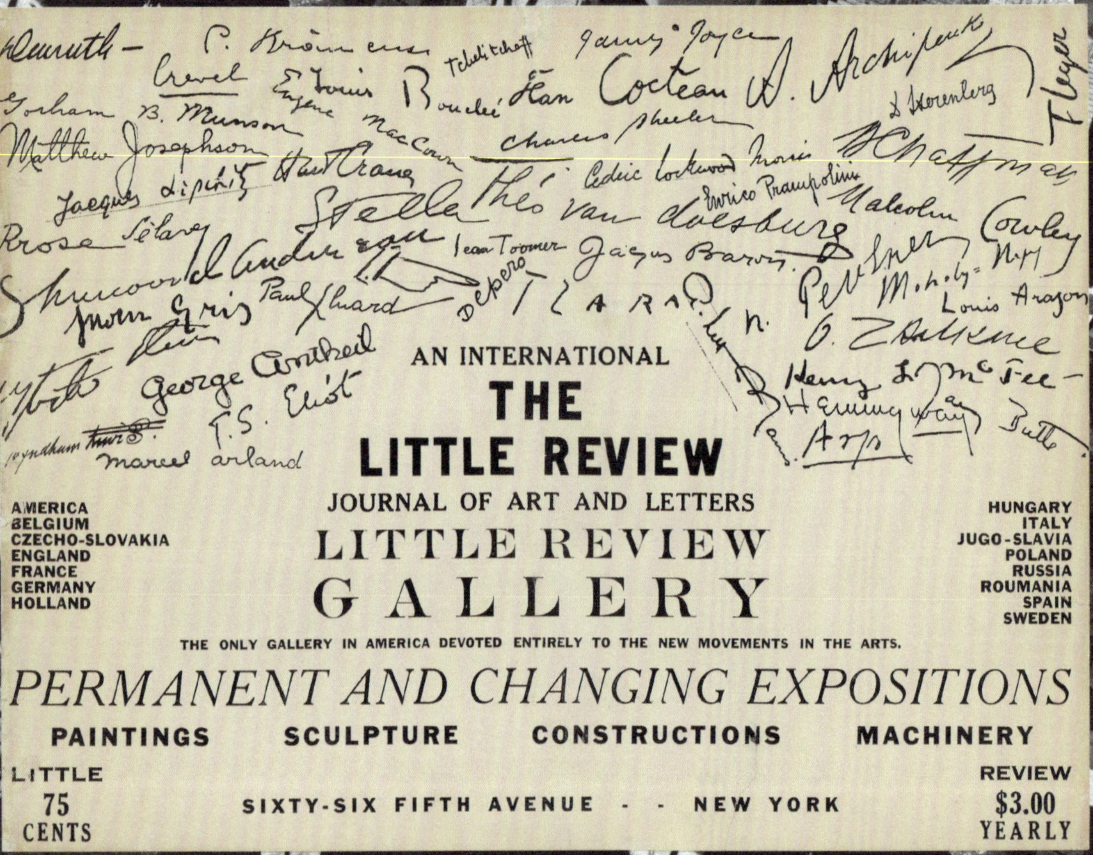

066 [Leaflet] *The Little Review. An International Journal of Art and Letters. Little Review Gallery*, New York, ca. 1925

067 *The Little Review: Quarterly Journal of Art and Letters*, no. 1, Autumn 1921, ed. Margaret Anderson, Ezra Pound,Francis Picabia, New York

068 *The Little Review. Quarterly Journal of Art and Letters*, no. 2, Spring 1922, ed. Margaret Anderson, Ezra Pound, Francis Picabia, New York

069 *The Little Review: Quarterly Journal of Art and Letters*, no. 1, Spring 1924, ed. Margaret Anderson, Jane Heap, Ezra Pound, New York

070 see 065

↓068 ↓067 ↑066

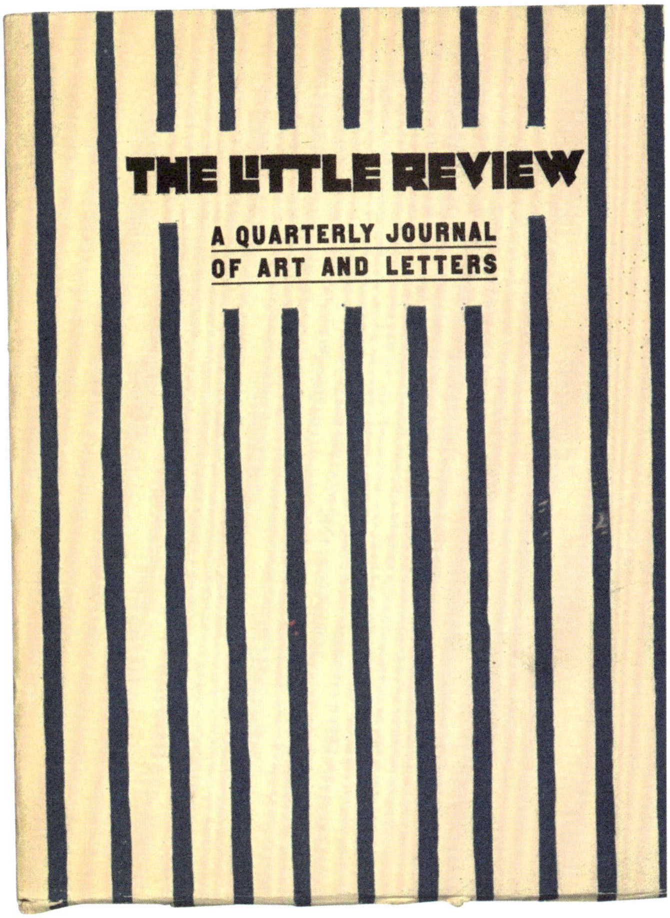

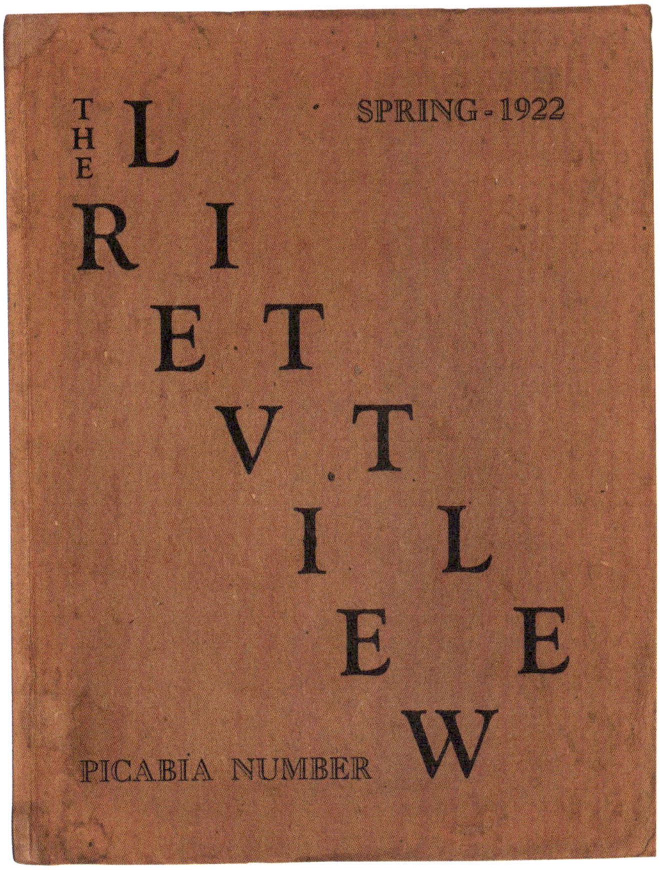

85

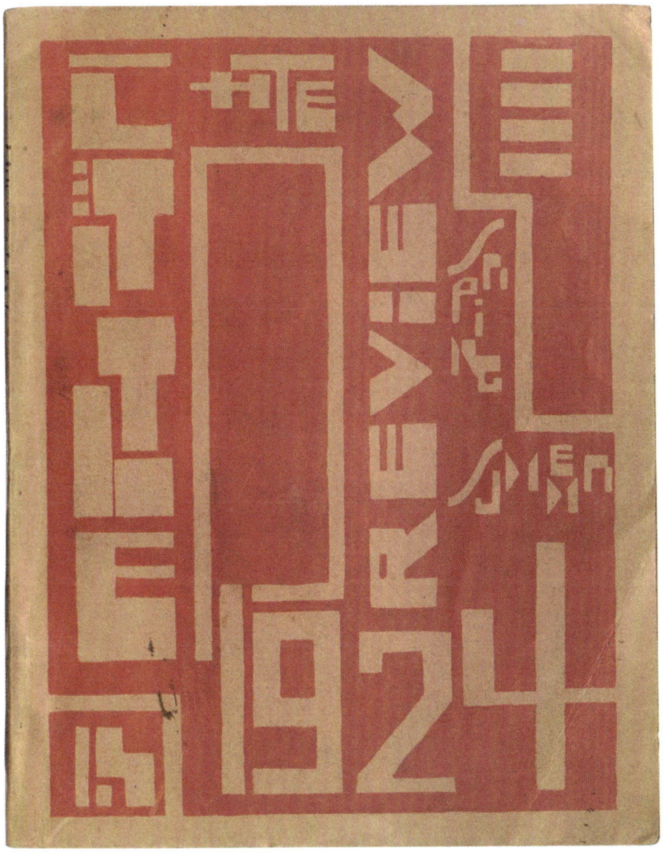

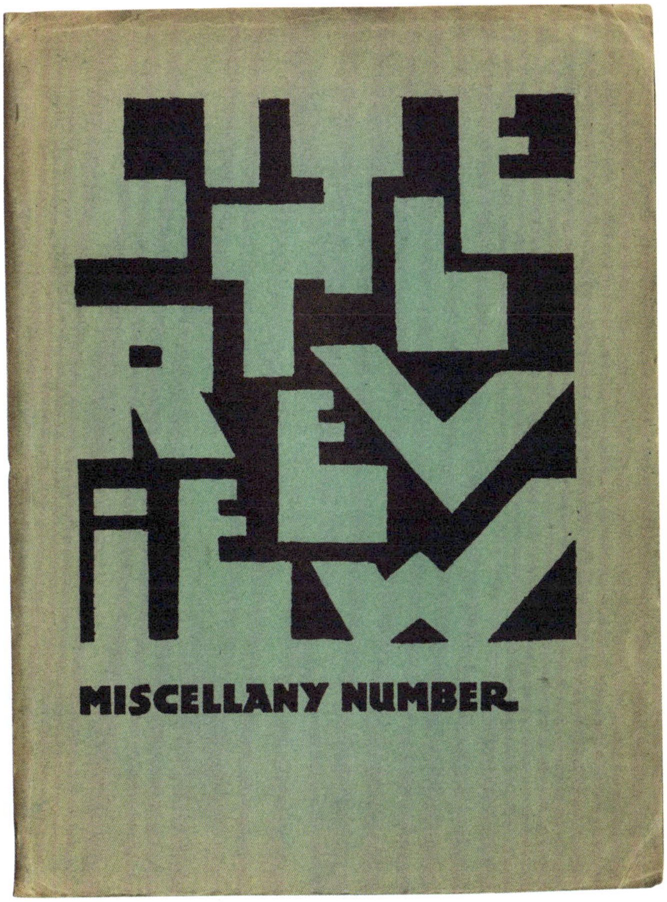

↓070 ↓069

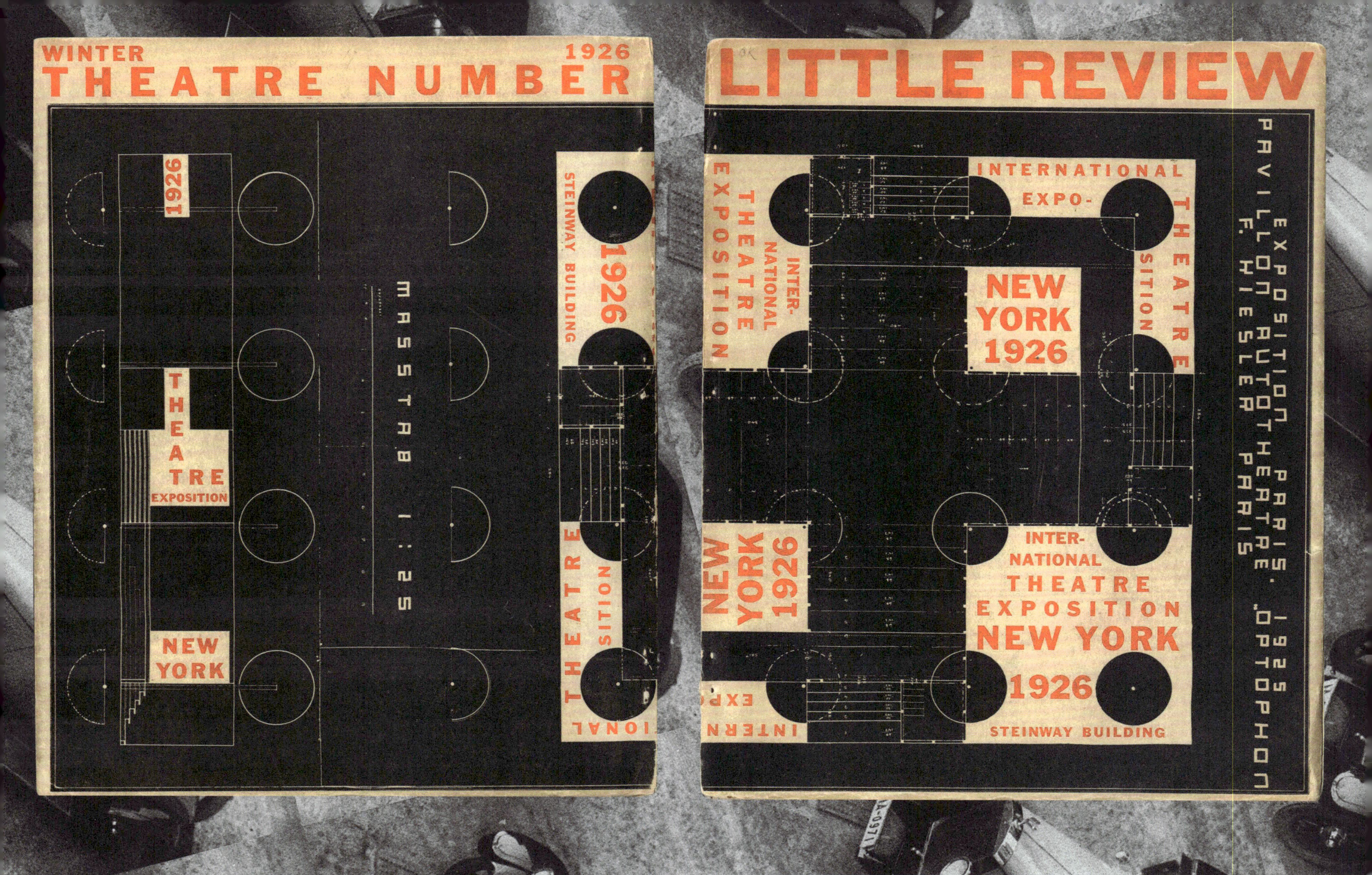

071 *The Little Review: Quarterly Journal of Art and Letters*, no. 2, Winter 1926, ed. Margaret Anderson, Jane Heap, New York, 1, Foreword by Friedrich Kiesler: *The theatre is dead*; cover by Friedrich Kiesler

F O R E W O R D

THE THEATRE IS DEAD.

WE ARE NOT WORKING FOR NEW DECORATION.

WE ARE NOT WORKING FOR NEW LITERATURE.

WE ARE NOT WORKING FOR NEW LIGHTING SYSTEMS.

WE ARE NOT WORKING FOR NEW MASKS.

WE ARE NOT WORKING FOR NEW STAGES.

WE ARE NOT WORKING FOR NEW COSTUMES.

WE ARE NOT WORKING FOR NEW ACTORS.

WE ARE NOT WORKING FOR NEW THEATRES.

WE ARE WORKING FOR THE THEATRE THAT HAS SURVIVED THE THEATRE.

WE ARE WORKING FOR THE SOUND BODY OF A NEW SOCIETY.

AND WE HAVE CONFIDENCE IN THE STRENGTH OF NEWER GENERATIONS THAT ARE AWARE OF THEIR PROBLEMS.

THE THEATRE IS DEAD.

WE WANT TO GIVE IT A SPLENDID BURIAL.

ADMISSION 75 CENTS.

KIESLER

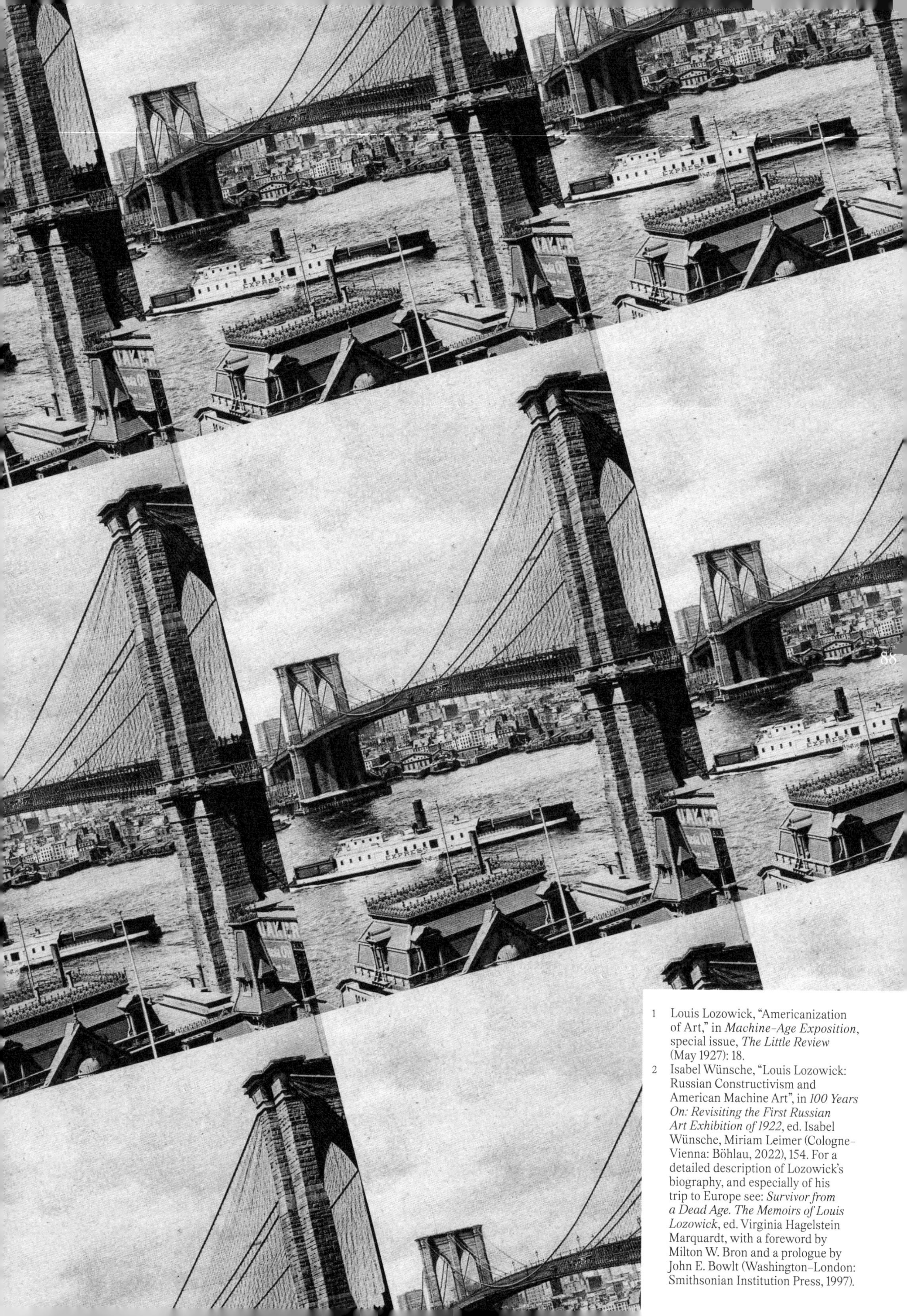

1 Louis Lozowick, "Americanization of Art," in *Machine-Age Exposition*, special issue, *The Little Review* (May 1927): 18.

2 Isabel Wünsche, "Louis Lozowick: Russian Constructivism and American Machine Art", in *100 Years On: Revisiting the First Russian Art Exhibition of 1922*, ed. Isabel Wünsche, Miriam Leimer (Cologne–Vienna: Böhlau, 2022), 154. For a detailed description of Lozowick's biography, and especially of his trip to Europe see: *Survivor from a Dead Age. The Memoirs of Louis Lozowick*, ed. Virginia Hagelstein Marquardt, with a foreword by Milton W. Bron and a prologue by John E. Bowlt (Washington–London: Smithsonian Institution Press, 1997).

Towards a Universal Art of the Machine Age. Machine Ornaments by Louis Lozowick in the 1920s

Przemysław Strożek

"The whole of mankind is vitally affected by industrial development and if the artist can make his work clear in its intention, convincing in its reality, inevitable in its logic, his potential audience will be practically universal."[1] Thus wrote Louis Lozowick, an American-Russian-Ukrainian-Jewish artist, in the catalog of the *Machine Age Exposition* which opened in New York in 1927. His article "Americanization of Art" referred to his own artistic exploration throughout the 1920s, when he had searched for a universal visual language of the Machine Age that would enable him to depict the essence of the industrialized world. To achieve this goal, he reflected on cultural developments within two discrete and contrasting geographical areas and political orders: those of the US, the capitalist country where he lived, and of the Soviet Union, the newly-founded communist country which he admired and felt attached to because of his Russian/Ukrainian roots. In his view, the project of creating a universal visual language for the modern times should focus on a fusion of American modernity and lifestyle with Soviet artistic experiments in the fields of typography, non-objective art, and the utopian visions of Constructivists. In this way, he based his work on cultural phenomena that would be regarded as opposed to one another: on the one hand, the capitalist agendas of the US, the rapid urbanization of American cities, radical consumerism, and the aesthetics of the Roaring Twenties; and on the other, the avant-garde experiments of Soviet Constructivism, post-revolutionary art, and the socio-political changes experienced in, and by, the first communist country.

In pursuit of the idea of a universal art of the Machine Age, Lozowick developed a set of works which he called Machine Ornaments—characteristic ink drawings combining mechanical and geometric imagery in single visual compositions. Created between 1923 and 1929, they formed the basis of his designs for stage sets, textiles, and all his work in print, ranging from book covers to advertisements and illustrations of the texts he wrote. They were inspired by the abstract, geometric style of Soviet and international Constructivism, but at the same time glorified the achievements of rapid American industrialization together with the Roaring Twenties aesthetic embodied by New York nightlife, neon and electric lights, and jazz and dancing clubs. From a socio-political perspective, Lozowick's idea of uniting the aesthetics of the American Machine Age with the avant-garde experiments of Soviet Constructivism in the form of a universal art mirrors the complex and complicated relations between art and the machine, activism, and pragmatism. And because of these complications, his idea could not be fully materialized and therefore could not fully succeed in terms of artistic practice. As I intend to show in this article, the Machine Ornaments did not fit the requirements of leftist propaganda either in terms of Soviet politics, or in addressing the needs of the proletariat. On the contrary, by creating this type of work, Lozowick always had to prioritize America, and could not escape the capitalist agendas of his new home country on the other side of the Atlantic. As a result, what he did was turn the stylistic features of Soviet Constructivism into an ornament of American Art Deco, with the major aim of highlighting the beauty of American modernity, through its cityscapes and key aspects of its popular culture.

SOVIET CONSTRUCTIVISM IN THE ARTISTIC CIRCLES OF NEW YORK: SOCIÉTÉ ANONYME AND *THE LITTLE REVIEW*

In the 1920s, by the time Lozowick had created his Machine Ornaments, he was not only an artist, but also the leading art critic informing the American audience about the recent developments in the Soviet avant-garde. His texts on Soviet Constructivism and his postulates of linking art with industry were published in exhibition catalogs edited by Société Anonyme, as well as in diverse American magazines, such as *Broom* and *The Little Review*. The interest in his texts exemplified a shared desire on the part of the artistic circles of Société Anonyme, led by Katherine S. Dreier, and of *The Little Review*, led primarily by Jane Heap from the mid-1920s. They were both eager to gain knowledge and to understand the post-revolutionary art of the first communist country. On the other hand, both Dreier and Heap were aware that Soviet Constructivism, which rejected traditional notion sculpture and painting, was far more advanced in its efforts to connect art with the machine, than any other American art trend of the time.

Lozowick established good contacts with the Constructivist avant-gardes in Europe and gained first-hand experience of Soviet art when he travelled to Berlin and Moscow in early 1920s.[2] He had been fourteen when his parents migrated from Ukraine (then part of the Russian Empire) to the US in 1906, settling in New Jersey, and after the end of the First World War he decided to come to Europe and revisit his home country. He stayed in Europe between 1920 and 1924, settling first in Paris and then in Berlin. While in Paris in 1920 he met Ivan Goll and Fernand Léger, who collaborated in the same year on the famous film-poem book *Die Chapliniade* (1920). In Berlin he met László Moholy Nagy, and the Soviet Contructivists El Lissitzky and Naum Gabo. He had had the opportunity by then to get acquainted

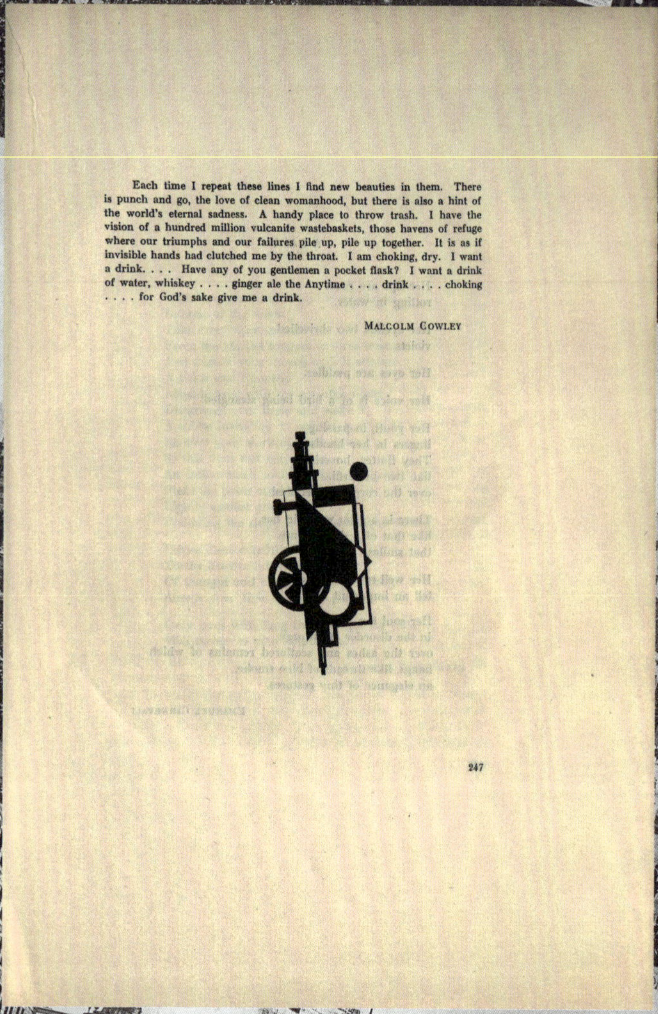

Each time I repeat these lines I find new beauties in them. There is punch and go, the love of clean womanhood, but there is also a hint of the world's eternal sadness. A handy place to throw trash. I have the vision of a hundred million vulcanite wastebaskets, those havens of refuge where our triumphs and our failures pile up, pile up together. It is as if invisible hands had clutched me by the throat. I am choking, dry. I want a drink. . . . Have any of you gentlemen a pocket flask? I want a drink of water, whiskey . . . . ginger ale the Anytime . . . . drink . . . . choking . . . . for God's sake give me a drink.

MALCOLM COWLEY

247

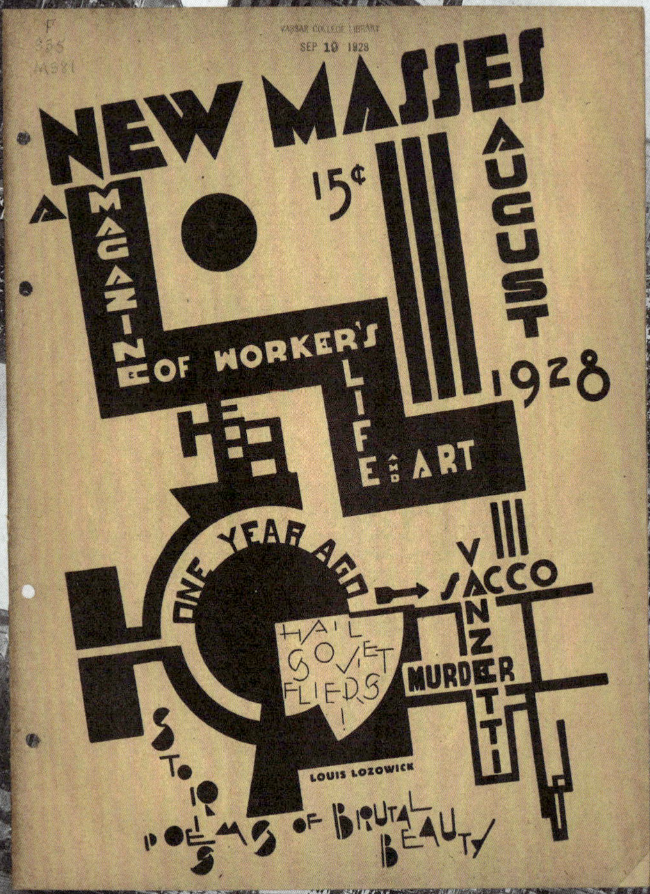

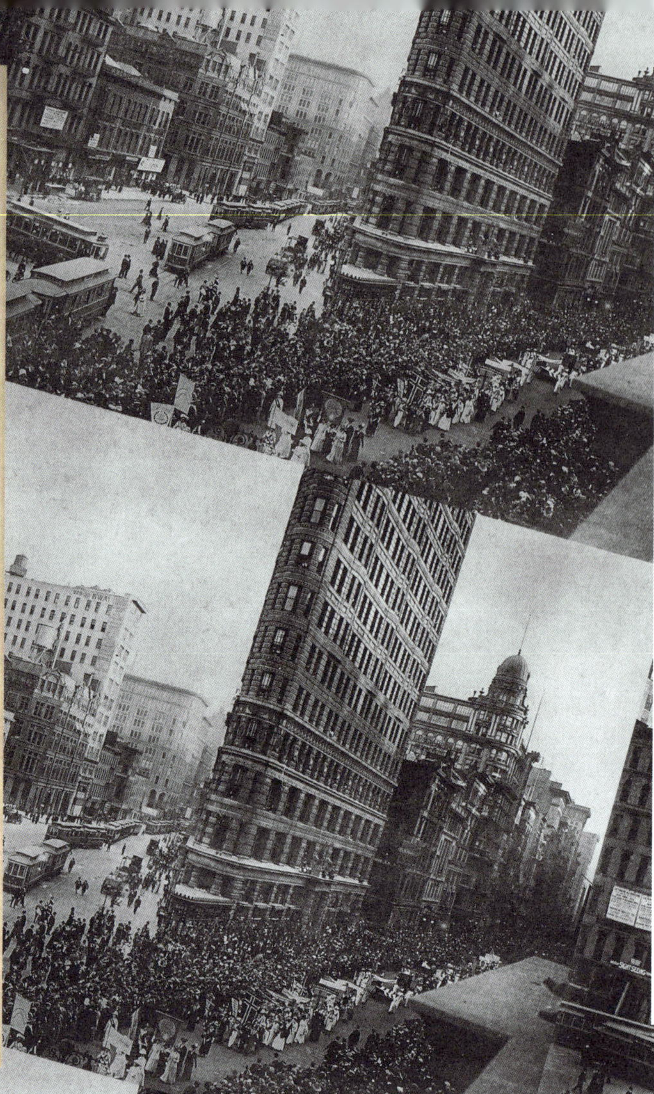

072 see 059, 247, illustration by Louis Lozowick
073 *New Masses*, no. 3, August 1928, ed. Michael Gold, Hugo Gellert, New York, cover by Louis Lozowick

3 Louis Lozowick, "The Russian Dadaists," *The Little Review* 8, no. 3 (September–December 1920): 72–73.
4 Nikolai Punin, "Tatlinova bashnia—Tour de Tatline," *Veshch / Object / Gegenstand*, 1, nos. 1–2 (March–April 1922): 22
5 Louis Lozowick, "Tatlin's Monument to the Third International," *Broom*, 3 no. 3 (October 1922): 232.
6 Louis Lozowick, "A Note on Modern Russian Art," *Broom* 4, no. 3 (February 1923): 202.
7 Louis Lozowick, [Drawing], *Broom* 4, no. 4 (March 1923): 247.
8 Jane Heap, "Independents," *The Little Review* 9, no. 2 (Winter 1922): 22
9 Katherine S. Dreier, *Western Art and the New Era*, (New York: Brentano's, 1923), 73.
10 Virginia Hagelstein Marquardt, "Louis Lozowick: From 'Machine Ornaments' to Applied Design," *The Journal of Decorative and Propaganda Arts* 8, (Spring 1988): 40.
11 Dreier's exhibition followed two minor exhibitions of Russian art organized by the art critic and dealer Christian Brinton in 1923 and 1924. Roann Barris, *Reclaiming and Redefining American Exhibitions of Russian Art*, (New York: Routledge, 2023), 19.
12 Isabel Wünsche, "Katherine S. Dreier and the Promotion of Russian Art in the United States," in *100 Years On: Revisiting the First Russian Art Exhibition of 1922*, 150.
13 *Survivor from a Dead Age*, 253.

↑ 072

with the magazine *Veshch-Objet-Gegenstand*, edited by El Lissitzky and Ilya Ehrenburg, which was issued in March–April (no. 1) and May (no. 2) of 1922, and which explained the theory and practices of Constructivism. In summer 1922 he arrived in Moscow, where he met some Soviet avant-garde artists.

While residing in Europe, Lozowick studied writings on Suprematism and Constructivism by Kazimierz Malewicz, Aleksandr Gan, Nikolai Punin, and Naum Gabo, and deepened his understanding of Lissitzky's concept of *proun*—the non-objective art labelled a utopian "Project for the Affirmation of the New." In 1920, he already intended to share his knowledge of the recent developments in the Russian avant-garde, and approached two American magazines: *The Little Review*, where he published a short text on "Russian Dadaists",[3] and *Broom*, where he wrote on Constructivism. In the article, he explained the principles of the work of Vladimir Tatlin to his American readership, based on Punin's text which Lozowick read in *Veshch.*[4] He wrote:

> The magic word in modern Russian art: Construction. Construction and not composition, teaches the new Gospel. Why? Because composition is inspired by the past, looks toward the past, and therefore, belongs to the past; because composition stands apart from life [...]. And construction? Construction is inspired by what is most characteristic of our epoch: industry, machinery, science.[5]

In his text written for the American audience he highlighted the connections between Constructivism and the machine. A few months later in February 1923, he reported in *Broom* on the newest experiments of the members of the First Group of Constructivists. In his view, the modern artist should follow Alexandr Rodchenko's path and "devote his organizing, creative faculties to the productive industrial processes and thus relinquish his parasitic existence."[6] As an example of the new artistic way being paved by Rodchenko and other Constructivists, he included his early type of Machine Ornament in the next issue of *Broom,* published in March 1923.[7]

The articles Lozowick published in *Broom* on Soviet Constructivism spread knowledge about this new artistic movement, which had hitherto been largely unknown in the US. In around 1922–1923, important ideas around linking modern art with machinery and industry were also being discussed in New York. These reflections on "mechanical art" were initiated by two of the most prominent popularizers of the European avant-garde: the aforementioned Jane Heap and Katherine S. Dreier. On the pages of *The Little Review* in Winter 1922, Heap reproduced an illustration of Tatlin Tower and wrote:

↑ 073

> What belief in the power of art, to be terrorized by the power of plumbing systems and engines. The artist must affiliate with the creative artist in the other arts and with the constructive men of his epoch; engineers, scientists, etc.[8]

Dreier, in turn, added in her influential book *Western Art and New Era* (1923) the observation that:

> It is only natural that the modern artist with his inherent love of the dynamic force, with his understanding of the powers of electricity, of the brilliant metal surface of a dynamo, the beauty to be felt in an engine room with its powerful steel engines and glossy surface, has little in common with an art which tries to repeat the past.[9]

Both Heap and Dreier expressed interest in the machine aesthetic as an "art of the new era", and they were understandably drawn to the artistic achievements of Soviet Constructivism, and especially in a practical sense, to understanding how Constructivist artists were framing the relationship between art and industry.

When Lozowick returned from his Paris-Moscow-Berlin sojourn to New York in early 1924,[10] he was immediately approached by Dreier to collaborate on the Société Anonyme's forthcoming exhibition on *Modern Russian Art* at the Heckscher Building in New York.[11] Ultimately, the exhibition was not strictly devoted to the Russian avant-garde and Soviet Constructivism, because it also featured works by some Hungarian artists, French Cubists, and Lozowick himself. In this way it presented a show on "Modern Russian Artists" to the American audience in the context of the wider international avant-garde.[12] Lozowick authored a book under the same title for the exhibition. According to Virginia Hagelstein Marquardt, it was "the first book on the subject of Russian Suprematist and Constructivist art published in the United States."[13]

Lozowick designed the cover, which was intentionally inspired by Lissitzky's cover for *Veshch-Objet-Gegenstand.* Lissitzky's project featured a combination of prouns, which are non-objective, geometric figures, and rational typographic composition. The design of the cover was constructed on a diagonal axis with the dominant shape of the letter L reversed, with the foot reaching to the left rather than the right. It combined words (title and publishing place), numbers (issue number and year), and pictorial images (prouns) in a non-hierarchical way which could be viewed as a coherent, interactive work. It was reminiscent of a famous design from his children's book *Pro dva Kvadrata* (About Two Squares, 1922) that incorporated geometric shapes, numbers, and words into new visual language that is not just read, but first of all seen, felt, heard, and experienced. The cover of *Veshch* expressed Lissitzky's

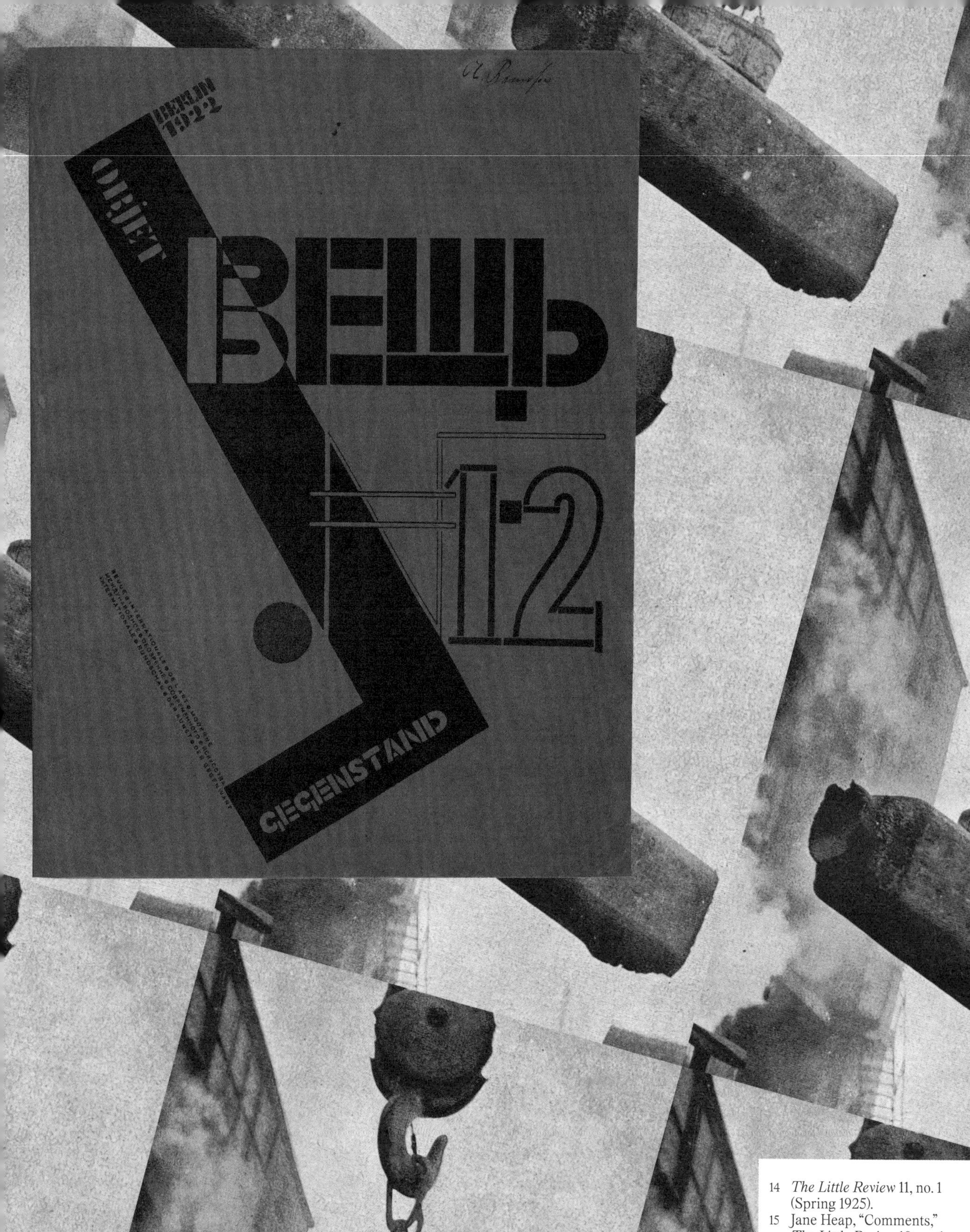

074 *Vesh/Objet/Gegenstand*, no. 1–2, March–April 1922, ed. El Lissitzky, Ilya Ehrenburg, Berlin, cover by El Lissitzky

14 *The Little Review* 11, no. 1 (Spring 1925).
15 Jane Heap, "Comments," *The Little Review* 10, no. 1 (Spring 1924): 57.
16 For more on Constructivism in *The Little Review*, see the first chapter in Barnaby Haran, *Watching the Red Dawn. The American Avant-Garde and the Soviet Union* (Manchester: Manchester University Press, 2016), 10–53.
17 Lozowick, "Americanization of Art," 18.
18 In the first issue of *New Masses*, Lozowick was described as the author of *Modern Russian Art* and a designer of the theatre sets for *Gas* in Chicago, "The Artists," *New Masses* 1, no. 1 (May 1926): 3.

↑ 074 strong beliefs that modern typography needs to address all the senses to convey the reality of industrialized society.

Lozowick's cover of *Modern Russian Art* followed Lissitzky's principles and directly referred to the composition of the cover of *Veshch*. However, there are some significant distinctions between the two covers. Lozowick's cover was based on a similar diagonal axis with a reversed L, and like *Veshch*, it included different fonts. He used a different font in the title, which in fact did not align with Soviet typography, instead resembling an American Art Deco neon advertisement with arrows, characteristic of a New York cityscape. Lozowick's cover was thus more decorative than Lissitzky's design, and turned the viewer's attention from non-objective proun-like experiments towards the more recognizable advertisement logos which could be seen in the cityscapes of American metropolises. In this way, it became more embedded in the aesthetics of the Roaring Twenties and American popular culture symbolized by modern electric lights, and less aligned with "Modern Russian Art".

In 1925, Lozowick's design for Société Anonyme's *Modern Russian Art* was advertised on the back cover of *The Little Review.*[14] Jane Heap, the leading editor of the magazine, had already popularized Soviet Constructivism in

New York by 1924.[15] As Dreier had done, she engaged Lozowick to collaborate with him in spreading the news about this movement. By the mid-1920s, she had invited him to work on her biggest exhibition project: *Machine Age Exposition* (1927), which presented a wide range of artistic positions linking art with industry. She exhibited avant-garde artists who explored notions of mechanical art, including Constructivist artists from the USSR, with the intention of stimulating discussion about Soviet society—that in her opinion had achieved the true union of arts and technology. The exhibition renewed discussion about Constructivism within New York's artistic circles, shifting them away from strict connections with 1910s Russian art. While Dreier's *Modern Russian Art* at Société Anonyme (1924) connected Constructivism to more traditional art, the *Machine Age Exposition* (1927) organized by Heap recontextualized Russian Constructivism into an American environment of industry and popular culture.[16] In the exhibition catalog, Lozowick expressed his views on creating a universal language of the Machine Age and called upon artists to give their "creative interpretation" of industrialized America.[17] Next to his text he included an example of his Machine Ornament along with photographs of a Steel Gyratory Crusher in the US and an Industrial Plant in the Soviet Union. His intended message was clear: that the concept of the American Machine Age mirrors the same industrialization processes of the USSR, and the Machine Ornament is a perfect embodiment of both principles.

MACHINE ORNAMENTS IN *NEW MASSES*: JAZZ ADVERTS AND CRITICISM OF AMERICA

By the time Lozowick had expressed his views in the catalog of *Machine Age Exposition*, he had already collaborated with the leftist American magazine *New Masses*, which issued its first number in New York in May 1926.[18] The magazine "recruited" avant-garde artists to become its illustrators. Many of them, like Lozowick, had worked with Katherine S. Dreier before, including migrants from USSR such as David Burluk and Constantin Alajálov, Czechoslovak artist Jan Matulka, and American Cubist Stuart Davis. They all exhibited with Société Anonyme and from 1926 collaborated with *New Masses*, merging the avant-garde tendencies of Futurism, Cubism, and Constructivism with the agendas of proletarian culture.

Almost every number of *New Masses* published between 1926 and 1928 reprinted Lozowick's Machine Ornaments, peculiar black and white semi-abstract compositions featuring geometric shapes resembling the images of the machines: levers, cranes, and machine vices. In August 1928, Lozowick featured a Machine Ornament on the cover of *New Masses* which included some political statements. The cover of *Modern Russian Art* had already experimented with Soviet Constructivist typography, but his cover of *New Masses* was probably the first to have directly glorified the success of Soviet Union ("Hail Soviet Fliers!") and expressed socio-political critique against the US justice system ("One Year Ago [arrow] Sacco Vanzetti Murder"). The "Soviet Fliers" were Airmen Semyon Shestakov and Dmitrii Fufaev, who successfully flew from Moscow to Tokyo in August 1928, while Sacco and Vanzetti were two Italian workers who had been sentenced to death and executed by electric chair in Charleston, Massachusetts for a crime they did not commit. The word "Murder" simply highlights the fact that both anarchists were wrongly sentenced to death, while the three vertical lines may have referred to the metal bars of prison. The killing of Sacco and Vanzetti on August 23, 1927, left a scar on American society and was a turning point in terms of viewing the US not only as a symbol of democracy and Roaring Twenties, but also as a country that violates fundamental human rights. Just as in the case of the cover of *Modern Russian Art*, the Machine Ornament on the cover of *New Masses* resembled a neon advertisement with arrows, characteristic of the New York cityscape. However, the content of both slogans: Soviet propaganda and criticism of the US, clashed with this type of composition, which had previously always been used to present the beauty of the American Machine Age. It also exemplified how easily the words and slogans included in Machine Ornaments could be viewed as simple advertising logos.

The cover from August 1928 that directly praised Soviet Union and criticized the actions of the US government

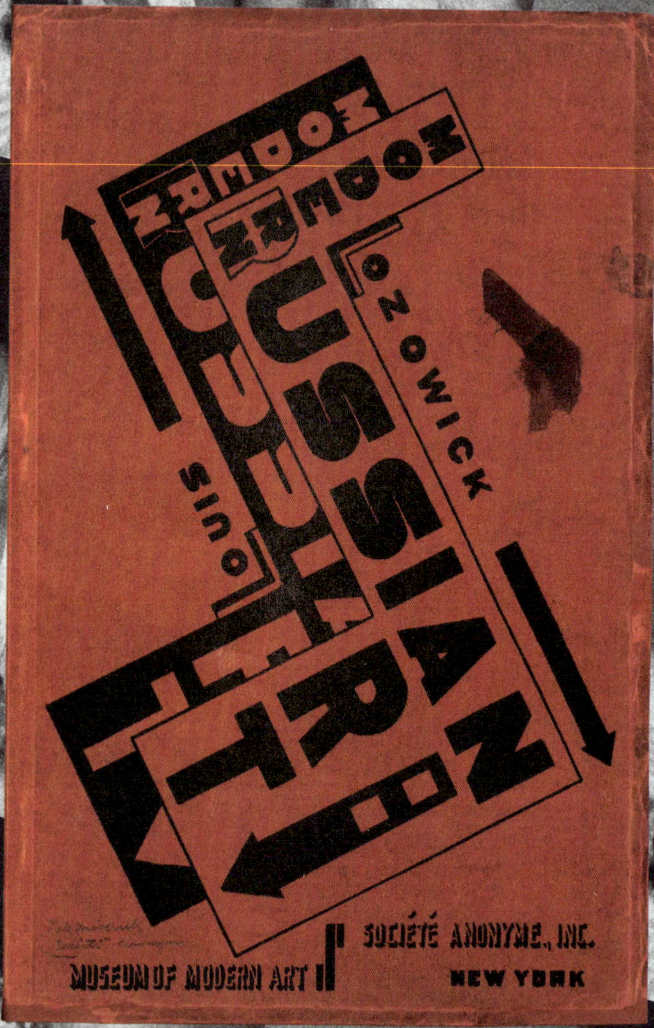

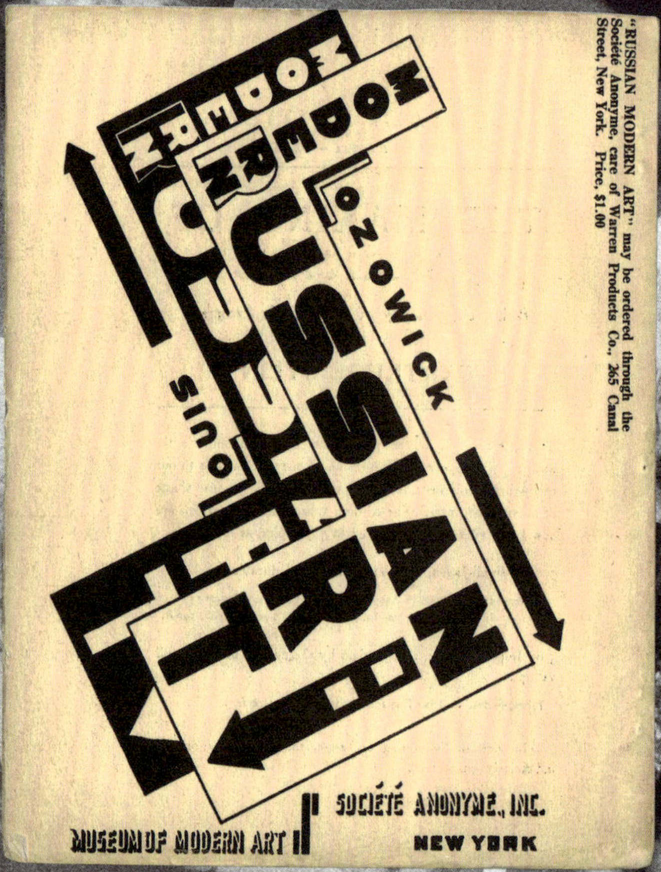

075 Louis Lozowick, *Modern Russian Art*, New York: Museum of Modern Art – Société Anonyme, Inc. 1925, cover by Louis Lozowick

076 *The Little Review. Quarterly Journal of Art and Letters*, no. 1, Spring 1925, Hg. Margaret Anderson, Jane Heap, New York, back cover with an illustration by Louis Lozowick

19 Louis Lozowick, "Machine Ornament (1929)," in *Survivor from Dead Age*, 284.

20 Marquardt, "Louis Lozowick: From 'Machine Ornaments' to Applied Design," 49.

21 "Machine art is Bourgeois," *New Masses* 4, no. 9 (Feb. 1929): 31.

22 [Bruno Jasieński], "Resolution on the Work of New Masses for 1931," quoted in Andrew Hemingway, *Artists on the Left: American Artists and the Communist Movement, 1926–1956*, (New Haven-London: Yale University Press, 2002), 30.

23 Andrew Hemingway, *Artists on the Left*, 31.

24 Louis Lozowick, "Art in the Service of the Proletariat" (1931), in *Survivor from a Dead Age*, 289

↑ 075 was most probably a singular case in Lozowick's Machine Ornaments. A few months later, in December 1928 and March 1929, he created two "Jazz adverts" for music events organized by *New Masses*, which turned out to be among the last examples of the type of work he had developed since 1923. Here, he openly praised the jazz aesthetics of the Roaring Twenties as the embodiment of the American Machine Age. In this case, Lozowick did not present his Machine Ornaments as his characteristic semi-abstract compositions, which were always focused on depicting cityscapes and machines and often deprived of any human interaction. Instead, he took on figurative representation exemplifying direct links between the machine aesthetics and jazz musicians and dancers. He also abandoned the proun principles and withdrew from the geometric shapes inspired by Soviet Constructivism. By depicting a male jazz musician whose figure merges with a saxophone, and a female dancer whose dress is filled with a machine-like design, he highlighted human involvement in the new music of the American Machine Age.

"MACHINE ART IS BOURGEOIS"

Between 1928 and 1929, Lozowick decided to write the theory of Machine Ornament, a work which he left unpublished. He regarded this type of artistic production as a development of historical ornament forms such as

the Egyptian lotus, Greek acanthus, and Indian crocodile. He wrote:

> The machine and its products open an inexhaustible source of new machine ornament based on the conventionalization of inorganic, mechanical geometric form. And just as older organic ornament—concentric, asymmetric, repetitive—used animals and plants in whole or in part (wings scales, leaves, figures), so can the new machine ornament use machinery in its parts (cams, wheels, shafts, cogs, screws) to achieve results similar in scope and application.[19]

According to Lozowick's own recollections, the article was scheduled to appear in *The Little Review*, but the magazine ceased publication in May 1929, which meant that the text ultimately never appeared in print.[20] At around the same time, he also decided to withdrew from creating any new Machine Ornaments and never returned to this type of works. Among the likely reasons why he distanced himself from his concepts was the condemnation of his work from leftist circles as promoting capitalist agendas. In the February issue of *New Masses* from 1929, Lozowick had an exchange with Pauline Zutringer under the headline "Machine Art is bourgeois". Zutringer wrote that "The machine artist as
↑ 076 well as the jazz composer are not serving the cause of the working masses, they are the opportunists in the world of art."[21] Lozowick took that opportunity to make a general statement about revolutionary art, responding that artists should recognize the importance of machinery for the revolution and in building the new society. He pointed out that living in a capitalist country determines that artists will inevitably be involved in capitalist institutions; however, this statement was unacceptable to radical leftist artists. In 1931, the Polish ex-Futurist and revolutionary poet Bruno Jasieński wrote:

> Very often, in the drawings published in the magazine [*New Masses*], we find revolutionary content sacrificed for esthetic innovations and experiments in form [...] together with a fetishistic approach to capitalist technique (Lozowick) and its underestimation of the consciousness and militancy of the revolutionary movement with corresponding overestimation of the might of American capitalism.[22]

Art historian Andrew Hemingway has suggested that "Lozowick did not become the model proletarian artist—in part because he was too cosmopolitan, too much the intellectual."[23] However, his intellectual approach to the concept of the Machine Ornament was not the only reason his work was rejected by revolutionary artists. His Machine Ornaments could not simply escape the aesthetics of American Art Deco, and they were too loaded with visualizations of his own experiences of living in American cityscapes. Lozowick was aware of this, and in 1931 even published an essay, "Art in the Service of the Proletariat", in the Soviet journal *Literature of the World Revolution* to explain and defend his earlier Machine Ornament approach. He outlined the difficulties of living in the US, where "the American worker inevitably lives and works with cities and machines."[24] By distancing himself from Machine Ornaments in the 1930s after withdrawing from this concept by 1929, he most probably realized that a universal artistic language of the Machine Age based on the fusion of American modernity with Soviet Constructivism would always remain a utopian project, because of inherent socio-political inconsistencies. But in the history of the avant-garde, his work from that decade remains a perfect example of attempts to transmit Constructivist experiments into the aesthetics of the Roaring Twenties. At the same time, this type of work was praised by the most innovative circles in the country in the form of Société Anonyme and *The Little Review*, and inevitably stimulated further developments within the American avant-garde.

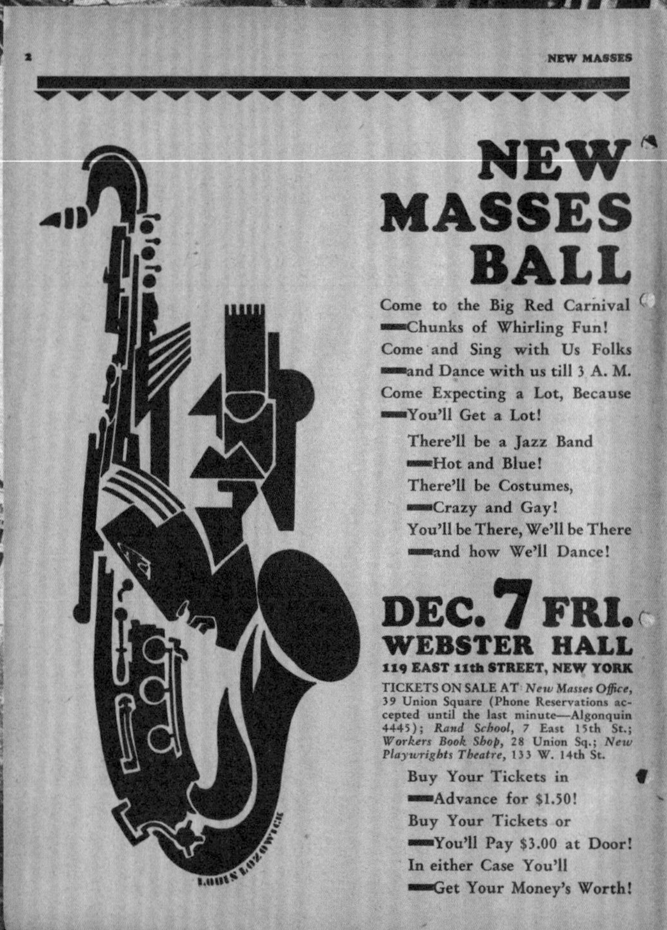

NEW MASSES BALL

Come to the Big Red Carnival
—Chunks of Whirling Fun!
Come and Sing with Us Folks
—and Dance with us till 3 A. M.
Come Expecting a Lot, Because
—You'll Get a Lot!

There'll be a Jazz Band
—Hot and Blue!
There'll be Costumes,
—Crazy and Gay!
You'll be There, We'll be There
—and how We'll Dance!

DEC. 7 FRI.
WEBSTER HALL
119 EAST 11th STREET, NEW YORK

TICKETS ON SALE AT *New Masses Office*, 39 Union Square (Phone Reservations accepted until the last minute—Algonquin 4445); *Rand School*, 7 East 15th St.; *Workers Book Shop*, 28 Union Sq.; *New Playwrights Theatre*, 133 W. 14th St.

Buy Your Tickets in
—Advance for $1.50!
Buy Your Tickets or
—You'll Pay $3.00 at Door!
In either Case You'll
—Get Your Money's Worth!

LOUIS LOZOWICK

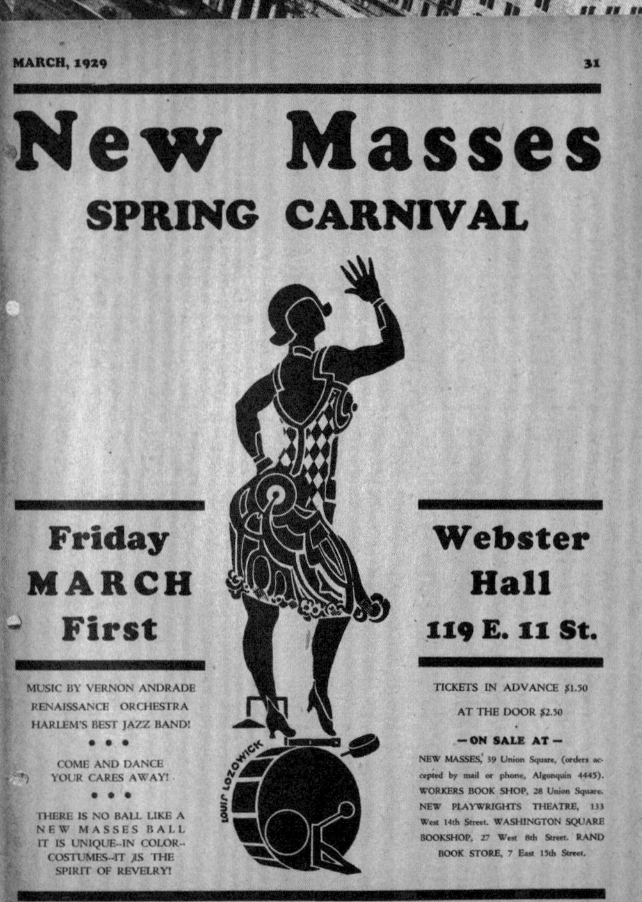

New Masses
SPRING CARNIVAL

Friday MARCH First

MUSIC BY VERNON ANDRADE
RENAISSANCE ORCHESTRA
HARLEM'S BEST JAZZ BAND!

• • •

COME AND DANCE
YOUR CARES AWAY!

• • •

THERE IS NO BALL LIKE A NEW MASSES BALL IT IS UNIQUE—IN COLOR—COSTUMES—IT IS THE SPIRIT OF REVELRY!

LOUIS LOZOWICK

Webster Hall 119 E. 11 St.

TICKETS IN ADVANCE $1.50
AT THE DOOR $2.50

— ON SALE AT —

NEW MASSES, 39 Union Square, (orders accepted by mail or phone, Algonquin 4445). WORKERS BOOK SHOP, 28 Union Square. NEW PLAYWRIGHTS THEATRE, 133 West 14th Street. WASHINGTON SQUARE BOOKSHOP, 27 West 8th Street. RAND BOOK STORE, 7 East 15th Street.

077 *New Masses*, no. 7, December 1928, ed. Michael Gold, New York, illustration by Louis Lozowick, 2
078 *New Masses*, no. 10, March 1929, ed. Michael Gold, New York, illustration by Louis Lozowick, 31

97

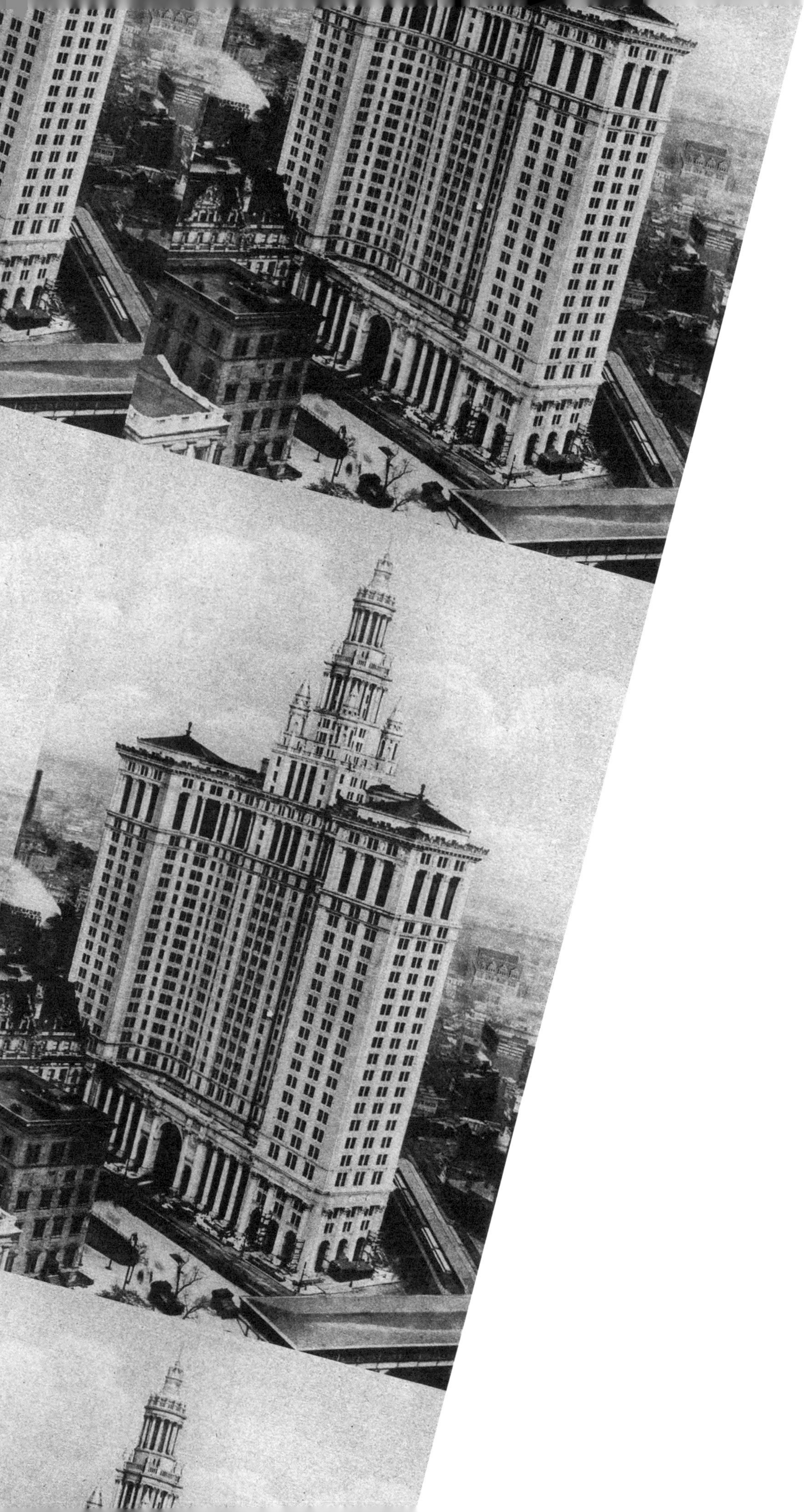

↑ 077

↑ 078

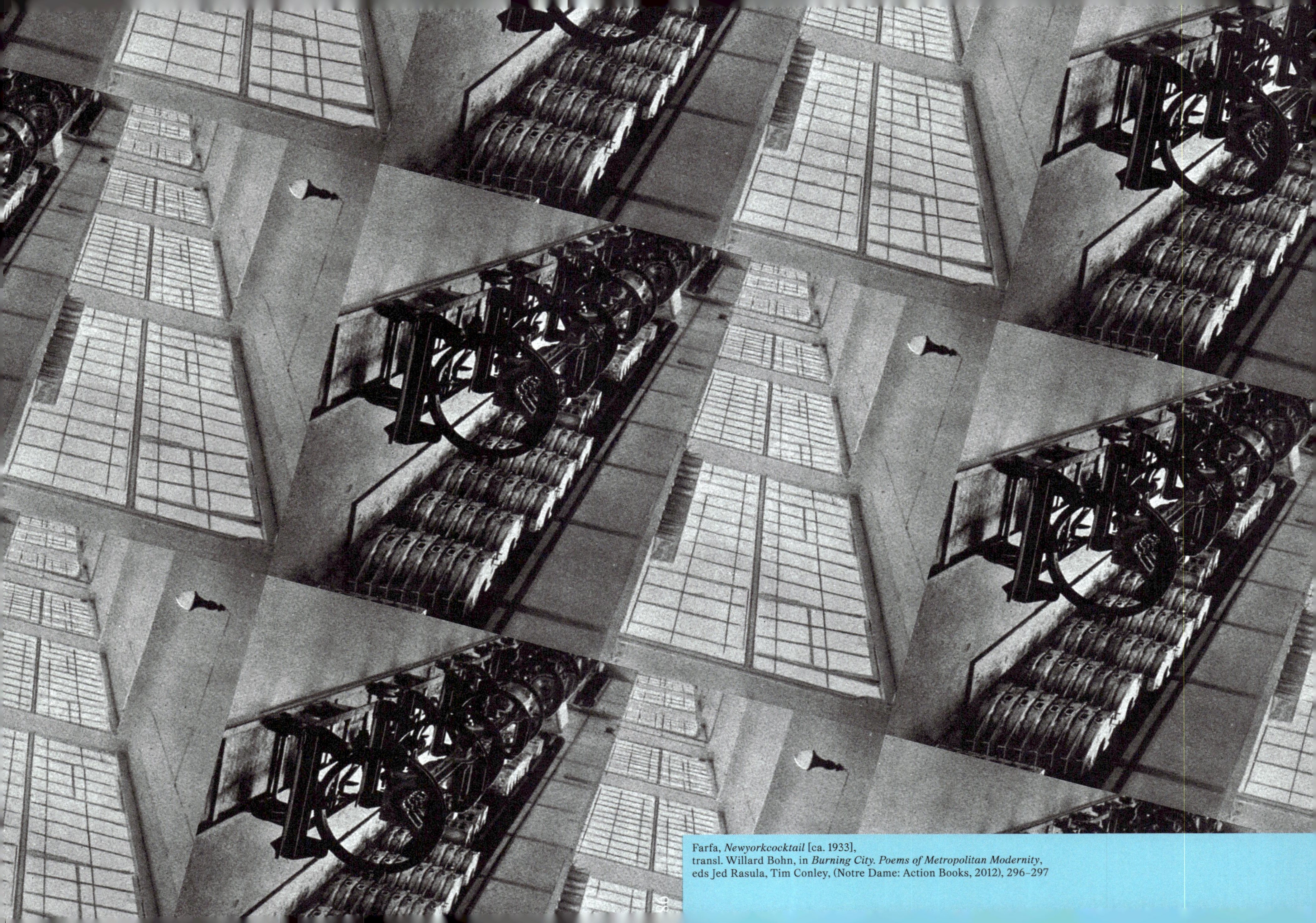

Farfa, *Newyorkcocktail* [ca. 1933],
transl. Willard Bohn, in *Burning City. Poems of Metropolitan Modernity*,
eds Jed Rasula, Tim Conley, (Notre Dame: Action Books, 2012), 296–297

Newyorkcocktail

If I could only live
one new york night
that skins women's clothing
and strips bodies
with stabbing reflections
cast by drunken
limnous advertising

marvellous geometropolis
clinging to manhattan
island's arm
and caressing the sun
with rectangular
skyscraper fingers

city of cities
I feel you a thousand times
more than chaotic paris
more than the prey
of any naked starving girl
at the folies bergére

capital of the sixty-three
cocktails enumerated
by Nathan
that corrosive American writer
strangely sensitive cocktail
of cerebralism

in the national drink
jazz band of taste
are dipped the starts
of the white flag
steeped in red
for the blue unity

cocktail
sublime mixture
liquid creature
with tuscan flavour
and prosciutto tint
my mind strives
to exalt you
above
the dry realm
since I have never seen you
nor tasted you
and thus have yet to know you

Envisioning America: Jazzbandism and Chaplinism

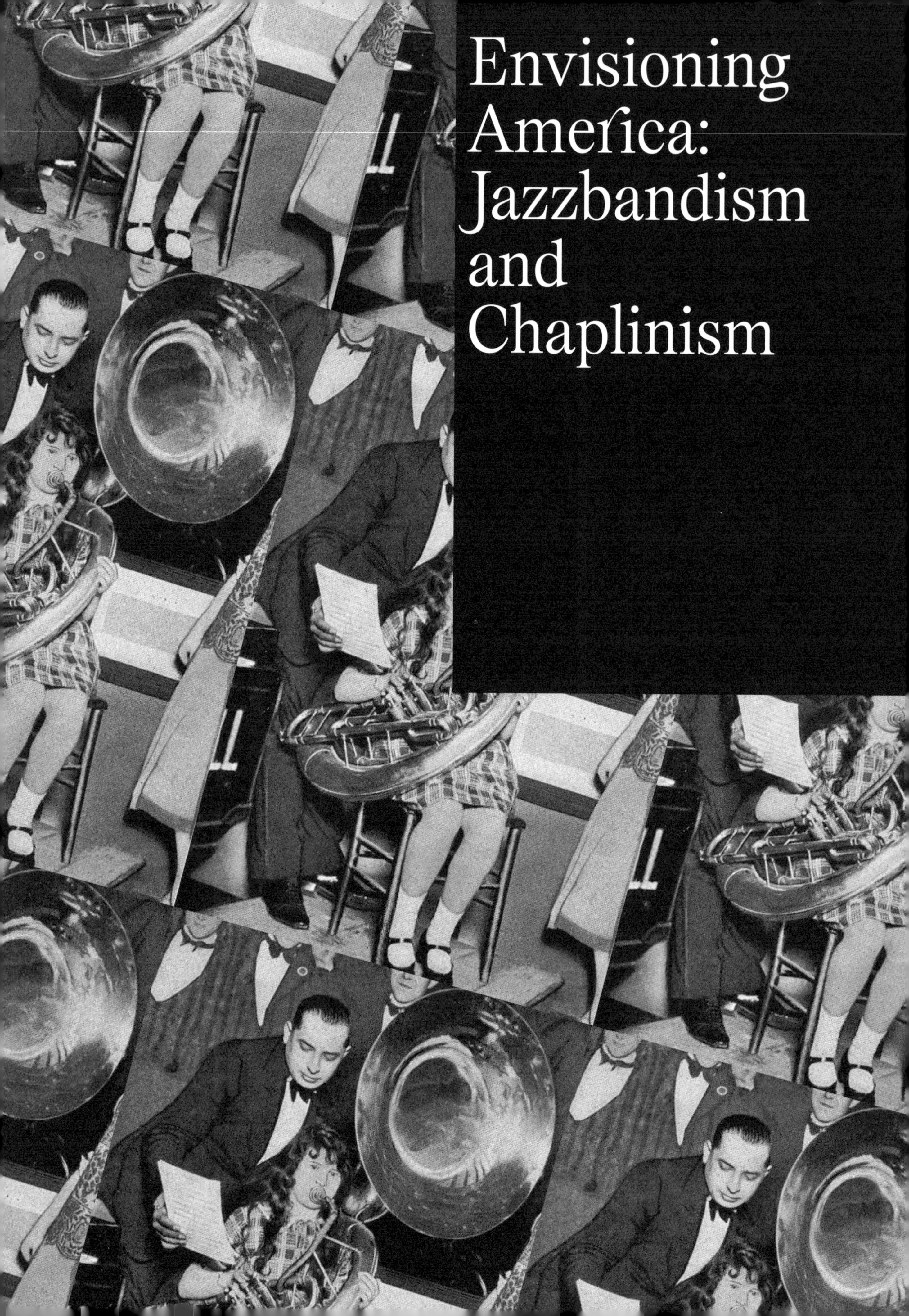

The decade of the 1920s was a time of rapid technological change, cultural innovation, economic growth, and new-found optimism that impacted everyday life on both sides of the Atlantic, in the US and post-First World War Europe. It was often described as the Roaring Twenties or Golden Twenties, and those names were often used interchangeably with the term Jazz Age. American writer F. Scott Fitzgerald coined the latter term to express the energy, freedom, and hedonistic culture of 1920s America, which became a model for the modern urban lifestyle around the globe, most notably in Europe. The common perception of America was by then inseparably associated with the economic boom, business, jazz, Hollywood, skyscrapers, dancing clubs, consumerism, Machine Age aesthetics, technological advancement, and cultural renewal directed against the conventions and traditions of the past, which were increasingly regarded as outdated. The new culture of jazz music and the Hollywood film industry were often identified with the carefree lifestyle of American society and were among the most important exports to Europe, which had been left in ruins by the devastating war. Indeed, at a time when countries such as Germany, Austria, France, and others were recovering from the nightmare of the First World War, the American way of life represented a phantasm of new, joyful energy and optimism. Jazz was the sound of modern America and enjoyment, while the films of Charlie Chaplin—the first global movie star—gave people in Europe hope that hard times could, and would, soon be overcome. Such images of America as a land of constant prosperity and progress were spread across the Atlantic, mainly through mass media, photography, and film, and defined what it really meant to be modern.

The aesthetics of American popular culture inevitably began to seep into the theories and practices of the European avant-gardes as a symbol of freedom, breaking the predetermined rules of the bourgeois and the age-old traditional culture of the Old Continent. "Art must not scorn the things that it can take from Americanism and assimilate into its principles" wrote Hugo Ball in 1916 in his Zurich diary, while two members of Berlin Dada, Georg Gross and Helmut Herzfeld, decided to Americanize their names and changed them to George Grosz and John Heartfield. In his introduction to the Berlin *Dada Almanac* (1920), Richard Huelsenbeck considered Dadaism "the American version of Buddhism." Tristan Tzara was even a regular correspondent for New York's *Vanity Fair*, and the American writer Walter C. Arensberg proclaimed in the Dadaist-Surrealist Parisian magazine *Littérature*, that "Dada is American." Similarly, Tzara wrote in Paris that "All New York is Dada", while Francis Picabia confided to Parisians that "in America everything is DADA."

Dadaists from Zurich, Berlin, and Paris praised the new American modes of life because they seemed to exemplify what they were fighting against, namely the bourgeoise traditions and establishment. "YESTERDAY—the culture of Europe. TODAY—the technology of America" wrote the Eccentrist group from the Soviet Union, thus showing that technological and cultural developments in the US fuelled the avant-garde imagination, not only in Paris or Berlin but also in Eastern Europe, and even in the world's first communist state. Simultaneously, the Devětsil group from Prague and Brno looked upon jazz and Hollywood as new forms of modern poetry that entered and aestheticized everyday life, end recognized them under the term Poetism.

It was perhaps for good reason that Spanish avant-garde writer Ramón Gómez de la Serna coined two terms, Jazzbandism and Charlotism (Chaplinism), and defined them as significant avant-garde "-isms" in his influential book *Ismos* (1931). He placed them next to other movements such as Futurism and Suprarealism, and alongside "one person movements" such as Lhotism (from a Cubist painter, André Lhote) and Archipenkism (from a Cubist sculptor, Alexander Archipenko). In Gómez de la Serna's views, both Jazzbandism and Charlotism linked avant-garde practices to mass entertainment and exemplified the common imagination of technological New America as a phenomenon directed against decadent Old Europe. It soon became clear that the Hollywood films and jazz music created on the other side of the Atlantic had pioneered new approaches towards sound and visual arts expressing the spirit of progress and modernity as opposed to European traditions. Josephine Baker, who embodied the energy of jazz music and dance, and Charlie Chaplin were not only two significant performing stars beloved by European audiences, but became truly transnational cultural phenomena that succeeded in affecting the masses and, at the same time, had a significant impact on avant-garde artists and movements such as Cubism, Purism, Dada, and Futurism.

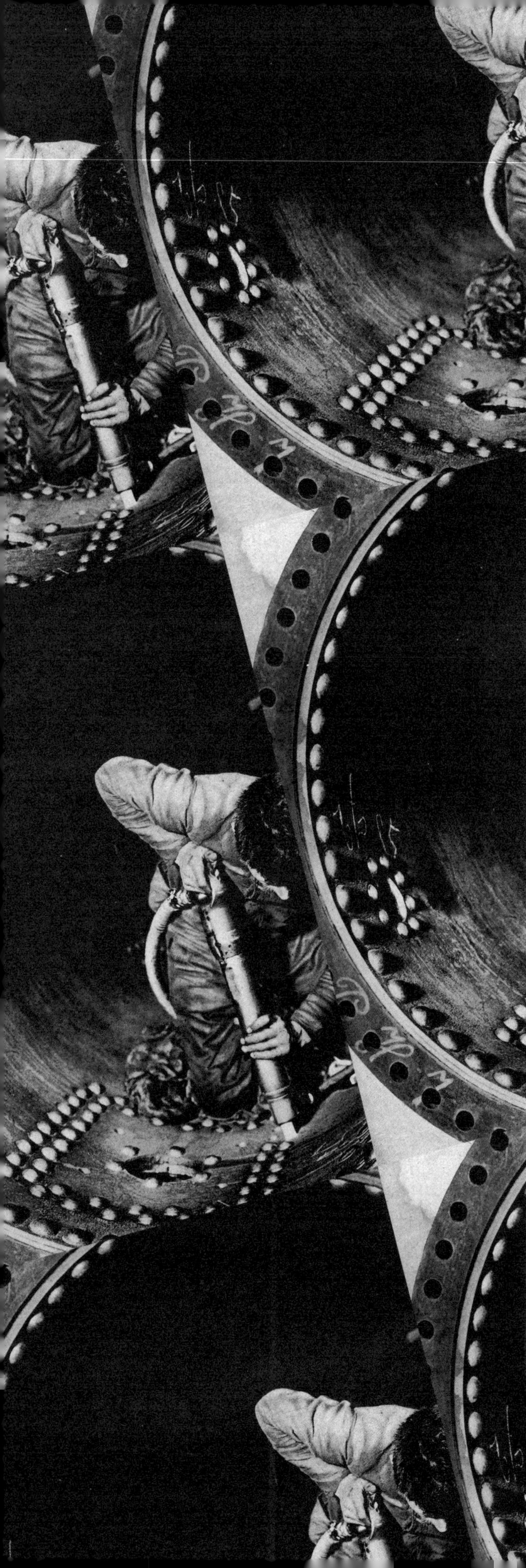

JAZZBANDISM

At the beginning of the twentieth century, the first signs of African American culture in the form of dances, ragtime, cakewalk, jazz, and the Charleston appeared in Europe as new, original forms of entertainment and music crazes. Often perceived as a synonym of modern Black culture, jazz soon became a generic signifier of modernism and was incorporated into the pronouncements and activities of the avant-garde, from Dada to Futurism, Constructivism, and Neo-plasticism.

Although no consensus has been reached on the precise date of the birth of jazz, the first recording by the Original Dixieland Jazzband from 1917 can be regarded as a turning point. Jazz has its roots in blues and ragtime, and first emerged as a fusion of those styles. Ragtime is a syncopated American popular music style going back to the Black folk music of the 1890s, with the first published composition denoted ragtime having appeared in 1897. A comedian, Harry Fox, popularized this music genre and in 1913 introduced a new dance accompanied by ragtime music, which became known as the foxtrot. Another important dance form of jazz was the Charleston, which originated the same year in South Carolina. It was a fast-paced, energetic, bouncy dance requiring many movements of the dancers' torso, arms, and legs. In Europe, the Charleston reached its apogee with the stunning success of Josephine Baker after she arrived in Paris from Harlem in 1925.

In the 1920s, jazz as modern music and jazz as modern dance had become extremely popular in Europe and attracted attention from some avant-garde composers including Eric Satie, Igor Stravinsky and Paul Hindemith. They were also affected by ragtime and incorporated this music style into their compositions. But jazz had not only had an impact on European avant-garde music. Another important question was: how to paint jazz? Avant-garde artists sought to express the rhythms of jazz in the visual arts and focused both on figurative (Ernesto Thayaht, Hugo Scheiber) and abstract, geometricized representations (Karel Teige, Piet Mondrian). In his 1931 book *Ismos*, Gómez de la Serna suggested a new "-ism" of Jazzbandism, which in his view had provided the present with a forceful image of primordial artistic expression, in contrast with the decadence of Western art. In the end, the cultural phenomenon of jazz was strictly connected to race, seen both as a liberating force and through clichéd visual representations of Black musicians and dancers as inseparably connected to the African continent.

↓080 ↓079

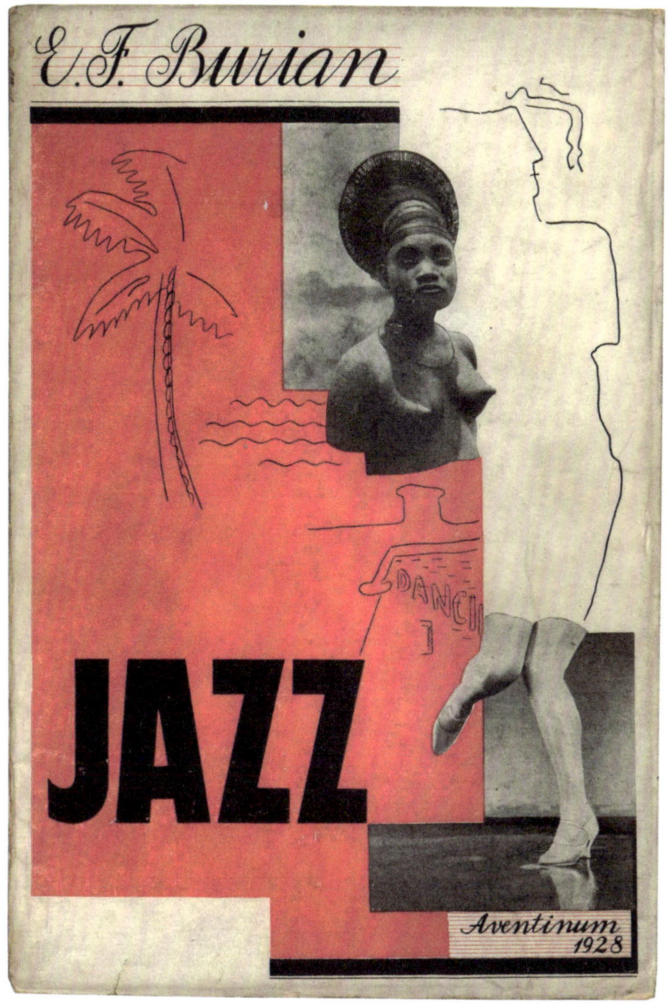

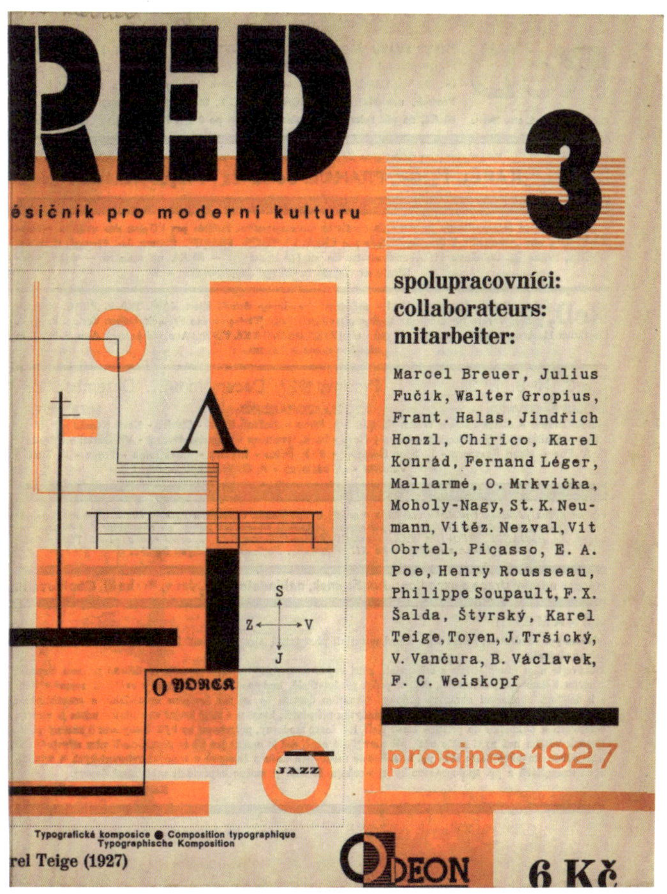

079 Emil František Burian, *Jazz*, Prague: Aventinum 1928, cover by Karel Šourek

080 *ReD [Revue Devětsil]. Měsíčník pro moderní kulturu*, no. 3, December 1927, cover by Karel Teige

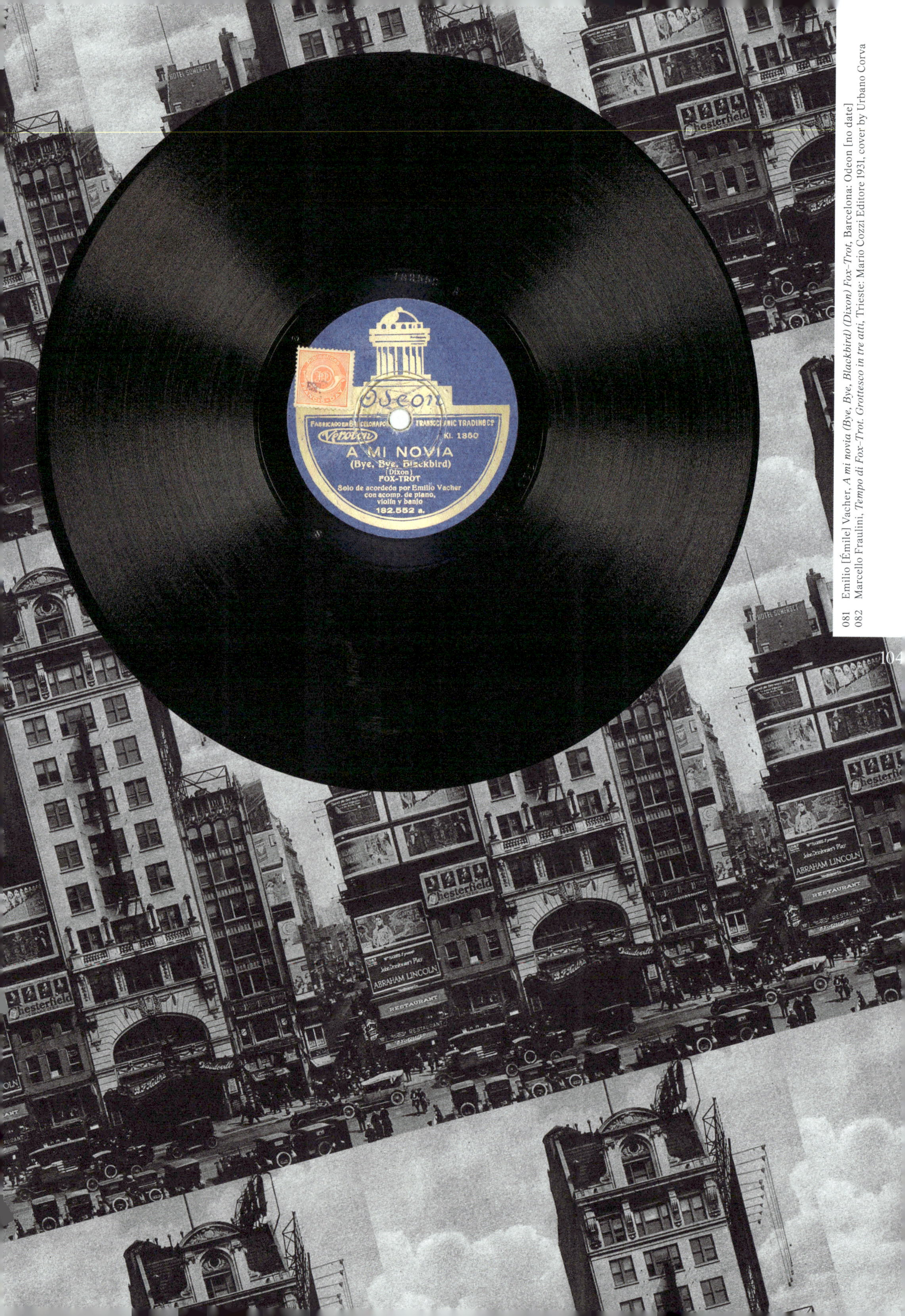

081 Emilio [Émile] Vacher, *A mi novia (Bye, Bye, Blackbird) (Dixon) Fox-Trot*, Barcelona: Odeon [no date]
082 Marcello Fraulini, *Tempo di Fox-Trot. Grottesco in tre atti*, Trieste: Mario Cozzi Editore 1931, cover by Urbano Corva

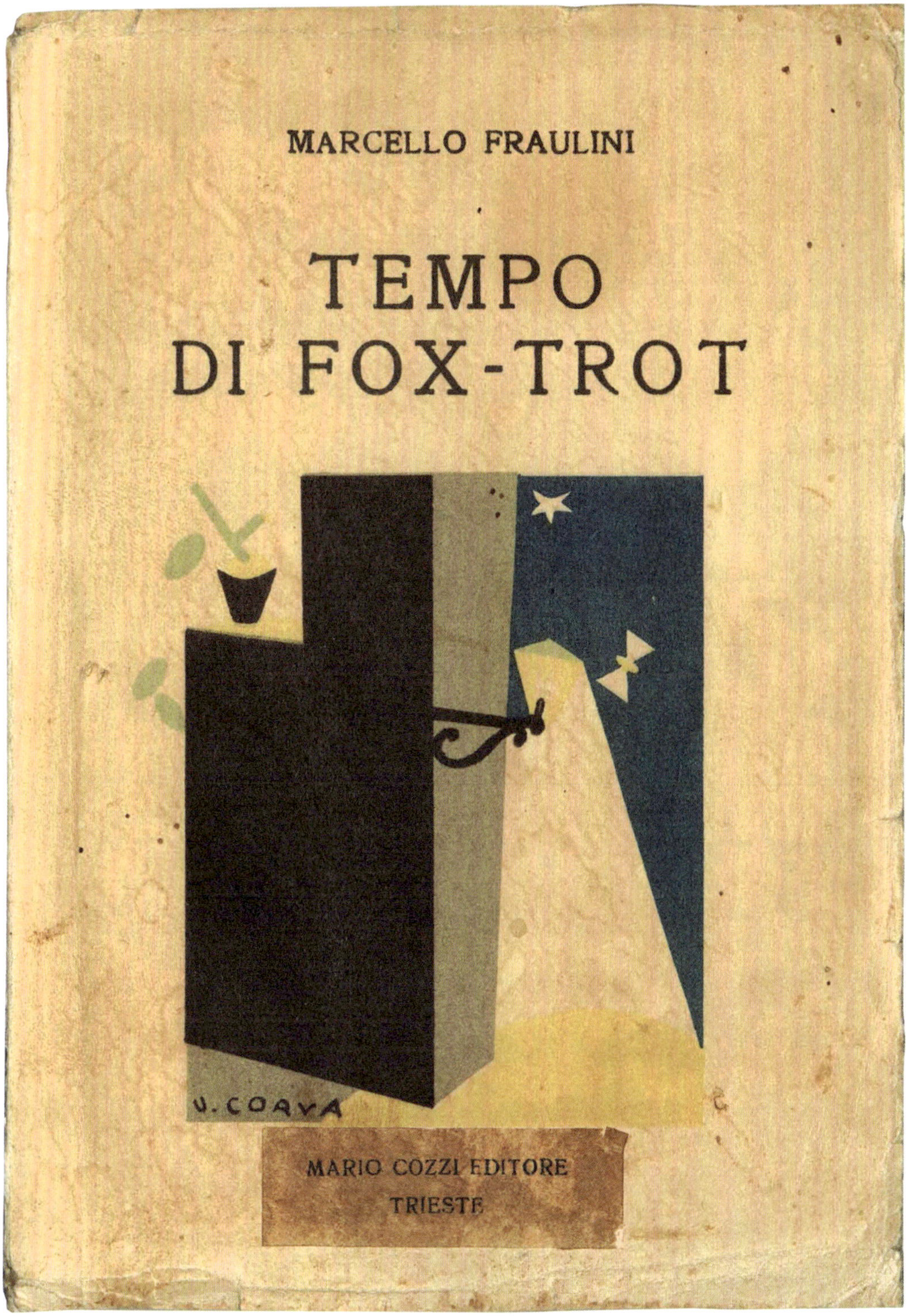
MARCELLO FRAULINI
TEMPO
DI FOX-TROT
MARIO COZZI EDITORE
TRIESTE

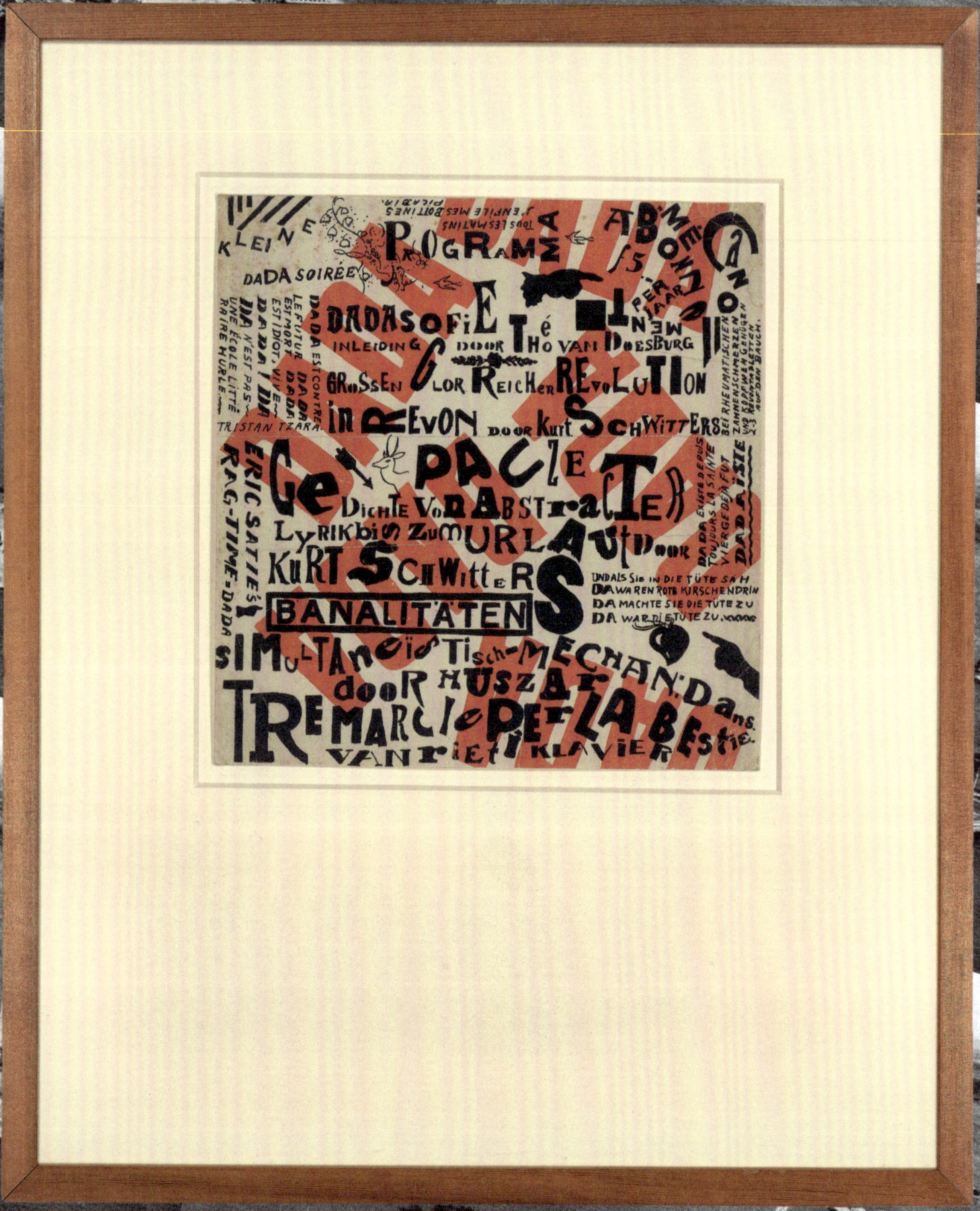

083 Kurt Schwitters, Theo van Doesburg, *Kleine Dada Soirée*, 1922
084 DaDa Beda [Fritz Löhner], Ober-DaDa Hajós [Karl Hajós], *DADA. Dadaistischer Fox-trot für Trottel und solche – die es noch werden wollen*, Vienna/Berlin: Wiener Bohème Verlag 1920, cover by Wolfgang Ortmann

↓084 ↑083

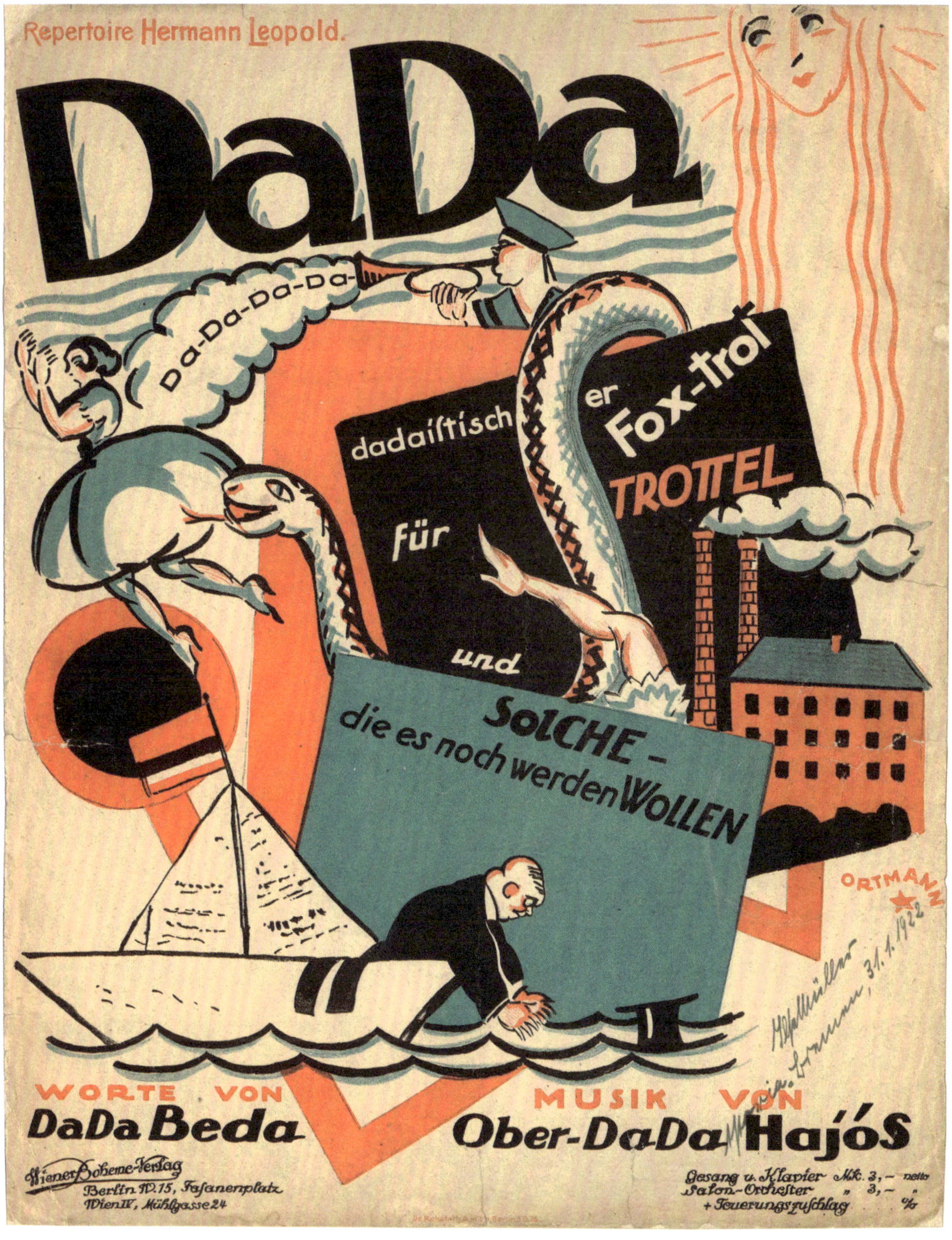
Repertoire Hermann Leopold.
DaDa
Da-Da-Da-Da-
Da-Da-Da-
dadaistischer Fox-trot
für TROTTEL
und
SOLCHE –
die es noch werden WOLLEN
ORTMANN
WORTE VON
DaDa Beda
MUSIK VON
Ober-DaDa Hajós
Wiener Boheme-Verlag
Berlin W. 15, Fasanenplatz
Wien IV, Mühlgasse 24
Gesang u. Klavier Mk. 3,– netto
Salon-Orchester „ 3,– „
+ Teuerungszuschlag %

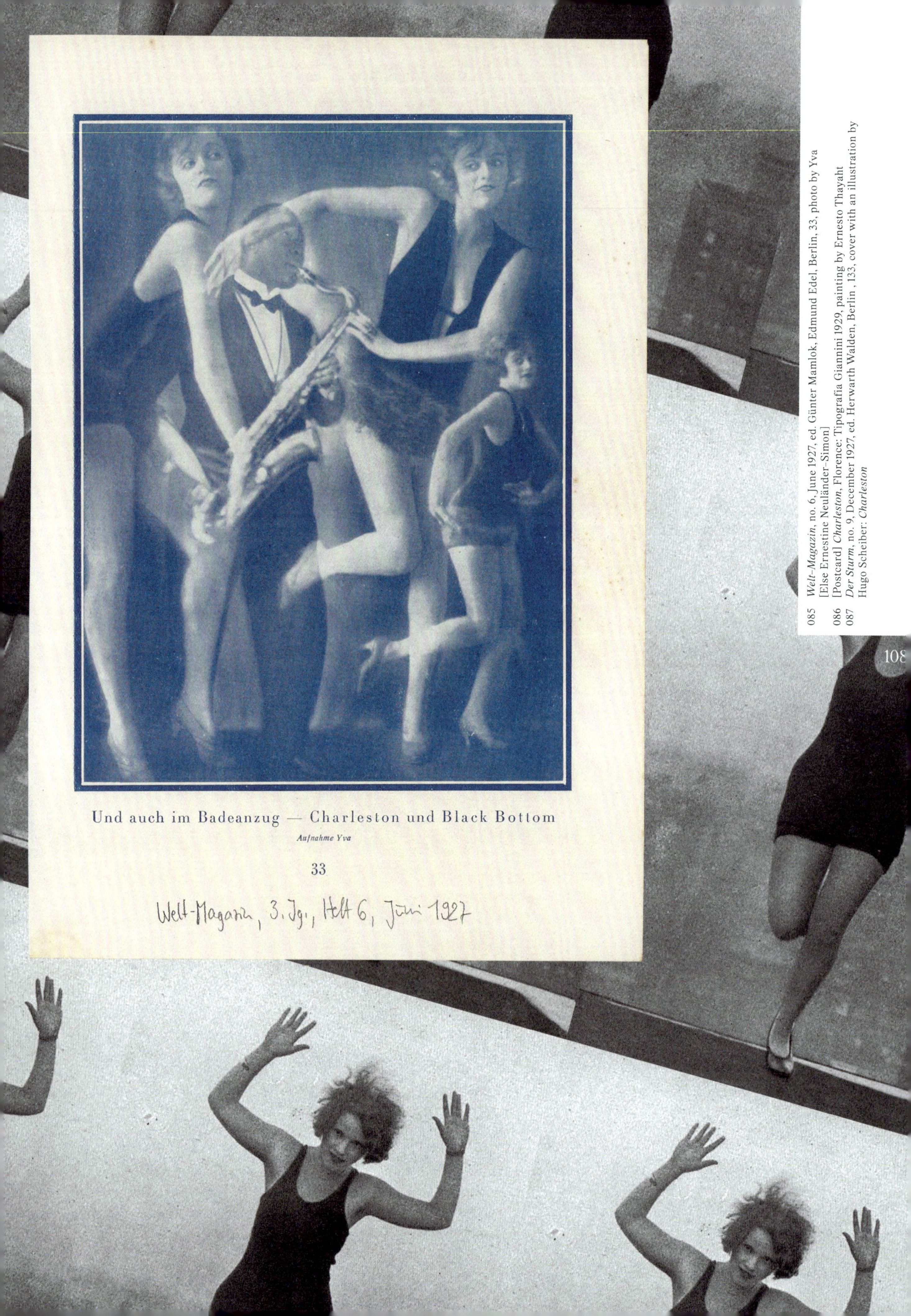

085 *Welt-Magazin*, no. 6, June 1927, ed. Günter Mamlok, Edmund Edel, Berlin, 33, photo by Yva [Else Ernestine Neuländer-Simon]
086 [Postcard] *Charleston*, Florence: Tipografia Giannini 1929, painting by Ernesto Thayaht
087 *Der Sturm*, no. 9, December 1927, ed. Herwarth Walden, Berlin , 133, cover with an illustration by Hugo Scheiber: *Charleston*

↓086 ↑085

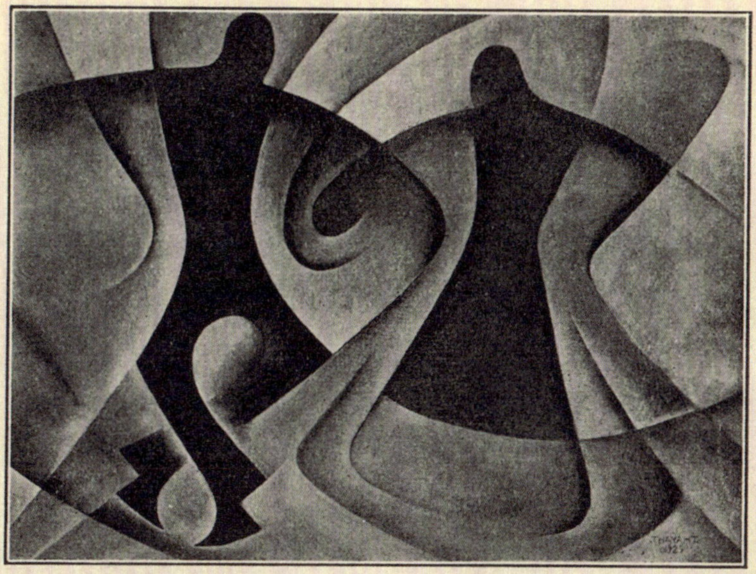

"CHARLESTON"

RITMO DI DANZA - Pittura a olio

ERNESTO THAYAHT Firenze 1927 - Anno V.

09

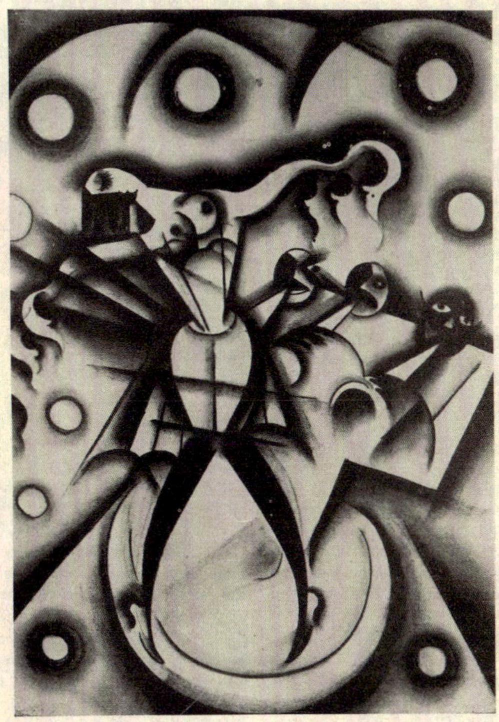

Hugo Scheiber: Charleston

133

↓087

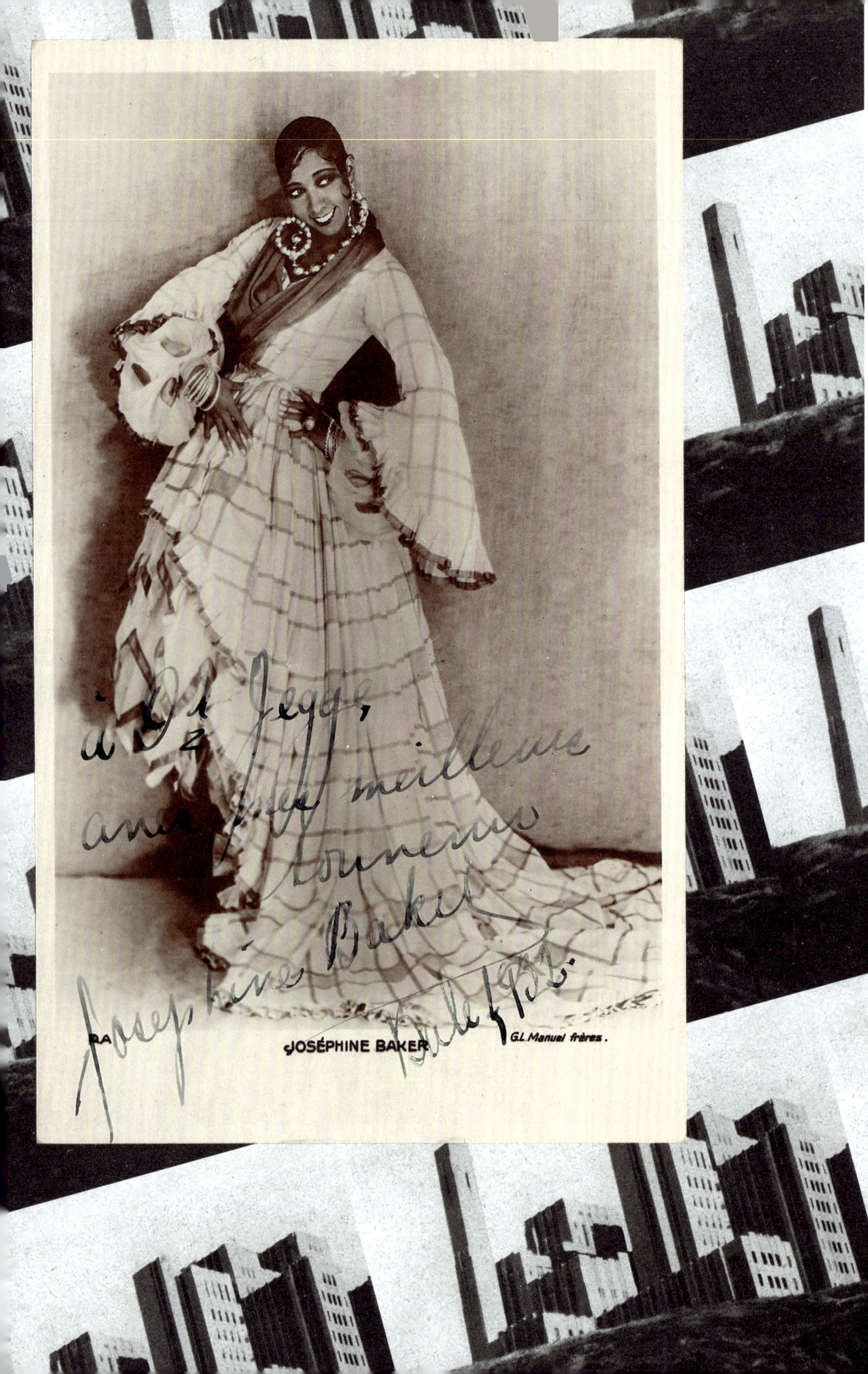

088 [Postcard] *Joséphine Baker*, presumably Paris, 1927–1932, photo by G.L. Manuel frères
089 *ReD* [*Revue Devětsil*]. *Měsíčník pro moderní kulturu*, no. 8, May 1928, ed. Karel Teige, Prague, 291, photo by Studio Waléry Paris: *Josephine Baker*

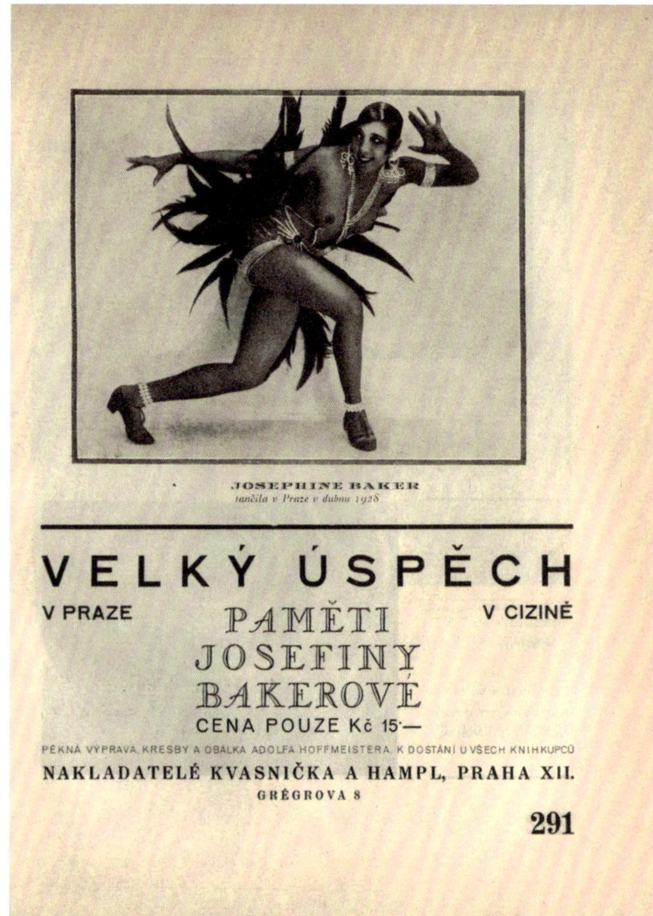

11

JOSEPHINE BAKER AND THE EUROPEAN AVANT-GARDES

At the age of thirteen, Josephine Baker headed to New York City, where she danced as a child at the Plantation Club. Her first success was in the Broadway revue *Shuffle Along* (1921), and she was later cast in Broadway musical *The Chocolate Dandies* (1924), before arriving in Paris in 1925. She came to the French capital right after the city's Worlds' Fair, which was intended to position Paris as the cosmopolitan capital of the world. She immediately became an unquestionable celebrity of *Revue Nègre* in the Théâtre des Champs-Élysées and toured around Europe from Paris to Prague, Bucharest, and Kraków. Her performances in a banana skirt exemplified clichés related to Africa, but at the same time, she positioned herself as a modern, self-confident woman who revolutionized dance and popularized the Charleston in Europe. She was a performing star beloved by avant-garde artists including Alexander Calder, Paul Colin, Kees van Dongen, and Enrico Prampolini. The latter made a sketch in which Baker's posture clearly resembles a muscular Futurist robot. Modernist architects, including Adolf Loos and Le Corbusier, also admired Baker. The former made plans for a (never realized) Baker House, while the second travelled with her to South America in 1929. On the return transatlantic trip from Rio de Janeiro to Bordeaux, he made a number of drawings of Baker and even drafted a libretto for a ballet in which she was meant to play a major role.

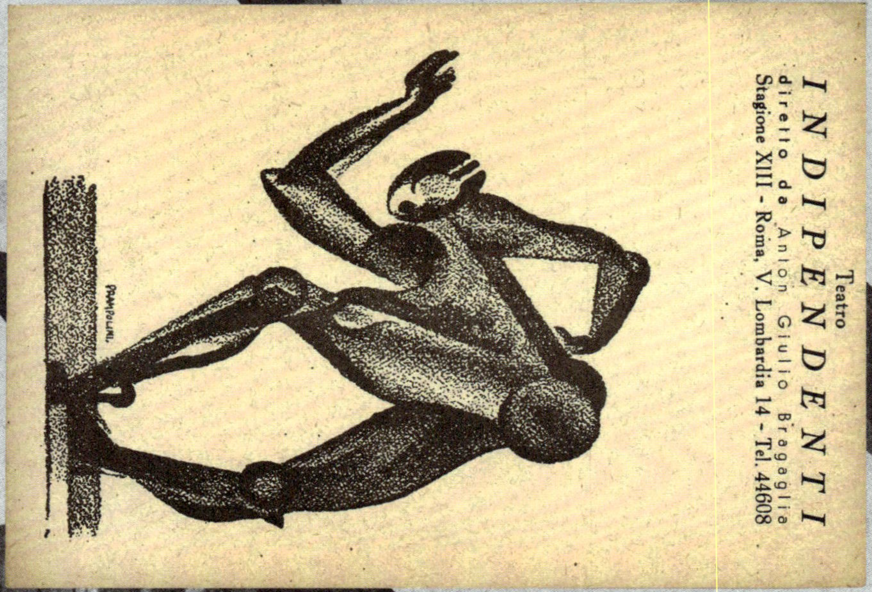

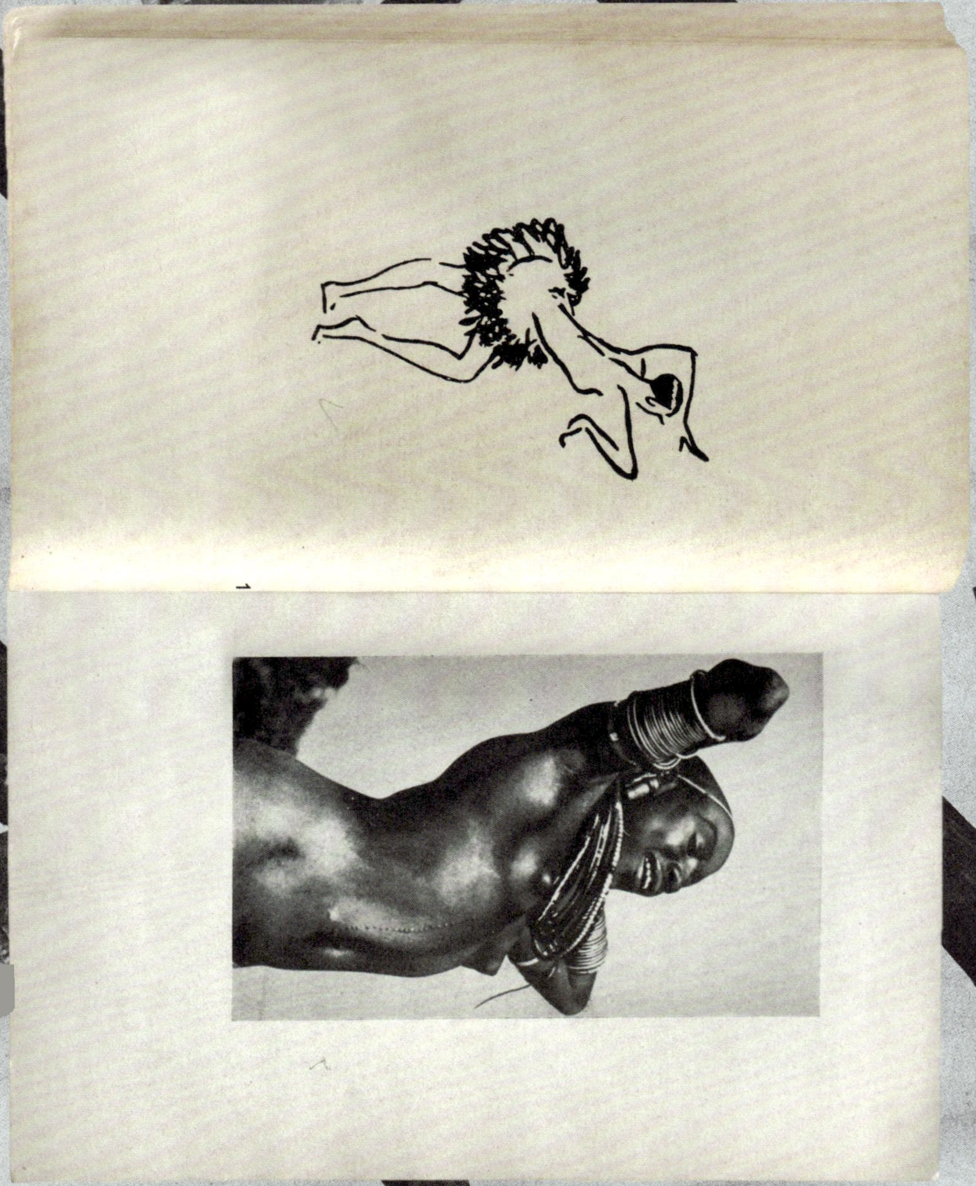

090 [Postcard] *Teatro Indipendenti*, Rome, 1928, illustration by Enrico Prampolini: *Joséphine Baker*
091 Emil František Burian, *Černošské tance. Obrazová knihovna, sv. 1*, Prague: Odeon 1929, [unpaginated], illustration by Paul Colin [Josephine Baker]
092 [photographer unknown], *Adolf Loos, Wohnhaus für Josephine Baker (Entwurf)*, in *Der Querschnitt*, no. 12, December 1930, ed. Hermann von Wedderkop, Berlin, 837

↓092 ↑090

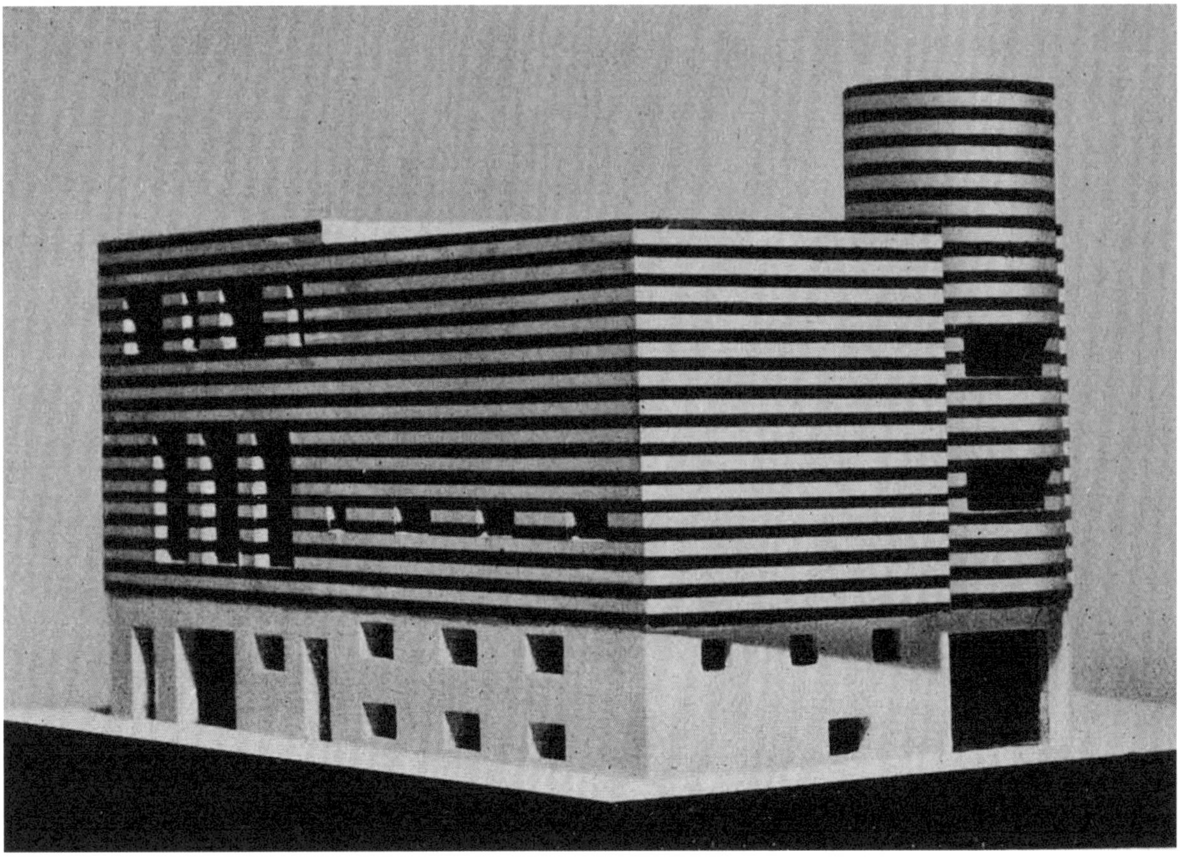

13

↑091

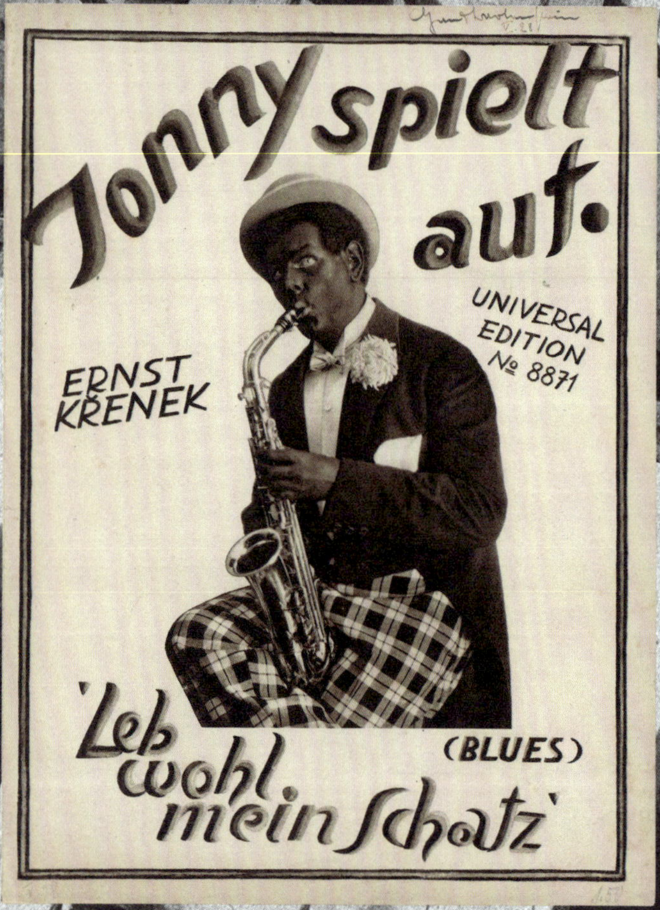

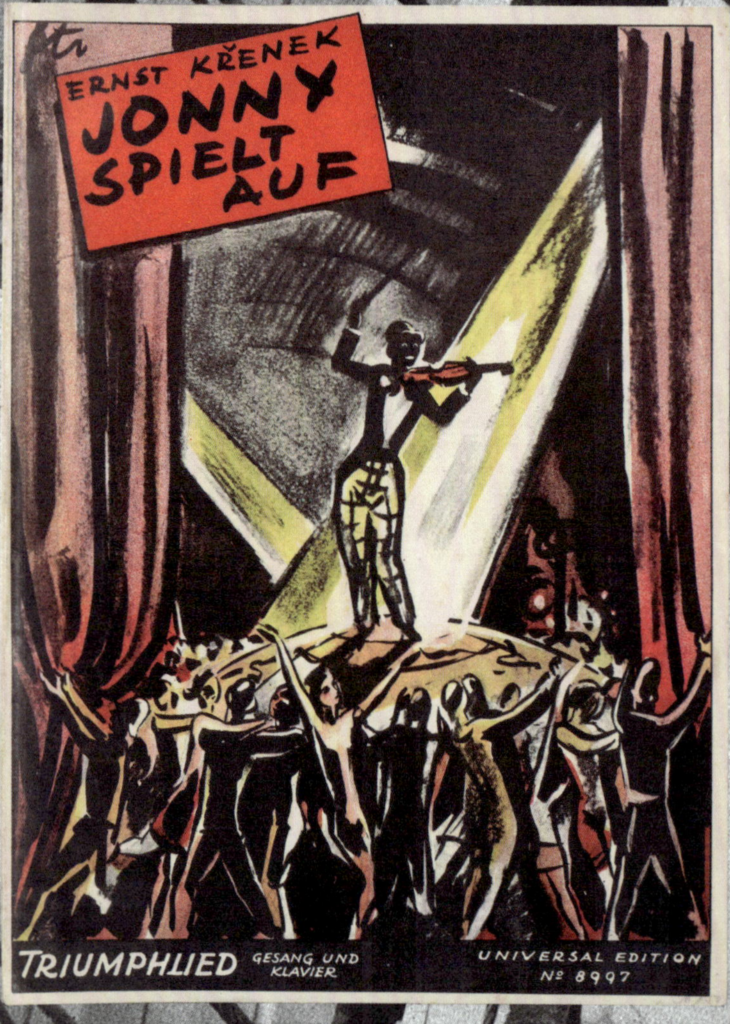

093 Ernst Křenek, *Leb' wohl mein Schatz. Blues aus der Oper „Jonny spielt auf"*, Vienna/Leipzig: Universal Edition A. G. 1927

094 Ernst Křenek, *2 Jonny-Songs aus der Oper „Jonny spielt auf"*, Vienna/Leipzig: Universal Edition A. G. 1927

095 *Bauhaus. Zeitschrift für Gestaltung*, no. 2–3, 1928, ed. Hannes Meyer, Dessau, 29, photo by T. Lux Feininger: *jonny–schawinsky spielt auf*

↓095 ↑093

(fritz kuhr)
am bauhaus sind, er lädt mich ein, auch dorthin zu kommen. es reizte mich kolossal, von kandinsky zu erfahren, was eigentlich seine bildwerke bedeuten sollten. nun, ich kam in weimar an, wurde von herrn kandinsky zuvorkommend empfangen. er erzählte mir einiges über die abstrakte malerei, was mir ziemlich unplausibel erschien, lieh mir sein buch „über das geistige in der kunst" und verabschiedete mich. ich wanderte zu moholy, dem ich im eifer der diskussion vorwarf, daß ich das, was ich an seiner atelierwand hängen sah (ein bild von moholy, ich wußte aber nicht, daß es von ihm war) für unfug und blödsinn halte, worauf mir moholy haarscharf bewies (in der beweisführung kamen die worte „spannungen" und „hemmungen" sehr oft vor), daß ich nicht berechtigt sei, etwas, was ich nicht verstehe, für unfug oder für blödsinn zu halten. das leuchtete mir ein. was los war, wußte ich immer noch nicht, jedenfalls imponierte mir die überzeugung, mit der moholy die abstrakte malerei verteidigte. auf seine veranlassung meldete ich mich dann in den vorkurs.

der vorkurs war gegliedert in theorie, elementare gestaltung und werkarbeit. die theorie kam von herrn kandinsky und herrn klee, die elementare gestaltung von herrn moholy und die werkarbeit wurde von herrn albers beaufsichtigt und beeinflußt. herr albers bemühte sich, mir meine mühsam konstruierten „gebrauchsgegenstände" auf ihren praktischen wert zu untersuchen und zu zerpflücken. und erzählte von ungeahnten möglichkeiten (von welchen ich bloß nichts merkte).

ich konstruierte dann rein theoretisch mit einer kameradin einen regenschirm aus aluminium (ganz-metall). wir wollten das leidige durchrosten der seide verhindern. aluminium wählten wir wegen des gewichtes. die ausführung dieses projektes verwarfen wir, weil die vorkurs-werkstatt nicht für derartige dinge eingerichtet war. eventuell hätten wir es der industrie überlassen, wenn wir nicht auf den gedanken gekommen wären, daß die industrie kein interesse an soliden haltbaren schirmen hat.

in der elementaren gestaltung ging es sehr schlecht vorwärts. wir bauten plastiken aus holz, haben die hölzchen sauber gesägt, geschliffen, zusammengesetzt, mal ein stück glas oder metall daran gehalten, aber immer mit dem bewußtsein, es ist eine sinnlose spielerei, es ist kohl. ich begreife doch nicht, was man hier will, es ist doch das beste, ich verschwinde wieder geräuschlos. das war so meine überzeugung.

dann kam aber das große, wichtige erlebnis.

mit der zweiten holzplastik hatte ich eine balance-übung verbunden, das hauptgewicht jedoch auf den ästhetischen reiz gelegt. bei der dritten plastik kam mir die anziehungskraft der erde zum bewußtsein, d. h. ich wußte schon von früher um diese anziehungskraft, aber jetzt erlebte ich erst, wissen sie, mit dem herzen, mit dem verstand, mit jedem nerv erlebte ich die anziehungskraft der erde. ich hoffe, daß sie wissen, wie das ist, wenn man etwas, was man schon vorher wußte, auf einmal, nicht so mir nichts dir nichts, sondern durchaus folgerichtig in allen etappen, bloß mit ungeheurer schnelligkeit und eindringlichkeit, so mit seinem ganzen selbst begreift. so baute ich meine vierte plastik, aus holz, eisen, blech, kupfer, glas, papier, aber

das sinnlose spiel mit dem material war nicht mehr sinnlos.

ich schuftete, verglich, wog, feilte, bohrte, pinselte, tupfte, zeichnete mit einem ernst und eifer an meiner plastik, die nur noch ein kind seiner arbeit entgegenbringen kann.

ich war so frei, so aufgelockert, so zufrieden-explodiert, wie nie in meinem leben. ich fühlte mich wie neugeboren.

eine form hatte die plastik nicht, überhaupt glaube ich, daß sie etwas unscheinbar aussah. ich nannte sie großspurig

„versuch einer vierdimensionalen plastik". nun aber stand es fest, daß ich vorläufig am bauhaus studieren würde. ich hatte den sinn des bauhauses begriffen. daß ich heute noch studierender des bauhauses bin, mögen sie als beweis dafür nehmen, daß für mich

die welt nur dann einen sinn hat, wenn sie ein „bauhaus" ist. „die ganze welt ein bauhaus"!

schluß des interviews in der nächsten nummer.

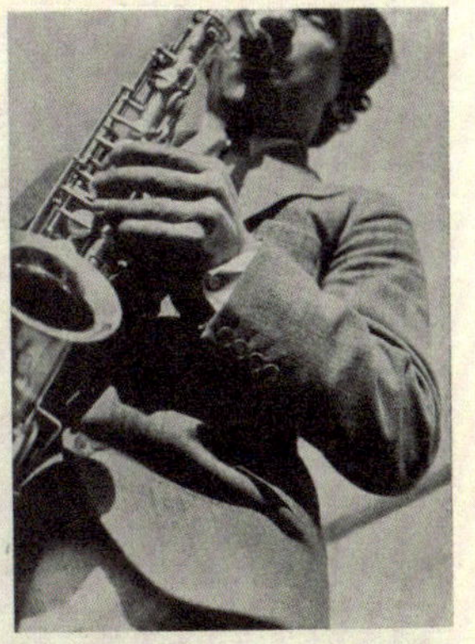

jonny-schawinsky spielt auf — foto lux feininger

imdu babauhaus!
venez étudier à bauhaus!
studiato nel bauhaus!
come and study at the bauhaus!
tanuljatok a bauhausnál!
studjnjcie w bauhausie!
studujete v bauhausu!
studiert am bauhaus!

vom 29. juli bis 12. august tagt in prag in der tschechoslowakei der

VI. internationale kongreß für zeichnen, kunstunterricht und angewandte graphik, mit welchem eine internationale ausstellung „erziehung zur bildenden kunst" verbunden ist.

informationen erteilt bereitwilligst das sekretariat prag-II, škola u sv. vojtécha.

29

JONNY SPIELT AUF—A JAZZ OPERA In the 1920s, the practice of blackfacing was very common in the context of jazz performance. One of the best-known examples was the first-ever sound movie *Jazz Singer* (1927), produced in Hollywood. The main protagonist, a Black singer, was played by a white actor, Al Jolson, wearing blackface. In the 1920s, blackfacing was not considered out of the ordinary or offensive, and it is important to emphasize that Jolson was a prominent civil rights advocate who helped to pave the way for African-American actors to find jobs in Hollywood. The same year, another example of blackfacing connected to jazz appeared during performances of *Jonny spielt auf* (Jonny Strikes Up the Band) composed by Austrian-Czech musician Ernst Křenek. This "jazz opera" premiered at the Neues Theater in Leipzig in 1927 and narrated the adventures of a love triangle between the Black musician Jonny, the white composer Max, and the singer Anita. The role of Jonny was played by an Austrian singer named Alfred Jerger in wearing blackface. In Germany, the opera was well received by the progressive environment of Bauhaus. Xanti Schawinsky modelled himself as "jonny-schawinsky spielt auf" in a photograph by T. Lux Feininger. However, it provoked outrage from right-wing sympathizers, who classified jazz as a form of so-called "degenerate art." After 1933, when the National Socialists came to power in Germany, performances of *Jonny spielt auf* were banned.

↑094

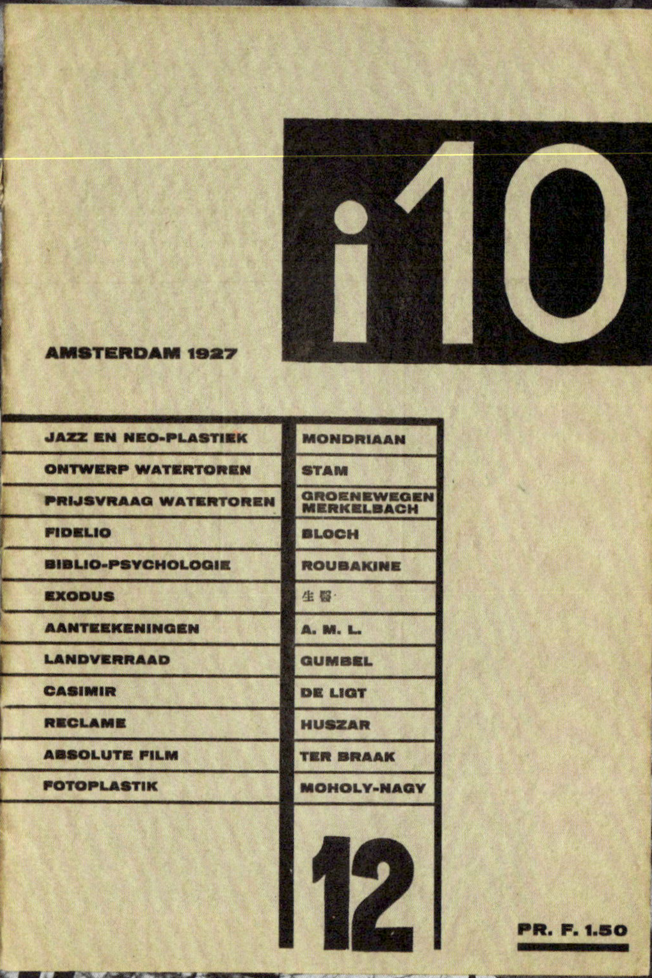

AMSTERDAM 1927

i10

JAZZ EN NEO-PLASTIEK	MONDRIAAN
ONTWERP WATERTOREN	STAM
PRIJSVRAAG WATERTOREN	GROENEWEGEN MERKELBACH
FIDELIO	BLOCH
BIBLIO-PSYCHOLOGIE	ROUBAKINE
EXODUS	生 腎
AANTEEKENINGEN	A. M. L.
LANDVERRAAD	GUMBEL
CASIMIR	DE LIGT
RECLAME	HUSZAR
ABSOLUTE FILM	TER BRAAK
FOTOPLASTIK	MOHOLY-NAGY

12

PR. F. 1.50

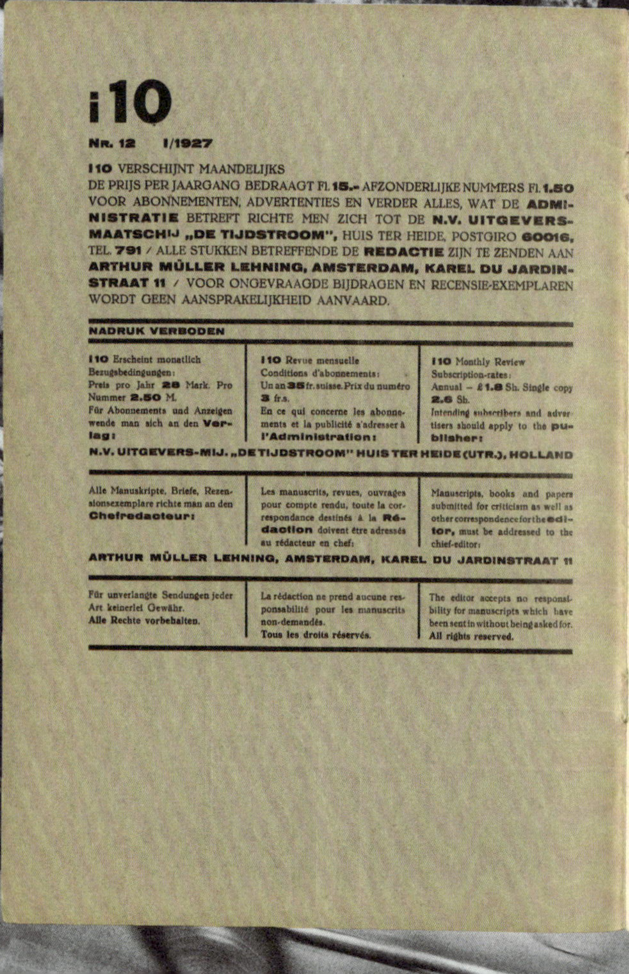

i10

NR. 12 I/1927

I10 VERSCHIJNT MAANDELIJKS
DE PRIJS PER JAARGANG BEDRAAGT Fl. **15.-** AFZONDERLIJKE NUMMERS Fl. **1.50** VOOR ABONNEMENTEN, ADVERTENTIES EN VERDER ALLES, WAT DE **ADMINISTRATIE** BETREFT RICHTE MEN ZICH TOT DE **N.V. UITGEVERS-MAATSCHIJ „DE TIJDSTROOM"**, HUIS TER HEIDE, POSTGIRO **60016**, TEL. **791** / ALLE STUKKEN BETREFFENDE DE **REDACTIE** ZIJN TE ZENDEN AAN **ARTHUR MÜLLER LEHNING, AMSTERDAM, KAREL DU JARDINSTRAAT 11** / VOOR ONGEVRAAGDE BIJDRAGEN EN RECENSIE-EXEMPLAREN WORDT GEEN AANSPRAKELIJKHEID AANVAARD.

NADRUK VERBODEN

I10 Erscheint monatlich Bezugsbedingungen: Preis pro Jahr **28** Mark. Pro Nummer **2.50** M. Für Abonnements und Anzeigen wende man sich an den **Verlag:**	**I10** Revue mensuelle Conditions d'abonnements: Un an **35** fr. suisse. Prix du numéro **3** fr.s. En ce qui concerne les abonnements et la publicité s'adresser à **l'Administration:**	**I10** Monthly Review Subscription-rates: Annual – £ **1.8** Sh. Single copy **2.6** Sh. Intending subscribers and advertisers should apply to the **publisher:**

N.V. UITGEVERS-MIJ. „DE TIJDSTROOM" HUIS TER HEIDE (UTR.), HOLLAND

Alle Manuskripte, Briefe, Rezensionsexemplare richte man an den **Chefredacteur:**	Les manuscrits, revues, ouvrages pour compte rendu, toute la correspondance destinés à la **Rédaction** doivent être adressés au rédacteur en chef:	Manuscripts, books and papers submitted for criticism as well as other correspondence for the **editor,** must be addressed to the chief-editor:

ARTHUR MÜLLER LEHNING, AMSTERDAM, KAREL DU JARDINSTRAAT 11

Für unverlangte Sendungen jeder Art keinerlei Gewähr. Alle Rechte vorbehalten.	La rédaction ne prend aucune responsabilité pour les manuscrits non-demandés. Tous les droits réservés.	The editor accepts no responsibility for manuscripts which have been sent in without being asked for. All rights reserved.

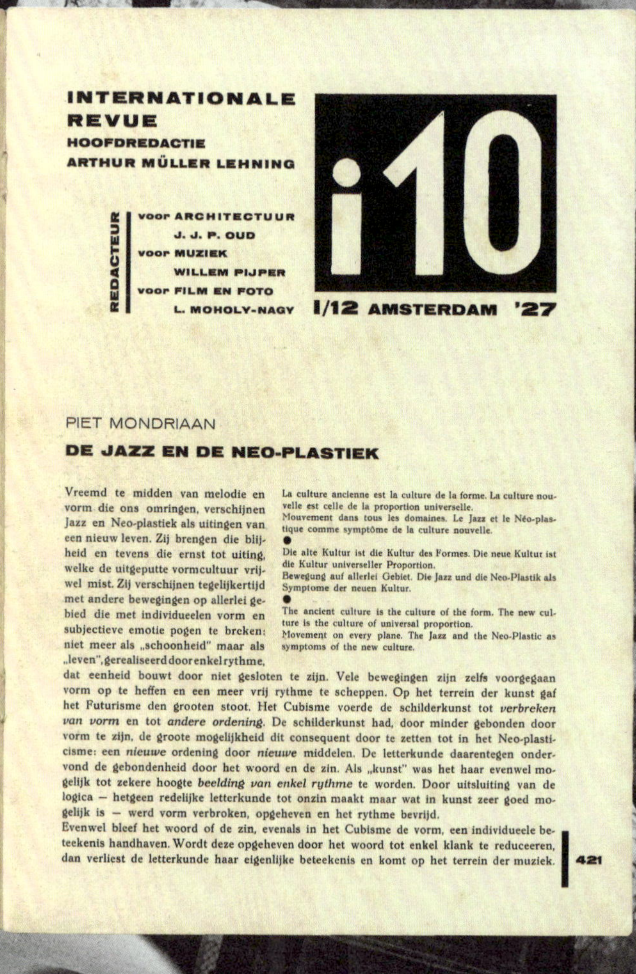

INTERNATIONALE REVUE
HOOFDREDACTIE
ARTHUR MÜLLER LEHNING

i10

REDACTEUR
voor ARCHITECTUUR J. J. P. OUD
voor MUZIEK WILLEM PIJPER
voor FILM EN FOTO L. MOHOLY-NAGY

I/12 AMSTERDAM '27

PIET MONDRIAAN

DE JAZZ EN DE NEO-PLASTIEK

La culture ancienne est la culture de la forme. La culture nouvelle est celle de la proportion universelle.
Mouvement dans tous les domaines. Le Jazz et le Néo-plastique comme symptôme de la culture nouvelle.

●

Die alte Kultur ist die Kultur des Formes. Die neue Kultur ist die Kultur universeller Proportion.
Bewegung auf allerlei Gebiet. Die Jazz und die Neo-Plastik als Symptome der neuen Kultur.

●

The ancient culture is the culture of the form. The new culture is the culture of universal proportion.
Movement on every plane. The Jazz and the Neo-Plastic as symptoms of the new culture.

Vreemd te midden van melodie en vorm die ons omringen, verschijnen Jazz en Neo-plastiek als uitingen van een nieuw leven. Zij brengen die blijheid en tevens die ernst tot uiting, welke de uitgeputte vormcultuur vrijwel mist. Zij verschijnen tegelijkertijd met andere bewegingen op allerlei gebied die met individueelen vorm en subjectieve emotie pogen te breken: niet meer als „schoonheid" maar als „leven", gerealiseerd door enkel rythme, dat eenheid bouwt door niet gesloten te zijn. Vele bewegingen zijn zelfs voorgegaan vorm op te heffen en een meer vrij rythme te scheppen. Op het terrein der kunst gaf het Futurisme den grooten stoot. Het Cubisme voerde de schilderkunst tot *verbreken van vorm* en tot *andere ordening*. De schilderkunst had, door minder gebonden door vorm te zijn, de groote mogelijkheid dit consequent door te zetten tot in het Neo-plasticisme: een *nieuwe* ordening door *nieuwe* middelen. De letterkunde daarentegen ondervond de gebondenheid door het woord en de zin. Als „kunst" was het haar evenwel mogelijk tot zekere hoogte *beelding van enkel rythme* te worden. Door uitsluiting van de logica – hetgeen redelijke letterkunde tot onzin maakt maar wat in kunst zeer goed mogelijk is – werd vorm verbroken, opgeheven en het rythme bevrijd.
Evenwel bleef het woord of de zin, evenals in het Cubisme de vorm, een individueele beteekenis handhaven. Wordt deze opgeheven door het woord tot enkel klank te reduceeren, dan verliest de letterkunde haar eigenlijke beteekenis en komt op het terrein der muziek.

421

096 *i10. Internationale Revue*, no. 12, 1927, ed. Arthur Müller Lehning, Amsterdam, cover by César Domela Nieuwenhuis; inside cover and 421 with a text by Piet Mondrian: *De Jazz en de Neo-Plastiek*; 426–427 with paintings by Piet Mondrian: *Neo-Plastisch Schilderij*

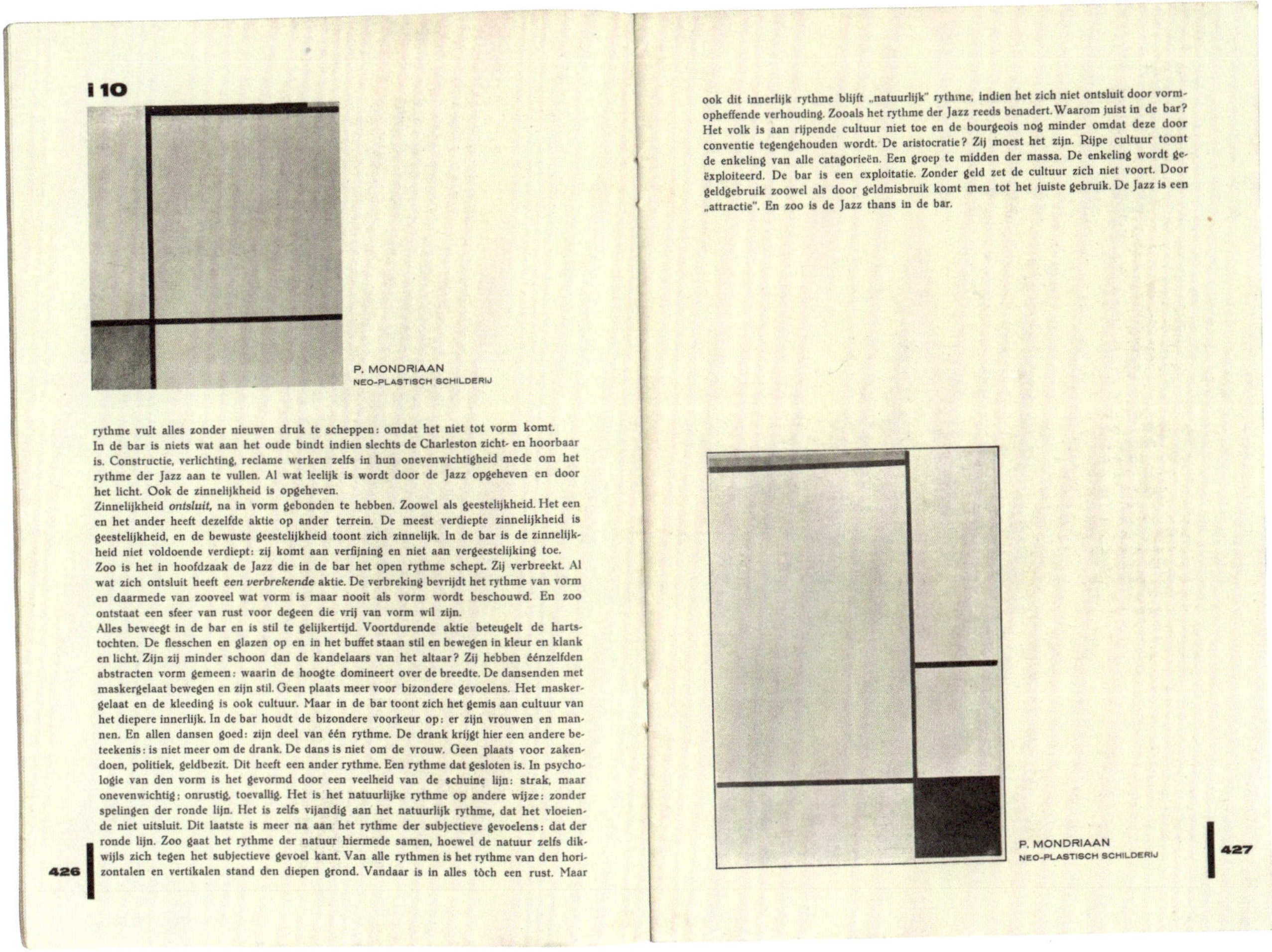

i10

P. MONDRIAAN
NEO-PLASTISCH SCHILDERIJ

rythme vult alles zonder nieuwen druk te scheppen: omdat het niet tot vorm komt.
In de bar is niets wat aan het oude bindt indien slechts de Charleston zicht- en hoorbaar is. Constructie, verlichting, reclame werken zelfs in hun onevenwichtigheid mede om het rythme der Jazz aan te vullen. Al wat leelijk is wordt door de Jazz opgeheven en door het licht. Ook de zinnelijkheid is opgeheven.
Zinnelijkheid *ontsluit*, na in vorm gebonden te hebben. Zoowel als geestelijkheid. Het een en het ander heeft dezelfde aktie op ander terrein. De meest verdiepte zinnelijkheid is geestelijkheid, en de bewuste geestelijkheid toont zich zinnelijk. In de bar is de zinnelijkheid niet voldoende verdiept: zij komt aan verfijning en niet aan vergeestelijking toe.
Zoo is het in hoofdzaak de Jazz die in de bar het open rythme schept. Zij verbreekt. Al wat zich ontsluit heeft *een verbrekende* aktie. De verbreking bevrijdt het rythme van vorm en daarmede van zooveel wat vorm is maar nooit als vorm wordt beschouwd. En zoo ontstaat een sfeer van rust voor degeen die vrij van vorm wil zijn.
Alles beweegt in de bar en is stil te gelijkertijd. Voortdurende aktie beteugelt de hartstochten. De flesschen en glazen op en in het buffet staan stil en bewegen in kleur en klank en licht. Zijn zij minder schoon dan de kandelaars van het altaar? Zij hebben éénzelfden abstracten vorm gemeen: waarin de hoogte domineert over de breedte. De dansenden met maskergelaat bewegen en zijn stil. Geen plaats meer voor bizondere gevoelens. Het maskergelaat en de kleeding is ook cultuur. Maar in de bar toont zich het gemis aan cultuur van het diepere innerlijk. In de bar houdt de bizondere voorkeur op: er zijn vrouwen en mannen. En allen dansen goed: zijn deel van één rythme. De drank krijgt hier een andere beteekenis: is niet meer om de drank. De dans is niet om de vrouw. Geen plaats voor zakendoen, politiek, geldbezit. Dit heeft een ander rythme. Een rythme dat gesloten is. In psychologie van den vorm is het gevormd door een veelheid van de schuine lijn: strak, maar onevenwichtig; onrustig, toevallig. Het is het natuurlijke rythme op andere wijze: zonder spelingen der ronde lijn. Het is zelfs vijandig aan het natuurlijk rythme, dat het vloeiende niet uitsluit. Dit laatste is meer na aan het rythme der subjectieve gevoelens: dat der ronde lijn. Zoo gaat het rythme der natuur hiermede samen, hoewel de natuur zelfs dikwijls zich tegen het subjectieve gevoel kant. Van alle rythmen is het rythme van den horizontalen en vertikalen stand den diepen grond. Vandaar is in alles tòch een rust. Maar

426

ook dit innerlijk rythme blijft „natuurlijk" rythme, indien het zich niet ontsluit door vormopheffende verhouding. Zooals het rythme der Jazz reeds benadert. Waarom juist in de bar? Het volk is aan rijpende cultuur niet toe en de bourgeois nog minder omdat deze door conventie tegengehouden wordt. De aristocratie? Zij moest het zijn. Rijpe cultuur toont de enkeling van alle catagorieën. Een groep te midden der massa. De enkeling wordt geëxploiteerd. De bar is een exploitatie. Zonder geld zet de cultuur zich niet voort. Door geldgebruik zoowel als door geldmisbruik komt men tot het juiste gebruik. De Jazz is een „attractie". En zoo is de Jazz thans in de bar.

P. MONDRIAAN
NEO-PLASTISCH SCHILDERIJ

427

HOW TO PAINT JAZZ? PIET MONDRIAN AND NEOPLASTICISM

Piet Mondrian is best known as a theoretician of neoplasticism, an avant-garde style associated with abstract art. He believed that painting should consist of a balanced composition of simple geometric shapes, right-angled relationships, primary colors (red, blue, yellow) and non-colors (black, white, grey). While writing his theory, he was influenced by the music played by jazz bands and listened to his gramophone, which he had placed in the centre of his studio. He had high praise for the African American dancer Josephine Baker after he first saw her performing in the *Revue Nègre* in Paris. Two years later, he published an essay on "Jazz and Neoplasticism" in a Dutch avant-garde magazine, *i10*, in which he outlined the affinities of his painterly concept with the exploration of jazz rhythm and dance. He intended to visualize jazz in painting, giving it an abstract form. He was convinced that rhythm, whether optically (neoplasticism) or musically (jazz), links life and art. He ultimately stated that "Jazz and Neo-Plasticism are highly revolutionary phenomena."

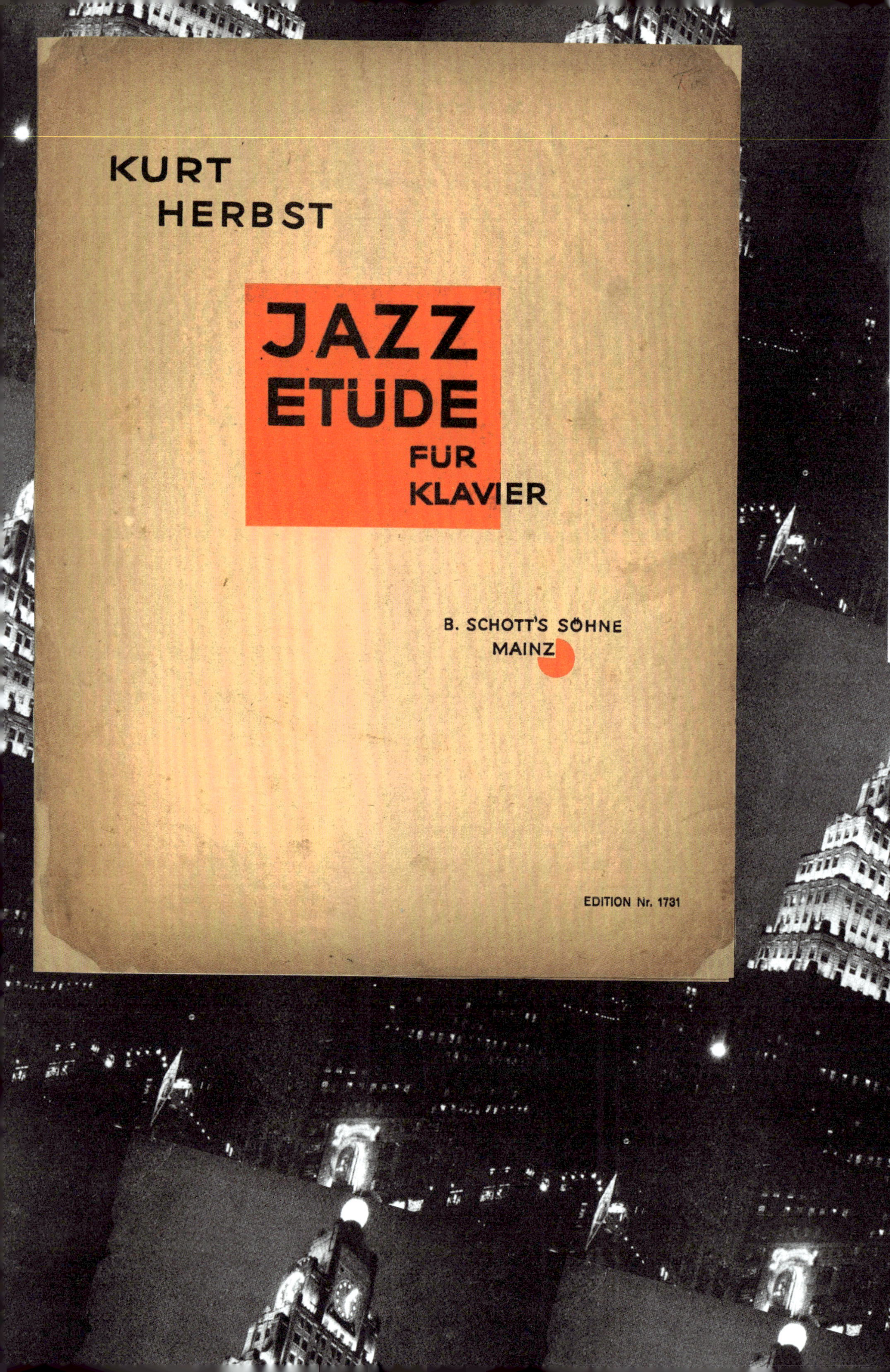

097 Kurt Herbst, *Jazz Etüde für Klavier*, Mainz: B. Schott's Söhne 1928, cover; 3

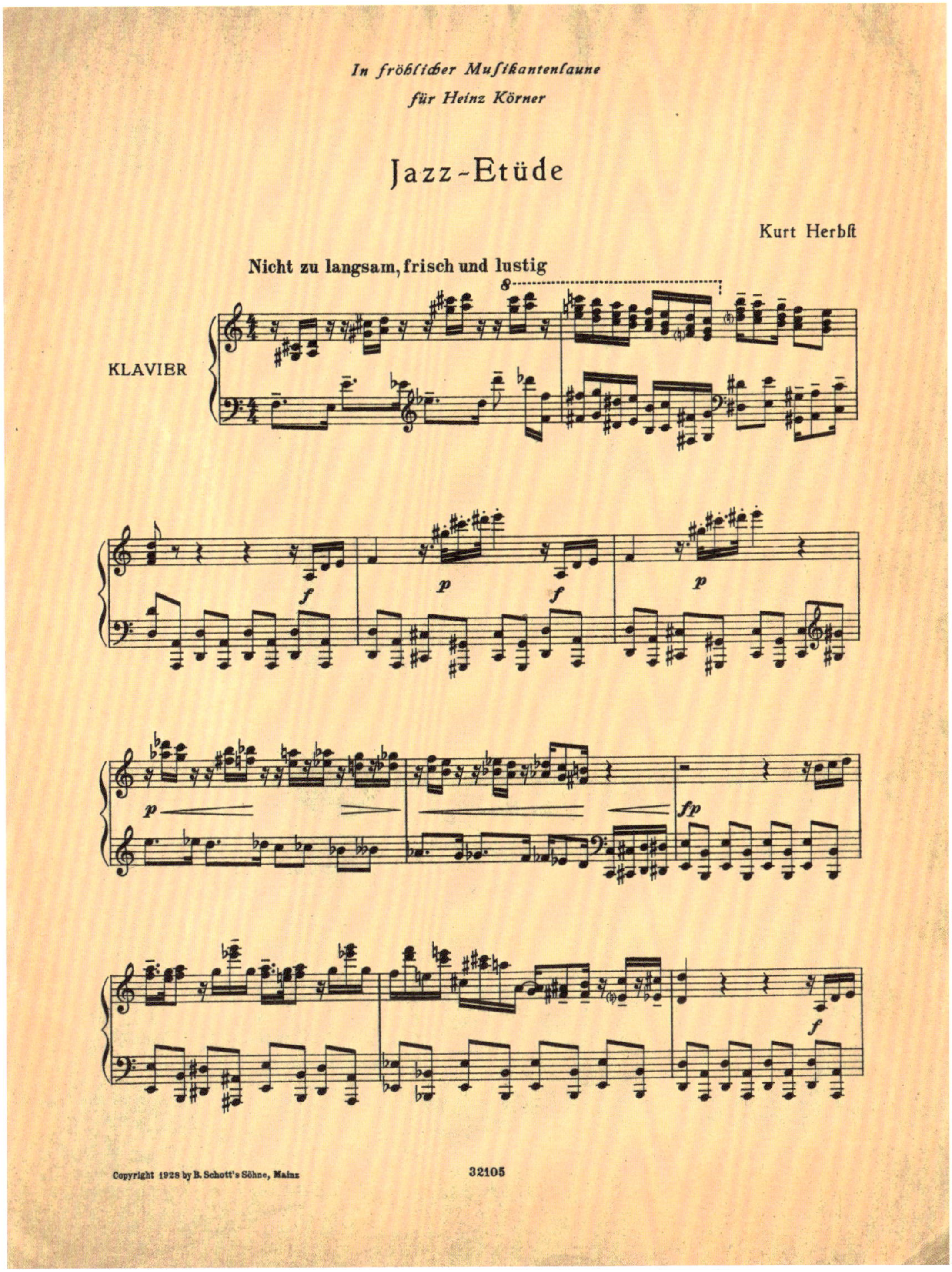
In fröhlicher Musikantenlaune
für Heinz Körner
Jazz-Etüde
Kurt Herbst
Nicht zu langsam, frisch und lustig
KLAVIER
Copyright 1928 by B. Schott's Söhne, Mainz
32105

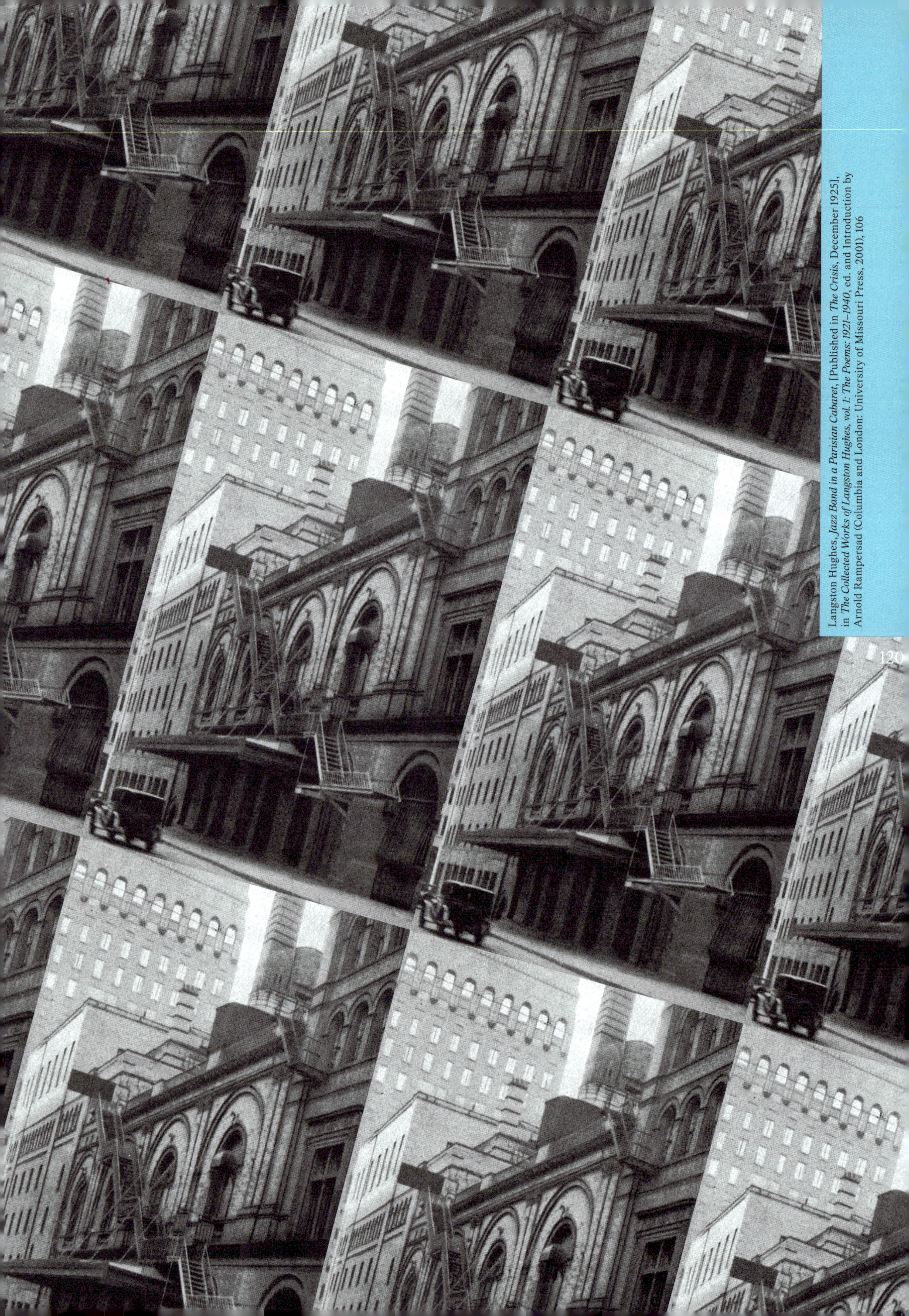

Langston Hughes, *Jazz Band in a Parisian Cabaret*, [Published in *The Crisis*, December 1925], in *The Collected Works of Langston Hughes, vol. 1: The Poems: 1921–1940*, ed. and Introduction by Arnold Rampersad (Columbia and London: University of Missouri Press, 2001), 106

Jazz Band in a Parisian Cabaret

Play that thing,
Jazz band!
Play it for the lords and ladies,
For the dukes and counts,
For the whores and gigolos,
For the American millionaires,
And the school teachers
Out for a spree.
Play it,
Jazz band!
You know that tune
That laughs and cries at the same time.
You know it.
        May I?
        Mais oui.
        Mein Gott!
        Parece una rumba.
Play it, jazz band!
You've got seven languages to speak in
And then some,
Even if you do come from Georgia.
Can I go home wid yuh, sweetie?
Sure.

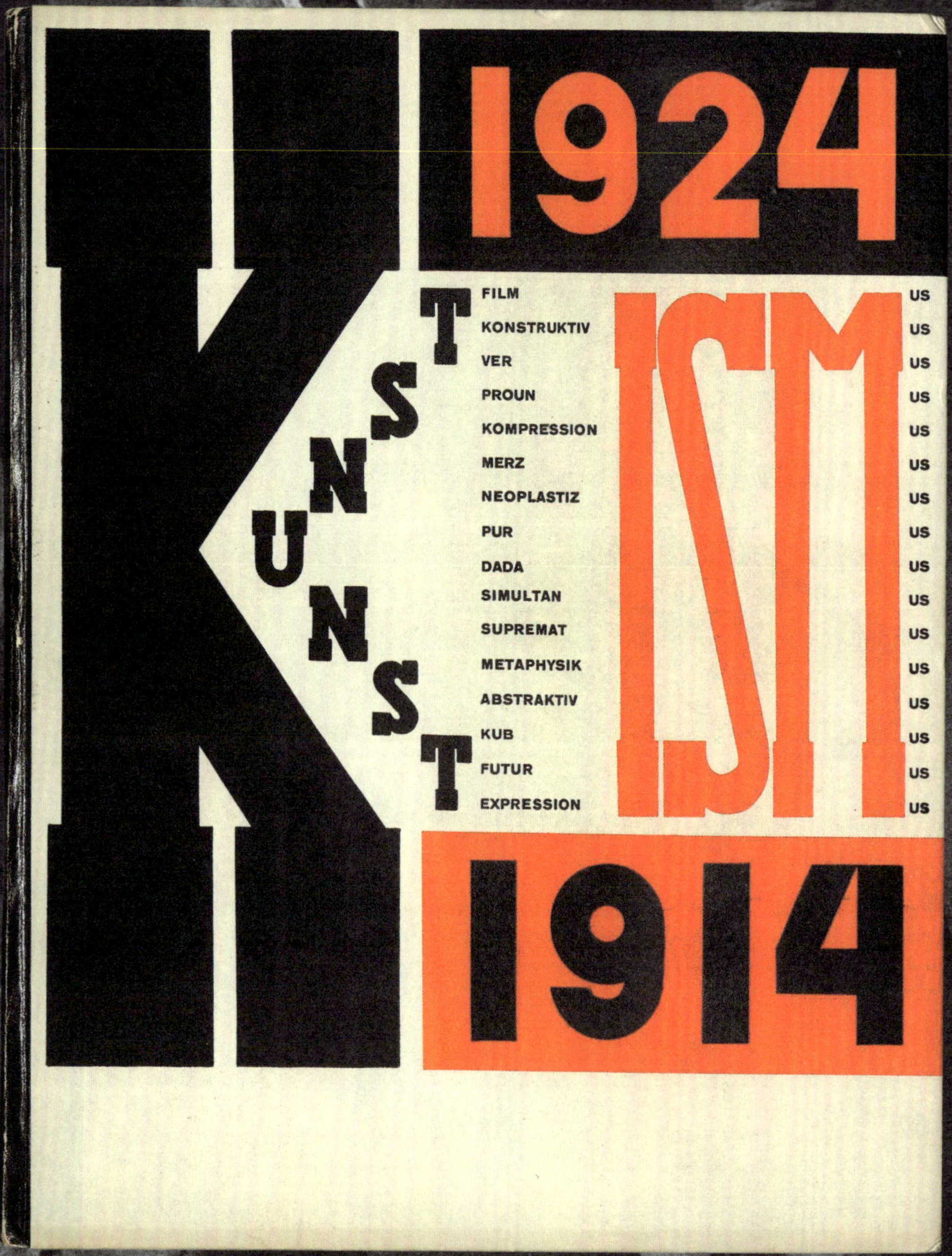

098 Hans [Jean] Arp, El Lissitzky, *Die Kunstismen 1914–1924*, Erlenbach-Zurich/Munich/Leipzig: Eugen-Rentsch-Verlag 1925, cover by El Lissitzky
099 Ramón Gómez de la Serna, *ISMOS*, Buenos Aires: Editorial Poseidon 1947 [first edition Madrid 1931], cover with a painting by Pablo Picasso

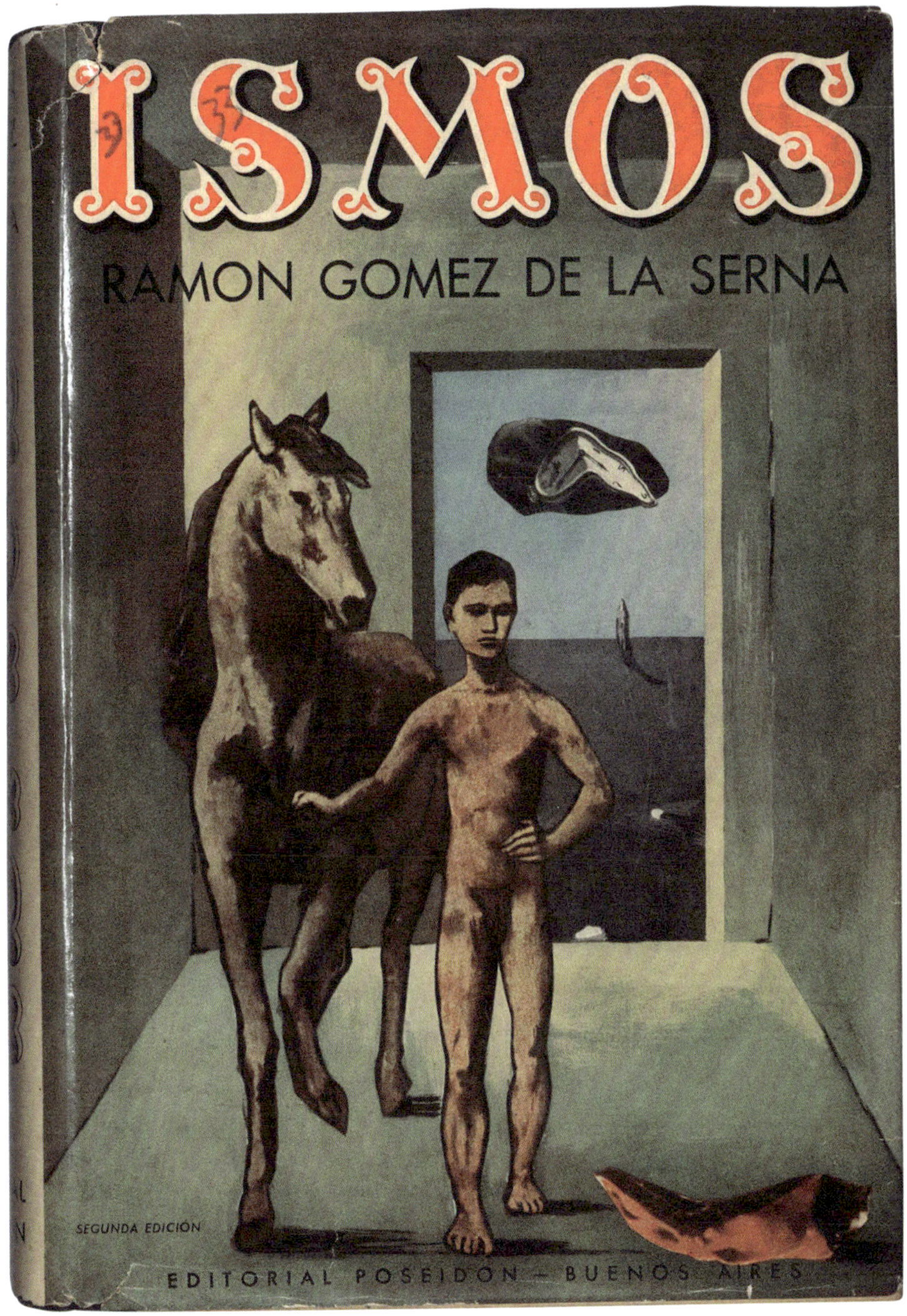
ISMOS
RAMON GOMEZ DE LA SERNA
SEGUNDA EDICIÓN
EDITORIAL POSEIDON – BUENOS AIRES

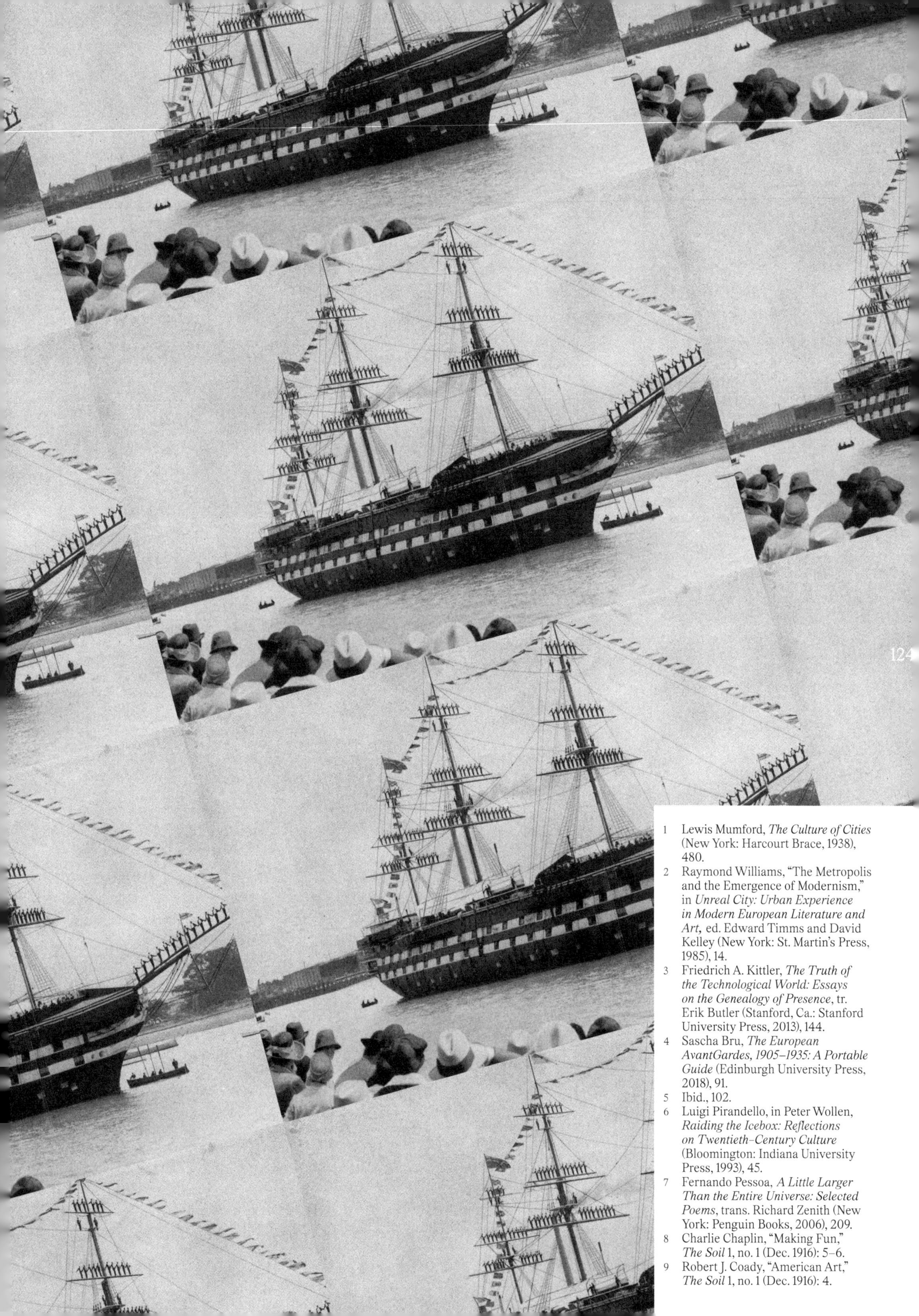

1 Lewis Mumford, *The Culture of Cities* (New York: Harcourt Brace, 1938), 480.
2 Raymond Williams, "The Metropolis and the Emergence of Modernism," in *Unreal City: Urban Experience in Modern European Literature and Art,* ed. Edward Timms and David Kelley (New York: St. Martin's Press, 1985), 14.
3 Friedrich A. Kittler, *The Truth of the Technological World: Essays on the Genealogy of Presence*, tr. Erik Butler (Stanford, Ca.: Stanford University Press, 2013), 144.
4 Sascha Bru, *The European AvantGardes, 1905–1935: A Portable Guide* (Edinburgh University Press, 2018), 91.
5 Ibid., 102.
6 Luigi Pirandello, in Peter Wollen, *Raiding the Icebox: Reflections on Twentieth-Century Culture* (Bloomington: Indiana University Press, 1993), 45.
7 Fernando Pessoa, *A Little Larger Than the Entire Universe: Selected Poems*, trans. Richard Zenith (New York: Penguin Books, 2006), 209.
8 Charlie Chaplin, "Making Fun," *The Soil* 1, no. 1 (Dec. 1916): 5–6.
9 Robert J. Coady, "American Art," *The Soil* 1, no. 1 (Dec. 1916): 4.

Esperanto Theatre: American Culture Comes to Europe

Jed Rasula

In 1938, Lewis Mumford enumerated the salient characteristics of the city as "a geographic plexus, an economic organization, an institutional process, a theatre of social action, and an esthetic symbol of collective unity."[1] As a theatre of social action, the modern city became a "transmitting metropolis"[2] as Raymond Williams called it, by which he meant not only in relation to communication technologies but also the cultural impact of urban activity. The transmission was two-way. Media theorist Friedrich Kittler reminds us that "The more one 'thinks' a capital like Paris, Valéry wrote, the more one knows that one is 'thought' by it oneself."[3] I offer these perspectives as prelude to Sascha Bru's suggestion that "there probably would have been no avant-gardes without the cities in which they thrived."[4] The European network of the avant-gardes extended from Paris, Berlin, Moscow, and St. Petersburg to Madrid, Lisbon, Milan, Prague, Zagreb, and more. As Bru suggests, "The idea of the city, rather than the real or given city, made it possible for avant-gardists to imagine, say, Paris, without ever having been to the city"—or, increasingly, New York, the specter that hovered over avant-garde self-reckoning.[5] As early as 1875 New York was already the world's third-largest city, then second by 1900, and the most populous by 1925. In 1900, three-quarters of the city's inhabitants were foreign-born, an immigrant population that helped to make New York the transmitting metropolis of America. By 1929, the Italian playwright Pirandello felt that "Americanism is swamping us. I think that a new beacon of civilization has been lit over there."[6] What, exactly, was this Americanism? Fernando Pessoa suggests an answer in his ode to that globally influential New Yorker, Walt Whitman: "The true modern poem is life without poems," he wrote. "It's the train itself and not verses that sing of it."[7]

What we have here is a European vanguardist coming to terms with art as artifice and artifact. Having long since established an aesthetic hegemony over much of the world, European culture found itself playing second fiddle to a young, brash, upstart culture with its skyscrapers, jazz, movies, cocktails, and other paraphernalia of a globalizing modernity. Avant-garde artists wrote poems and made artworks about these phenomena, even as they warily suspected that skyscrapers and jazz trumped modest mimesis. But what was at stake was not subject matter. Rather, being modern involved a recalibration of the senses—such was the protocol internalized, for so many artists, by that mercurially engaging figure known in Europe as Charlot (Charlie Chaplin). He was the engine, "not the verses that sing of it."

Chaplin was aware of the role he played in the global context. In 1916, after disclosing his considerable wealth, he confided that: "I wasn't paid that salary because I can amuse the American public alone." Rather, "we have discovered, through the medium of the film, that elusive touch of nature that makes the whole world kin—the sort of stuff that makes everybody laugh."[8] Chaplin was unique in that he was not just a lovable comedian, nor just another film star, but the star whose name became shorthand for "the movies" around the world, and as the image of the little tramp circumnavigated the globe, the movies became endemically indexically tied to America. In short, Chaplin + film = Americanism in a new world order.

Chaplin's "Making Fun" appeared in the first issue of a little magazine, *The Soil*, edited by Robert J. Coady, proprietor of the Washington Square Gallery in New York. Although subtitled "A Magazine of Art," Coady's mission was to celebrate what we now call popular culture, and it was a coup to persuade Chaplin to contribute to his modest enterprise. *The Soil* was short lived, publishing its fifth and final issue in July 1917. In retrospect, it looks like a charter of the American cultural ascendancy which would emerge after the First World War. Coady filled page after page in "American Art," not so much an essay as a panoramic catalogue, with "The Panama Canal, the Sky-scraper and Colonial Architecture, The East River" and on through "Rag-time, the Buck and Wing and the Clog," Chaplin, Motorcycles, Gertrude Stein, Cigar Store Indians, electric signs and movie posters, Coney Island, Deadwood Dick, "Madison Square Garden on a fight night" and "The Clowns, the Jugglers, the Bareback and the Rough Riders." This lavish retinue culminates with America's industrial claim on the world's attention: "The Cranes, the Plows, the Drills, the Motors, the Thrashers, the Derricks, Steam Hammers, Stone Crushers, Steam Rollers, Grain Elevators, Trench Excavators, Blast Furnaces—This is American Art."[9]

Coady's advocacy of an American art spanning industry and popular culture, highbrow and lowbrow, tacitly resisted Eurocentric models. His message was premature in the United States, but it was about to be embraced abroad. It took on a programmatic air in Zurich, where refugees from the war launched Dada by disavowing the prestige of "Art," attuned instead to the overlooked and underestimated collateral of everyday life. While Dada is best known for its caterwauling tactics of confrontation, it owed its hospitable outlook to the *Blue Rider Almanac* (1912), edited by Wassily Kandinsky and Franz Marc, with its expanded repertoire of artistic activities. Children's drawings, artifacts

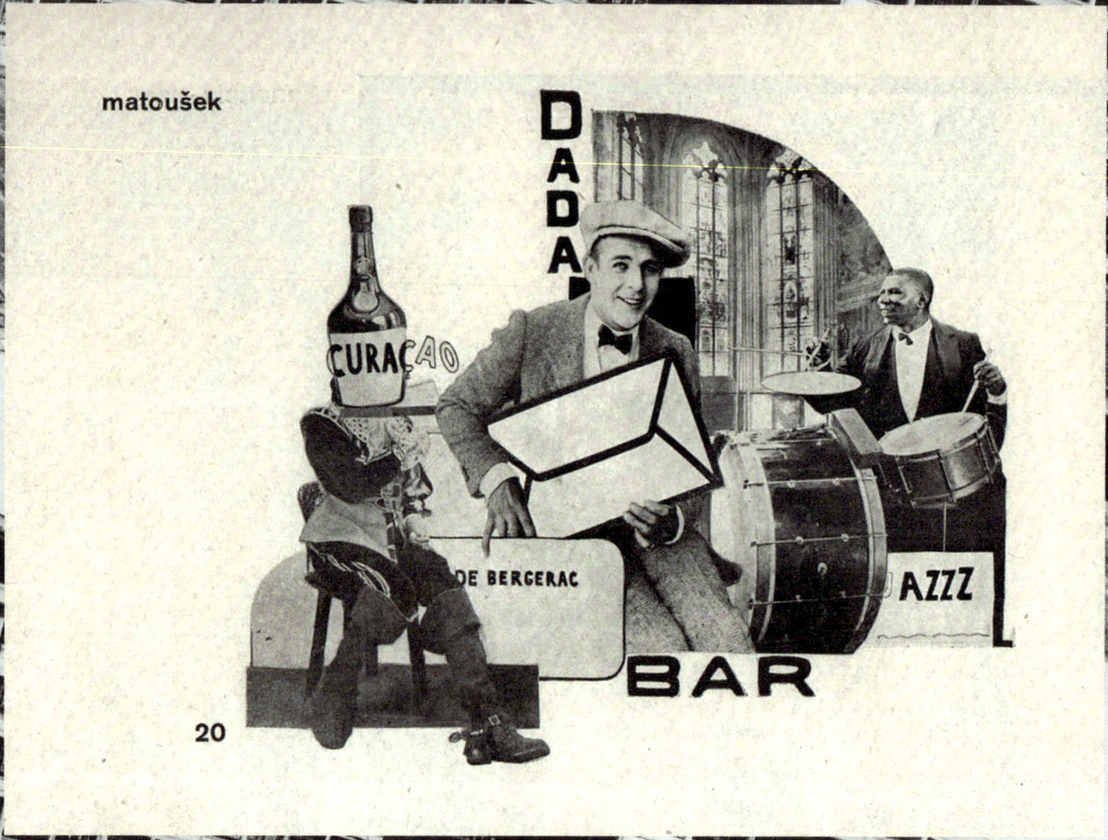

100 František Matoušek, [Dada Jazzz Bar], in *Fronta. Internationaler Almanach der Aktivität der Gegenwart*, no. 1, 1927, ed. František Halas, Bedřich Václavek, Zdeněk Rossmann, Brno

10 Arthur Cravan, "New York," *The Soil* 1, no. 1 (Dec. 1916): 36. Cravan's ellipses

11 Victoria Kingham, "'Audacious Modernity'," *The Oxford Critical and Cultural History of Modernist Magazines, Volume II: North America 1894–1960*, ed. Peter Brooker and Andrew Thacker (Oxford: Oxford University Press, 2012), 411.

12 Henri Bergson, *Matter and Memory*, tr. N. M. Paul and W. S. Palmer (New York: Zone, 1988), 208.

13 *Eccentrism Turns 100: FEKS and the Early Soviet AvantGarde, A Centenary Anthology*, ed. Ian Christie (London: Animatograph, 2023), 13.

14 Georgy Kozintsov, Georgy Kryzhitsky, Leonid Trauberg, Sergei Yutkevich, "Eccentrism," *The Drama Review* 19, no. 4 (1975): 98.

15 Frederick Brown, *An Impersonation of Angels: A Biography of Jean Cocteau* (New York: Viking, 1968), 128–129.

16 Oskar Schlemmer, *The Letters and Diaries*, ed. Tut Schlemmer, tr. Krishna Winston (Middletown: Wesleyan University Press, 1972), 185.

↑100

from Africa, Oceania, and America, Russian folk icons, and Bavarian glass paintings were all juxtaposed with masterworks of Western art. The *Almanac* was a global portfolio of visual activity unconstrained by canons of inherited taste, and while its eclecticism did not yet extend to America, it set the stage for a European receptivity generated during and after the war.

Coady was probably unaware of Dada when he produced *The Soil*, but in the first issue he printed a poem by Arthur Cravan, a nephew of Oscar Wilde infamous for his Parisian journal *Maintenant* which had skewered everyone in the art world. He made enough money boxing former world champion Jack Johnson to travel to New York, where Coady interviewed him about the fight. Cravan's poem envisions, from the distant French port of Le Havre, "New York! New York! I should like to inhabit you!"

> I see there science married
> To industry,
> In an audacious modernity,
> And in the palaces,
> Globes,
> Dazzling to the retina
> By their ultra-violet rays;
> The American telephone,
> 27 And the softness
> Of elevators ...[10]

Cravan's yearning for America was shared by many Europeans disaffected by the war, including George Grosz and other Berlin Dadaists. Cravan became a regular in the New York Dada scene, where he met poet Mina Loy, whom he eventually married in Mexico City before he vanished.

Coady's enthusiasms were so inclusive as to baffle even those inclined to share his eclecticism. William Carlos Williams, for instance, found *The Soil* to be "a fine lively magazine" but complained that in it, "there is no discrimination."[11] Williams himself would soon face the same charge when he published *Kora in Hell*, a hellbent rollercoaster inspired by Dada. It turned out that no discrimination could be a strategic gambit amidst the flood tide of modernity. As a form of life, American modernism embodies the cognitive posture identified by Henri Bergson: "we seize, in the act of perception, something which outruns perception itself."[12] Early in the twentieth century, it seemed as though modernity was outrunning perception, inciting an enthrallment with hectic multiplicity registered in avant-garde journals and events. The 1922 Soviet pamphlet *Eccentrism* summarized its outlook in a simple formula: "YESTERDAY—the culture of Europe. TODAY—the technology of America."[13] In their 1921 manifesto, the Eccentrics boldly proclaimed:

> "WE'LL USE AMUSEMENT PARKS, DEVIL'S WHEELS AND ROLLER-COASTERS TO TEACH THE NEW GENERATION THE TRUE TEMPO OF OUR EPOCH. TAP-DANCE RHYTHMS, CRACKLING CINEMA. PINKERTON. ROLLERCOASTER SHENANIGANS. THE RED-HEADED CLOWN'S WHOMPING CRUNCHES. POETRY EQUALS 'TIME IS MONEY'!"[14]

Petersburg's Eccentrics were as keen on American novelties as Jean Cocteau was in Paris, when he provided composer Eric Satie with a suggestive roster of atmospheric ingredients for the ballet *Parade*:

> The Titanic—"Nearer My God To Thee"—elevators—the sirens of Boulogne—submarine cables—ship-to-shore cables—Brest—tar—varnish—steamship apparatus—*The New York Herald*—dynamos—airplanes—short circuits—palatial cinemas—the sheriff's daughter—Walt Whitman—the silence of stampedes—cowboys with leather and goatskin chaps—the telegraph operator from Los Angeles who marries the detective at the end—the 144 express—the Sioux—the cordillera of the Andes—Negroes picking maize—jail—the reverberation—beautiful Madame Astor—the declarations of President Wilson—torpedo boats—mines—the tango—Vidal Lablanche—mercury globes—projectors—arc lamps—gramophones—typewriters—the Eiffel Tower—the Brooklyn Bridge—huge automobiles of enamel and nickel—Pullman cars which cross the virgin forest—bars—saloons—ice-cream parlors—roadside taverns—Nick Carter—Helene Boodge—the Hudson and its docks—the Carolinas—my room on the seventeenth floor—panhandlers—posters—advertising—Charlie Chaplin—Christopher Columbus—metal landscapes—the list of the victims of the Lusitania—women wearing evening gowns in the morning—the isle of Mauritius—*Paul et Virginie*[15]

This smorgasbord was Cocteau's evocation of a single character, the Little American Girl. It reveals how much America was transmitted abroad by movies, and his "silence of stampedes" is a poignant reflection of cinema before the talkies.

Grand gestures like Cocteau's were soon refined. Oskar Schlemmer, theatre director at the Bauhaus, found the school convulsed with "the latest, the most modern, up-to-the-minute, Dadaism, circus, *variété*, jazz, hectic pace, movies, America, airplanes, the automobile."[16] With similar concision, Bertolt Brecht listed the ingredients for a proposed revue on the subject of Americanism: "Record, Girl, Smiling, Advertising, Boxing Match, Revue,

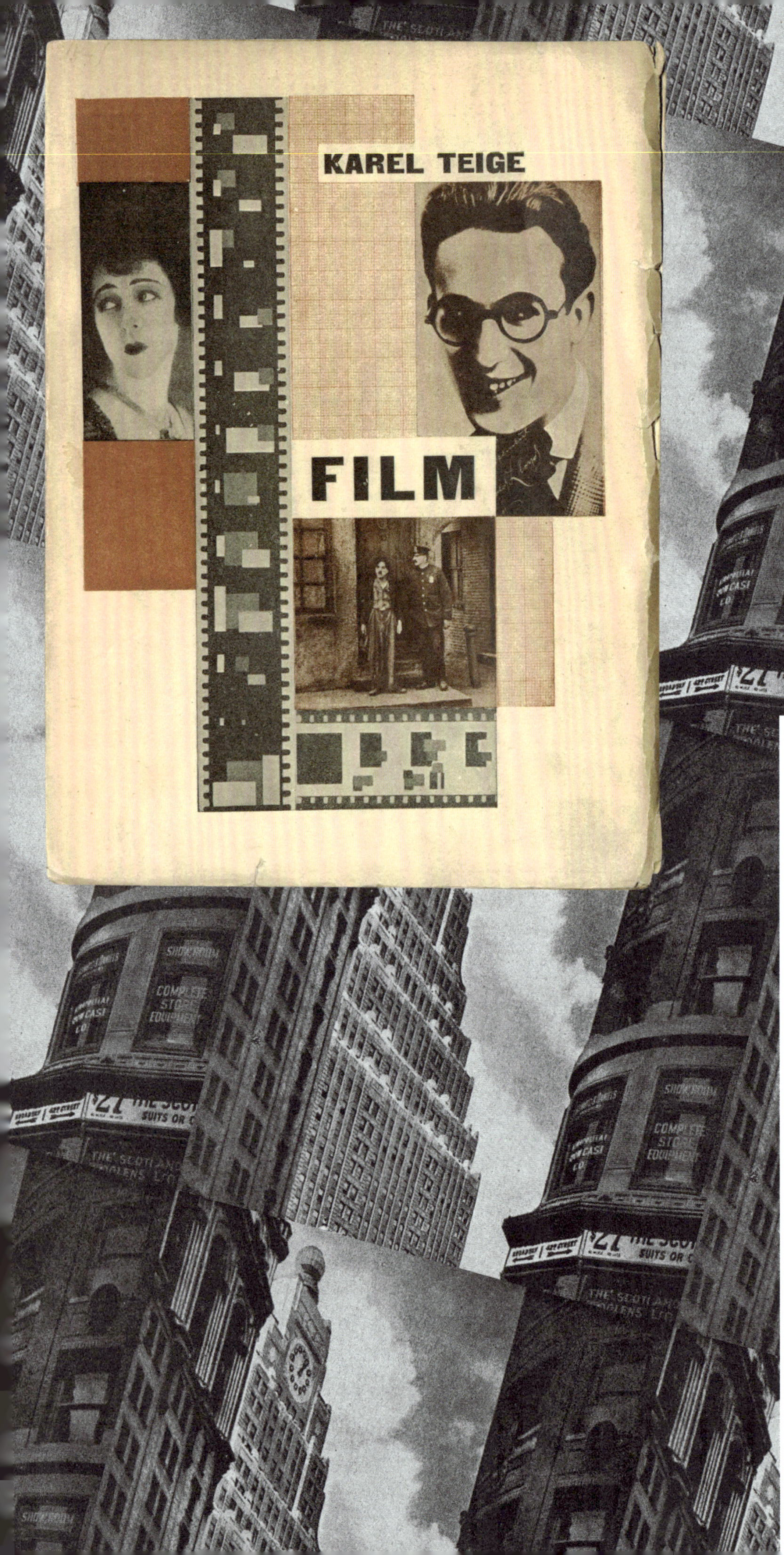

101 Karel Teige, *Film*, Prague: Petr Václav 1925, cover by Karel Teige

17 Bertolt Brecht, in Beeke Sell Tower, *Envisioning America: Prints, Drawings, and Photographs by George Grosz and his Contemporaries 1915–1933* (Cambridge, MA: Busch-Reisinger Museum, 1990), 14.

18 *The New Art—The New Life: The Collected Writings of Piet Mondrian*, ed. and tr. Harry Holtzman and Martin S. James (Boston: G. K. Hall, 1986), 126.

19 *Aviones Plateados: 15 Poetas Futuristas Latinoamericanos*, ed. Juan Bonilla (Málaga: Puerta del Mar, 2009), 267. Rasula translation.

20 Saşa Pană in *Burning City: Poems of Metropolitan Modernity*, ed. Jed Rasula and Tim Conley (Notre Dame, Ind.: Action Books, 2012), 27.

21 Joseph Audner, *A Schoenberg Reader: Documents of a Life* (New Haven: Yale University Press, 2003), 47.

22 Aleksandr Rodchenko, *Experiments for the Future: Diaries, Essays, Letters and Other Writings*, ed. Alexander N. Lavrentiev, tr. Jamey Gambrell (New York: Museum of Modern Art, 2005), 247.

23 Beeke Sell Tower, *Envisioning America: Prints, Drawings, and Photographs by George Grosz and his Contemporaries 1915–1933* (Cambridge, MA: Busch-Reisinger Museum, 1990), 14.

24 Pierre Loti, in Charles Ammerson, *1913: In Search of the World Before the Great War* (New York: Public Affairs, 2014), 165.

25 T. S. Elliot, *Waste Land* (New York: Boni and Liveright, 1922), v. 374–376.

26 Armando Mazza, in *Burning City*, 371.

27 Bruno Corra, in *Burning City*, 45.

28 Eugène Jolas, in *Burning City*, 504.

↑101 Tarzan, Sixday Races, Slow Motion Film, Business, Radio."[17] Such checklists were the lingua franca of artistic striving. Itemization was a way of registering the pace of modern life, assimilated in the sort of corporeal collage which Piet Mondrian exercised in his account of "Le Grands Boulevards" of Paris: "Negro head, widow's veil, Parisienne's shoes, soldier's legs, cart wheel, Parisienne's ankles, piece of pavement, part of a fat man, walking-stick nob, piece of newspaper, lamp post base, red feather."[18]

Itemization was also a mental cigarette which moderns couldn't resist. A bare list of names could function as poetic carburetor, as in Brazilian poet Luis Aranha's "Cocktail":

> Shaken in a metal tube
> Cold and strong
> Cocktail
> Cocteau
> Cendrars
> Rimbaud
> Cabaret'd
> Spontaneity
> Simultaneity[19]

Such rhetorical bouquets, itemized, could dispense with
29 the usual rhetoric of manifestos altogether, as in Saşa Pană's journal *Unu* in 1928:

> M ANIFESTO
>
> "readers, disinfect your brains!"
> kettledrum cry
> airplane
> wireless telegraphy—radio
> television
> 76 h.p.
> marinelli
> *s* breton
> vinea
> *a* tzara
> ribemont-dessaignes
> *ş* argnezi
> *a* brancusi
> theo van doesburg
> huraaaah hurraaaaa hurraaaaaa[20]

Playful transcriptions like this conform to Gustav Mahler's advice when Arnold Schoenberg complained of being distracted by funeral bells from the local church. "Surely that doesn't disturb you," the older composer advised. "Just compose the bells in!"[21] This is what Charles Ives did in compositions like *Central Park in the Dark*, picking up ambient sounds from the environment as compositional prerogatives, much as Pablo Picasso was doing in his Cubist collages—or, most influentially, Chaplin's approach on his film sets, where "he could do everything he needs to with his bowler derby and cane," playing around with whatever came to hand.[22]

Play is the province of childhood, and Chaplin was a child-like free spirit marooned in his oversized outfit. Georg Grosz, on his first visit to New York, approvingly noted that Americans were like carefree children. American youth was acknowledged as a catalyst in Europe, evident in jazz, cocktails, shop windows, and cinema, which were then folded into a broader palette of Americanism noted for its heavy industry, Taylorism, skyscrapers, and advertising. Americanism was "a mirage that Europe created as a vision of its own future."[23] Here, the term mirage usefully suggests that America was less a travel destination and more a source of beguiling exports. Jazz bands and movie stars excited fantasies about America that could be corroborated by those, like Darius Milhaud, who visited nightclubs in Harlem, or Le Corbusier, who thrilled at Manhattan's skyscrapers up close. Pierre Loti, mesmerized by New York, declared it the "capital of modernism." After experiencing it, he reflected, "Paris is going to seem like a nice old-fashioned little place."[24]

Paris—the reigning capital of modernity—would have to adjust. This was reflected in a trope increasingly deployed in poetry, the thumbnail evocation of urban topoi. Although the "unreal" cities of T. S. Eliot's *The Waste Land* are the most famous, it was atypical in its bleakness as well as its historical range:

> Jerusalem Athens Alexandria
> Vienna London
> Unreal[25]

This sparse gesture reads like a formula. Others were more explicitly formulaic. Armando Mazza's "Oceanliner" notices, like an electromagnetic pulse, "polarized desires Paris—New York."[26] In "Futurist Hope," Bruno Corra feels "Paris London New York monstrously engaged."[27] Eugène Jolas traces a scintillating frenzy as "Michigan Boulevard cries / and Broadway shakes with lust / and Montmartre smears caricatures onto the stars."[28]

Lajos Kassák, having walked from his native Hungary to France, finds that "the new poets can rejoice as they sing the face of the new times coming: / in Rome, Paris, Moscow, Berlin, London, and Budapest." Franz Richard Behrens sees in Danish film star Asta Nielsen a beacon of these new times in "The Asta Ode," tracking her sold-out screenings from Stockholm to New York, California, Greenland, China and Australia. "All the cinemas in the

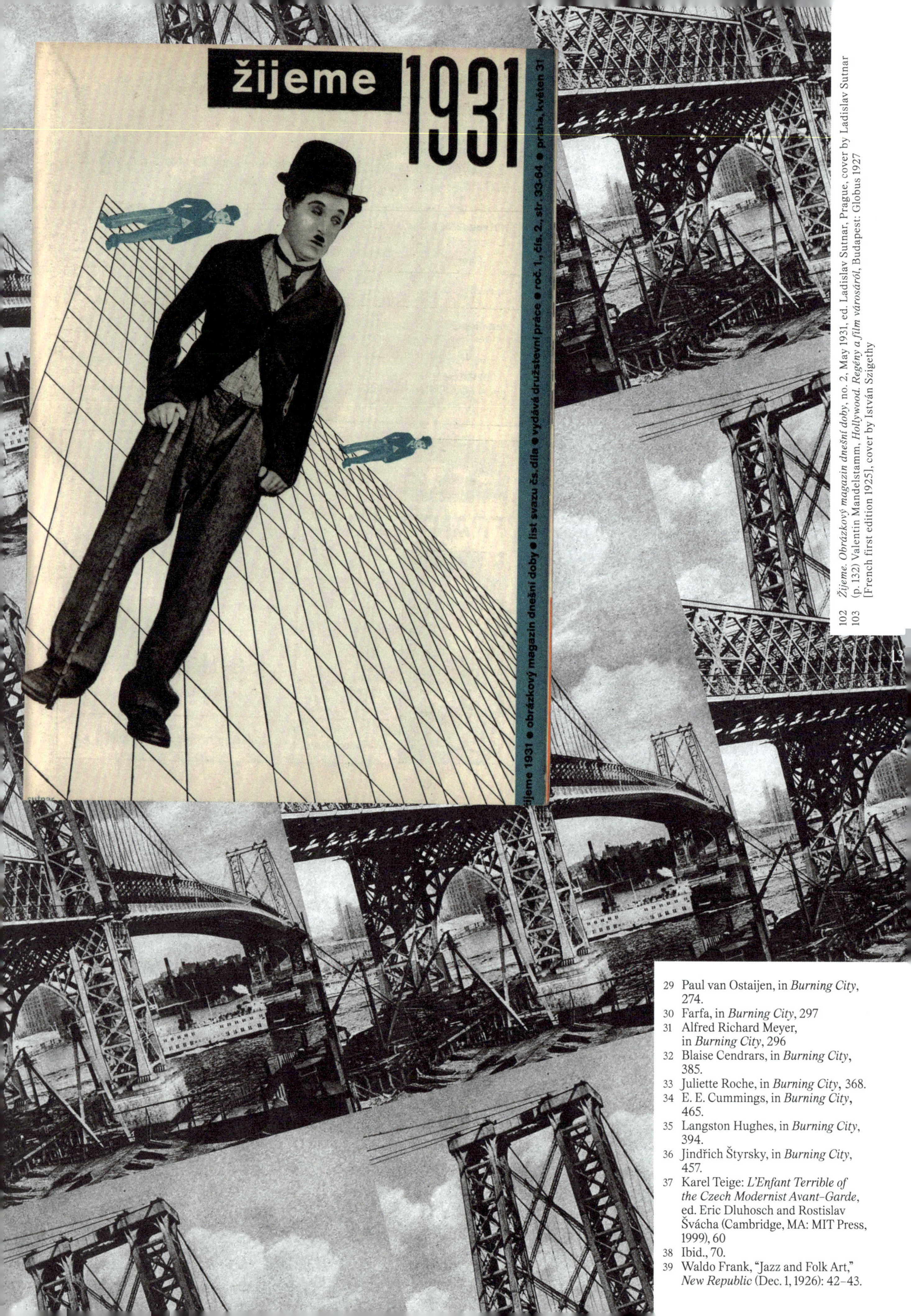

102 *Žijeme. Obrázkový magazin dnešní doby*, no. 2, May 1931, ed. Ladislav Sutnar, Prague, cover by Ladislav Sutnar (p. 132)
103 Valentin Mandelstamm, *Hollywood. Regény a film városáról*, Budapest: Globus 1927 [French first edition 1925], cover by István Szigethy

29 Paul van Ostaijen, in *Burning City*, 274.
30 Farfa, in *Burning City*, 297
31 Alfred Richard Meyer, in *Burning City*, 296
32 Blaise Cendrars, in *Burning City*, 385.
33 Juliette Roche, in *Burning City*, 368.
34 E. E. Cummings, in *Burning City*, 465.
35 Langston Hughes, in *Burning City*, 394.
36 Jindřich Štyrsky, in *Burning City*, 457.
37 Karel Teige: *L'Enfant Terrible of the Czech Modernist Avant-Garde*, ed. Eric Dluhosch and Rostislav Švácha (Cambridge, MA: MIT Press, 1999), 60
38 Ibid., 70.
39 Waldo Frank, "Jazz and Folk Art," *New Republic* (Dec. 1, 1926): 42–43.

world sing the Asta aria." Asta presages a kind of venereal trail, her image on the silver screen infecting moviegoers worldwide with primal compulsions. Asta Nielsen also appears in Paul van Ostaijen's *Occupied City*, where the buoyant typography traces the international route of "legs thighs breasts Berlin ***Germany*** BRUSSELS Amsterdam Bucharest ***London*** PARIS."[29]

Cosmopolitan nightlife was fueled by that "national drink / jazz band of taste" in Farfa's "Newyorkcocktail."[30] Alfred Richard Meyer provides the recipe:

> Vermouth from Turin, take it: dry!
> The whiskey: American!
> Blend these two into one!
> Skyscrapingly satanic:
> Manhattan! Manhattan! Geechy Manitou!
> Mannahatta! And you—Susquehanna![31]

The circulation of these emblematic American concoctions, jazz and cocktails, paralleled the experience of globetrotters like Blaise Cendrars, whose disorientation presages today's higher altitude jet setters:

> Finally we pull into the station
> São Paulo
> I think I'm in the station at Nice
> ◀31 Or disembarking at Charing Cross in London[32]

The experience also involves a kind of voyaging Esperanto, as Juliette Roche realized: "She read Chinese poets in Swiss hotels and Russian novels in Spanish trains."[33]

This worldly wanderlust did not lead to a metropolitan hub like Rome, but it did prompt reflections on the texture of modern experience. E. E. Cummings summons the whole panorama of Americanism in one of his wise guy voices:

> guys talks big
> about Lundun Burlin an gay Paree
> some guys claims der never was
> nutn like Nooer Leans Shikahgo Sain
> Looey Noo York an San Franc Dictaphones
> wireless subways vacuum
> cleaners pianolas funnygraphs skyscrapers an
> safetyrazors[34]

Another American, the consummate globetrotter Langston Hughes, reflects on the lessons of distant destinations:

> I know now
> That Venice is a church dome
> And a net-work of canals
> Tangiers a whiteness under sun.
> I thought
> It was Tangiers I wanted
> Or the gargoyles of Notre Dame,
> Or the Crystal Palace in Antwerp,
> O the golden palm-grove moon in Africa,
> Or a church dome and a net-work of canals.[35]

An image that captures this peripatetic itinerary is the Dadaist Georges Ribbemont-Dessaignes's "Poetic Circulation". The title threading through scattered dominoes suggests what was involved in navigating the global spaces of modernity, tracking cultural stimuli in search of affiliations, as reflected in Jindřich Štyrský's "Picture":

> Goll: The Chaplin Saga (cinema).—Černik: Joys of the Electric Century.—Nezval: The Wisdom of Foolhardy Merriment.—Krejcar: Americanism.—Birot: Outdoor Poetry.—Teige: Paris.—Seifert: Paris.—Picasso-Seurat: Circus. The Third International.—Film (music hall, circus).[36]

Štyrský was a participant in Poetism, the Czech movement defined by Karel Teige as an "*art of living and enjoying*." It aspired to be an incubator of all the arts, including poetry and film, along with "avionics, radio, technical, optical, and auditory inventions (optophonetics), sport, dance, circus and music hall, places of perpetual improvisation."[37] Significantly, Teige proposed that "Clowns and Dadaists taught us this aesthetic skepticism" in which jazz and Charlie Chaplin took pride of place.[38] Chaplin appears on the cover of Teige's book on the popular culture of modernity, and frequently in the movement's *Devětsil* anthology, including in several pieces by Fernand Léger, who constructed a mobile wooden Chaplin puppet for the film *Ballet mécanique*, and illustrated Ivan Goll's play *Die Chapliniade.*

For Poetism, as for the avant-garde in general, Chaplin's spasmodic acrobatics were a cinematic corollary to the off-kilter provocations of jazz and its novelty instruments like the kazoo, the comb, and the "goofus," Adrian Rollini's nickname for the couesnophone, a toy keyboard activated by air blown through a rubber tube. Novelty effects could also be produced on familiar instruments, with examples including the "gas-pipe" style of playing clarinet, the wa-wa mutes of brass instruments, and trap drum sets. It was the saxophone that successfully transitioned from novelty to mainstay, becoming an icon of the new sensibility.

Jazz was sometimes accused of being a mindless, mechanistic response to modernity. "Jazz is not so much a folk music—like the spirituals—as a folk accent in music," wrote Waldo Frank in 1926. "It expresses well a mass response to our world of piston-rods, cylinders and mechanized laws."[39] Decades later, Marshall McLuhan pondered the "folklore of industrial man" in *The Mechanical Bride*,

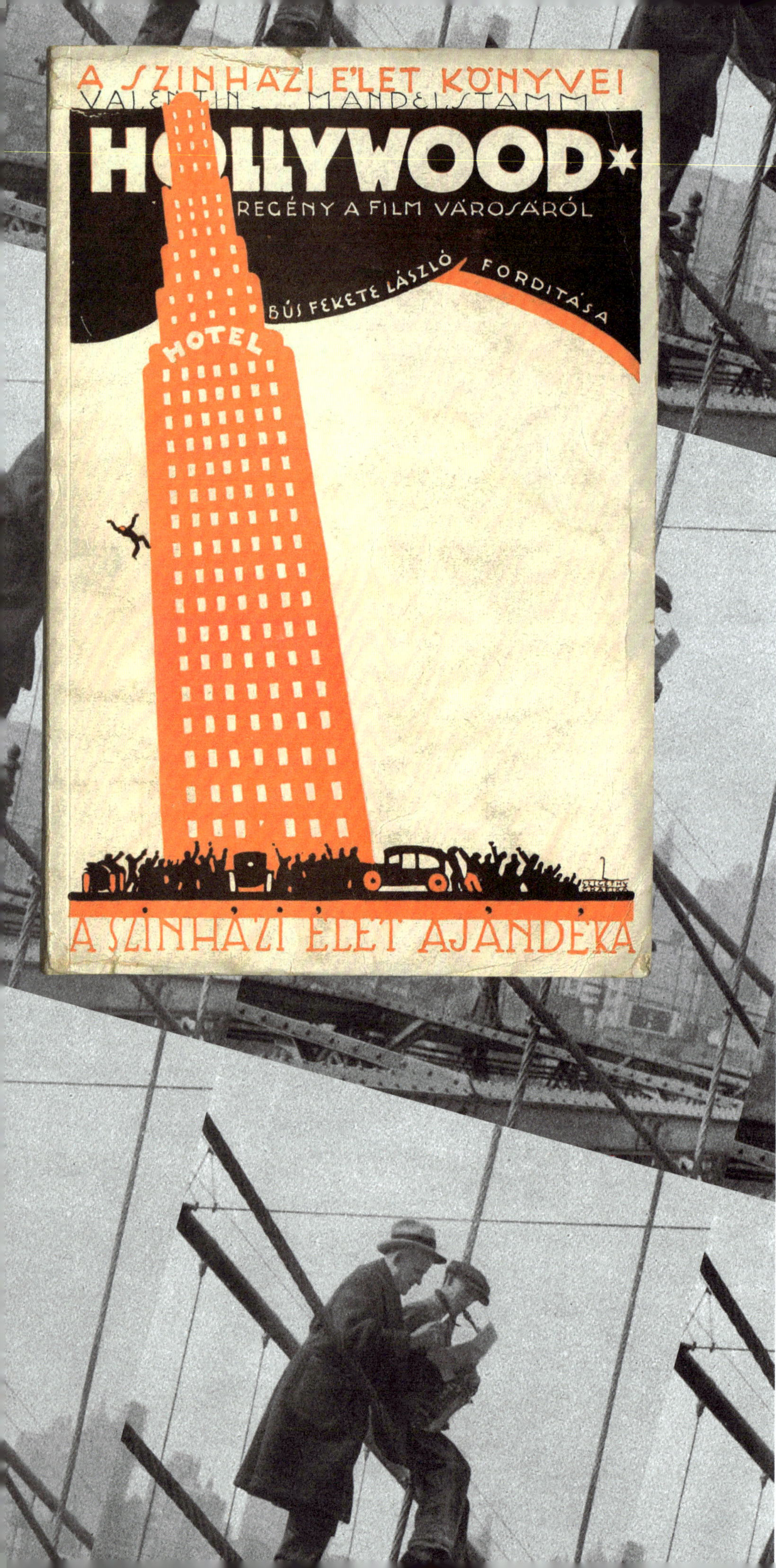

40 Marshall McLuhan, *The Mechanical Bride: Folklore of Industrial Man* (New York: Vanguard Press, 1951), 113.

41 *The Collected Writings of Salvador Dalí*, ed. and tr. Haim Finkelstein (New York: Cambridge University Press, 1994), 70.

42 Tokin authored the *Manifesto of Zenithism* with Ljubomir Micić and Yvan Goll. Tokin assimilated prevailing vanguards into components of a single movement: "Barbarian + aristocrat + metacosmician + surrealist = zenithist." Ljubomir Micić, *Zenithism: A Yugoslav Avant-Garde Anthology, 1921–1927*, ed. Aleksandar Bošković and Steven Teref (Brookline, MA.: Academic Studies Press, 2023), 77. Published in 1921, this reference to surrealists was Tokin's response to a term Goll was developing into a movement, his journal *Surréalisme* being published shortly before André Breton snatched it away with his own manifesto in 1924.

43 Élie Faure, "The Art of Charlie Chaplin," tr. Walter Pach, New England Review 19, no. 2 (Spring 1998): 146.

44 Ljubomir Micić, Ibid., 19 of the facsimile of the original typography.

45 Charlie Chaplin in David F. Kuhns, *German Expressionist Theatre: The Actor and the Stage* (Cambridge University Press, 1997), 112.

46 Siegfried Kracauer, "Two Chaplin Sketches," tr. John MacKay, *Yale Journal of Criticism* 10, no. 1 (1997): 116.

47 Viktor Shklovsky, *Literature and Cinematography*, tr. Irina Masinovsky (Champaign, Ill.: Dalkey Archive, 2008), 64.

48 Walter Benjamin, *Selected Writings, Volume 3: 1935–1938*, ed. Howard Eiland and Michael W. Jennings (Cambridge, MA: Harvard University Press, 2002), 94.

49 *Léger: Modern Art and the Metropolis*, ed. Anna Vallye (Philadelphia: Philadelphia Museum of Art, 2013), 153.

50 Gilbert Seldes, *The Seven Lively Arts* (New York: Harper, 1924), 43.

51 T. S. Eliot, *The Complete Prose, Volume 2: The Perfect Critic, 1919–1926*, ed. Anthony Cuda and Ronald Schuchard (Baltimore: Johns Hopkins University Press, 2021), 435.

52 John Dos Passos, *Orient Express* (New York: Harper, 1927), 165. Dos Passos introduced Cendrars to the American public with his 1931 translation of the poems.

53 Jean Cocteau, "Carte Blanche," in *French Film Theory and Criticism: A History/ Anthology 1907–1939. Volume 1: 1907–1929*, ed. Richard Abel (Princeton, NJ: Princeton University Press, 1988), 173.

↑103

suggesting that "much of the industrial world's entertainment and public expression is just as unconsciously expressive of its inner life ... as any old ballad is of a past way of life."[40] Salvador Dalí agreed, observing: "the best thing about Chaplin is his primitive MECHANISM, not his transcendental sentimentalism."[41] Dismissing sentiment in favor of mechanism opened up a space for improvisation both on the silver screen and in the jazz band.

Boško Tokin's "Cinema Poems" detects the pulse of jazz filling in the aural vacancy of early film. The first of the poems reflects the experience of a Yugoslavian living in Paris while assimilating and estimating the consequences of modern and American provocations.

> Life: buildup of power.
> Thwarted power is worked off daily.
> American, our—life—certainly three films:
> *Charlie Chaplin, Douglas, Rio Jim.*
> Our America, three triumphs:
> life (being alive), struggle (struggling), creation.
> Accumulated powers, emotions, creating, raging,
> the jazzband rages.
> Owing to the play of Romanticism—mourning:
> Thirsting after freedom in my dreams
> Seeking new men, crazed, through the world.
> When will my work see the light of the world?
> 33 The jazzband rages.
> Our film (title: *The Standard Intensity of Life*) is
> projected.
> Our America: *wins.*[42]

For Tokin, "Our America" has Chaplin as its north star. Elie Faure applauded Chaplin for having rendered the world as a "poème cinéplastique," "a visible symphony into which enter the rhythm of the dance and the mysterious changes of a musical poem."[43] A cineplastic poem is among the many attempts by artists to come to terms with a new art form, like the concept of *photogenie* favored by Germaine Dulac and Jean Epstein. In his cinépoem *Damn Your Hundred Gods* (1922), Ljubomir Micić declared that "Film is Esperanto".[44] The reference is to the aspirational quest to establish an international tongue, which had been inaugurated in 1887 by a Polish Jew. The important connection here is that the Esperanto of cinema in the United States was largely the creation of Jewish immigrants (leading to the erroneous assumption by some that Chaplin was Jewish).

For Chaplin, "gesture rules speech, indeed creates it."[45] Siegfried Kracauer lauded Chaplin's "mastery of the language of gesture, a mastery that reduces the spoken word to shame."[46] Viktor Shklovsky observed that by rejecting "photoplays" and forfeiting nearly all alphabetic cues, Chaplin "works with the cinematic material instead of translating himself from theatrical into screen language."[47] The mechanics of Chaplin's gestural vocabulary inspired Walter Benjamin's ruminations on mechanical reproduction. In an unpublished fragment from 1935, he observed that with Chaplin,

> the human being is integrated into the film image by way of his gestures—that is, his bodily and mental posture. The innovation of Chaplin's gestures is that he dissects the expressive movements of human beings into a series of minute innervations. Each single movement he makes is composed of a succession of staccato bits of movement. Whether it is his walk, the way he handles his cane, or the way he raises his hat—always the same jerky sequence of tiny movements applies the law of the cinematic image sequence to human motorial functions.[48]

Léger, who produced some of the most widely disseminated renderings of the little tramp, succinctly noted that Chaplin was "acting the 'mobile image.'"[49] Gilbert Seldes, in his influential *Seven Lively Arts* (1924), emphasized Chaplin's early Keystone films when he "began to live in another world, with a specific rhythm of his own, as if the pulse-beat in him changed and was twice or half as fast as those who surrounded him."[50] Meanwhile, T. S. Eliot appreciated Chaplin for having "escaped in his own way from the realism of the cinema and invented a *rhythm*."[51] Chaplin's gestural rhythm was part of a mass media transfiguration of the public sphere, along with jazz and other stimuli, casting the spell of a "fascinating rhythm," to use the title of Gershwin's perennially catchy melody.

As the pulse of life accelerated, jazz and Chaplin provided the cultural acrobatics most adept at the modern pace, the fabled American pep, get up and go. They were arts in which the instant prevailed. It made sense that among the keenest respondents were the pioneers of *simultanéisme*. Of one, Blaise Cendrars, John Dos Passos wrote:

> From Paris has spread in every direction a certain Esperanto of the arts that has "modern" for its trademark. Blaise Cendrars is an itinerant Parisian well versed in this as in many other dialects. He is a kind of medicineman trying to evoke the things that are our cruel and avenging gods. Turbines, triple-expansion engines, dynamite, high tension coils. Navigation, speed, flight, annihilation. No medicine has been found strong enough to cope with them; in cubist Paris they have invented some fetishes and gris-gris that many are finding useful.[52]

As though fluttering on a banner above the surging avant-gardes, we find the figure of Chaplin, "the modern Punch" of whom Cocteau said, "He addresses all of us, everywhere. Esperanto laughter."[53]

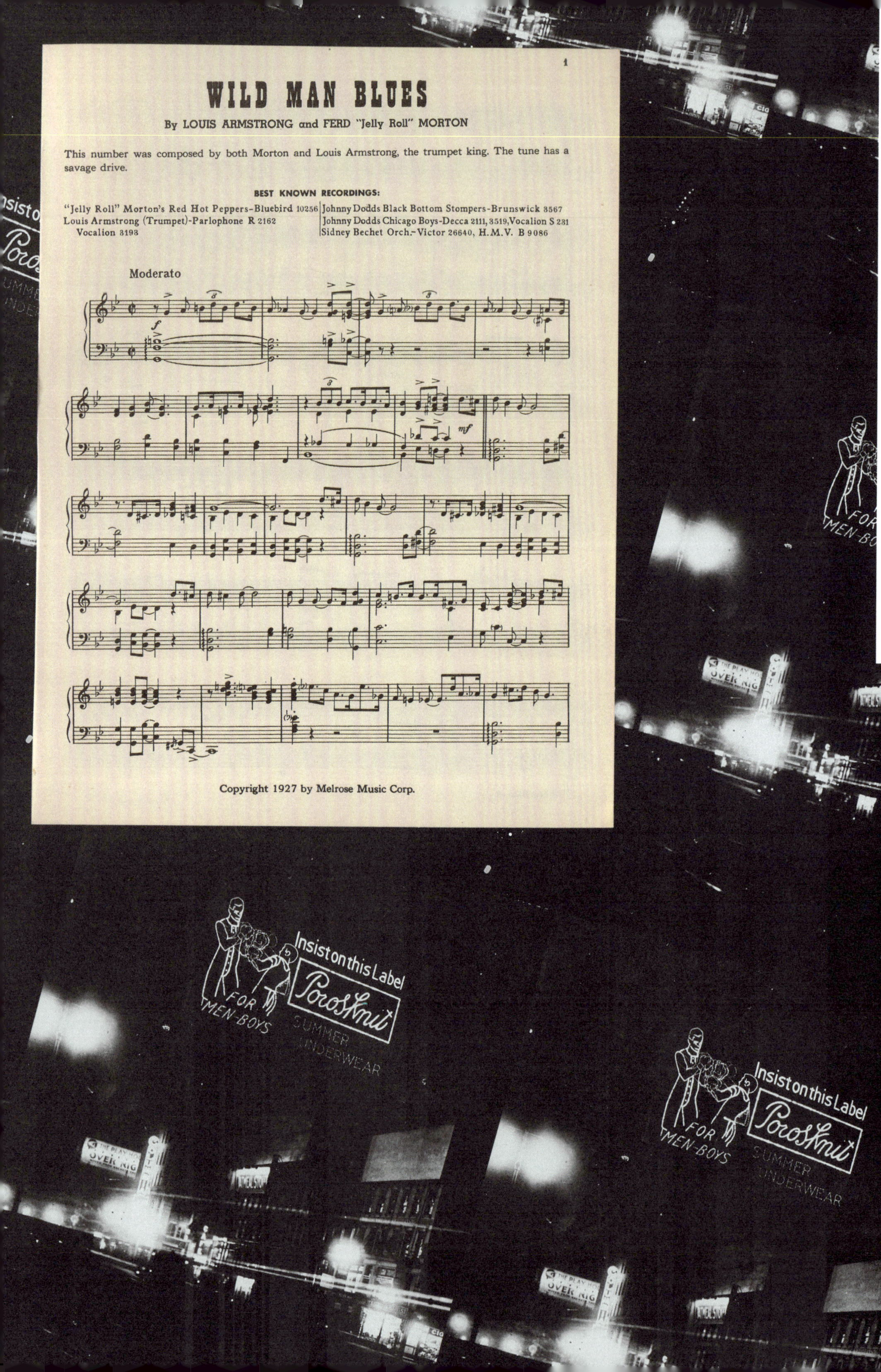

1

WILD MAN BLUES

By LOUIS ARMSTRONG and FERD "Jelly Roll" MORTON

This number was composed by both Morton and Louis Armstrong, the trumpet king. The tune has a savage drive.

BEST KNOWN RECORDINGS:

"Jelly Roll" Morton's Red Hot Peppers-Bluebird 10256
Louis Armstrong (Trumpet)-Parlophone R 2162
Vocalion 3193
Johnny Dodds Black Bottom Stompers-Brunswick 3567
Johnny Dodds Chicago Boys-Decca 2111, 3519, Vocalion S 231
Sidney Bechet Orch.-Victor 26640, H.M.V. B 9086

104 Jelly Roll Morton, *Jelly Roll Morton's Famous Series of Blues & Stomps for Piano, Book 2*, London: Herman Darewski Music Publishing Co., after 1927, 1

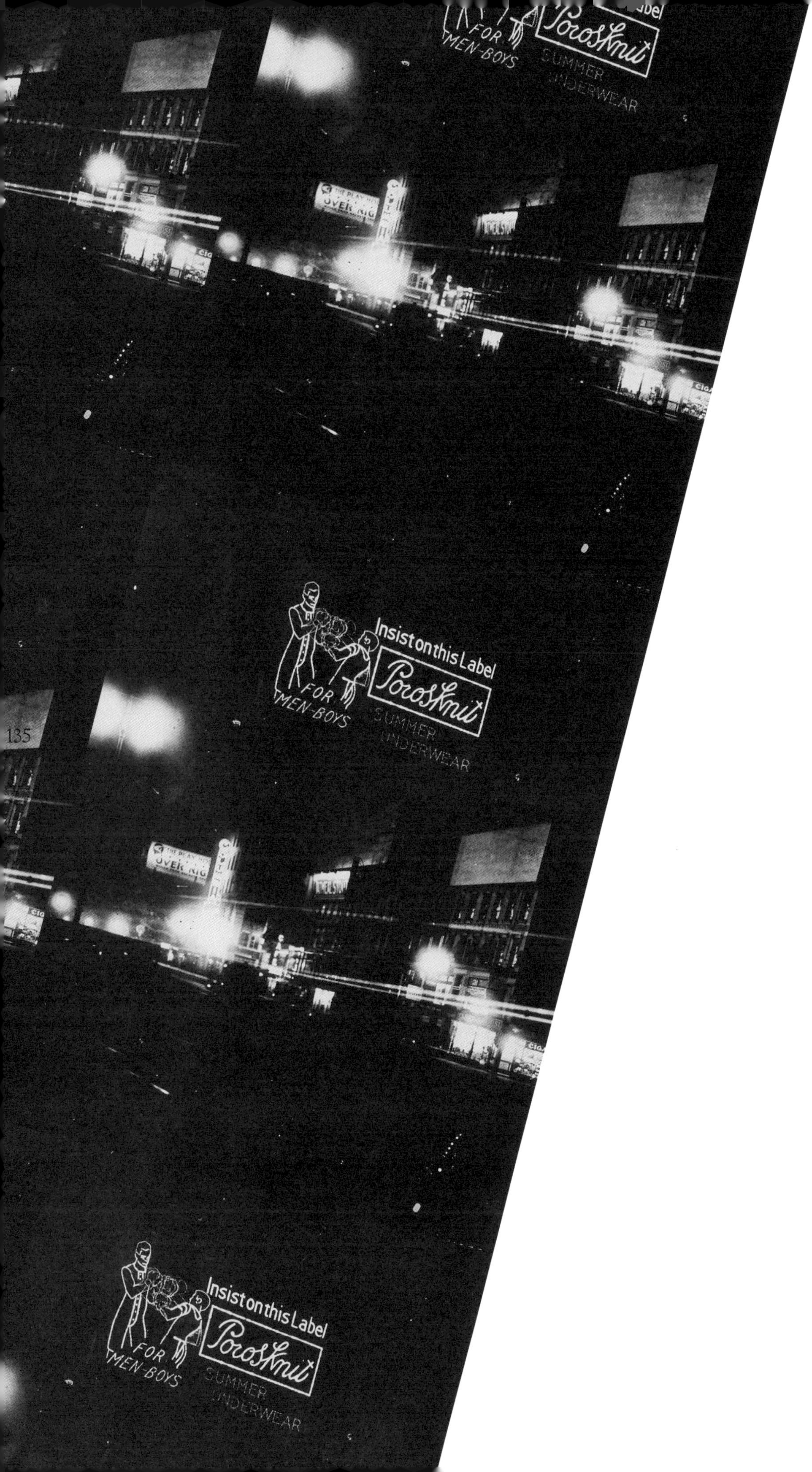
Insist on this Label
PorosKnit
FOR
MEN-BOYS
SUMMER
UNDERWEAR
135

↑104

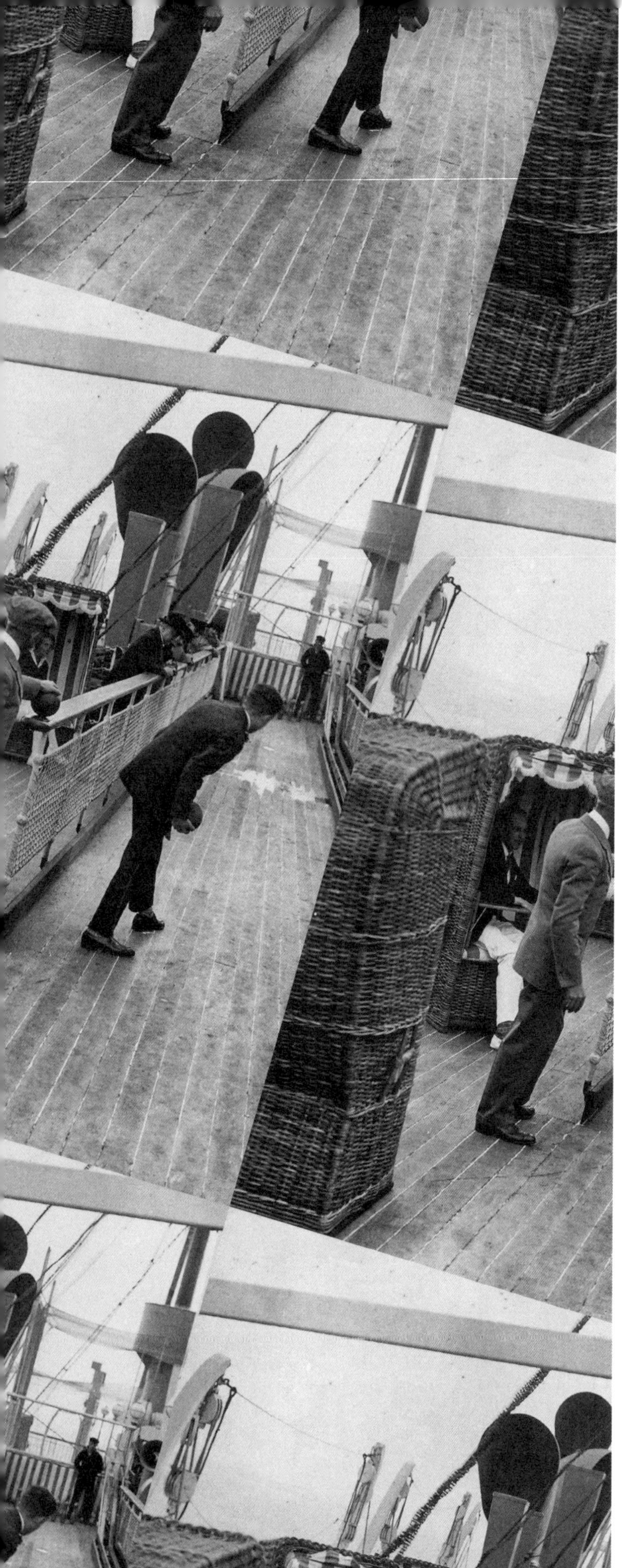

CHAPLINISM IN PARIS AND BERLIN

One of the major exports of American popular culture to Europe was the iconic figure of Charlie Chaplin—the first global movie star. The great popularity of his filmic image of the little tramp, the instantly recognizable figure of a poor fellow in torn trousers and ill-fitting shoes, wearing a bowler hat and carrying a walking cane, proved how widely his persona resonated among the working classes and international artistic circles alike.

The first movie in which Chaplin appcarcd as the famous little tramp premiered in 1914. Not long after, his first movies arrived in war-torn Europe, and from 1915, Parisian avant-garde circles became fascinated by his filmic persona. Members of the Dadaist group announced that he had joined the Dada movement, even listing him as one of the "Presidents of Dada." The magazine *Littérature*, edited by André Breton, Louis Aragon and Philippe Soupault, assigned numerical grades to a range of authors and artists according to their perceived creative merit, and Chaplin received one of the highest marks. In Germany, Chaplin became a highly political figure. Berlin Dadaists were not able to watch his movies because of a ban imposed on the importation of American films, which remained in force in Weimar Germany until 1921. In that period, George Grosz created a *Self-Portrait for Charlie Chaplin* (1919), and Johannes Baader exhibited his *Homage Portrait to Chaplin* at the *International Dada Fair* (1920). The third number of *Der Dada* magazine published in Berlin in 1920 called for a protest of the ban on Chaplin movies in Germany. It was signed not only by the members of the Dada group, but also by other avant-garde artists, including Erwin Blumenfeld (Bloomfield), who proclaimed himself a Chaplinist.

Throughout the 1920s, Chaplin's figure was admired by members of all the avant-garde movements and groups across Europe, including the Dadaist group in Yugoslavia, the Devětsil group in Czechoslovakia, Italian Futurists, Soviet Constructivists, and French Surrealists. Among them was Phillippe Soupault, who saw a new form of modernity in American films which he believed are capable of regenerating poetry. He published many articles on Chaplin, and according to Walter Benjamin, attempted "the first definition of Chaplin as a historical phenomenon." In 1931, Ramón Gómez de la Serna included the term Charlotism (Chaplinism), which he had initially coined in 1924, among other avant-garde movements in his theoretical book *Ismos*.

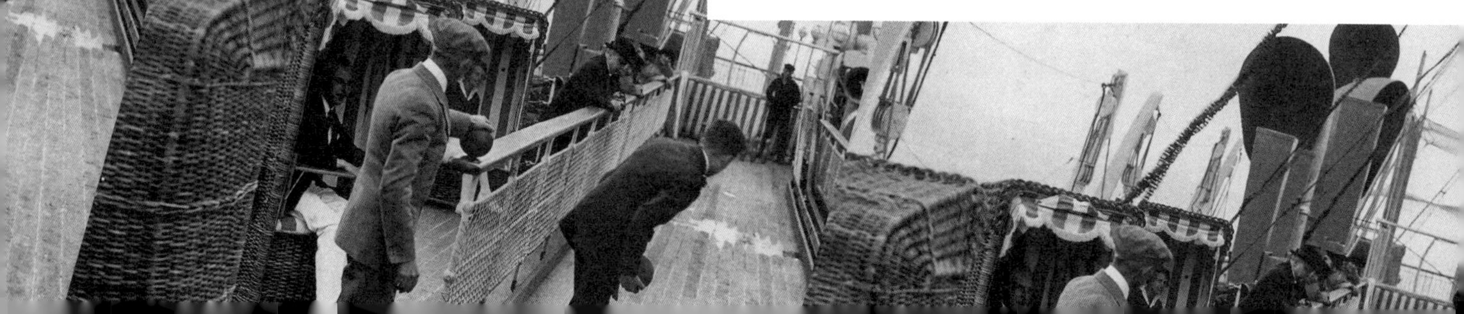

137

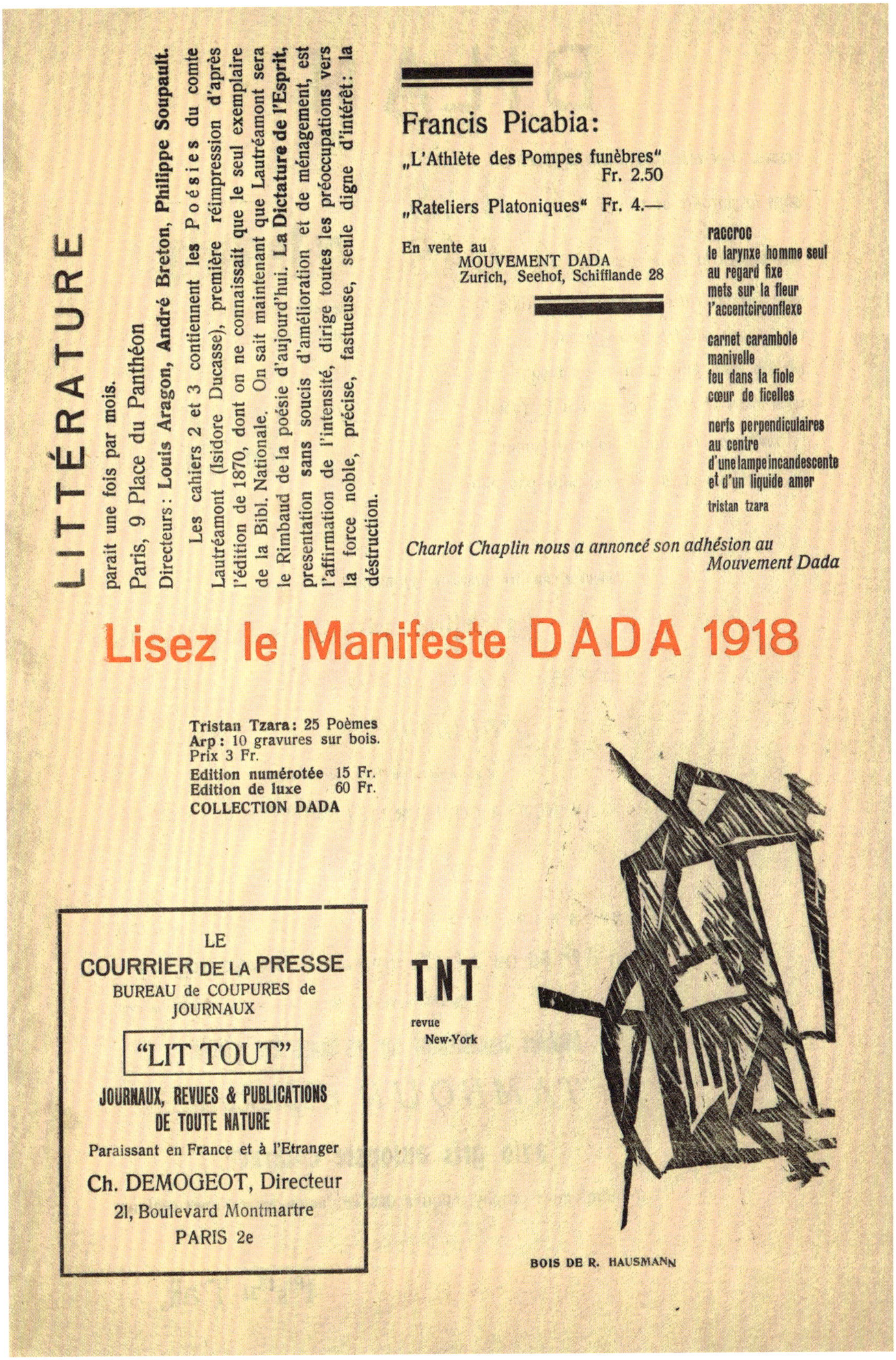

LITTÉRATURE

parait une fois par mois.

Paris, 9 Place du Panthéon

Directeurs: **Louis Aragon, André Breton, Philippe Soupault.**

Les cahiers 2 et 3 contiennent les P o é s i e s du comte Lautréamont (Isidore Ducasse), première réimpression d'après l'édition de 1870, dont on ne connaissait que le seul exemplaire de la Bibl. Nationale. On sait maintenant que Lautréamont sera le Rimbaud de la poésie d'aujourd'hui. **La Dictature de l'Esprit,** presentation sans soucis d'amélioration et de ménagement, est l'affirmation de l'intensité, dirige toutes les préoccupations vers la force noble, précise, fastueuse, seule digne d'intérêt: la déstruction.

Francis Picabia:

„L'Athlète des Pompes funèbres" Fr. 2.50

„Rateliers Platoniques" Fr. 4.—

En vente au
MOUVEMENT DADA
Zurich, Seehof, Schifflande 28

raccroc
le larynxe homme seul
au regard fixe
mets sur la fleur
l'accentcirconflexe

carnet carambole
manivelle
feu dans la fiole
cœur de ficelles

nerfs perpendiculaires
au centre
d'une lampe incandescente
et d'un liquide amer

tristan tzara

Charlot Chaplin nous a annoncé son adhésion au Mouvement Dada

Lisez le Manifeste DADA 1918

Tristan Tzara: 25 Poèmes
Arp: 10 gravures sur bois.
Prix 3 Fr.
Edition numérotée 15 Fr.
Edition de luxe 60 Fr.
COLLECTION DADA

LE
COURRIER DE LA PRESSE
BUREAU de COUPURES de
JOURNAUX
"LIT TOUT"
JOURNAUX, REVUES & PUBLICATIONS
DE TOUTE NATURE
Paraissant en France et à l'Etranger
Ch. DEMOGEOT, Directeur
21, Boulevard Montmartre
PARIS 2e

TNT
revue
New-York

BOIS DE R. HAUSMANN

105 *Anthologie Dada*, ed. Tristan Tzara, Zurich: Mouvement Dada 1919, illustration by Raoul Hausmann, [unpaginated]

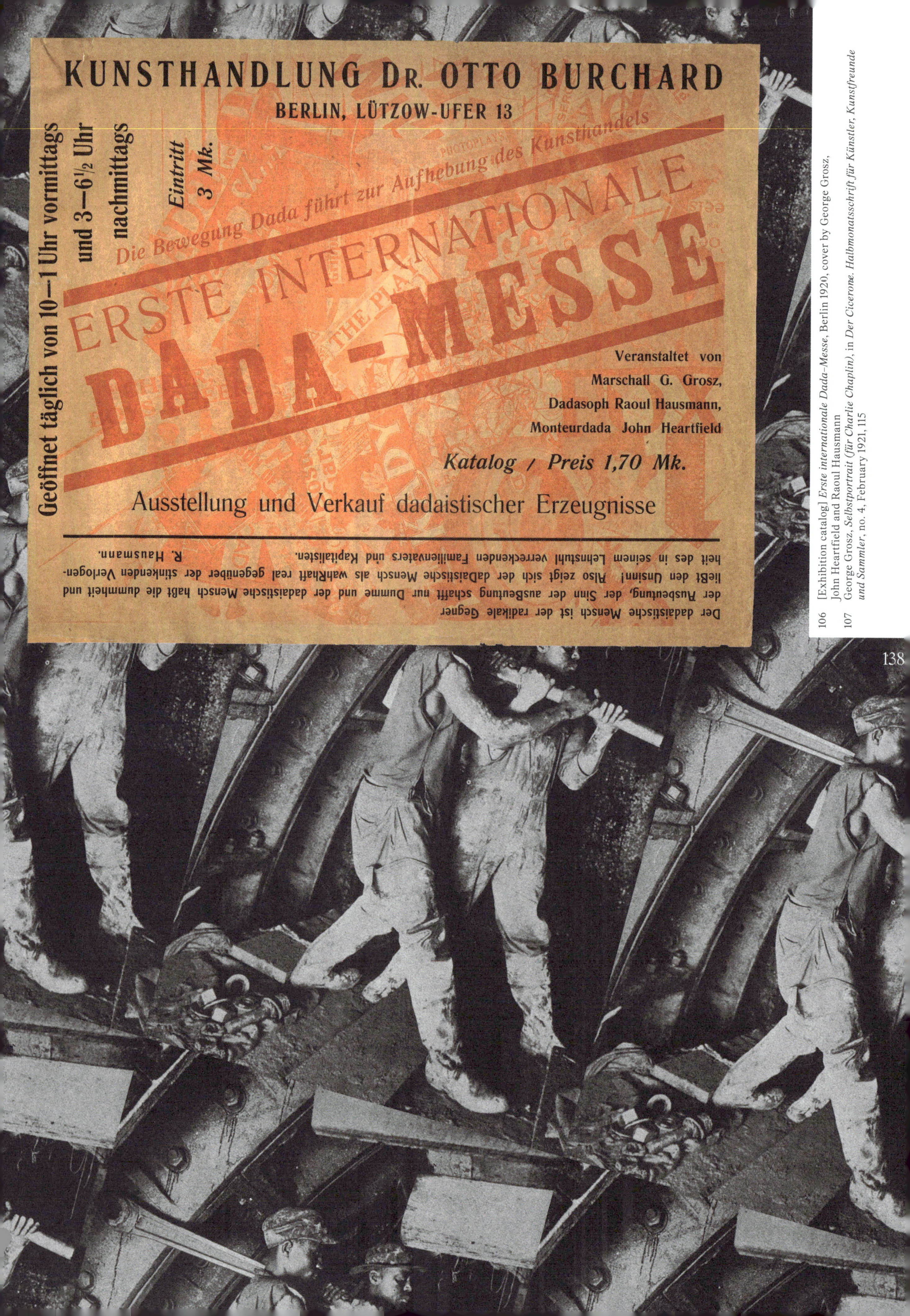

106 [Exhibition catalog] *Erste internationale Dada-Messe*, Berlin 1920, cover by George Grosz, John Heartfield and Raoul Hausmann

107 George Grosz, *Selbstportrait (für Charlie Chaplin)*, in *Der Cicerone. Halbmonatsschrift für Künstler, Kunstfreunde und Sammler*, no. 4, February 1921, 115

↓107 ↑106

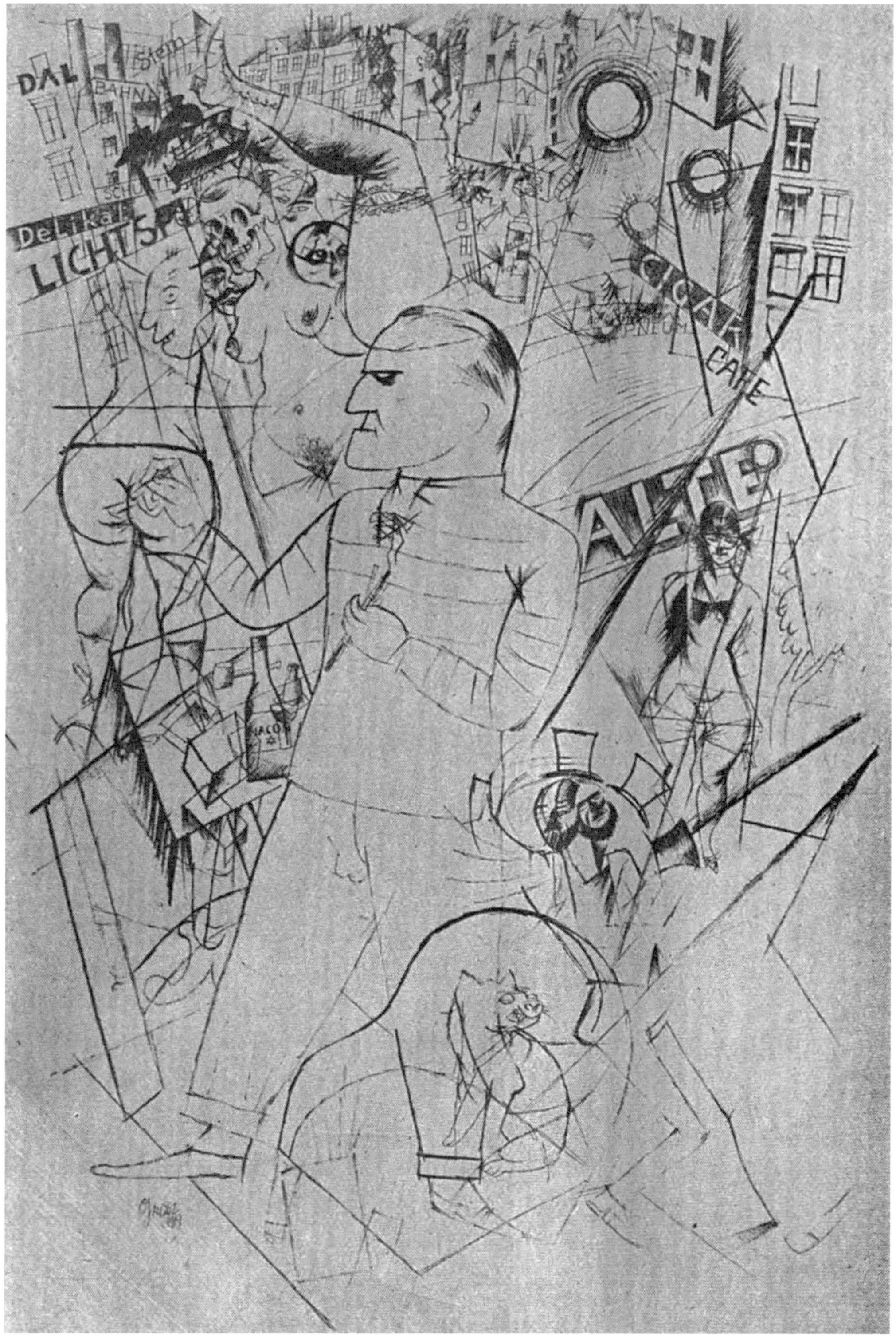

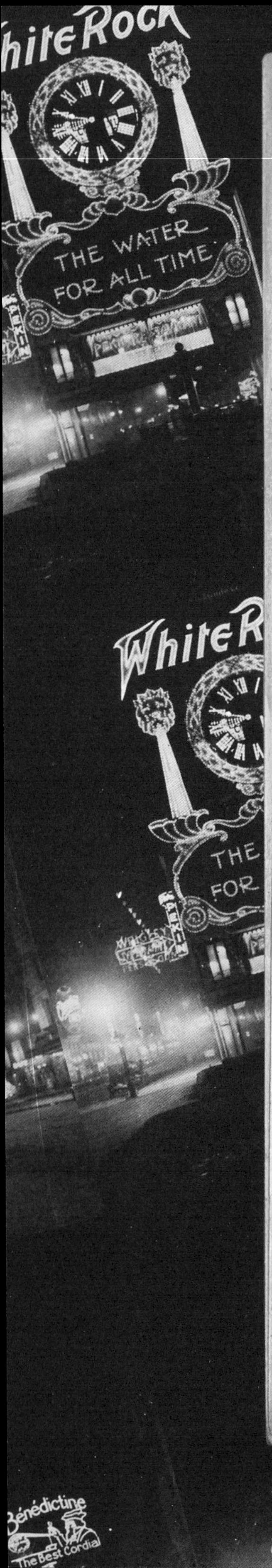

	Louis Aragon	André Breton	Gabrielle Buffet	Pierre Drieu la Rochelle	Paul Eluard	T. Fraenkel	Benjamin Péret	Georges Ribemont-Dessaignes	Jacques Rigaut	Philippe Soupault	Tristan Tzara	Moyenne
Briand	-15	10	0	10	-2	-1	-15	0	5	-1	-25	**-3,09**
Byron	11	7	20	9	-10	-20	-10	1	-20	2	-25	**-3,18**
Caillaux	12	10	0	9	-25	10	11	16	10	16	-25	**4,00**
Carpentier	-20	-20	0	-1	10	-20	4	0	5	2	-15	**-5,00**
Cendrars	10	4	0	7	-24	-12	5	3	5	3	2	**0,27**
Cervantès	0	-25	0	0	15	-13	0	0	-1	0	-25	**-4,27**
Cézanne	0	-1	-25	15	13	9	0	0	-20	-3	-25	**-3,36**
Chateaubriand	12	9	0	16	-20	1	6	0	5	11	-25	**1,27**
Chagall	12	12	0	0	12	13	10	0	8	3	0	**6,36**
Charlot	16	17	20	20	17	18	17	15	16	11	10	**16,09**
Chirico	12	14	0	3	16	15	15	-10	7	11	-25	**5,27**
Claudel	2	-22	-25	14	16	7	-5	0	5	2	-25	**-2,81**
Clémenceau	-12	1	-25	18	15	-20	6	-23	7	3	-20	**-4,54**
Colette	1	-5	0	7	-25	1	-10	0	1	-12	0	**-3,81**
Condillac	3	4	10	0	-18	-20	4	8	10	-23	-25	**-4,27**
Constant	2	17	0	15	3	-20	3	0	16	3	-25	**1,27**
Corbière	0	2	0	5	11	-15	0	0	1	-3	-25	**-2,18**
Corneille	2	-25	0	20	-25	-20	-10	-25	-13	8	-25	**-10,27**
Corot	0	6	-25	-5	-22	1	0	0	5	11	-25	**-4,90**
Coulon (Johnie)	1	1	0	-1	14	0	3	0	14	0	2	**3,09**
Cravan	2	3	20	1	12	-4	9	0	10	2	4	**5,36**
Curel	-1	-20	10	0	-25	-1	-15	-24	-1	-22	-25	**-11,27**
Dante	10	2	20	20	-20	-20	-10	0	5	1	-25	**-1,54**
Daudet (Léon)	-12	-25	-25	1	15	3	3	0	1	0	-25	**-5,81**
Debussy	10	-19	-25	13	-25	8	-20	5	-23	0	-25	**-9,18**
Delacroix	10	-5	0	8	-15	6	-10	-21	-20	-22	-25	**-8,54**
Derain	17	18	0	10	14	16	10	-21	10	12	-20	**6,00**
Deschanel	1	2	20	-25	8	2	0	0	2	0	-25	**-1,36**

108 *Littérature*, no. 18, March 1921, ed. Louis Aragon, André Breton, Philippe Soupault, Paris, 2–3

	Louis Aragon	André Breton	Gabrielle Buffet	Pierre Drieu la Rochelle	Paul Eluard	T. Fraenkel	Benjamin Péret	Georges Ribemont-Dessaignes	Jacques Rigaut	Philippe Soupault	Tristan Tzara	Moyenne
Dostoïevski	15	13	0	20	19	15	14	19	15	2	-25	**9,72**
Drieu la Rochelle	18	14	0		4	7	7	12	12	5	8	**8,70**
Duçasse	18	20	10	1	19	17	17	14	18	18	5	**14,27**
Duchamp	12	10	20	0	-3	10	9	19	12	0	12	**9,18**
Duval (Bonnet rouge)	14	10	20	0	17	10	11	20	11	2	0	**10,45**
Edison	14	12	20	1	0	-20	15	13	9	-25	5	**4,00**
Einstein	16	15	0	5	0	13	15	15	14	2	10	**9,54**
Eluard	17	17	20	5		19	14	17	14	16	12	**15,10**
Ernst	11	14	20	0	0	4	10	14	9	2	10	**8,54**
Eschyle	1	3	20	20	-1	14	0	13	5	0	-25	**4,54**
Euripide	0	-15	0	16	-3	-20	0	12	-20	-14	-25	**-6,27**
Fatty	0	11	20	-20	8	4	10	0	9	12	9	**5,72**
Fairbanks	-18	-19	20	2	1	-8	-10	-7	-7	-12	0	**-5,27**
Flaubert	1	-1	20	1	0	-20	-10	0	-25	-1	-25	**-5,45**
Foch	-20	-25	-25	1	16	-20	-25	-25	-25	-25	-25	**-18,00**
Fort (Paul)	-19	-25	-25	-10	-3	-2	-25	-25	-1	-22	-25	**-16,54**
Fraenkel	15	16	0	1	15		9	0	10	9	8	**8,30**
France	-20	-25	-25	1	1	-20	-20	-25	-25	-25	-25	**-18,00**
Freud	15	16	10	1	8	16	14	0	14	1	0	**8,63**
Gide	6	12	0	-20	4	9	3	-13	4	6	-20	**-0.81**
Gobineau	13	12	0	2	16	14	5	-1	6	9	-25	**4,63**
Gœthe	19	6	0	20	16	13	10	4	11	10	-25	**7,63**
Greco	-10	-7	20	0	13	14	0	12	7	10	-25	**3,09**
Guillaume II	0	-5	0	9	-25	0	0	13	7	3	-25	**-2,09**
Guitry (Sacha)	0	-25	-25	1	1	-18	0	-6	0	-22	-25	**-10,81**
Guynemer	-1	-24	-25	-1	8	-20	0	-21	-20	-25	-25	**-14,00**
Hamsun (Knut)	16	14	0	0	16	8	8	0	5	11	-25	**4,81**
Hart (W)	2	-24	20	-1	16	-20	0	18	-10	3	8	**1,18**

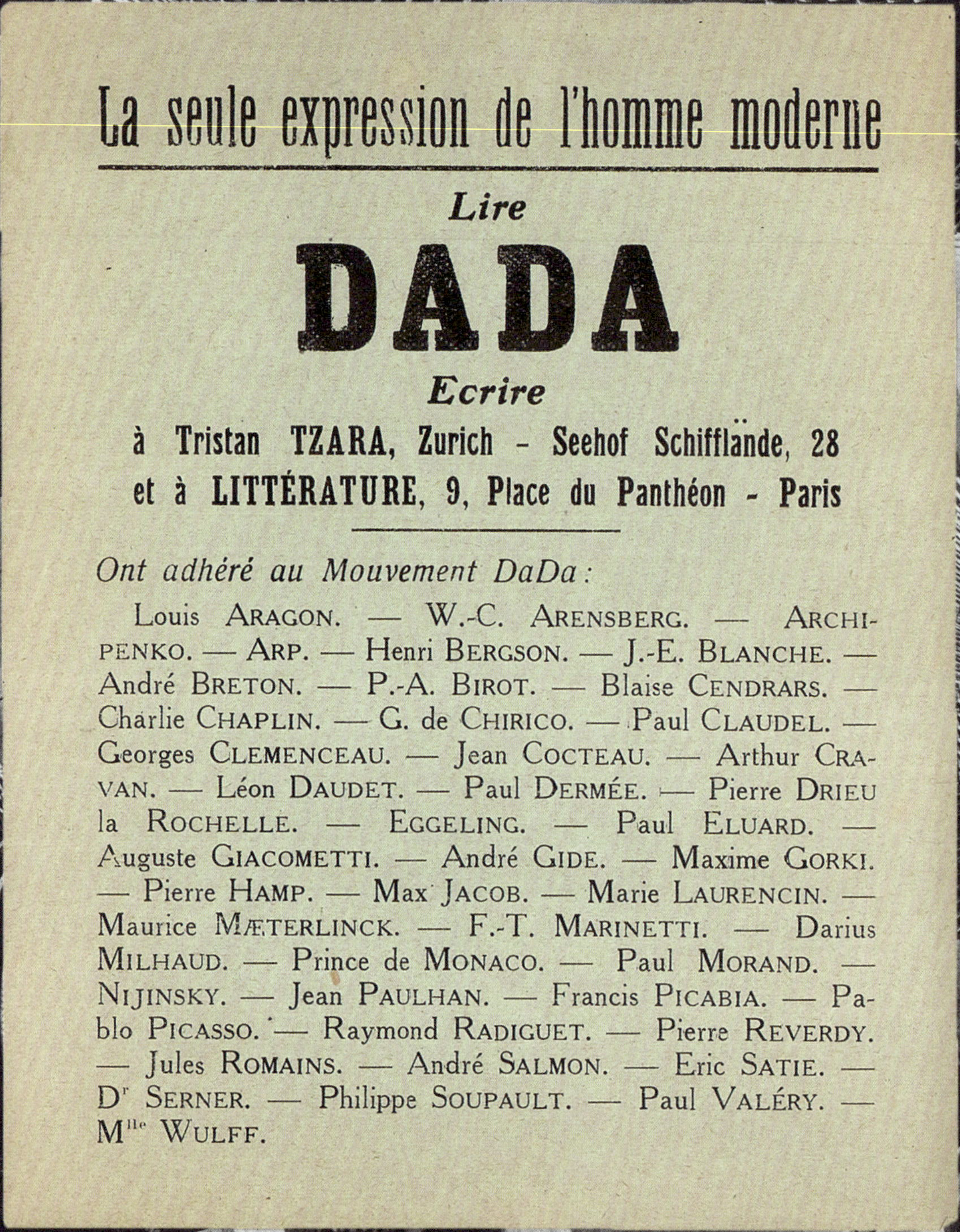

La seule expression de l'homme moderne

Lire

DADA

Ecrire

à Tristan TZARA, Zurich - Seehof Schiffländе, 28
et à LITTÉRATURE, 9, Place du Panthéon - Paris

Ont adhéré au Mouvement DaDa :

Louis ARAGON. — W.-C. ARENSBERG. — ARCHIPENKO. — ARP. — Henri BERGSON. — J.-E. BLANCHE. — André BRETON. — P.-A. BIROT. — Blaise CENDRARS. — Charlie CHAPLIN. — G. de CHIRICO. — Paul CLAUDEL. — Georges CLEMENCEAU. — Jean COCTEAU. — Arthur CRAVAN. — Léon DAUDET. — Paul DERMÉE. — Pierre DRIEU la ROCHELLE. — EGGELING. — Paul ELUARD. — Auguste GIACOMETTI. — André GIDE. — Maxime GORKI. — Pierre HAMP. — Max JACOB. — Marie LAURENCIN. — Maurice MÆTERLINCK. — F.-T. MARINETTI. — Darius MILHAUD. — Prince de MONACO. — Paul MORAND. — NIJINSKY. — Jean PAULHAN. — Francis PICABIA. — Pablo PICASSO. — Raymond RADIGUET. — Pierre REVERDY. — Jules ROMAINS. — André SALMON. — Eric SATIE. — Dr SERNER. — Philippe SOUPAULT. — Paul VALÉRY. — Mlle WULFF.

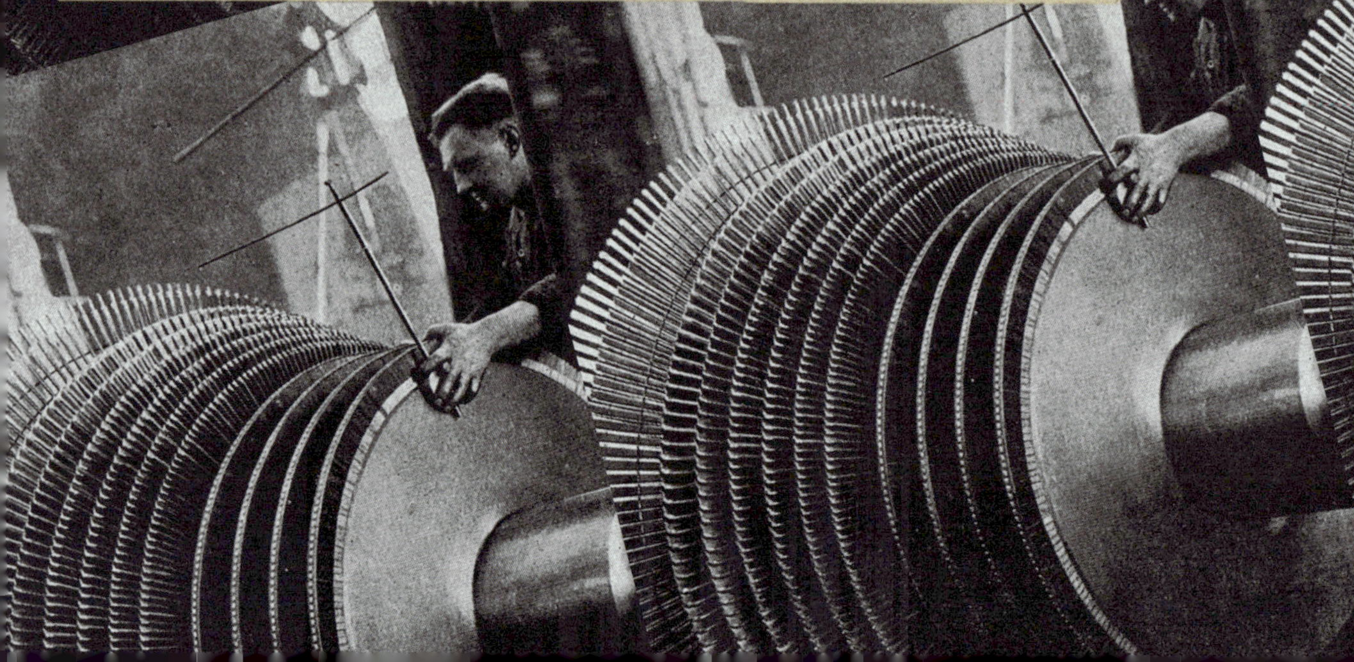

109 [Leaflet], *Le seule expression de l'homme moderne. Lire DADA*, Zürich/Paris 1920, attributed to Tristan Tzara
110 *Dada-Almanach*, ed. Richard Hülsenbeck, Berlin: Erich Reiss Verlag 1920, cover by Otto Schmalhausen

43

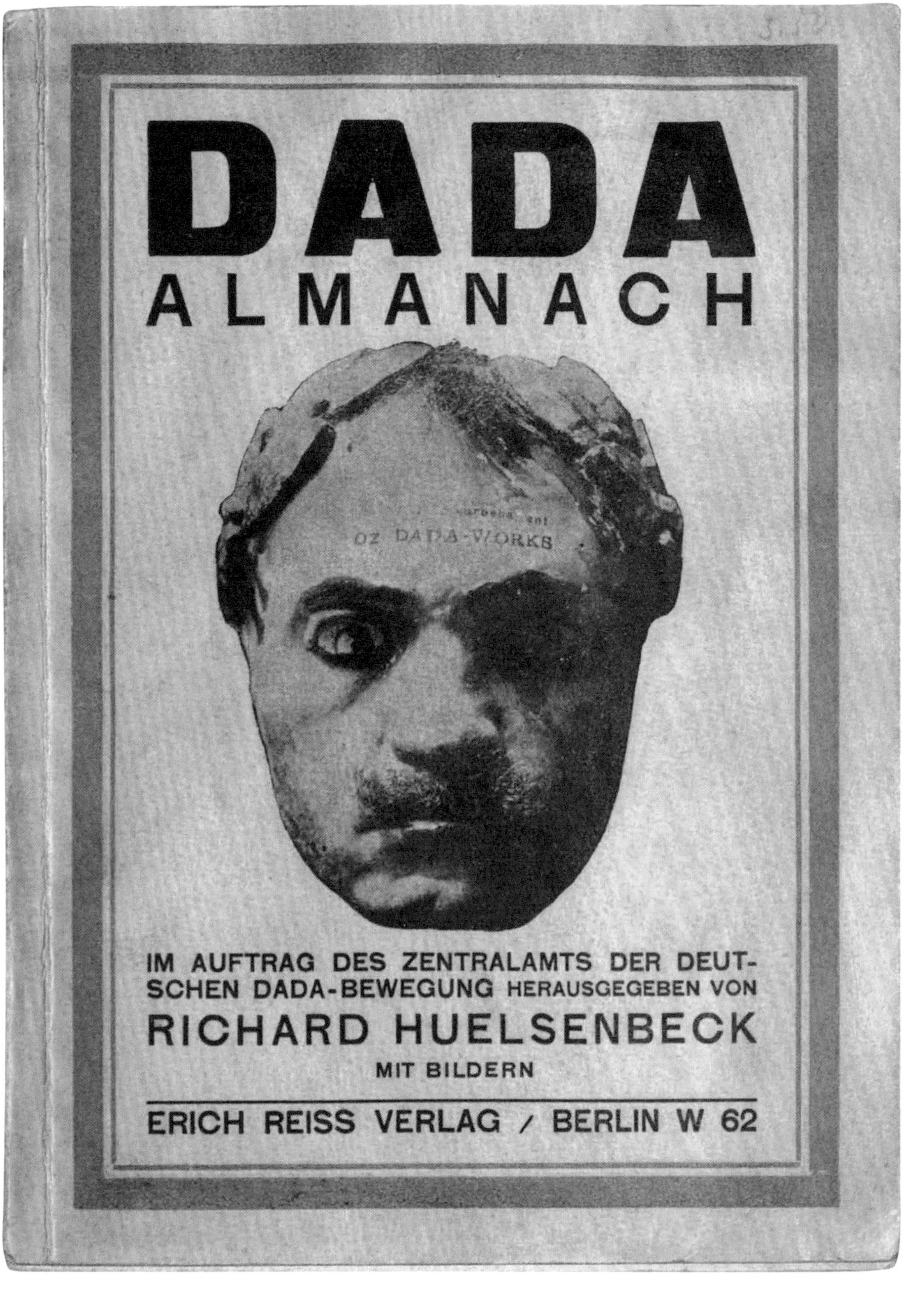
DADA
ALMANACH
OZ DADA-WORKS
IM AUFTRAG DES ZENTRALAMTS DER DEUTSCHEN DADA-BEWEGUNG HERAUSGEGEBEN VON
RICHARD HUELSENBECK
MIT BILDERN
ERICH REISS VERLAG / BERLIN W 62

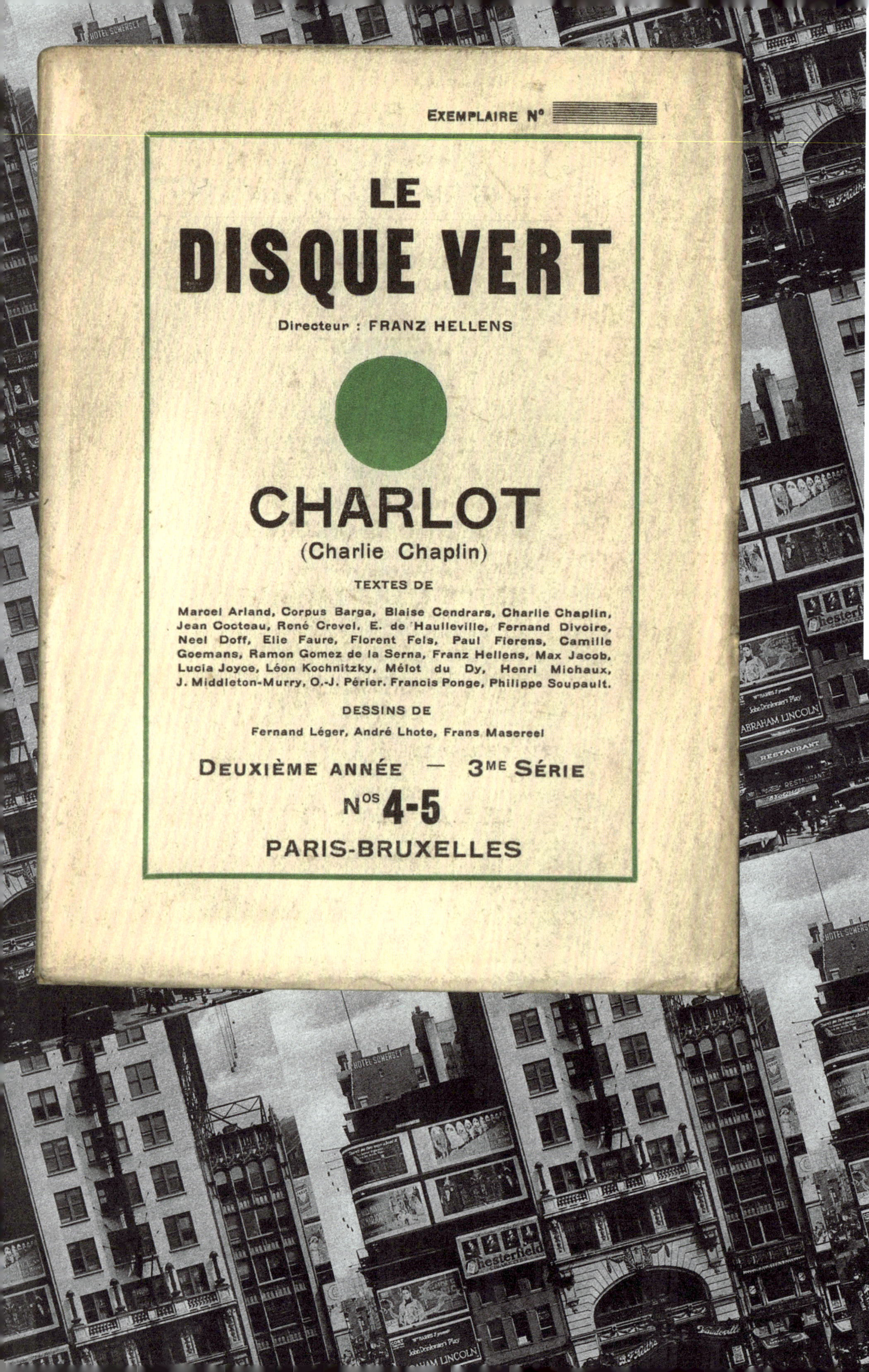

EXEMPLAIRE N°

LE DISQUE VERT

Directeur : FRANZ HELLENS

CHARLOT
(Charlie Chaplin)

TEXTES DE

Marcel Arland, Corpus Barga, Blaise Cendrars, Charlie Chaplin, Jean Cocteau, René Crevel, E. de Haulleville, Fernand Divoire, Neel Doff, Elie Faure, Florent Fels, Paul Fierens, Camille Goemans, Ramon Gomez de la Serna, Franz Hellens, Max Jacob, Lucia Joyce, Léon Kochnitzky, Mélot du Dy, Henri Michaux, J. Middleton-Murry, O.-J. Périer. Francis Ponge, Philippe Soupault.

DESSINS DE

Fernand Léger, André Lhote, Frans Masereel

DEUXIÈME ANNÉE — 3ME SÉRIE

Nos 4-5

PARIS-BRUXELLES

111 *Le Disque vert*, no. 4–5, 1924, ed. Franz Hellens, Paris/Brussels
112 Louis Delluc, *Charlie Chaplin* [*Charlot*], Paris: Maurice de Brunoff 1921 [8th edition]
113 Philippe Soupault, *La grande fable. Chroniques des personnages imaginaires 3. Charlot*, Paris: Librairie Plon 1931

↓113 ↓112 ↑111

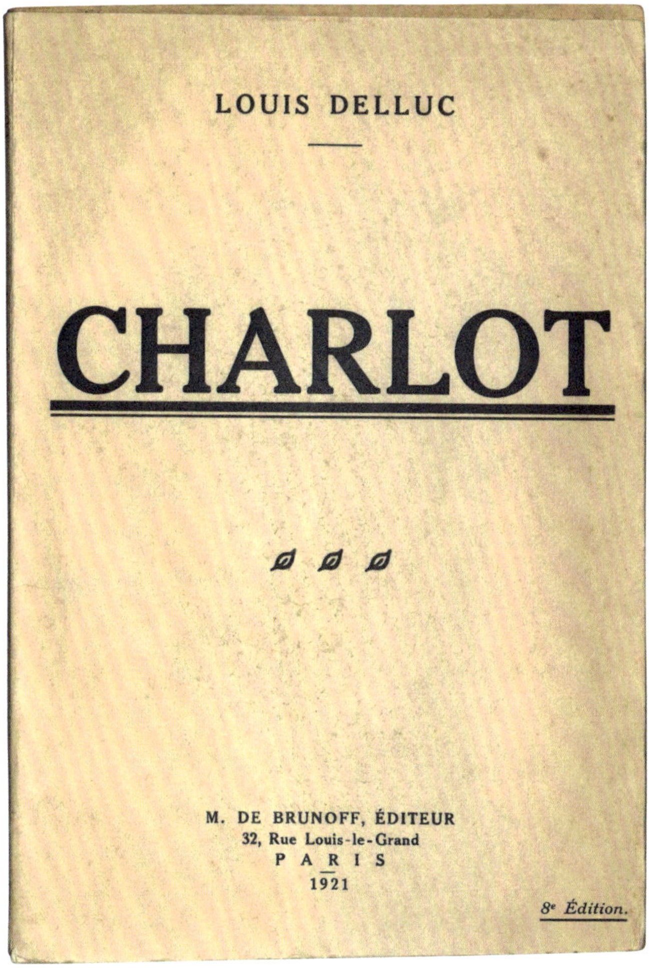
LOUIS DELLUC
CHARLOT
M. DE BRUNOFF, ÉDITEUR
32, Rue Louis-le-Grand
PARIS
1921
8e Édition.

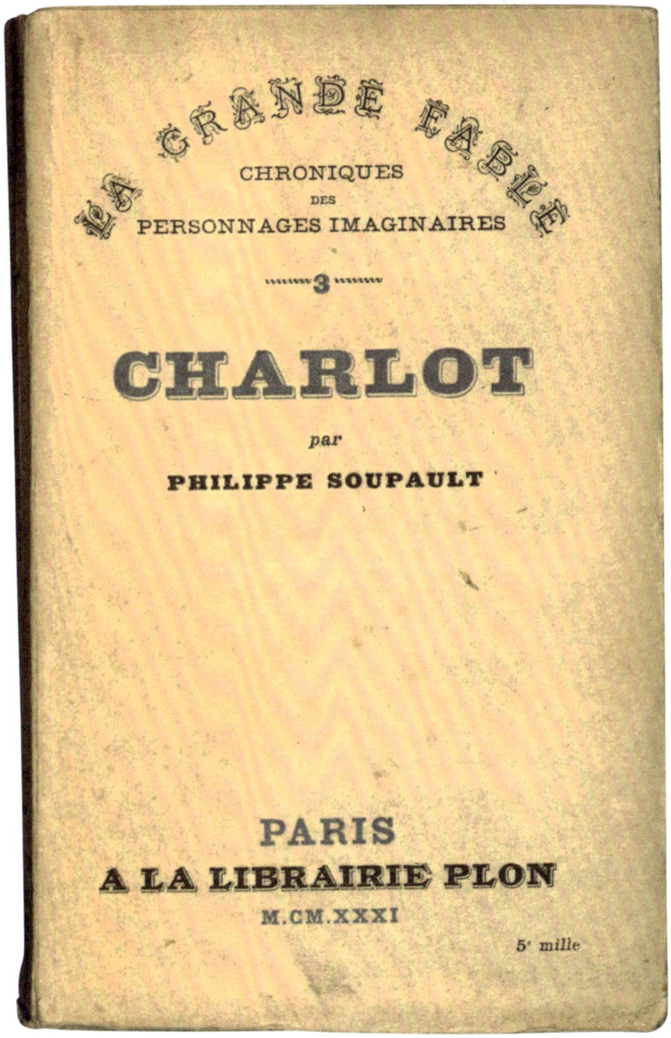
LA GRANDE FABLE
CHRONIQUES
DES
PERSONNAGES IMAGINAIRES
3
CHARLOT
par
PHILIPPE SOUPAULT
PARIS
A LA LIBRAIRIE PLON
M.CM.XXXI
5e mille

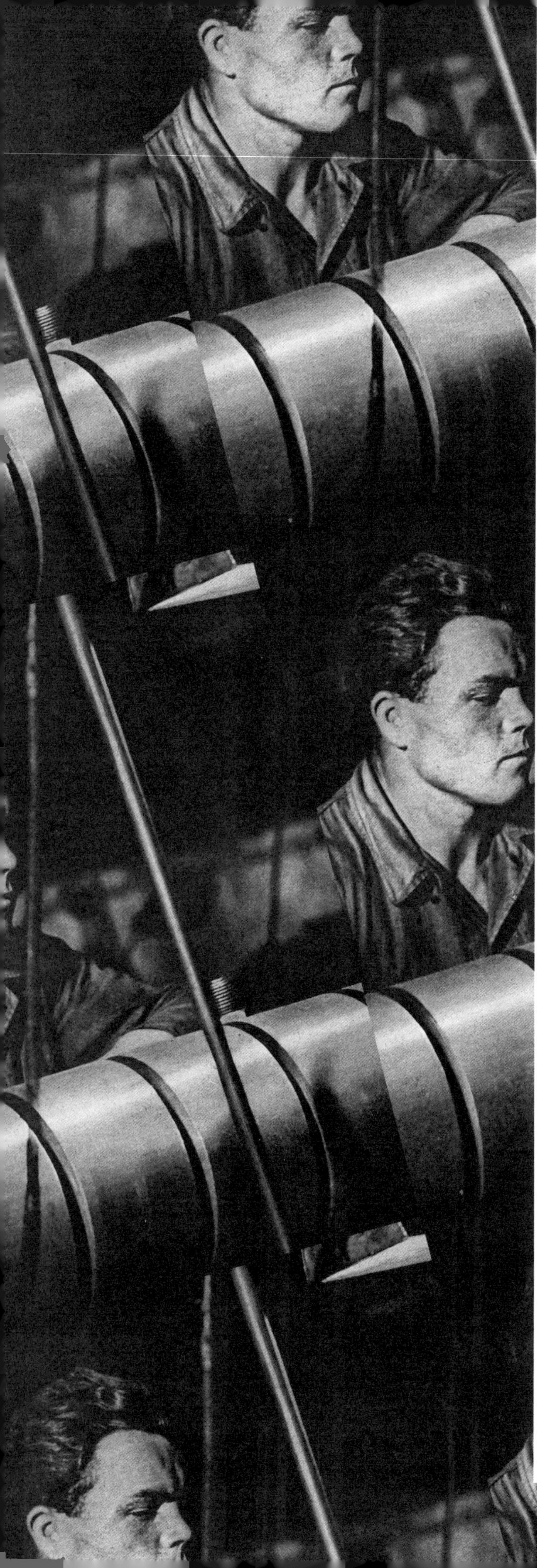

THE CHAPLINIADE

Ivan Goll was a left-wing writer and one of the first authors to reflect in his literary work on the cultural and socio-political importance of Charlie Chaplin. In the 1910s, he studied in Germany, where he encountered Expressionism in Berlin, and he later spent the First World War in Switzerland, where he befriended Dadaists from Zurich. In around 1919, upon moving to France, he had the chance to watch Chaplin films in movie theatres. His films were banned in Germany at that time because of the embargo on American movies that lasted till 1921. Goll was in contact with cultural magazines and publishing houses in Germany and his writings escaped censorship, meaning that his was the first to discuss the comedian's work in the country. First, he published the text "Charlot's Apology" in *Die Neue Schaubühne* (The New Stage, February 1920), and later that same year he wrote *Die Chapliniade* (The Chapliniade), published in Dresden.

The Chapliniade is a film-poem that cites short vignettes from Chaplin's movies. It depicts a poetical variation on the adventures of the famous tramp and is divided into six episodes, starting with the story of Chaplin, who descends from a film poster and starts to live his own life. He decides to become a poet and departs on a train, then is crowned like Jesus Christ and becomes a revolutionary figure who intends to bring the socialist revolution to the masses. Wandering through cities, the countryside, and journeying to the center of the Earth, he triggers various events before returning to the poster from where he started his journey.

The Chapliniade includes Fernand Léger's four illustrations of *Charlot Cubiste* which were created especially for the book. These figures of Chaplin exemplify the connections between the avant-garde tradition of Cubism and modern cinematic culture. They gained wide recognition around the world, from Dresden to Paris, Moscow, Prague, and Montevideo, expressed in a number of avant-garde books such as *A vse taki ona vertitsja* by Ehrenburg (Berlin, 1922), Goll's collection *Le Nouvel Orphée* (Paris, 1923), the Czech translation of Louis Delluc's *Charlie Chaplin* (1924), *Film* (1925) and *Svět, který se směje* (1928) by Karel Teige in Prague, and *El sueño de Chaplin* by Uruguayan avant-garde writer Ildefons Pereda Valdes (1930). They also became a sort of viral image in numerous international avant-garde periodicals published between 1922 and 1924, including *Veshch/Objet/Gegenstand* (Berlin), *Kino-Fot* (Moscow), *Broom* (Rome-Berlin-New York), *Le Disque vert* (Brussels/Paris), *La Vie des Lettres* (Paris), *Devětsil* (Prague), and *Život* (Prague). In 1924, Léger included an animated *Charlot Cubiste* in the famous avant-garde movie *Ballet mécanique* which he created with American filmmaker Dudley Murphy.

↓114

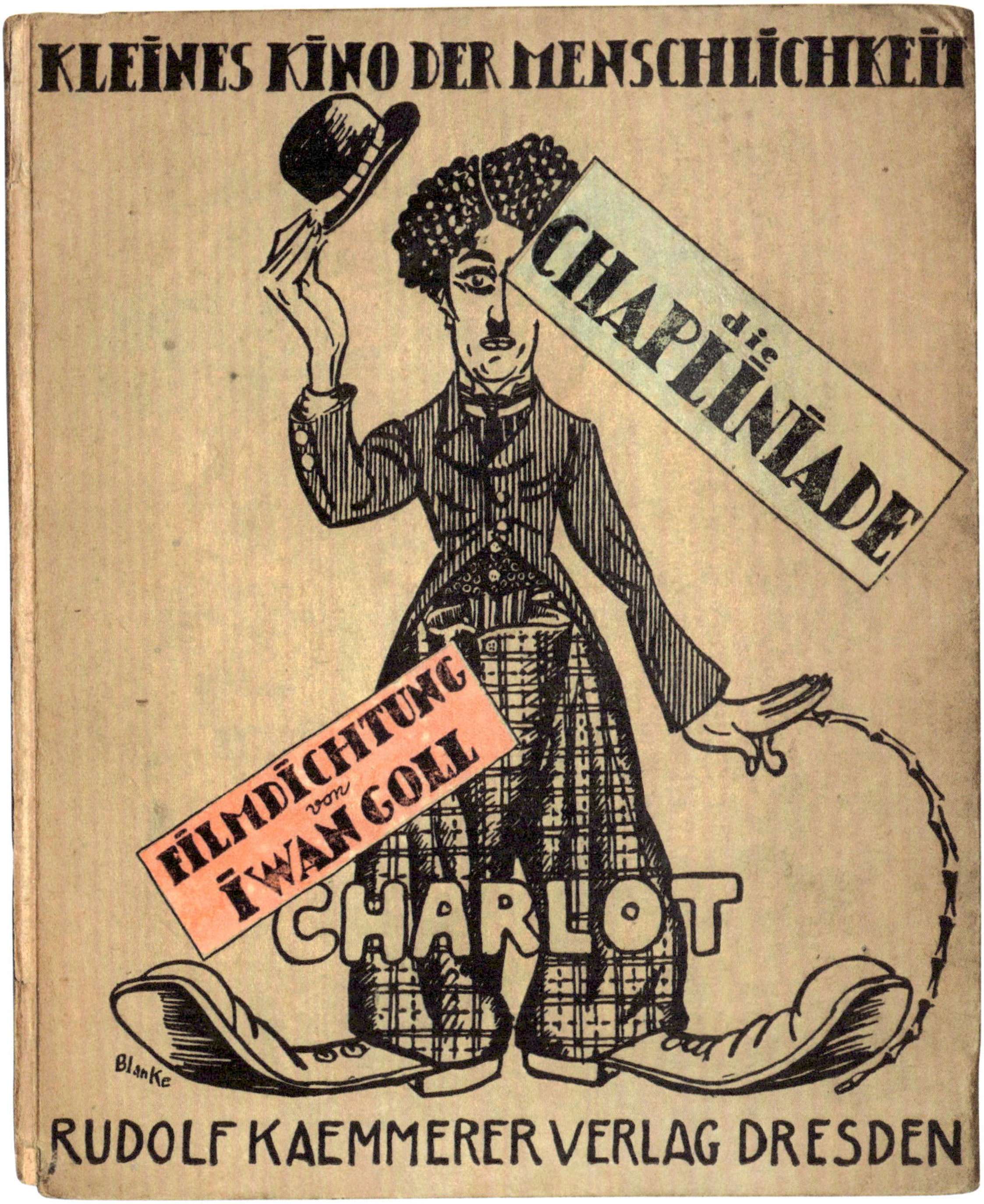

114 Iwan [Ivan] Goll, *Die Chapliniade. Eine Kinodichtung*, Dresden: Rudolf Kaemmerer Verlag 1920, cover by Hans Blanke

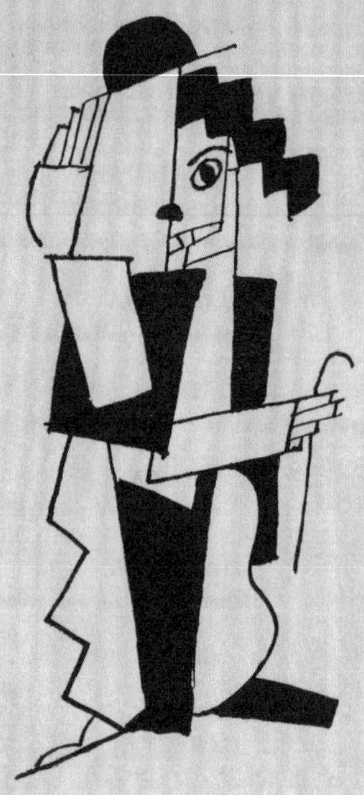

9

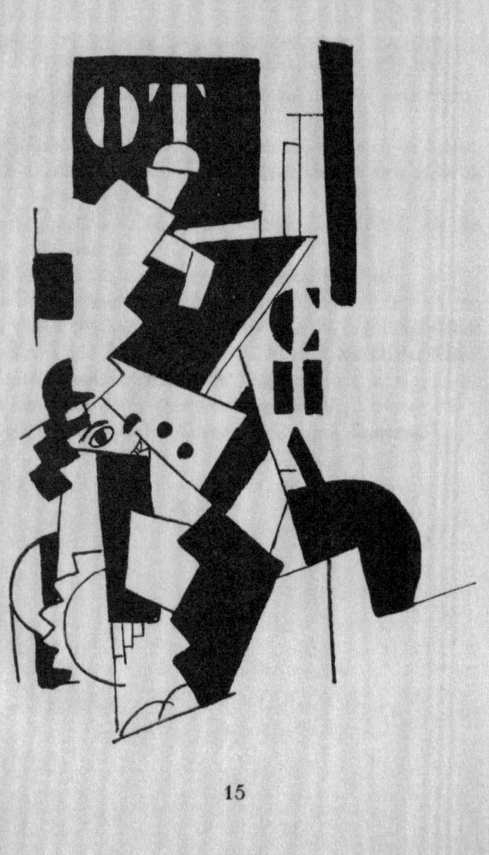

15

115 see pages in the book 114: 9, 13, 31, 37, illustrations by Fernand Léger: *Charlot Cubiste*

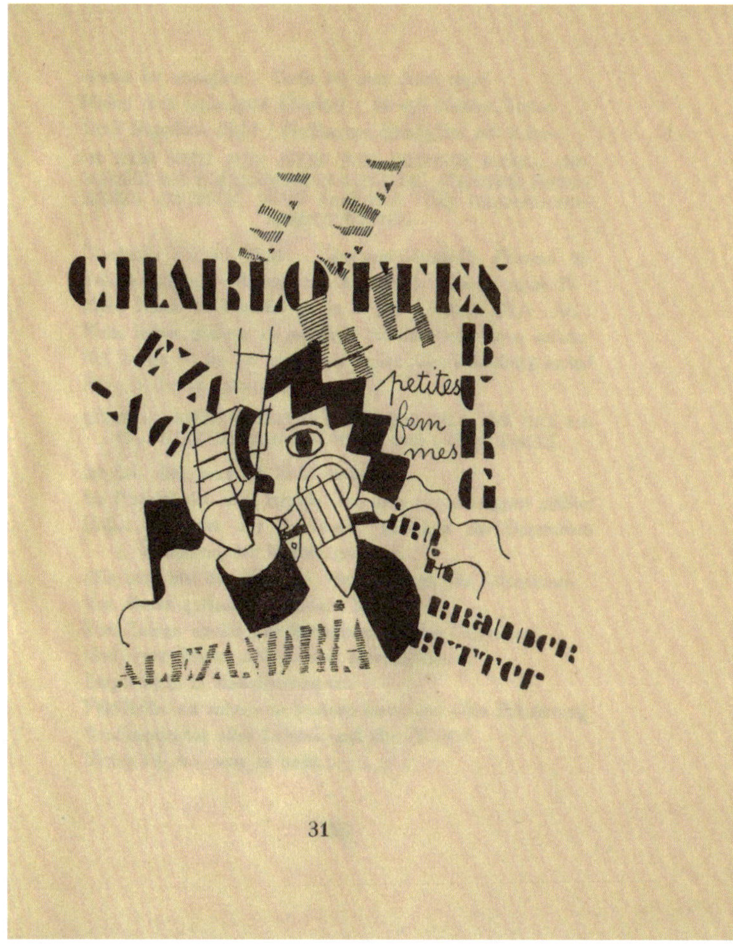

49

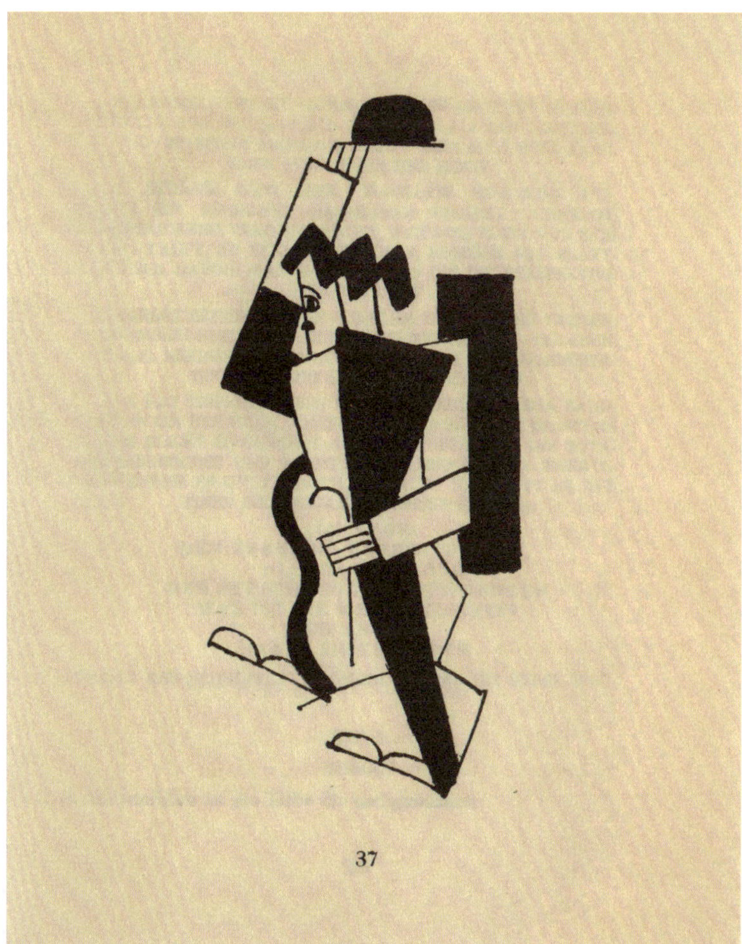

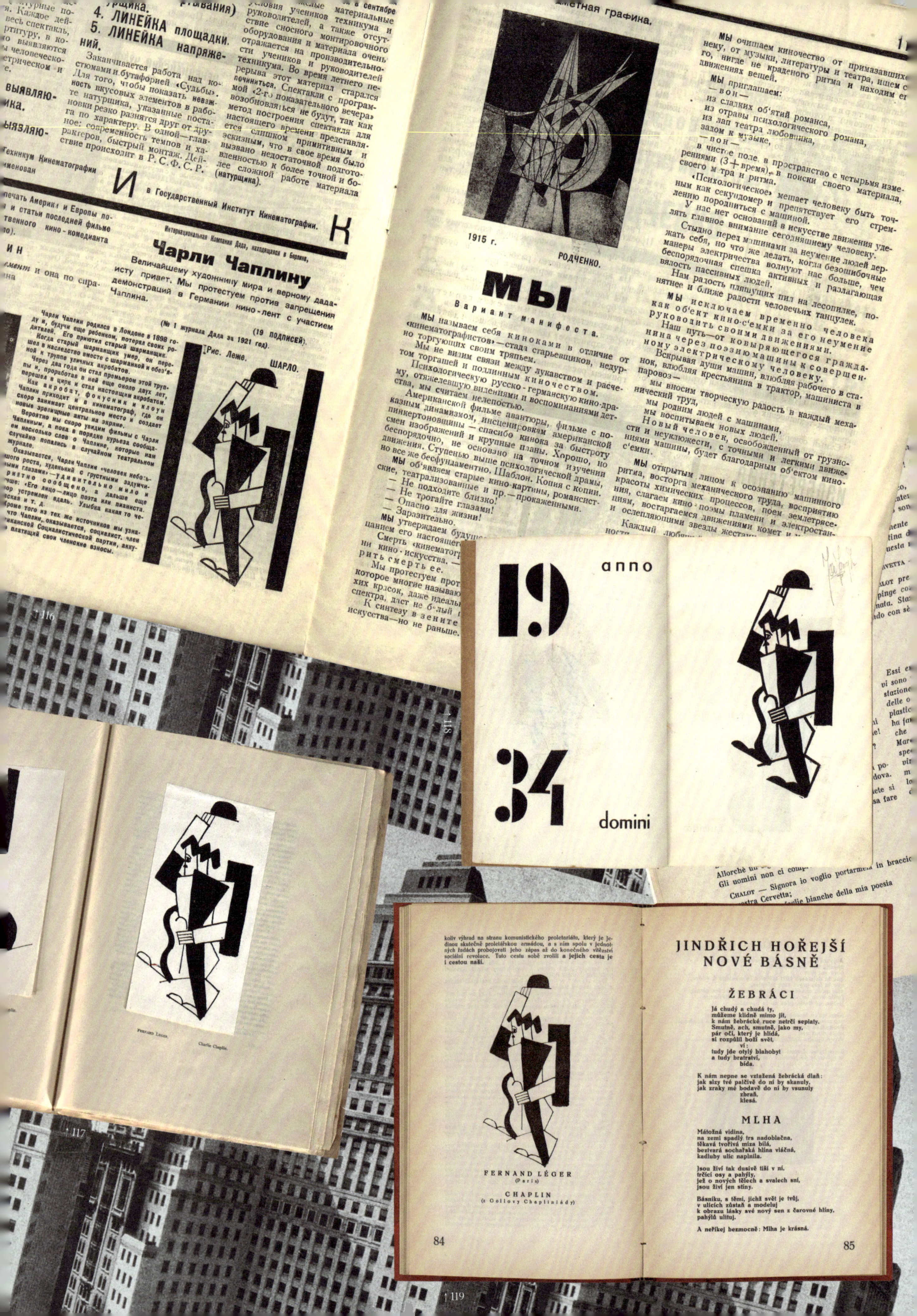

4. ЛИНЕЙКА площадки.
5. ЛИНЕЙКА напряжений.
в Государственный Институт Кинематографии.
Интернациональная Компания Дада, находящаяся в Берлине,
Чарли Чаплину
Величайшему художнику мира и верному дада-исту привет. Мы протестуем против запрещения демонстраций в Германии кино-лент с участием Чаплина.
(№ 1 журнала Дада за 1921 год). (19 ПОДПИСЕЙ)
Рис. Леже.
ШАРЛО.
1915 г.
РОДЧЕНКО.
МЫ
Вариант манифеста.
19
34
anno
domini
Fernand Léger
Charlie Chaplin
JINDŘICH HOŘEJŠÍ
NOVÉ BÁSNĚ
ŽEBRÁCI
MLHA
FERNAND LÉGER
(Paris)
CHAPLIN
(z Gollovy Chapliniády)
84
85
116
117
118
119

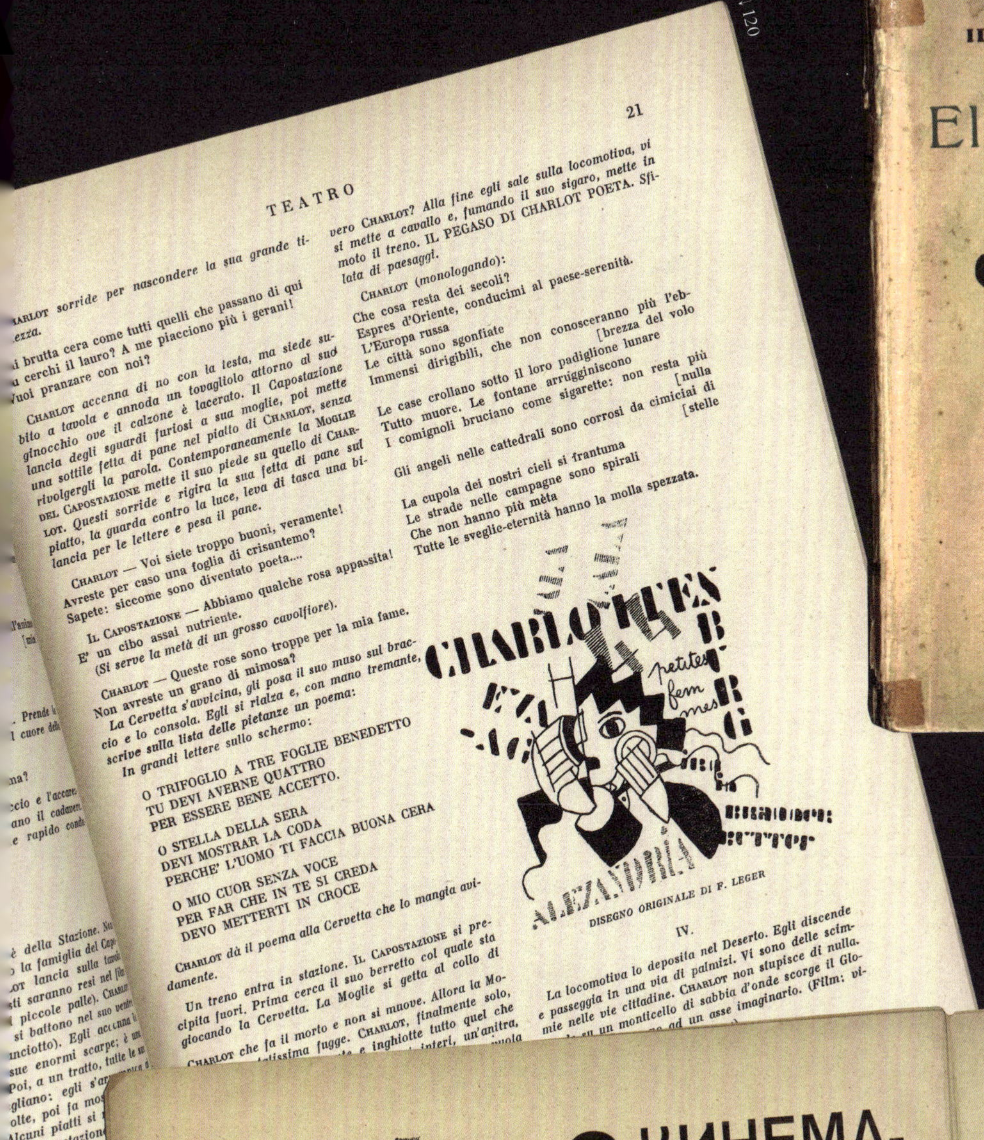

TEATRO 21

CHARLOT sorride per nascondere la sua grande ti-
[...]ezza.

[...]i brutta cera come tutti quelli che passano di qui
[...]u cerchi il lauro? A me piacciono più i gerani!
[...]Vuoi pranzare con noi?

CHARLOT *accenna di no con la testa, ma siede su-
bito a tavola e annoda un tovagliolo attorno al suo
ginocchio ove il calzone è lacerato. Il Capostazione
lancia degli sguardi furiosi a sua moglie, poi mette
una sottile fetta di pane nel piatto di* CHARLOT, *senza
rivolgergli la parola. Contemporaneamente la* MOGLIE
DEL CAPOSTAZIONE *mette il suo piede su quello di* CHAR-
LOT. *Questi sorride e rigira la sua fetta di pane sul
piatto, la guarda contro la luce, leva di tasca una bi-
lancia per le lettere e pesa il pane.*

CHARLOT — Voi siete troppo buoni, veramente!
Avreste per caso una foglia di crisantemo?
Sapete: siccome sono diventato poeta....

IL CAPOSTAZIONE — Abbiamo qualche rosa appassita!
E' un cibo assai nutriente.
(Si serve la metà di un grosso cavolfiore).

CHARLOT — Queste rose sono troppe per la mia fame.
Non avreste un grano di mimosa?

*La Cervetta s'avvicina, gli posa il suo muso sul brac-
cio e lo consola. Egli si rialza e, con mano tremante,
scrive sulla lista delle pietanze un poema:*

In grandi lettere sullo schermo:

O TRIFOGLIO A TRE FOGLIE BENEDETTO
TU DEVI AVERNE QUATTRO
PER ESSERE BENE ACCETTO.

O STELLA DELLA SERA
DEVI MOSTRAR LA CODA
PERCHE' L'UOMO TI FACCIA BUONA CERA

O MIO CUOR SENZA VOCE
PER FAR CHE IN TE SI CREDA
DEVO METTERTI IN CROCE

CHARLOT *dà il poema alla Cervetta che lo mangia avi-
damente.*

Un treno entra in stazione. IL CAPOSTAZIONE *si pre-
cipita fuori. Prima cerca il suo berretto col quale sta
giocando la Cervetta. La Moglie si getta al collo di*
CHARLOT *che fa il morto e non si muove. Allora la Mo-
[...]tissima fugge.* CHARLOT, *finalmente solo,
[...] e inghiotte tutto quel che
[...] interi, un'anitra,*

vero CHARLOT? *Alla fine egli sale sulla locomotiva, vi
si mette a cavallo e, fumando il suo sigaro, mette in
moto il treno.* IL PEGASO DI CHARLOT POETA. *Sfi-
lata di paesaggi.*

CHARLOT *(monologando):*

Che cosa resta dei secoli?
Espres d'Oriente, conducimi al paese-serenità.
L'Europa russa
Le città sono sgonfiate
Immensi dirigibili, che non conosceranno più l'eb-
[brezza del volo

Le case crollano sotto il loro padiglione lunare
Tutto muore. Le fontane arrugginiscono
I comignoli bruciano come sigarette: non resta più
[nulla

Gli angeli nelle cattedrali sono corrosi da cimiciai di
[stelle

La cupola dei nostri cieli si frantuma
Le strade nelle campagne sono spirali
Che non hanno più mèta
Tutte le sveglie-eternità hanno la molla spezzata.

DISEGNO ORIGINALE DI F. LEGER

IV.

*La locomotiva lo deposita nel Deserto. Egli discende
e passeggia in una via di palmizi. Vi sono delle scim-
mie nelle vie cittadine.* CHARLOT *non stupisce di nulla.
[...] un monticello di sabbia d'onde scorge il Glo-
[...] ad un asse imaginario. (Film: vi-*

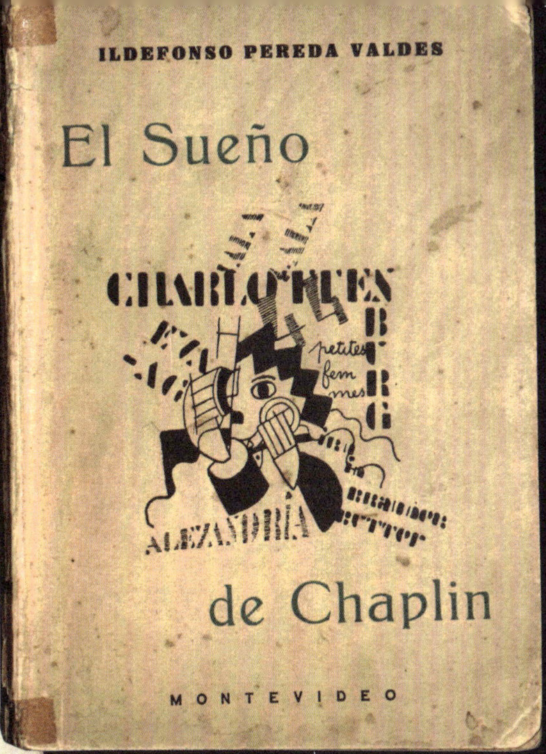

ILDEFONSO PEREDA VALDES

El Sueño de Chaplin

MONTEVIDEO

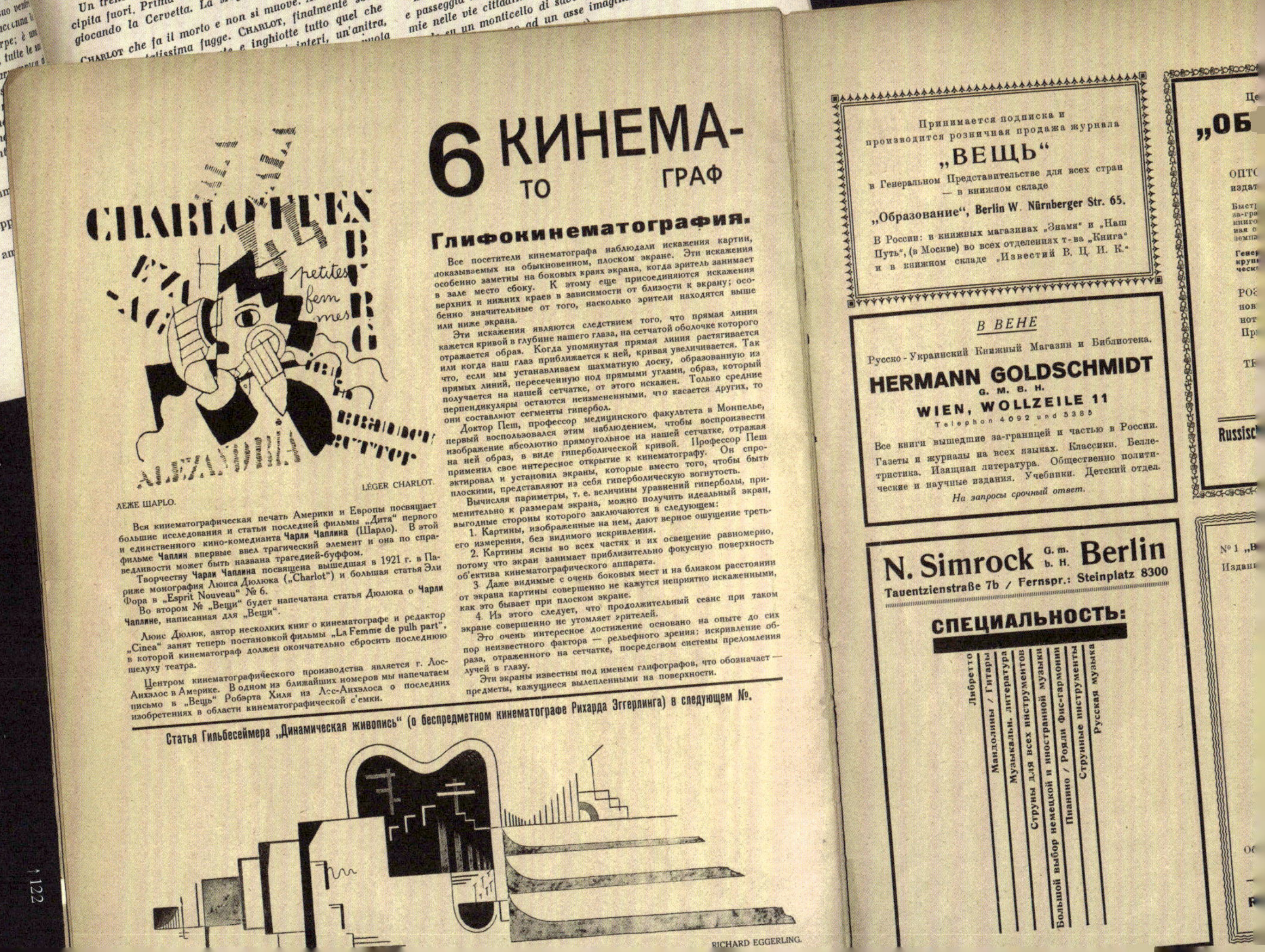

LÉGER CHARLOT.

ЛЕЖЕ ШАРЛО.

Вся кинематографическая печать Америки и Европы посвящает большие исследования и статьи последней фильмы „Дитя" первого и единственного кино-комедианта **Чарли Чаплина** (Шарло). В этой фильме **Чаплин** впервые ввел трагический элемент и она по справедливости может быть названа трагедией-буффом.

Творчеству **Чарли Чаплина** посвящена вышедшая в 1921 г. в Париже монография Люиса Дюлюка („Charlot") и большая статья Эли Фора в „Esprit Nouveau" № 6.

Во втором № „Вещи" будет напечатана статья Дюлюка о **Чарли Чаплине**, написанная для „Вещи".

Люис Дюлюк, автор несколких книг о кинематографе и редактор „Cinea" занят теперь постановкой фильмы „La Femme de pulh part", в которой кинематограф должен окончательно сбросить последнюю шелуху театра.

Центром кинематографического производства является г. Лос-Анхэлос в Америке. В одном из ближайших номеров мы напечатаем письмо в „Вещь" Робэрта Хиля из Лос-Анхэлоса о последних изобретениях в области кинематографической с'емки.

6 КИНЕМА-ТО ГРАФ

Глифокинематография.

Все посетители кинематографа наблюдали искажения картин, показываемых на обыкновенном, плоском экране. Эти искажения особенно заметны на боковых краях экрана, когда зритель занимает в зале место сбоку. К этому еще присоединяются искажения верхних и нижних краев в зависимости от близости к экрану; особенно значительные от того, насколько зрители находятся выше или ниже экрана.

Эти искажения являются следствием того, что прямая линия кажется кривой в глубине нашего глаза, на сетчатой оболочке которого отражается образ. Когда упомянутая прямая линия растягивается или когда наш глаз приближается к ней, кривая увеличивается. Так что, если мы устанавливаем шахматную доску, образованную из прямых линий, пересеченную под прямыми углами, образ, который получается на нашей сетчатке, от этого искажен. Только средние перпендикуляры остаются неизмененными, что касается других, то они составляют сегменты гипербол.

Доктор Пеш, профессор медицинского факультета в Монпелье, первый воспользовался этим наблюдением, чтобы воспроизвести изображение абсолютно прямоугольное на нашей сетчатке, отражая на ней образ, в виде гиперболической кривой. Профессор Пеш применил свое интересное открытие к кинематографу. Он спроэктировал и установил экраны, которые вместо того, чтобы быть плоскими, представляют из себя гиперболическую вогнутость.

Вычисляя париметры, т. е. величины уравнений гиперболы, применительно к размерам экрана, можно получить идеальный экран, выгодные стороны которого заключаются в следующем:

1. Картины, изображенные на нем, дают верное ощущение третьего измерения, без видимого искривления.

2. Картины ясны во всех частях и их освещение равномерно, потому что экран занимает приблизительно фокусную поверхность об'ектива кинематографического аппарата.

3. Даже видимые с очень боковых мест и на близком расстоянии от экрана картины совершенно не кажутся неприятно искаженными, как это бывает при плоском экране.

4. Из этого следует, что продолжительный сеанс при таком экране совершенно не утомляет зрителей.

Это очень интересное достижение основано на опыте до сих пор неизвестного фактора — рельефного зрения: искривление образа, отраженного на сетчатке, посредством системы преломления лучей в глазу.

Эти экраны известны под именем глифографов, что обозначает — предметы, кажущиеся вылепленными на поверхности.

Статья Гильбесеймера „Динамическая живопись" (о беспредметном кинематографе Рихарда Эггерлинга) в следующем №.

RICHARD EGGERLING.

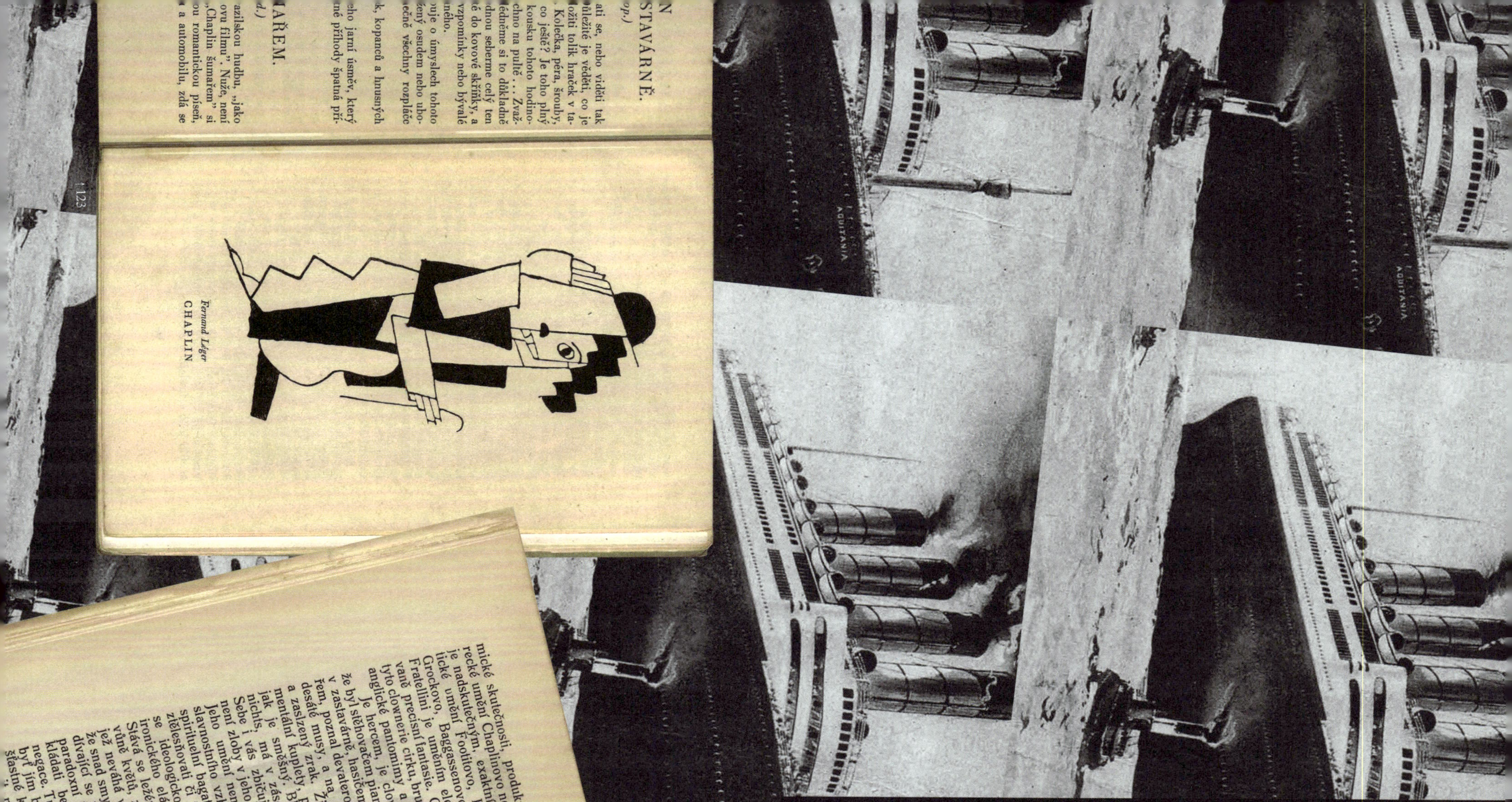

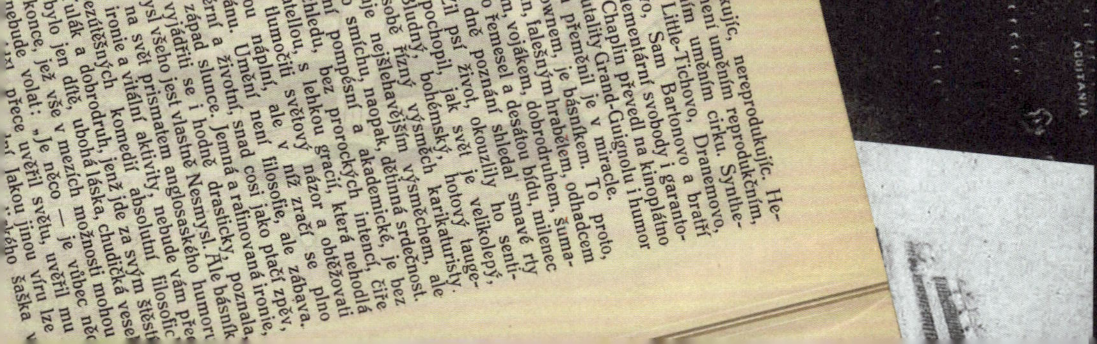

116 *Kino-Fot*, no. 1, August 1922, ed. Aleksej Gan, Moscow, 10–11
117 *Broom*, no. 3, January 1922, ed. Harold A. Loeb, Alfred Kreymburg, Rome/New York/London, 232–233
118 Friedrich Robert August Henkels, Ate Johannes Zuithoff, *Kampkweel*, Groningen: Christelijke Jeugd Organisatie 1934, 2–3
119 *Devětsil*, ed. Jaroslav Seifert, Karel Teige, Prague: Vortel 1922, 84–85
120 *Teatro. Rivista d'arte*, no. 6–7, June–July 1926, ed. Nino della Casa, Milan, 20–21
121 Ildefonso Pereda Valdés, *El Sueño de Chaplin*, Montevideo: Editorial Rio de la Plata 1930, cover
122 *Veshch Objet Gegenstand*, no. 1–2, March–April 1922, ed. El Lissitzky, Ilya Ehrenburg, Berlin, 28–29
123 Louis Delluc, *Charlie Chaplin*, Prague: Lidováknihovna Aventina Sv. 7, 1924, 34–35
124 Ivan Goll, *Le Nouvel Orphée*, Paris: Éditions de la Sirène 1923, 12–13
125 see 101, 56–57
126 *14 Rue du Dragon*, no. 1, March 1933, ed. Christian Zervos, Paris, [unpaginated]
*All illustrations by Fernand Léger: *Charlot Cubiste*

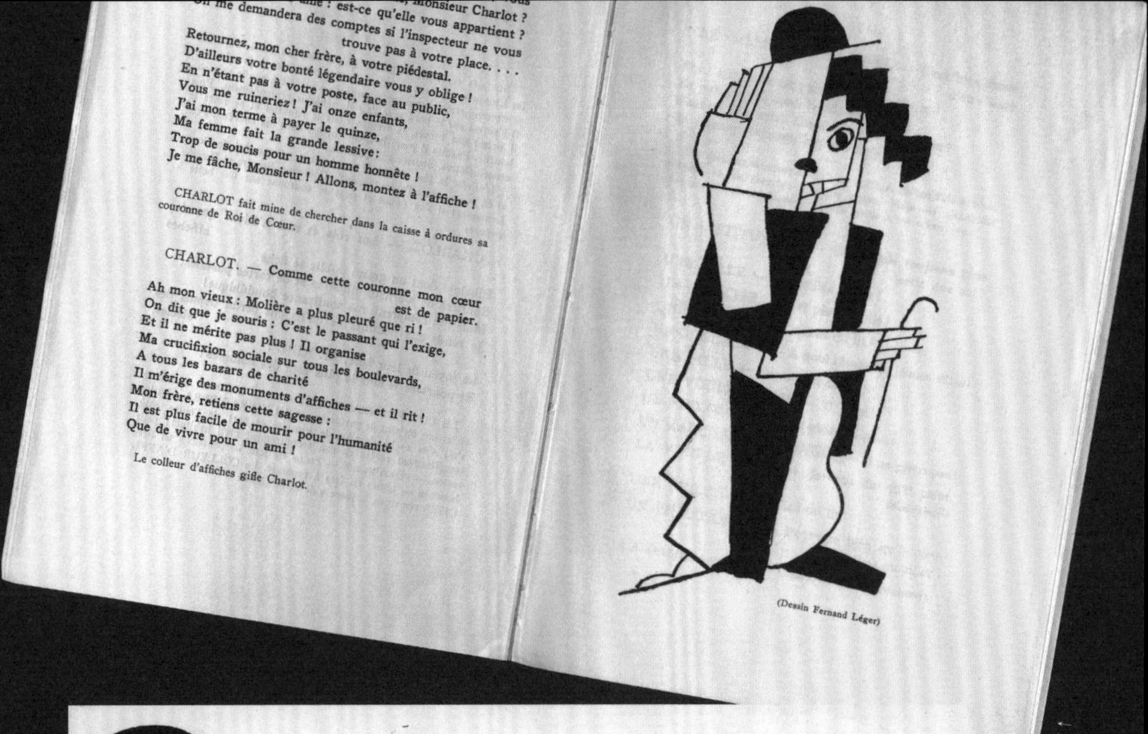
On me demandera des comptes si l'inspecteur ne vous
trouve pas à votre place. . . .
Retournez, mon cher frère, à votre piédestal.
D'ailleurs votre bonté légendaire vous y oblige !
En n'étant pas à votre poste, face au public,
Vous me ruineriez ! J'ai onze enfants,
J'ai mon terme à payer le quinze,
Ma femme fait la grande lessive:
Trop de soucis pour un homme honnête !
Je me fâche, Monsieur ! Allons, montez à l'affiche !
CHARLOT fait mine de chercher dans la caisse à ordures sa couronne de Roi de Cœur.
CHARLOT. — Comme cette couronne mon cœur est de papier.
Ah mon vieux : Molière a plus pleuré que ri !
On dit que je souris : C'est le passant qui l'exige,
Et il ne mérite pas plus ! Il organise
Ma crucifixion sociale sur tous les boulevards,
A tous les bazars de charité
Il m'érige des monuments d'affiches — et il rit !
Mon frère, retiens cette sagesse :
Il est plus facile de mourir pour l'humanité
Que de vivre pour un ami !
Le colleur d'affiches gifle Charlot.
(Dessin Fernand Léger)

↓124

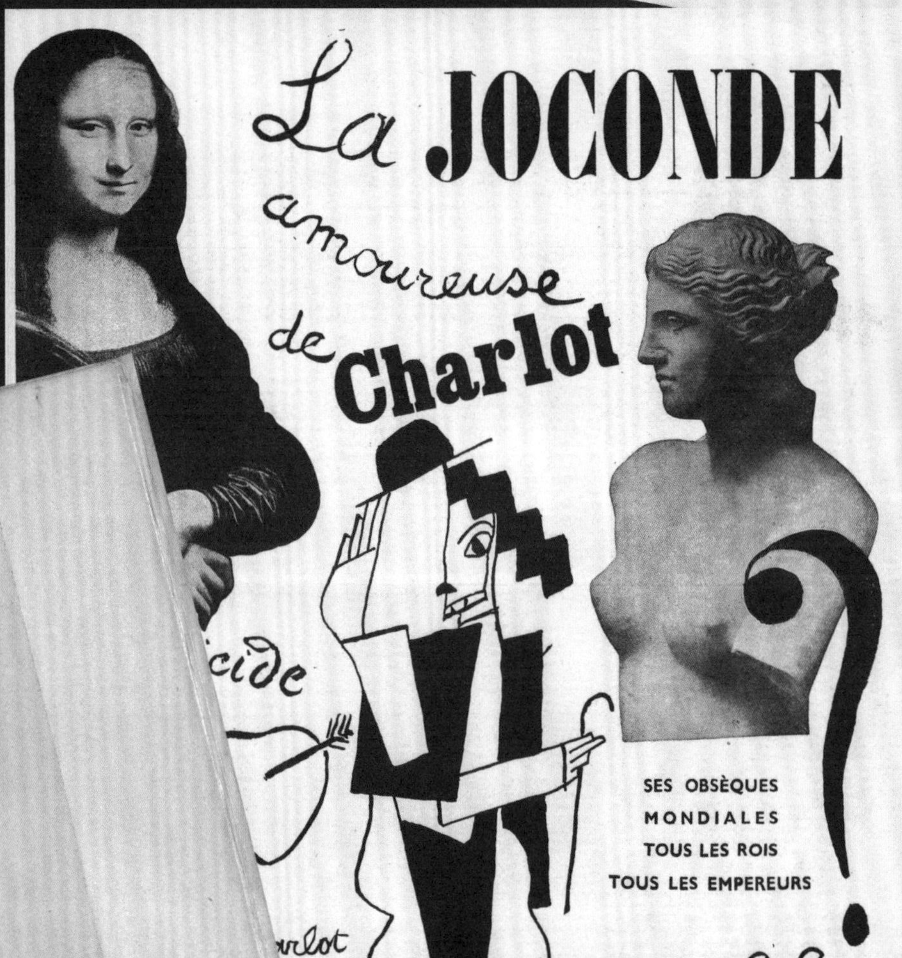
La JOCONDE
amoureuse
de Charlot
SES OBSÈQUES
MONDIALES
TOUS LES ROIS
TOUS LES EMPEREURS
Fernand Léger
A SUIVRE

↓126

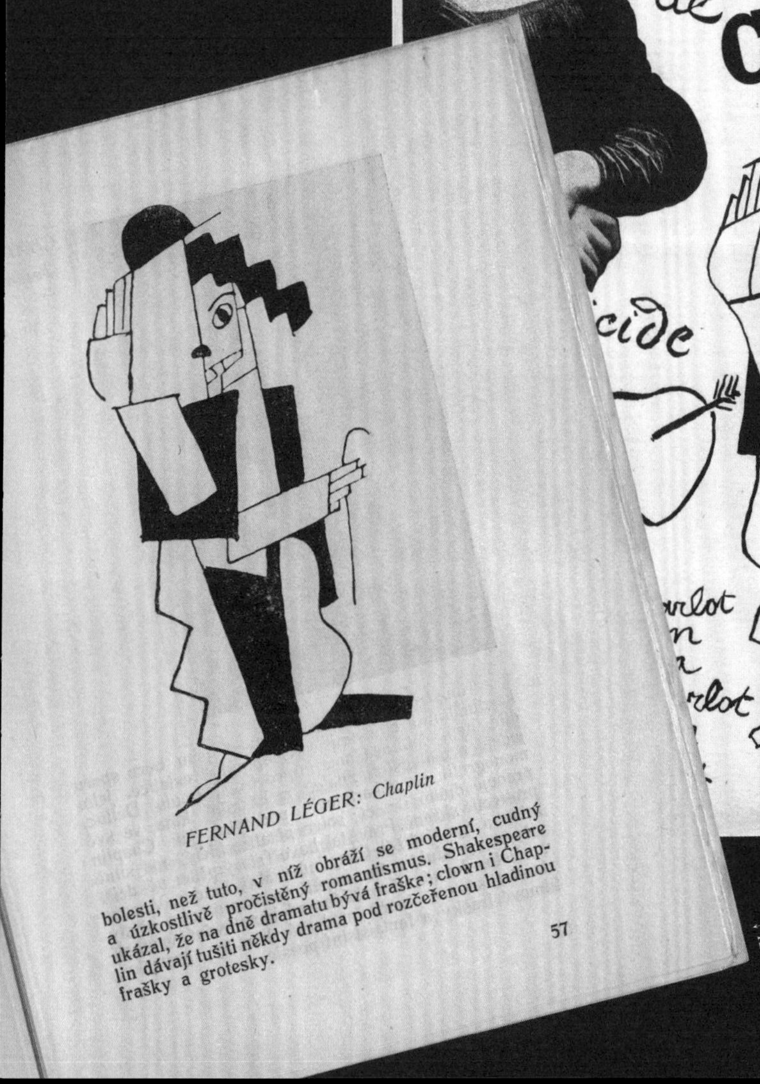
FERNAND LÉGER: Chaplin
bolestí, než tuto, v níž obráží se moderní, cudný a úzkostlivě pročistěný romantismus. Shakespeare ukázal, že na dně dramatu bývá fraška; clown i Chaplin dávají tušiti někdy drama pod rozčeřenou hladinou frašky a grotesky.
57

↓125

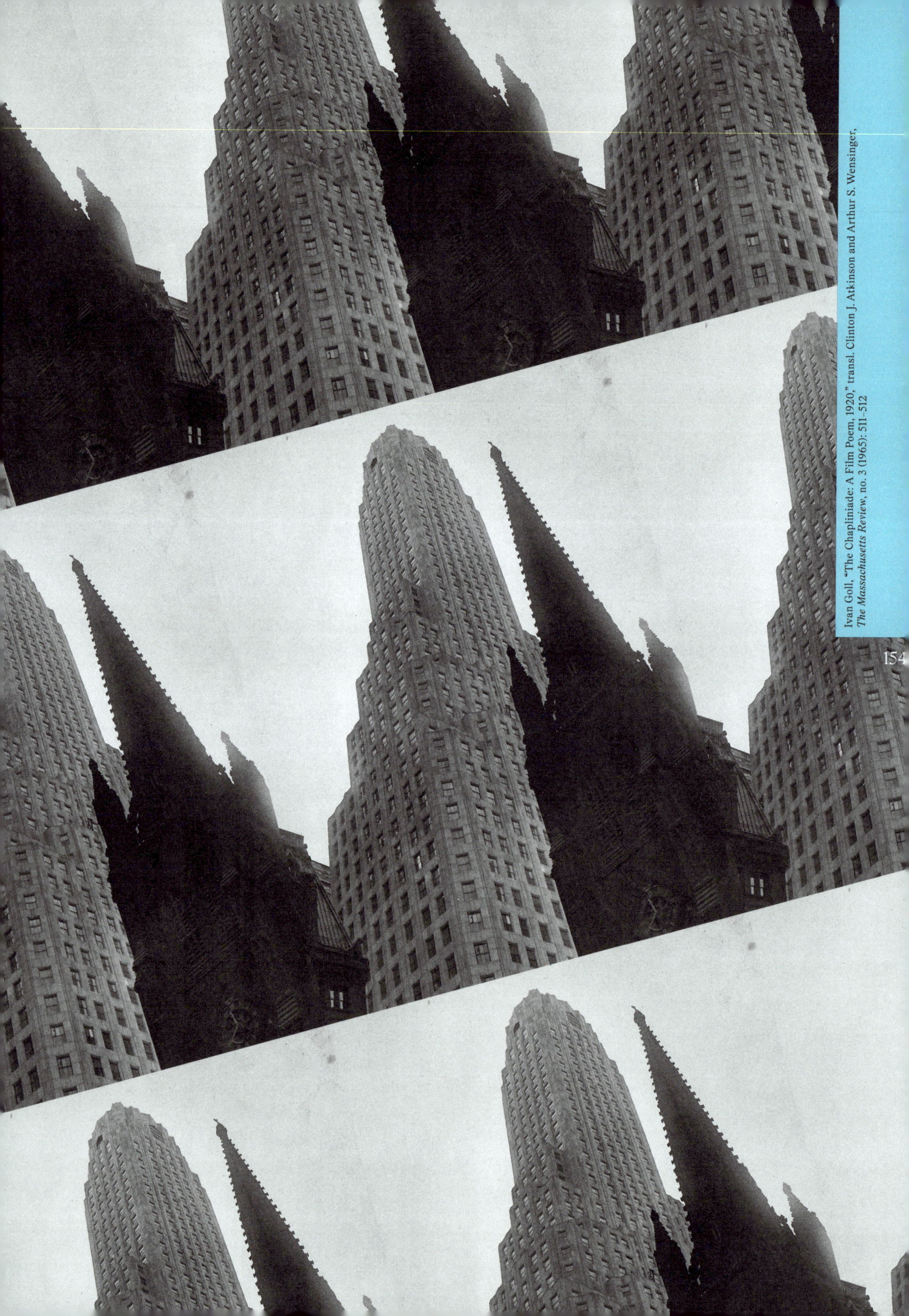

Ivan Goll, "The Chapliniade: A Film Poem, 1920," transl. Clinton J. Atkinson and Arthur S. Wensinger, *The Massachusetts Review*, no. 3 (1965): 511–512

Iwan Goll

The Chapliniade [fragment]

[...] Chaplin escapes his attackers and is seen suddenly first in a public square in Cairo and then in a street in Hong Kong.
Then the same street in Marseilles.
From one side a new mob comes forward with a placard: "Intellectual Wanted! Earn a Million!" The leader of the mob dashes up to Chaplin and kneels before him:

> Ave Charlot!
> Hail to the one who has liberated us from a
> century's
> work!
> Lead us back again to ourselves!
> Rare brother of the deer, prophet of the desert
> nomads,
> Here we languish and thirst for your healing art,
> Beat at the rocky wellspring of our breast!
> Give us back our laughter
> And pour the heavens back into our eyes.
> We can no longer think!
> We can no longer recognize ourselves!
> Release us from work! Bring us the Communism
> of the Soul!

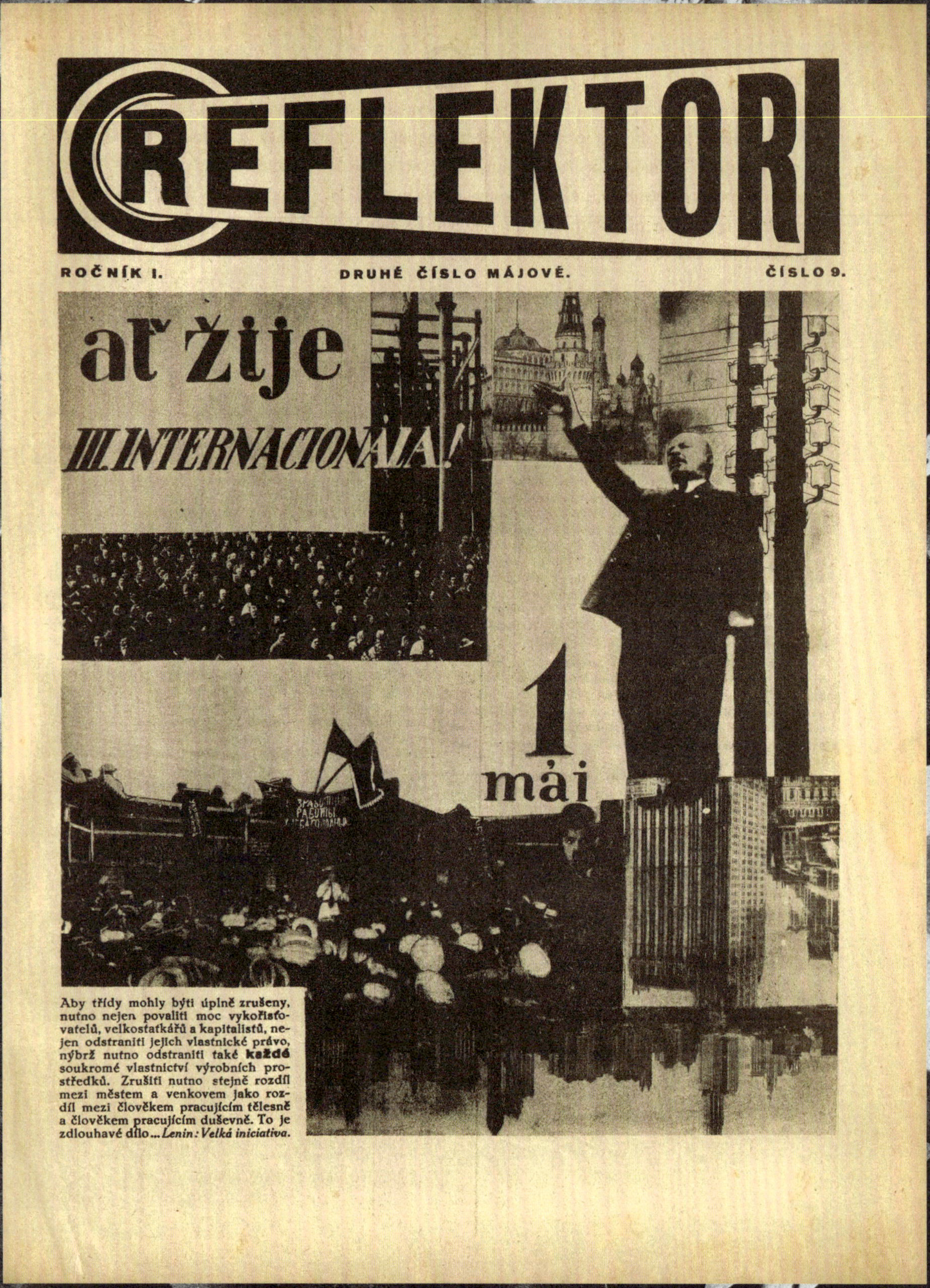

REFLEKTOR

ROČNÍK I. DRUHÉ ČÍSLO MÁJOVÉ. ČÍSLO 9.

ať žije

III. INTERNACIONÁLA!

1 máj

Aby třídy mohly býti úplně zrušeny, nutno nejen povaliti moc vykořisťovatelů, velkostatkářů a kapitalistů, nejen odstraniti jejich vlastnické právo, nýbrž nutno odstraniti také **každé** soukromé vlastnictví výrobních prostředků. Zrušiti nutno stejně rozdíl mezi městem a venkovem jako rozdíl mezi člověkem pracujícím tělesně a člověkem pracujícím duševně. To je zdlouhavé dílo... *Lenin: Velká iniciativa.*

127 *Reflektor*, no. 9, May 1925, ed. Stanislav K. Neumann, Prague, cover by Karel Teige

128 Karel Teige, *Svět, který se směje*, Prague: Odeon 1928, cover by Karel Teige

↓128 ↑127

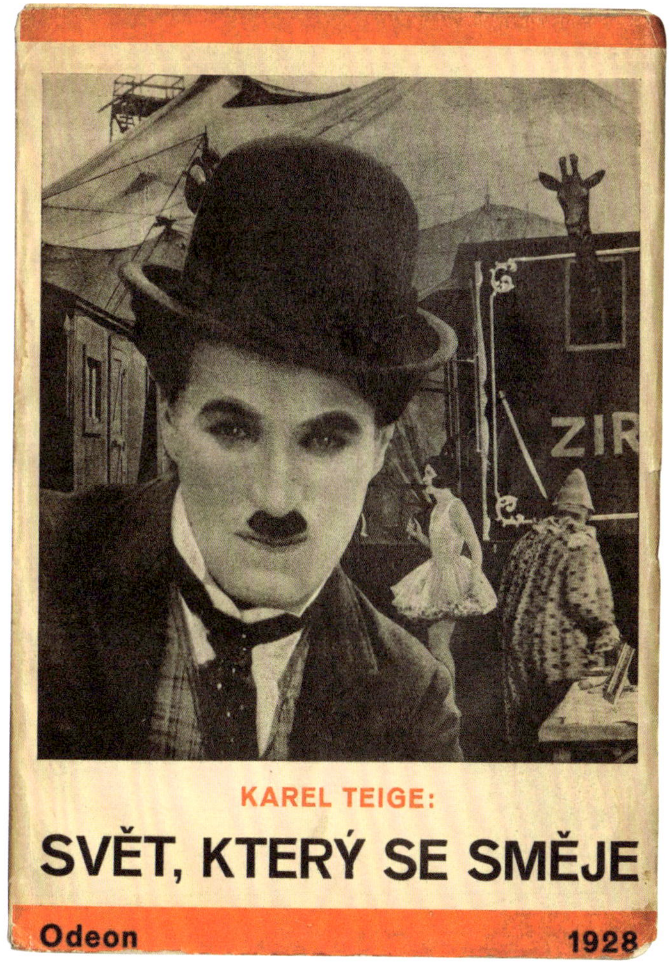

57

CHAPLIN AS A POLITICAL FIGURE In Charlie Chaplin's movies, the character of the little tramp was always portrayed in dire straits, as a homeless, starving vagrant and immigrant. He expressed criticism of the bourgeoise and the clergy (for example, in his movie *Pilgrim*, 1923). In this way, his movies fitted the strategies of leftist propaganda as he ridiculed the ruling class and capitalism while always managing to get out of even the biggest trouble. "Who is today the most popular man in France, England, Italy, and other countries? There are two: Lenin and Chaplin" wrote the Soviet modernist author, Ilya Ehrenburg, in 1922. This stance was not an isolated one, as Lenin and Chaplin were sometimes viewed in the 1920s as leaders of the fighting proletariat, and the avant-garde left elevated them both as heroes of the working class. Further evidence of this can be found on the cover of an issue of *Reflektor* magazine in Czechoslovakia, which included a photomontage by Karel Teige (no. 9, 1925). It depicts a proletarian crowd during the Labor Day celebrations with two recognizable silhouettes among the masses—those of Lenin and Chaplin—both placed next to a sign reading "Long live the 3rd International." Chaplin's image also features in *Europa* (1929), written in Warsaw by Anatol Stern with illustrations by a Construcivist artist, Mieczyslaw Szczuka. On the opening page of this Polish artbook, he is depicted laughing at the hedonistic bourgeoise and rural class that had led Europe towards a catastrophic fall.

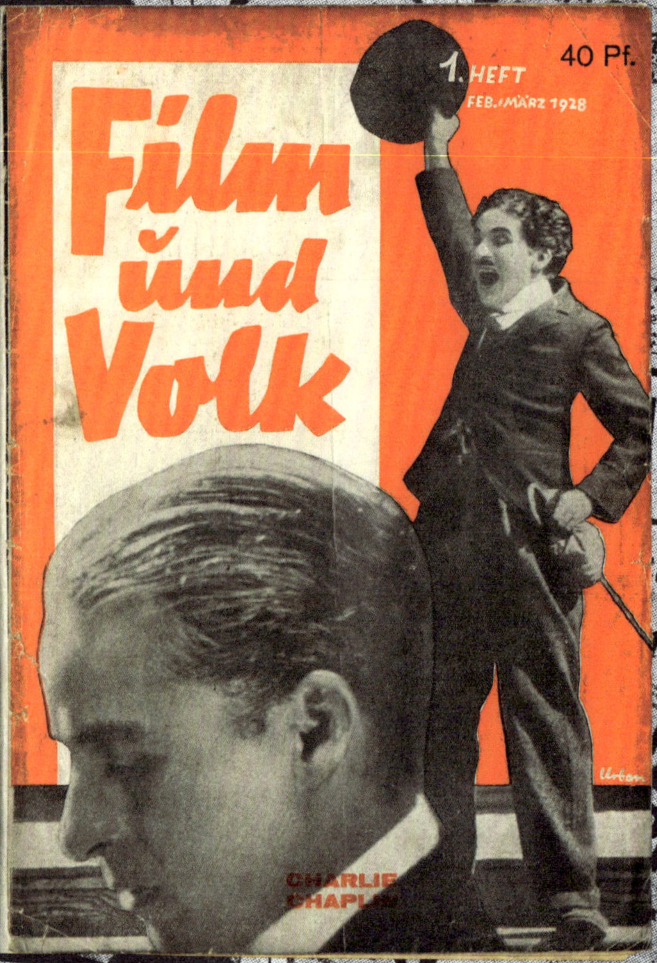

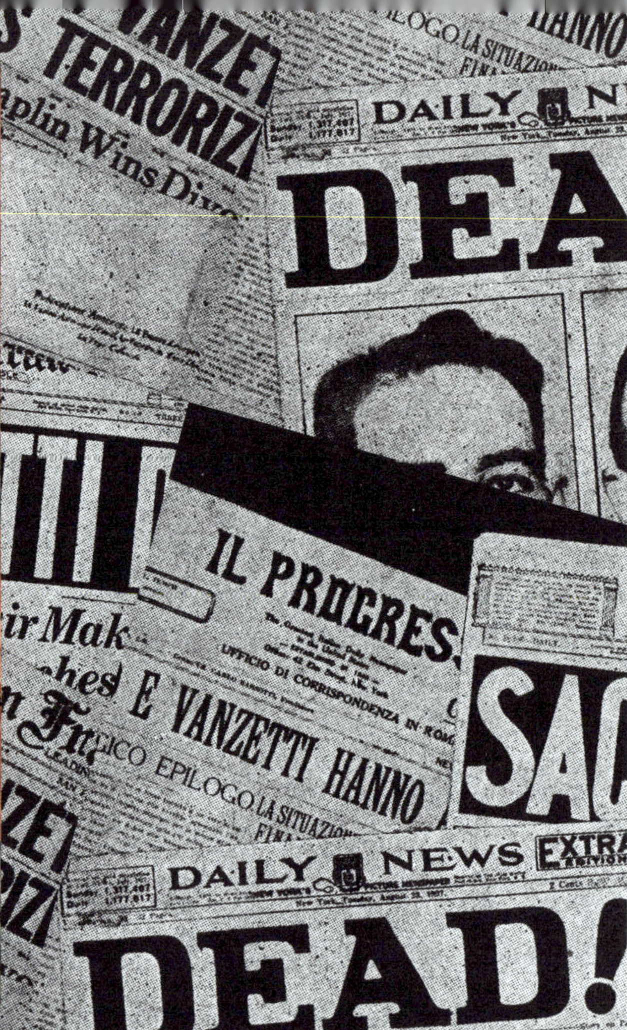

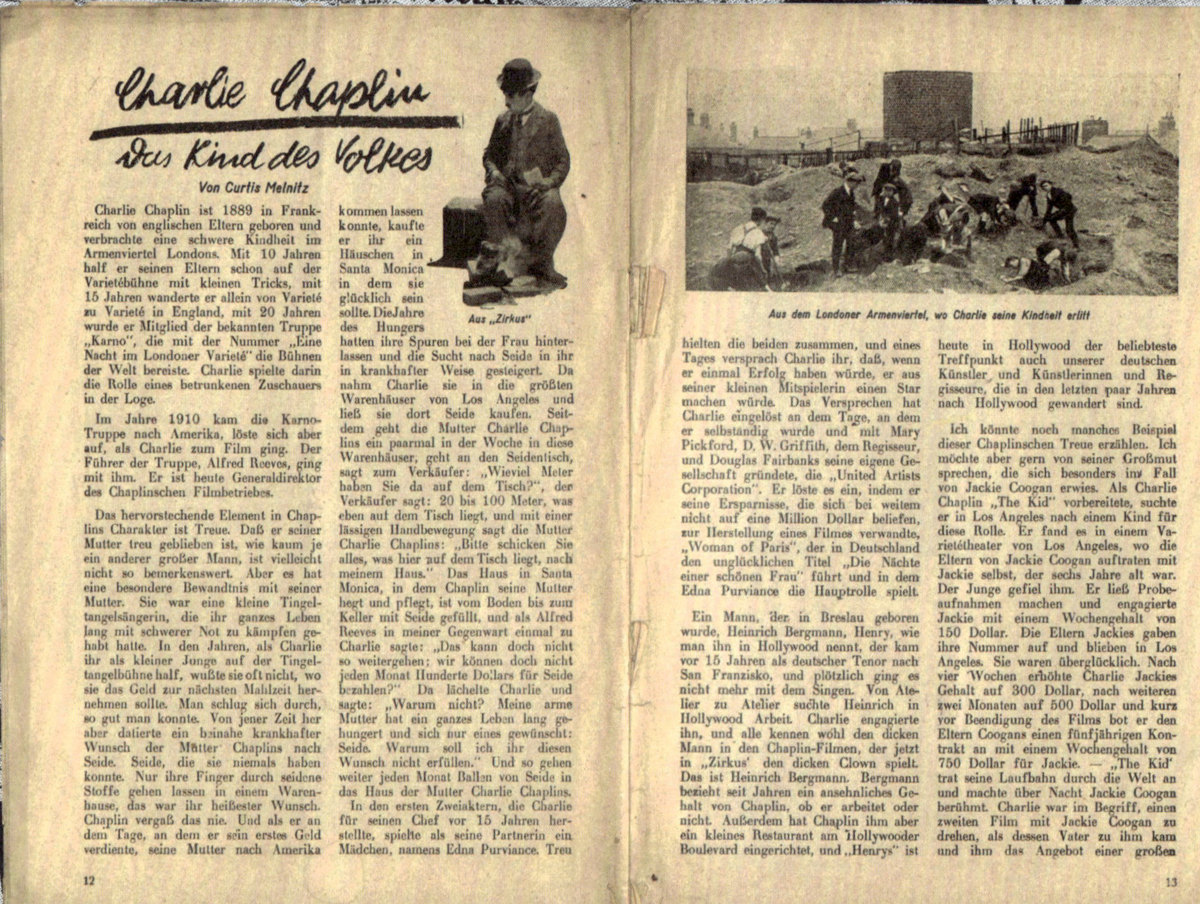

Charlie Chaplin

Das Kind des Volkes

Von Curtis Melnitz

Charlie Chaplin ist 1889 in Frankreich von englischen Eltern geboren und verbrachte eine schwere Kindheit im Armenviertel Londons. Mit 10 Jahren half er seinen Eltern schon auf der Varietébühne mit kleinen Tricks, mit 15 Jahren wanderte er allein von Varieté zu Varieté in England, mit 20 Jahren wurde er Mitglied der bekannten Truppe „Karno", die mit der Nummer „Eine Nacht im Londoner Varieté" die Bühnen der Welt bereiste. Charlie spielte darin die Rolle eines betrunkenen Zuschauers in der Loge.

Im Jahre 1910 kam die Karno-Truppe nach Amerika, löste sich aber auf, als Charlie zum Film ging. Der Führer der Truppe, Alfred Reeves, ging mit ihm. Er ist heute Generaldirektor des Chaplinschen Filmbetriebes.

Das hervorstechende Element in Chaplins Charakter ist Treue. Daß er seiner Mutter treu geblieben ist, wie kaum je ein anderer großer Mann, ist vielleicht nicht so bemerkenswert. Aber es hat eine besondere Bewandtnis mit seiner Mutter. Sie war eine kleine Tingeltangelsängerin, die ihr ganzes Leben lang mit schwerer Not zu kämpfen gehabt hatte. In den Jahren, als Charlie ihr als kleiner Junge auf der Tingeltangelbühne half, wußte sie oft nicht, wo sie das Geld zur nächsten Mahlzeit hernehmen sollte. Man schlug sich durch, so gut man konnte. Von jener Zeit her aber datierte ein beinahe krankhafter Wunsch der Mutter Chaplins nach Seide. Seide, die sie niemals haben konnte. Nur ihre Finger durch seidene Stoffe gehen lassen in einem Warenhause, das war ihr heißester Wunsch. Chaplin vergaß das nie. Und als er an dem Tage, an dem er sein erstes Geld verdiente, seine Mutter nach Amerika kommen lassen konnte, kaufte er ihr ein Häuschen in Santa Monica in dem sie glücklich sein sollte. Die Jahre des Hungers hatten ihre Spuren bei der Frau hinterlassen und die Sucht nach Seide in ihr in krankhafter Weise gesteigert. Da nahm Charlie sie in die größten Warenhäuser von Los Angeles und ließ sie dort Seide kaufen. Seitdem geht die Mutter Charlie Chaplins ein paarmal in der Woche in diese Warenhäuser, geht an den Seidentisch, sagt zum Verkäufer: „Wieviel Meter haben Sie da auf dem Tisch?", der Verkäufer sagt: 20 bis 100 Meter, was eben auf dem Tisch liegt, und mit einer lässigen Handbewegung sagt die Mutter Charlie Chaplins: „Bitte schicken Sie alles, was hier auf dem Tisch liegt, nach meinem Haus." Das Haus in Santa Monica, in dem Chaplin seine Mutter hegt und pflegt, ist vom Boden bis zum Keller mit Seide gefüllt, und als Alfred Reeves in meiner Gegenwart einmal zu Charlie sagte: „Das kann doch nicht so weitergehen; wir können doch nicht jeden Monat Hunderte Dollars für Seide bezahlen?" Da lächelte Charlie und sagte: „Warum nicht? Meine arme Mutter hat ein ganzes Leben lang gehungert und sich nur eines gewünscht: Seide. Warum soll ich ihr diesen Wunsch nicht erfüllen." Und so gehen weiter jeden Monat Ballen von Seide in das Haus der Mutter Charlie Chaplins.

Aus „Zirkus"

In den ersten Zweiaktern, die Charlie für seinen Chef vor 15 Jahren herstellte, spielte als seine Partnerin ein Mädchen, namens Edna Purviance. Treu hielten die beiden zusammen, und eines Tages versprach Charlie ihr, daß, wenn er einmal Erfolg haben würde, er aus seiner kleinen Mitspielerin einen Star machen würde. Das Versprechen hat Charlie eingelöst an dem Tage, an dem er selbständig wurde und mit Mary Pickford, D. W. Griffith, dem Regisseur, und Douglas Fairbanks seine eigene Gesellschaft gründete, die „United Artists Corporation". Er löste es ein, indem er seine Ersparnisse, die sich bei weitem nicht auf eine Million Dollar beliefen, zur Herstellung eines Filmes verwandte, „Woman of Paris", der in Deutschland den unglücklichen Titel „Die Nächte einer schönen Frau" führt und in dem Edna Purviance die Hauptrolle spielt.

Aus dem Londoner Armenviertel, wo Charlie seine Kindheit erlitt

Ein Mann, der in Breslau geboren wurde, Heinrich Bergmann, Henry, wie man ihn in Hollywood nennt, der kam vor 15 Jahren als deutscher Tenor nach San Franzisko, und plötzlich ging es nicht mehr mit dem Singen. Von Atelier zu Atelier suchte Heinrich in Hollywood Arbeit. Charlie engagierte ihn, und alle kennen wohl den dicken Mann in den Chaplin-Filmen, der jetzt in „Zirkus' den dicken Clown spielt. Das ist Heinrich Bergmann. Bergmann bezieht seit Jahren ein ansehnliches Gehalt von Chaplin, ob er arbeitet oder nicht. Außerdem hat Chaplin ihm aber ein kleines Restaurant am Hollywooder Boulevard eingerichtet, und „Henrys" ist heute in Hollywood der beliebteste Treffpunkt auch unserer deutschen Künstler und Künstlerinnen und Regisseure, die in den letzten paar Jahren nach Hollywood gewandert sind.

Ich könnte noch manches Beispiel dieser Chaplinschen Treue erzählen. Ich möchte aber gern von seiner Großmut sprechen, die sich besonders im Fall von Jackie Coogan erwies. Als Charlie Chaplin „The Kid" vorbereitete, suchte er in Los Angeles nach einem Kind für diese Rolle. Er fand es in einem Varietétheater von Los Angeles, wo die Eltern von Jackie Coogan auftraten mit Jackie selbst, der sechs Jahre alt war. Der Junge gefiel ihm. Er ließ Probeaufnahmen machen und engagierte Jackie mit einem Wochengehalt von 150 Dollar. Die Eltern Jackies gaben ihre Nummer auf und blieben in Los Angeles. Sie waren überglücklich. Nach vier Wochen erhöhte Charlie Jackies Gehalt auf 300 Dollar, nach weiteren zwei Monaten auf 500 Dollar und kurz vor Beendigung des Films bot er den Eltern Coogans einen fünfjährigen Kontrakt an mit einem Wochengehalt von 750 Dollar für Jackie. — „The Kid' trat seine Laufbahn durch die Welt an und machte über Nacht Jackie Coogan berühmt. Charlie war im Begriff, einen zweiten Film mit Jackie Coogan zu drehen, als dessen Vater zu ihm kam und ihm das Angebot einer großen

12 13

129 *Film und Volk*, no. 1, February–March 1928, ed. Volksverband für Filmkunst, Berlin, cover; 12–13
130 *Arbeiterbühne und Film*, no. 4, April 1931, ed. Arbeiter-Theater-Bund Deutschlands e.V., Berlin, cover; 28–29, photo of Charlie Chaplin in *City Lights*

↓130 ↑129

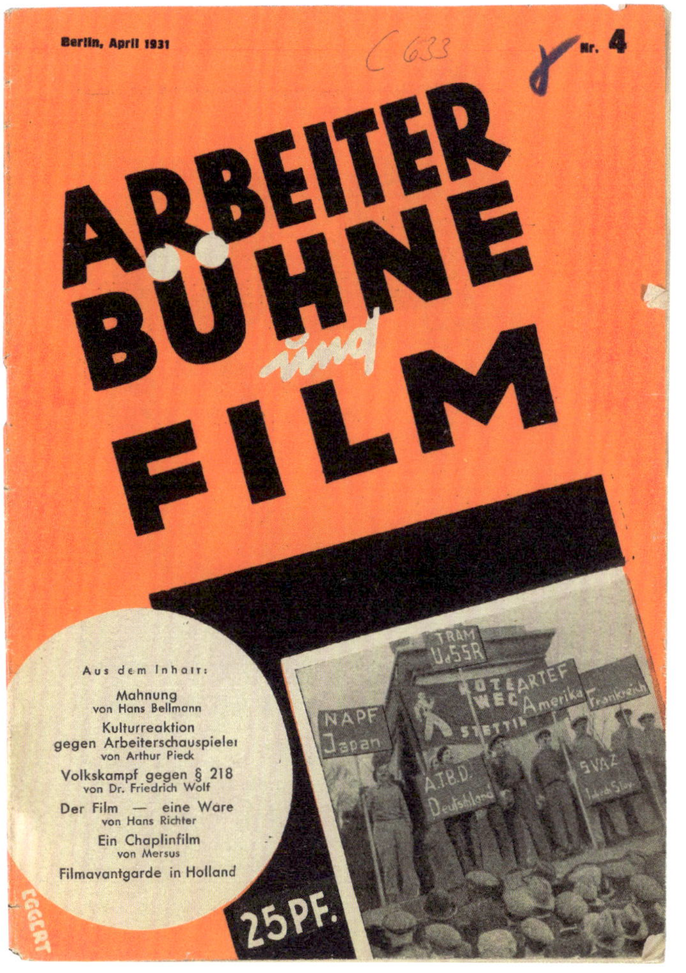

59

Charlie Chaplin

Charlie Chaplin ist einige Tage lang in Berlin gewesen. Die gesamte bürgerliche Presse hat anläßlich seines Besuches einen widerlichen Klamauk in Szene gesetzt und spaltenlang in allen Arten von Rührseligkeit und Sensationsmache geschwelgt. Weit davon entfernt, bei diesem ebenso unsympathischen wie bezeichnenden Rummel mittun zu wollen, halten wir es doch für richtig, die Gelegenheit der an sich unwichtigen Europareise Chaplins und die schon wichtigere der bevorstehenden Uraufführung seines Films „Lichter der Großstadt" zu benutzen, um ausführlich über den großen amerikanischen Filmkünstler zu sprechen, dem ein beträchtlicher Teil des proletarischen Kinopublikums sehr freundlich gesinnt ist. — In einer kleinen „Plauderei" soll versucht werden, die Möglichkeiten und Grenzen der Chaplin'schen Kunst darzustellen. Der Verfasser hat sich dabei dem Stil der Chaplin-Filme absichtlich angepaßt. Man darf daher nicht glauben, wenn in dem sehr witzigen und interessanten Beitrag vom „lieben Gott" und Zubehör die Rede ist, daß wir, durch die donnernden Reden des Herrn Reichsinnenministers Wirth eingeschüchtert, plötzlich fromm geworden sind! Zuvor jedoch noch zwei kurze Auszüge aus der Tagespresse. *„Die Rote Fahne"* hat in Verbindung mit erwerbslosen Filmschauspielern und Komparsen, die in einer RGO-Gruppe organisiert sind, eine Delegation zu Chaplin gesandt, der es gelungen ist, ein Interwiev zu bekommen, das sich auffallend von den Interwievs der bürgerlichen Presse unterscheidet. Wir zitieren aus der „Roten Fahne" vom 13. März 1931:

„Der Kontakt mit Chaplin war sofort gegeben. Angesichts der vor ihm stehenden erwerbslosen Berufskollegen, und weil Chaplin über die Arbeitslosigkeit im internationalen Maßstäbe gut unterrichtet ist, galt seine erste Frage der politischen Lage in Deutschland und der Stoßkraft der deutschen Arbeiterschaft. Im selben Atemzuge wollte er wissen: „Und die ‚Rote Fahne' — welche Richtung der Arbeiterbewegung vertritt sie?"
„Wir sind die einzige revolutionäre Arbeiterpartei in Deutschland! Die KPD! In Berlin haben wir die meisten Stimmen!"
„Also revolutionär, ja?"
„Ja, dadurch unterscheiden wir uns von den anderen Parteien, die sich als Arbeiterparteien hinstellen."
„Oh, I see!" Und nach einigem Nachdenken entgegnet Chaplin: „Aber die Arbeiter Deutschlands haben doch schon einmal Revolution gemacht?! Ist nur ein Personenwechsel vor sich gegangen?"
„Das stimmt, Herr Chaplin. Die Arbeiter Deutschlands hatten schon einmal eine Revolution, aber sie ist verraten worden."
„Verraten?!" fragt Chaplin erstaunt, „wie das? Von wem denn?"
„Von den sozialdemokratischen Führern."
Chaplin mit lebhaftem Interesse, mit bewegter Gebärde: „Aber wie war so etwas möglich?"
Und nach einer Pause, während welcher sein Gesicht sich nachdenklich zusammenzieht: „Ja, wenn man eine Revolution macht, dann muß man sie ganz machen. Das darf kein bloßer Personenwechsel sein, nicht wahr?"

Im schroffen Gegensatz zu der sachlichen und sympathischen Stellungnahme der „Roten Fahne" steht ein Artikel „Chaplinade" aus Hitlers *„Völkischem Beobachter"* vom 21. März 1931, der in ekelerregender Weise gegen den . . . Juden Charlie Chaplin hetzt. Wir drucken den Schluß dieses jämmerlichen Erzeugnisses nationalsozialistischen „Geistes" ab, weil es die „Kultur" des „herannahenden Dritten Reiches" außerordentlich gut charakterisiert, daß seine „Propheten" *für einen der bedeutendsten Künstler der Welt nichts anderes übrig haben als wüste Drohungen und gemeine Beschimpfungen:*

„Jedoch wir sind ehrlich genug, auch dem Clown Chaplin den schuldigen Tribut bereits schon früher gezahlt zu haben — durch das Lachen, das uns dieser kleine, krummbeinige, plattfußbehaftete Filmfritze Chaplin abzwang allein durch die Zurschaustellung seiner rassisch bedingten Eigenart!
Bleiben Sie, Herr Chaplin, in Berlin, solange es Ihnen behagt; aber wir raten Ihnen, den hiesigen Aufenthalt nicht bis zur Heraufkunft des Dritten Reiches auszudehnen! Aus wohlgemeinten Gründen, Herr Chaplin!"

Was sagen *die noch nicht völlig verblödeten* „Anhänger" der „Nationalen Idee", die Charlie Chaplin sicherlich genau so lieben wie viele klassenbewußten Proleten es mit Recht tun, zu dieser Blüte völkischer „Kunstkritik"?

28

St. Charlie oder Ein Chaplinfilm, der nie gedreht wird.

Um die Stellung Chaplins heute in der Epoche der zugespitzten Klassengegensätze und der ungeheuerlichen Krisen der bürgerlichen Gesellschaft zu kennzeichnen, werde ich euch jetzt einen Film erzählen, den ich mir einmal für Charlie ausgedacht habe.

*

Vielleicht würde sich dieser Film „St. Charlie" betiteln. Also Charlie ist gestorben und, wie das nur recht und billig ist, holen sie ihn gleich im Lift hinauf. Ja, da wäre er nun im Lande der Seligen. Er, der unselige kleine Landstreicher, der ewige Vagabund mit den riesigen Schuhen und den weiten Hosen, dem Stöckchen, der schwarzen Melone auf den krausen Locken. Chaplin im Himmel, das kann natürlich nicht gut ausgehen. Selbstverständlich findet der Engel Arsenalverwalter nur ein paar erbärmliche mottenzerfressene Flügel für ihn, die Charlie jeden Morgen, wenn er sie anlegt, nicht ohne Rührung betrachtet und bürstet. Ganz natürlich bringt Charlie in kurzer Zeit den ganzen Himmel in Aufruhr. Absichtslos, versteht sich. Er nimmt nacheinander die verschiedensten himmlischen Aemter ein. Man kann den lieben Gott verstehen, wenn ihm die Sache schließlich doch zu bunt wird. Er muß sich dieses tölpischen kleinen Engels mit dem liebevollen Herzen irgendwie entledigen. Charlie wird vorgeladen und man überträgt ihm das verantwortungsvolle Amt eines Schutzengels, das ihn in vierundzwanzigstündigem Dienst an die Erde fesselt. Chaplin wird also wieder hinuntergeschickt, und Ruhe, Ordnung und göttlicher Friede lagern sich abermals über dem himmlischen Reich.

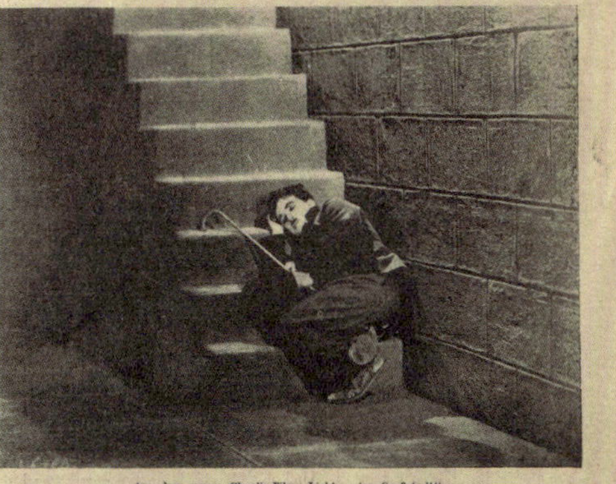

Aus dem neuen Chaplin-Film „Lichter der Großstadt"

29

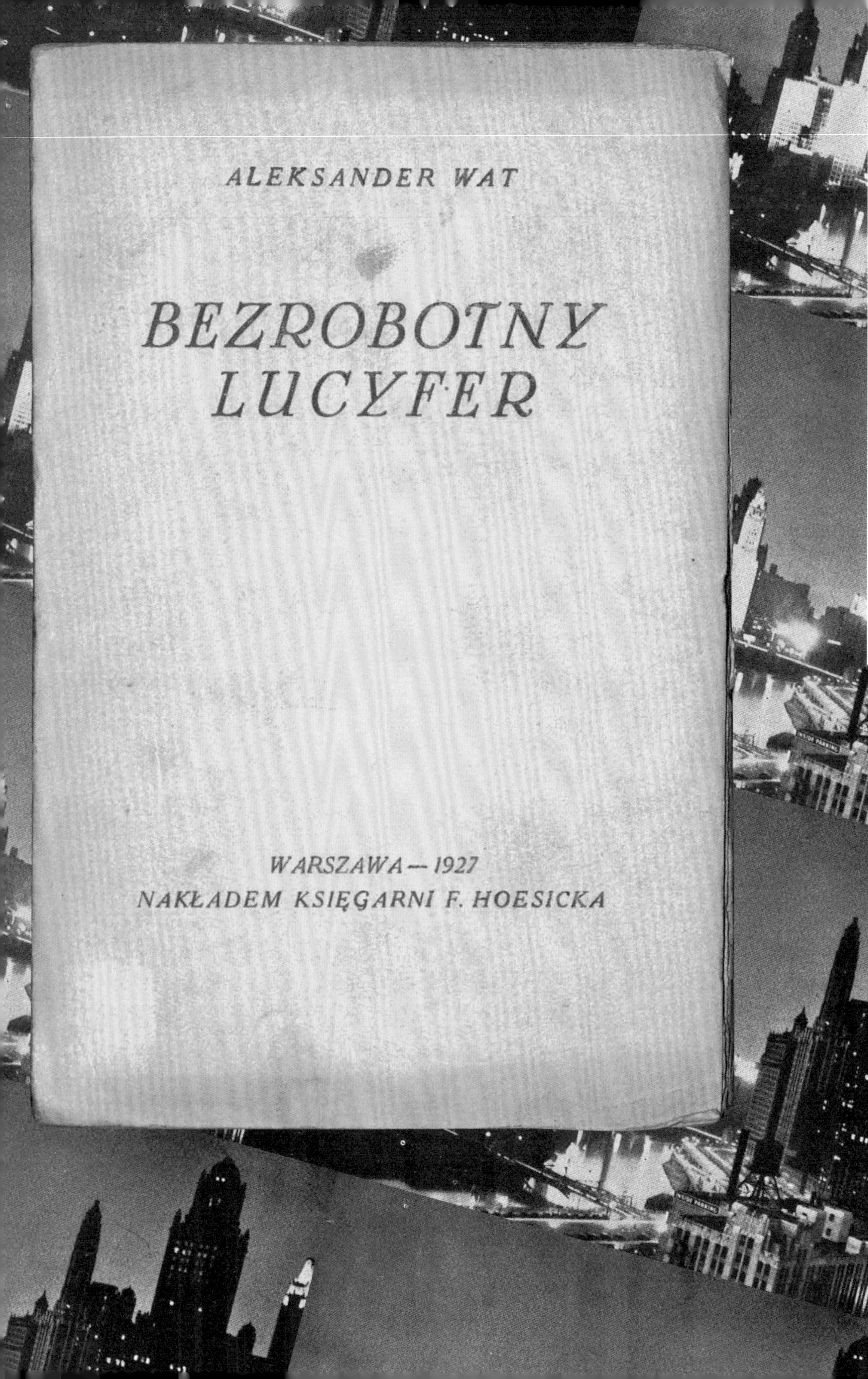

131 Aleksander Wat, *Bezrobotny Lucyfer*, Warsaw: Księgarnia F. Hoesicka 1927
132 *A-I-Z* [Arbeiter-Illustrierte-Zeitung], no. 2, 1930, ed. Willi Münzenberg, Berlin, cover with Charlie Chaplin in *The Pilgrim*

↓132 ↑131

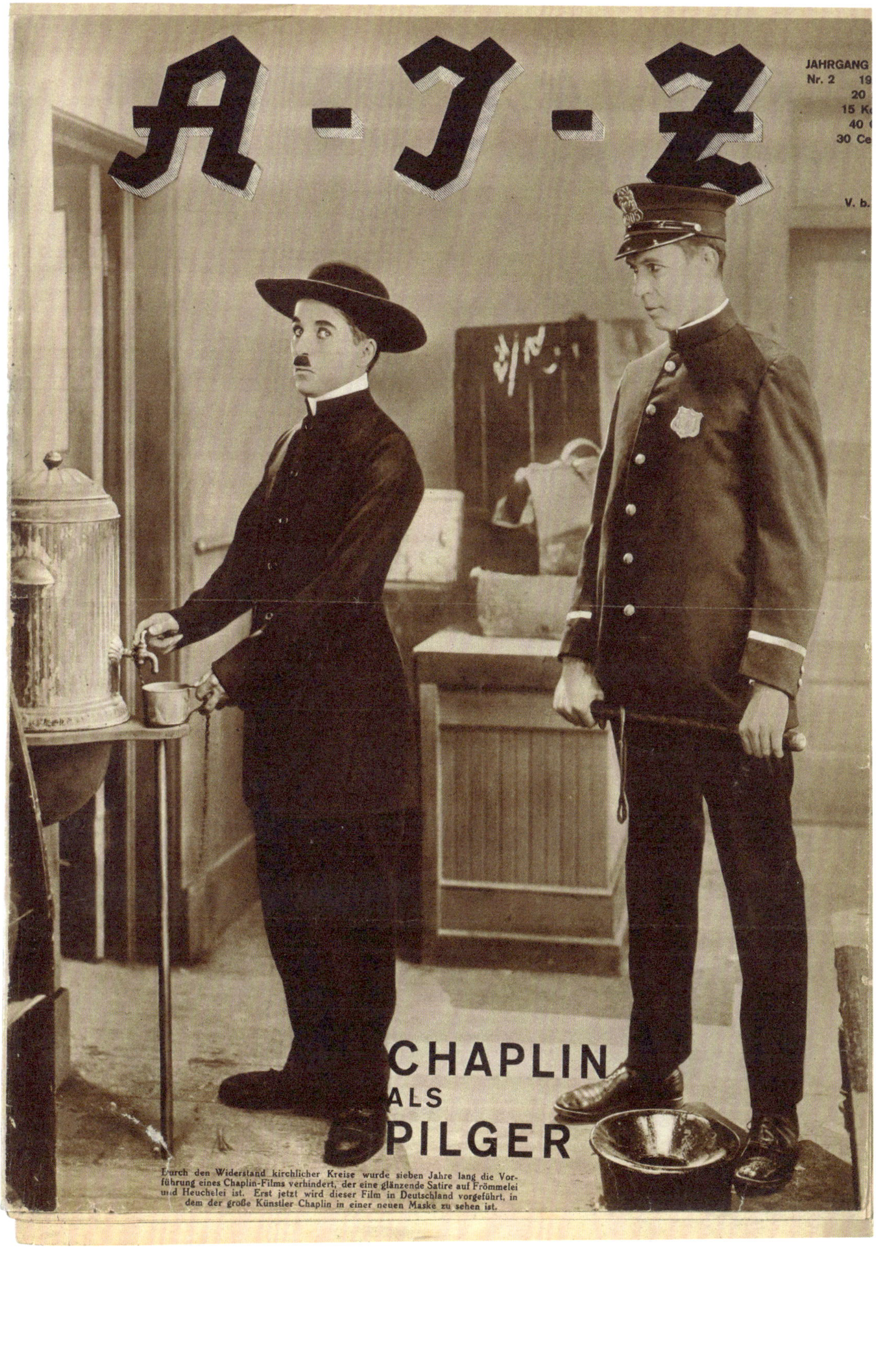

A-I-Z
JAHRGANG
Nr. 2 19
20
15 K
40
30 Ce
V. b.
CHAPLIN
ALS
PILGER
Durch den Widerstand kirchlicher Kreise wurde sieben Jahre lang die Vorführung eines Chaplin-Films verhindert, der eine glänzende Satire auf Frömmelei und Heuchelei ist. Erst jetzt wird dieser Film in Deutschland vorgeführt, in dem der große Künstler Chaplin in einer neuen Maske zu sehen ist.

61

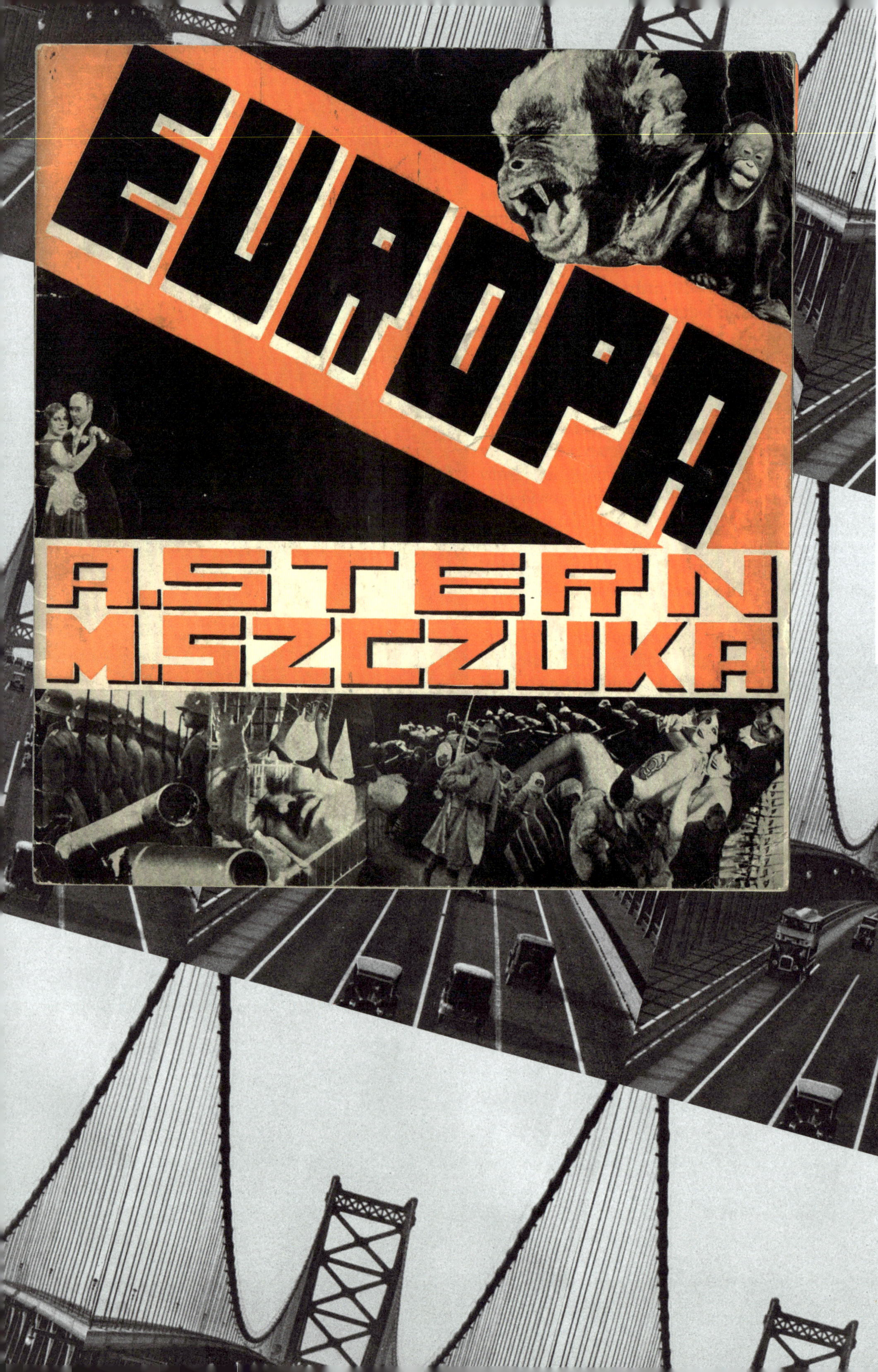

133 Anatol Stern, Mieczysław Szczuka, *Europa*, Warsaw: Księgarnia F. Hoesicka 1929, cover by Teresa Żarnowerówna; layout by Mieczysław Szczuka [unpaginated]

abecadło rzezi
brudu wesz pożarów
i miłosierdzia
stany zjednoczone
i argentyna brazylja chili
państwa walczące
fenomen i noumen
wieczność i nicość —
dwaj wypasieni bokserzy
którzy zawsze wygrają!
my
żrący mięso
raz na miesiąc
my
oddychający
siarką
kosztowną siarką
jak powietrzem —
my
wlokący ulicami
rząd zapadłych brzuchów
z bezsilnemi pięściami
wypychającemi kieszenie —
my —
przegramy
przegramy
przegramy
jak zwykle!!

63

Aleksander Wat, *Lucifer Unemployed* [1927], translated by Lillian Vallee (Evanston, Ill: Northwestern University Press, 1990), 121–123

Lucifer Unemployed [fragment]

"[...] I do not believe that you who are so endowed with talent and experience need to commit suicide because of unemployment, I believe that we can find even you an occupation. I've got it!" he said after a moment's silence. "You have been a viewer of the history of humanity from its inception. Finding yourself at a certain distance, however, you saw it but didn't hear it. Or, to put it another way: you were the viewer of a photographic history of the world, a viewer of a historical film. That being the case, it is impossible that you should not have acquired photogenic qualities. I am certain that you would make a first-rate film artist. Film is a great thing. Film gives you unmatched popularity. Finally, film is the first universal theatre of the imagination in centuries, and a place where it will be easy to make contact with humanity. I see you more clearly now: the spirit of restlessness, the spirit of anarchy—you will fight with order, with organization, with the machine. You will be their battle, their magic dissonance, melancholy, their buffoon, their dance. You will be an anarchist dancing with a machine—an ingenious metaphor for the present day. You will be a hundred-story slaughterhouse from Chicago, filled with refinements of a dozen Louvres. You will be the Eiffel Tower of the spirit, advertising Citroens. The eternal nihilist and corrupter, your face will express sadness and despair, metaphysics and goodness, the depth of cosmic melancholy, the soul, soul of humanity, which is your true essence. O Lucifer! your hands will be America, a machine, Taylorism, a biomecanic. And this discrepancy between the tragic soul of your face and your mechanized movements will show people their caricature. A consistent anarchist, you will negate not just laws but things. A watch brought to a pawnshop, for example, will be treated like a patient. You will check its reflexes and pump it full of gas like a car. On the screen you will treat the watch the way you treated the great watch of the world. For you are sufficiently wise to understand that humanity demands anarchy to the end.

"And so your wish since the beginning of time will be granted—for, by negating things, you will become equal to God who created them in ac of affirmation."

The stranger vanished just as miraculously, unexpectedly, and fantastically as he had appeared.

Lucifer looked at the revolver that lay next to him on the marble tabletop.

"Oh, well" he muttered to himself, "it would not have done any good anyway. I forgot I am immortal."

He returned the revolver to his pocket, paid his bill and left. The day—a foggy, autumn day—was well underway. Throngs of workers hurried like so many gray coulds to the factories. Newspaper vendors shouted the short names of the city's morning prayers.

Lucifer became a film artist.

We all know him.

He's Charlie Chaplin.

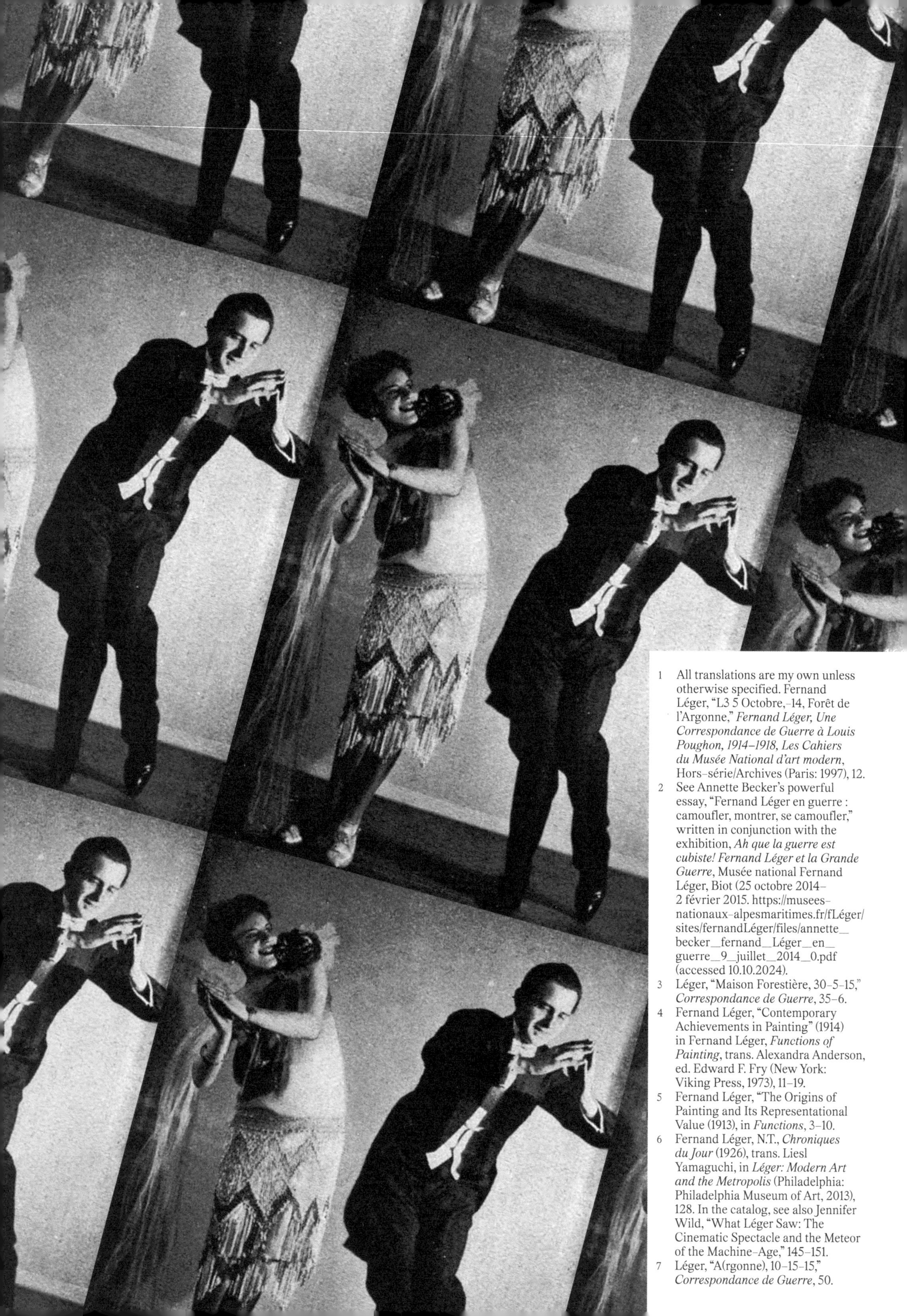

1 All translations are my own unless otherwise specified. Fernand Léger, "L3 5 Octobre,-14, Forêt de l'Argonne," *Fernand Léger, Une Correspondance de Guerre à Louis Poughon, 1914–1918, Les Cahiers du Musée National d'art modern*, Hors-série/Archives (Paris: 1997), 12.

2 See Annette Becker's powerful essay, "Fernand Léger en guerre : camoufler, montrer, se camoufler," written in conjunction with the exhibition, *Ah que la guerre est cubiste! Fernand Léger et la Grande Guerre*, Musée national Fernand Léger, Biot (25 octobre 2014– 2 février 2015. https://musees-nationaux-alpesmaritimes.fr/fLéger/sites/fernandLéger/files/annette_becker_fernand_Léger_en_guerre_9_juillet_2014_0.pdf (accessed 10.10.2024).

3 Léger, "Maison Forestière, 30-5-15," *Correspondance de Guerre*, 35–6.

4 Fernand Léger, "Contemporary Achievements in Painting" (1914) in Fernand Léger, *Functions of Painting*, trans. Alexandra Anderson, ed. Edward F. Fry (New York: Viking Press, 1973), 11–19.

5 Fernand Léger, "The Origins of Painting and Its Representational Value (1913), in *Functions*, 3–10.

6 Fernand Léger, N.T., *Chroniques du Jour* (1926), trans. Liesl Yamaguchi, in *Léger: Modern Art and the Metropolis* (Philadelphia: Philadelphia Museum of Art, 2013), 128. In the catalog, see also Jennifer Wild, "What Léger Saw: The Cinematic Spectacle and the Meteor of the Machine-Age," 145–151.

7 Léger, "A(rgonne), 10-15-15," *Correspondance de Guerre*, 50.

American Salvo
Fernand Léger, Charlie Chaplin, and The Mechanical Spectacle of the Great War

Jennifer J. Wild

By November 1915, Fernand Léger had already been fighting on the Western Front in the First World War for fourteen months. During that time and after, he steadily wrote to his friend Louis Poughon describing his everyday experience on the front as a "poilu," or the vernacular term for a common soldier. In his early letters, Léger often described the fellow members of his squad and his sense of social isolation from them. Léger felt especially estranged from the professional soldiers for whom the war had fewer worries than civilian life did. These were soldiers for whom wine and food were the most valuable currencies, followed by items such as buttons and socks. Léger wrote about them with curiosity and admiration, at times noting what he had learned within their perilous milieu: "Money no longer existing here, all these first materials take on an enormous value. There is bread, meat, potatoes and wine [...]. I know what it is to choose potatoes. I learned not to waste bread," he wrote in a letter dated October 5, 1914.[1]

In other letters, Léger recounted his experience as a stretcher-barer (*brancardier*), such as when he carried a wounded soldier on his back, the soldier's blood running down Léger's body. The atrocious sight of human remains, he wrote, appeared to be nearly "mummified" by layers of mud.[2] But despite witnessing these and other war-time horrors, in his first year on the front Léger nevertheless continued to discuss his art practice in his letters to Poughon even while also complaining of the colorless quality of both his daily life and his drawing materials.

In a letter written during a rare moment of calm on the front in 1915, Léger drew an important parallel between the formal principles of Cubism and the violent abstraction of daily life by the organization, implementation, and mechanization of warfare:

> I am writing to you in the middle of a forest, under artillery fire and not on my knees as you might believe but sitting very comfortably under a charming arbor that opens on to a beautiful panorama. The artillerymen 'proved' (*"prouvé")* to me that I was at an angle such that no shell could reach me... they perfectly know their métier and I have the fullest confidence in them. It is, at any rate, a very curious war .... It's a perfect orchestration of all the ways of ancient and modern killing. It's intelligent down to its fingernails... It's linear and dry like a geometry problem... Everything is set off mechanically. It's pure abstraction, purer than Cubist Painting 'itself.'... It is certain that this here war couldn't be waged except by the modern folks who are waging it. [3]

Léger's elegant, if momentary, reflection on Cubism here recalls his many pre-war publications on the intellectual and formal stakes, methods, and objectives of "Contemporary Achievements in Painting"—which was the title of his 1914 address at the Academy Wassilieff (Paris), published the same year in Guillaume Apollinaire's journal, *Les Soirées de Paris*.[4] Léger had already declared in 1913 that "modern mechanical achievements such as color photography, the motion-picture camera, the profusion of more or less popular novels" had done away with all "visual, sentimental, representational, and popular subject matter in art."[5] From this starting point, we can follow the artist's changing perception of modern mechanization and its consequences, both for human life and the work of art, across his war letters. From these accounts, we can say that by around 1916 the "giant spectacle" of war had indelibly directed his approach towards a modern form (and the related concepts of modern beauty and composition), as his style unsparingly, perhaps even violently, became more rational, reduced, and "mechanized." [6]

But the industrialized timing and execution of warfare was also a dangerously monotonous force. Léger's mood in mid-November 1915 was exasperated and desperate:

> How sad everything is! How bored I am all alone in this shriveled (*ratatiné*) world and with no one to talk to about life. All newness has disappeared. We do the same gestures in the same locations, it's a mechanization, where all emotion is excluded and all this without seeing the end, without seeing even a sliver of promising light. [7]

Upon his arrival in Paris in late August 1916 on one of his few official leaves (*permission*) from duty, Léger was unaware that he would soon have an encounter with a powerful ray of light. Having been steeped in the front's morbid, desperate atmosphere, in which he and his fellow soldiers were reduced to automated killing machines, Léger one day went to a Parisian cinema venue where he first encountered the humor, gestures, movement, body, liberty, spirit, and plasticity of Charlie Chaplin and the unjust American worlds of his filmic persona, known in France as "Charlot."

Back home in the city, Charlot's performative style hit Léger right in the gut, so to speak. This film comedian, imported from the USA, had a physical comedy style that

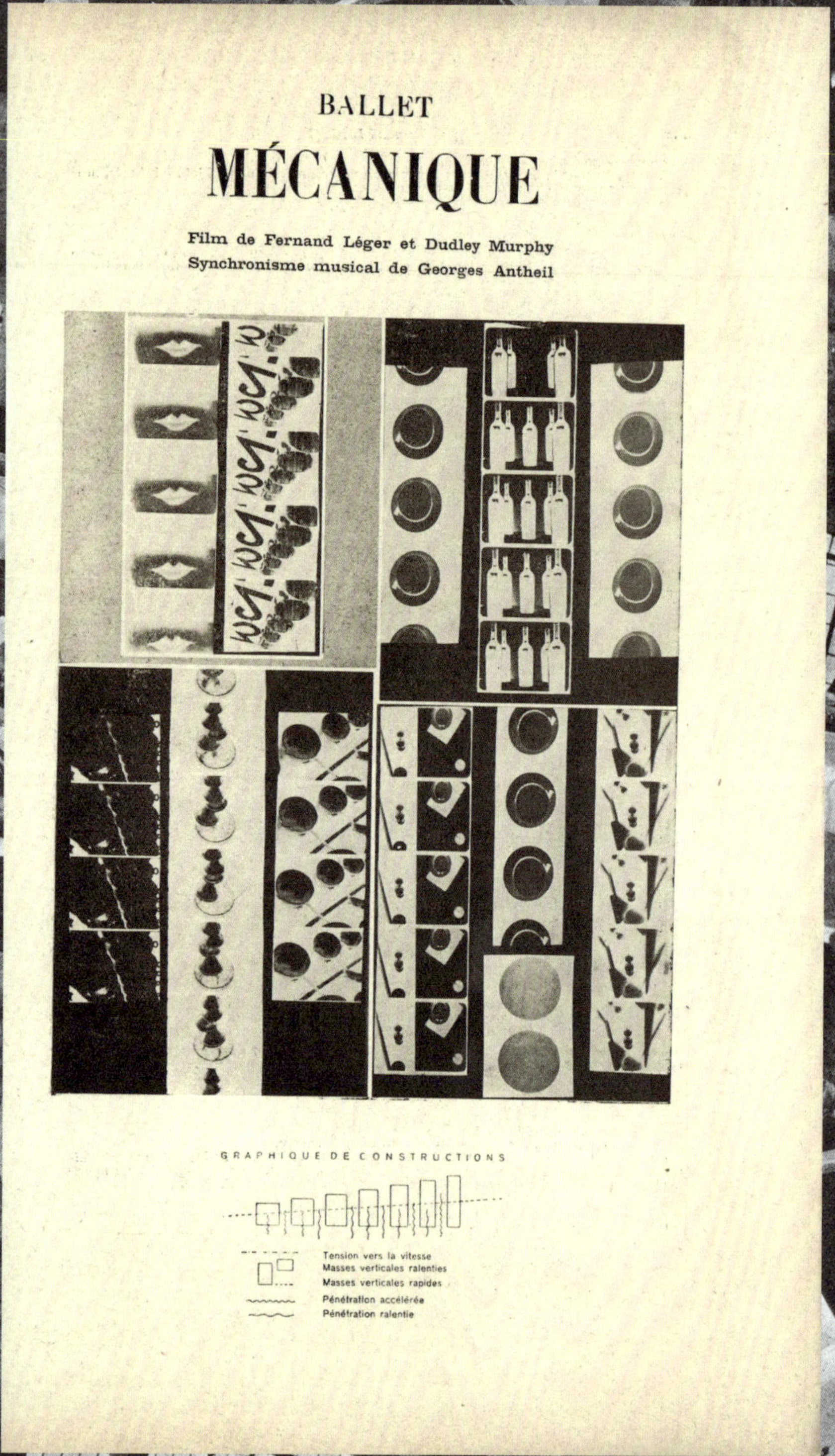

134 *L'Esprit Nouveau*, no. 28, January 1925, ed. Amédée Ozenfant, Charles-Édouard Jeanneret-Gris [Le Corbusier], Paris, 23, image by Fernand Léger: *Ballet mécanique*

8 Léger, *Chroniques du Jour*.
9 David Hunter, *Apollinaire in the Great War 1914–1918* (London: Peter Owen, 2014), 238.
10 See Jennifer Wild, *The Parisian Avant-Garde in the Age of Cinema, 1900–1924* (Berkeley, CA: University of California Press, 2015).
11 Sabine Hake, "Chaplin Reception in Weimar Germany," *New German Critique* 51 (Fall, 1990): 87–88. Hake's account is essential reading for anyone interested in these subjects, or in the historiography of the avant-garde and cinema.

infused mechanized motion with human vulnerability and emotion—a quality that had made Chaplin the first international film star. In Léger's eyes, however, Charlot's expressive filmic image also seemed to resolve a painterly problem: Léger saw Charlot as something akin to a "pure" form.

As Léger recounted in 1926, he had met up with Apollinaire, his art-world friend and fellow soldier, who had had to convince Léger to go to the movies. "We were of the opinion that everything was happening 'over there'—that life was collected on the [front] 'lines,' that the civilian zone was boredom and death."[8] And with good reason: in July, Léger had been gassed and grazed by shrapnel. Apollinaire had it even worse. Back in March he had received a serious head wound from a shell fragment and had since undergone months of medical treatment, including trepanation. When he met Léger, he is likely to have just moved back into his apartment on the Boulevard Saint-Germain des Près (7th arr.) after months of treatment in different hospitals.[9] Apollinaire went on to publish *The Poet Assassinated*, a short novel, just months later in October.

Aside from a debilitating wartime fatigue, Léger's initial reticence to go to the movies may also have been due to the lackluster offerings and atmosphere of most Parisian
69 cinema venues by wartime. Parisian cinema culture by 1914 had been utterly transformed from its early days (1900–1910) when it was a wild, largely unregulated industry for making and, importantly, showing and seeing "movies."[10] In that decade, nothing was predictable about what would be seen, or how or where one saw it. In part to compete with American and other international rivals in the new, rapidly expanding capitalist industry of moving pictures, the different arms of the French film industry (production, distribution, and exhibition) strived in tandem to define and develop a specifically French film product and experience. There were also campaigns within and outside the French film industry beginning in around 1910 that sought to transform the new leisure time technology of *le cinema* into a "real art," with adaptations of great, patrimonial works of French literature and theater.

These and other efforts to "tame," uplift or gentrify, and thereby stabilize the early cinema certainly succeeded. However, in its efforts to remake the new entertainment form into a bourgeois experience to be centered ultimately on the "masterpieces" of literature and theater, the *le cinématographe* lost its radical, disruptive appeal for much of the Parisian avant-garde. Léger grew up during the earliest and wildest days of *le cinématographe*, having been born in 1881, well before the first public screenings of moving images in 1895. By the time Léger departed for the front in 1914 at the age of thirty-three, "going to the cinema" probably felt more like "going to the theater" with precise start-times for what might be a two-and-a-half-hour film.

But suddenly, *CHARLOT*! His short films deluged screens in Paris and elsewhere across Europe, except, of course, for Germany, where Chaplin's films had started to trickle in only in 1921. While news of Charlot's films (and his image) must surely have crossed the border before then, in 1920 the Dresden publishing house Rudolf Kaemmerer released Ivan Goll's *Die Chapliniade*, illustrated by Léger. In this iconic collaboration, Goll's text, formulated as a "ciné-poème" alongside Léger's first "Cubist" distillation of Chaplin's moving image, radiantly broadcast the post-war project of the avant-garde in vibrantly cinematic terms. There is little doubt that *Die Chapliniade* was intrinsic to the "distribution" of Charlie Chaplin or Charlot among members of the German intelligentsia and the avant-garde. The scholar Sabine Hake has wonderfully described this encounter and its dénoument as a long-standing "love affair between Chaplin and an entire generation of German left-liberal intellectuals," which included Siegfried Kracauer, Walter Benjamin, Rudolf Arnheim, and many others. [11]

The censorship in Germany which had restricted Chaplin's work also meant that much of the public may not have experienced the arrival of *WESTERNS*! *Cowboys*! *Tom Mix! William Hart! Fatty! Mac Sennett and Mary Pickford!* In these American films and their heroes and heroines, French and other European audiences encountered acting and filming styles, and also landscapes, that were vastly different from contemporary European productions. The great Sessue Hayakawa introduced French audiences to a new kind of male Hollywood glamour and sex appeal with his appearance in Cecil B. DeMille's *The Cheat* (1915). For French filmmakers, DeMille's film illuminated another, altogether more modern, approach to filming, lighting, and editing (and even casting) film narratives. Most importantly, war-torn Germans missed out on the ebullient effect of Chaplin's films that had percolated across much of the rest of the war-torn European public, for Charlot's comedy and image did not discriminate in its address. Charlot was, in effect, capable of drawing in and annihilating *everyone* with laughter: from children to mothers to plumbers to soldiers on leave, from the average worker to avant-garde writers and artists and waiters alike. Charlot arrived just about everywhere to introduce a modern audience to the cinema as though for the first time.

What made Chaplin's work, and other American films, so novel in the power of their address, was that they did not aim to uplift their spectators toward the higher, contemplative realm of national "quality" with literary

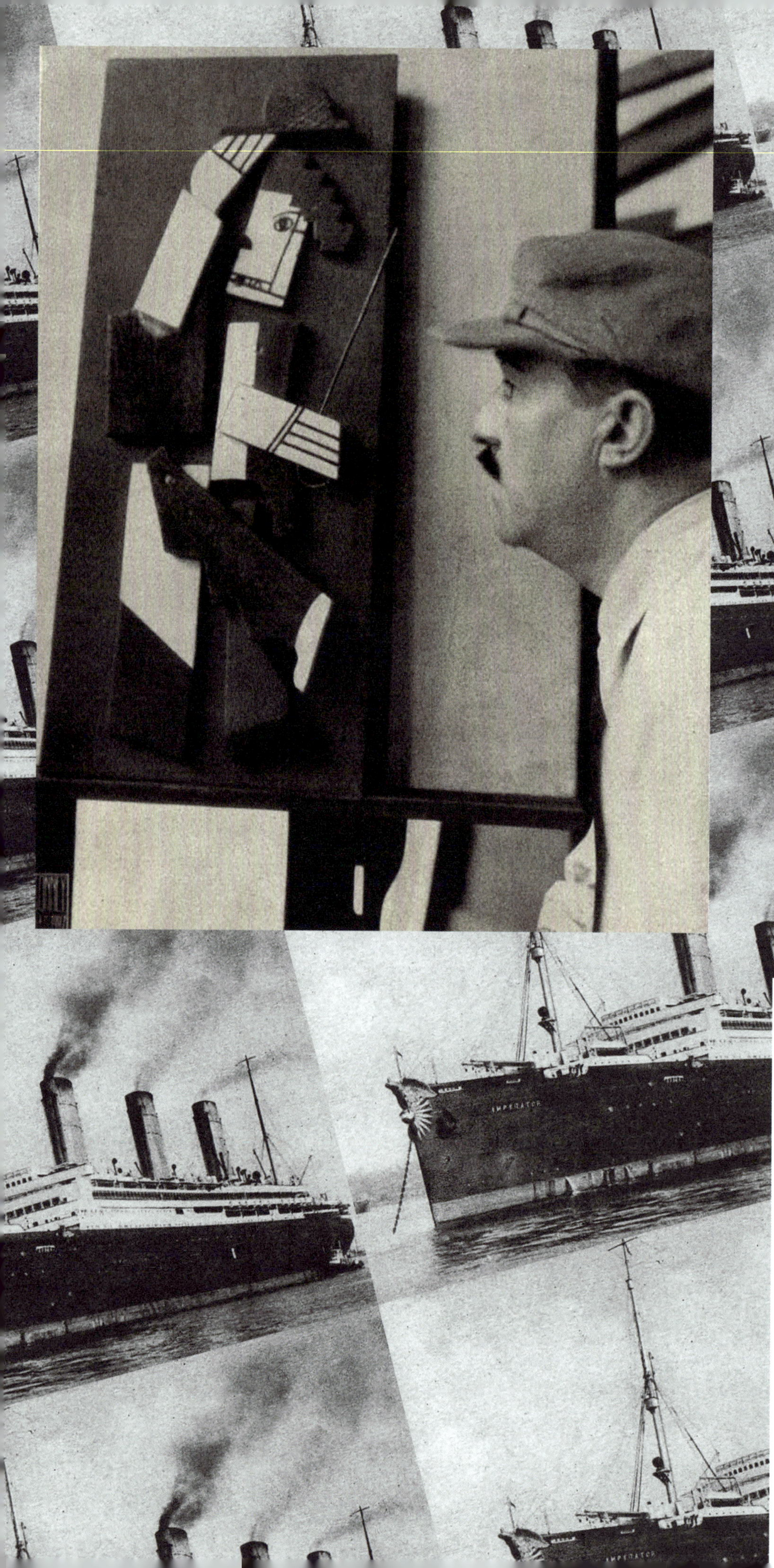

135 Thérèse Bonney, *Fernand Léger vor seinem Chaplin-Bild*, in *Der Querschnitt*, no. 8, August 1929, ed. Hermann von Wedderkop, Berlin, 552

12 Henri Michaux, “Notre frère Charlie,” *Le Disque vert* 2, numéro consacré à “Charlot (Charlie Chaplin)” no. 4–5 (1924): 17.

13 Léger, *Les Chroniques du jour*, here quoted from Gordon Hughes’ translation in “Fernand Léger’s Cinema of Pictorial Equivalence (and the Return to Disorder) *Oxford Art Journal* 44, no. 1 (2021): 69. Hughes’s essay is an important new account of Léger’s use of Chaplin in *Ballet mécanique*.

14 See Rae Beth Gordon’s groundbreaking study, *Why the French Love Jerry Lewis: From Cabaret to Early* Cinema (Stanford, CA: Stanford University Press, 2001).

15 See Di San Lazzaro, Gualtieri, “Bon à Tirer,” *Les Chroniques du Jour* 7, numéro double consacré à Charlie Chaplin (Dec. 31, 1926): 202.

16 Blaise Cendrars, *Les Chroniques du Jour*, 1926, quoted in Henry Poulaille, *Charles Chaplin* (Paris: Bernard Gasset, 1927), 114–15.

17 Léger, *Chroniques*.

18 Quoted in Hake, “Chaplin Reception in Weimar Germany,” 87–88.

19 See Nantes Museum; and Musée National Fernand Léger, *Léger et le Cinéma* (2021).

↑135

adaptations or the language of legitimate theater. Instead, American film aesthetics in this period were categorically unconcerned with addressing the spectator using tools drawn from the other arts. American films were equally unconcerned with recreating the spectator's social attitude associated with "legitimate" or "high art." Instead, and with the help of the international apparatus of American film distribution, American films in this wartime period assailed audiences with their direct address, their speed, daring, slapstick timing, their "exotic" characters and locales, on-location shooting, and the surprise and shock and laughter that was loudest when Chaplin was on screen.

Chaplin is the best, most iconic example of how the appeal of American films, like a missile that does not discriminate with its explosive power, cut across all social categories and divides in Europe and the USA alike, across all contemporary categories of class, gender, and age, or civilian versus soldier. The visual language capable of such a sweeping address came from the new medium of film. The plastic mobility of Chaplin's comic style, which allowed him to embody the misfit, the tramp, and the beggar, but also the cop, the dancer, the drunk, the cross-dresser, the waiter, the bandit, the janitor, the ice-skater, or the husband, made this English-born vaudevillian and immigrant into both a symbol of, and a figure for, the utopian promises of a modern life in American film terms. As the Belgian poet Henri Michaux wrote, "Brick layer, policeman, he is of all these professions—inside them, he is a modern soul."[12]

Chaplin's impact on audiences around the world was often profoundly transformative, not least on Léger, who affirmed "uncontestably" in 1926 that "[Charlot] was something since it helped me cope with the enormous spectacle I had just left for seven days."[13] Léger was not alone in finding solace, relief, and comfort in Chaplin, whose film comedy often struck other *poilus* similarly, delivering joyous respite in the form of sometimes uncontrollable, full-body laughter. The soldier/author Blaise Cendrars, Léger's close friend and collaborator, first heard about the Chaplin phenomenon ("Chaplinitis") while stationed on the front.[14] His remarkably vivid memory recounted below was first published in 1926, alongside Léger's account in the same issue of *Les Chroniques du Jour* devoted to "consecrating" Chaplin:[15]

> Charlot was born in the trenches (*né au front*)! I'll never forget the first time I heard about him. It was in the Bois de la Vache, an autumn evening, rainy and stormy. We were trudging in the mud [...] when Garnier, who we called Warm-piss (*Chaude-Pisse),* joined us upon returning from leave. It was 1915.... The whole night he only talked to us about Charlot.... From that night on and for every eight to fifteen days, every group of soldiers returning from leave would ram us full of new stories about Charlot.... The whole front only talked about Charlot. On the go, refueling himself, doing the water or wine errand, as the telephone operator on the end of the line, as the liaison to the .... Charlot, Charlot, Charlot.... On the left on the right, and the whole line of *poilous* behind us, we were shimmying. Charlot, Charlot, Charlot.[16]

But the comedian's visual buoyancy and plasticity on the early cinema screen was not simply a soothing distraction or a salve for Léger's war wounds. Chaplin's film-image vitally nourished Léger's concepts concerning formal composition and the human form, which became the foundation for many of his future works including his 1924 film, *Ballet mécanique,* made with the American director Dudley Murphy. Most important here is how Chaplin's image offered Léger a new model that "had nothing of theater about him." Rather, Charlot was a visual entity of pure "invention" rather than of "imitation;" he was a "mobile image" whose existence depended solely on the invention of *le cinématographe*. "[T]hey were born together, manufactured together," Léger explained. And although Léger predicted that Chaplin would not be the last American cinematographic invention to possess such power, he warned that the young country must not "become contaminated by the frightful "good taste" of the French. There lies the danger."[17]

On the one hand, Chaplin quickly became a humorous weapon in the French wartime context of the Western Front, as his character, likeness, and attitude were disseminated in military publications such as *La Baionnette,* whose authors mocked the German leader while also celebrating the absence of Chaplin's films across enemy lines. "The Germans lost the war because they didn't get to know Charlot in time," Cendrars once quipped.[18] On the other hand, throughout the 1920s Chaplin proliferated as a motif in countless works related to the international avant-garde, appearing in novels, paintings, poems, drawings, *papiers collés*, photomontage, scenarios, and still other forms. Léger's drawings for Goll's *Die Chapliniade* no doubt nourished this proliferation of Chaplin as motif.

As the recent French exhibitions and conferences on Léger have reinforced with rigor, Chaplin's body, humor, appearance, nimbleness, and comic irreverence fueled countless works of modern art, poetry, and literature whose modernism hinged on Chaplin's (and the cinema's) "low" popular culture and the experience only it afforded.[19] In a world torn asunder by the war and its mechanized means of murder, and where international exiles in Zürich devised their own anti-nationalist weapons in the Dada movement, we might say that Chaplin and his image circulated as the modern lingua franca of both the masses *and* the avant-garde.

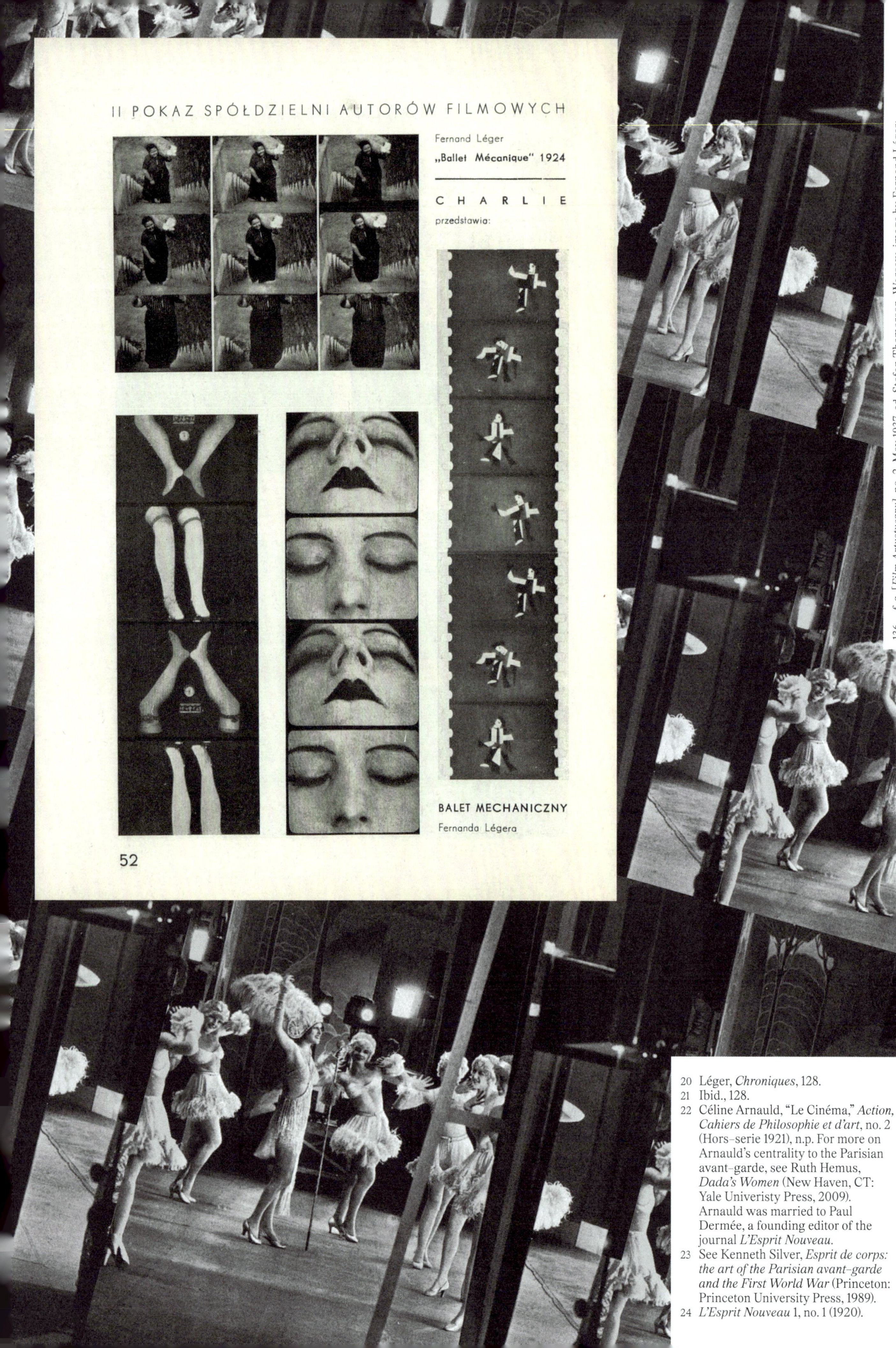
II POKAZ SPÓŁDZIELNI AUTORÓW FILMOWYCH

Fernand Léger
„Ballet Mécanique" 1924

C H A R L I E
przedstawia:

BALET MECHANICZNY
Fernanda Légera

52

136 *f.a.* [*Film Artystyczny*], no. 2, May 1937, ed. Stefan Themerson, Warsaw, image by Fernand Léger: *Balet Mechaniczny*, 52

20 Léger, *Chroniques*, 128.
21 Ibid., 128.
22 Céline Arnauld, "Le Cinéma," *Action, Cahiers de Philosophie et d'art*, no. 2 (Hors-serie 1921), n.p. For more on Arnauld's centrality to the Parisian avant-garde, see Ruth Hemus, *Dada's Women* (New Haven, CT: Yale Univeristy Press, 2009). Arnauld was married to Paul Dermée, a founding editor of the journal *L'Esprit Nouveau*.
23 See Kenneth Silver, *Esprit de corps: the art of the Parisian avant-garde and the First World War* (Princeton: Princeton University Press, 1989).
24 *L'Esprit Nouveau* 1, no. 1 (1920).

↑136 To fully appreciate how Léger's artistic practice evolved with the impact of the "discovery" of modern warfare alongside "Charlot," it is also important to address his more critical attitudes toward Chaplin and the American cinema star. These thoughts are from the same 1926 article quoted above:

> 'Cinema begins with Charlot'—it will live as long as there are Charlots for stars; but reliance upon a star, even the brightest of them, is the standard mistake.
>
> It is stars who "bring in the money," but it is also stars who bury the possibilities of cinema, killing it—preventing it from becoming a significant art form equal to the others. Charlot's weakness is that he is a star; were it within his powers to bring his whole troupe up to his level, to be the director of an ensemble rather than an "individual case," were he able to resist sacrificing the whole troupe to his personality, he might have been the greatest artistic event of our time. [20]

Here, Léger identifies the phenomenon of film stardom by underscoring that "Charlot and Charlie Chaplin are two different things."[21] In so doing, he also transmits his post-war perception of the failures of the modern regime of American film stardom: specifically, its inevitable
73 overshadowing and eventual consumption of the original, utopian promise of the cinematographic experience that was first made visible by Charlot's "arrival" onto French screens in around 1915. Although Léger stops short of indicting Hollywood by name (indeed, he never mentions the industry's Los Angeles base), he nevertheless criticizes Chaplin for, in essence, failing to sacrifice his relationship with stardom, or what can only be called the official currency of Hollywood or American industrial cinema.

While Léger's words may reveal a hierarchy governing his own aesthetic values (here with respect to the picture plane versus the effects of the Hollywood star-machine), other avant-garde artists were even more critical of Chaplin's evolution in the 1920s when his films grew longer and more grounded in the formal templates of Hollywood narrative and visual style, or mise-en-scène. Writing about *The Kid* (1921), Céline Arnauld, Dadaist and active avant-garde writer, was strident in her distaste of Chaplin's film: "This smells strongly of bad literature!"[22] At this time, Chaplin's star power also grew so monumental—so official—that by 1921 it could eclipse the memory of that guy "Charlot," from the trenches, as it were. Indeed, when Charles Chaplin visited Paris in 1921 for the release of *The Kid*, he also acted in an official capacity. He was raising money for the French state's post-war reconstruction efforts, apparently meeting only with dignitaries and aristocrats and visiting storied, patrimonial venues such as *la Comédie Française*. Whereas Chaplin's image once stood for the radical disorder of war-time absurdity and resistance, increasingly in the post-First World War era, his star-body was transformed into a more stable, often "consecrated" figure of post-war humanism, decorum, and, arguably, the order of the State.

For Léger and his generation of veterans, however, Chaplin's image remained tightly bound up with war-time experience and the formal development of modern painting, especially after Cubism. Works belonging to Léger's "Chaplin archive," or works that explicitly depict Charlot, largely relate to the creative processes associated with the film *Ballet mécanique*. Scholars agree that Léger's illustrations for Goll's *Die Chapliniade* were likely a preparatory step for his 1924 wood assemblages, titled *Charlot Cubiste*. These, in turn, were likely used to create the animated sequence "Charlot Cubiste Présent" that opens Léger's and Murphy's film. Léger's approach to mechanical bodily form that he first developed in drawings done at the front, and then revised for Goll's project, are still resonant in *Charlot Cubiste*. Like his earlier war-time sketches, the assemblage retains the suggestion of movement or motion, especially considering the balanced use of black and white colored segments.

To understand the Parisian artistic milieu in the post-war period, it is important to remember that it percolated with competing arguments regarding how to advance the avant-garde project in the post-war and "post-Cubist" era. This position was taken up in the 1918 essay "Après le Cubism" (After Cubism) by the artist-architect Charles-Edouard Jeanneret (or Le Corbusier) and artist-writer Amédée Ozenfant. Two years later in 1920, the two would initiate the Purist movement with their journal *L'Esprit Nouveau,* which served to amplify their voice in the post-war, avant-garde debates. Today, Purism's legacy belongs to a more general "return to order" (*retour à l'ordre*) trend among French artists after the war, who turned to more classical pictorial and compositional values.[23] Specific to Purism's and *L'Esprit Nouveau*'s system of orderly form and value was the positive valuation of the machine and all that was mechanical or mechanized. The journal's three-part opening salvo to its readers consisted of a declaration ("L'ESPRIT NOUVEAU EST LA PREMIERE REVUE DU MONDE VRAIMENT CONSACRÉE A L'ESTHETIQUE VIVANTE"); a statement ("DOMAINE DE L'ESPRIT NOUVEAU"); and a detailed examination of Purism's primary aesthetic concerns, the first of which was "L'ESTHETIQUE MÉCANIQUE" (The Mechanical Aesthetic).[24] Every aspect of modern life was subjected to the editors' query into "the new spirit," from urbanism and architecture to music, dance, the cinema, literature, and even physics. The Purist enterprise continually turned on examining

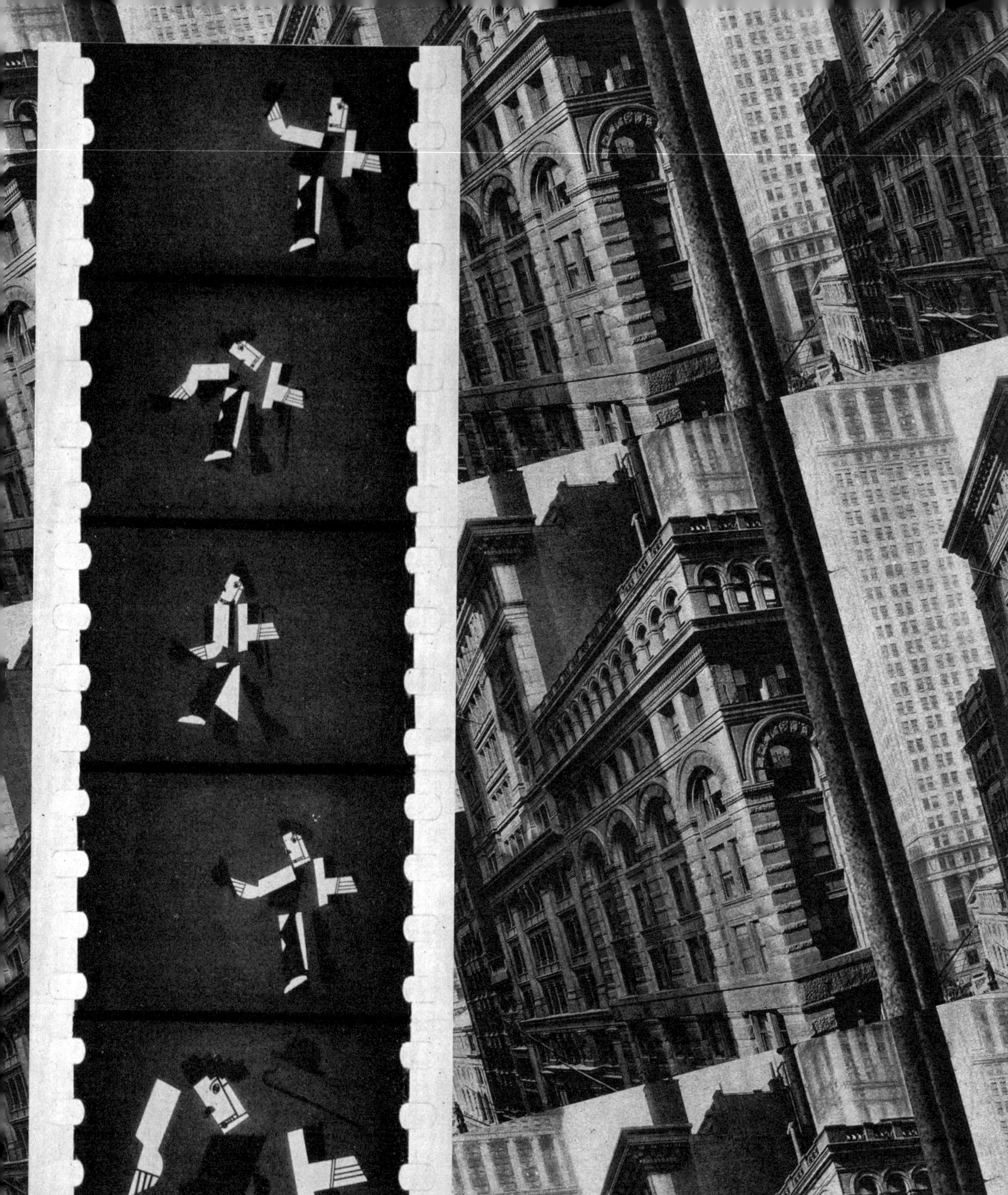

137 Fernand Léger, *Mechanisches Ballet*, in Hans Richter, *Filmgegner von Heute – Filmfreunde von Morgen*, Berlin: Verlag Hermann Reckendorf 1929, 9

25 *L'Esprit Nouveau* 4, no. 18 (1923).
26 See François Albera, "Fernand Léger et 'l'affiche-arrêt': la Roue, l'Inhumaine," *1895*, no. 81 (2017).
27 Elie Faure, "Charlot", *L'Esprit Nouveau* 2, no. 6 (1921): 657–666.
28 Fernand Léger, "Ballet Mecanique," *L'Esprit Nouveau* 6, no. 28 (1925).
29 Amédée Ozenfant and Charles Édouard Jeanneret, "Le Purisme," *L'Esprit Nouveau* 1, no. 4 (1920): 369–386.
30 Fernand Léger, "The Machine Aesthetic: Geometric Order and Truth" (1925), in *Functions of Painting*.
31 Maurice Raynal, "F. Léger," *L'Esprit Nouveau* 1, no. 4 (1920): 429.

the principles of mechanical rationality, even as it was expressed in systems, nature, movement, institutions, and institutionality.

Léger's post-war painting was featured prominently in *L'Esprit Nouveau* as early as 1920. The journal then tracked his 1923 collaboration with the Ballets Suédois's theatrical production of Cendrars' *La Création du Monde*.[25] By this time, Léger had already become a very active collaborator within the French film industry, designing posters, sets, or mise-en-scène for Abel Gance's and Marcel l'Herbier's large-scale, "experimental" narrative productions.[26] Even as *L'Esprit Nouveau* often published articles on the cinema including, for example, articles devoted to Chaplin by the prominent art historian Elie Faure, Ozenfant and Jeanneret ignored Léger's creative contributions to the French film industry.[27] They did, however, pay special attention to Léger's and Murphy's film *Ballet mécanique* with a two-page illustrated feature in 1925. Curiously, Léger seemingly designed the pages to function like a press release and a manual for how to understand this non-narrative, arguably Purist film experiment. In keeping with the rational tone of Purist thought, Léger's statement on the film is organized as a series of explanations about film shot scale, the different shutter speeds of the film footage, and his combined (and collaborative) strategies for the editing and composition "of similar object-images, or those of the same nature." [28]

In these pages of *L'Esprit Nouveau*, Léger presents a radically scaled-down version of *Ballet mécanique,* in what was at the time an utterly singular example of a painter's artistic exploration with the medium of film. In his written and visual account in the journal, Léger reduces the film to an array of mechanical and cinematographic principles, including their effects. He thereby casts it as a Purist "system," or an architecture for achieving "sensations" in the viewer by way of form. We might say that Léger frames the film, in the words of Jeanneret and Ozenfant, as "an artificial formation which, by appropriate means, should lead to the objectification of an entire world." [29]

One consequence of Léger's intellectual approach here is that Chaplin or Charlot are never mentioned. In fact, Charlot's singularly identifiable image, which importantly opens the film in what can only be understood as an animated homage to Charlot's epic wartime power, has apparently been absorbed into the film's mechanical processes. We might note that Léger's effacement of Chaplin within his scientifically dry, theoretical presentation of *Ballet mécanique* is consistent with his point of view a few years later: that Chaplin's greatest failure was in remaining an "individual case" within a performative and formal ensemble. As Léger explained, in the end Charlot was simply incapable of forgoing the effects of Hollywood stardom to achieve the stricter aesthetic goals of absolute formal unity, equity, balance, and democracy in the materials and motifs of an art work or film.

In these terms, had Léger directly included Chaplin's name or image, especially in the Purist context of *L'Esprit Nouveau* , Charlot's star power would have garnered all the attention. It would have effaced Léger and his precise work in advancing the avant-garde project beyond Cubism into a yet undiscovered future of formal purity and filmic practice. Otherwise, *Ballet mécanique* might easily have become just another advertisement for a new Chaplin film; or, like Goll's modernist experiment, it may have been registered in history primarily as another paean to the democratic power of the cinematic machine that Chaplin represented as a prolific avant-garde motif.

These outcomes were never Léger's goal, of course, in doing the deeply collaborative work of shooting and editing celluloid in the early 1920s, and in opening *Ballet mécanique* with the animated sequence, "Charlot Cubiste." In all of his experiments—in *Ballet mécanique* and in those that had earlier taken place on paper and canvas from his 1916 discovery of Charlot onward—Léger strived with insistence and severity to transform the brutal lessons from the front into a corresponding procedure for organizing and composing his tableau and its subject matter: "A nail, a stub of candle, a shoelace can cost a man's life or a regiment's... *there is no longer anything of negligible value*. Everything counts, everything competes, and the scale of ordinary and conventional values is overturned," he wrote in 1925.[30] The resulting style was one that severely "stripped itself down," as Maurice Raynal, the prolific champion of avant-garde art and early film critic, wrote in *L'Esprit Nouveau* (1920), attributing this post-war evolution in Léger's canvases both to his survival of the war itself, and "[t]he hypertrophic development of the individual" that it encouraged.[31]

In the simplest terms, the highest ambition behind Léger's restraint in the post-war period was the complete and radical democratization of all forms—from bodies to machines to objects and nature. In this order of values, there simply couldn't be any "stars" in the presentation of *Ballet mécanique* to the readers of *L'Esprit Nouveau* in 1925—neither Chaplin nor Léger could claim this status (he was emphatic about the collaborative nature of the project). In 1916, Charlot's comedy no doubt erupted memorably from the screen to overtake the bodies of war-weary soldiers, artists, and civilians alike during the exponential growth of Chaplin, the star. But Léger's omission of Charlot from a taut, diagrammatic presentation of the film in such a prominent avant-garde journal reminds us that Charlot may never have been a "weapon"

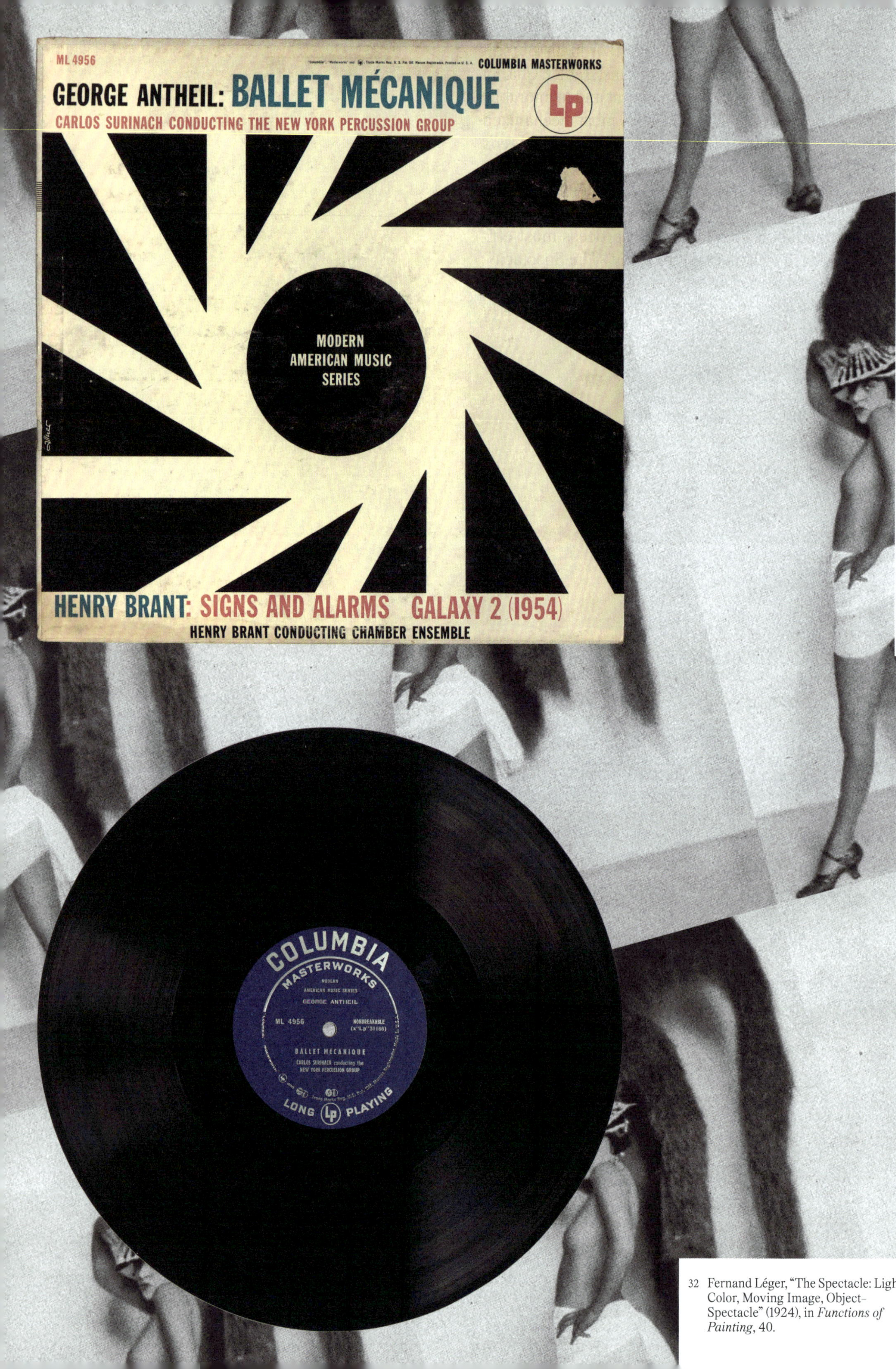

138 George Antheil, *Ballet mécanique*, Henry Brant, *Signs and Alarms / Galaxy 2 (1954)*, New York: Columbia Records 1955, sleeve; vinyl record

32 Fernand Léger, "The Spectacle: Light, Color, Moving Image, Object-Spectacle" (1924), in *Functions of Painting*, 40.

↑138

in Léger's war against sentimental art, or in his pursuit for the unequivocal liberation of all forms. Rather, Charlot may have been just one (albeit important and memorable) *form* from Léger's life at the front—the most mechanized and powerfully violent spectacle of his lifetime. Léger's exclusion of Charlot from his introduction of *Ballet mécanique* in the journal might be best understood as an expression—or step—in his process of modern aesthetic democratization. He explained this process most efficiently and elegantly in his 1924 essay "The Spectacle": "Very gently make the 'little fellow' disappear. I swear to you that the stage will not be empty, for we are going to make *the objects act.*"[32]

Taylorism, Fordism, and Anti-Capitalist Views: America as Utopia and Dystopia

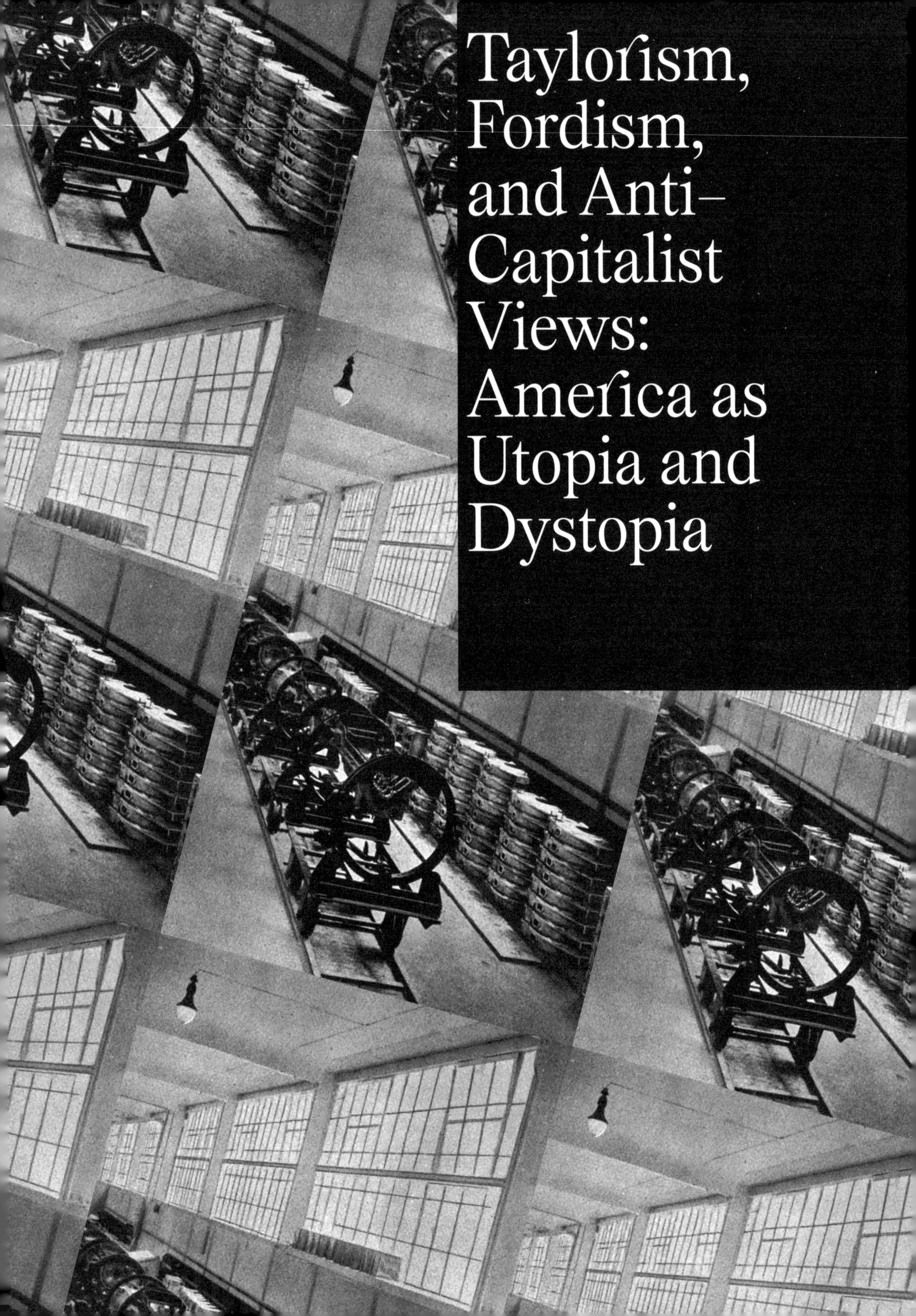

In the early 1900s, Taylorism and Fordism changed the working system in US factories and defined a new approach towards interactions between workers and machines. Taylorism, conceived by American engineer Frederick Winslow Taylor, was a method of work organization and discipline based on scientific investigations of labor efficiency. He detailed a division of labor in time-and-motion studies and proposed a wage system based on performance. Taylorism soon became the dominant scientific-technical way of organizing work in Henry Ford's car factory in Detroit. Ford's methods, labelled Fordism, were characterized by rationalization, industrial mass production, and the standardisation of work on the assembly line. Ford promised higher wages for workers and created a working environment conducive to manufacturing affordable cars at low cost. Taylorism and Fordism thus strengthened the belief that social problems and class inequalities could be solved through capitalist enterprise.

Fiat's operations at its European car factory were inspired by Ford's organizational and production methods. The company applied Taylorist principles of time management and boasted the longest production line in Europe with the latest manufacturing machinery. The new Fiat Factory building in Lingotto, completed in 1923, was hailed for its architecture, with an oval open-air rooftop track which could be used to test run the newly assembled cars. Photographs of the factory circulated in avant-garde publications such as the magazine *L'Esprit Nouveau*, edited by Purists in Paris, and the magazine *G*, published by the Berlin-based group of Constructivists. Associates of both magazines recognized the cultural importance of Taylorism as a fundamental component of social renewal. They were interested in how the application of Fordism in car production could contribute to the new patterns of avant-garde practices and modernist architecture.

In Weimar Germany, meanwhile, the hopes for prosperity and corresponding expectations of Fordist production methods were strictly embodied in a phenomenon known as *Amerikanismus* (Americanism). This term, which originated in the mid-1920s, was an expression of the concept of America as a symbol of freedom and democracy, a place where a new, modern, popular culture and lifestyle were inseparably linked to industrial-technical modernity and the economic boom that had been made possible by Taylorism and Fordism. *Amerikanismus* also had a political aspect connected to the Dawes Plan, which had authorized a large loan from American banks to help stabilize and stimulate the German economy, which had been left in ruins at the end of the war. At the same time, this new US-oriented phenomenon was critically viewed from the perspective of German leftist movements. The circles of the artistic left were initially interested in the new American systems of work, because Henry Ford had raised his workers' salaries. However, they soon realized that Fordism was closely linked to the exploitation of the working class. Anti-capitalist and anti-Fordist sentiments, which were directed against the idealized concept of Roaring Twenties America, gradually spread among left-leaning artists both in the US and in Europe. These sentiments were strengthened in 1927 by the executions by electric chair of two Italian workers, Nicola Sacco and Bartolomeo Vanzetti, who had been unjustly convicted. Their deaths caused a global outrage against the undemocratic system of justice in the US. The so-called Sacco and Vanzetti case was largely commented upon in the leftist press, including *New Masses* in New York and *Arbeiter-Illustrierte-Zeitung* (Workers' Illustrated Newspaper) in Berlin. The global support for freeing the convicted men can be regarded as one of the earliest examples of transatlantic activism against the unjust capitalist system.

Avant-garde artists were faced with the stark choice of whether to follow capitalism and the technological methods of rationalization derived from new systems of work provided by Taylorism and Fordism, or to dismiss the idealized image of America, where the values of freedom and democracy were being disrespected. From the mid-1920s, leftist and socially engaged avant-garde artists in Europe often adopted a critical stance against American politics and lifestyle and the exploitation of the working class through the capitalist system, for which Taylorism and Fordism were regarded as models. The socio-political problems of the 1920s culminated in the 1929 global crash and continued during the times of the Great Depression, which shifted the idealized concept of America towards negative connotations, with an emphasis on racial problems, exploitation, backwardness, homelessness, and imperialist ambitions. The icon of the Roaring Twenties—Charlie Chaplin—would best present this image in his famous 1936 movie *Modern Times*, which offered a critique of Taylorism and Fordism and simultaneously of the idealized Machine Age aesthetics.

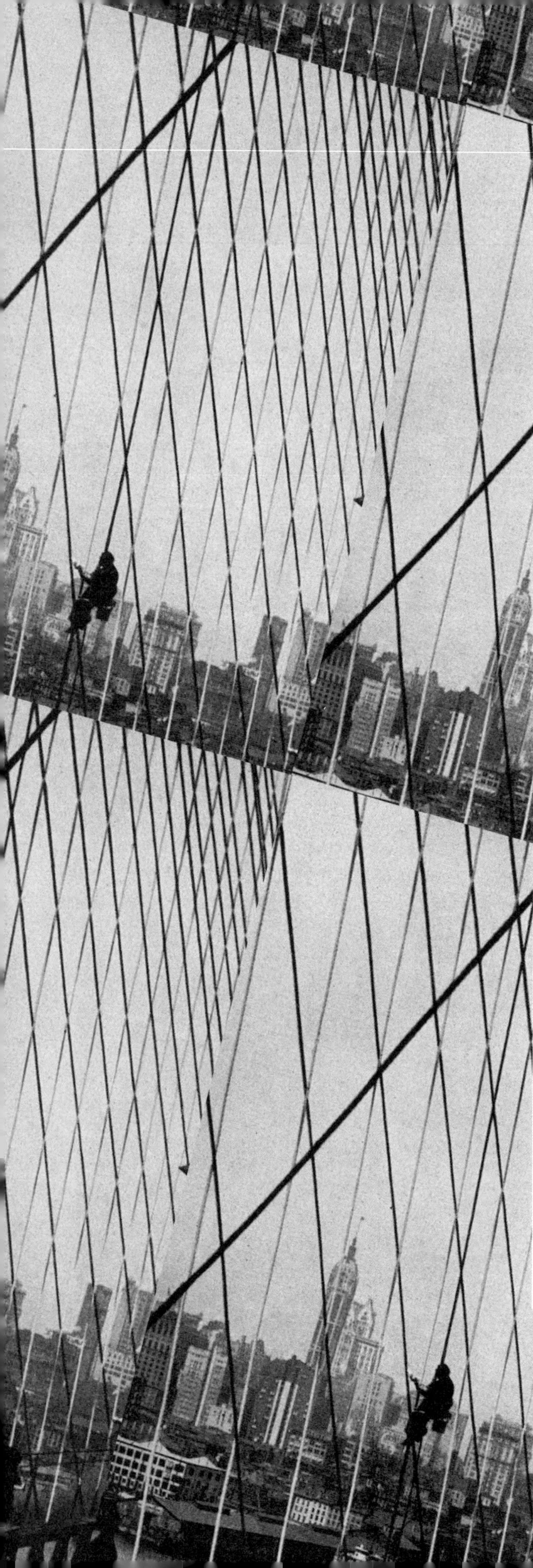

TAYLORISM-FORDISM AS A MODEL FOR MACHINE AGE AVANT-GARDES

"A roaring motorcar, which seems to race on like machine-gun fire, is more beautiful than the Winged Victory of Samothrace." This famous statement, from Filippo Tommaso Marinetti's *Manifesto of Futurism* (1909), defined the beginnings of the first avant-garde movement. The shift from an interest in automobiles in arts and literature towards a focus on automobile production in industry became visible in the new artistic vanguards that emerged in the 1920s: French Purism, and Constructivism in Germany, Czechoslovakia, and Poland. Some members of these groups were highly aware of the cultural importance of car production, both in socio-political and aesthetic terms. They often treated the automobile as the result of the collective work of inventors, engineers, designers, and workers. At the same time, Fordist production methods were recognized as the perfect model of rationalized, economical, and efficient work organization, which, as some avant-garde artists called for, had to be applied to art.

In the early 1920s, Taylorism and Fordism became models for Purist and Constructivist avant-garde practices in Europe. American theories of scientific management and the invention of conveyor belt production inspired such artists and architects as Le Corbusier, Ludwig Hilberseimer, and Władysław Strzemiński, who linked artistic practice to efficient and collective work. Photographs of cars and car parts often circulated via avant-garde magazines and publications, in which they were presented as symbols of the new beauty of the Machine Age. They appeared in the early 1920s in the Purist magazine *L'Esprit Nouveau* in Paris, and in Constructivist magazines in Central and Eastern Europe: *G* in Berlin, *Život* in Prague, and *Blok* in Warsaw. Some artists connected to these avant-garde groups highlighted the car as a perfect model of modern creation and design. Some of them also believed that thanks to the new methods of organization and rationalization of work, the problems of unemployment and the exploitation of the working class could be systemically and comprehensively solved. However, in the years to come, the Constructivist groups linked to the artistic left increasingly criticized these methods as modes of exploitation of the working class.

↓140 ↓139

139 see 117, cover by Fernand Léger
140 *Broom*, no. 3, October 1922, ed. Harold A. Loeb, Berlin/New York/London, cover by Enrico Prampolini

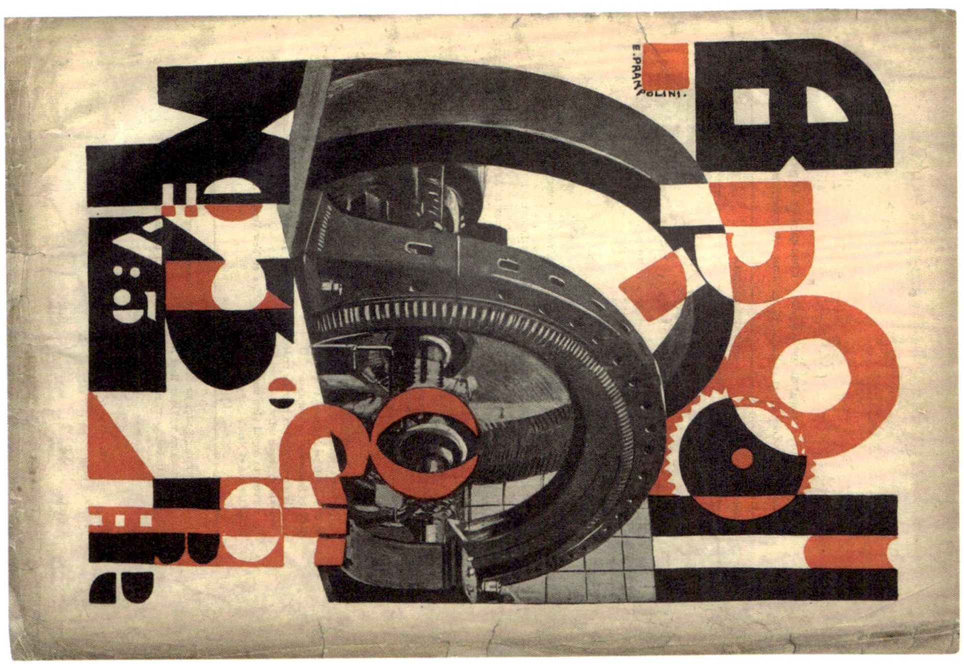

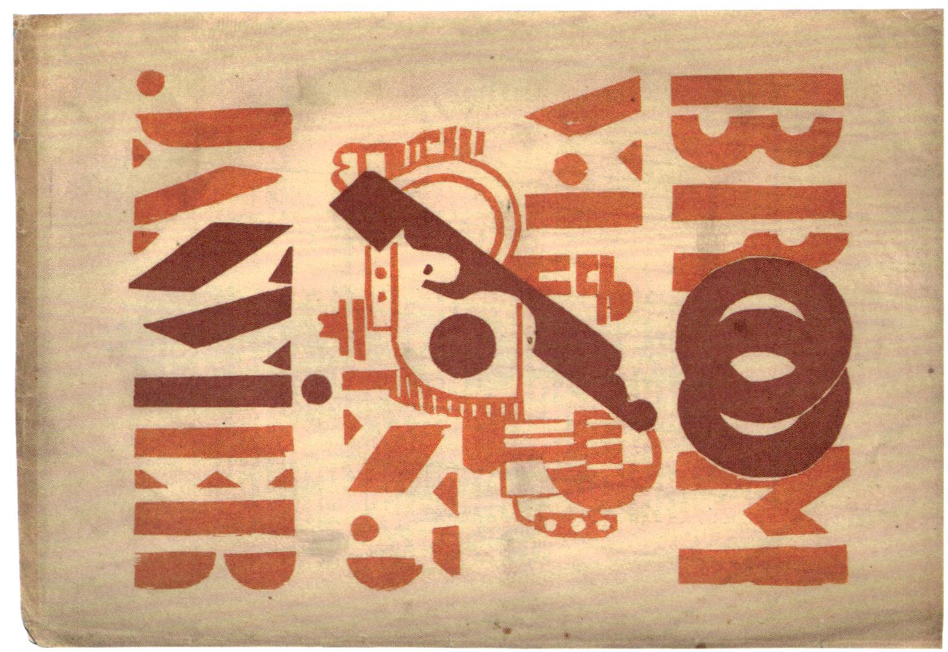

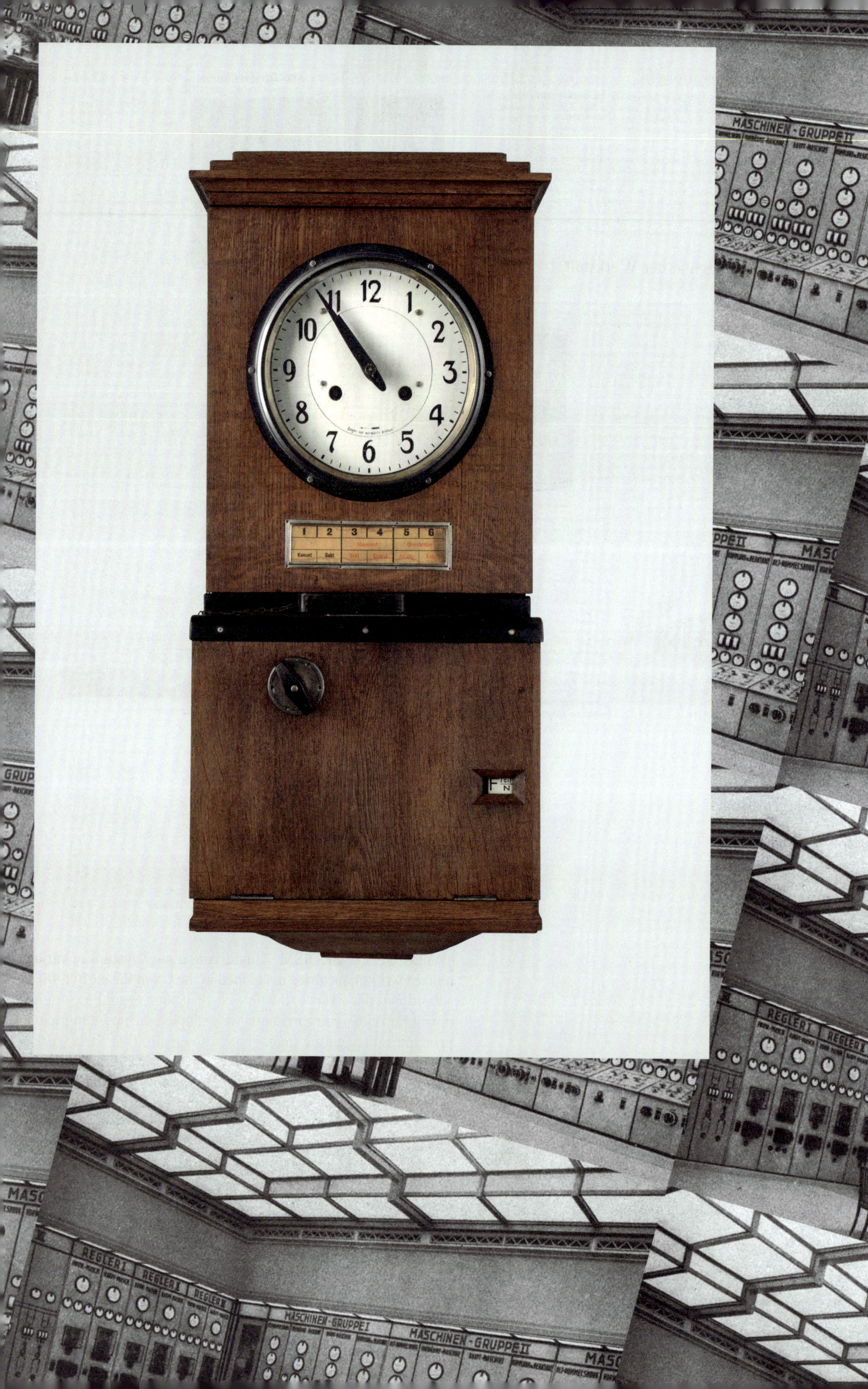

141 AEG [Allgemeine Elektricitäts-Gesellschaft Berlin], *Arbeiter-Kontrolluhr, P. L. No. 4181, Typ RH 2*, presumably from 1921

142 *AEG-Mitteilungen*, no. 7, July 1927, ed. Allgemeine Elektricitäts-Gesellschaft, Berlin, 302–303

↓142 ↑141

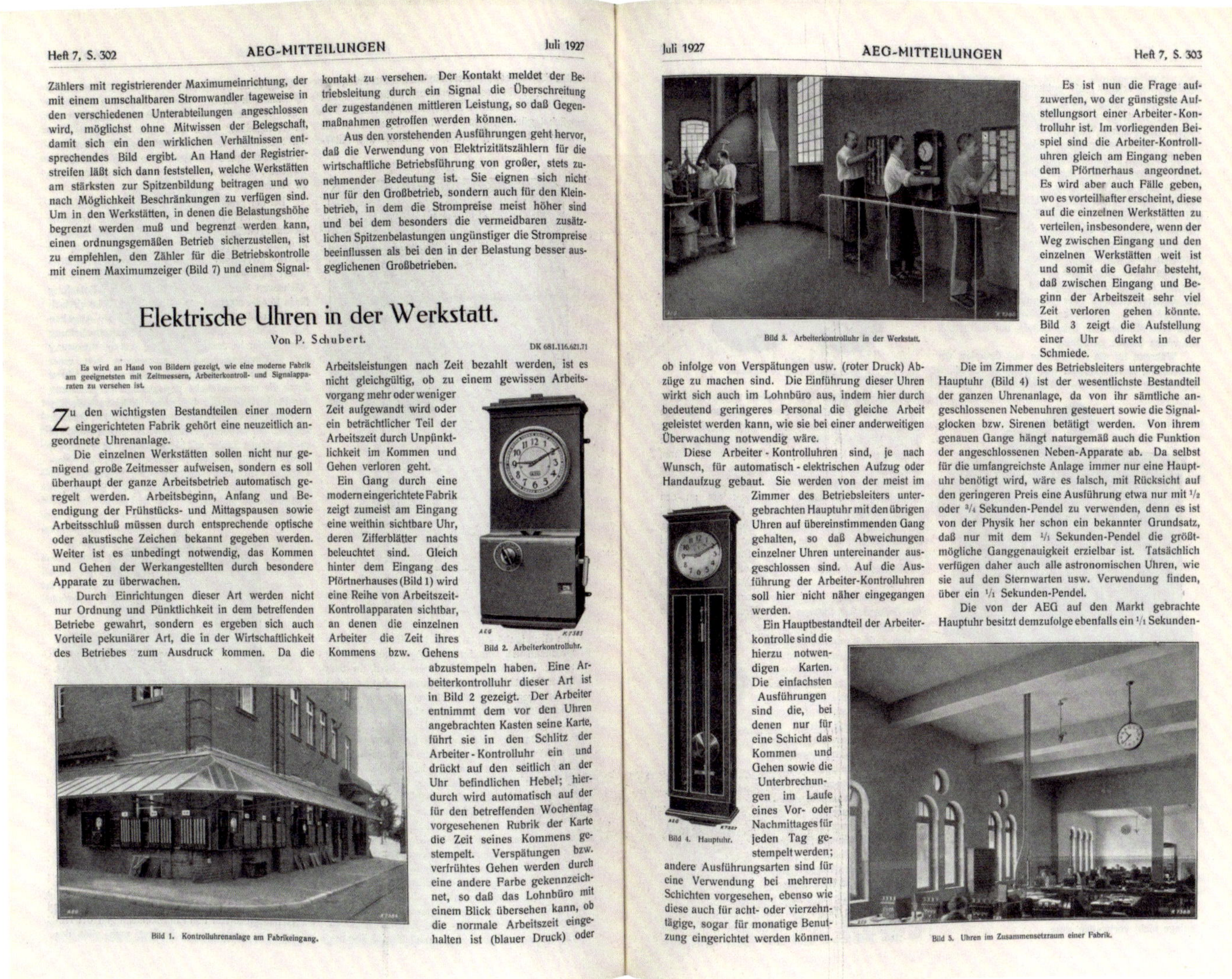

Zählers mit registrierender Maximumeinrichtung, der mit einem umschaltbaren Stromwandler tageweise in den verschiedenen Unterabteilungen angeschlossen wird, möglichst ohne Mitwissen der Belegschaft, damit sich ein den wirklichen Verhältnissen entsprechendes Bild ergibt. An Hand der Registrierstreifen läßt sich dann feststellen, welche Werkstätten am stärksten zur Spitzenbildung beitragen und wo nach Möglichkeit Beschränkungen zu verfügen sind. Um in den Werkstätten, in denen die Belastungshöhe begrenzt werden muß und begrenzt werden kann, einen ordnungsgemäßen Betrieb sicherzustellen, ist zu empfehlen, den Zähler für die Betriebskontrolle mit einem Maximumzeiger (Bild 7) und einem Signalkontakt zu versehen. Der Kontakt meldet der Betriebsleitung durch ein Signal die Überschreitung der zugestandenen mittleren Leistung, so daß Gegenmaßnahmen getroffen werden können.

Aus den vorstehenden Ausführungen geht hervor, daß die Verwendung von Elektrizitätszählern für die wirtschaftliche Betriebsführung von großer, stets zunehmender Bedeutung ist. Sie eignen sich nicht nur für den Großbetrieb, sondern auch für den Kleinbetrieb, in dem die Strompreise meist höher sind und bei dem besonders die vermeidbaren zusätzlichen Spitzenbelastungen ungünstiger die Strompreise beeinflussen als bei den in der Belastung besser ausgeglichenen Großbetrieben.

Elektrische Uhren in der Werkstatt.

Von P. Schubert.

DK 681.116.621.71

Es wird an Hand von Bildern gezeigt, wie eine moderne Fabrik am geeignetsten mit Zeitmessern, Arbeiterkontroll- und Signalapparaten zu versehen ist.

Zu den wichtigsten Bestandteilen einer modern eingerichteten Fabrik gehört eine neuzeitlich angeordnete Uhrenanlage.

Die einzelnen Werkstätten sollen nicht nur genügend große Zeitmesser aufweisen, sondern es soll überhaupt der ganze Arbeitsbetrieb automatisch geregelt werden. Arbeitsbeginn, Anfang und Beendigung der Frühstücks- und Mittagspausen sowie Arbeitsschluß müssen durch entsprechende optische oder akustische Zeichen bekannt gegeben werden. Weiter ist es unbedingt notwendig, das Kommen und Gehen der Werkangestellten durch besondere Apparate zu überwachen.

Durch Einrichtungen dieser Art werden nicht nur Ordnung und Pünktlichkeit in dem betreffenden Betriebe gewahrt, sondern es ergeben sich auch Vorteile pekuniärer Art, die in der Wirtschaftlichkeit des Betriebes zum Ausdruck kommen. Da die Arbeitsleistungen nach Zeit bezahlt werden, ist es nicht gleichgültig, ob zu einem gewissen Arbeitsvorgang mehr oder weniger Zeit aufgewandt wird oder ein beträchtlicher Teil der Arbeitszeit durch Unpünktlichkeit im Kommen und Gehen verloren geht.

Ein Gang durch eine modern eingerichtete Fabrik zeigt zumeist am Eingang eine weithin sichtbare Uhr, deren Zifferblätter nachts beleuchtet sind. Gleich hinter dem Eingang des Pförtnerhauses (Bild 1) wird eine Reihe von Arbeitszeit-Kontrollapparaten sichtbar, an denen die einzelnen Arbeiter die Zeit ihres Kommens bzw. Gehens abzustempeln haben. Eine Arbeiterkontrolluhr dieser Art ist in Bild 2 gezeigt. Der Arbeiter entnimmt dem vor den Uhren angebrachten Kasten seine Karte, führt sie in den Schlitz der Arbeiter-Kontrolluhr ein und drückt auf den seitlich an der Uhr befindlichen Hebel; hierdurch wird automatisch auf der für den betreffenden Wochentag vorgesehenen Rubrik der Karte die Zeit seines Kommens gestempelt. Verspätungen bzw. verfrühtes Gehen werden durch eine andere Farbe gekennzeichnet, so daß das Lohnbüro mit einem Blick übersehen kann, ob die normale Arbeitszeit eingehalten ist (blauer Druck) oder ob infolge von Verspätungen usw. (roter Druck) Abzüge zu machen sind. Die Einführung dieser Uhren wirkt sich auch im Lohnbüro aus, indem hier durch bedeutend geringeres Personal die gleiche Arbeit geleistet werden kann, wie sie bei einer anderweitigen Überwachung notwendig wäre.

Bild 2. Arbeiterkontrolluhr.

Bild 1. Kontrolluhrenanlage am Fabrikeingang.

Bild 3. Arbeiterkontrolluhr in der Werkstatt.

Diese Arbeiter-Kontrolluhren sind, je nach Wunsch, für automatisch-elektrischen Aufzug oder Handaufzug gebaut. Sie werden von der meist im Zimmer des Betriebsleiters untergebrachten Hauptuhr mit den übrigen Uhren auf übereinstimmenden Gang gehalten, so daß Abweichungen einzelner Uhren untereinander ausgeschlossen sind. Auf die Ausführung der Arbeiter-Kontrolluhren soll hier nicht näher eingegangen werden.

Ein Hauptbestandteil der Arbeiterkontrolle sind die hierzu notwendigen Karten. Die einfachsten Ausführungen sind die, bei denen nur für eine Schicht das Kommen und Gehen sowie die Unterbrechungen im Laufe eines Vor- oder Nachmittages für jeden Tag gestempelt werden; andere Ausführungsarten sind für eine Verwendung bei mehreren Schichten vorgesehen, ebenso wie diese auch für acht- oder vierzehntägige, sogar für monatige Benutzung eingerichtet werden können.

Bild 4. Hauptuhr.

Es ist nun die Frage aufzuwerfen, wo der günstigste Aufstellungsort einer Arbeiter-Kontrolluhr ist. Im vorliegenden Beispiel sind die Arbeiter-Kontrolluhren gleich am Eingang neben dem Pförtnerhaus angeordnet. Es wird aber auch Fälle geben, wo es vorteilhafter erscheint, diese auf die einzelnen Werkstätten zu verteilen, insbesondere, wenn der Weg zwischen Eingang und den einzelnen Werkstätten weit ist und somit die Gefahr besteht, daß zwischen Eingang und Beginn der Arbeitszeit sehr viel Zeit verloren gehen könnte. Bild 3 zeigt die Aufstellung einer Uhr direkt in der Schmiede.

Die im Zimmer des Betriebsleiters untergebrachte Hauptuhr (Bild 4) ist der wesentlichste Bestandteil der ganzen Uhrenanlage, da von ihr sämtliche angeschlossenen Nebenuhren gesteuert sowie die Signalglocken bzw. Sirenen betätigt werden. Von ihrem genauen Gange hängt naturgemäß auch die Funktion der angeschlossenen Neben-Apparate ab. Da selbst für die umfangreichste Anlage immer nur eine Hauptuhr benötigt wird, wäre es falsch, mit Rücksicht auf den geringeren Preis eine Ausführung etwa nur mit $^{1}/_{2}$ oder $^{3}/_{4}$ Sekunden-Pendel zu verwenden, denn es ist von der Physik her schon ein bekannter Grundsatz, daß nur mit dem $^{1}/_{1}$ Sekunden-Pendel die größtmögliche Ganggenauigkeit erzielbar ist. Tatsächlich verfügen daher auch alle astronomischen Uhren, wie sie auf den Sternwarten usw. Verwendung finden, über ein $^{1}/_{1}$ Sekunden-Pendel.

Die von der AEG auf den Markt gebrachte Hauptuhr besitzt demzufolge ebenfalls ein $^{1}/_{1}$ Sekunden-

Bild 5. Uhren im Zusammensetzraum einer Fabrik.

TAYLORISM–FORDISM Taylorism, a new system of rationalized work in factories developed in the US in the early 1900s, subordinated workers to the time clock. It soon caught the attention of European entrepreneurs, who adapted the new American principles of scientific management to ensure that their workers would be more productive and efficient. Before the First World War, the Zeiss Company was the first German adopter of Taylor's scientific management, and other companies, such as AEG, Bosch, Borsig, and Siemens were also urged to follow American methods of work organization in factories. Around the time of the First World War, Taylorism heavily influenced the German and Italian car industries and became inseparably associated with Fordism. In 1920, the Fiat factory in Turin witnessed a huge wave of protests from workers in the famous "clock hand strike" directed against the time-management system. The general strike began after a worker was dismissed for turning back the clock. One of the best-known criticisms of Taylorist-Fordist concepts of work regulation later became a major theme in Chaplin's *Modern Times* (1936), which dealt with the negative effects of automobile work in factories.

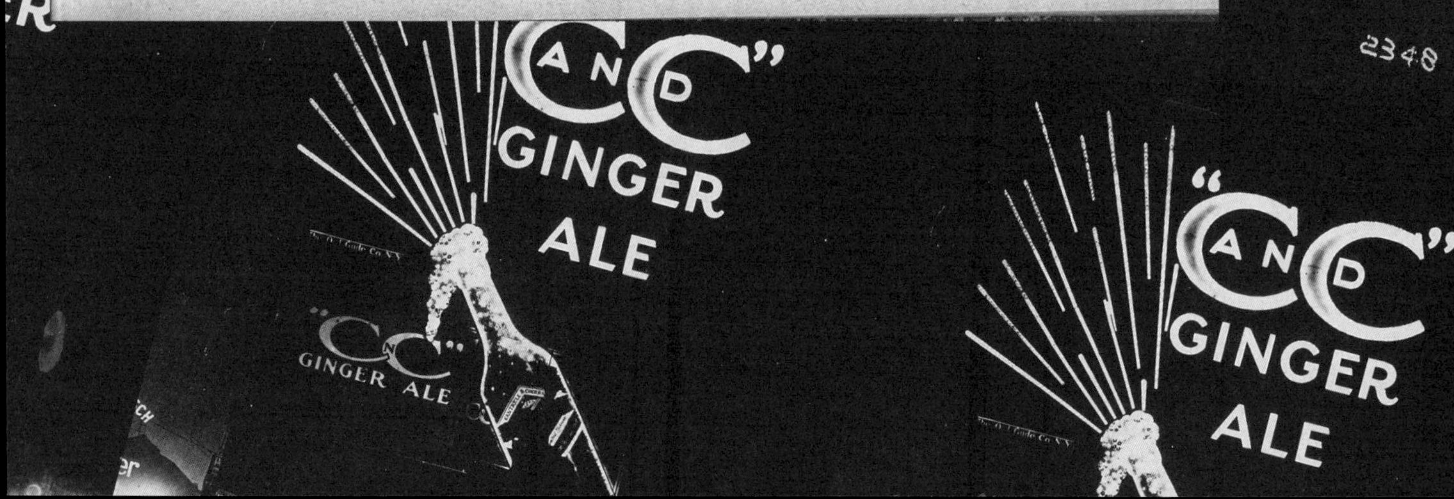

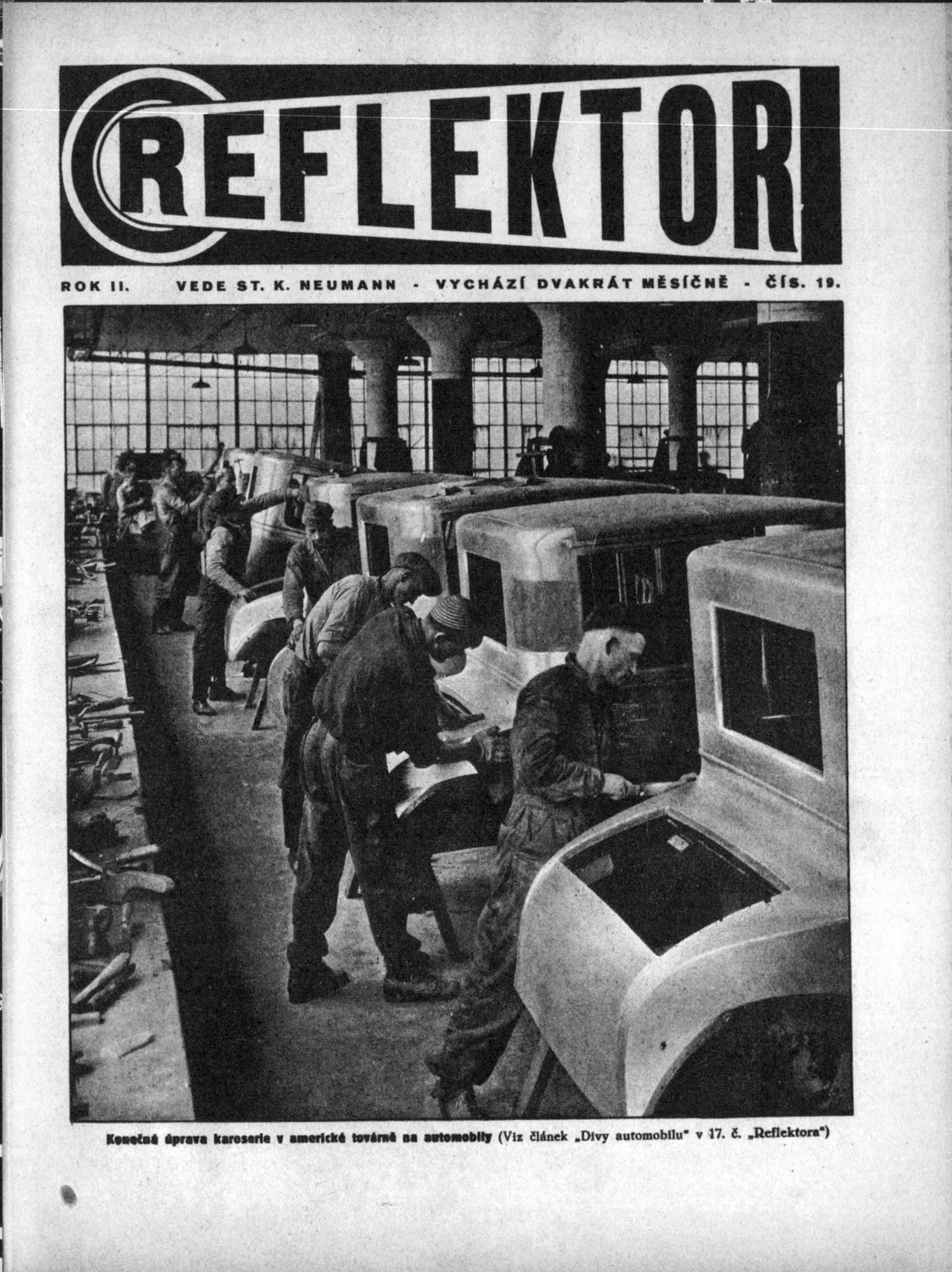

REFLEKTOR

ROK II. VEDE ST. K. NEUMANN - VYCHÁZÍ DVAKRÁT MĚSÍČNĚ - ČÍS. 19.

Konečná úprava karoserie v americké továrně na automobily (Viz článek „Divy automobilu" v 17. č. „Reflektora")

143 *Reflektor*, no. 19, October 1926, ed. Stanislav K. Neumann, Prague
144 Albert Renger-Patzsch, *Industrie. Spannknechte-anreißen und bohren einer Nietplatte*, 1920s
145 Albert Renger-Patzsch, *Industrie. Drückvorrichtung für Bohrmuffen*, 1920s

↓144 ↑143

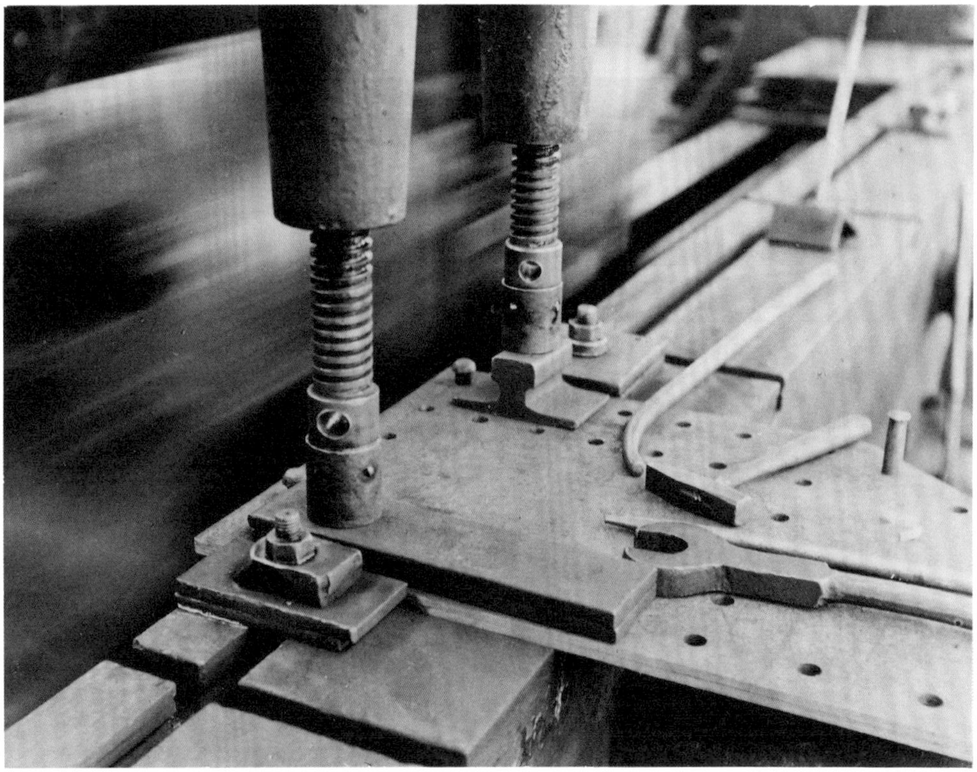

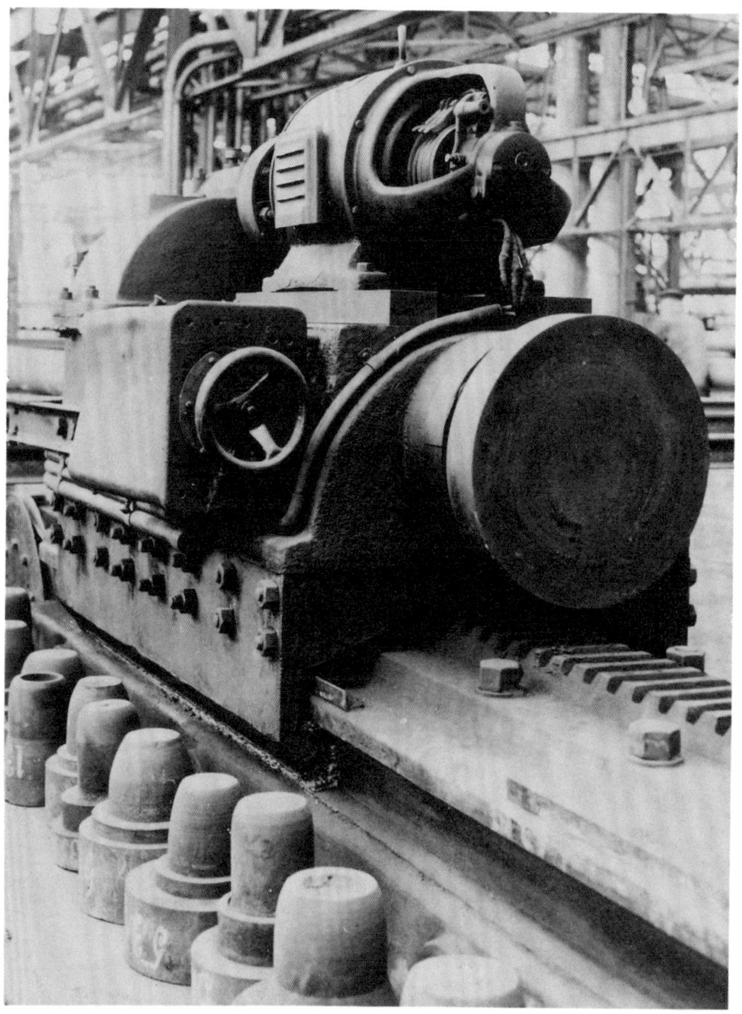

↓145

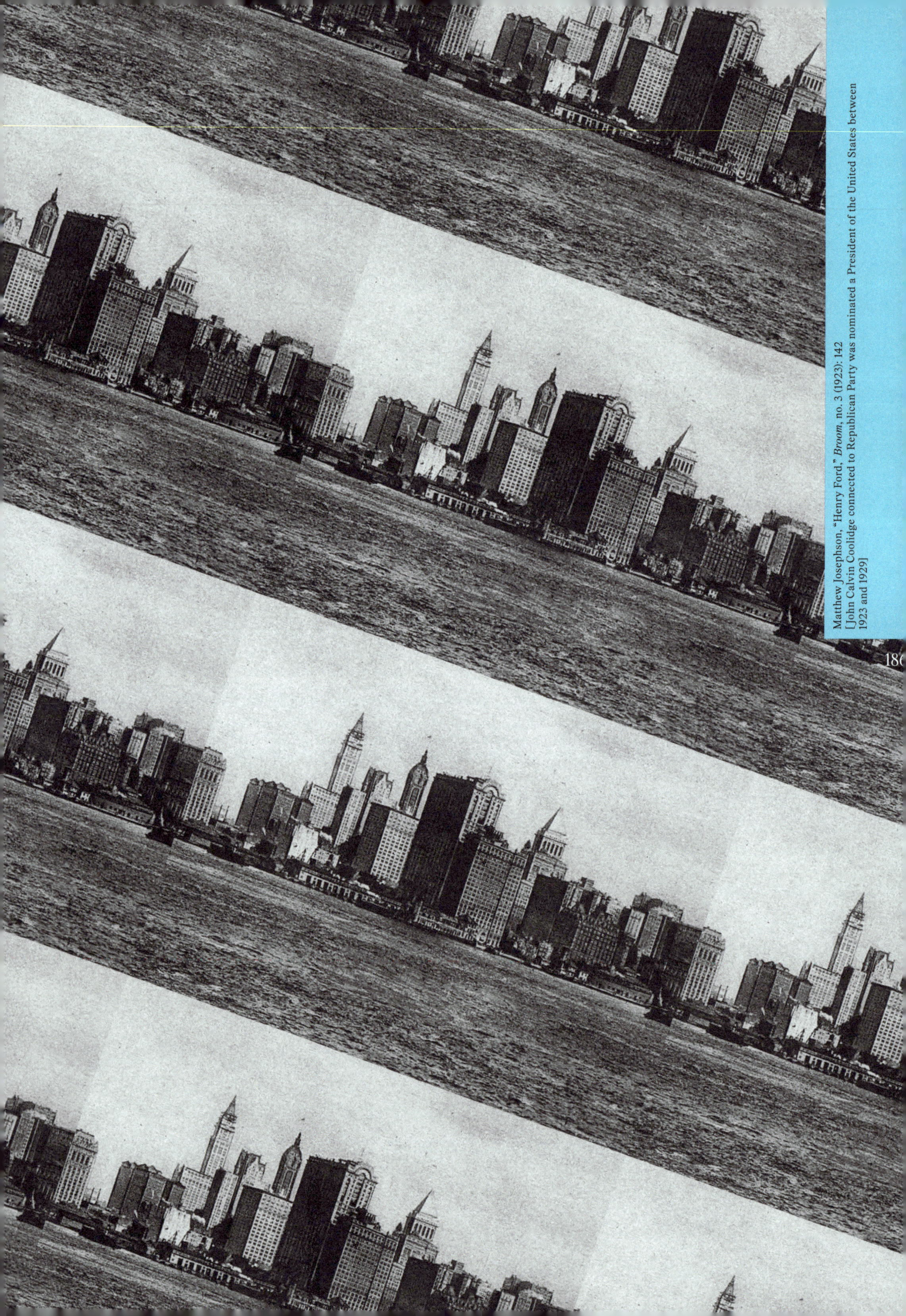

Matthew Josephson, "Henry Ford," *Broom*, no. 3 (1923): 142
[John Calvin Coolidge connected to Republican Party was nominated a President of the United States between 1923 and 1929]

Henry Ford [fragment]

[...] Mr. Ford, ladies and gentlemen, is not a human creature. He is a principle, or better, a relentless process. Away with waste and competitive capitalism. Our bread, butter, tables, chairs, beds, houses, and also our homebrew shall be made in Ford factories. There shall be one great Power-house for the entire land, and ultimately a greater one for the whole world. Mr. Ford, ladies and gentlemen, is not a man.

Let Ford be President. Let him assemble us all into his machine. Let us be properly assembled. Let us all function unanimously. Let the wheels turn more swiftly. [John Calvin] Coolidge! Bah, what is Coolidge! A rococo Yankee lawyer.

Ford means action.	Coolidge means procrastination.
Ford, higher wages.	Coolidge, the ten-hour day.
Ford, standardization.	Coolidge, inefficiency.
Ford, higher wheat market.	Coolidge, farm mortgages.
Ford, lower freight.	Coolidge, the Pork barrel!

VOTE FOR PEOPLE'S CANDIDATE. A veritale crusade has sprung up spontaneously throughout the country to place this man in the white house. The vast and effective Ford organization in every city and every hamlet of the continent is behind it.

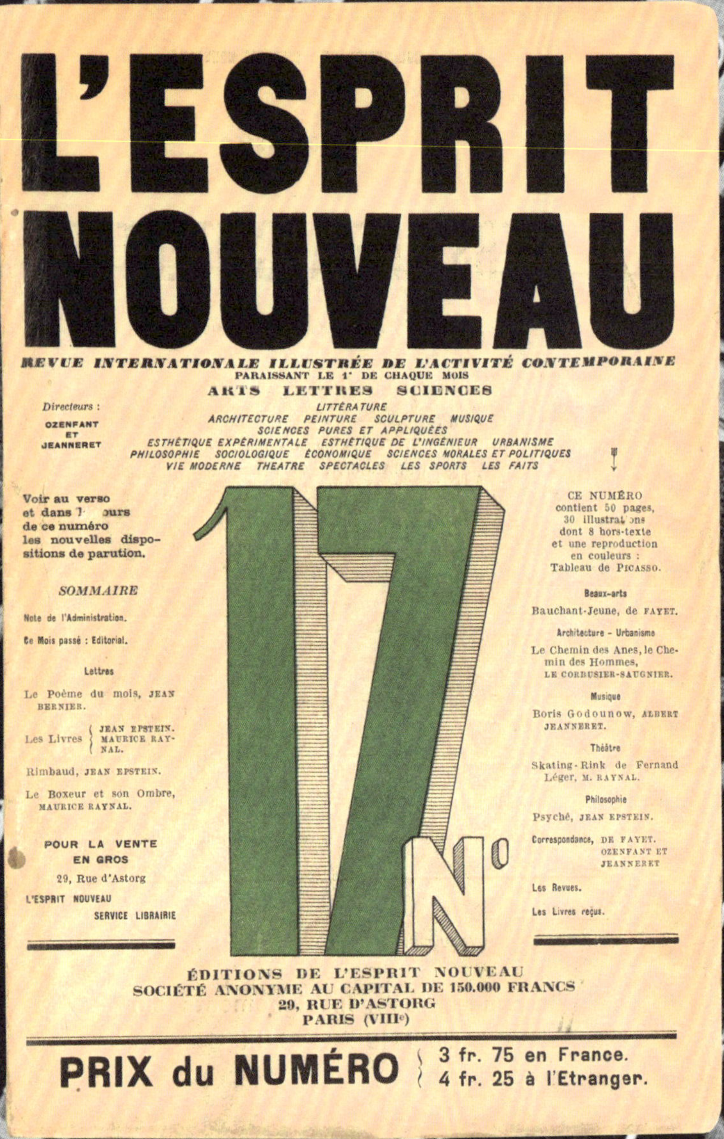

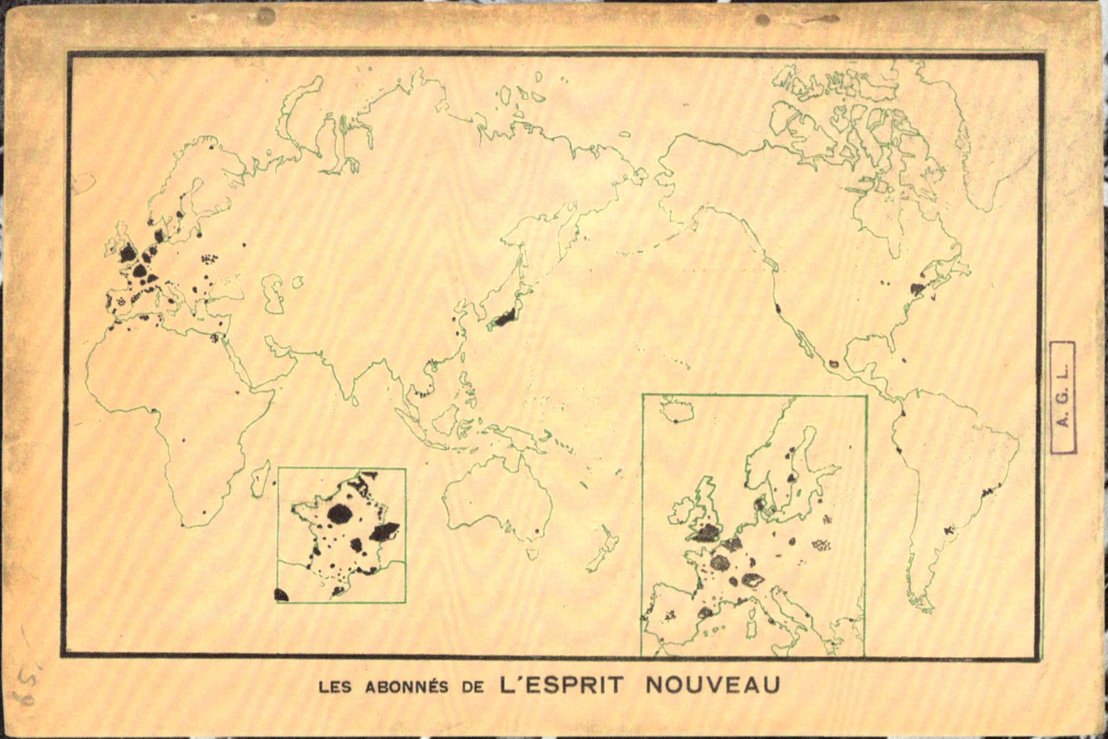

146 *L'Esprit Nouveau*, no. 17, June 1922, ed. Amédée Ozenfant, Charles-Édouard Jeanneret-Gris [Le Corbusier], Paris, cover and back cover by Le Corbusier
147 Le Corbusier, *Vers une architecture*, Paris: Les Éditions G. Crès et Cie 1924, cover; 106–107

↓147 ↑146

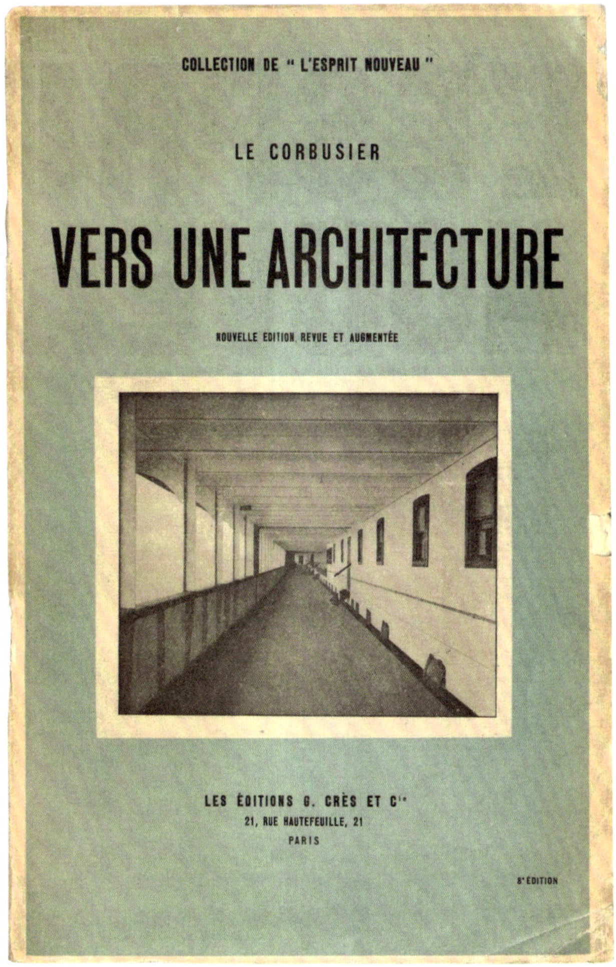

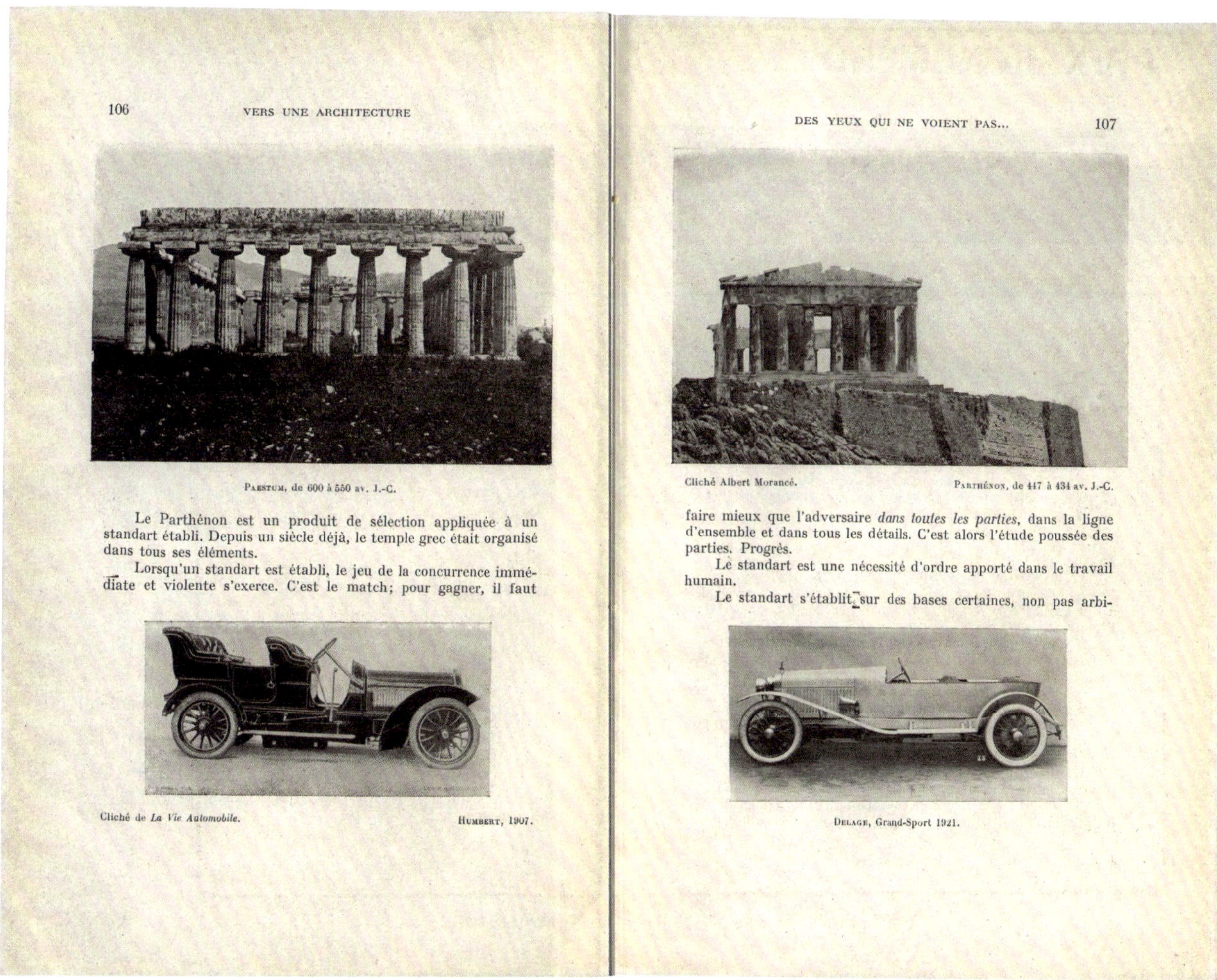

106 VERS UNE ARCHITECTURE

PAESTUM, de 600 à 550 av. J.-C.

Le Parthénon est un produit de sélection appliquée à un standart établi. Depuis un siècle déjà, le temple grec était organisé dans tous ses éléments.

Lorsqu'un standart est établi, le jeu de la concurrence immédiate et violente s'exerce. C'est le match; pour gagner, il faut

Cliché de *La Vie Automobile*. HUMBERT, 1907.

DES YEUX QUI NE VOIENT PAS... 107

Cliché Albert Morancé. PARTHÉNON, de 447 à 434 av. J.-C.

faire mieux que l'adversaire *dans toutes les parties*, dans la ligne d'ensemble et dans tous les détails. C'est alors l'étude poussée des parties. Progrès.

Le standart est une nécessité d'ordre apporté dans le travail humain.

Le standart s'établit sur des bases certaines, non pas arbi-

DELAGE, Grand-Sport 1921.

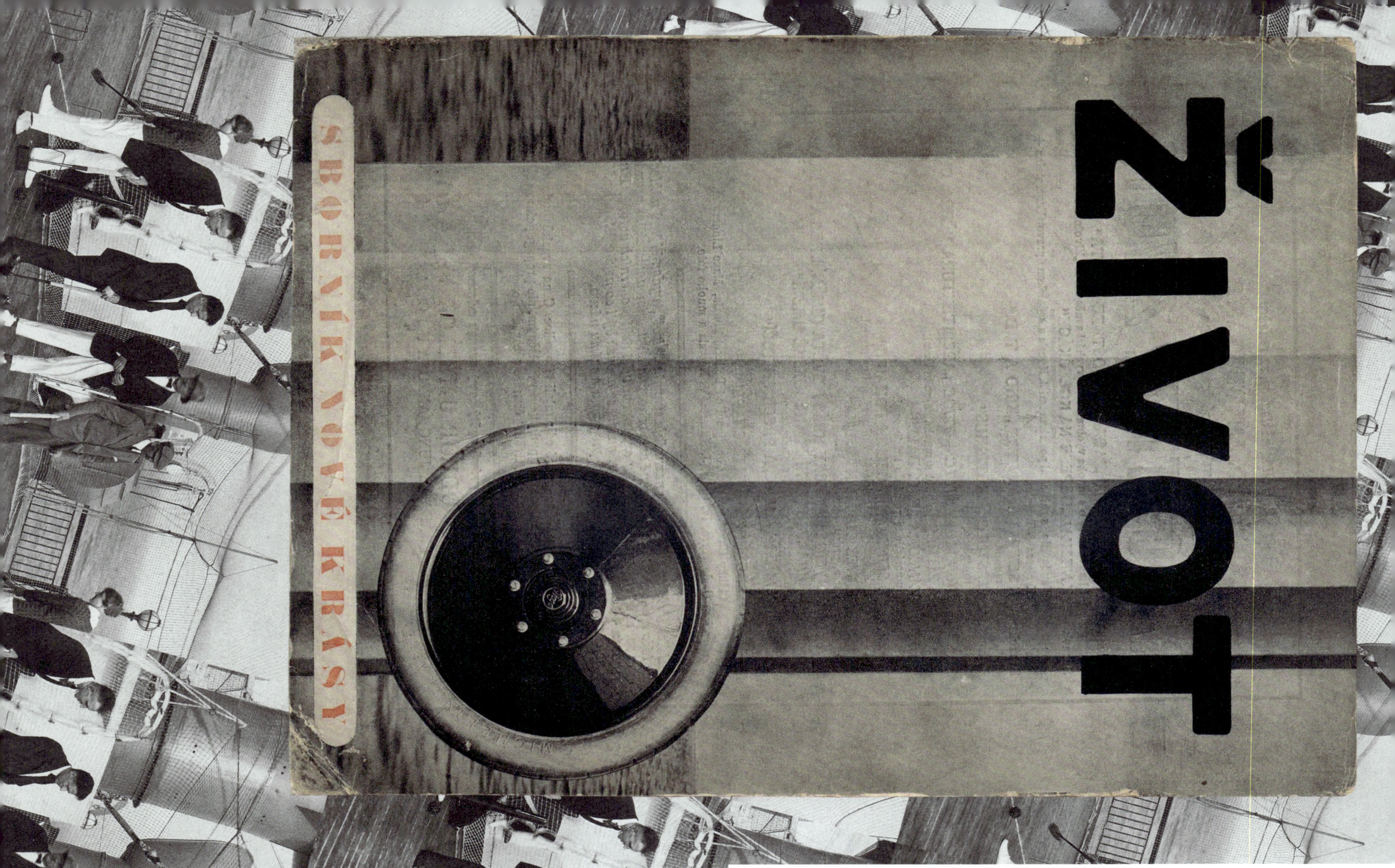

148 see 003, cover by Jaromír Krejcar, Karel Teige, Josef Šíma and Bedřich Feuerstein
149 László Moholy-Nagy, *Malerei Fotografie Film* [Bauhausbücher 8], Munich: Albert Langen Verlag 1927 [second, modified edition, first edition 1925], cover by László Moholy-Nagy; 105, photomontage by Paul Citroen: *Die Stadt*, 109; photoplastic by Vanity Fair: *Amerikanische Pneureklame*

↓149 ↑148

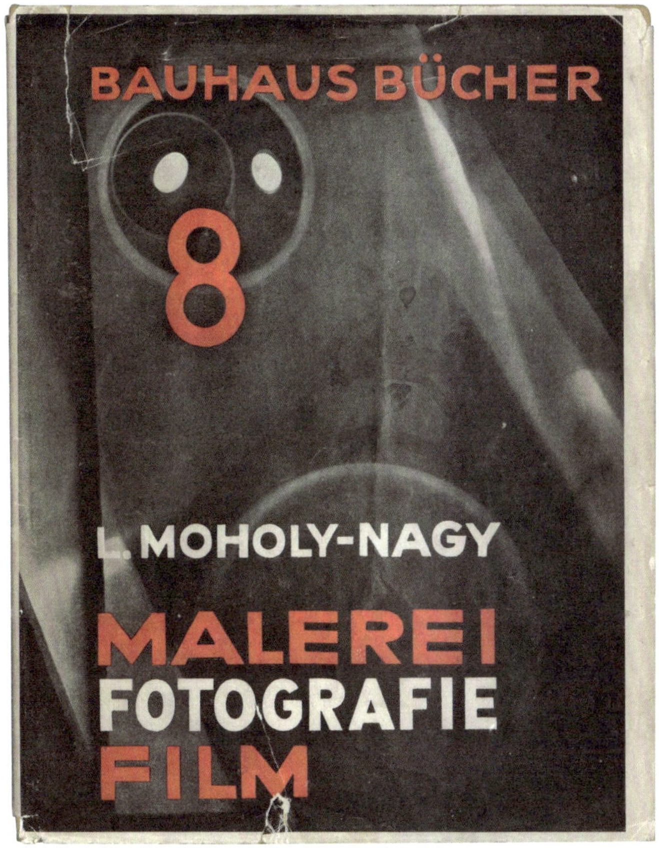

91

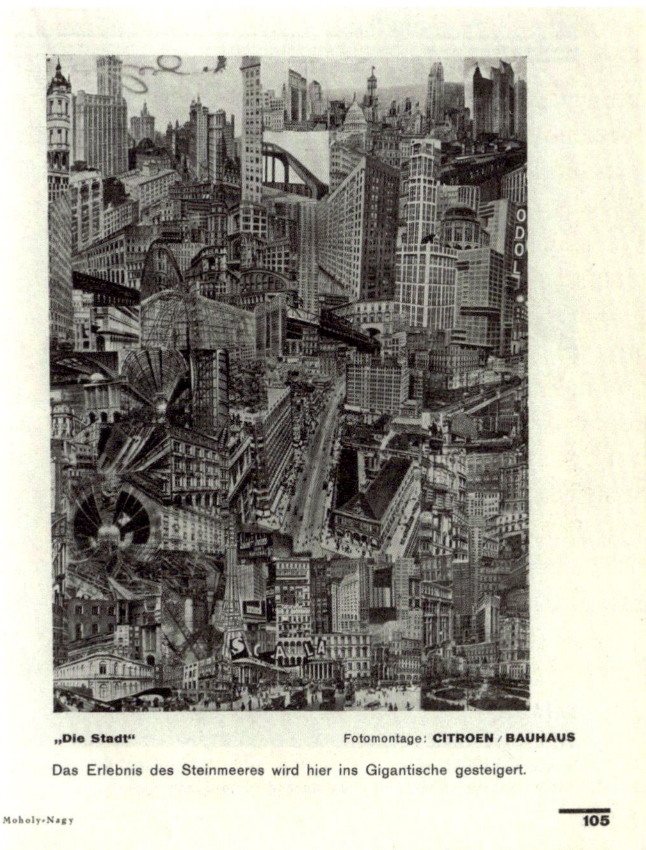

„Die Stadt" Fotomontage: CITROEN / BAUHAUS

Das Erlebnis des Steinmeeres wird hier ins Gigantische gesteigert.

L. Moholy-Nagy 105

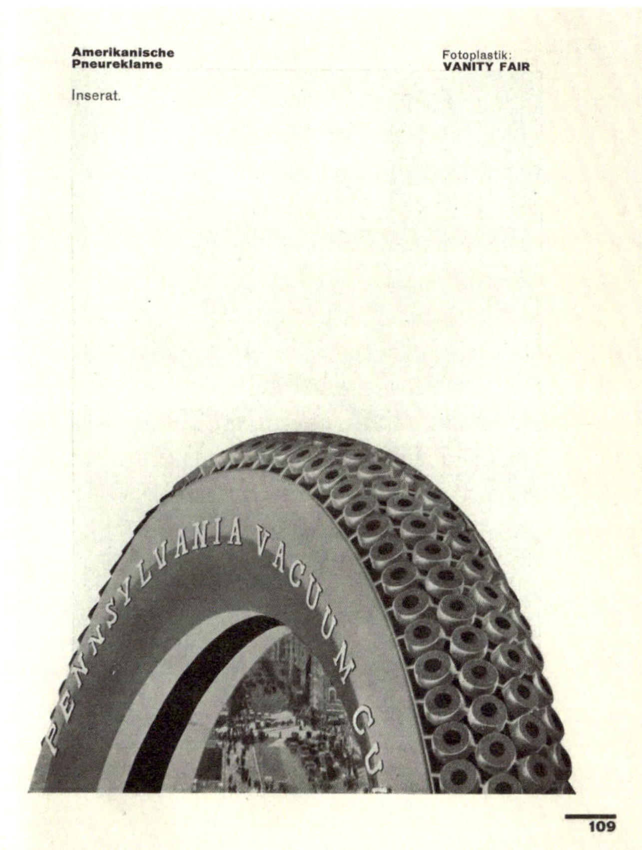

Amerikanische Pneureklame

Fotoplastik: VANITY FAIR

Inserat.

109

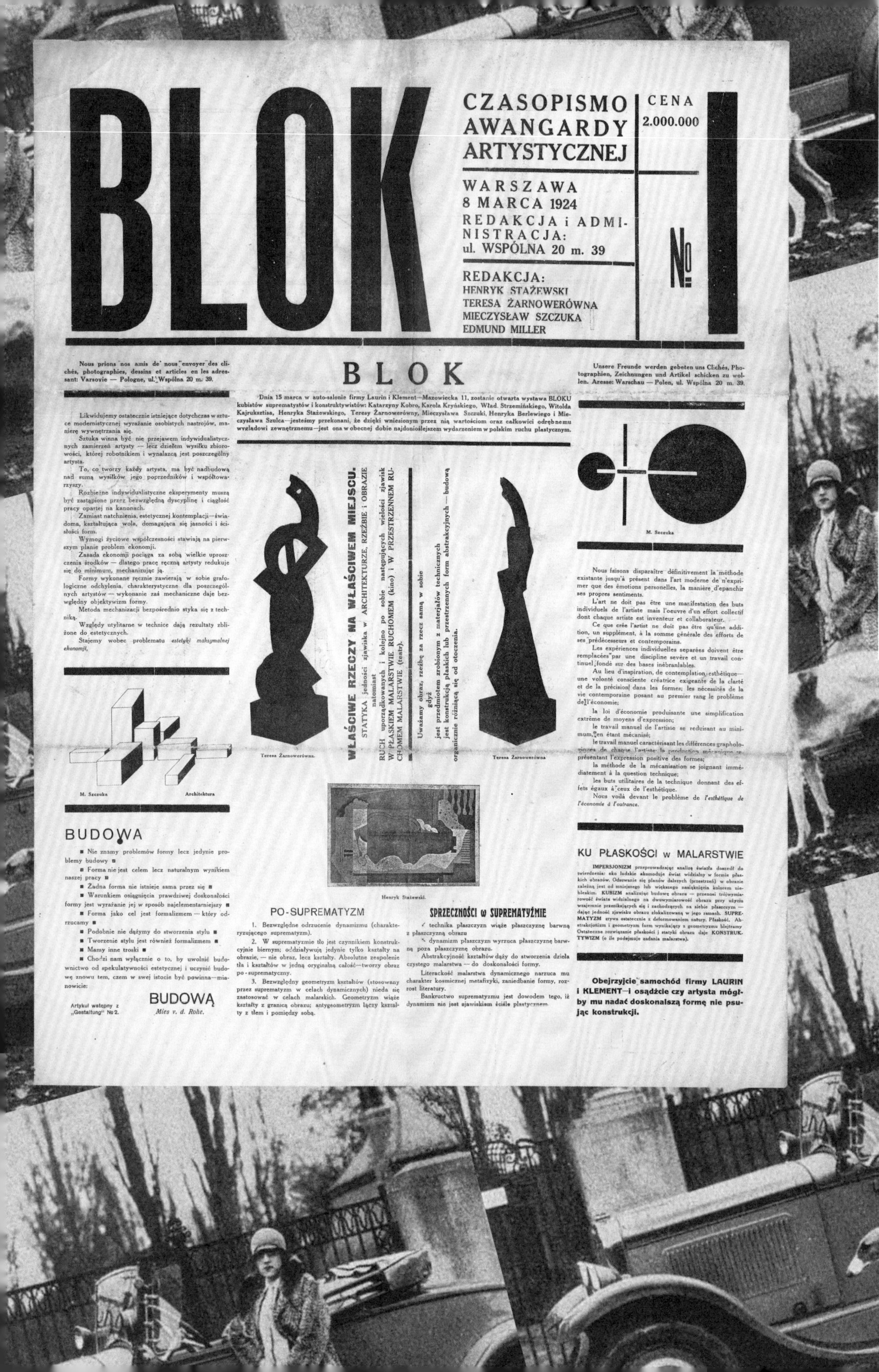

BLOK

CZASOPISMO AWANGARDY ARTYSTYCZNEJ

CENA 2.000.000

WARSZAWA 8 MARCA 1924

REDAKCJA i ADMINISTRACJA: ul. WSPÓLNA 20 m. 39

REDAKCJA:
HENRYK STAŻEWSKI
TERESA ŻARNOWERÓWNA
MIECZYSŁAW SZCZUKA
EDMUND MILLER

№ I

Nous prions nos amis de nous envoyer des clichés, photographies, dessins et articles en les adressant: Varsovie — Pologne, ul. Wspólna 20 m. 39.

BLOK

Dnia 15 marca w auto-salonie firmy Laurin i Klement—Mazowiecka 11, zostanie otwarta wystawa BLOKU kubistów suprematystów i konstruktywistów: Katarzyny Kobro, Karola Kryńskiego, Wład. Strzemińskiego, Witolda Kajruksztisa, Henryka Stażewskiego, Teresy Żarnowerówny, Mieczysława Szczuki, Henryka Berlewiego i Mieczysława Szulca—jesteśmy przekonani, że dzięki wniesionym przez nią wartościom oraz całkowici odrębnemu wyglądowi zewnętrznemu—jest ona w obecnej dobie najdonioślejszem wydarzeniem w polskim ruchu plastycznym.

Unsere Freunde werden gebeten uns Clichés, Photographien, Zeichnungen und Artikel schicken zu wollen. Aresse: Warschau — Polen, ul. Wspólna 20 m. 39.

Likwidujemy ostatecznie istniejące dotychczas w sztuce modernistycznej wyrażanie osobistych nastrojów, manierę wywnętrzania się.

Sztuka winna być nie przejawem indywidualistycznych zamierzeń artysty — lecz dziełem wysiłku zbiorowości, której robotnikiem i wynalazcą jest poszczególny artysta.

To, co tworzy każdy artysta, ma być nadbudową nad sumą wysiłków jego poprzedników i współtowarzyszy.

Rozbieżne indywidualistyczne eksperymenty muszą być zastąpione przez bezwzględną dyscyplinę i ciągłość pracy opartej na kanonach.

Zamiast natchnienia, estetycznej kontemplacji—świadoma, kształtująca wola, domagająca się jasności i ścisłości form.

Wymogi życiowe współczesności stawiają na pierwszym planie problem ekonomji.

Zasada ekonomji pociąga za sobą wielkie uproszczenia środków — dlatego pracę ręczną artysty redukuje się do minimum, mechanizując ją.

Formy wykonane ręcznie zawierają w sobie grafologiczne odchylenia, charakterystyczne dla poszczególnych artystów — wykonanie zaś mechaniczne daje bezwględny objektywizm formy.

Metoda mechanizacji bezpośrednio styka się z techniką.

Względy utylitarne w technice dają rezultaty zbliżone do estetycznych.

Stajemy wobec problematu *estetyki maksymalnej ekonomji.*

M. Szczuka Architektura

Teresa Żarnowerówna.

WŁAŚCIWE RZECZY NA WŁAŚCIWEM MIEJSCU.

STATYKA jedności zjawiska w ARCHITEKTURZE, RZEŹBIE i OBRAZIE
natomiast
RUCH uporządkowanych i kolejno po sobie następujących wielości zjawisk W PŁASKIEM MALARSTWIE RUCHOMEM (kino) i W PRZESTRZENNEM RUCHOMEM MALARSTWIE (teatr).

Uważamy obraz, rzeźbę za rzecz samą w sobie
gdyż
jest przedmiotem zrobionym z materjałów technicznych
jest konstrukcją płaskich lub przestrzennych form abstrakcyjnych — budową organicznie różniącą się od otoczenia.

Teresa Żarnowerówna

M. Szczuka

Nous faisons disparaître définitivement la méthode existante jusqu'à présent dans l'art moderne de n'exprimer que des émotions personelles, la manière d'epanchir ses propres sentiments.

L'art ne doit pas être une manifestation des buts individuels de l'artiste mais l'oeuvre d'un effort collectif dont chaque artiste est inventeur et collaborateur.

Ce que crée l'artist ne doit pas être qu'une addition, un supplément, à la somme générale des efforts de ses prédécesseurs et contemporains.

Les expériences individuelles separées doivent être remplacées par une discipline sevère et un travail continuel fondè sur des bases inébranlables.

Au lieu d'inspiration, de contemplation esthètique—une volontè consciente crèatrice exigeante de la clarté et de la précision dans les formes; les nécessités de la vie contemporaine posant au premier rang le problème de l'économie;

la loi d'économie produisante une simplification extrême de moyens d'expression;

le travail manuel de l'artiste se reduisant au minimum, en étant mécanisé;

le travail manuel caractérisant les différences graphologiques de chaque l'artiste; la production mécanique représentant l'expression positive des formes;

la méthode de la mécanisation se joignant immédiatement à la question technique;

les buts utilitaires de la technique donnant des effets égaux à ceux de l'esthétique.

Nous voilà devant le problème de *l'esthétique de l'économie à l'outrance.*

BUDOWA

■ Nie znamy problemów formy lecz jedynie problemy budowy ■

■ Forma nie jest celem lecz naturalnym wynikiem naszej pracy ■

■ Żadna forma nie istnieje sama przez się ■

■ Warunkiem osiągnięcia prawdziwej doskonałości formy jest wyrażanie jej w sposób najelementarniejszy ■

■ Forma jako cel jest formalizmem — który odrzucamy ■

■ Podobnie nie dążymy do stworzenia stylu ■

■ Tworzenie stylu jest również formalizmem ■

■ Mamy inne troski ■

■ Chodzi nam wyłącznie o to, by uwolnić budownictwo od spekulatywności estetycznej i uczynić budowę znowu tem, czem w swej istocie być powinna—mianowicie:

BUDOWĄ

Mies v. d. Rohe.

Artykuł wstępny z „Gestaltung" № 2.

Henryk Stażewski.

PO-SUPREMATYZM

1. Bezwzględne odrzucenie dynamizmu (charakteryzującego suprematyzm).

2. W suprematyzmie tło jest czynnikiem konstrukcyjnie biernym; oddziaływują jedynie tylko kształty na obrazie, — nie obraz, lecz kształty. Absolutne zespolenie tła i kształtów w jedną oryginalną całość—tworzy obraz po-suprematyczny.

3. Bezwzględny geometryzm kształtów (stosowany przez suprematyzm w celach dynamicznych) nieda się zastosować w celach malarskich. Geometryzm wiąże kształty z granicą obrazu; antygeometryzm łączy kształty z tłem i pomiędzy sobą.

SPRZECZNOŚCI w SUPREMATYŹMIE

↙ technika płaszczyzn wiąże płaszczyznę barwną z płaszczyzną obrazu

↖ dynamizm płaszczyzn wyrzuca płaszczyznę barwną poza płaszczyznę obrazu.

Abstrakcyjność kształtów dąży do stworzenia dzieła czystego malarstwa — do doskonałości formy.

Literackość malarstwa dynamicznego narzuca mu charakter kosmicznej metafizyki, zaniedbanie formy, rozrost literatury.

Bankructwo suprematyzmu jest dowodem tego, iż dynamizm nie jest zjawiskiem ściśle plastycznem.

KU PŁASKOŚCI w MALARSTWIE

IMPERSJONIZM przeprowadzając analizę światła doszedł do twierdzenia: oko ludzkie akomoduje świat widzialny w formie płaskich obrazów. Odsuwanie się planów dalszych (przestrzeń) w obrazie zależną jest od mniejszego lub większego nasiąknięcia kolorem niebieskim. **KUBIZM** analizując budowę obrazu — przenosi trójwymiarowość świata widzialnego na dwuwymiarowość obrazu przy użyciu wzajemnie przenikających się i zachodzących na siebie płaszczyzn — dając jedność zjawisku obrazu zlokalizowaną w jego ramach. **SUPREMATYZM** zrywa ostatecznie z deformowaniem natury. Płaskość. Abstrakcjonizm i geometryzm form wynikający z geometryzmu blejtramy Ostateczne rozwiązanie płaskości j statyki obrazu daje **KONSTRUKTYWIZM** (o ile podejmuje zadania malarstwa).

Obejrzyjcie samochód firmy LAURIN i KLEMENT—i osądźcie czy artysta mógłby mu nadać doskonalszą formę nie psując konstrukcji.

150 *Blok: Czasopismo awangardy artystycznej*, no. 1, March 1924, ed. Henryk Stażewski, Teresa Żarnowerówna, Mieczysław Szczuka, Edmund Miller, Warsaw, cover with illustrations by the editors; back cover

L. HILBERSEIMER
Przedruk
z „Gestaltung" № 2.

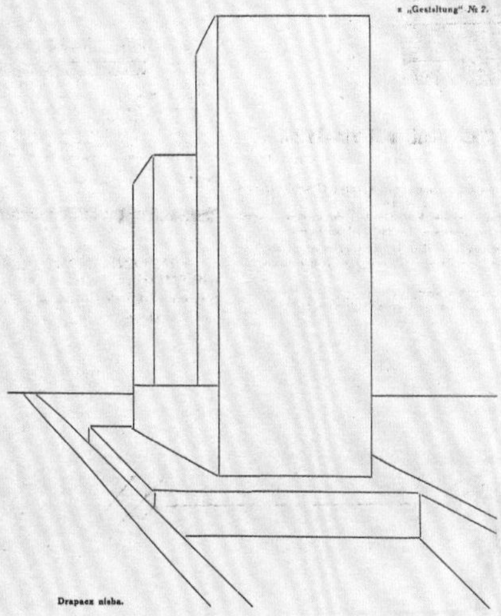

Drapacz nieba.

L. HILBERSEIMER
Przedruk z „Gestaltung" № 2.

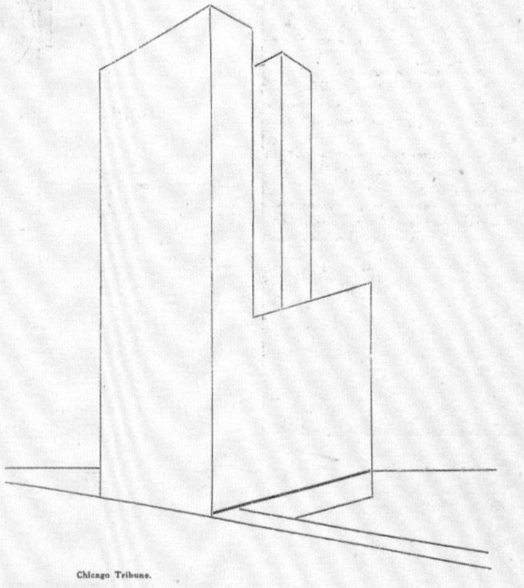

Chicago Tribune.

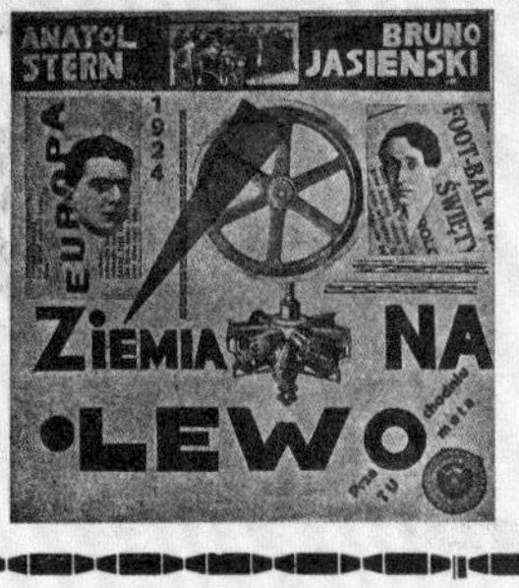

DO NABYCIA WE WSZYSTKICH KSIĘGARNIACH.

Obojętna jest kwestja zdolności — o skutkach decyduje wyłącznie wola i metodyczna praca.

Im doskonalszy jest twór techniki tem mniej jest w nim wolnego miejsca dla sztuki i artysty.

Z chwilą gdy sztuka zbliża się ku utylitaryzacji — przekreśla sama siebie.

Konstruktywizm nie stara się naśladować maszyny lecz konstruować każdą rzecz według jej własnych zasad — więc w swej dziedzinie jest logiczny jak maszyna.

APEL DO UCZNIÓW SZKÓŁ SZTUKI

Jako pismo, torujące drogę Nowej Sztuce, tworzące podstawy nowej kultury plastycznej, — zwracamy się do Was z gorącem wezwaniem o jaknajdalej idące poparcie naszej akcji.

Bratnie Pomoce Waszych szkół przez poparcie materjalne naszego pisma, tudzież przez intensywną agitację i kolportaż mogą nam tę akcję ułatwić, dając tem możność uczniom szkół sztuki korzystania z materjałów, jakie pismo nasze gromadzić będzie w zakresie sztuki europejskiej.

Nasze hasła znalazły już dostęp do Was i w większości szkół spotykają się z entuzjazmem i szczerem uznaniem.

Popieranie zatem pisma leży we własnym waszym interesie.

PRZEGLĄD CZASOPISM POLSKICH

Zwrotnica redaktor: T. Peiper, Kraków, Jagiellońska 5.
Blok. Warszawa, Wspólna 20 m. 39.

PRZEGLĄD CZASOPISM ZAGRANICZNYCH

De Stijl redaktor: Theo van Doesburg Holland — Aja — Klimopstraat, 18.
Ma redaktor: L. Kassak, Wiedeń 8—Amalienstrasse 26/11.
Manomètre redaktor: E. Malespine, Lion—49 Cours Gambetta
Disk redaktorzy: Krejcur-Seifert-Teige, Praga II, Cerna Ulice 12a.
Farbe und Form redaktor: Von Dietrich, Berlin W. 39—Landshuterstrasse 38.
Der Sturm redaktor: Herwardt Walden — Berlin W 9, Potsdamerstrasse 134a.
Het Owerzicht redaktorzy: F. Berckelaerg e S. Peeters — Belgia — Antwerpja — Turnhoutschebaun 106.
Contimporanul Rumunja — Bucarest — Str. Trinidatea 29.
„noi" redaktor: Enrico Prampolini, Roma via Tronto 89.
„G" redaktorzy: Hans Richter, Gräff, Mies v. d. Rohe, Berlin — Friedenau Eschenstr. 7.
Mecano redaktorzy: I. K. Bonset i T. van Doesburg. Hang — Klimopstraat 10, Holland.
Espagna Prado, 11, 2 Madrid Apartado 139.
La Vie des Lettres et des Arts redaktorzy: N. Beauduin W. Speth, Paris — 20 rue de Chartres — Neully.
7. Arts Boulevard Leopold II 271 Brüssel.
Stavba redakcja: Czernarty, Feuersteih, Jira, Koula, Kysela-Stary, Teige. Praga — Kolkovna 5.
Merz redaktor: Kurt Schwitters — Hannower, Waldhausenstr. 5.

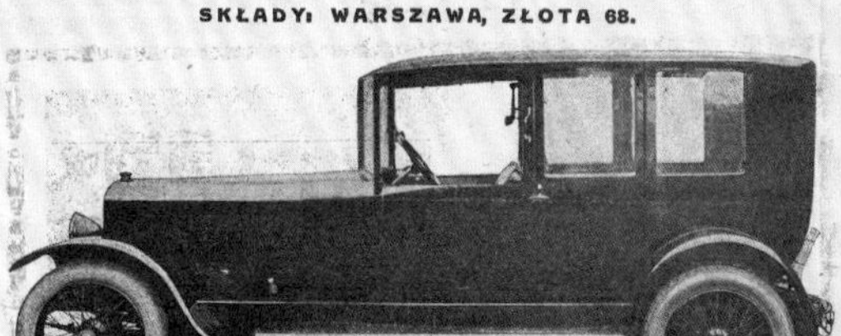

KRONIKA UJEMNA.

Dowiadujemy się, że dyrektor Warsz. Szkoły Sztuk Pięknych pan Józef Czajkowski zerwał część jednej z dekoracji na balu tejże szkoły, nie rozumiejąc, że w ten sposób niszczy całość kompozycji. Zerwana część zawierała napis „Zwrotnica". Bez komentarzy.

Zwracamy uwagę opinji społecznej, że udział Polski w wystawie nowoczesnej sztuki dekoracyjnej grozi po raz wtóry zupełną kompromitacją. Założeniem wystawy jest dawanie rzeczy, które nie są powtórzeniem tego co było, żadnych stylów, jakie kiedykolwiek istniały. Charakter jaki chcą nadać polskiemu pawilonowi, jego organizatorowie zapowiada, że wystawa będzie dowodem zupełnego braku twórczości w Polsce i zastąpieniem jej przez naśladownictwo dawno umarłych stylów.

Wydawnictwo „BLOK". Redaktor odpowiedzialny Henryk Stażewski, ul. Piękna 46 m. 4. „Drukarnia Krajowa" w Warszawie, Żelazna 89, tel. 188-70.

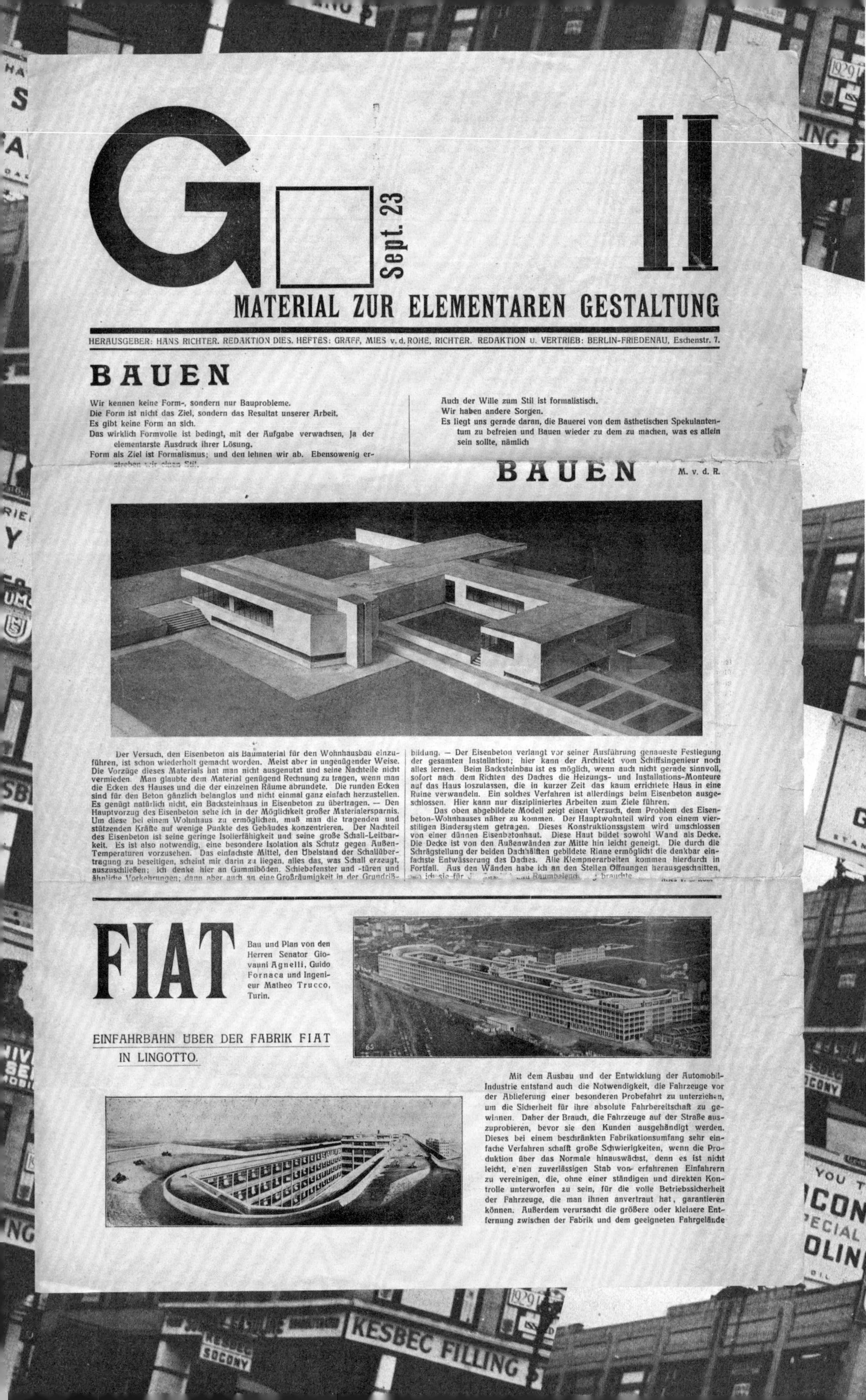

G

Sept. 23

II

MATERIAL ZUR ELEMENTAREN GESTALTUNG

HERAUSGEBER: HANS RICHTER. REDAKTION DIES. HEFTES: GRÄFF, MIES v. d. ROHE, RICHTER. REDAKTION u. VERTRIEB: BERLIN-FRIEDENAU, Eschenstr. 7.

BAUEN

Wir kennen keine Form-, sondern nur Bauprobleme.
Die Form ist nicht das Ziel, sondern das Resultat unserer Arbeit.
Es gibt keine Form an sich.
Das wirklich Formvolle ist bedingt, mit der Aufgabe verwachsen, ja der elementarste Ausdruck ihrer Lösung.
Form als Ziel ist Formalismus; und den lehnen wir ab. Ebensowenig erstreben wir einen Stil.
Auch der Wille zum Stil ist formalistisch.
Wir haben andere Sorgen.
Es liegt uns gerade daran, die Bauerei von dem ästhetischen Spekulantentum zu befreien und Bauen wieder zu dem zu machen, was es allein sein sollte, nämlich

BAUEN

M. v. d. R.

Der Versuch, den Eisenbeton als Baumaterial für den Wohnhausbau einzuführen, ist schon wiederholt gemacht worden. Meist aber in ungenügender Weise. Die Vorzüge dieses Materials hat man nicht ausgenutzt und seine Nachteile nicht vermieden. Man glaubte dem Material genügend Rechnung zu tragen, wenn man die Ecken des Hauses und die der einzelnen Räume abrundete. Die runden Ecken sind für den Beton gänzlich belanglos und nicht einmal ganz einfach herzustellen. Es genügt natürlich nicht, ein Backsteinhaus in Eisenbeton zu übertragen. — Den Hauptvorzug des Eisenbeton sehe ich in der Möglichkeit großer Materialersparnis. Um diese bei einem Wohnhaus zu ermöglichen, muß man die tragenden und stützenden Kräfte auf wenige Punkte des Gebäudes konzentrieren. Der Nachteil des Eisenbeton ist seine geringe Isolierfähigkeit und seine große Schall-Leitbarkeit. Es ist also notwendig, eine besondere Isolation als Schutz gegen Außen-Temperaturen vorzusehen. Das einfachste Mittel, den Übelstand der Schallübertragung zu beseitigen, scheint mir darin zu liegen, alles das, was Schall erzeugt, auszuschließen; ich denke hier an Gummiböden, Schiebefenster und -türen und ähnliche Vorkehrungen; dann aber auch an eine Großräumigkeit in der Grundrißbildung. — Der Eisenbeton verlangt vor seiner Ausführung genaueste Festlegung der gesamten Installation; hier kann der Architekt vom Schiffsingenieur noch alles lernen. Beim Backsteinbau ist es möglich, wenn auch nicht gerade sinnvoll, sofort nach dem Richten des Daches die Heizungs- und Installations-Monteure auf das Haus loszulassen, die in kurzer Zeit das kaum errichtete Haus in eine Ruine verwandeln. Ein solches Verfahren ist allerdings beim Eisenbeton ausgeschlossen. Hier kann nur diszipliniertes Arbeiten zum Ziele führen.

Das oben abgebildete Modell zeigt einen Versuch, dem Problem des Eisenbeton-Wohnhauses näher zu kommen. Der Hauptwohnteil wird von einem vierstiligen Bindersystem getragen. Dieses Konstruktionssystem wird umschlossen von einer dünnen Eisenbetonhaut. Diese Haut bildet sowohl Wand als Decke. Die Decke ist von den Außenwänden zur Mitte hin leicht geneigt. Die durch die Schrägstellung der beiden Dachhälften gebildete Rinne ermöglicht die denkbar einfachste Entwässerung des Daches. Alle Klempnerarbeiten kommen hierdurch in Fortfall. Aus den Wänden habe ich an den Stellen Öffnungen herausgeschnitten, wo ich sie für [illegible] Raumbeleuch[illegible] brauchte.

Mies v. d. Rohe

FIAT

Bau und Plan von den Herren Senator Giovanni Agnelli, Guido Fornaca und Ingenieur Matheo Trucco, Turin.

EINFAHRBAHN ÜBER DER FABRIK FIAT IN LINGOTTO.

Mit dem Ausbau und der Entwicklung der Automobil-Industrie entstand auch die Notwendigkeit, die Fahrzeuge vor der Ablieferung einer besonderen Probefahrt zu unterziehen, um die Sicherheit für ihre absolute Fahrbereitschaft zu gewinnen. Daher der Brauch, die Fahrzeuge auf der Straße auszuprobieren, bevor sie den Kunden ausgehändigt werden. Dieses bei einem beschränkten Fabrikationsumfang sehr einfache Verfahren schafft große Schwierigkeiten, wenn die Produktion über das Normale hinauswächst, denn es ist nicht leicht, einen zuverlässigen Stab von erfahrenen Einfahrern zu vereinigen, die, ohne einer ständigen und direkten Kontrolle unterworfen zu sein, für die volle Betriebssicherheit der Fahrzeuge, die man ihnen anvertraut hat, garantieren können. Außerdem verursacht die größere oder kleinere Entfernung zwischen der Fabrik und dem geeigneten Fahrgelände

151 *G. Material zur elementaren Gestaltung*, no. 2, September 1923, ed. Hans Richter, Werner Graeff, Ludwig Mies van der Rohe, Berlin

152 *G. Zeitschrift für elementare Gestaltung*, no. 3, June 1924, ed. Hans Richter, Werner Graeff, Friedrich Kiesler, *Ludwig Mies van der Rohe*, Berlin, 18–19

↓152 ↑151

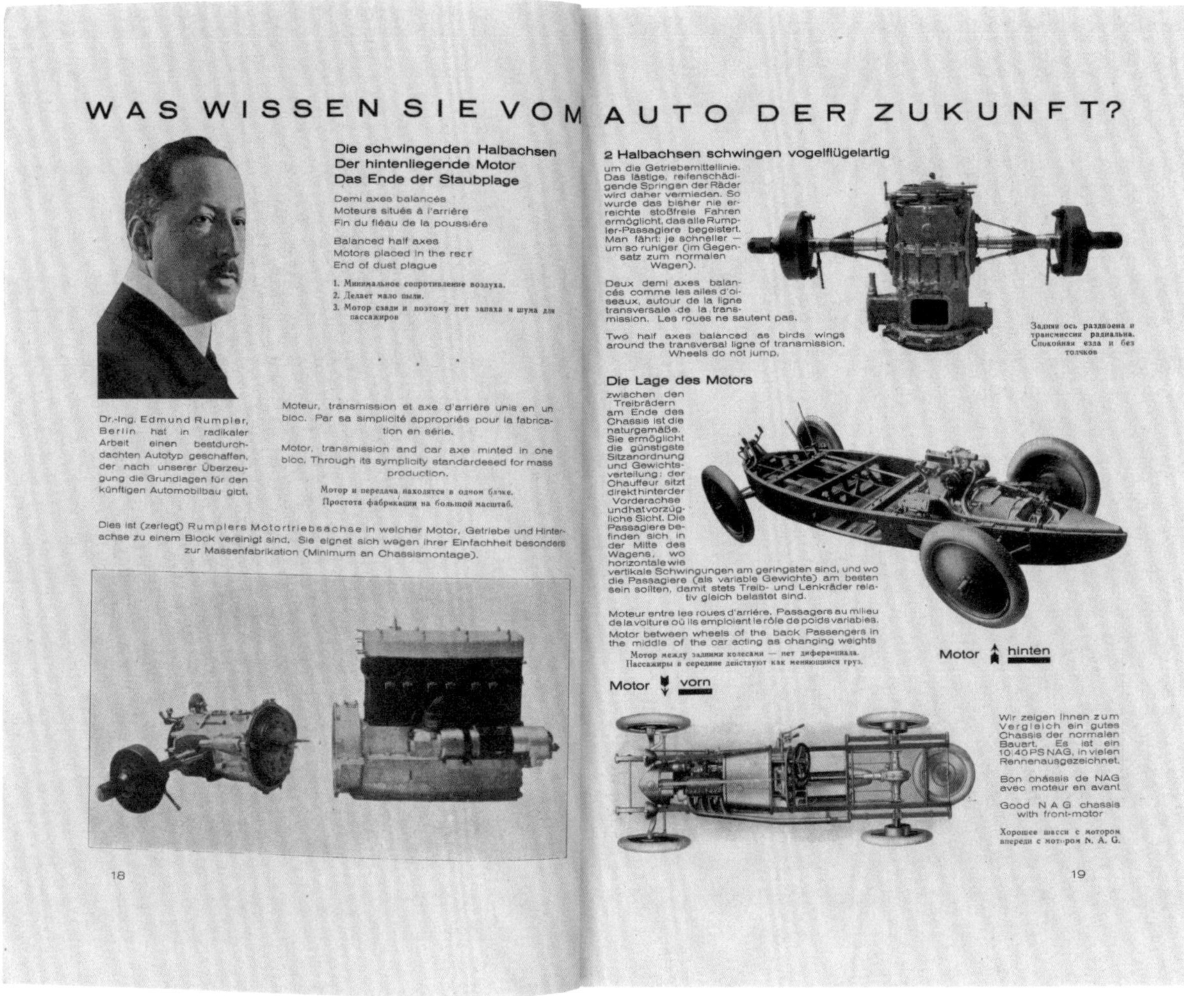

WAS WISSEN SIE VOM AUTO DER ZUKUNFT?

Die schwingenden Halbachsen
Der hintenliegende Motor
Das Ende der Staubplage

Demi axes balancés
Moteurs situés à l'arrière
Fin du fléau de la poussiére

Balanced half axes
Motors placed in the rear
End of dust plague

1. Минимальное сопротивление воздуха.
2. Делает мало пыли.
3. Мотор сзади и поэтому нет запаха и шума для пассажиров

Dr.-Ing. Edmund Rumpler, Berlin hat in radikaler Arbeit einen bestdurchdachten Autotyp geschaffen, der nach unserer Überzeugung die Grundlagen für den künftigen Automobilbau gibt.

Moteur, transmission et axe d'arrière unis en un bloc. Par sa simplicité appropriés pour la fabrication en série.

Motor, transmission and car axe minted in one bloc. Through its symplicity standardesed for mass production.

Мотор и передача находятся в одном блоке. Простота фабрикации на большой масштаб.

Dies ist (zerlegt) Rumplers Motortriebsachse in welcher Motor, Getriebe und Hinterachse zu einem Block vereinigt sind. Sie eignet sich wegen ihrer Einfachheit besonders zur Massenfabrikation (Minimum an Chassismontage).

18

2 Halbachsen schwingen vogelflügelartig
um die Getriebemittellinie. Das lästige, reifenschädigende Springen der Räder wird daher vermieden. So wurde das bisher nie erreichte stoßfreie Fahren ermöglicht, das alle Rumpler-Passagiere begeistert. Man fährt: je schneller – um so ruhiger (im Gegensatz zum normalen Wagen).

Deux demi axes balancés comme les ailes d'oiseaux, autour de la ligne transversale de la transmission. Les roues ne sautent pas.

Two half axes balanced as birds wings around the transversal ligne of transmission. Wheels do not jump.

Задняя ось раздвоена и трансмиссия радиальна. Спокойная езда и без толчков

Die Lage des Motors
zwischen den Treibrädern am Ende des Chassis ist die naturgemäße. Sie ermöglicht die günstigste Sitzanordnung und Gewichtsverteilung: der Chauffeur sitzt direkt hinter der Vorderachse und hat vorzügliche Sicht. Die Passagiere befinden sich in der Mitte des Wagens, wo horizontale wie vertikale Schwingungen am geringsten sind, und wo die Passagiere (als variable Gewichte) am besten sein sollten, damit stets Treib- und Lenkräder relativ gleich belastet sind.

Moteur entre les roues d'arrière. Passagers au milieu de la voiture où ils emploient le rôle de poids variables.

Motor between wheels of the back Passengers in the middle of the car acting as changing weights

Мотор между задними колесами — нет диференциала. Пассажиры в середине действуют как меняющийся груз.

Motor hinten

Motor vorn

Wir zeigen Ihnen zum Vergleich ein gutes Chassis der normalen Bauart. Es ist ein 10|40 PS NAG, in vielen Rennen ausgezeichnet.

Bon châssis de NAG avec moteur en avant

Good N A G chassis with front-motor

Хорошее шасси с мотором впереди с мотором N. A. G.

19

CAR PRODUCTION AND ARTISTIC PRACTICE: PURISM AND CONSTRUCTIVISM In the early 1920s, French Purists Amédée Ozenfant and Le Corbusier believed that industry, the rationality of the machine, and advanced technology were key elements in creative work which should be applied in art and architecture. The automobile was recognized by Le Corbusier as the perfect product of rationalized, economical, and efficient work organization. A similar approach towards car production can be observed in the work of Ludwig Hilberseimer, who followed Le Corbusier by linking Fordist methods of manufacturing cars to methods of designing apartments and housing estates. The editor of Berlin-based Constructivist magazine *G*, Werner Graeff, wrote about artists' tasks as new engineers who should look at car production as a model. The Polish Constructivist Blok group shared a similar idea and linked principles of manufacturing cars to collective artistic practices. In Warsaw in 1924 they organized their first exhibition at the automobile showroom of the Czechoslovak brand Laurin & Klement, and wrote in one of their statements that "Art must not be a manifestation of the artists' individualism, but the result of an effort by the collective in which the artist is the worker and inventor."

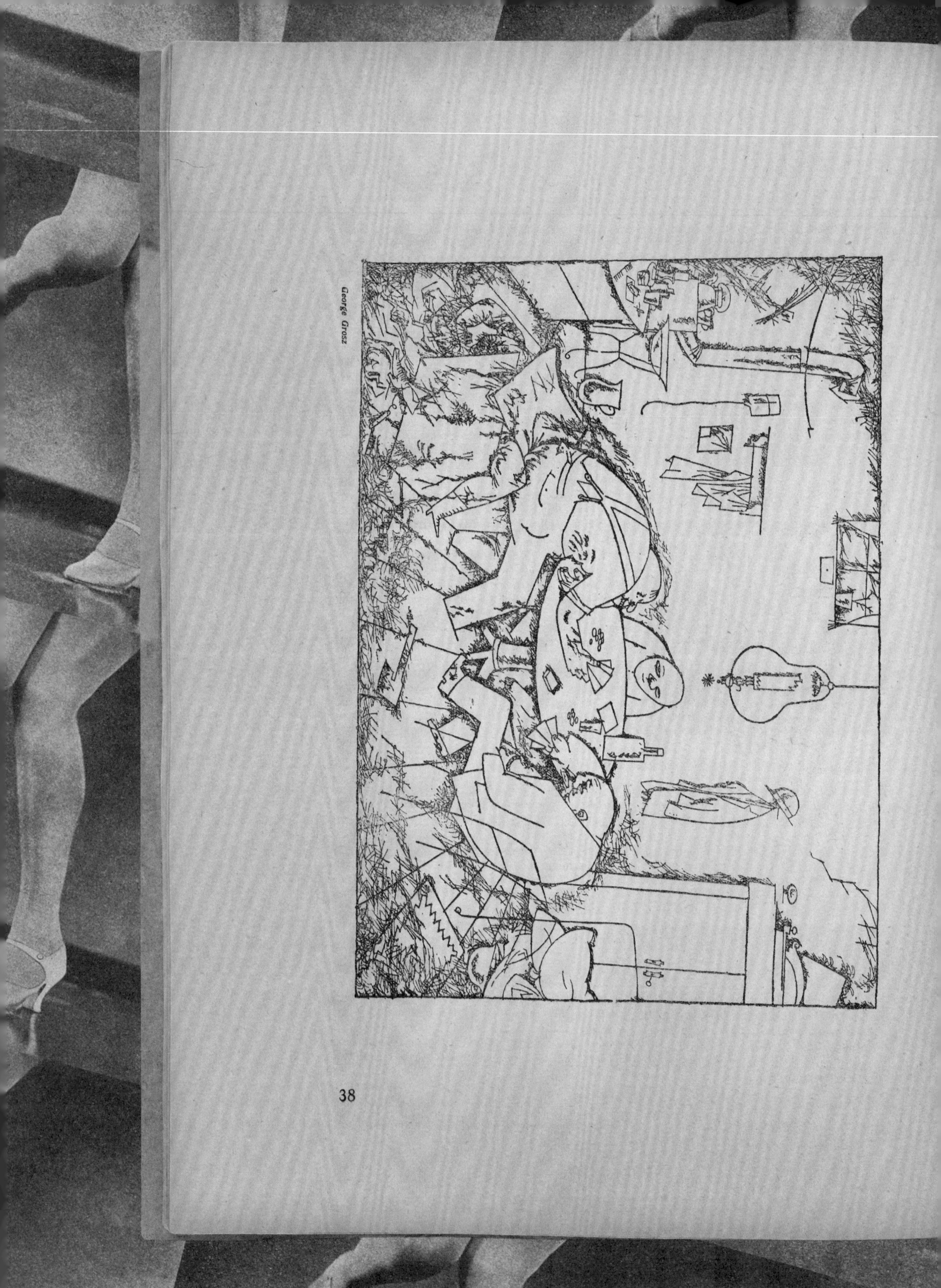

153 *Periszkop*, no. 4, June–July 1925, ed. György Szántó, Arad, 38–39, illustration by George Grosz, text by Erich Roederer: *Ford*

FORD

Von

ERICH ROEDERER

Was ist Ford? Ein Name, ein Begriff, eine Gefahr? Es ist schwer zu sagen, fest steht jedoch dass die amerikanische Gefahr, von der seit Jahren in den Kreisen der deutschen Automobilindustrie gesprochen wird, aufs engste mit dem Namen Ford verknüpft ist. Henry Ford ist nicht nur einer der reichsten Männer der Welt, wenn nicht gar der reichste, sondern auch der bedeutendste Automobilfabrikant, ein Mann, der sein Unternehmen aus kleinsten Anfängen heraus bis zu einer für europäischen Begriffe geradezu unbegreiflichen Höhe gebracht hat.

Wenn vir uns hier etwas eingehender mit Henry Ford beschäftigen, so geschieht es, weil der Mann und sein Werk wirklich interessant und bezeichnend für amerikanische Verhältnisse sind, und weil wir glauben, dass die amerikanische Gefahr, soweit sie mit dem Namen Ford verknüpft ist, nicht viel mehr ist als ein Schreckgespens, trotz der unleugbaren Erfolge, die Ford dank einer geschickten, ser grosszügigen Organisation in den letzten Jahren auch in Europa zu verzeichnen hatte.

In der Stärke Fords und seines Systems liegt auch seine Schwäche. Der Humorist Roda Roda, der im vergangenen Jahre in den Vereinigten Staaten war und auch die Ford-Werke besuchte, erzählt folgende Anekdote von ihm: Irgend ein deutscher Automobiltechniker kam zu Ford, um ihm eine technische Verbeserung anzubieten. Die Verbesserung kostete nur einen halben Dollar pro Wagen, aber Ford lehnte die Erfindung ab, weil er den Preis seiner Wagen nicht erhöhen wollte. An einer Verbesserung der Qualität seines Wagens war ihm nämlich nichts gelegen, wenn dadurh zugleich seine Einnahmen verringert wurden.

Hierin liegt der Wesensunterschied zwischen dem deutschen und dem amerikanischen Wagen. Der deutsche Wagen ist ein Qualitätswagen, ein Erzeugnis wirklicher, echter Werkmansarbeit, der amerikanische — mit Ausnahmen geviss — ein Fabrikat, das soundsoviele Dollars einbringen soll und das man nach ein paar Jahren auf den Schutthaufen wirft, wen es aus dem Leim geht.

Wir haben ja heute auch schon in Deutschland zahlreiche Typen eines billigen Volkswagens, und die Prese werden immer mehr herabgehen, je leistungsfähiger unsere Industrie infolge der erhöhten Nachfrage werden wird. Die amerikanische Gefahr, die noch vor einem Jahre zu drohen schien, ist heute mehr akut, und wenn wir uns im nachfolgenden mit Ford und seiner Organisation befassen, so geschieht es nicht zuletzt aus dem Grunde, dem Leser einen Begriff davon zu geben, in welcher Weise Ford versucht, den Weltmarkt zu erobern.

Dem Sport-Tagblat in Wien wird aus New-Xork geschrieben: Zum erstenmal lässt jetzt die Ford Motor Company Ozeanschiffe laufen, indem der Dampfer „Oneinda", nachdem er hier 5000 Automobile an Bord genommen hat, nach Jacksonville (Florida), New-Orleans und Houston (Texas) in See gegangen ist. Die „Onondaga" mit Automobilen für Südamerika wird folgen. Im Sommer wurden diese beiden Fahrzeuge sowie auch die beiden andern Dampfer der Flotte zum Erztransport auf den grossen Seen verwendet. Die Gesellschaft hat erst im letzten Jahr den Wassertransport begonnen, nachdem sie ein Jahr vorher durch Übernahme der Detroit, Toledo und Ironton Rail roade inen eigenen Anschluss an die grossen Stammbahnen des Landes gefunden hatte, wodurch sie von der Ford Motor Company noch weiteres hören, namentlich, wenn ihre ambitiösen Pläne in Europa verwirklicht werden können.

Ungeachtet der besonders in der Atomobilbranche scharf empfundenen Rückschläge der Wirtschaftskonjunktur im letzten Jahre bis Anfang November hat die Gesellschaft nicht einen Augenblick gezögert, die schon gemachten Pläne für die Ausdehnung der Betriebe programmgemäss durchzuführen. Den Anlagen in den Vereinigten Staaten sind nicht weniger als 40 Prozent Fläche zugefügt worden, das heisst, die Werke sind von 1450 Millionen Quadratfuss Raum auf 25 Millionen gekommen. Neue Anlagen wurden in Memphis (Texas), Charlotte (N. C.) Jacksonville (Florida), Dallas (Texax) und Lousville (Kentucky) geschaffen. Manche der älteren Werke wurden bedeutend erweitert, so dass zum Beispiel die in St. Paul (Minn.) in Chicago je 500 Wagen pro Tag montieren können.

Die Auslandswerke haben einen Zuwachs von 230.000 Quadratfuss erhalten. Während des Jahres eine neue Filiale in Santiago (Chile) errichtet, ferner wurden solche in Rotterdam und Stockholm eröffnet und die in Kopenhagen und Sao Paolo (Brasilien) erweitert.

Die Gesellschaft wendet neuerdings der Errichtung von hydro-elektrischen Anlagen sehr viel Aufmerksamkeit zu. Ein Wasserwerk in St. Paul (Minn.) und ein kleineres in Iron Mountain (Mich.) mit zusammen 34.000 Pferdekräften, sind kürzlich fertiggestellt worden, für ein weiteres in Ypsilanti (Mich.) sind die Pläne entworfen. Bekannt sind die Bestrebungen Henry Fords, die Regierung zur Abschliessung eines 99-Jahre-Pachtvertrages für die sogenannten „Muscle Shoals"-Stromschnellen in Alabama zu bewegen. Die Sache schwebt noch im Kongress, wo grosse Opposition entstanden ist, obwohl Ford den Farmer billigeren Dünger garantieren will, sofern ihm die Ausbeutung dieser ungeheuren Wasserkraft übertragen wird.

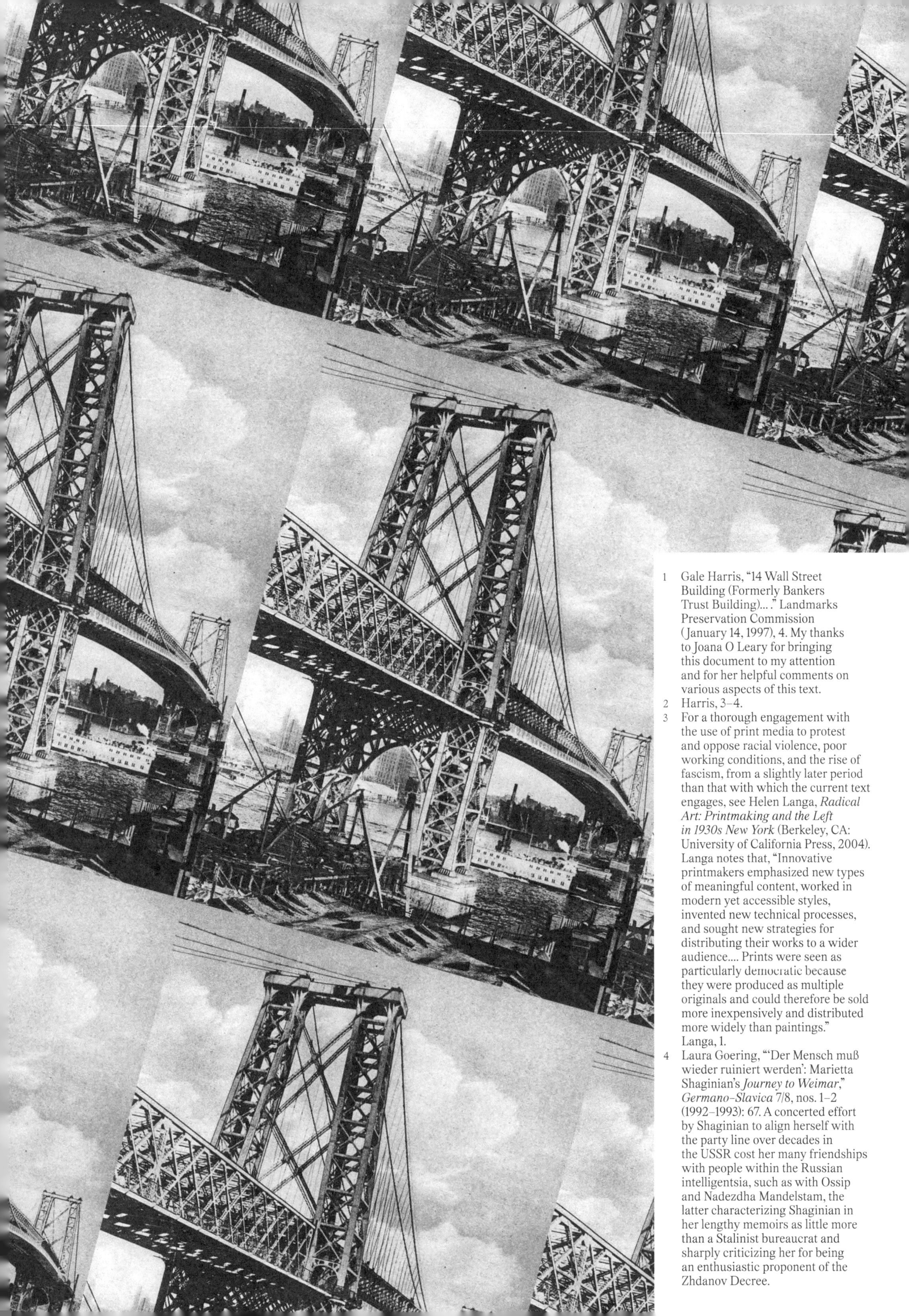

1 Gale Harris, "14 Wall Street Building (Formerly Bankers Trust Building)… ." Landmarks Preservation Commission (January 14, 1997), 4. My thanks to Joana O Leary for bringing this document to my attention and for her helpful comments on various aspects of this text.

2 Harris, 3–4.

3 For a thorough engagement with the use of print media to protest and oppose racial violence, poor working conditions, and the rise of fascism, from a slightly later period than that with which the current text engages, see Helen Langa, *Radical Art: Printmaking and the Left in 1930s New York* (Berkeley, CA: University of California Press, 2004). Langa notes that, "Innovative printmakers emphasized new types of meaningful content, worked in modern yet accessible styles, invented new technical processes, and sought new strategies for distributing their works to a wider audience.... Prints were seen as particularly democratic because they were produced as multiple originals and could therefore be sold more inexpensively and distributed more widely than paintings." Langa, 1.

4 Laura Goering, "'Der Mensch muß wieder ruiniert werden': Marietta Shaginian's *Journey to Weimar*," *Germano-Slavica* 7/8, nos. 1–2 (1992–1993): 67. A concerted effort by Shaginian to align herself with the party line over decades in the USSR cost her many friendships with people within the Russian intelligentsia, such as with Ossip and Nadezdha Mandelstam, the latter characterizing Shaginian in her lengthy memoirs as little more than a Stalinist bureaucrat and sharply criticizing her for being an enthusiastic proponent of the Zhdanov Decree.

"Who Does Not Work Does Not Eat": Reflections in Print of Solidarity for Labor Movements in the United States, Mexico, and Czechoslovakia in the 1920s

Meghan Forbes

In 1923, the Czech poet Jaroslav Seifert put out his second volume of poetry, titled *Samá láska* (Sheer Love). It is a slim book, with a photomontage reproduced on the cover by artist Otakar Mrkvička. At first glance, the cover art is a celebration of the industry and commodity culture which is indelibly connected with the United States. In the foreground is the Bankers Trust Company Building, originally erected in 1910–1912 in the financial district of New York City, which quickly "became an iconic symbol of American capitalism."[1] Other symbols of modernity—a gramophone record, an airplane, and an ocean liner—firmly situate the composition in a technologically advanced and trans-Atlantic context. But, on closer contemplation, something else is at work here. The Bankers Trust building is without its iconic stone pyramid that was a source of "enormous pride," seen as a "trademark" that asserted the bank building as a "'Tower of Strength'," and is, instead, irreverently capped with the red star of communism.[2] An outsized vase with flowers curiously climbs halfway up the face of the American skyscrapers. The shiny new buildings are also divorced from their context at the epicenter of capitalism and placed instead along Wenceslas Square in Prague, leading up to the National Museum. Mrkvička's photomontage, like Seifert's book of poems, is not an unfettered, jubilant depiction of innovation in the West, but rather a claim for the place of Prague (and the Devětsil group of which both the artist and poet were members) within the unfolding twentieth century story of industrial progress.

The cover of *Sheer Love* is evocative of the ambiguous way in which the Czech Left of the 1920s viewed developments on the American continent in the years immediately after the First World War. Book and periodical publications originating in Prague in this timeframe shine a light on the complicated reception of a "Western" modernity in Central Europe within the atmosphere of optimism that emerged from the devastation of the war; an atmosphere which, however, was quickly dissipated by the rise of fascism and economic instability that would characterize the 1930s. I show this through a selection of visual examples drawn from the forms of photography and photomontage, illustration, block printing and lithography, and mural painting, which were reproduced in the serial publications *Reflektor* in Prague and the far more famous *New Masses* in New York. These periodicals, which began publication in the mid-1920s on either side of the Atlantic, utilized accessible print media to critically address the conditions of a rapidly industrializing workforce in urban centers as well as those laboring in rural, agricultural environments.[3] They also make visible, both deliberately and sometimes inadvertently, the implications of imperialism on Indigenous life in the Americas.

Reflektor was an explicitly communist magazine first published in 1925, running until 1929 under the editorship of poet and political activist S. K. Neumann. Of an older generation than the Devětsil members, Neumann was something of a father figure to the likes of Seifert, who was for a time also an editor at *Reflektor*. Devětsil's leading members, including Seifert and his peers Karel Teige and Vítězslav Nezval, originally modeled their group's production on that of Neumann, then later worked in opposition to him and quarreled with him both in public and private. To a far greater extent than can be seen on the pages of Devětsil publications (such as those of what was perhaps their best-known periodical, *ReD*, which ran from 1927–1931), the orientation of *Reflektor* is consistently and ardently aligned in its sympathies towards a world proletariat that is being abused by European and US might, while also overlooking certain instances of violences and inequalities and expressing some political sympathies that would later prove misguided.

Where Devětsil members are platformed in *Reflektor*, this typically occurs in relation to the group's more overtly political outputs. For instance, another montage by Mrkvička is featured in volume one, issue thirteen, this time in collaboration with Teige: a reproduction of the book cover for *Mess Mend: Američané v Leningradě* (Mess Mend: A Yankee in Leningrad). Here, as on the cover of *Sheer Love*, are the symbols of modern forms of transportation, layered with architectural features and human figures. A statue of Lenin with his back turned to the viewer raises an arm in the direction of a figure who looks like a terrified, deranged businessman. In his other hand, Lenin holds a stone likeness of Karl Marx. A large, disembodied, and open hand bears the insignia "MM"—a reference to the book's title, that is also an uncanny precursor of the poster for Fritz Lang's famous 1931 film *M*.

The original book, published in Russian by Marietta Shaginian, the daughter of an Armenian doctor living in Moscow, is described by Laura Goering as "revolutionary-satirical," and thus rather at odds in its detective story format with the author's later Socialist Realist work.[4] The wandering plot pits the proletariat, unified as a transnational organization known as "Mess Mend," against the world's wealthiest man, an American. In *Reflektor*, a brief promotional text for the book presents

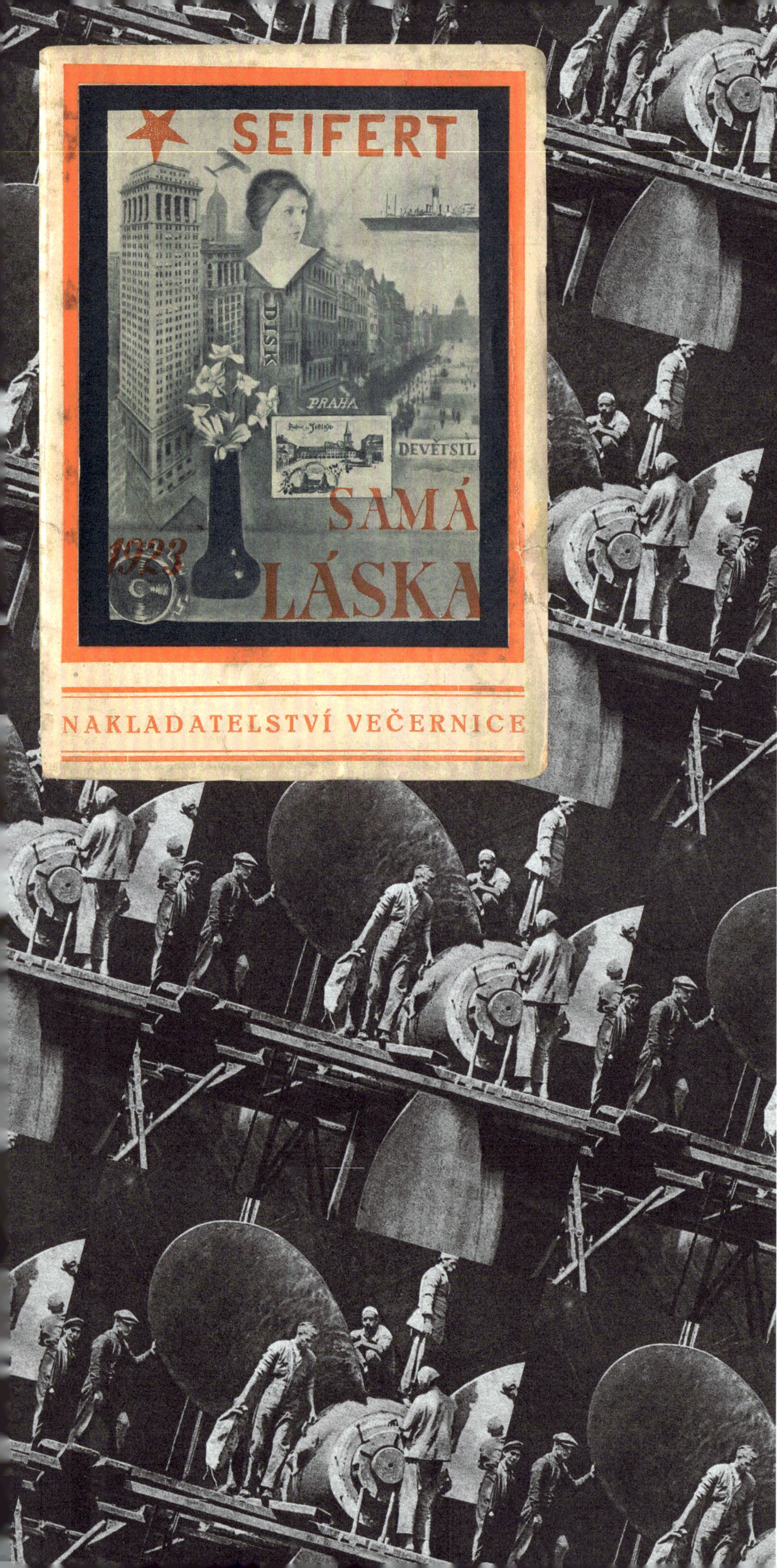

 Jaroslav Seifert, *Samá Láska*, Prague: Nakladatelství Večernice 1923, cover by Otakar Mrkvička

5 Unsigned, "Američané v Leningradě čili Mess Mend," *Reflektor* 1, no. 6 (1925): 14. Unless otherwise noted, all translations from the Czech in this text are my own.

6 Unsigned, "Vlk v rouše beránčím," *Reflektor* 1, no. 3 (1925): 2. Unattributed article, with the original source listed only as "*Spectator*."

7 For a summary of the proceedings in English, see Alois Neurath(?), "The Organisations of Kladno and Brünn on the Decisions of the Enlarged Executive," *International Press Correspondence* 5, no. 43 (May 14, 1925): 563.

8 Devětsil, untitled afterword in Seifert, *Samá láska* by Jaroslav Seifert (Prague: Večernice, V. Vortel and R. Rejman, 1923), 62. Translation published as "Afterword," in Seifert, *The Early Poetry of Jaroslav Seifert*, trans. Dana Loewy (Evanston, IL: Northwestern University Press, 1997), 93. The translation is my own, however.

9 In Moravia, the town of Zlín, where the shoemaker Baťa had set up shop, built workers' housing, and offered recreational activities, can serve as a foil to the situation as represented in Kladno. In "High Modernism in Theory and Practice: Karel Teige and Tomáš Baťa," Jessica Merrill sees more similarities than differences between the socialist-oriented rhetoric of the Czechoslovak avant-garde centered around Teige, and a burgeoning capitalist workers' economy in the countryside, which was on view in the town of Zlín. See "High Modernism in Theory and Practice: Karel Teige and Tomáš Baťa," *Slavic Review* 76, no. 2 (Summer 2017): 428–454. A recent article in Czech on the interactions between the political left and the avant-garde is by Marek Krejčí, "Kultura radikální levice ve stínu politiky dvacátých let," *Paginae Historiae* 1 (2024): 167–176.

the novel as a socialist counterpoint to the bourgeoise detective novel, and claims that its revolutionary potential lies precisely in its capacity to captivate a wide audience. Its description reads, “New and newer people, crowds, New York, salons of millionaires, secret meetings of workers, fascists, a doctor’s office, a crazy man, secrets signs, secret passageways, perversion and love—Leningrad, working factories, radium city, a meeting of doctors, intricacies of counter revolution and an astonishing end—life in the novel is truly adventurous […].”[5] *Mess Mend* was published in serial form in Moscow in ten volumes across the year 1924, featuring photomontage covers by the Soviet artist Aleksandr Rodchenko. It was a popular success, but was also criticized for lacking a serious social message. On account of its fame and ostensibly anti-capitalist bent, it was of immediate interest to the leftist avant-garde in Prague, and was almost simultaneously published in Czech translation, by Josef Hora, in 1925. That same year, *Mess Mend* was also published in German, similarly featuring a photomontage on its front and back covers.

Reflektor also platformed the actually existing conditions of the working class, at home in Czechoslovakia as well as to the East and West. Also in 1925, a *Reflektor* photospread focused on the Ford Motor Company illustrates this succinctly, and gives real-life context as to how an
•01 evil capitalist such as the fictionalized protagonist in *Mess Mend* might accumulate vast wealth by exploiting the laboring masses in the US. In an accompanying article, titled “A Wolf in Sheep’s Clothing,” the following conclusion is made:

> Ford is the unwitting accomplice to the revolutionary proletariat, in his revolutionization of the production process and technology, and in his struggle against the financial capital of Wall Street (Morgan, Rockefeller, etc.).
>
> Ford is also however the most dangerous enemy of the revolutionary proletariat, because he ensnares workers in a “golden cage,” where one “pecks from the hand” and is entirely tamed.[6]

The didactic photomontage, far less sophisticated in its layout than Mrkvička and Teige’s collaboration, illustrates this sentiment. It shows the men of the Ford Motor Company gathered at work, in training, and at leisure. There is very little chance for individuality to be registered in these masses surrounded by factory buildings, save for the inclusion of a couple of photographs of distinct workers operating machines; they are, however, focused on the job at hand and do not acknowledge the photographer. By way of contrast, a man in suit and cap is seated in the earliest Ford Model T and faces the viewer from his vehicle. What is more, Henry Ford himself gazes out, benignly inactive, in a photograph cut and pasted below a headline from his own newspaper about employees receiving bonuses. While it is not Ford who appears at the center of Teige and Mrkvička’s montage for *Mess Mend* from the same year, the two men bear some resemblance, in the guise of wealthy US industrialists.

Shortly after the Ford montage publication, a double-page spread in a subsequent issue of *Reflektor* depicts life in another factory town: that of Kladno, an industrial center some thirty kilometers from Prague, which was once a site for logging, then coal mining, before finally becoming a center for steel manufacture in the post-war era. The Communist Party had held a Congress in Kladno in April of 1925, and aimed to build a strong proletarian front against a backdrop of rising costs and job loss.[7] Photographs of the buildings around the mines emphasize the heavy architecture of the facilities, and almost wholly lack human figures, in stark contrast to images of the town square. A large oval cutout in the middle of the visual field encompasses a mass gathering of men, women, and children, all apparently marching in a demonstration. To the right and below, the group is captured from a different perspective, now with their backs turned to the viewer. Just to the left of this frame, centered at the bottom of the montage, the crowd stands in a semi-circle facing forward while carrying flags in a street demonstration, as small children advance in the foreground. Together, these photographs take on a cinematic dimension, as though they are tracing the movement of a procession. The people of Kladno, these montaged photographs suggest, are not only the engine of the mines, but also of socialism.

These two photo spreads—one depicting US industry, the other factory/life in Kladno—together recall a line in a collective statement, signed simply “Devětsil” in Seifert’s *Sheer Love*: “In these poems lives Kladno, also New York — Paris lives in the them, as does Jičín and Prague, the whole world.”[8] Czechoslovakia was a major industrial center in 1920s Europe, and placing its cities and towns in this list alongside New York and Paris—famous cities known by the “whole world”—is a strategy that simultaneously lifts the status of the smaller country and humbles those Western centers as just some among many sites of industrialization and modernity. The photomontage from Kladno suggests that the city would be nothing without its workers, and that the people have made this clear; on the other hand, the Ford photomontage warns that while the same could be true in Detroit or Grand Rapids, Ford has successfully coerced his employees into compliance by offering them ice skating rinks and the promise of bonuses.[9]

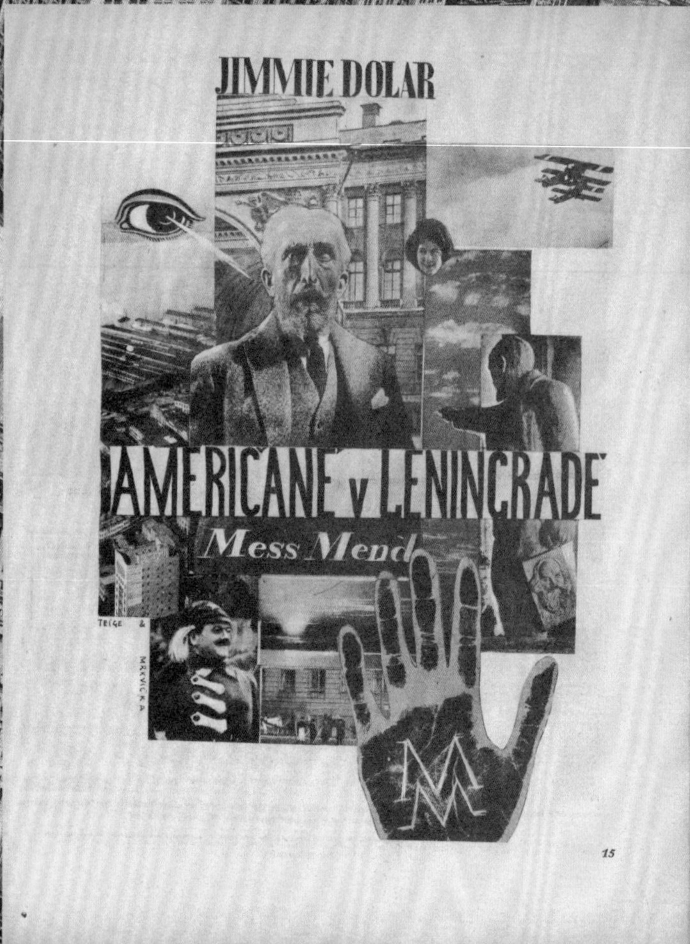

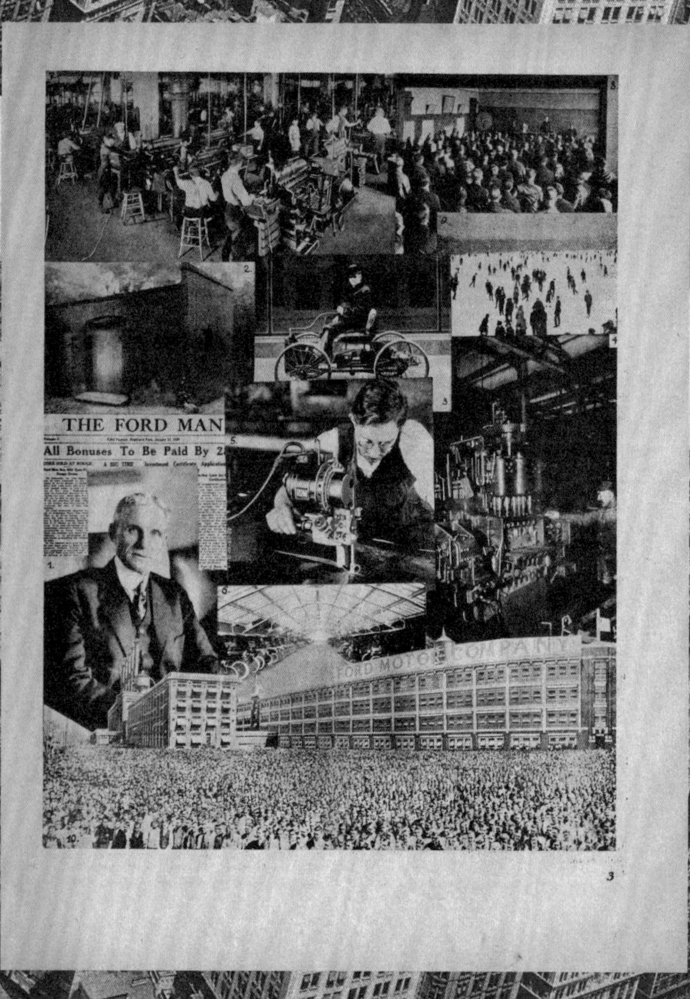

155 *Reflektor*, no. 13, July 1925, ed. Stanislav K. Neumann, Prague, 15, collage by Karel Teige and Otakar Mrkvička [*Jimmie Dollar, Američané v Leningradě*]

156 *Reflektor*, no. 3, February 1925, ed. Stanislav K. Neumann, Prague, 3, [The Ford Man]

10 Benjamin Madley, *An American Genocide: The United States and the California Indian Catastrophe, 1846–1873* (New Haven: Yale University Press, 2016), 194. The US government subsidized this massacre by paying colonial "volunteers" to murder Indigenous people.

11 A.V. Frič, "Mexické kapitoly, I. Země vulkánů," *Reflektor* 1, no. 6 (1925): 7.

12 See David Craven, "The Ministry of Education Murals (1923–1928) and the New Mass Politics," in *Art and Revolution in Latin America, 1910–1990* (New Haven: Yale University Press, 2002), 37–45; and María Estela Duarte, "Chronology: Diego Rivera's Artistic Trajectory," in *Diego Rivera: Art and Revolution* (Mexico: Instituto Nacional de Bellas Artes: Landucci Editores, 1999), 387; published in conjunction with an exhibition of the same name at The Cleveland Museum of Art, February 14–May 2, 1999; Los Angeles County Museum of Art, May 30–August 16, 1999; Museum of Fine Arts, Houston, September 19–November 28, 1999; Museo de Arte Moderno, INBA, Mexico City, December 17, 1999–March 19, 2000. Famously, in the midst of the Great Depression, Edsel Ford, son of Henry Ford, commissioned Rivera to produce a mural for the newly-opened Detroit Institute of Art. Rivera's seemingly unlikely Detroit Industry Murals, produced in 1932–1933, include motifs reminiscent of this production in Mexico City from the decade prior.

13 Craven, 40. Also, Rivera produced a revised detail from this painting in the US in 1932, titled *Open Air School*, which was printed as a lithograph in an edition of 100 copies by Georg Miller for the Weyhe Gallery, New York. *Diego Rivera*, 285.

14 Craven, 40.

15 Langa, 85.

16 See "Cronología," in *Xavier Guerrero: 1896–1974* (Mexico City: Museo Nacional de Arte, 2012), 111–114.

↑155 A year later, in volume two of *Reflektor*, an article titled "The Wonders of the Automobile" and related photographic documentation across several issues together produce a statement that is rather less emphatic in its criticism of US-based industrialization. The potential use-value of tractors for agricultural work is noted for instance, while also reflecting on the low chance that the auto worker will ever have access to the luxury goods he produces. One page features a photograph of a large vehicle driving tourists through a hole cut in a tree, in what one might assume to be obvious fodder ridiculing the bourgeoise (an opportunity often taken up with relish in the pages of *Reflektor*). However, there is no indication of critique in the accompanying caption or page layout with this documentation of the Wawona Tree Tunnel in the Yosemite National Park in California, so the purpose of the photograph appears merely to be to present the potential for amusement of the modern automobile. Perhaps the intended spectacle of the image disguises what is, in fact, in plain view: an arrogant disrespect of nature and the genocide of Indigenous people by white settlers in the region. Euro-Americans first arrived in the area in the 1850s, and in the Spring of 1851, as Benjamin Madley records, "in no fewer than seven separate incidents, they [the so-called Mariposa Battalion] killed at least twenty-four to thirty Ahwahnees and perhaps many more. By systematically torching villages and food stores, the battalion also made survival difficult for retreating Ahwahnee survivors."[10] In 1864, Abraham Lincoln signed a bill granting Yosemite the status of a state park; it became a National Park in 1890. From 1927 up to the present day, the luxury Ahwahnee Hotel within the park has been named after the area's earlier inhabitans—not in memorium, but rather in a cruel erasure of the violent history of the place. So even as an aggressive domination over nature is clearly evident in the photo in *Reflektor*, it is perhaps unsurprising that the story of colonization in North America which is also embedded in it seems to have been entirely lost on the editors.

The magazine *Reflektor* was markedly international in its scope and did not limit its view of the Americas to the United States, as it also followed movements in Latin America, aiming to keep an eye on labor movements there; for instance, it traced those connected with the Mexican Revolution (1910–1940). The Czech botanist and ethnographer A.V. Frič, who traveled extensively in the Americas, made unfavorable comparisons between Mexico and the United States, claiming that whereas people in the former country were disparagingly called "bandits and Bolsheviks," the real crooks are to be found on Wall Street, against which the proletariat in Mexico stands as the first line of defense.[11] The twentieth and twenty-first numbers of volume one subsequently ↑156 feature works by Diego Rivera. They are two reproductions of murals produced for the Ministry of Education in Mexico City, where Rivera had created a series of 235 panels over the course of five years from 1923–1928, collectively titled the *Political Vision of the Mexican People*, that reflect various aspects of socio-political life in the artist's home country.[12] In one of the images we see men at work in a foundry, the words (in Czech) "The Proletariat in Art" imposed in capital letters in the upper-right corner. The other image foregrounds a circle of women, seated outdoors in a study circle. David Craven highlights the significance of this mural, *La muestra rural* (The Rural Teacher), for its representation of women "on the front lines of conflict," and identifies the model for the teacher in the painting as Luz Jiménez, "a young indigenous woman aspiring to be a literary brigadista."[13] An armed union cadre on horseback is stationed behind the women, as men labor in the fields in the background; the painting is thus a "superb embodiment of the distinctive radicalism of the educational program in Mexico," notable for its depiction of the rural teacher as integral to this movement amidst "the intense class struggle that marked the contest over land reform in a period when the haciendas were slowly being broken up."[14] In *Reflektor*, the image is captioned "A liberated country," perhaps with a glint of irony, or simply as an optimistic reference to the contemporary revolutionary moment in Mexico that Rivera was depicting with his murals.

In 1926, in volume two of *Reflektor*, the work of another figure in the Mexican Mural Movement of the 1920s, Xavier Guerrero, is printed. Though the artist is not credited in the caption in *Reflektor*, the image source is attributed to the magazine *New Masses*, which is described as "a revolutionary American magazine"—evidence that this new monthly from New York was making its way to Prague. *New Masses* had first appeared in May 1926, having been created in response to (and distinct from) previous leftist-socialist New York periodicals *The Masses* (1911–1917) and *The Liberator* (1918–1924), and alongside *The Crisis* (founded in 1910 by W.E.B. du Bois). Like *Reflektor,* it contained polemical essays, poetry and prose, as well as visual art, and sought to reach a working-class audience. Helen Langa writes that *New Masses* reproduced lithographs and pen-and-ink drawings in its first couple of years of operation to depict labor issues and police violence "in an abstracted mechanical style inspired by Cubism and Russian Constructivism. This openness to varied styles was somewhat suppressed when the editors turned to stricter proletarian perspectives in 1929 and 1930."[15] Guerrero's poster art (which made its way into *Reflektor*) had been first reproduced in *New Masses* in September 1926 and the artist was represented in the magazine again in the subsequent month, likely the outcome of meeting the American author John Dos Passos, who was a regular contributor.[16] Both reproductions in *New Masses* reflect the workers' struggle and revolutionary times in Mexico. In the former,

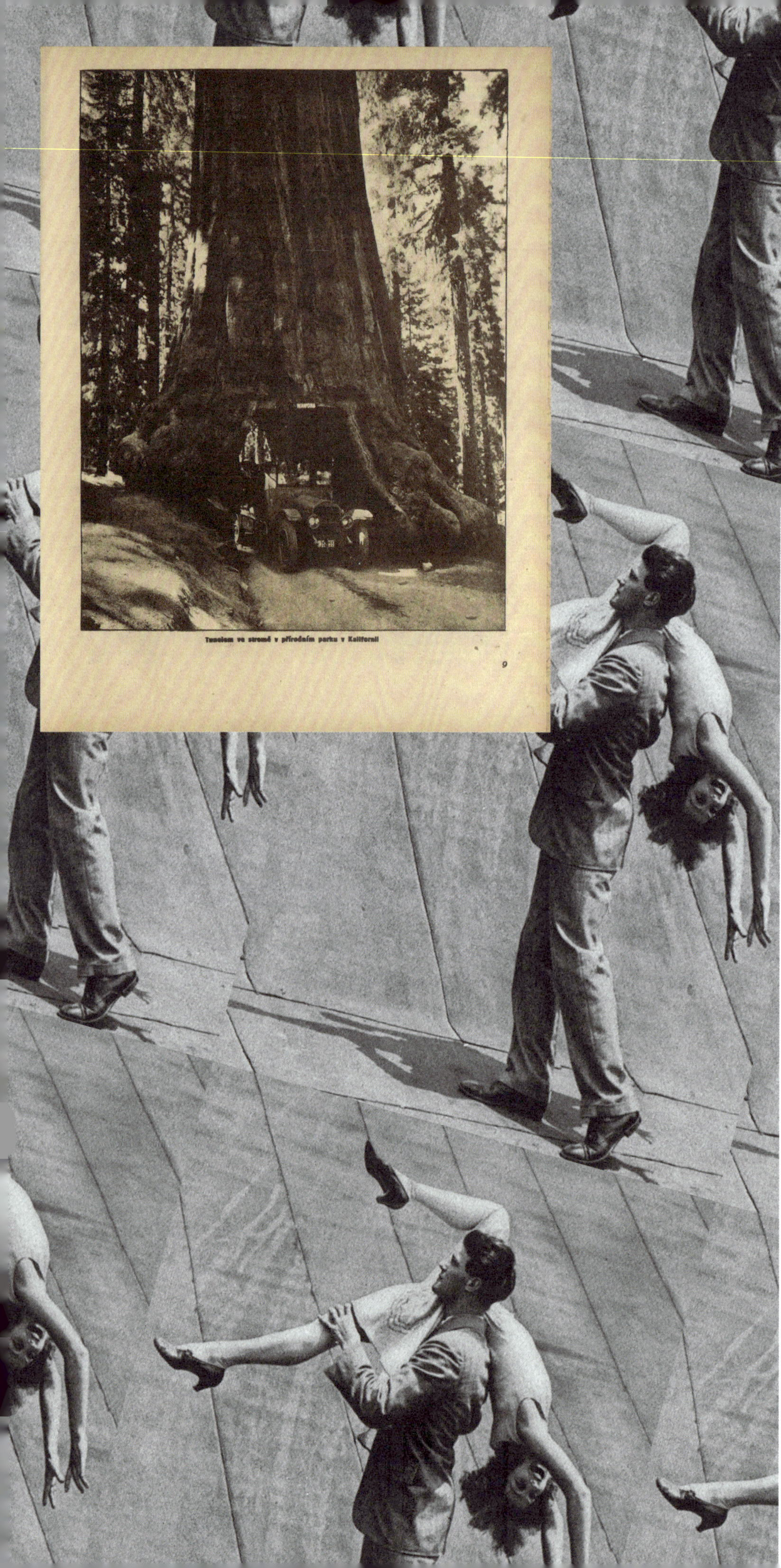

Reflektor, no. 17, September 1926, ed. Stanislav K. Neumann, Prague, 9, [photo of the Wawona Tree Tunnel, Yosemite National Park]

17 The iconography and messaging is reminiscent of that employed in a woodcut Guerrero created for the masthead for *El Machete*, a periodical of the Mexican Artists' Union founded in 1924, which only existed for one year.

18 Biographical details on Matulka were referenced in *Jan Matulka 1890–1972* (Washington, D.C.: Smithsonian Institution, 1980), published in con-junction with an exhibition of the same name at the Whitney Museum of American Art, New York, December 18–February 24, 1980; the Houston Museum of Fine Arts, April 3–June 1, 1990; the Birmingham Museum of Art, Alabama, June 15–October 1, 1980; and the National Collection of Fine Arts, Smithsonian Institution, Washington, D.C., November 21, 1980–February 8, 1981; and in *Jan Matulka* (Chicago: Thomas McCormick Gallery, 1999); and Whitney Rugg, "The Global Modernist," in *Jan Matulka: The Global Modernist* (Chicago: TMG Projects, 2004), 12–18; published in conjunction with an exhibition of the same name organized with the estate of Jan Matulka and the Montclair Art Museum, September 2004–June 2006.

19 For the most part, Matulka in *New Masses* engaged with the machinations of US systems of power, such as the two-party political system, racial segregation, urbanization, the prospects of the working class, and income inequality. He also produced more abstract, modernist cityscapes.

20 Ironically, as he advocated for fair wages in both publications, it seems he was not paid for his contributions in either of them. He was largely supported by his wife, Lida Jiroušková-Matulka, as her decades-long career with the New York Public Library was their primary source of income. Henry Adams, "Jan Matulka," in *Jan Matulka*, 17.

21 The reproduction that would ultimately appear in *New Masses* originated as a conté crayon drawing, later re-worked as a lithograph by Matulka once he was back in New York.

22 Frič, 7.

an armed man faces forward surrounded by the iconography of both urban industry and rural agriculture, and key communist symbols (a star with a hammer and sickle) are shown at the top of the frame. While one hand holds a gun, the other is held up, palm outward, in front of which two small banners bear a slogan in Spanish: "El que no trabaja no come" (subsequently translated into Czech and English: "Who does not work does not eat"). The second image, printed above the table of contents in *New Masses,* shows men, women, and children gathered under a union banner, whose caption reads: "Workers of the World Unite! A Mexican Labor Poster."[17]

In the context of Czechoslovak leftist politics in the 1920s, and its relationship or response to the socio-political climate in the US, one contributor to *New Masses* particularly stands out: Jan Matulka. Born in Bohemia in 1890, Matulka emigrated with his family to New York in 1907.[18] Though infrequently exhibited today, Matulka was active in the New York art scene of the first half of the twentieth century—Katherine S. Dreier championed his work and initiated his solo show at the Art Center in 1926 (though their relationship was volatile). In the 1930s, Matulka was on the faculty of the Art Students League alongside another infer Czech immigrant, Vaclav Vytlacil, as well as George Grosz. Matulka had spent much of the first half of the 1920s in Europe, living mainly in Paris

and Prague (where he aligned himself not with Devětsil, but an older generation of artists), and by the time he contributed to the *New Masses*—for which he ultimately produced 24 illustrations—he reflected issues related to labor conditions and income inequality on both the American and European continents.[19] While collaborating with *New Masses*, Matulka simultaneously served as art advisor to the Czech-American publication *Dělník kalendář* (Worker's Almanac).[20]

In January 1927, a work titled "Czecho-Slovak Peasants" was printed in *New Masses.* Influenced by his travels outside Prague, and specifically to the Slovak town of Turie Pole, Matulka rendered this portrait of three people who sit forlornly in a field. Against a backdrop of rolling hills with a cow just behind them, two women in headscarves hold sickles on their laps, while a man at their side sits looking fatigued with hands crossed, his tool upturned at his feet.[21] Whereas the works of Rivera and Guerrero in *New Masses* reflect a dynamic moment of revolution in Mexico, Matulka's depiction of life for rural laborers in Czechoslovakia is bleaker, suggesting no real prospect of change. The sickles in the hands of the women, and their resolute if skeptical gazes, may hint at other, burgeoning pathways. Still, though, it is a far more ambiguous rendering than, for instance, Vera Mukhina's sculpture *The Worker and Collective Farm Woman*, which would be unveiled a decade later at the USSR Pavilion at the 1937 Paris World's Fair, in which a young woman steps forward stridently, her sickle raised aloft, joined by a young man who likewise holds his hammer high. The inclusion of women in depictions of worker's struggles by Rivera, Guerrero, and Matulka renders something which is persistently absent in illustrations of labor conditions in the interwar period generally.

By the end of the 1920s, it was increasingly clear on both sides of the Atlantic that the utopian visions early in the decade were to be foreclosed by the banks and blocked by the rise of right-wing politics. Now that a century has passed, the peoples of Europe and the United States find themselves in the midst of arguably a rather similar political position, which is perhaps the outcome of a refusal to see what the editors of periodicals like *Reflektor*, *New Masses*, and others were showing: that is, the fabricated mythology of US democracy and freedom. A.V. Frič wrote with bitter irony nearly one hundred years ago that the US is "not the country of bandits and Bolsheviks, but rather a democratic republic under the reign of Wall Street, prohibition, and the Ku-Klux-Klan. It's a respectable country, occupied by 'good' people."[22] The contributors to *Reflektor* and *New Masses* sought to expose the hypocrisy of the rhetoric of freedom and democracy at the service of capitalism in the US—that "wolf in sheep's clothing"—that has become increasingly tenuous in our own times. The final chapter in the story of the Wawona Tree Tunnel was already a striking evocation of this: after a hole was cut out of the massive 2000-year-old tree in 1881 for the amusement of tourists, less than a century later, in the late 1960s, the giant sequoia fell.

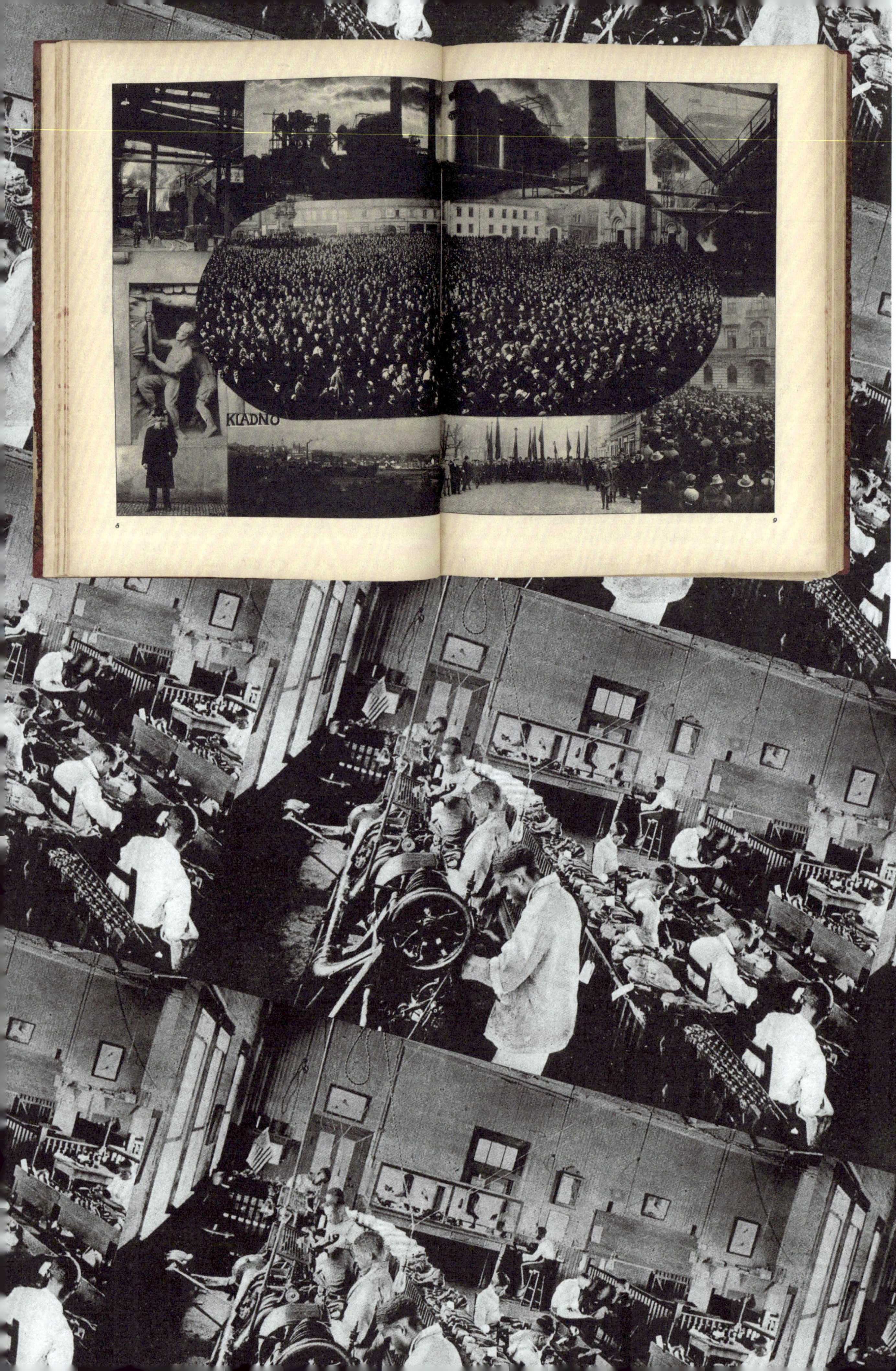

158 *Reflektor*, no. 5, March 1925, ed. Stanislav K. Neumann, Prague, 8–9, [Kladno]

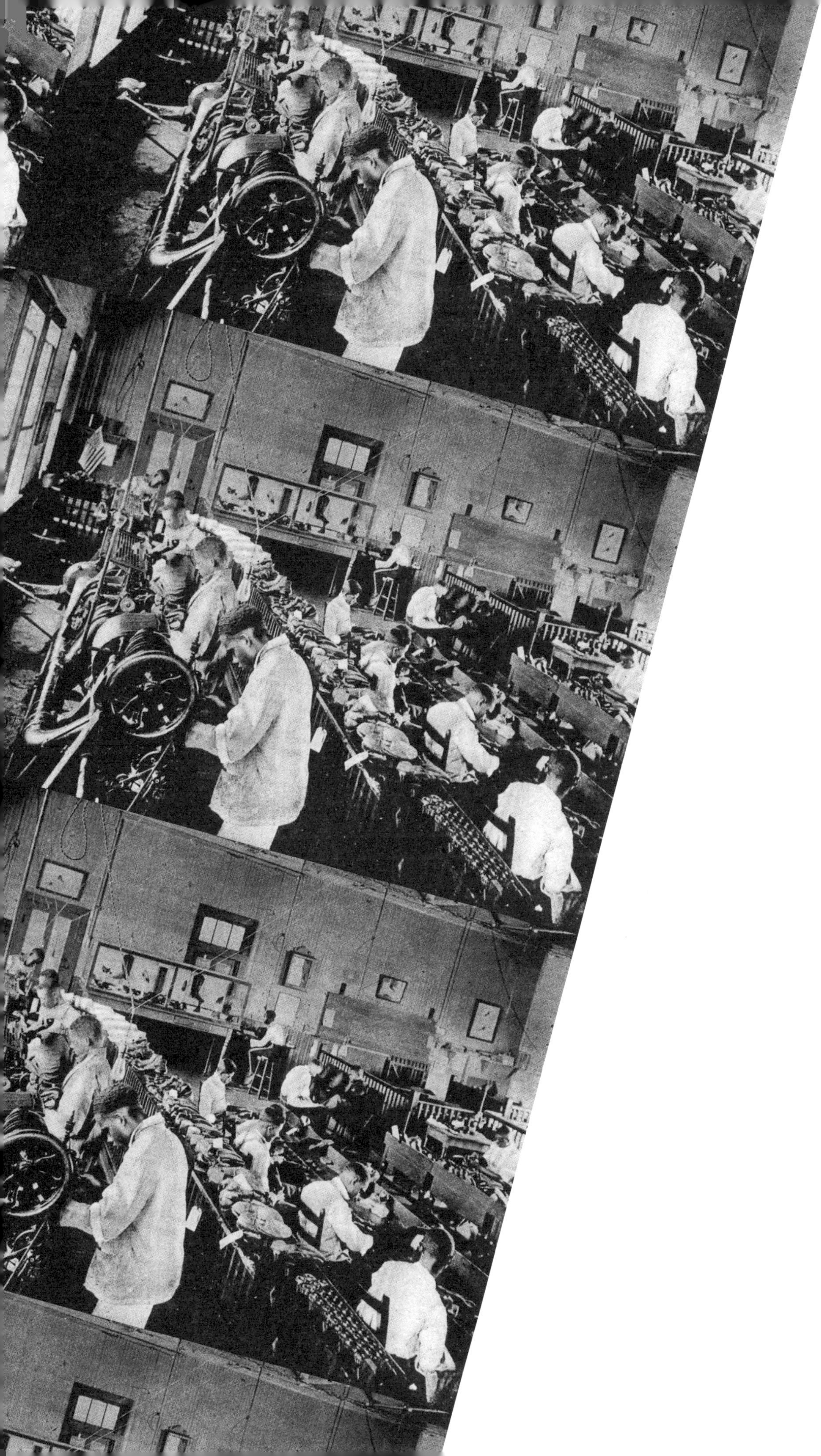

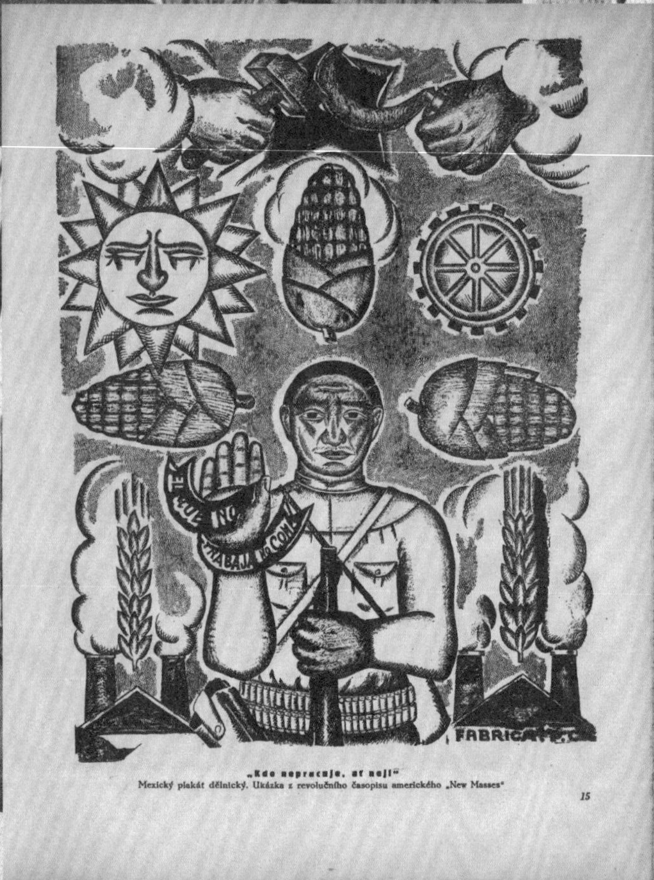

„Kdo nepracuje, ať nejí"
Mexický plakát dělnický. Ukázka z revolučního časopisu amerického „New Masses"

15

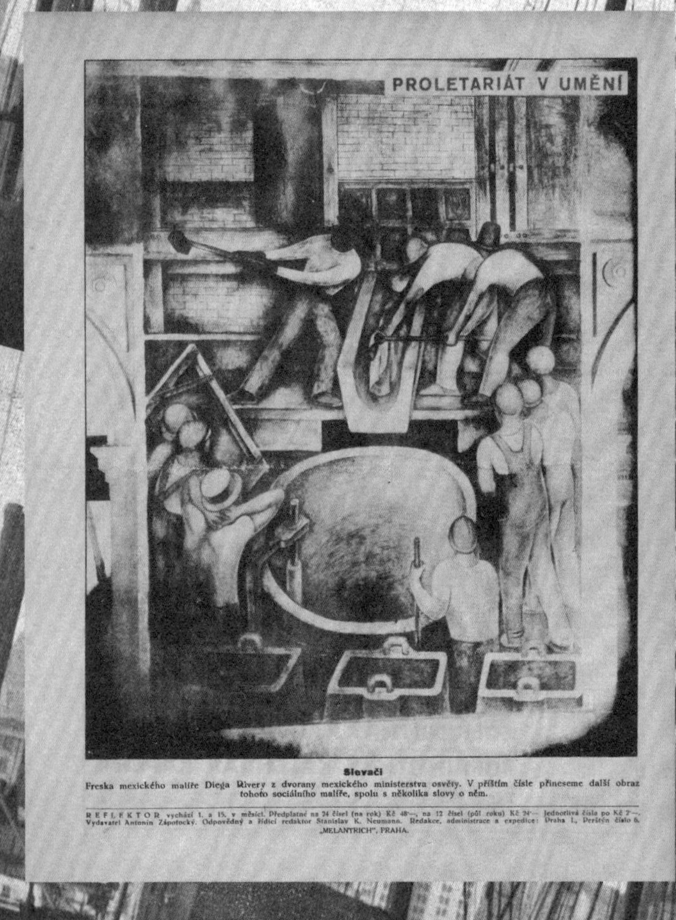

PROLETARIÁT V UMĚNÍ

Slévači

Freska mexického malíře Diega Rivery z dvorany mexického ministerstva osvěty. V příštím čísle přineseme další obraz tohoto sociálního malíře, spolu s několika slovy o něm.

REFLEKTOR vychází 1. a 15. v měsíci. Předplatné na 24 čísel (na rok) Kč 48'—, na 12 čísel (půl roku) Kč 24'—. Jednotlivá čísla po Kč 2'—. Vydavatel Antonín Zápotocký. Odpovědný a řídící redaktor Stanislav K. Neumann. Redakce, administrace a expedice: Praha I., Perštýn číslo 6. „MELANTRICH", PRAHA.

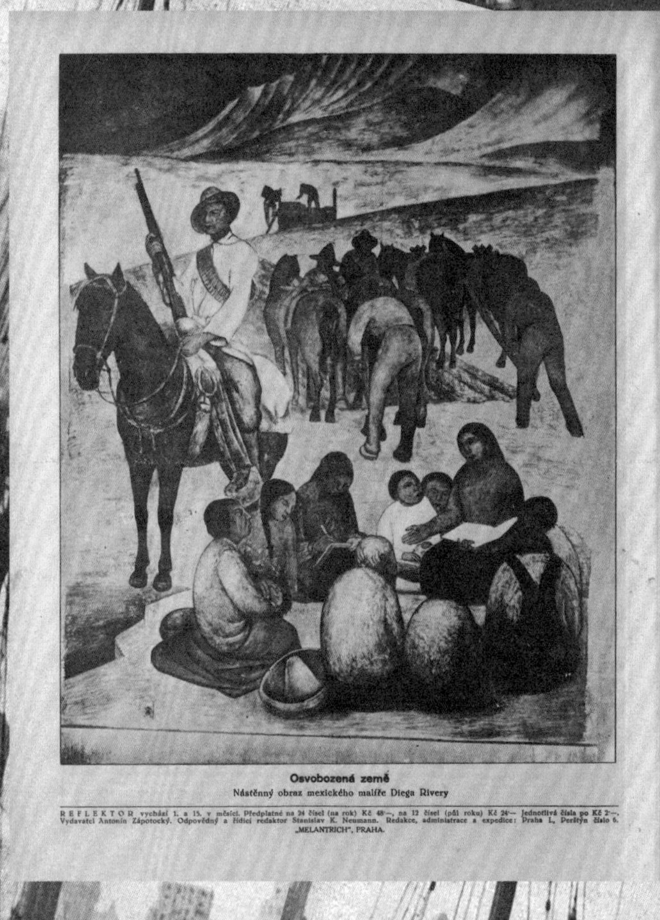

Osvobozená země

Nástěnný obraz mexického malíře Diega Rivery

REFLEKTOR vychází 1. a 15. v měsíci. Předplatné na 24 čísel (na rok) Kč 48'—, na 12 čísel (půl roku) Kč 24'—. Jednotlivá čísla po Kč 2'—. Vydavatel Antonín Zápotocký. Odpovědný a řídící redaktor Stanislav K. Neumann. Redakce, administrace a expedice: Praha I., Perštýn číslo 6. „MELANTRICH", PRAHA.

159 see 143.15, illustration by Xavier Guerrero
160 *Reflektor*, no. 20, October 1925, ed. Stanislav K. Neumann, Prague, back cover, mural by Diego Rivera
161 *Reflektor*, no. 21, November 1925, ed. Stanislav K. Neumann, Prague, back cover, mural by Diego Rivera: *La muestra rural*
162 *New Masses*, no. 3, August 1929, ed. Michael Gold, New York, cover by Rufino Tamayo: *Mexican Worker With Machete*
163 *New Masses*, no. 3, January 1927, ed. Egmond Arens, Hugo Gellert, Michael Gold, New York, cover by Rufino Tamayo

↓162 ↑159

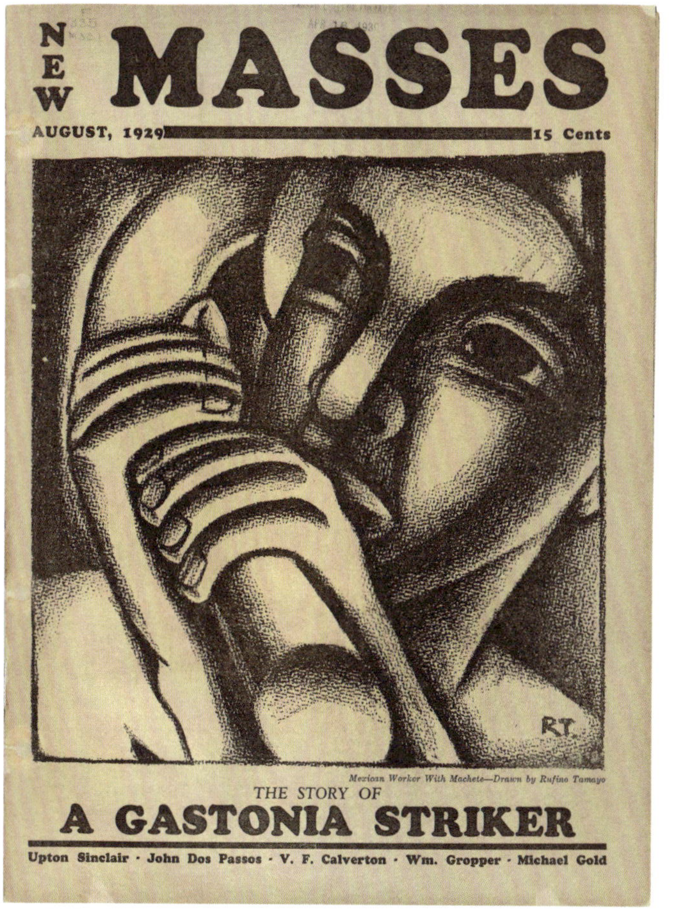

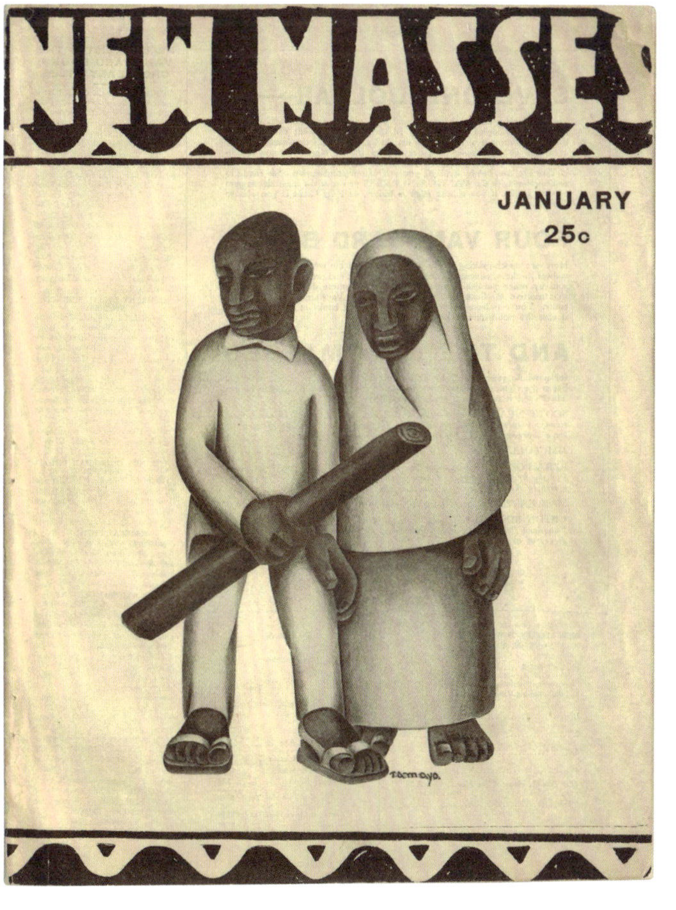

↓163 ↑161 ↑160

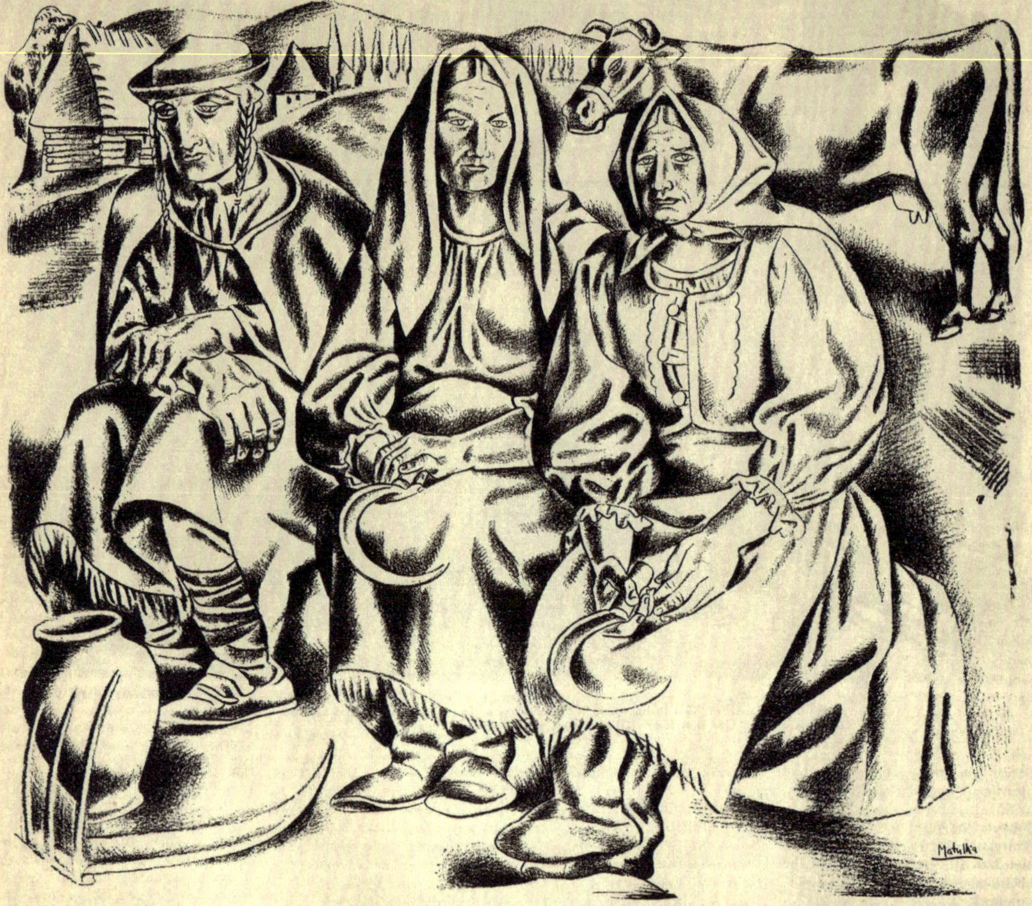

From a Lithograph by Jan Matulka

CZECHO - SLOVAK PEASANTS

surely not serious enough to warrant their resorting to unions.

As for "artistic advancement," it is certainly true that artists can benefit by coming together in groups in which they can work at their problems together and profit by each other's experience. Such a group were the Italian painters of the Renaissance; such another was the group of novelists which vibrated between the two poles of Flaubert and Zola in France in the last century; and such another was the Irish revival of Synge and Yeats and Lady Gregory and the rest. We have no such groups in America, except on a very small scale—the Stieglitz group, Mencken and Nathan, the disbanded vers-librists and imagists—and I believe that it would be a good thing if we had.

8. ***May society properly demand of the artist, not merely good craftsmanship and good reporting, but the "transvaluation of values"—the creation of new social values.***

JEFFERS: Society may properly wish for it, but it would be fatuous to demand what there is only the most exceptional chance of getting.

SINCLAIR: To say that the artist shall not be a creator, but merely a craftsman is to turn him from a man into a monkey.

TAGGARD: Hell!

CHASE: This is too esoteric for me. A sound artist does what he has to, regardless of social values. Read *The Constant Nymph.* Sanger kicked social values in the face, but it was worth the booting.

SEAVER: It is the vision that counts. . . . Vision means the breaking down of stale concepts into its living components. It means the formation of new values in the alembic of the creative imagination.

KRUTCH: I do not think it will do society any good to demand of the artist anything he does not feel like giving. Shakespeare is Shakespeare, even if he isn't Shaw. Even a conservative may be sincere. Why try to make a hypocrite of him by *demanding* that he be a revolutionary? Isn't that just as bad as demanding that he be a conservative?

BROUN: Society has a nerve even if it demands anything of the artist. It should take what he gives it and be properly humble and thankful. In a certain sense every creative person is a reformer, but this does not mean that he must be in his work a propagandist for good roads, shorter hours and a low tariff. All these are excellent things but they need not be the concern of the artist.

DEUTSCH: An enlightened society will not demand anything of its artists beyond good craftsmanship. It is the artist's business to create, with material abstracted from the actual world, images which live and move and have their being in a world of their own. Since he is constantly drawing upon life in creating these images, he cannot but affect in some sort the life about him. But the effect of his work is indirect and sometimes slow, and in any case it is not by this that his performance is to be judged. The artist must have his roots in the social soil, and it may well be that his genius drops

164 see 163, 7, lithograph by Jan Matulka
165 *New Masses*, no. 2, July 1929, ed. Michael Gold, New York, cover with a painting by Eitarō Ishigaki: *Undefeated Arm*
166 *New Masses*, no. 9, February 1929, ed. Michael Gold, New York

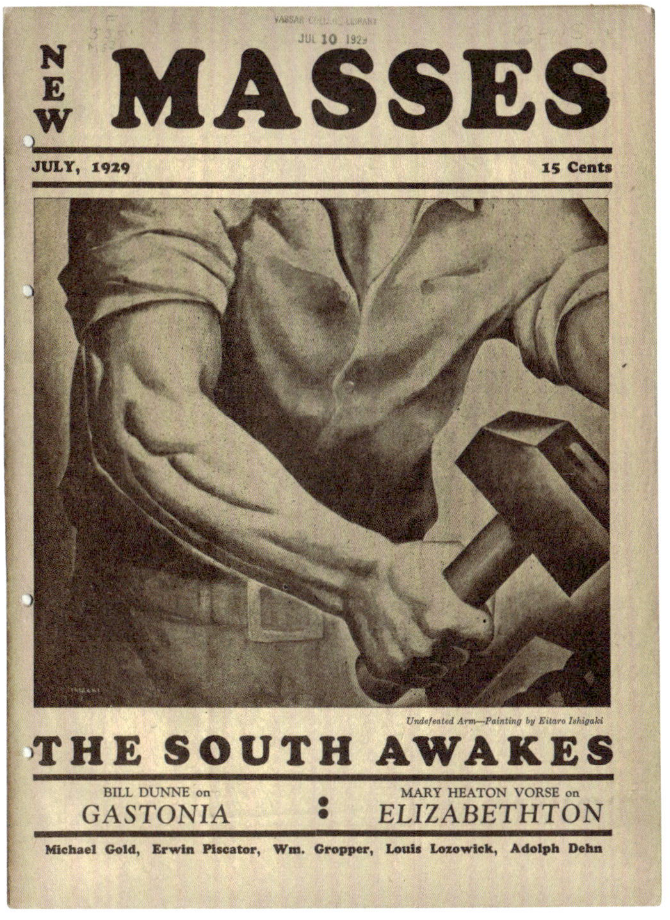

NEW MASSES

JULY, 1929 15 Cents

Undefeated Arm—Painting by Eitaro Ishigaki

THE SOUTH AWAKES

BILL DUNNE on GASTONIA : MARY HEATON VORSE on ELIZABETHTON

Michael Gold, Erwin Piscator, Wm. Gropper, Louis Lozowick, Adolph Dehn

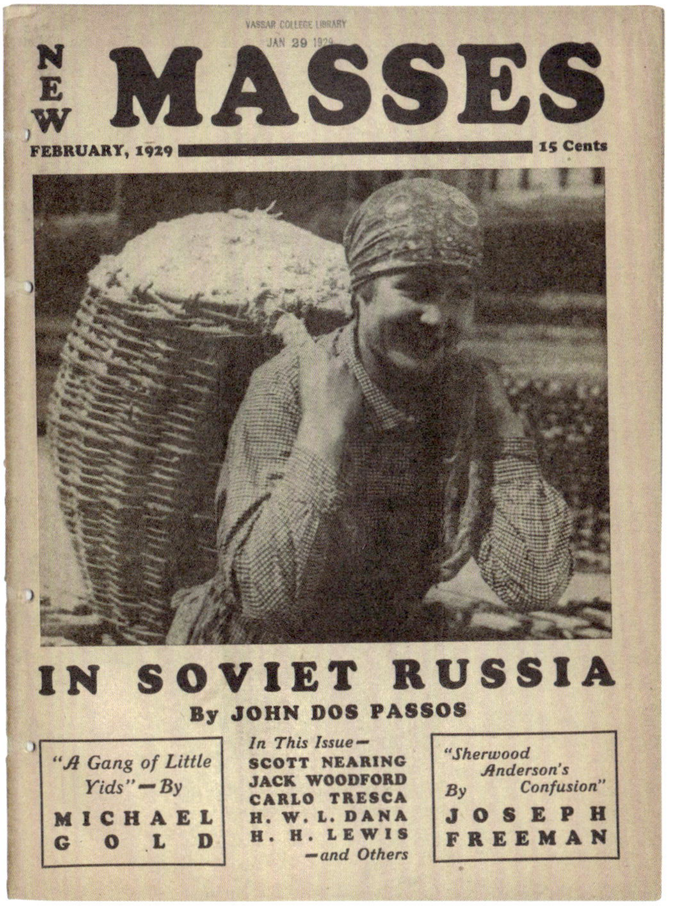

NEW MASSES

FEBRUARY, 1929 15 Cents

IN SOVIET RUSSIA
By JOHN DOS PASSOS

"A Gang of Little Yids"—By MICHAEL GOLD

In This Issue—
SCOTT NEARING
JACK WOODFORD
CARLO TRESCA
H. W. L. DANA
H. H. LEWIS
—and Others

"Sherwood Anderson's Confusion" By JOSEPH FREEMAN

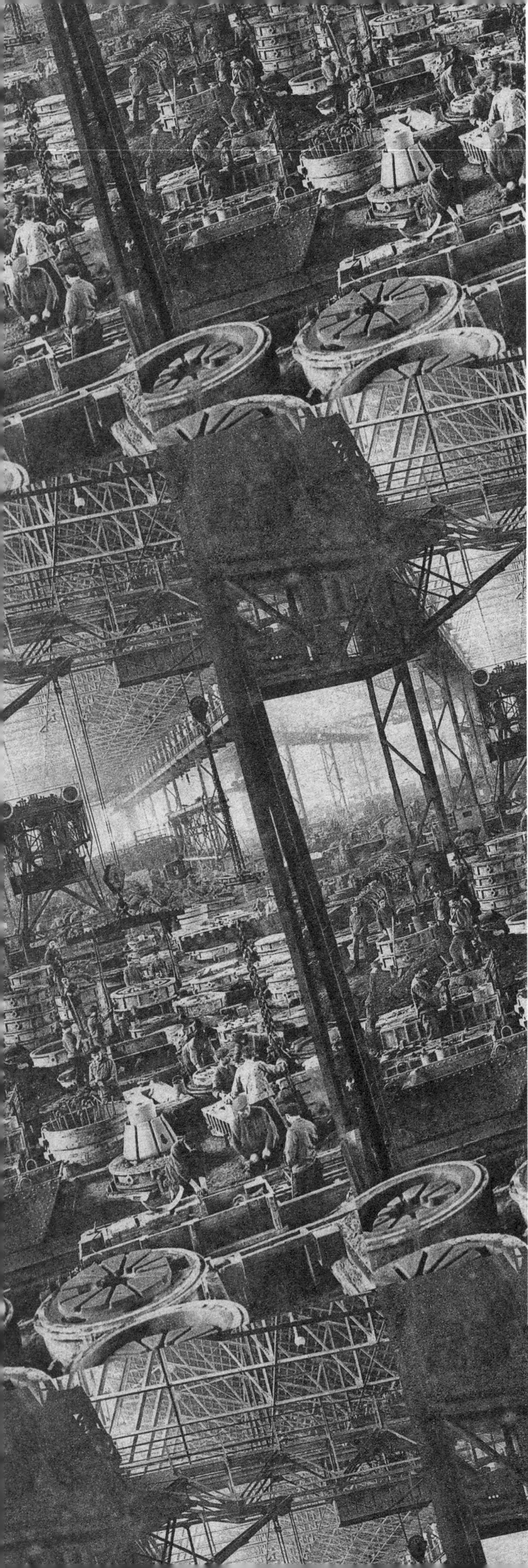

ANTI-CAPITALIST VIEWS BETWEEN NEW YORK AND BERLIN: *NEW MASSES*—*A-I-Z*—MALIK VERLAG

Avant-garde artists often worked as illustrators for leftist illustrated magazines and publishing houses. Visible evidence of this can be found in the magazines *New Masses* and *Arbeiter-Illustrierte-Zeitung* (Worker Illustrated Newspaper, A-I-Z), published in the 1920s on each side of the Atlantic, in New York and Berlin, respectively. *New Masses* was founded as a monthly magazine of leftist cultures in May 1926, following the model of two earlier socialist American journals, *The Masses* and *The Liberator*. In its first two years, it engaged many avant-garde artists as illustrators, such as Cubist artists Stuart Davis and Jan Matulka, Constructivist Louis Lozowick, and Rufino Tamayo. The political views of the magazine became more radical after Mike Gold took over as the sole chief editor in May 1928. From that point onwards militant activism took precedence, and the magazine was transformed into a platform for the writings of young workers. In 1929, the eight staff members of *New Masses* established an influential John Reed Club in New York for writers and artists with the aim of maintaining contact with the American revolutionary labor movement and a focus on spreading communist propaganda by praising the Soviet Union as a model.

In Weimar Germany, *A-I-Z magazine* had a political scope similar to that of *New Masses*. It was founded in 1921 by Willi Münzenberg, a Comintern associate, and outlined anti-capitalist views, often expressing harsh social criticism against US politics. Münzenberg viewed America's imperialist ambitions, racism, and capitalism as threats to peace in the world. He highlighted inequality between the ruling class and the working class, racism, and the rise of the right-wing ideology of the Ku Klux Klan. In the 1920s, a former Dada artist, John Heartfield, started to work with *A-I-Z*, for which he created many political photomontages. He engaged in the social critique of the Weimar Republic, which had blindly embraced *Amerikanismus* as an economic and cultural model. At the same time, Heartfield worked as a graphic designer for Malik Verlag in Berlin, which translated and published works by Upton Sinclair, a California-based American writer, and social, political, and cultural reformer who provided a new perspective on activism and made strong critiques of the American ruling class.

↓167

13

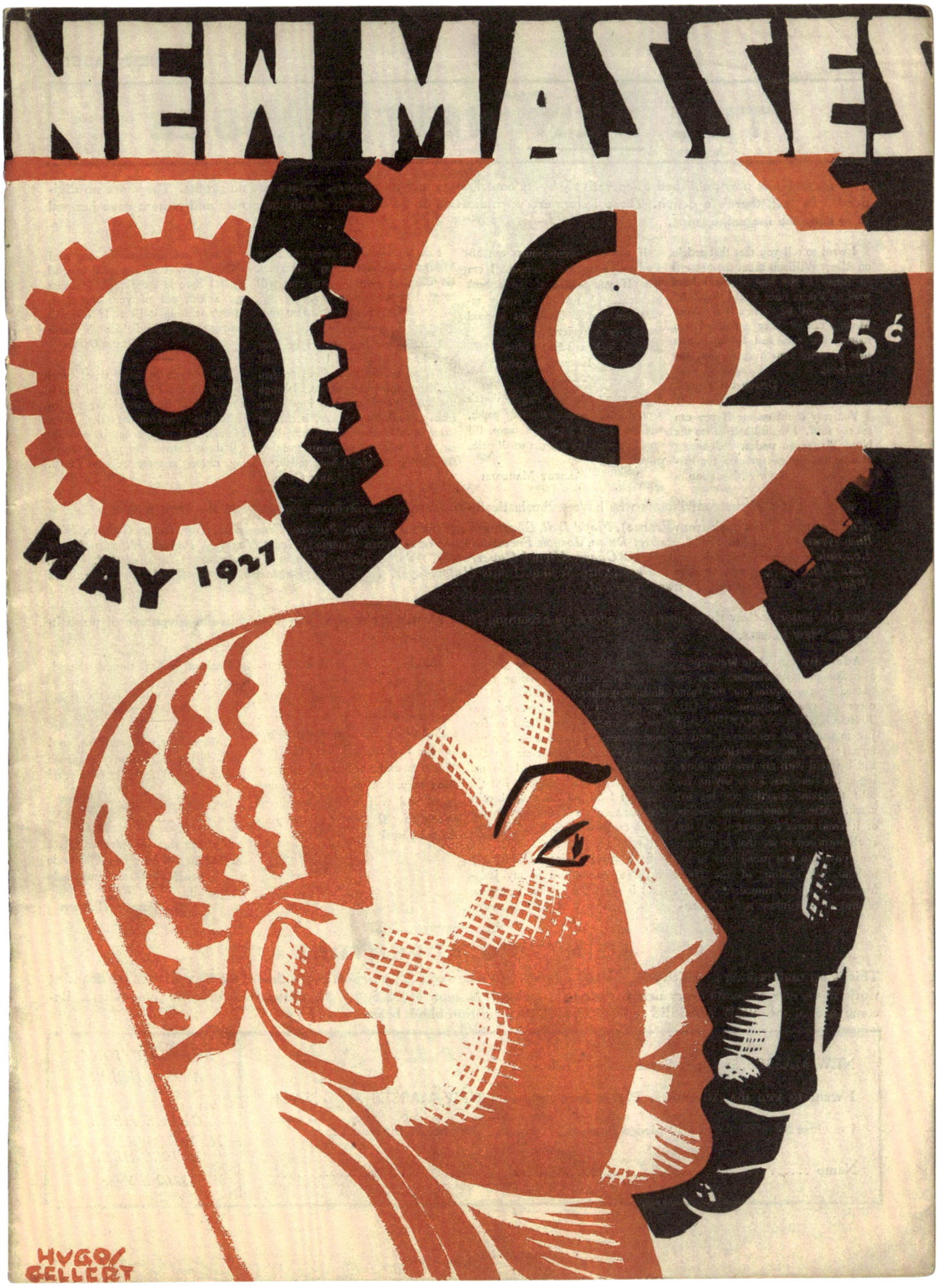

167 *New Masses*, no. 1, May 1927, ed. Michael Gold, Hugo Gellert, New York, cover by Hugo Gellert

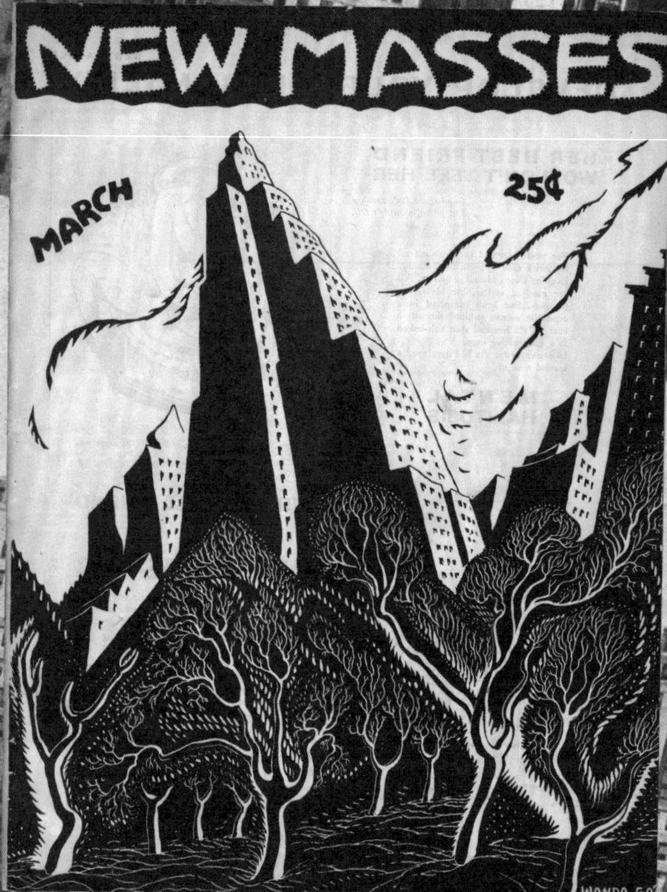

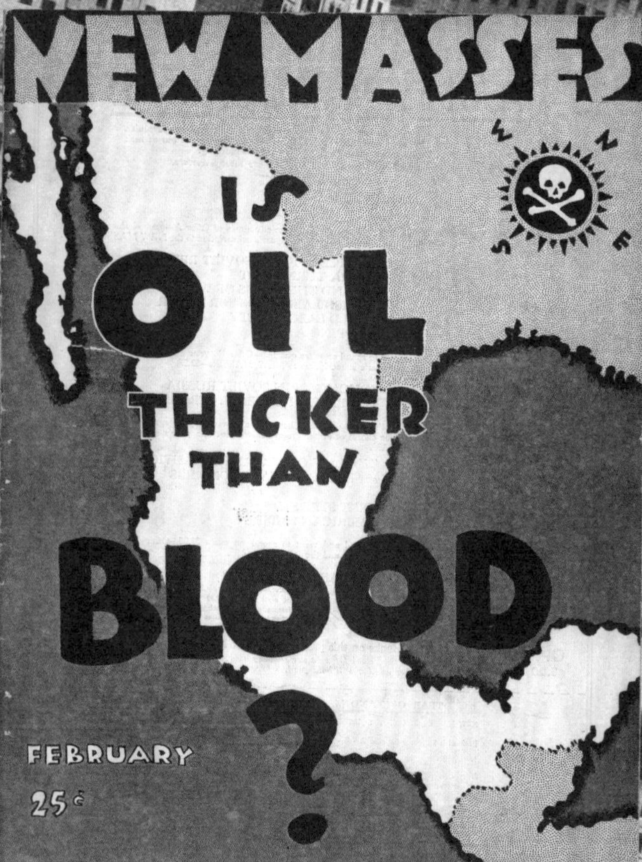

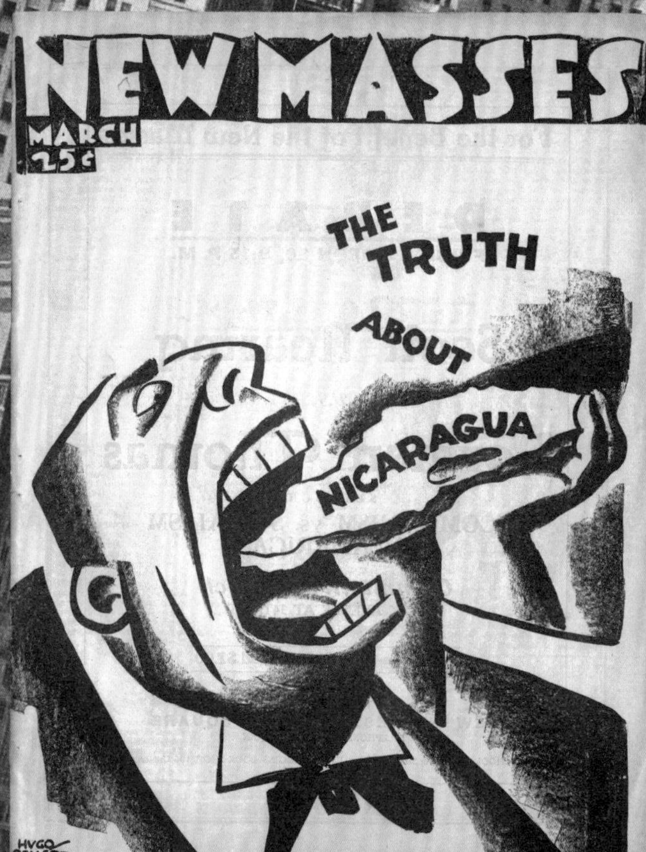

168 *New Masses*, no. 11, March 1928, ed. Egmont Arens, Joseph Freeman, Hugo Gellert, Willam Gropper, Michael Gold, New York, cover by Hugo Gellert

169 *New Masses*, no. 4, February 1927, ed. Egmont Arens, Hugo Gellert, William Gropper, Michael Gold, New York, cover by Hugo Gellert

170 *New Masses*, no. 5, March 1927, ed. Egmont Arens, Hugo Gellert, William Gropper, Michael Gold, New York, cover by Wanda Gág

171 *New Masses*, no. 2, July 1928, ed. Michael Gold, Hugo Gellert, New York, cover with a painting by Maximo Pacheco

172 *New Masses*, no. 8, January 1929, ed. Michael Gold, New York, cover by Hernandez, from a drawing by Xavier Guerrero

173 *New Masses*, no. 12, May 1929, ed. Michael Gold, New York, cover by Gan Kolski

↓172 ↓171 ↑168

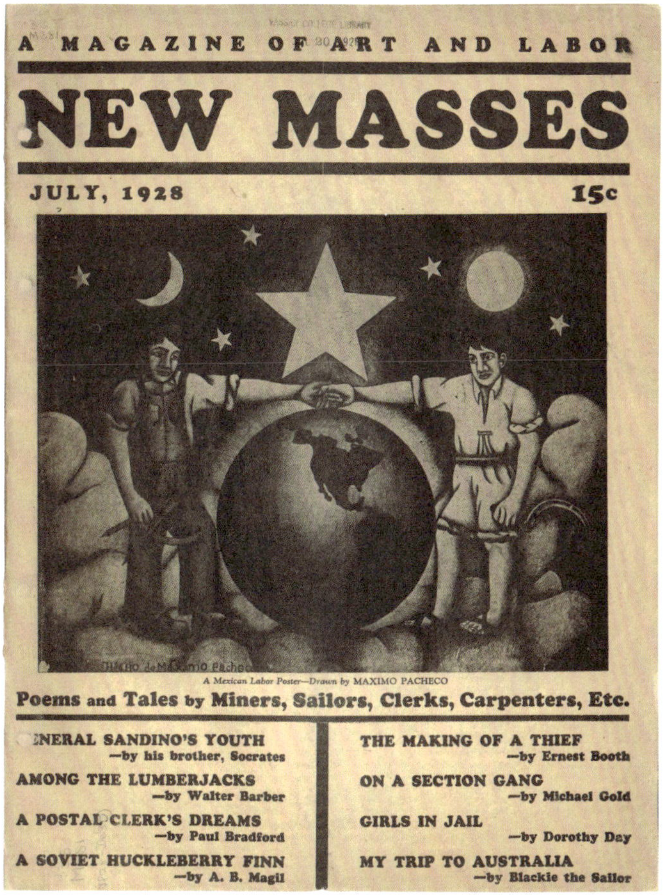

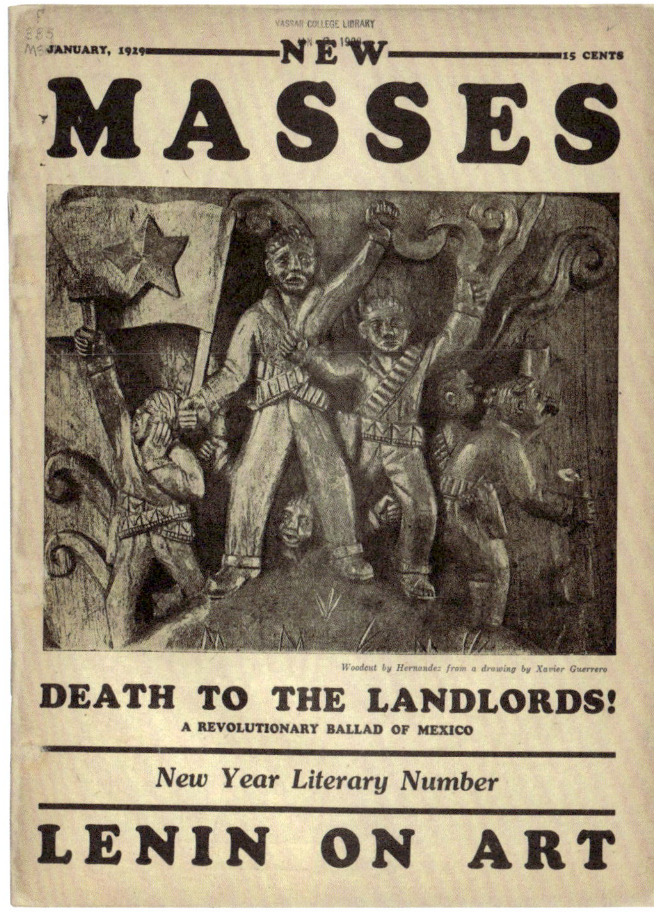

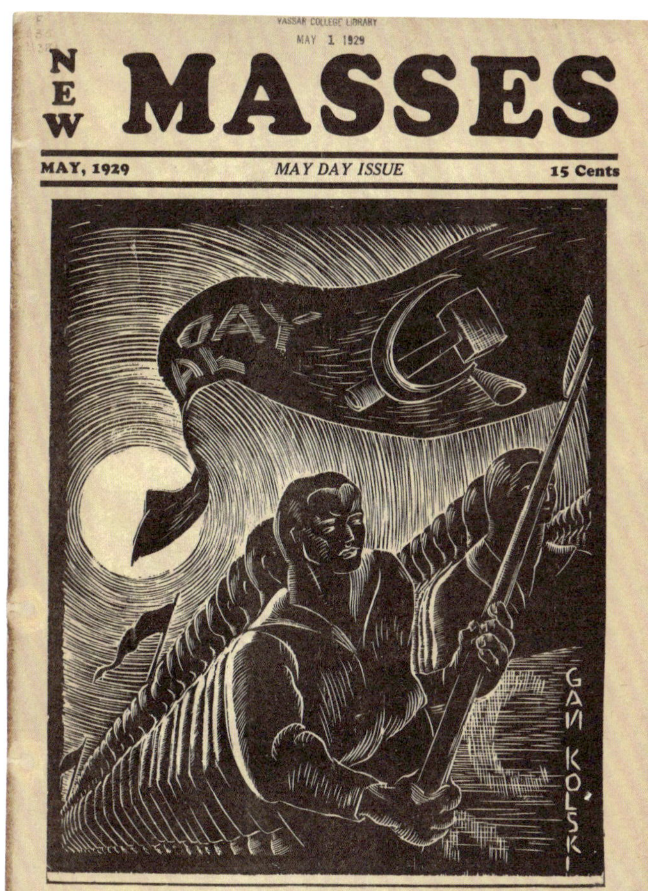

↓173 ↑170 ↑169

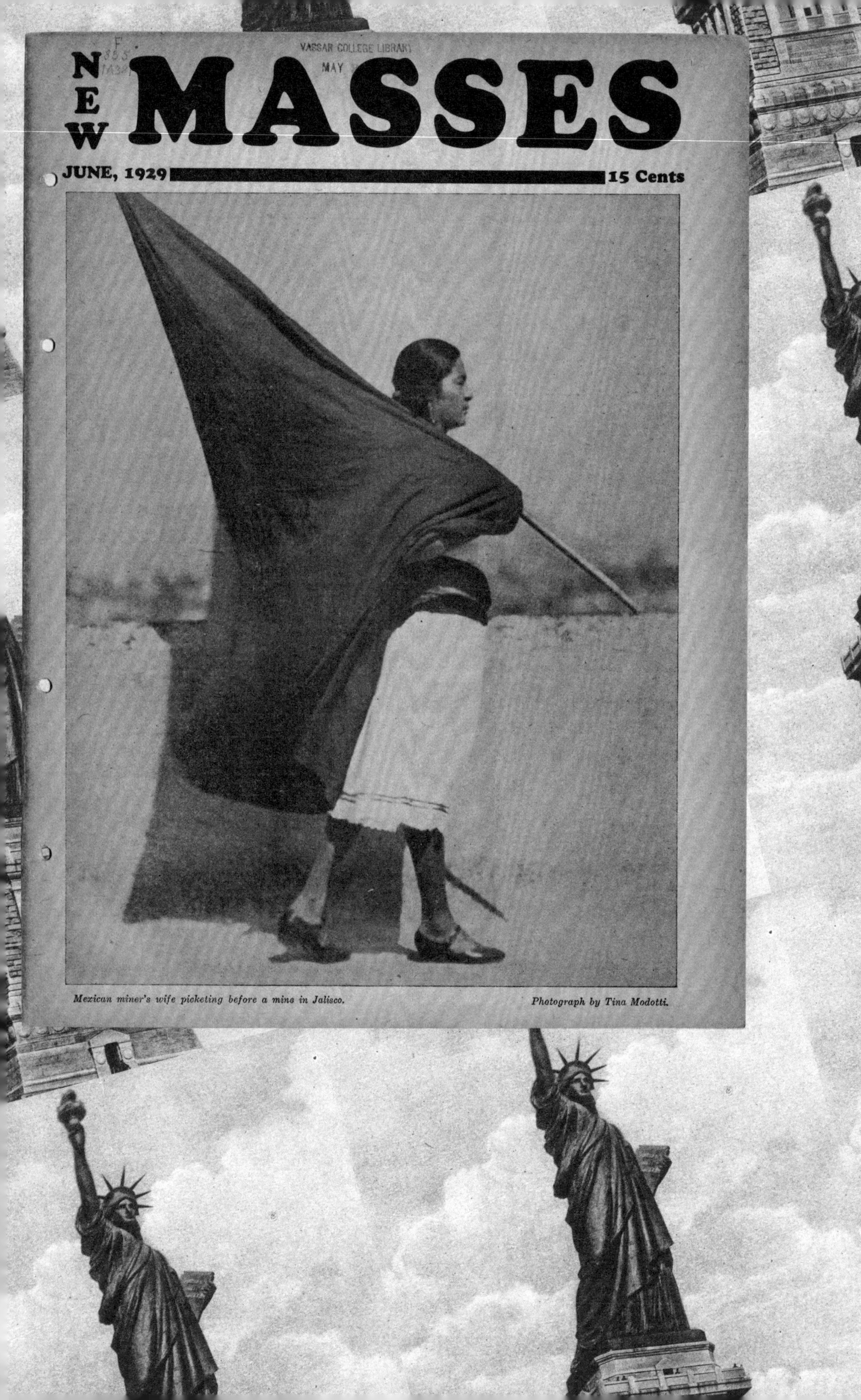

NEW MASSES

JUNE, 1929 — 15 Cents

Mexican miner's wife picketing before a mine in Jalisco.

Photograph by Tina Modotti.

174 *New Masses*, no. 1, June 1929, ed. Michael Gold, New York, cover with a photo by Tina Modotti: *Mexican miner's wife picketing before a mine in Jalisco*

175 *A-I-Z* [*Arbeiter-Illustrierte-Zeitung*], no. 17, 1931, ed. Josef Wildner, Berlin, cover with a photo by Tina Modotti: *Mexikanische Bergarbeiterfrau*

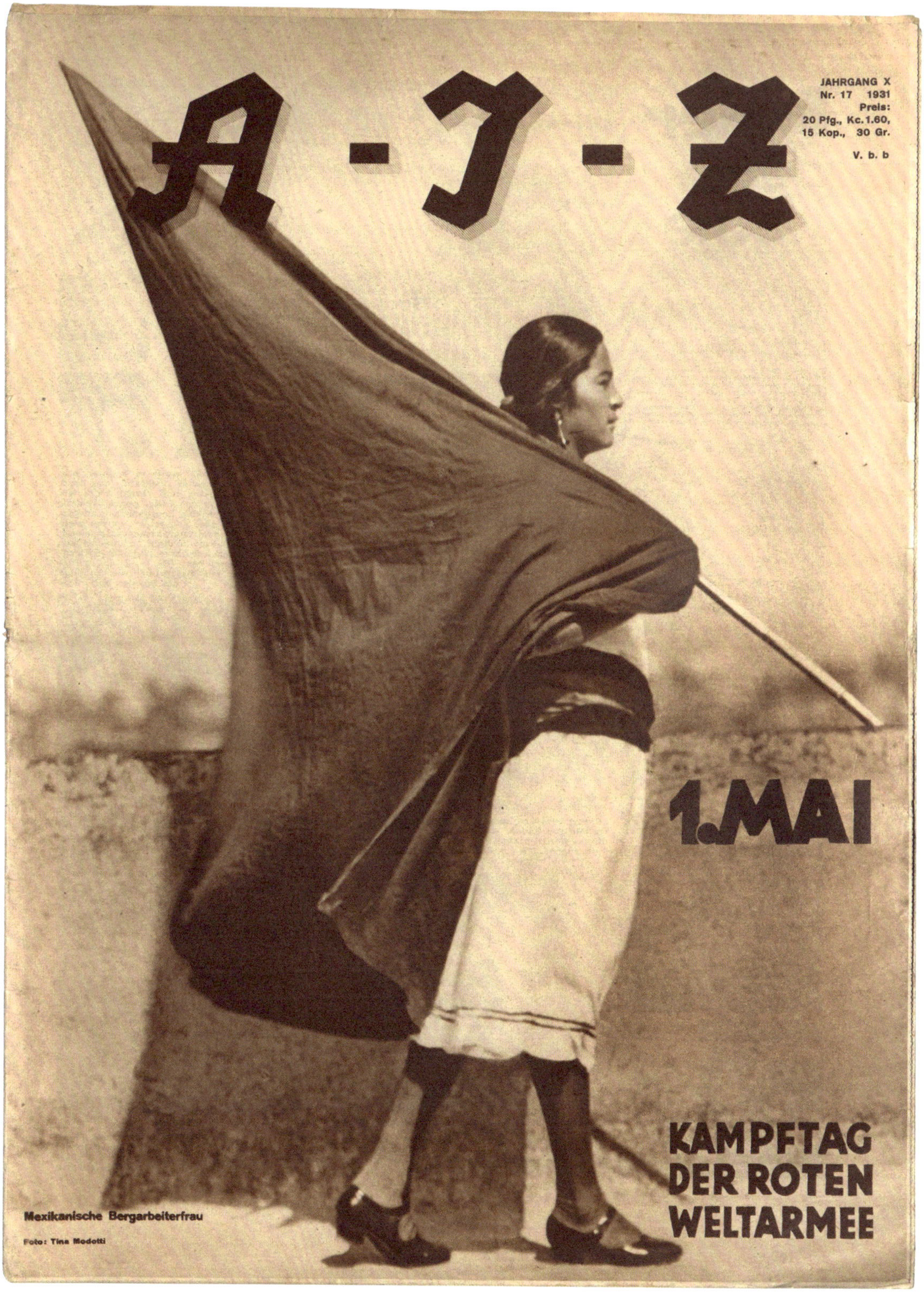
A-I-Z
JAHRGANG X
Nr. 17 1931
Preis:
20 Pfg., Kc.1.60,
15 Kop., 30 Gr.
V. b. b
1. MAI
KAMPFTAG
DER ROTEN
WELTARMEE
Mexikanische Bergarbeiterfrau
Foto: Tina Modotti

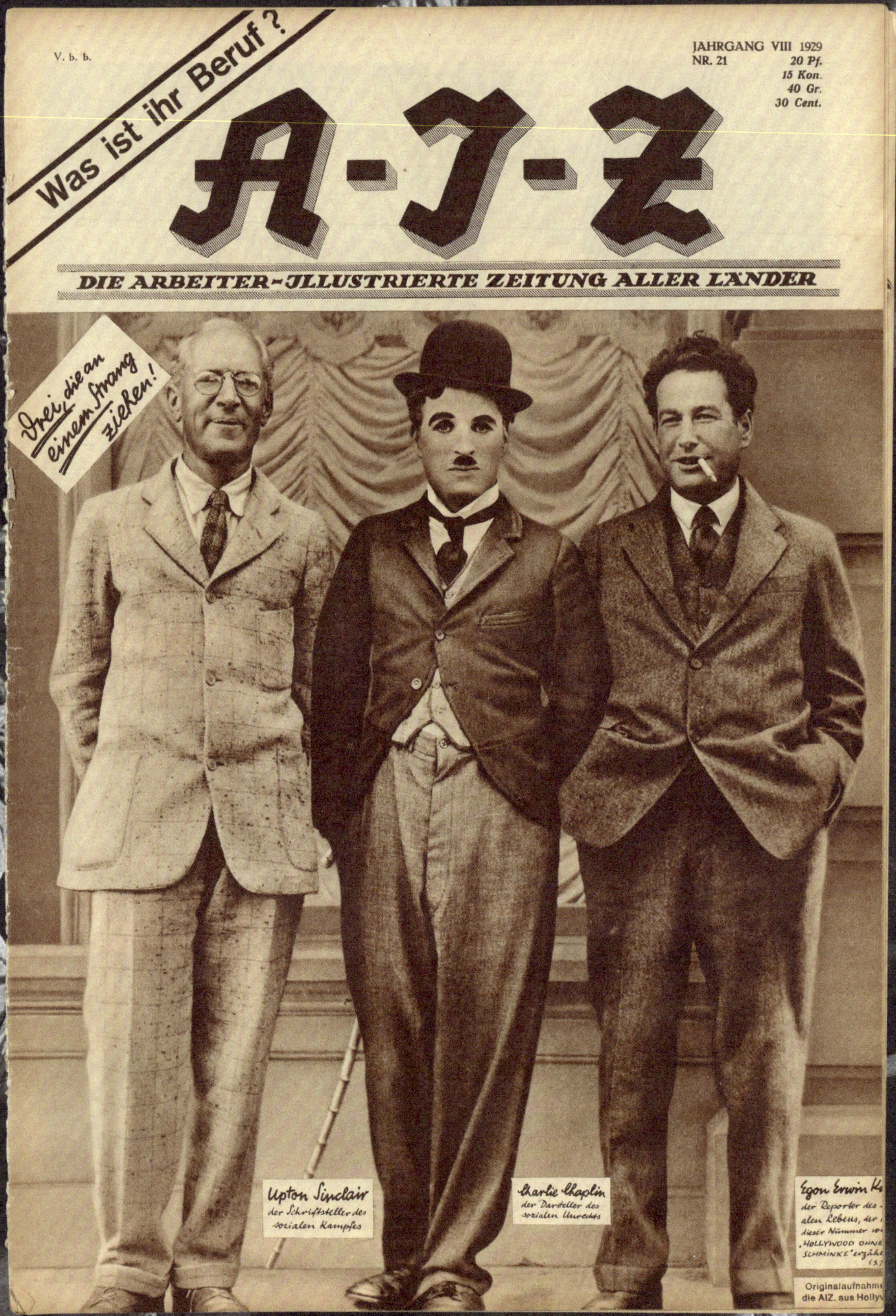

V. b. b.

Was ist ihr Beruf?

JAHRGANG VIII 1929
NR. 21
20 Pf.
15 Kon.
40 Gr.
30 Cent.

A-J-Z

DIE ARBEITER-JLLUSTRIERTE ZEITUNG ALLER LÄNDER

Drei, die an einem Strang ziehen!

Upton Sinclair
der Schriftsteller des sozialen Kampfes

Charlie Chaplin
der Darsteller des sozialen Unrechts

Egon Erwin K
der Reporter des
alen Lebens, der
dieser Nummer
„HOLLYWOOD OHNE
SCHMINKE" erzäh

Originalaufnahme
die AIZ. aus Hollyw

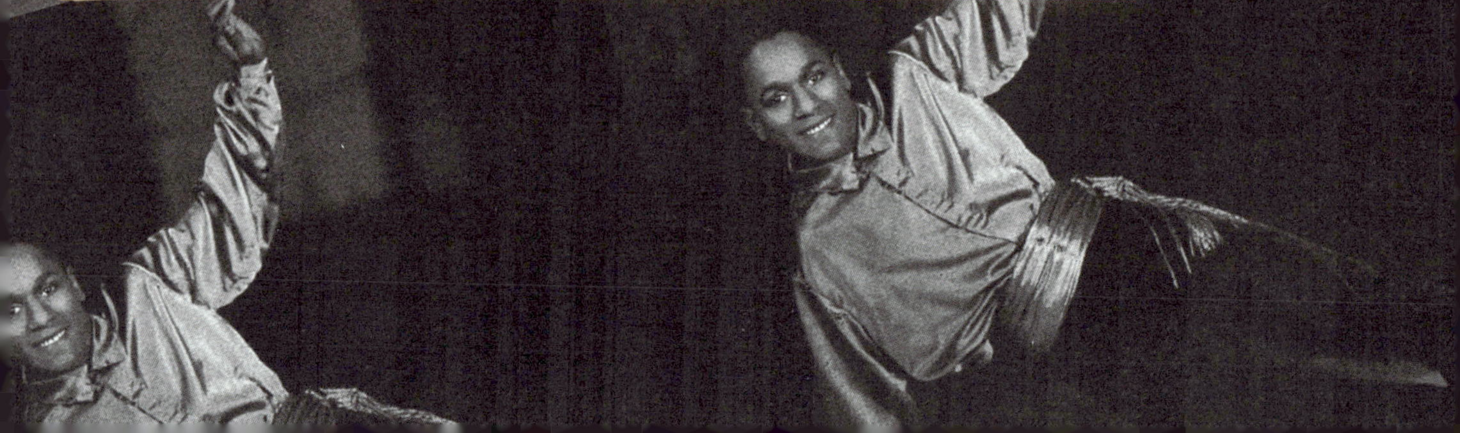

176 *A-I-Z* [*Arbeiter-Illustrierte-Zeitung*], no. 21, 1929, ed. Willi Münzenberg, Berlin, on the cover: Upton Sinclair, Charlie Chaplin and Egon Erwin Kisch

177 Egon Erwin Kisch, *Raj Amerika. Knjiga Prva*, Belgrade: Nolit 1930 [German first edition 1930: *Paradies Amerika*], cover by P. Bihaly

178 Egon Erwin Kisch, *Raj Amerika. Knjiga Druga*, Belgrade: Nolit 1930 [German first edition 1930: *Paradies Amerika*], cover by P. Bihaly

↓178 ↓177 ↑176

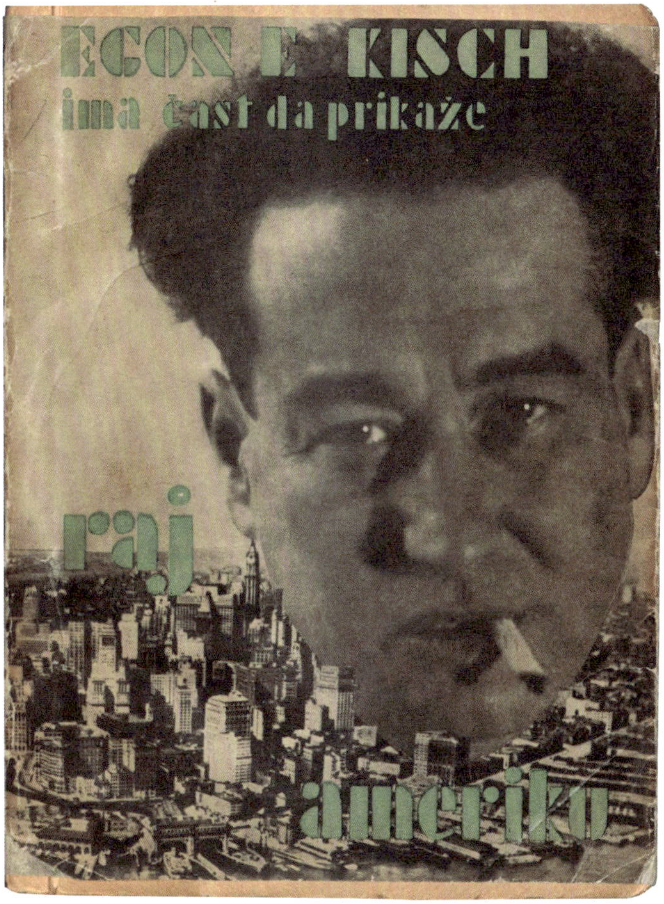

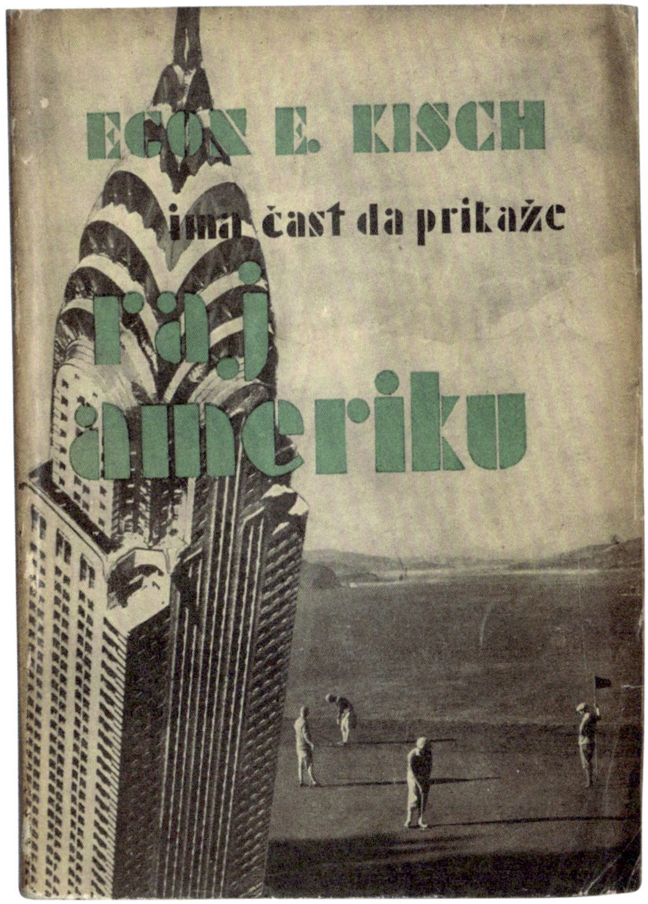

EGON ERWIN KISCH IN AMERICA On 30 October 1928, leftist writer and journalist Egon Erwin Kisch boarded the trans-atlantic liner Olympic to arrive in the United States. He remained there until April 1929, preparing *Paradies Amerika* (Paradise America), a volume comprising forty-one sketches, which was published in December of that year. It was a widely popular piece of reportage, appealing to readers from across the political spectrum in Weimar Germany. However, it had leftist leanings. Kisch was affiliated with the Communist Party, which he had joined in 1925. In *Paradies Amerika*, he described many places he had visited from the moment he embarked on the liner to encounters with New York, Detroit, and Hollywood. During his journey to Detroit, he described the working conditions in the Ford automobile factory. He took a stand against the effects of exploitation, and criticized the consequences that the demands of a single owner, Ford, had for thousands of nameless workers. While visiting California and Hollywood, he met Upton Sinclair, who shared his social and political views, and Charlie Chaplin at around the time the latter was preparing the movie *City Lights* (prem. 1931). Kisch named him a true socialist who understood the problems of the working class.

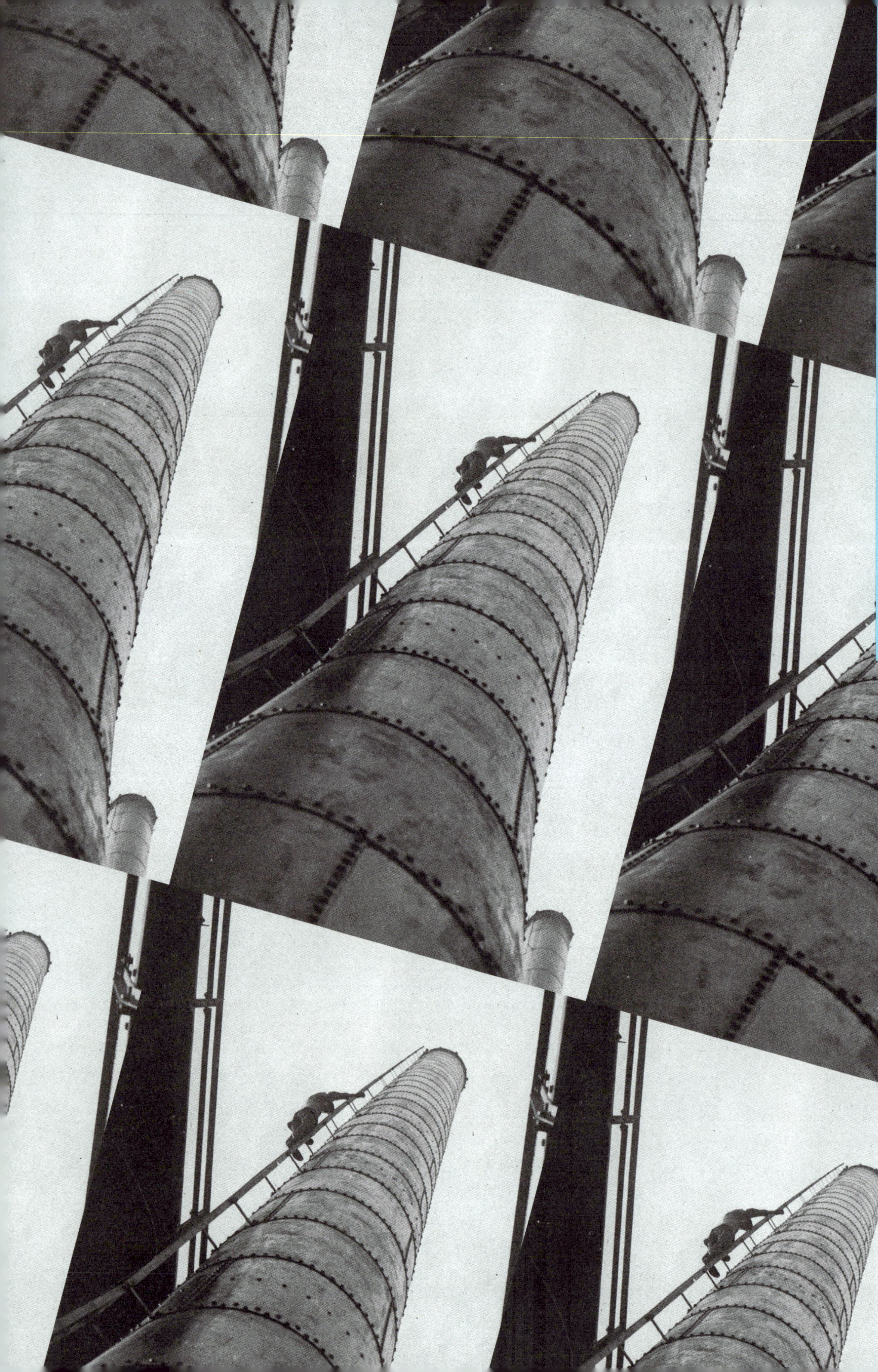

Egon Erwin Kisch, *At Ford's Place in Detroit* [from *America Paradise* 1929], transl. Sheila Skaff, in *Michigan Historical Review*, no. 1 (2003): 125, 130–131

Egon Erwin Kisch

At Ford's Place in Detroit [fragment]

On your first visit to the Ford plant it is, first of all, hard not to notice that almost all of the workers have swollen cheeks. You ask yourself: "How come?" An echo replies: "That's right, Mister Ford doesn't smoke."

That means he cannot stand smokers. Oh, not only during work?—a worker busy on the assembly line doesn't have time to take a drag on a cigarette. But smoking is also forbidden before and after work?—in the departments, where no flammable materials are used (which are full of dust or poisonous gas anyway), outside the halls, on the streets, in the plazas, and in the teeming swamplands between the factory buildings, in spite of the smoke-puffing trains that run there. Smoking is not allowed in the bus that takes foreign visitors to see the manufacturing activities or in the cafeteria, where engineers and officials eat lunch. [...]

21 The "Final Assembly Line," the last conveyor belt, is not just a small stream but a river 268 meters in length with many tributaries. From a vat of enamel varnish the rear axle rises to the surface; the wheels, already equipped with tires, rotate; the mudguards rise above them; the chassis appears; the motor is mounted in the frame; the radiator is tightened; the painters spray everything with paint, while the body of the car with its leather seats, windows, and headlights comprises the whole automobile. It only needs to be screwed tightly together.

Now it turns out that the conveyer belt sets the tempo for the work, and not the work for the conveyer belt. Only a few workers stand on the edge of it. Many move along with their automobile parts, sitting on tiny thirty-centimeter-high carts, transformed into footless beggars. The worker's legs slide along the floor, and he must catch up with his automobile part in order to smooth it out and polish it, in order to finish it up as it moves.

The sum of the parts more and more resembles the idea of an automobile. Suddenly a man swings into the driver's seat, honks the horn—the cry of a newborn—and a live being speeds off the steeply sloping belt, detaches itself from the revolving umbilical cord, and bursts into the hall carrying the name of "A."

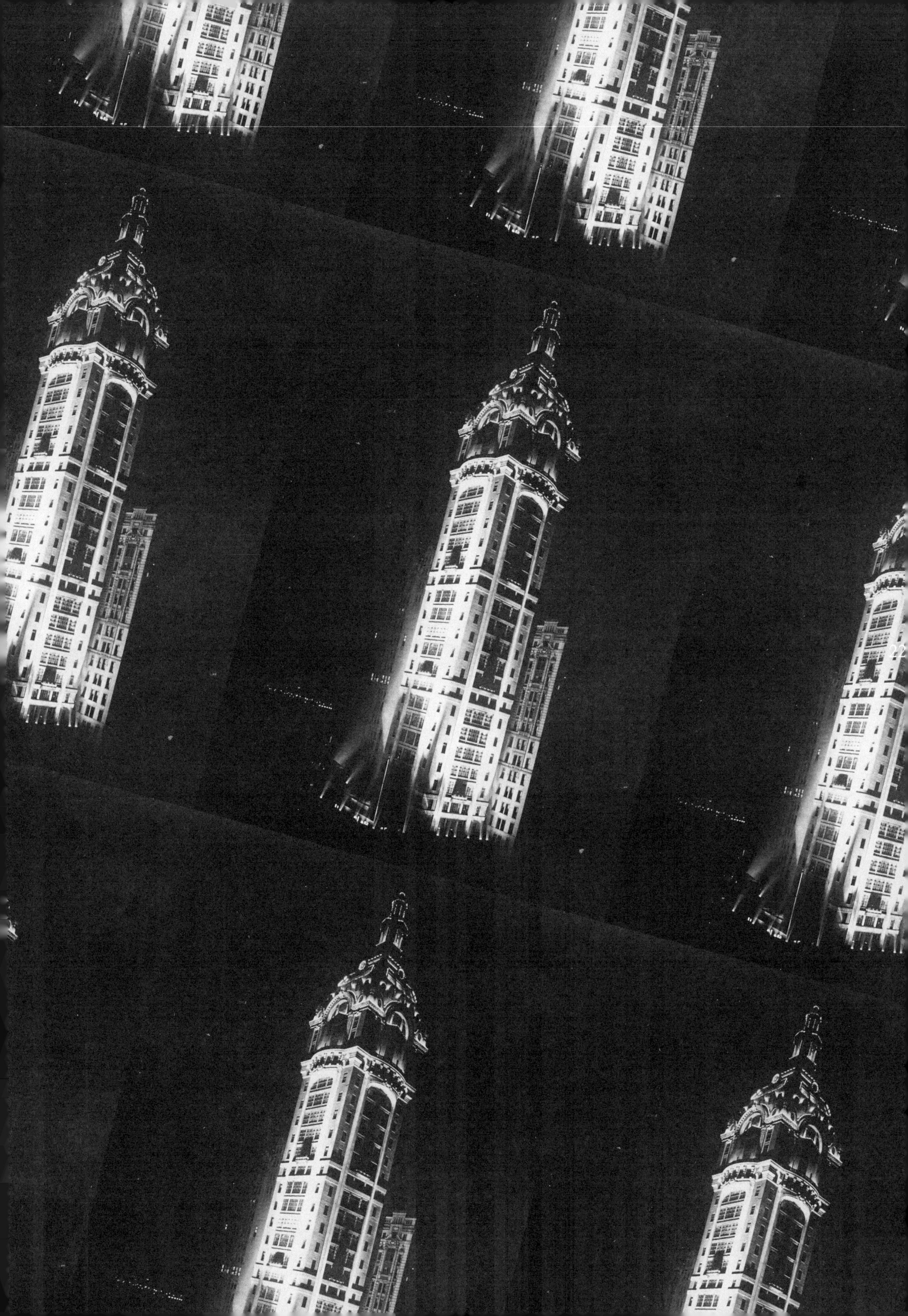

Eight inspectors check out and look over the auto. The door handles are put to the test, windshields, radiators, tires. Five hundred and fifty autos enter the world here daily. Car dealers and their employees wait with the automobiles' numbers in hand, have the gas tanks filled, and drive home in their newly born cars.

In another part of Dearborn, which also can only be called Ford's Dearborn operations, is an airstrip and its airplane factory. One hangar and two others, which are really workshops. No conveyor belt, no Taylorism, no Fordism are to be seen here. Using the same methods as every airplane factory, the metallic Ford Tri-Motor, Stout-Type, with capacity for fourteen passengers and a price of $65,000, is made here.

Nevertheless, this serves as a sightseeing attraction, and so there are some museum pieces there, such as the "Pride of Detroit" airplane that flew around the world making 193 stops, Captain Byrd's Arctic expedition airplane, and one biplane with which Blériot crossed the English Channel in 1909 ...

But why the sightseeing? The visitors are strongly urged by the guides to take an excursion over Detroit for the price of eight dollars.

On each side of the entrance to the gigantic Ford factory complex, right and left, is a heaped-up mound of iron—the remains of four hundred warships, "Eagle Boats" from the U.S.A. Shipping Board, which were delivered to Mister Ford for demolition. Parts [of this consignment] will be used to produce specialty steel used for building the automobiles; the rest serve as transport ships on the Rouge River and Detroit River.

Once one is past this rusty-red dike, Ford's most closely controlled territory is at an end. You may now, in the car or waiting for your trolley, light a cigarette and head home through the east side of Detroit—of this city, which produces more crime than Chicago, more murders, killings, manslaughters, and holdups than any other city on the globe. But Mister Ford doesn't smoke.

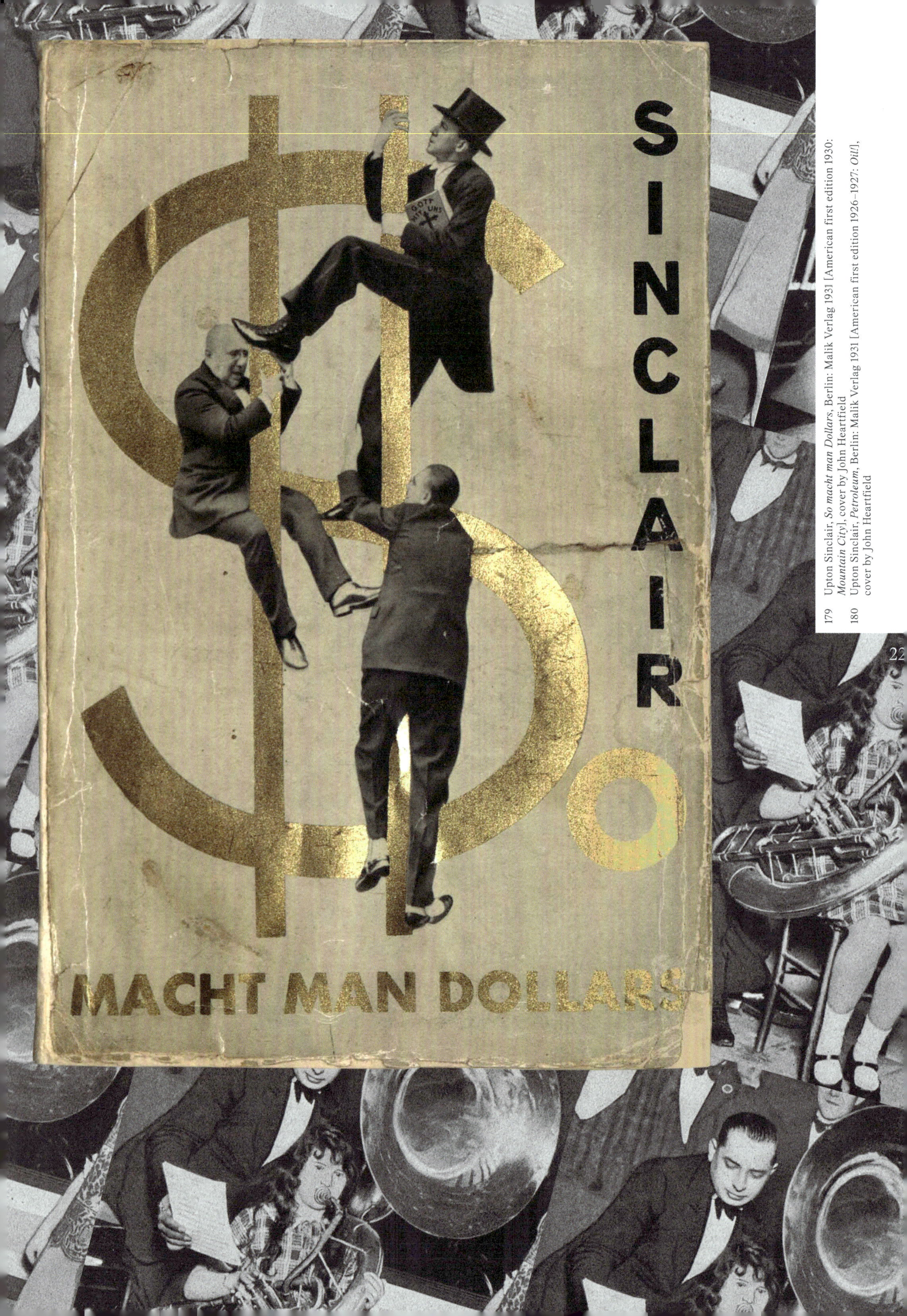

179 Upton Sinclair, *So macht man Dollars*, Berlin: Malik Verlag 1931 [American first edition 1930: *Mountain City*], cover by John Heartfield
180 Upton Sinclair, *Petroleum*, Berlin: Malik Verlag 1931 [American first edition 1926–1927: *Oil!*], cover by John Heartfield

↓180 ↑179

25

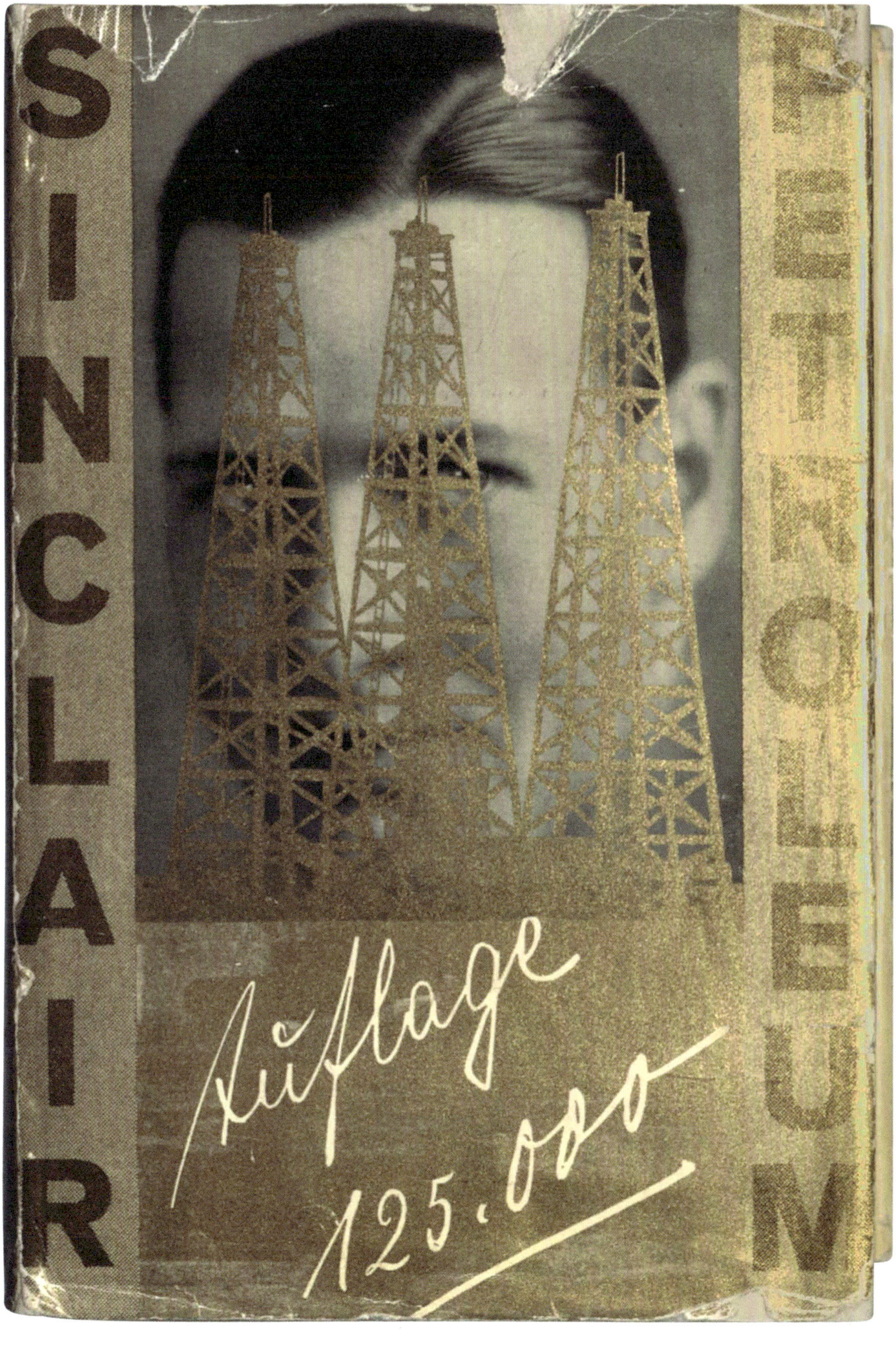

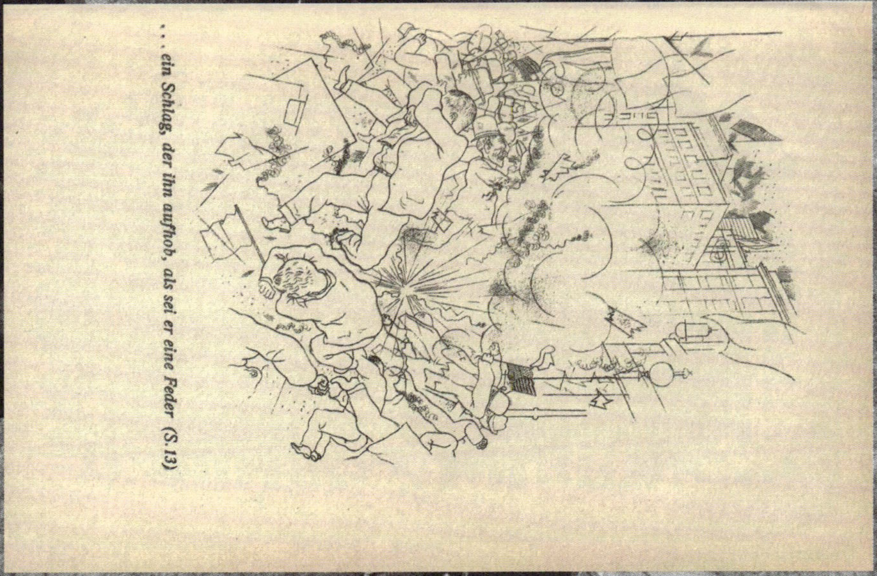

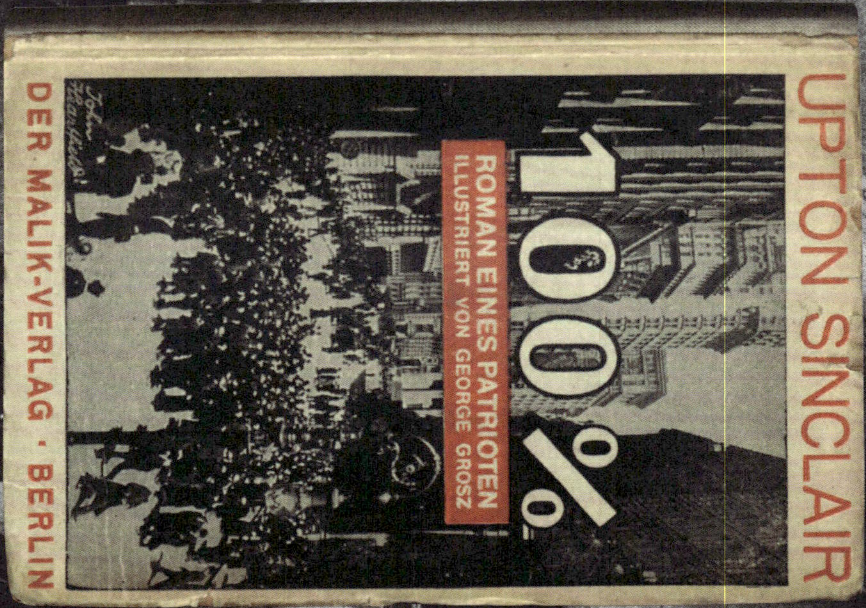

181 Upton Sinclair, *100%. Roman eines Patrioten*, Berlin: Malik Verlag 1921 [American first edition 1920: *100%. The Story of a Patriot*], cover by John Heartfield; illustration by George Grosz [unpaginated]

182 Upton Sinclair, *Jimmie Higgins*, Berlin: Malik Verlag 1924 [American first edition 1918: *Jimmie Higgins goes to War*], cover by John Heartfield

183 Upton Sinclair, *Der Sündenlohn. Eine Studie über den amerikanischen Journalismus*, Berlin: Malik Verlag 1929 [American first edition 1919: *The Brass Check*], cover by John Heartfield

184 Upton Sinclair, *König Kohle*, Berlin: Malik Verlag 1931 [American first edition 1917: *King Coal*], cover by John Heartfield

185 Upton Sinclair, *Der Sumpf*, Berlin: Malik Verlag 1924 [American first edition 1906: *The Jungle*], cover by John Heartfield

↓183 ↓182 ↑181

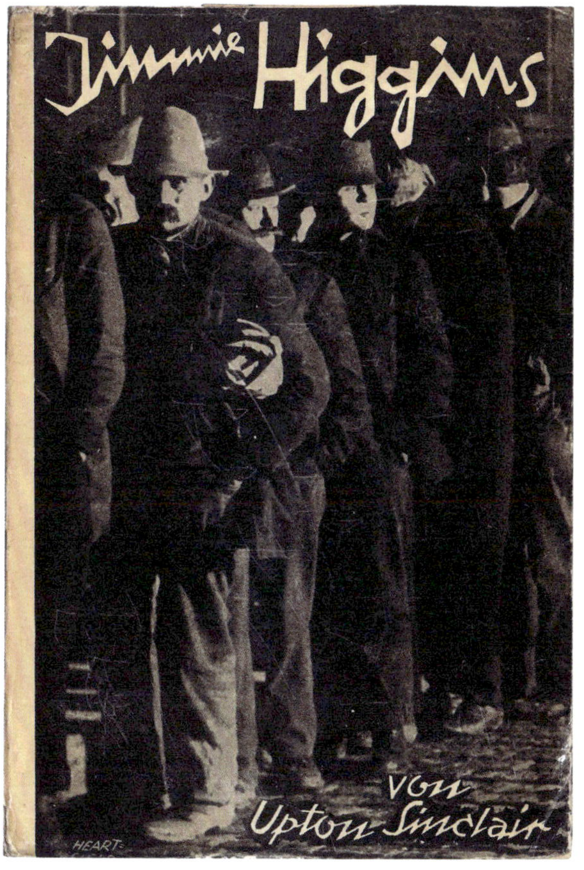

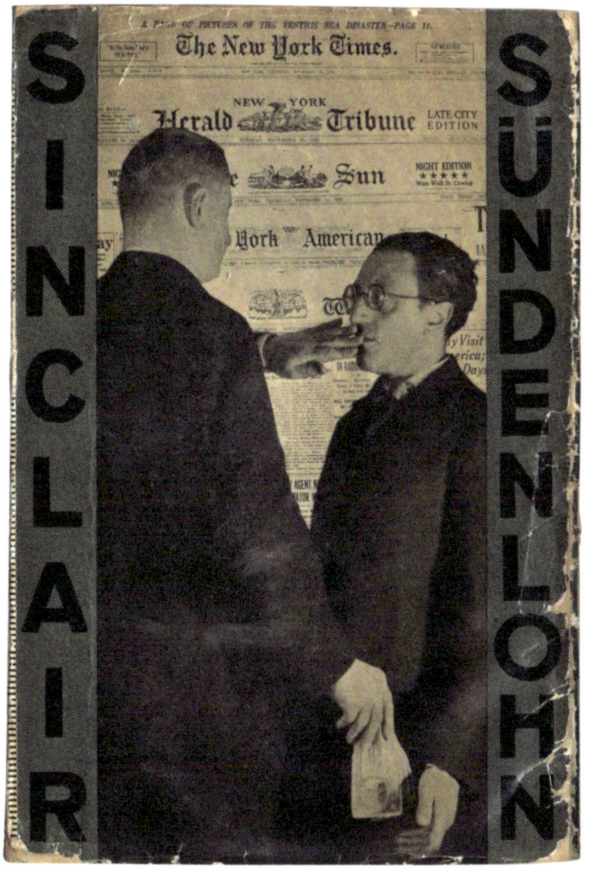

27

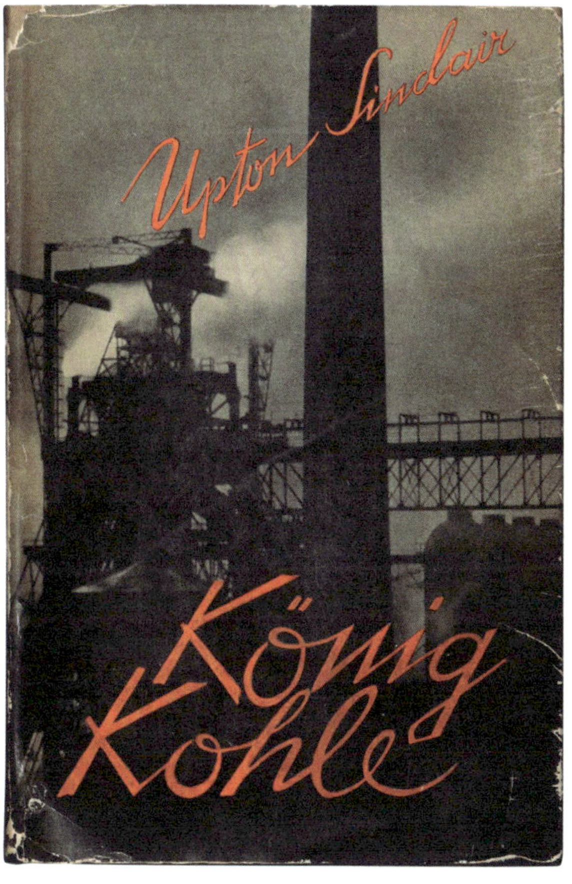

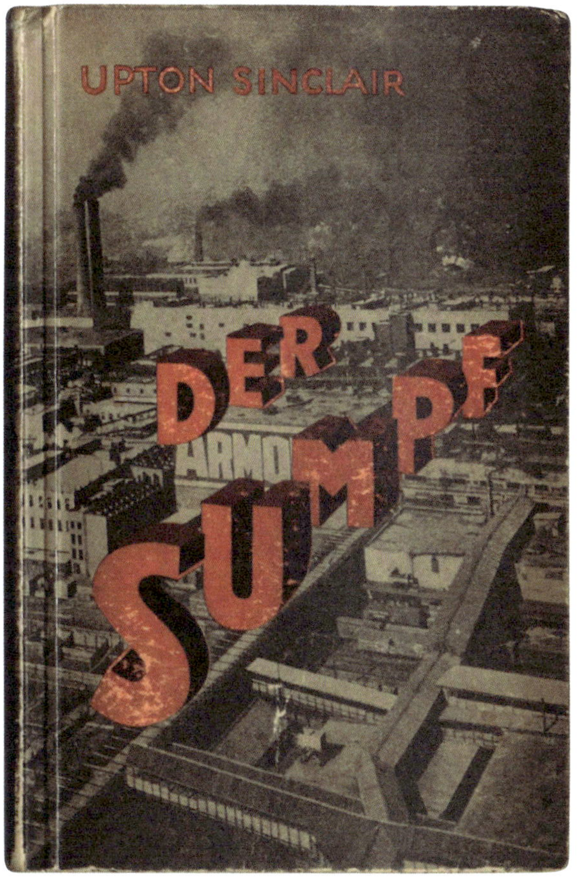

↓185 ↓184 ↑181

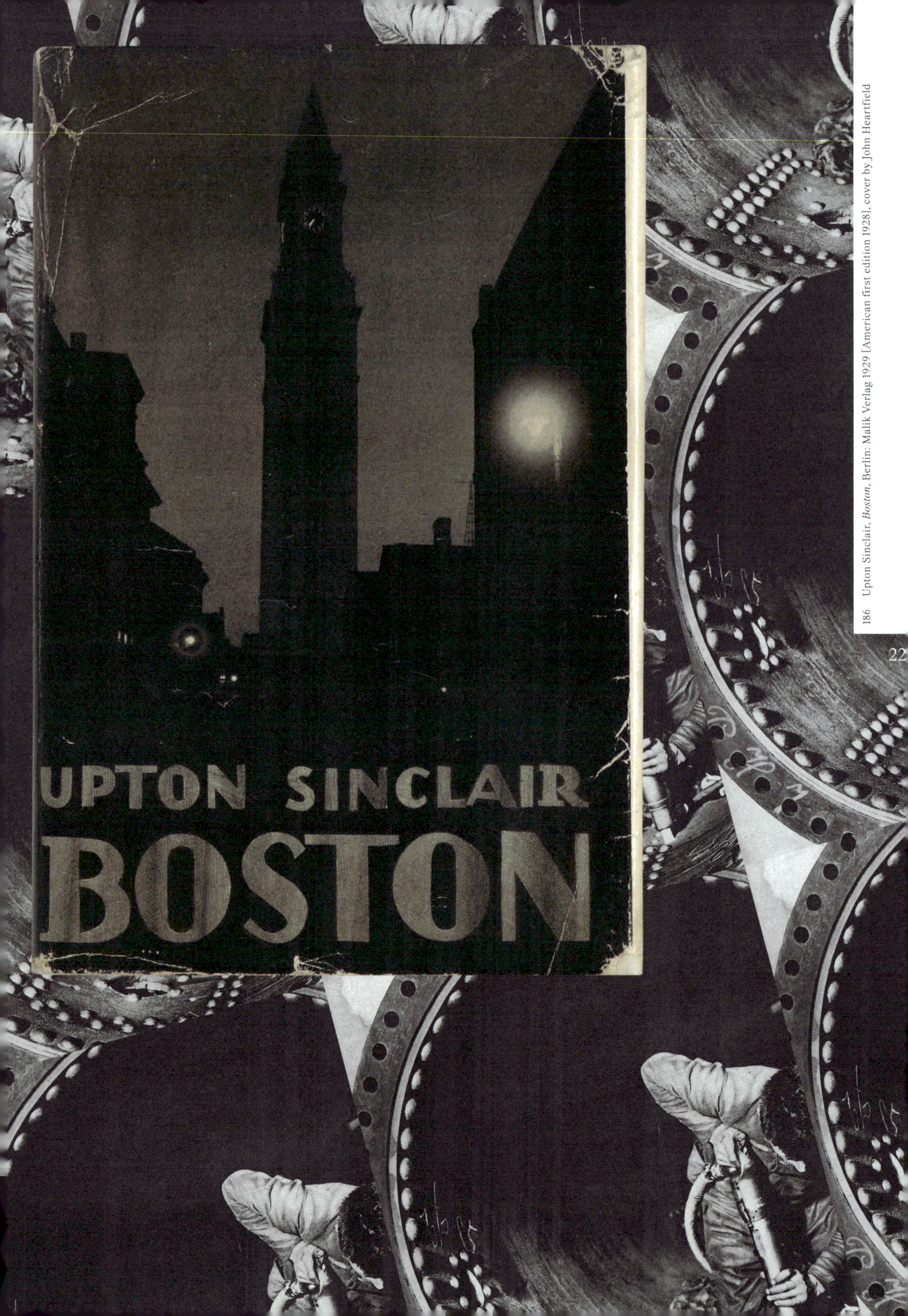

186 Upton Sinclair, *Boston*, Berlin: Malik Verlag 1929 [American first edition 1928], cover by John Heartfield

↓↑ 186

29

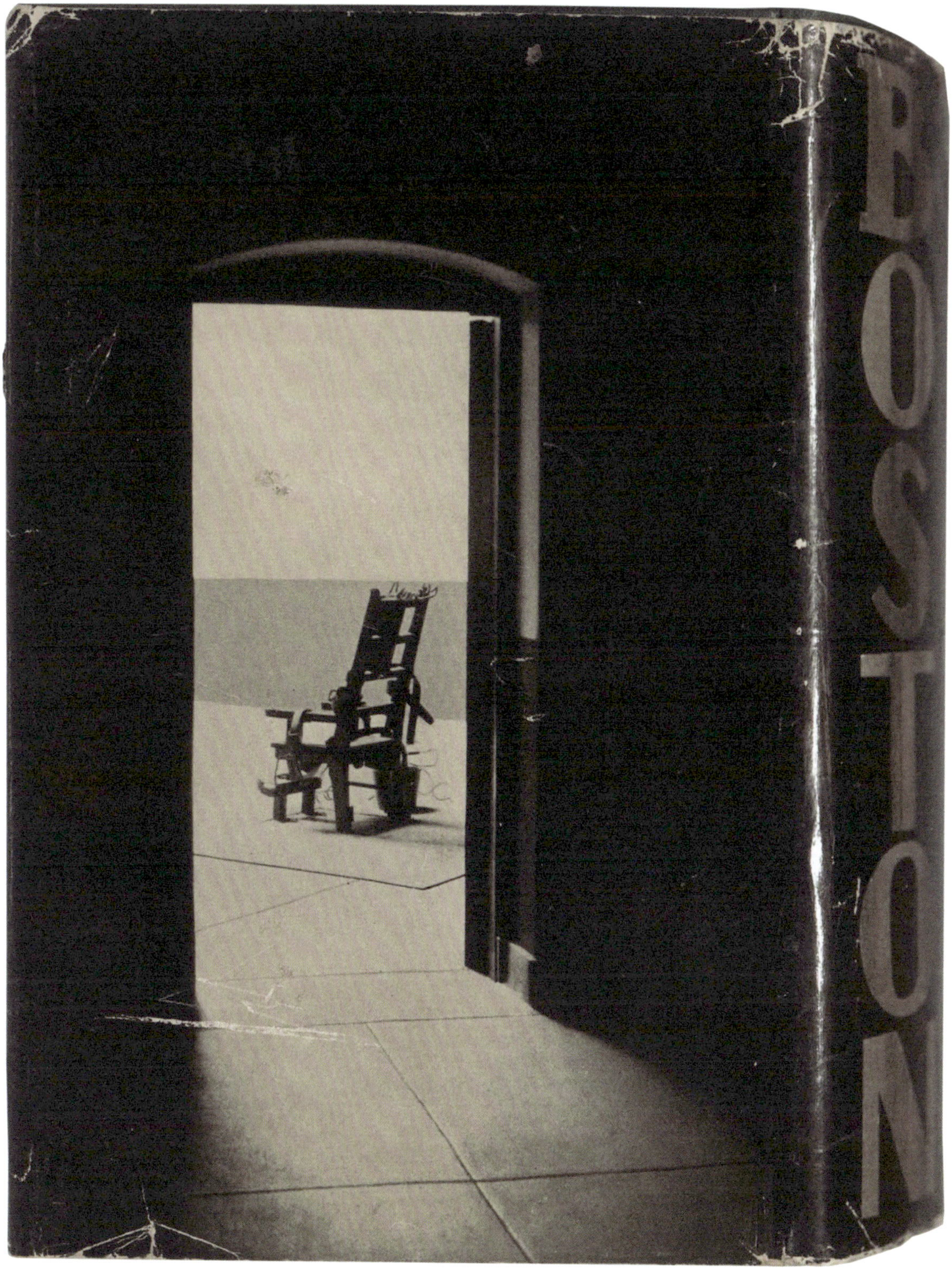

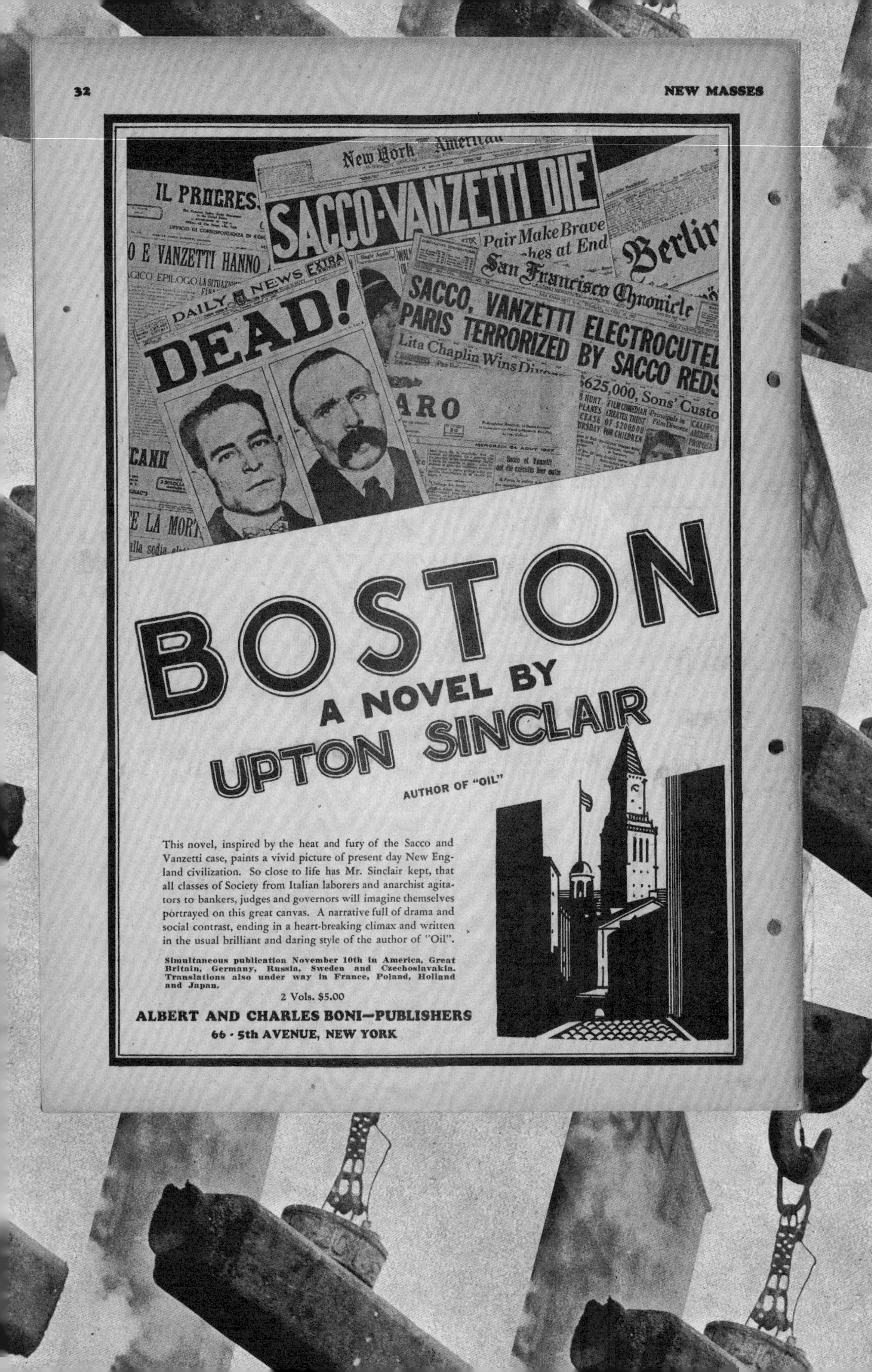

187 *New Masses*, no. 6, November 1928, ed. Michael Gold, New York, 32
188 see 161, 2

SHALL SACCO *and* VANZETTI HAVE DIED IN VAIN?

Help Smash the Gastonia Murder Frame-Up!

THE RIGHT OF THE WORKERS IN THE SOUTH TO ORGANIZE AND BETTER THEIR CONDITIONS IS MENACED!

THE STRUGGLE OF THE SOUTHERN TEXTILE WORKERS IS

YOUR CAUSE!

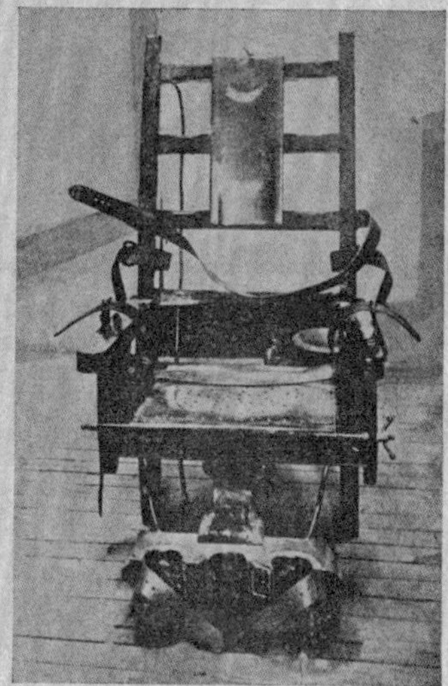

15 TEXTILE WORKERS OF GASTONIA FACE THE

ELECTRIC CHAIR!

8 OTHER MEMBERS OF THE NATIONAL TEXTILE WORKERS UNION FACE LONG YEARS IN PRISON!

RALLY TO THE DEFENSE OF THESE HEROIC STRIKERS!

EVERY GASTONIA DEFENDANT MUST BE SAVED FROM THE ELECTRIC CHAIR!

NO PRISON SENTENCE FOR ANY DEFENDANT

Unconditional Release of all 23 of these innocent men and women.

RALLY TO THE DEFENSE

I hereby enclose $........................ *for the Gastonia Defense.*

I pledge $.................... *per week.*

Name ....

Address ....

City & State ....

THOUSANDS OF DOLLARS are needed to Defend the 23 Strikers.

The readers of the NEW MASSES—millions of workers must contribute—and demonstrate—to save and free them.

RUSH ALL FUNDS TO

INT'L LABOR DEFENSE

80 East 11th Street, Room 402, New York City.

If you must ruin this copy of the Masses to send the blank—we'll be glad to send you another. Tell us you want one.

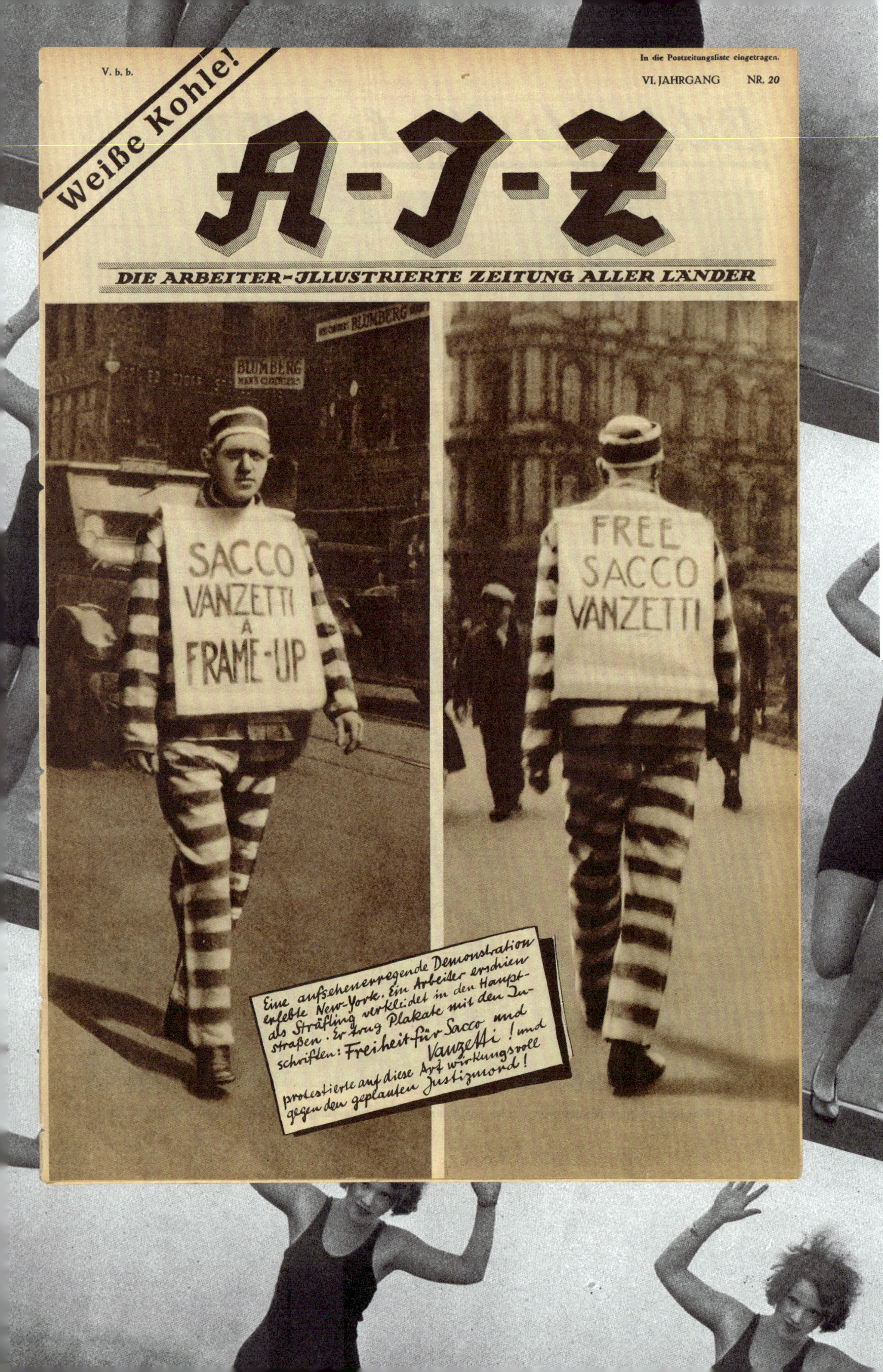

189 *A-I-Z* [*Arbeiter-Illustrierte-Zeitung*], no. 20, 1927, ed. Willi Münzenberg, Berlin
190 *Die Weltbühne*, no. 38, September 1927, ed. Kurt Tucholsky, Berlin, 442–443

↓190 ↑189

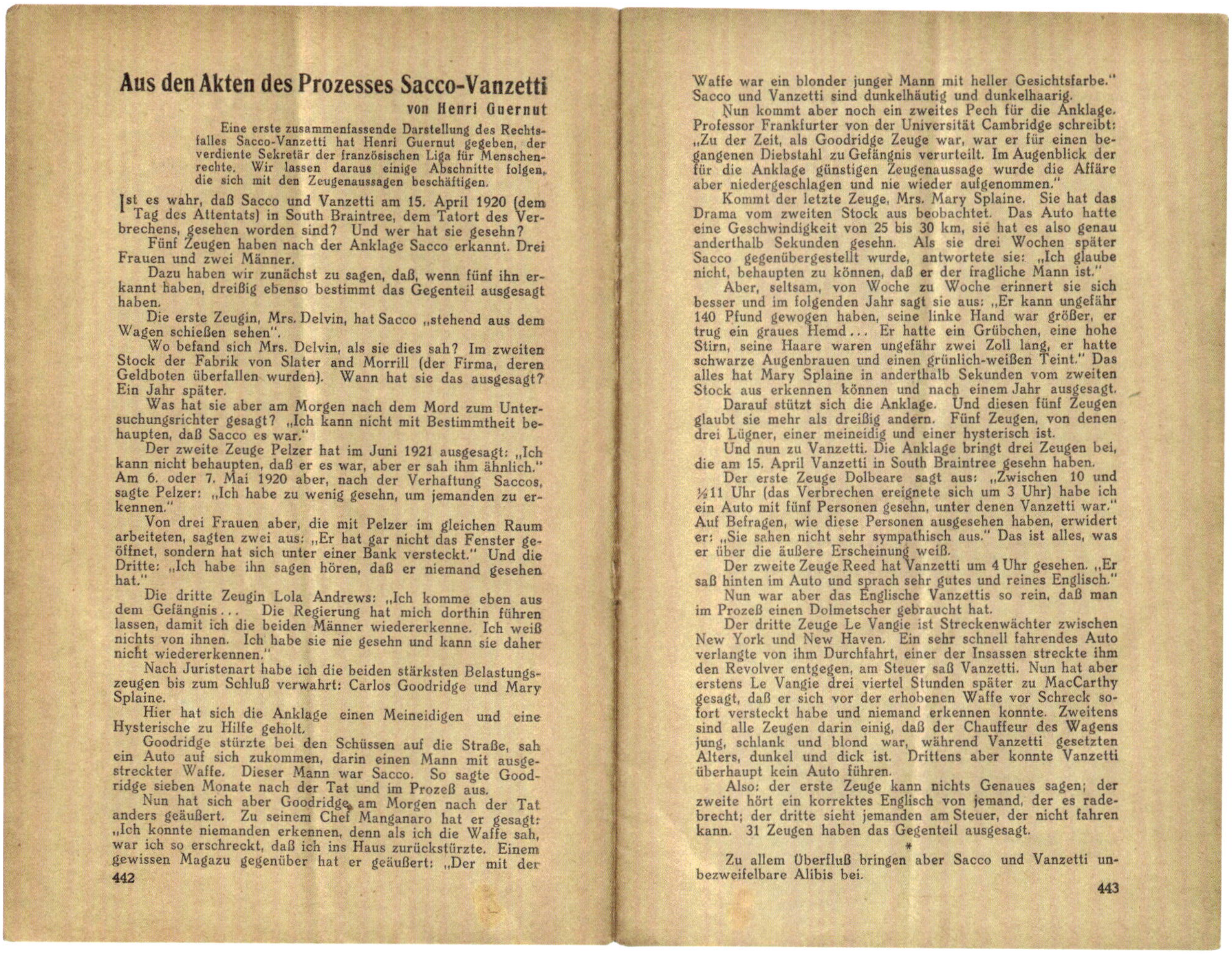

Aus den Akten des Prozesses Sacco-Vanzetti

von Henri Guernut

Eine erste zusammenfassende Darstellung des Rechtsfalles Sacco-Vanzetti hat Henri Guernut gegeben, der verdiente Sekretär der französischen Liga für Menschenrechte. Wir lassen daraus einige Abschnitte folgen, die sich mit den Zeugenaussagen beschäftigen.

Ist es wahr, daß Sacco und Vanzetti am 15. April 1920 (dem Tag des Attentats) in South Braintree, dem Tatort des Verbrechens, gesehen worden sind? Und wer hat sie gesehn?

Fünf Zeugen haben nach der Anklage Sacco erkannt. Drei Frauen und zwei Männer.

Dazu haben wir zunächst zu sagen, daß, wenn fünf ihn erkannt haben, dreißig ebenso bestimmt das Gegenteil ausgesagt haben.

Die erste Zeugin, Mrs. Delvin, hat Sacco „stehend aus dem Wagen schießen sehen".

Wo befand sich Mrs. Delvin, als sie dies sah? Im zweiten Stock der Fabrik von Slater and Morrill (der Firma, deren Geldboten überfallen wurden). Wann hat sie das ausgesagt? Ein Jahr später.

Was hat sie aber am Morgen nach dem Mord zum Untersuchungsrichter gesagt? „Ich kann nicht mit Bestimmtheit behaupten, daß Sacco es war."

Der zweite Zeuge Pelzer hat im Juni 1921 ausgesagt: „Ich kann nicht behaupten, daß er es war, aber er sah ihm ähnlich." Am 6. oder 7. Mai 1920 aber, nach der Verhaftung Saccos, sagte Pelzer: „Ich habe zu wenig gesehn, um jemanden zu erkennen."

Von drei Frauen aber, die mit Pelzer im gleichen Raum arbeiteten, sagten zwei aus: „Er hat gar nicht das Fenster geöffnet, sondern hat sich unter einer Bank versteckt." Und die Dritte: „Ich habe ihn sagen hören, daß er niemand gesehen hat."

Die dritte Zeugin Lola Andrews: „Ich komme eben aus dem Gefängnis... Die Regierung hat mich dorthin führen lassen, damit ich die beiden Männer wiedererkenne. Ich weiß nichts von ihnen. Ich habe sie nie gesehn und kann sie daher nicht wiedererkennen."

Nach Juristenart habe ich die beiden stärksten Belastungszeugen bis zum Schluß verwahrt: Carlos Goodridge und Mary Splaine.

Hier hat sich die Anklage einen Meineidigen und eine Hysterische zu Hilfe geholt.

Goodridge stürzte bei den Schüssen auf die Straße, sah ein Auto auf sich zukommen, darin einen Mann mit ausgestreckter Waffe. Dieser Mann war Sacco. So sagte Goodridge sieben Monate nach der Tat und im Prozeß aus.

Nun hat sich aber Goodridge am Morgen nach der Tat anders geäußert. Zu seinem Chef Manganaro hat er gesagt: „Ich konnte niemanden erkennen, denn als ich die Waffe sah, war ich so erschreckt, daß ich ins Haus zurückstürzte. Einem gewissen Magazu gegenüber hat er geäußert: „Der mit der

442

Waffe war ein blonder junger Mann mit heller Gesichtsfarbe." Sacco und Vanzetti sind dunkelhäutig und dunkelhaarig.

Nun kommt aber noch ein zweites Pech für die Anklage. Professor Frankfurter von der Universität Cambridge schreibt: „Zu der Zeit, als Goodridge Zeuge war, war er für einen begangenen Diebstahl zu Gefängnis verurteilt. Im Augenblick der für die Anklage günstigen Zeugenaussage wurde die Affäre aber niedergeschlagen und nie wieder aufgenommen."

Kommt der letzte Zeuge, Mrs. Mary Splaine. Sie hat das Drama vom zweiten Stock aus beobachtet. Das Auto hatte eine Geschwindigkeit von 25 bis 30 km, sie hat es also genau anderthalb Sekunden gesehn. Als sie drei Wochen später Sacco gegenübergestellt wurde, antwortete sie: „Ich glaube nicht, behaupten zu können, daß er der fragliche Mann ist."

Aber, seltsam, von Woche zu Woche erinnert sie sich besser und im folgenden Jahr sagt sie aus: „Er kann ungefähr 140 Pfund gewogen haben, seine linke Hand war größer, er trug ein graues Hemd... Er hatte ein Grübchen, eine hohe Stirn, seine Haare waren ungefähr zwei Zoll lang, er hatte schwarze Augenbrauen und einen grünlich-weißen Teint." Das alles hat Mary Splaine in anderthalb Sekunden vom zweiten Stock aus erkennen können und nach einem Jahr ausgesagt.

Darauf stützt sich die Anklage. Und diesen fünf Zeugen glaubt sie mehr als dreißig andern. Fünf Zeugen, von denen drei Lügner, einer meineidig und einer hysterisch ist.

Und nun zu Vanzetti. Die Anklage bringt drei Zeugen bei, die am 15. April Vanzetti in South Braintree gesehn haben.

Der erste Zeuge Dolbeare sagt aus: „Zwischen 10 und ½11 Uhr (das Verbrechen ereignete sich um 3 Uhr) habe ich ein Auto mit fünf Personen gesehn, unter denen Vanzetti war." Auf Befragen, wie diese Personen ausgesehen haben, erwidert er: „Sie sahen nicht sehr sympathisch aus." Das ist alles, was er über die äußere Erscheinung weiß.

Der zweite Zeuge Reed hat Vanzetti um 4 Uhr gesehen. „Er saß hinten im Auto und sprach sehr gutes und reines Englisch."

Nun war aber das Englische Vanzettis so rein, daß man im Prozeß einen Dolmetscher gebraucht hat.

Der dritte Zeuge Le Vangie ist Streckenwächter zwischen New York und New Haven. Ein sehr schnell fahrendes Auto verlangte von ihm Durchfahrt, einer der Insassen streckte ihm den Revolver entgegen, am Steuer saß Vanzetti. Nun hat aber erstens Le Vangie drei viertel Stunden später zu MacCarthy gesagt, daß er sich vor der erhobenen Waffe vor Schreck sofort versteckt habe und niemand erkennen konnte. Zweitens sind alle Zeugen darin einig, daß der Chauffeur des Wagens jung, schlank und blond war, während Vanzetti gesetzten Alters, dunkel und dick ist. Drittens aber konnte Vanzetti überhaupt kein Auto führen.

Also: der erste Zeuge kann nichts Genaues sagen; der zweite hört ein korrektes Englisch von jemand, der es radebrecht; der dritte sieht jemanden am Steuer, der nicht fahren kann. 31 Zeugen haben das Gegenteil ausgesagt.

*

Zu allem Überfluß bringen aber Sacco und Vanzetti unbezweifelbare Alibis bei.

443

33

SACCO AND VANZETTI CASE The Sacco and Vanzetti case refers to the killing of two Italian anarchists who were living in Massachusetts, Nicola Sacco and Bartolomeo Vanzetti. They were tried and found guilty of a fatal bank robbery and executed in 1927. Their fate sparked global solidarity movements and led to worldwide condemnation of the American system of justice, most notably from left-wing artistic circles. Books and mass media publicized the matter and helped to unite intellectuals and artists across the globe, including Albert Einstein, Marie Skłodowska Curie, Tina Modotti, and Diego Rivera, to directly appeal to free Sacco and Vanzetti and to condemn their killing. The case had huge global resonance, with thousands of people protesting on the streets of cities around the world, from Warsaw to Mexico City. The leftist circles of Weimar Germany, including Kurt Tucholsky, Erich Mühsam, and the editors of communist-linked *Arbeiter-Illustrierte-Zeitung* also addressed the subject. The chief editor of *A-I-Z*, Willy Münzenberg, organized international committees, congresses, and movements to protest Sacco and Vanzetti's executions. Also, the Comintern—the Communist International—organized the Sacco and Vanzetti Defense Committee. Among the literary works that addressed the case was Upton Sinclair's *Boston*, which was translated and published in Weimar Germany by Malik Verlag in 1929 with a cover design by John Heartfield.

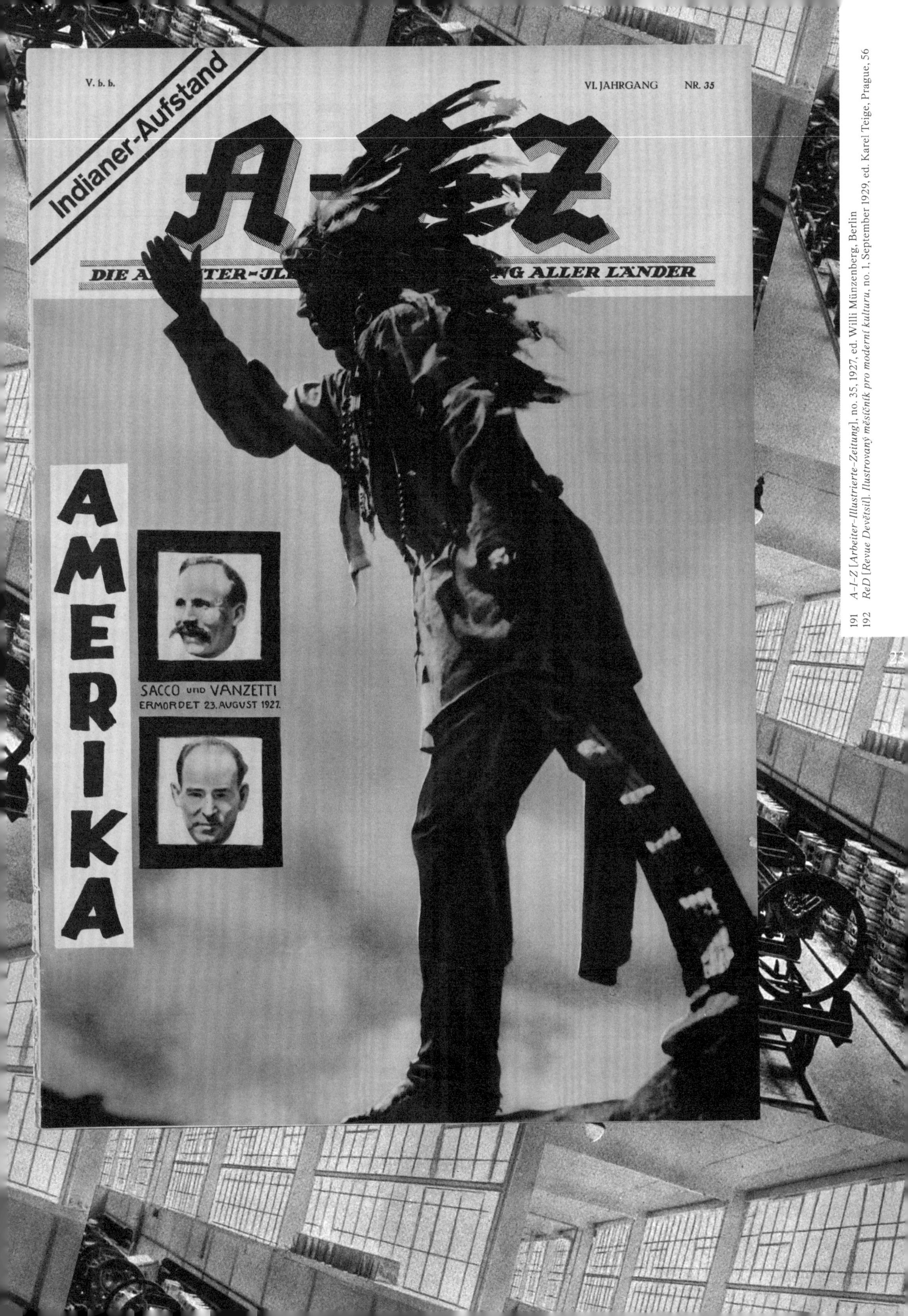

191 *A-I-Z* [*Arbeiter-Illustrierte-Zeitung*], no. 35, 1927, ed. Willi Münzenberg, Berlin
192 *ReD* [*Revue Devětsil*]. *Ilustrovaný měsíčník pro moderní kulturu*, no. 1, September 1929, ed. Karel Teige, Prague, 56

Symboly Ameriky

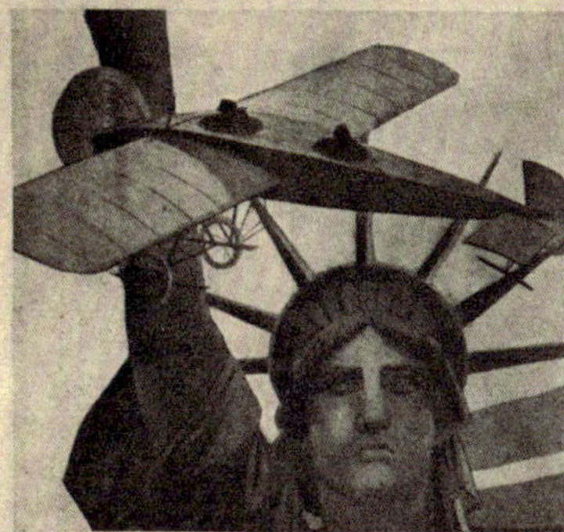

Socha svobody

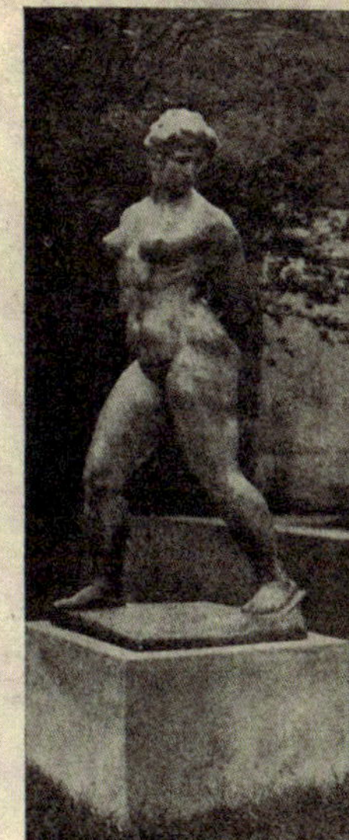

A. Maillol:
Spoutaná svoboda

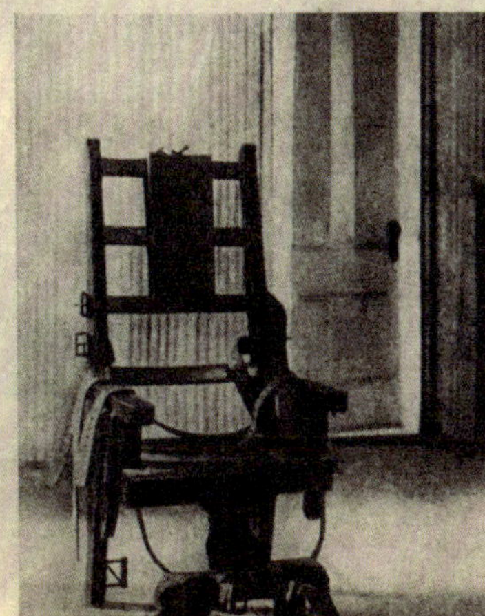

Elektrické křeslo, na jakém byli zavražděni Sacco a Vanzetti a jaké zlo přichystáno pro textilní dělníky z Gastonie.

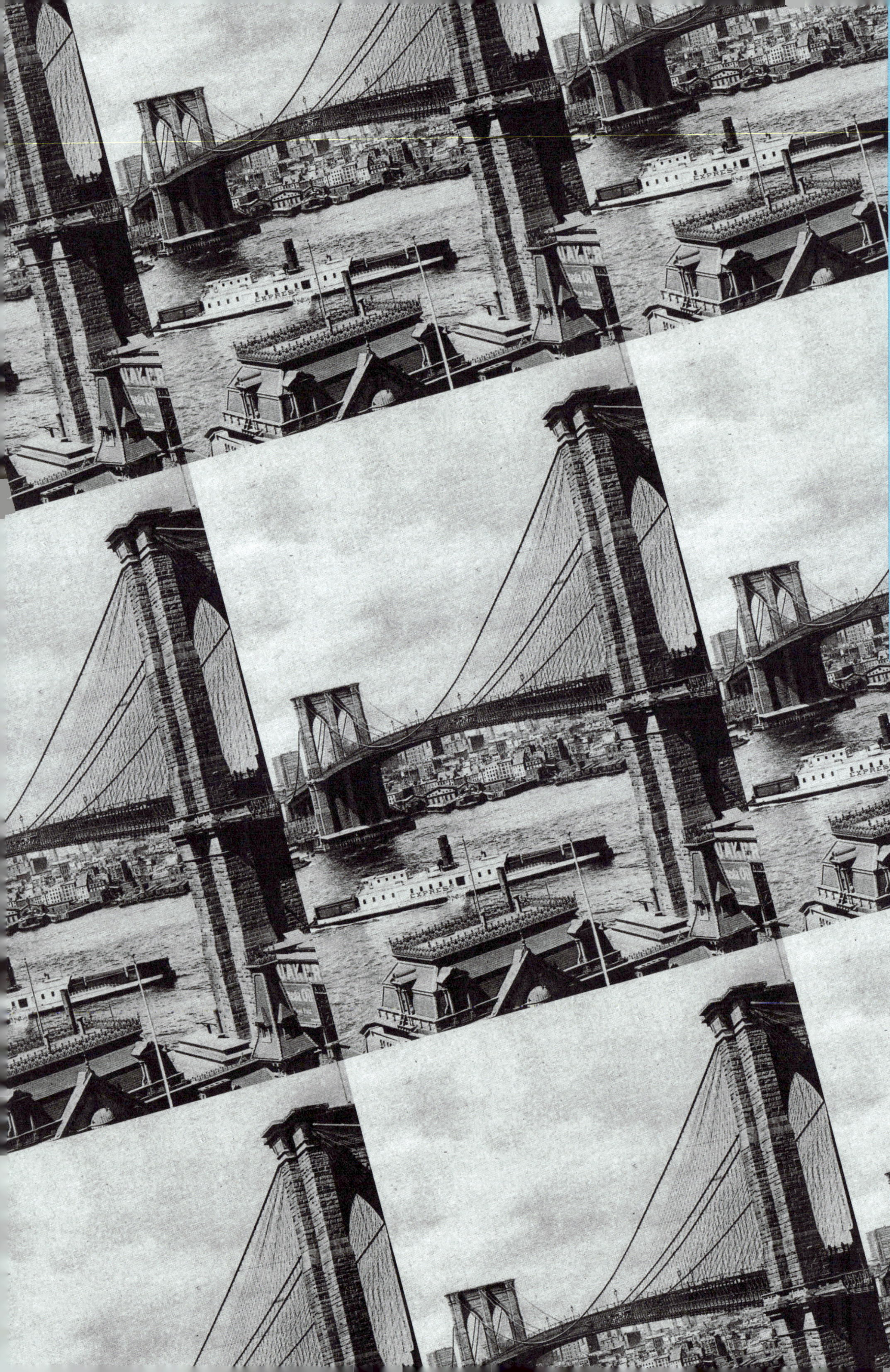

John dos Passos, "They Are Dead Now—," *New Masses*, no. 6 (October 1927): 7

John Dos Passos

“They Are Dead Now—”

This isn’t a poem
This is two men in grey prison clothes.
One man sits looking at the sick flesh of his hands—
hands that haven’t worked for seven years.
Do you know how long a year is?
Do you know how many hours there are in a day
when a day is twenty-three hours on a cot in a cell,
in a cell in a row of cells in a tier of rows of cells
all empty with the choked emptiness of dreams?
Do you know the dreams of men in jail?
They are dead now
The black automatons have won.
They are burned up utterly
their flesh has passed into the air of Massachusetts their dreams
have passed into the wind.
“They are dead now,” the Governor’s secretary nudges the Governor,
“They are dead now,” the Superior Court Judge nudges
the Supreme Court Judge,
“They are dead now” the College President nudges
the College President
A dry chuckling comes up from all the dead:
The white collar dead; the silkhatted dead;
the frockcoated dead
They hop in and out of automobiles
breathe deep in relief
as they walk up and down the Boston streets.
they are free of dreams now
free of greasy prison denim
their voices blow back in a thousand lingoes
singing one song
to burst the eardrums of Massachusetts
Make a poem of that if you dare!

List of Works

001 Franz Kafka, *Amerika* [*Der Verschollene*], Munich: Kurt Wolff Verlag 1927, 19,6 × 15 cm, ADA Inv. AdA-E-303

002 Arnaldo Fraccaroli, *New York. Ciclone di Genti*, Milan: Fratelli Treves Editori 1929, 19 × 12,7 cm, ADA Inv. AdA-E-119

003 *Život. Nové umění—konstrukce, soudobá intelektuelní aktivita*, no. 2, 1922, ed. Jaromír Krejcar, Prague, 25,3 × 18,5 cm, ADA Inv. I 582

004 *ReD* [*Revue Devětsil*]. *Měsíčník pro moderní kulturu*, vol. 1 [bound edition], October 1927–July 1928, ed. Karel Teige, Prague, 23,1 × 18,5 cm, ADA Inv. I 566

005 Hyacinthe Dubreuil, *Arbeiter in U.S.A.*, Leipzig: Bibliographisches Institut 1930, 18,2 × 12,5 cm, ADA Inv. AdA-E-320

006 Америка [America], ed. R. A. Rosenthal, Moscow: Biblioteka Krasnoj Nivy 1924, 23,9 × 16,1 cm, ADA Inv. AdA-E-300

007 Erich Mendelsohn, *Amerika. Bilderbuch eines Architekten*, Berlin: Rudolf Mosse Buchverlag 1926 [3rd edition], 35 cm × 24,1 cm, ADA Inv. AdA-E-312

008 Erich Mendelsohn, *Amerika. Bilderbuch eines Architekten*, Berlin: Rudolf Mosse Buchverlag 1928 [6th modified edition], 34,5 × 24,4 cm, ADA Inv. AdA-E-313

009 see 007

010 see 008

011 Richard J. Neutra, *Amerika. Die Stilbildung des neuen Bauens in den Vereinigten Staaten* [*Neues Bauen in der Welt*. Band 2], Vienna: Verlag Anton Schroll & Co 1930, 28,9 × 22,5 cm, ADA Inv. AdA-E-314

012 Otto Haeckel, *West 42te Strasse vom Broadway aus gesehen*, ca. 1924, black and white photography, 12,9 × 17,7 cm, ADA Inv. C 1/Kerbs 201, 10

013 Otto Haeckel, *Die Front eines der vielen Theater, hell erleuchtet*, ca. 1924, black and white photography, 12,7 cm × 17,7 cm, ADA Inv. C 1/Kerbs 201, 20

014 [Fortunato Depero on the transatlantic ship Augustus], ca. 1928, black and white photography, 14 × 9 cm, ADA Inv. F 3253

015 *New-York. Film vissuto. Primo libro parolibero sonoro. Fortunato Depero 1931*, Rovereto 1931, 19,9 × 22,1 cm, ADA Inv. A 1/Fut 8, 1

016 Fortunato Depero, *Inaffiatore* [*delle strade*] *di New York*, 1930, black and white photography and colored pencil on paper, 29,6 × 23,6 cm, ADA Inv. A 1/Fut 34, 13/1

017 *Prenotazione libraria. New York film vissuto. Primo libro parolibero sonoro*, ca. 1931, 16,9 × 12,3 cm, ADA Inv. A 1/Fut 8, 34

018 Fortunato Depero, *Depero Futurista. 1913–1927*, Milan: Edizione Italiana della Dinamo Azari [1927], 24,2 × 31,8 cm, Archiv Marzona

019 *Depero. Futurist House. New York City*, New York 1929, 5,9 × 10 cm, ADA Inv. A 4/Fut 8, 23

020 *Fortunato Depero. Opening New York Studio*, New York 1928–1930, 9,7 × 12,2 cm, ADA Inv. A 1/Fut 8, 17

021 Fortunato Depero, *Coney Island N. Y.*, 1929, colored pencil on paper, 24,2 × 30 cm, ADA Inv. Z 589

022 Fortunato Depero, [Variation of the poem *Subway*], ca. 1930, black and red ink on paper, 25,2 × 37,6 cm, ADA Inv. Z 479

023 Armando Mazza, *Transatlantico*, Italy 1930s, 14,1 × 9,2 cm, ADA Inv. A 1/Fut 4, 4

024 [Photographer unknown], *Golfspiel auf dem Sportdeck des neuen Hapagdampfer Hamburg*, Photographisches Atelier der Hamburg-Amerika 1920s, black and white photography, 16,9 × 23,1 cm, ADA Inv. C 1/Kerbs 209, 70

025 *Katherine S. Dreier. Lecturer and Painter*, New York after 1933, 7,8 × 10,5 cm, ADA Inv. A 1/SoAnon 1, 17

026 *Western Art and the New Era. An Introduction to Modern Art by Katherine S. Dreier*, New York: Bretano's Publishers 1923, 22,8 × 15,8 cm, ADA Inv. A 1/SoAnon 1, 23

027 *4 Painters. Albers, Dreier, Drewes, Kelpe*, presumably New York 1936, 17,9 × 13,2 cm, ADA Inv. A 1/SoAnon 2, 18

028 Katherine S. Dreier, *Marcel Duchamp*, 1918, charcoal on paper, laminated on paper, 61,2 × 45,8 cm, ADA Inv. Z 126

029 Marcel Duchamp, *La Mariée mise à nu par ses célibataires, même* [Boîte Verte], Paris: Editions Rrose Sélavy, 1934, no. 193/300, 93 facsimiles of notes and photographs in a green box in a green cardboard slipcase, 34,5 × 30 × 4 cm, ADA Inv. MW 228

030 Société Anonyme, Inc., *Report 1920–1921*, New York: Société Anonyme, Inc. 1921, 25,7 × 17 cm, ADA Inv. AdA-E-309

031 Man Ray, *Lampshade. Return to Reason*, 1920, thin cardboard, 45 × 13 × 13 cm, ADA Inv. K 285

032 *391*, no. 13, July 1920, ed. Francis Picabia, Paris, 49 × 32,2 cm, Archiv Marzona

033 *Its Why & its Wherefore*, New York: Société Anonyme, Inc. 1923, 25,5 × 16,7 cm, ADA Inv. A 1/SoAnon 2, 16

034 *Societe Anonyme, Inc. open its First Exhibition of Modern Art* [...], New York 1920, 15,8 × 17,1 cm, ADA Inv. A 1/SoAnon 2, 29

035 *Société Anonyme, Inc. opens its 3rd Exhibition of Modern Art* [...], New York 1920, 16,1 × 17,5 cm, ADA Inv. A 1/SoAnon 2, 26

036 *Societe Anonyme Inc. (Museum of Modern Art) Presents the Works of Schwitters—Campendonk—Paul Klee—Molzahn—Tour Donas—Stuckenberg*, New York 1921, 15,8 × 17,1 cm, ADA Inv. A 1/SoAnon 2, 5

037 *Societe Anonyme Inc. (Museum of Modern Art) Presents the First Exhibition in New York, of the Works of Alexandre Archipenko (Russian Sculptor)*, New York 1921, 15,9 × 17,1 cm, ADA Inv. A 1/SoAnon 2, 6

038 *Societe Anonyme Inc. (Museum of Modern Art) Presents the First Exhibition in New York, of the Works of Dorothea A. Dreier (American Painter)*, New York 1921, 15,8 × 17,1 cm, ADA Inv. A 1/SoAnon 2, 8

039 *Societe Anonyme Inc. (Museum of Modern Art) Announces its Last Exhibition For the Season 1920–1921* [...], New York 1921, 15,9 × 16,9 cm, ADA Inv. A 1/SoAnon 2, 7

040 see 030

041 Jennings Tofel, *Form in Painting*, New York: Société Anonyme, Inc. 1921, 25,8 × 16,5 cm, ADA Inv. A 1/SoAnon 2, 31

042 Jennings Tofel, *Expression*, New York: Société Anonyme, Inc. 1923, 25,5 × 16,7 cm, ADA Inv. A 1/SoAnon 2, 30

043 *Kandinsky*, New York: Société Anonyme, Inc. 1923, 25,6 × 16,7 cm, ADA Inv. A 1/Bau 37, 18

044 *Fernand Leger*, New York: Société Anonyme, Inc., Anderson Galleries 1925, 26,1 × 33 cm, ADA Inv. A 1/Kub 15, 44

045 *Archipenko*, New York: Société Anonyme. Inc. 1921, 25,5 × 16,5 cm, ADA Inv. A 1/Kub 1, 14

046 *Stella*, New York: Société Anonyme, Inc.1923, 25,5 × 16,1 cm, ADA Inv. A1/SoAnon 2, 32

047 *International Exhibition of Modern Art, arranged by Société Anonyme for the Brooklyn Museum*, New York: Société Anonyme, Inc.-Museum of Modern Art 1926, 25,5 × 19 cm, ADA Inv. AdA-E-308

048 Société Anonyme, Inc., *Modern Art at the Sesqui-Centennial Exhibition*, New York: Société Anonyme, Inc. – Museum of Modern Art 1926, 26,5 × 22 cm, ADA Inv. AdA-E-310

049 *Brochure Quarterly*, no. 1, July 1928, ed. Société Anonyme, Inc., New York, 26,6 × 17,2 cm, ADA Inv. A 1/SoAnon 2, 38

050 *Brochure Quarterly*, no. 2, October–January 1928–1929, ed. Société Anonyme, Inc., New York, 25,3 × 15,9 cm, ADA Inv. A 1/SoAnon 2, 37

051 [no title], New York: Société Anonyme, Inc., presumably 1927, 27,8 × 21,5 cm, ADA Inv. A 1/SoAnon 2, 39

052 *Broom*, no. 1, November 1921, ed. Harold A. Loeb, Alfred Kreymborg, Rome/New York, 32,2 × 24,2 cm, ADA Inv. I 609

053 *Broom*, no. 4, February 1922, ed. Harold A. Loeb, Alfred Kreymborg, Rome/New York/London, 32,4 × 22,9 cm, ADA Inv. I 610

054 *Broom*, no. 1, December 1922, ed. Harold A. Loeb, Berlin/New York, 33,5 × 23,2 cm, ADA Inv. I 615

055 *Broom*, no. 1, August 1922, ed. Harold A. Loeb, Rome/New York/London, 32,7 × 23,4 cm, ADA Inv. I 613

056 *Broom*, no. 3, June 1922, ed. Harold A. Loeb, Rome/New York/London, 32,7 × 23,4 cm, ADA Inv. I 612

057 *Broom*, no. 2, September 1922, ed. Harold A. Loeb, Rome/New York/London, 32,8 × 23,5 cm, ADA Inv. I 614

058 *Broom*, no. 1, April 1922, ed. Harold A. Loeb, Rome/New York/London, 32,6 × 23,8 cm, ADA Inv. I 611

059 *Broom*, no. 4, March 1923, ed. Harold A. Loeb, Berlin/New York, 33,5 × 23,3 cm, ADA Inv. I 455

060 *Broom*, no. 3, October 1923, ed. Harold A. Loeb, New York, 27,8 × 20,3 cm, ADA Inv. I 616

061 *Futurist Aristocracy*, no. 1, April 1923, ed. Nanni [Giovanni] Leone Castelli, New York, 22,8 × 15,7 cm, ADA Inv. A 1/Fut 48, 27/2

062 *transition: An International Quarterly for Creative Experiment*, no. 13, Summer 1928, ed. Eugène Jolas, Paris, 22,8 × 16,8 cm, ADA Inv. I 588

063 *transition: An International Quarterly for Creative Experiment*, no. 16–17, June 1929, ed. Eugène Jolas, Paris, 21,7 × 16,40 cm, ADA Inv. I 589

064 *The Little Review. A Magazine of the Arts*, no. 9, January 1918, ed. Margaret Anderson, Ezra Pound, New York/London, 22,3 × 14,8 cm, ADA Inv. I 618

065 *The Little Review. Quarterly Journal of Art and Letters*, no. 2, Winter 1922, ed. Margaret Anderson, Jane Heap, Ezra Pound, Francis Picabia, 24,7 × 19 cm, ADA Inv. I 634

066 *The Little Review. An International Journal of Art and Letters. Little Review Gallery*, New York ca. 1925, 22,1 × 30 cm, ADA Inv. A 1/Dada 51, 35

067 *The Little Review: Quarterly Journal of Art and Letters*, no. 1, Autumn 1921, ed. Margaret Anderson, Ezra Pound, Francis Picabia, New York, 24,4 × 19,3 cm, ADA Inv. I 633

068 *The Little Review. Quarterly Journal of Art and Letters*, no. 2, Spring 1922, ed. Margaret Anderson, Ezra Pound, Francis Picabia, New York, 24,5 × 19,3 cm, ADA Inv. I 619

069 *The Little Review: Quarterly Journal of Art and Letters*, no. 1, Spring 1924, ed. Margaret Anderson, Jane Heap, Ezra Pound, New York, 24,6 × 19,8 cm, ADA Inv. I 620

070 see 065

071 *The Little Review: Quarterly Journal of Art and Letters*, no. 2, Winter 1926, ed. Margaret Anderson, Jane Heap, New York, 24,4 × 19,3 cm, ADA Inv. I 621

072 see 059

073 *New Masses*, no. 3, August 1928, ed. Michael Gold, Hugo Gellert, New York, 29,8 × 22,5 cm, ADA Inv. I 595

074 *Veshch/Objet/Gegenstand*, no. 1–2, March–April 1922, ed. El Lissitzky, Ilya Ehrenburg, Berlin, 30,9 × 23,5 cm, ADA Inv. A 1/oSo 2, 2

075 Louis Lozowick, *Modern Russian Art*, New York: Museum of Modern Art – Société Anonyme, Inc. 1925, 26,2 × 17,2 cm, ADA Inv. AdA-E-311

076 *The Little Review. Quarterly Journal of Art and Letters*, no. 1, Spring 1925, Hg. Margaret Anderson, Jane Heap, New York, 24,4 × 19,3 cm, ADA Inv. I 425

077 *New Masses*, no. 7, December 1928, ed. Michael Gold, New York, 29,8 × 22,3 cm, ADA Inv. I 608

078 *New Masses*, no. 10, March 1929, ed. Michael Gold, New York, 29,9 × 22,2 cm, ADA Inv. I 597

079 Emil František Burian, *Jazz*, Prague: Aventinum 1928, 25,4 × 17,4 cm, ADA Inv. AdA-E-301

080 see 004

081 Emilio [Émile] Vacher, *A mi novia (Bye, Bye, Blackbird) (Dixon) Fox-Trot*, Barcelona: Odeon [no date], shellac record, 25 cm diameter, ADA Inv. I 667

082 Marcello Fraulini: *Tempo di Fox-Trot. Grottesco in tre atti*, Trieste: Mario Cozzi Editore 1931, 18,5 × 13 cm, ADA Inv. AdA-E-124

083 Kurt Schwitters, Theo van Doesburg, *Kleine Dada Soirée*, 1922, color lithograph, 30,2 × 30,2 cm, ADA Inv. DG 105

084 DaDa Beda [Fritz Löhner], Ober-DaDa Hajós [Karl Hajós], *DADA. Dadaistischer Fox-trot für Trottel und solche – die es noch werden wollen*, Vienna/Berlin: Wiener Bohème Verlag 1920, 34 × 27 cm, ADA Inv. A 1/Dada 52, 1

085 *Welt-Magazin*, no. 6, June 1927, ed. Günter Mamlok, Edmund Edel, Berlin, 24,3 × 16,8 cm, ADA Inv. A 4/Foto 114, 3

086 Ernesto Thayaht, *Charleston*, Florence: Tipografia Giannini 1929, 9,2 × 14,3 cm, ADA Inv. A 1/Fut 45, 60

087 *Der Sturm*, vol. 18 [bound edition], April–May 1927–March 1928, ed. Herwarth Walden, Berlin, 24,5 × 19,5 cm, ADA Inv. I 617

088 *Joséphine Baker*, presumably Paris 1927–1932, 18 × 10,9 cm, ADA Inv. A 4/Tanz 2, 11

089 see 004

090 Enrico Prampolini, *Teatro Indipendenti*, Rome 1928, 15,1 × 10,5 cm, Archiv Marzona

091 Emil František Burian, *Černošské tance. Obrazová knihovna, sv. 1*, Prague: Odeon 1929, 17,9 × 12,1 cm, ADA Inv. AdA-E-316

092 *Der Querschnitt*, no. 12, Dezember 1930, ed. Hermann von Wedderkop, Berlin, 24,5 × 17,9 cm, ADA Inv. I 666

093 Ernst Křenek, *Leb' wohl mein Schatz. Blues aus der Oper „Jonny spielt auf"*, Vienna/Leipzig: Universal Edition A. G. 1927, 31,7 × 24 cm, ADA Inv. A 4/Mus 124, 16

094 Ernst Křenek, *2 Jonny-Songs aus der Oper „Jonny spielt auf"*, Vienna/Leipzig: Universal Edition A. G. 1927, 30,5 × 23,3 cm, ADA Inv. A 4/Mus 124, 17

095 *Bauhaus. Zeitschrift für Gestaltung*, no. 2–3, 1928, ed. Hannes Meyer, Dessau, 29,5 × 20,9 cm, ADA Inv. A 8/Zeit 38, 24

096 *i10. Internationale Revue*, no. 12, 1927, ed. Arthur Müller Lehning, Amsterdam, 30 × 21 cm, ADA Inv. I 590

097 Kurt Herbst, *Jazz Etüde für Klavier*, Mainz: B. Schott's Söhne 1928, 30,9 × 24 cm, ADA Inv. A 4/Mus 50, 28

098 Hans [Jean] Arp, El Lissitzky, *Die Kunstismen 1914–1924*, Erlenbach-Zurich/Munich/Leipzig: Eugen-Rentsch-Verlag 1925, 29 × 23 cm, ADA Inv. I 548

099 Ramón Gómez de la Serna, *ISMOS*, Buenos Aires: Editorial Poseidon 1947, 23,5 × 17 cm, Archiv Marzona

100 *Fronta. Internationaler Almanach der Aktivität der Gegenwart*, no. 1, 1927, ed. František Halas, Bedřich Václavek, Zdeněk Rossmann, Brno, 30,5 × 23,5 cm, ADA Inv. AdA-E-326

101 Karel Teige, *Film*, Prague: Petr Václav 1925, 19,3 × 14,5 cm, ADA Inv. AdA-E-323

102 *Žijeme. Obrázkový magazin dnešní doby*, vol. 1 [bound edition], April 1931–March 1932, ed. Ladislav Sutner, Prague, 24,7 × 18,2 cm, ADA Inv. I 569

103 Valentin Mandelstamm, *Hollywood. Regény a film városáról*, Budapest: Globus 1927, 19,7 × 13,6 cm, ADA Inv. AdA-E-305

104 Jelly Roll Morton, *Jelly Roll Morton's Famous Series of Blues & Stomps for Piano, Book 2*, London: Herman Darewski Music Publishing Co. after 1927, 27,4 × 21,7 cm, ADA Inv. A 4/Mus 107, 15

105 *Anthologie Dada*, ed. Tristan Tzara, Zurich: Mouvement Dada 1919, 28 × 19 cm, Archiv Marzona

106 [Exhibition catalog] *Erste internationale Dada-Messe*, Berlin 1920, 30,5 × 37,5 cm, Archiv Marzona

107 *Der Cicerone. Halbmonatsschrift für Künstler, Kunstfreunde und Sammler*, vol. 13 [bound edition], January–December 1921, 27,2 × 21,2 cm, ADA Inv. I 583

108 *Littérature*, no. 18, March 1921, ed. Louis Aragon, André Breton, Philippe Soupault, Paris, 21,7 × 13,2 cm, ADA Inv. I 565

109 *Le seule expression de l'homme moderne. Lire DADA*, Zurich/Paris, 1920, 13,8 × 11 cm, attributed to Tristan Tzara, ADA Inv. A 1/Dada 37, 19

110 *Dada-Almanach*, ed. Richard Hülsenbeck, Berlin: Erich Reiss Verlag 1920, 18,1 × 13,3 cm, ADA Inv. AdA-E-321

111 *Le Disque vert*, no. 4–5, 1924, ed. Franz Hellens, Paris/Brussels, 18,5 × 14,20 cm, ADA Inv. I 560

112 Louis Delluc, *Charlie Chaplin [Charlot]*, Paris: Maurice de Brunoff 1921 [8th edition], 17 × 11,5 cm, Archiv Marzona

113 Philippe Soupault, *La grande fable. Chroniques des personnages imaginaires 3. Charlot*, Paris: Librairie Plon 1931, 19 × 12,5 cm, Archiv Marzona

114 Iwan [Yvan] Goll, *Die Chapliniade. Eine Kinodichtung*, Dresden: Rudolf Kaemmerer Verlag 1920, 22,5 × 19 cm, Archiv Marzona

115 see 114

116 *Kino-Fot*, no. 1, August 1922, ed. Aleksej Gan, Moscow, 29,5 × 22,2 cm, ADA Inv. A 1/Kon 49, 35

117 *Broom*, no. 3, January 1922, ed. Harold A. Loeb, Alfred Kreymburg, Rome/New York/London, 32,5 × 23,5 cm, ADA Inv. I 558

118 Friedrich Robert August Henkels, Ate Johannes Zuithoff, *Kampkweel*, Groningen: Christelijke Jeugd Organisatie 1934, 19,7 × 13,5 cm, Archiv Marzona

119 *Revoluční sborník Devětsil*, 1922, ed. Jaroslav Seifert, Karel Teige, Prague: V. Vortel, 23,8 × 16 cm, ADA Inv. I 561

120 *Teatro. Rivista d'arte*, no. 6–7, June–July 1926, ed. Nino della Casa, Milan, 29,4 × 22,3 cm, Archiv Marzona

121 Ildefonso Pereda Valdés, *El Sueño de Chaplin*, Montevideo: Editorial Rìo de la Plata 1930, 19,3 × 15 cm, Archiv Marzona

122 *Veshch/Objet/Gegenstand*, no. 1–2, March–April 1922, ed. El Lissitzky, Ilya Ehrenburg, Berlin, 30,9 × 23,5 cm, ADA Inv. A 1/oSo 2, 2

123 Louis Delluc, *Charlie Chaplin*, Prague: Lidováknihovna Aventina Sv. 7, 1924, Archiv Marzona

124 Ivan Goll, *Le Nouvel Orphée*, Paris: Éditions de la Sirène 1923, 19,8 × 14,2 cm, ADA Inv. AdA-E-318

125 see 101

126 *14 Rue du Dragon*, no. 1, March 1933, ed. Christian Zervos, Paris, 29 × 23 cm, ADA Inv. I 557

127 *Reflektor*, vol. 1 [bound edition], January–December 1925, ed. Stanislav K. Neumann, Prague, 30,5 × 24,5 cm, ADA Inv. I 567

128 Karel Teige, *Svět, který se směje*, Prague: Odeon 1928, 19,8 × 14 cm, Archiv Marzona

129 *Film und Volk*, no. 1, February–March 1928, ed. Volksverband für Filmkunst, Berlin, 24 × 17 cm, ADA Inv. A 4/Film 17, 11

130 *Arbeiterbühne und Film*, no. 4, April 1931, ed. Arbeiter-Theater-Bund Deutschlands e. V., Berlin, 23,8 × 17 cm, ADA Inv. A 8/Zeit 6, 8

131 Aleksander Wat: *Bezrobotny Lucyfer*, Warsaw: Księgarnia F. Hoesicka 1927, 18,7 × 12,5 cm, Archiv Marzona

132 *A–I–Z [Arbeiter-Illustrierte-Zeitung]*, no. 2, 1930, ed. Willi Münzenberg, Berlin, 36,5 × 27,4 cm, ADA Inv. A 8/Zeit 80, 51

133 Anatol Stern, Mieczysław Szczuka, *Europa*, Warsaw: Księgarnia F. Hoesicka 1929, 29,5 × 27,5 cm, Archiv Marzona

134 *L'Esprit Nouveau*, no. 28, January 1925, ed. Amédée Ozenfant, Charles-Édouard Jeanneret-Gris [Le Corbusier], Paris, 25,2 × 16,5 cm, Archiv Marzona

135 *Der Querschnitt*, no. 8, August 1929, ed. Hermann von Wedderkop, Berlin, 24,7 × 18,3 cm, ADA Inv. I 676

136 *f. a. [Film Artystyczny]*, no. 2, May 1937, ed. Stefan Themerson, Warsaw, 24 × 19 cm, Archiv Marzona

137 Hans Richter, *Filmgegner von Heute – Filmfreunde von Morgen*, Berlin: Verlag Hermann Reckendorf 1929, 26 × 19,5 cm, ADA Inv. AdA-E-25

138 George Antheil, *Ballet mécanique*, Henry Brant, *Signs and Alarms / Galaxy 2 (1954)*, New York: Columbia Records 1955, vinyl record in paper sleeve, 31 × 31 cm, ADA Inv. AV 204

139 see 117

140 *Broom*, no. 3, October 1922, ed. Harold A. Loeb, Berlin/New York/London, 33 × 23,5 cm, ADA Inv. I 559

141 AEG [Allgemeine Elektricitäts-Gesellschaft Berlin], *Arbeiter-Kontrolluhr, P. L. No. 4181, Typ RH 2*, [presumably from 1921], oak wood, metal, glas, 90 × 38 × 30 cm, ADA Inv. PD 176

142 *AEG-Mitteilungen*, no. 7, July 1927, ed. Allgemeine Elektricitäts-Gesellschaft, Berlin, 29,5 × 21,8 cm, ADA Inv. I 376

143 *Reflektor*, vol. 2 [bound edition], January-December 1926, ed. Stanislav K. Neumann, Prague, 30,3 × 24 cm, ADA Inv. I 587

144 Albert Renger-Patzsch, *Industrie. Spannknechte-anreißen und bohren einer Nietplatte*, 1920s, 15,3 × 20 cm, black and white photography, ADA Inv. A 4/Foto 46, 99

145 Albert Renger-Patzsch, *Industrie. Drückvorrichtung für Bohrmuffen*, 1920s, black and white photography, 20,1 × 15,3 cm, ADA Inv. A 4/Foto 46, 105

146 *L'Esprit Nouveau*, no. 17, June 1922, ed. Amédée Ozenfant, Charles-Édouard Jeanneret-Gris [Le Corbusier], Paris, 25 × 16,7 cm, ADA Inv. I 586

147 Le Corbusier, *Vers une architecture*, Paris: Les Éditions G. Crès et Cie 1924, 24,5 × 16 cm, Archiv Marzona

148 see 003

149 László Moholy-Nagy, *Malerei Fotografie Film* [Bauhausbücher 8], Munich: Albert Langen Verlag 1927 [second, modified edition], 23,7 × 18,7 cm, ADA Inv. AdA-E-302

150 *Blok: Czasopismo awangardy artystycznej*, no. 1, March 1924, ed. Henryk Stażewski, Teresa Żarnowerówna, Mieczysław Szczuka, Edmund Miller, Warsaw, 61,2 × 45,5 cm, ADA Inv. I 639

151 *G. Material zur elementaren Gestaltung*, no. 2, September 1923, ed. Hans Richter, Berlin, 45,5 × 29,2 cm, Archiv Marzona

152 *G. Zeitschrift für elementare Gestaltung*, no. 3, June 1924, ed. Hans Richter, Berlin, 25,2 × 17,5 cm, ADA Inv. I 563

153 *Periszkop*, no. 4, June-July 1925, ed. György Szántó, Arad, 30,6 × 24 cm, ADA Inv. AdA-E-315

154 Jaroslav Seifert, *Samá Láska*, Prague: Nakladatelství Večernice 1923, 19,4 × 14 cm, ADA Inv. AdA-E-299

155 see 127

156 see 127

157 see 143

158 see 127

159 see 143

160 see 127

161 see 127

162 *New Masses*, no. 3, August 1929, ed. Michael Gold, New York, 29,7 × 22,2 cm, ADA Inv. I 605

163 *New Masses*, no. 3, January 1927, ed. Egmond Arens, Hugo Gellert, Michael Gold, New York, 31,5 × 24 cm, ADA Inv. I 592

164 see 163

165 *New Masses*, no. 2, July 1929, ed. Michael Gold, New York, 29,7 × 22,2 cm, ADA Inv. I 604

166 *New Masses*, no. 9, February 1929, ed. Michael Gold, New York, 29,8 × 22,2 cm, ADA Inv. I 599

167 *New Masses*, no. 1, May 1927, ed. Michael Gold, Hugo Gellert, New York, 31,4 × 23,5 cm, ADA Inv. I 591

168 *New Masses*, no. 11, March 1928, ed. Egmont Arens, Joseph Freeman, Hugo Gellert, Willam Gropper, Michael Gold, New York, 31,7 × 24,4 cm, ADA Inv. I 673

169 *New Masses*, no. 4, February 1927, ed. Egmont Arens, Hugo Gellert, William Gropper, Michael Gold, New York, 31,7 × 24,4 cm, ADA Inv. I 668

170 *New Masses*, no. 5, March 1927, ed. Egmont Arens, Hugo Gellert, William Gropper, Michael Gold, New York, 31,5 × 24 cm, ADA Inv. I 669

171 *New Masses*, no. 2, July 1928, ed. Michael Gold, Hugo Gellert, New York, 29,8 × 22,5 cm, ADA Inv. I 594

172 *New Masses*, no. 8, January 1929, ed. Michael Gold, New York, 29,8 × 22,5 cm, ADA Inv. I 598

173 *New Masses*, no. 12, May 1929, ed. Michael Gold, New York, 29,8 × 22,2 cm, ADA Inv. I 602

174 *New Masses*, no. 1, June 1929, ed. Michael Gold, New York, 29,9 × 22,5 cm, ADA Inv. I 603

175 *A-I-Z* [*Arbeiter-Illustrierte-Zeitung*], no. 17, 1931, ed. Josef Wildner, Berlin, 38,4 × 28,3 cm, ADA Inv. I 456

176 *A-I-Z* [*Arbeiter-Illustrierte-Zeitung*], no. 21, 1929, ed. Willi Münzenberg, Berlin, 42 × 29,7 cm, ADA Inv. A 8/Zeit 79, 32

177 Egon Erwin Kisch, *Raj Ameriku. Knijiga Prva*, Belgrade: Nolit 1930, 19,3 × 14,7 cm, ADA Inv. AdA-E-306

178 Egon Erwin Kisch, *Raj Ameriku. Knijiga Druga*, Belgrade: Nolit 1930, 20,3 × 14,8 cm, ADA Inv. AdA-E-307

179 Upton Sinclair, *So macht man Dollars*, Berlin: Malik Verlag 1931, 18,8 × 12,8 cm, ADA Inv. AdA-E-297

180 Upton Sinclair, *Petroleum*, Berlin: Malik Verlag 1931, 18,8 × 12,8 cm, ADA Inv. AdA-E-294

181 Upton Sinclair, *100%. Roman eines Patrioten*, Berlin: Malik Verlag 1921, 18 × 13 cm, ADA Inv. AdA-E-328

182 Upton Sinclair, *Jimmie Higgins*, Berlin: Malik Verlag 1924, 18,9 × 13 cm, ADA Inv. AdA-E-298

183 Upton Sinclair, *Der Sündenlohn. Eine Studie über den amerikanischen Journalismus*, Berlin: Malik Verlag 1929, 19 × 12,9 cm, ADA Inv. AdA-E-295

184 Upton Sinclair, *König Kohle*, Berlin: Malik Verlag 1931, 18,9 × 12,6 cm, ADA Inv. AdA-E-296

185 Upton Sinclair, *Der Sumpf*, Berlin: Malik Verlag 1924, 19,2 × 13 cm, ADA Inv. AdA-E-329

186 Upton Sinclair, *Boston*, Berlin: Malik Verlag 1929, 19,1 × 13 cm, ADA Inv. AdA-E-292

187 *New Masses*, no. 6, November 1928, ed. Michael Gold, New York, 30 cm × 22 cm, ADA Inv. I 596

188 see 161

189 *A-I-Z* [*Arbeiter-Illustrierte-Zeitung*], no. 20, 1927, ed. Willi Münzenberg, Berlin, 42,8 × 29,5 cm, ADA Inv. A 8/Zeit 71, 20

190 *Die Weltbühne*, no. 38, September 1927, ed. Kurt Tucholsky, Berlin, 21,3 × 14,5 cm, ADA Inv. I 635

191 *A-I-Z* [*Arbeiter-Illustrierte-Zeitung*], no. 35, 1927, ed. Willi Münzenberg, Berlin, 42,7 × 29,7 cm, ADA Inv. A 8/Zeit 71, 35

192 *ReD* [*Revue Devětsil*]. *Ilustrovaný měsíčník pro moderní kulturu*, vol. 3 [bound edition], September 1929-July 1931, ed. Karel Teige, Prague, 22,60 × 19 cm, ADA Inv. I 679

IMPRINT

This Publication accompanies the exhibition
Modern Times. The American Dream and the Avant-Gardes of the 1920s
Archiv der Avantgarden – Egidio Marzona, Staatliche Kunstsammlungen Dresden
11 April–10 August 2025

ARCHIV DER AVANTGARDEN – EGIDIO MARZONA [ADA]

Director ADA
Rudolf A. Fischer

Project Idea and Research
Przemysław Strożek

Curatorial and Research Team
Przemysław Strożek und David Wittinghofer

Project Coordinator
Clemens A. Ottenhausen

Publication series
Antonella B. Meloni

Program and Public Relations
Nina Schwarzenberger

Education and Art Mediation
Isabell Baldermann

Archivists
Barbara Tlusty, Eleni Trupis

Collection Management
Ilka Stern

Inventory and Provenance Research
Franziska Graßl, Stefanie Recsko

Library
Claudia Decker-Diestel

House Technician (GMI)
Joachim Kleinert

Light Design and Media Technique (GMI)
Ralph Kunze, Kai-Uwe Metzler

Restoration
ZFB Zentrum für Bucherhaltung GmbH Leipzig

Production
Daniel Kunze (KKS Architektur + Gestaltung Dresden)

Art Handling
A-Team Dresden, Fißler & Kollegen Leipzig

STAATLICHE KUNSTSAMMLUNGEN DRESDEN [SKD]

Director General ad interim
Marius Winzeler

Director of Finance
Cornelia Rabeneck and Team

Accounting and Controlling
Elke Ullmann and Team

Marketing
Doreen Scherfke and Team

Event Management
Anne Böttger and Team

Press and Communication
Holger Liebs; Nina Schwarzenberger, Andreas Diesend

Digital Systems
Martin Zavesky; Bianca Schubert

Program and International Relations
Jiří Fajt and Team

Technical Service
Michael John and Team

Personnel Management
Romy Herold and Team

CATALOG

Edited by
Staatliche Kunstsammlungen Dresden, Archiv der Avantgarden – Egidio Marzona
Przemysław Strożek, Rudolf A. Fischer, Antonella B. Meloni in collaboration with David Wittinghofer

Postfach 120 551, 01006 Dresden
+49 351 491 420 00
besucherservice@skd.museum
www.skd.museum

ADA series publishers
Marius Winzeler (ad interim), Rudolf A. Fischer,
Antonella B. Meloni (Managing Editor)

Greetings, Introduction
Marius Winzeler,
Staatliche Kunstsammlungen Dresden
Rudolf A. Fischer,
Archiv der Avantgarden – Egidio Marzona, SKD

Authors of Essays
Przemysław Strożek,
Archiv der Avantgarden – Egidio Marzona, SKD
Jed Rasula, University of Georgia
Jennifer J. Wild, University of Southern California
Meghan Forbes, independent researcher

Author of introductions to chapters and
accompanying texts
Przemysław Strożek,
Archiv der Avantgarden – Egidio Marzona, SKD

Editing
Antonella B. Meloni and Team ADA

Copyediting
Colin Cumming and Team ADA

Translation
Clemens A. Ottenhausen

Graphic Design
Helen Stelthove

Final artwork production
Daniel Vandré

Conceptual support for the book series
Jan Wenzel

Published by
Spector Books OHG
Harkortstraße 10
D-04107 Leipzig
+49 341 264 510 12
mail@spectorbooks.com
www.spectorbooks.com

Reprography, Picture Editing
ScanColor Reprostudio GmbH

Printing
Druckhaus Sportflieger, Berlin

Reproductions
Herbert Boswank: 003, 004, 009, 010, 021, 028, 029, 031, 065, 083, 091, 098, 117, 118, 119, 120, 141, 152, 153, 158

Courtesy
Conrad R. Feininger: T. Lux Feininger;
Mary Ryan Gallery: Hugo Gellert, Louis Lozowick;
Tom McCormick: Jan Matulka;
Massimo Prampolini: Enrico Prampolini;
Riccardo Mihahelles: Thayaht

Cover
Fernand Léger: *Mechanisches Ballet*, in: Hans Richter, *Filmgegner von Heute – Filmfreunde von Morgen*, Berlin: Verlag Hermann Reckendorf 1929, 9

Left-sided background montages (public domain)
Der Querschnitt, diverse numbers, 1926–1930, ed. Hermann von Wedderkopp, Berlin; *A-I-Z* [*Arbeiter-Illustrierte-Zeitung*], diverse numbers,

1928–1930, ed. Willi Münzenberg, Berlin; *Volk und Zeit*, 1927, ed. Ludwig Lessen, Berlin; *New Masses*, diverse numbers, 1927–1929, ed. Michael Gold et al., New York; *transition: An International Quarterly for Creative Experiment*, no. 16–17, June 1929, ed. Eugène Jolas, Paris; *Reflektor*, diverse numbers, 1925–1926, ed. Stanislav K. Neumann, Prague; *Schaubücher 3. Technische Schönheit*, ed. Emil Schaeffer, Zurich/Leipzig: Orell Füssli Verlag, 1929; *Schaubücher 15. Riesenbauten Amerikas*, ed. Emil Schaeffer, Zurich/Leipzig: Orell Füssli Verlag, 1930; *Schaubücher 33. Hollywood wie es wirklich ist*, ed. Emil Schaeffer, Zurich/Leipzig: Orell Füssli Verlag, 1930; *Rotogravure Album of New York*, New York: Rotoprint Gravure Co., 1921

The Deutsche Nationalbibliothek lists this publication in the Deutsche Nationalbibliografie; detailed bibliographic data are available online at: http://dnb.dnb.de

Printed in Germany 2025
ISBN 978-3-95905-886-5

DISTRIBUTION

Germany, Austria
GVA, Gemeinsame Verlagsauslieferung Göttingen
GmbH & Co. KG, www.gva-verlage.de

Switzerland
AVA Verlagsauslieferung AG
www.ava.ch

France, Belgium
Interart Paris
www.interart.fr

UK
Central Books Ltd
www.centralbooks.com

USA, Canada, Central and South America, Africa:
ARTBOOK / D.A.P.
www.artbook.com

Japan
twelvebooks
www.twelve-books.com

South Korea
The Book Society
www.thebooksociety.org

Australia, New Zealand
Perimeter Distribution
www.perimeterdistribution.com